Puzzles, Paradoxes, and Problems

A READER FOR INTRODUCTORY PHILOSOPHY

D0061102

Puzzles, Paradoxes, and Problems

A READER FOR INTRODUCTORY PHILOSOPHY

PETER A. FRENCH
Lennox Distinguished Professor
Trinity University

CURTIS BROWN
Assistant Professor
Trinity University

St. Martin's Press   New York

Acknowledgments

"De Anima," by Richard Taylor. In the *American Philosophical Quarterly*, vol. 10, no. 1 (1973), pp. 61–64.
"Where Am I?" by Daniel C. Dennett, from *Brainstorms* by Daniel C. Dennett. Copyright © 1978 by Bradford Books, Publishers. All rights reserved. Reprinted by permission of MIT Press.
"*Meditations* II and VI," by Rene Descartes, from *Meditations*, translated by John Veitch (1853).
"Leviathan," by Thomas Hobbes, from the Introduction and Chapters I, VI, XXXIV, XLIV, and XLVI of *Leviathan* (1651).
"Personal Identity," by Charles B. Daniels. From *Philosophers in Wonderland* ed. Peter A. French. © 1975 by Peter A. French. Reprinted by permission of the author.
"Personal Identity," by Derek Parfit, In *Philosophical Review* (1971), pp. 3–27.
"Personal Identity," by John Locke, from Book II, Chapter 27 of *An Essay Concerning Human Understanding*, Second Edition (1694).
"Of Personal Identity," by Joseph Butler, from the first appendix to *The Analogy of Religion* (1736).
"Conditions of Personhood," by Daniel Dennett. In Amelie Rorty, *The Identities of Persons* (1976). © 1976 The Regents of the University of California, reprinted by permission of the University of California Press.
"Computing Machinery and Intelligence," by A. M. Turing. Excerpt from "Computing Machinery and Intelligence," *Mind* (1950), vol. LIX, no. 236. Reprinted by permission of Oxford University Press.
"The Corporation as a Moral Person," by Peter A. French. In the *American Philosophical Quarterly*, vol. 16, no. 3 (1979), pp. 207–15.
"*Discourse on Method* Part V," by Rene Descartes, from *Discourse on Method*, translated by John Veitch (1850).
"Letters to the Marquis of Newcastle and Henry More," by Rene Descartes, from *The Philosophy of Descartes*, selected and translated by Henry A. P. Torrey (1892).
"Truth in Fiction," by David Lewis. In the *American Philosophical Quarterly*, vol. 15, no. 1 (1978), pp. 37–46.
"How Remote are Fictional Worlds from the Real World?" by Kendall L. Walton. In the *Journal of Aesthetics and Art Criticism*, vol. 37 (1978), pp. 11–23.
"Of Names," by John Stuart Mill, from Book I, Chapter II of *A System of Logic* (1843).
"On Sense and Nominatum," by Gottlob Frege, from the translation by Herbert Feigl in Herbert Feigl and Wilfrid Sellars, eds., *Readings in Philosophical Analysis* (New York: Appleton-Century-Crofts, 1949).
"—All You Zombies—", by Robert A. Heinlein. In *The Unpleasant Profession of Jonathan Hoag* by Robert A. Heinlein. Copyright 1959 by Robert A. Heinlein. Reprinted by permission of the author.

Acknowledgments continue at the back of the book beginning on page 533, which constitutes an extension of the copyright page.

Contents

viii   Contents

Part XI. *The Sceptical Challenge*   *493*

Preface

Philosophy has a long and rich history of analyses and arguments from which a student can begin to grasp the philosophic enterprise. It is perhaps unnecessary to examine the treatises and arguments, the meditations and essays of the great philosophers of the past to achieve an understanding of philosophy. The current philosophical scene is alive with an intriguing and stimulating array of discussions and debates by highly skilled and creative philosophers. But, if the student intends truly to come to grips with the discipline of philosophy, both its past and present must be experienced. The issues around which we have organized this book are discussed in both classical and contemporary works. That should not be surprising. Philosophical problems have not altered much through the centuries, though scientific, cultural, and intellectual changes have sharpened the focus on some issues and blurred that on others. The deeper issues of philosophy are perennial, receiving new interpretations and applications with each new era. Progress consists not so much in solving them as in learning ever more from studying them.

Reading excerpts from the important works of the history of philosophy, from Aristotle, Descartes, Hobbes, Locke, Hume, Kant, Mill, Marx, and so on, may prove difficult for an introductory student, not because the subject matter is uninteresting, but because of differences in the styles characteristic of the various ages in which those philosophers wrote. Students need to be highly motivated to carry on the difficult work of trying to understand and evaluate the philosophical theories of the great classical authors. That fact challenges the professor who would introduce philosophy to the contemporary student. Rather than organize this reader along lines common in introductory texts, where the fashion has been to offer the student first a selection of materials from the classical texts and then provide contemporary applications, we have sought to begin with the present, to engage a student's imagination and curiosity with contemporary analyses of very intriguing issues, and then offer classical texts to which a student can turn to broaden his or her understanding of philosophy. Excerpts from the classical texts often require a good deal of "stage-setting" that can be provided by the instructor, but the issues can be grasped and discussed by students on the basis of readings from contemporary authors.

The contemporary papers in this book do have technical aspects. Some, no doubt, will seem as technical as, if not more difficult than, the classical works. That should be expected. Philosophy has always been a vigorous and vibrant and difficult intellectual and academic discipline. By and large, however, the contemporary essays in this collection keep technical apparatus to a minimum. Where technicalities are not explained, that is because they are in general use in the philosophical community and the professor can be expected to provide what is necessary for the student to gain an adequate understanding of the argument. No service is done either to the student of philosophy or to philosophy itself if superficial, journalistic, or shallow work is offered as representative of philosophy.

Our primary interest is to provide students who are first confronting philosophy with a collection of readings that reveals the broad interests, the richness, and the sheer intellectual excitement of the field. The focus of the book is on selected conceptual puzzles, thought experiments, and problems that are currently much discussed by philosophers. These are provocative issues that can be expected to intrigue and stimulate a student's native reflective interests.

We have not tried to represent all of the traditional areas of philosophical study. It will be recognized that many of the problems around which the parts are organized properly fall within the field of metaphysics. Issues in ethics are less fully represented, and issues in aesthetics not at all. The suggestion of a comprehensive introductory survey has been deliberately avoided. Our experience is that introductory philosophy is less an introduction to the real enterprise of philosophy the more it is an attempt to survey all of the various fields, or schools, or historical periods of philosophy.

Nevertheless, the interconnections among philosophical issues are such that the instructor will find few traditional problems which cannot be approached from the material represented here. For example, there is no section on the problem of induction, but the section on the skeptical challenge provides a natural route into that problem.

What ought a student learn about philosophy at the introductory level? Our answer is that students ought to learn something of what is involved when one tries to analyze critically fundamental assumptions and concepts. We believe that students learn about philosophical thinking when they are encouraged to allow their own intellectual curiosity, reflections, and analytical talents to range over legitimate philosophical puzzles and problems that almost immediately stimulate their imaginations. The topics emphasized here are those most students find intellectually absorbing, even exciting. They are also topics that "carry over" into after-class discussions and into other intellectual pursuits, such as the study of physics, biology, religion, medicine, law, politics, anthropology, and mathematics.

The selections that appear in this book, as previously mentioned, are not here to represent the kaleidoscope of philosophical opinion and methodology. The primary criteria of selection have been that the work be well-argued; that it open the doors to those who would continue the pursuit of the issues, especially by examining the classical analyses of the concepts; that it be focused on some provocative puzzle, paradox, or problem relevant to what have historically been the most characteristically philosophical of issues; and that it be written by a significant contributor to the philosophical literature whom students may be expected to en-counter again if they continue to study philosophy.

The prospect of enticing introductory students to participate actively in the enterprise of philosophy motivated the organization of this reader. By drawing their attention to some of the more lively issues of contemporary philosophy and providing historically important viewpoints, analyses, and arguments, we hope to engage students in critically evaluating the philosophical views of others and beginning carefully and responsibly to work out their own.

Although this reader is a joint product, the editors have to some extent divided their responsibility. The Table of Contents was developed by both from an initial list prepared by French. Of the editorial material, French was principally responsible for the Preface and Parts II, III, IV, VI, VIII, and X; Brown was principally responsible for the General Introduc-tion and Parts I, V, VII, IX, and XI. We welcome advice, criticism, and other comments from teachers using the text.

A NOTE ON THE ORGANIZATION OF THE BOOK

We have preferred not to impose an explicit structure on this work beyond its division into parts. The parts do not presuppose one another, but their topics intertwine in a multitude of ways; as a result, a wide variety of orderings might prove useful and illuminating in the classroom.

Nevertheless we do think that our own ordering clearly recommends itself. We begin with three parts that cluster around issues in the philoso-phy of mind. The first, "Mind-Body Puzzles," opens the book with puzzles about the relation between mind and body, and about whether any useful purpose is served by supposing that people are endowed with nonphysical minds or souls. Some of the articles in this section explicitly link these puzzles with problems about what makes the various periods in a person's life periods in the *same* life—that is, with the problem of personal identity, and this is the topic of Part II. Part I also has interesting connections with the question of what counts as a person, of how broad the category of persons is or can be made to be. Daniel Dennett raises this issue in his piece in Part I, and it is explored further in Part III, which opens with a paper by Dennett.

In Part IV we turn to a consideration of a central issue in the philoso-phy of language, the nature of reference, which we approach initially by discussions of real or apparent reference to fictional creatures. This is a change of subject from the first sections, but the rhetorical transition is smooth, since a character in a work of fiction might be thought of as a sort of artificially created person. Insofar as these referential issues also involve metaphysical matters, especially concerning the interpretation of the notion of possible worlds, a bridge is constructed between this section and the three more specifically metaphysics-oriented sections that follow.

Part V uses problems surrounding the notion of time travel as an entry into metaphysical issues about the nature of time. This transition from the previous section is rhetorically natural, since time travel is a favorite fictional device.

Issues about the possibility of time travel and the nature of time have obvious connections with the issue of backward causation; in Part VI we use this issue as a means of approaching the consideration of the nature of causation and the relationship of the concept of cause to most of the central concepts that govern the way we try to understand and explain our experiences. The possibilities of time travel and backward causation also have intriguing connections with the problem of free agency and fatalism, connections explicitly discussed by David Lewis and Michael Dummett. In Part VII these problems are addressed in detail, and in a way which makes their connection with earlier sections clear; in particular Gilbert Ryle appeals to a view of time also discussed by David Lewis, and both John Stuart Mill and A. J. Ayer appeal to a Humean view of causation.

Parts VII–X are primarily concerned with issues in value theory. Part VII explores one of the most heated issues in the philosophy of religion: the apparent threat to rational religious belief in an omnipotent, omniscient, and omnibenevolent God posed by the existence of evil. Since the chief response to this threat involves the view that human beings are free agents, this section has very explicit connections with the preceding one.

Part IX turns to a consideration of ethics. The contemporary selections in this section focus on possible conflicts between being a good person and doing one's duty; the substantial classical selections represent Aristotle's development of a moral view which emphasizes good character and Kant's development of an extremely influential moral view that emphasizes duty or right conduct. (Utilitarianism is not represented in this section, but a utilitarian account of just distribution is presented in Mill in Part X.)

In Part X we enter the realm of social and political philosophy, focusing on one of the most hotly disputed problems in this area: what makes any particular distribution of wealth, goods, and scarce resources just or unjust. A wide range of political and philosophical views is included, from Marx's communism to Robert Nozick's libertarianism.

The book concludes with a chapter on epistemology: Part XI, "The Sceptical Challenge." Some teachers will want to begin with this section, and the book will certainly lend itself to this use. Our own preference is to conclude with epistemological problems about knowledge and justification. Throughout the course, the student will have been striving to see which philosophical views are better justified than others, and in this way to acquire knowledge of a particularly deep and satisfying sort. This seems to us to be a good time for the student to look back over the course and consider, at a higher level of abstraction, the activity he or she has been engaged in—to consider whether knowledge is possible at all, and how in general beliefs are to be justified.

This is our justification for the way we have organized the book. But the interconnections among these problems are endless. What moral obligations would we have toward artificially created persons? Could a computer have free will? What makes the person who steps out of a time machine in ancient Greece the same person who steps into the machine in the twenty-first century United States? Is free will compatible with materialism? How is it possible for us to refer to God? These questions and many more illustrate the inevitable and complex criss-crossing of the puzzles, paradoxes, and problems of philosophy, and of philosophers' attempts to solve them.

GENERAL INTRODUCTION

W hat is philosophy? This is naturally one of the first questions which strikes someone taking an introductory course in philosophy. It would seem to be a good idea to begin by answering it. But this is surprisingly difficult. The question of the nature of philosophy is itself a philosophical question, and one on which philosophers differ. Philosophy is above all a kind of practice or activity; the best way to discover the nature of philosophy is to begin reading philosophical works, carrying on philosophical discussions, and writing philosophical prose—just as the best way to find out how to ride a bicycle, or to cook, or to speak in public is to begin doing it. And, as with other practices, the best practitioners of philosophy may be at a loss to say with precision just what it is they are doing.

Still, it is possible to say a few relatively uncontroversial things by way of an introduction to philosophy. Philosophy is distinctive both in its subject matter and in its approach. We begin, then, by exploring some of the features of philosophical problems and methods.

An important feature of philosophical problems is their *generality*. In going about our day-to-day business, we take a great many things for granted. The questions we ordinarily are concerned about are quite specific, and in answering them we simply accept without question a framework of beliefs and attitudes which enables us to get on with our enquiry. But philosophy makes us stop short and examine more carefully those fundamental, general, taken-for-granted concepts and beliefs.

Some examples may help make this difference between ordinary and philosophical questions clear.[1] A historian might ask when the French Revolution took place. Such a historian will know very well how to go about answering this question. But in answering it, he or she takes for granted the notion of time, a notion the philosopher will want to explore further. The philosopher is interested in such questions as: Does it make sense to talk of the universe itself as having a beginning in time? Does time move? Is time part of the objective nature of things, or is it merely a feature of our subjective experience of the world? (See Part V for an exploration of such questions.)

Again, we ordinarily wonder a great deal about the attitudes of others. Does he or she really love me? Does he really believe that Hitler is still alive, or is he kidding? Is she as happy as she seems, or is she covering

1

up a secret sorrow? The philosopher asks a more general sort of question: Can we ever really know what goes on in someone else's mind? If so, how, given that we can't directly experience the contents of other people's minds? (Such issues are a focus of discussion in Part XI.)

We often find ourselves asking practical questions about what we ought to do in a specific situation, given that we have a certain goal in mind. What is the best way to stop my car from burning oil? How can I keep my roommate away long enough to set the room up for her surprise party? But the philosopher is interested less in how to achieve particular goals than in the more general question of what goals we ought to have, of how we ought to live our lives and what sort of people we ought to be. (These issues are discussed in Part IX.)

A second feature of philosophical problems is due in part to their generality: *evidence* typically bears only indirectly on philosophical issues. You cannot simply perform an experiment and thereby discover whether time moves, or whether you ought to be concerned about the welfare of others, or whether you can know anything about other people's minds. This is a difference of degree rather than of kind. Evidence of all sorts is relevant to philosophical issues, though it rarely settles them conclusively; and even in science the bearing of evidence on problems is often much less direct than the novice would suspect. But in general the bearing of observation, experience, and experiment on philosophical problems is less direct than their bearing on ordinary or scientific problems.

Philosophers sometimes say that science is concerned with finding the truth about the world, while philosophy is concerned instead with revealing the meanings of our most basic concepts. Again, some philosophers say that in science and in everyday life we work within a framework of assumptions and beliefs, and that philosophy tries to understand and, where appropriate, criticize this framework. These claims, if taken too literally, are controversial, since many philosophers think that there is no sharp distinction between questions of meaning and questions of fact, or between framework beliefs or assumptions and more ordinary ones. But if we treat these distinctions as matters of degree, then the claims just considered may be helpful. Certainly philosophy tries to understand, criticize, and provide alternatives to beliefs we typically take for granted. As a result of philosophical reflection, people change even their most fundamental beliefs and attitudes about the world.

We have been considering the nature of philosophical problems. We now turn to the methods philosophers use in thinking about such problems.

The chief tools of the philosopher are creativity and critical argument. Discovering philosophical puzzles, proposing solutions to them, devising theories—all are creative endeavors in the fullest sense. But it is crucial that philosophers are not merely engaged in creative theory construction. In that case their views would be of interest as artistic creations but would not make serious claims on our belief. Philosophers do not just invent views, they argue for them.

The arguments in question are often critical. Philosophers expose viewpoints to various kinds of attack—they find inconsistencies, dissect arguments that do not work, reveal inexplicit and dubious premises, discover counterexamples. Philosophy progresses in large part by weeding out or modifying views which do not stand up to such criticism. Philosophical views thus go through a process analogous to Darwinian natural selection.

One historically proven and fruitful way to engage in the enterprise of philosophy is to investigate rather fantastic scenarios, or highly imaginative thought experiments. By carefully examining such intellectual puzzles, philosophers expose aspects and implications of ordinary assumptions that typically go unrecognized because our ordinary experience does not challenge them. Indeed such concepts and assumptions may constitute the very foundation of our ordinary experience. Focusing on such puzzles, paradoxes, and problems can free the intellect to explore to their very boundaries our cornerstone concepts and beliefs.

The essays which we have gathered in this book explore a variety of such puzzles. They are written by many of the very best philosophers, both contemporary and classical. They are not easy reading: the most rewarding writing is seldom easy. But neither are they obscure. They are written with care and precision. They deserve a careful and attentive reading—indeed several careful and attentive readings. In return, they will reward the serious reader with a deep and reflective understanding of fascinating and important issues which lie at the roots of our beliefs, attitudes, and actions.

NOTE

1. This paragraph and the next have been influenced by Isaiah Berlin's introduction to *The Age of Enlightenment* (New York: New American Library, 1956), pp. 11–12.

Part I. Mind-Body Puzzles

Our abilities to think, perceive, feel, decide, and act are really rather strange and marvelous. Most of us have felt at one time or another—perhaps when stretched out on the bed, watching our toes from several feet away—how peculiar and even faintly disturbing it is that we can *make them move*. Between our toes and ourselves there seems to be both a sharp divide and an intimate connection, and perhaps it is the tension between these two which is the source of our wonder and unease.

These feelings of wonder usually come only at odd moments. For the most part we take our mental lives, and their connection with our bodies, for granted. But, as Nietzsche reminds us in *The Gay Science*, we must not mistake familiarity for understanding:

> [The philosophers] think that the known is at least *more easily understood* than the strange; that, for example, it is methodically ordered to proceed outward from the "inner world," from "the facts of consciousness," because it is the world which is *better known to us!* Error of errors! The known is the accustomed, and the accustomed is the most difficult of all to "understand."

There are many puzzles about the relation between mind and body, but perhaps the most basic is simply this: What am I, anyway? Am *I* just the same thing as my body? Or am I perhaps a part of my body? Or am I something wholly distinct from my body but closely connected with it? The selections in this section are concerned in one way or another with these questions, and especially with the last-mentioned possibility.

There are a number of apparent differences between mental and physical phenomena. For instance, it seems that any physical object has a clear and precise location, but it is not at all clear how to locate mental events like emotions and beliefs. Again, physical objects can be chopped in two, while it seems bizarre to think of a belief being chopped in two.

We need to be cautious about just how much these apparent contrasts between mental and physical phenomena really show. Perhaps they are more accurately described as contrasts between more and less complex physical phenomena, or between more and less abstract levels of description of physical phenomena. (The development of computers and of the terminology needed to describe what they do leads to many of the same

5

oddities that discussion of mental phenomena seems to lead to, yet no one thinks that computers are more than physical entities.)

Such apparent differences as the ones just considered nevertheless led Rene Descartes to formulate a view of the relation between the mind and the body which has had an enormous influence on our thought about the mind. Although most philosophers are now inclined to believe that Descartes's view is mistaken, it is a view which has become deeply entrenched in common sense.

Descartes's view is elaborated in a selection in this chapter. In brief, Descartes defends a view known as mind-body *dualism*. This is the view that there are two fundamentally different sorts of substance in the universe: mental or "spiritual" substance and physical substance. Thoughts and feelings are then thought to be attributes of mental substance, while our physical features, like height or weight or hair color, are attributes of physical substance. Minds, then, are thought to be entirely nonphysical; a person is made up of two components: a physical body, and a nonphysical mind.

We often think of ourselves in this Cartesian way—as essentially a nonphysical thing with intimate connections to a particular physical body. This conception is involved in Delmore Schwartz's memorable description of his body as "the heavy bear who goes with me." His poem of the same title reads, in part:

That inescapable animal walks with me,
Has followed me since the black womb held,
Moves where I move, distorting my gesture,
A caricature, a swollen shadow,
A stupid clown of the spirit's motive,
Perplexes and affronts with his own darkness,
The secret life of belly and bone,
Opaque, too near, my private, yet unknown,
Stretches to embrace the very dear
With whom I would walk without him near,
Touches her grossly, although a word
Would bare my heart and make me clear,
Stumbles, flounders, and strives to be fed
Dragging me with him in his mouthing care,
Amid the hundred million of his kind,
The scrimmage of appetite everywhere.

Especially poignant here is Schwartz's image of his body getting in the way of an ideal spiritual communion with his loved one. If only we could leave our bodies behind, we sometimes think, and communicate mind-to-mind; if only we could be *really* together, without our bodies bumping into each other and preventing any closer contact.

But this dream may be not merely impossible, but incoherent. So, at least, *materialists* would claim. Materialism is the view that there is only one sort of substance in the world, physical substance; there is no such thing as the "spiritual substance" invoked by the Cartesians. People, then, are *not* compounds consisting of a physical body *and* an immaterial, nonphysical mind. People are *just* bodies, just complicated physical organisms. Not that the materialist thinks that people do not have beliefs or wishes or tickles or fears. The materialist is as much a believer in mental events as anyone, but thinks that Descartes had a mistaken view of the *nature* of mental events. Materialism is defended by Thomas Hobbes in this chapter, and it is the predominant view among contemporary philosophers.

There are difficulties with dualism, and these difficulties are in large part what has led people to reject the view. One of the principal difficulties is one which was posed to Descartes himself by a princess with whom he corresponded: If the mind is wholly nonphysical, how does it ever get the body to do anything? With what does it push? How does it get leverage? It seems utterly mysterious how a nonphysical entity could produce a physical result. Furthermore, if we are looking for the causes of an action, and we have traced the *physical* causes back some distance (e.g., my arm moved because my muscles flexed, the muscles flexed because they received neural impulses from the brain, . . .), it seems obstructionist at any point to say "OK, we've got all the physical causes now; the next step back must be the nonphysical mind." It seems unlikely that we will ever reach a point in the chain of causes at which this seems like the right thing to say.

The contemporary selections in this section raise various intriguing puzzles about the relation between mind and body. Richard Taylor makes a surprising analogy and Daniel Dennett tells a sort of science-fiction story. Both may be read as posing difficulties for dualism. But it is necessary to read them carefully. Taylor claims to assume that people have immaterial minds or souls, and Dennett at one point claims to have proven that the soul is immaterial. But these statements are ironic. If we took them at their word we would be missing the point, just as one misses the point of Jonathan Swift's famous "A Modest Proposal" if one takes Swift *really* to be advocating that babies should be eaten. Swift wants to jar us into examining his arguments and seeing that something is seriously wrong—and so do Taylor and Dennett, despite their deadpan delivery.

Both articles may be read as suggesting that there are certain questions which *would* have answers if people were essentially immaterial minds, but which in some describable cases do not in fact have answers. For Taylor, the question is "which organism is parent and which is offspring?" For Dennett, it is "where am I?" If these questions are really unanswerable in some cases, that is a strong argument against dualism.

Both articles also raise issues which will be taken up later, in Parts II and III. If we see an amoeba, or a person, on Monday, and then see an amoeba, or a person, on Tuesday, what determines whether they were the same amoeba or the same person? This is the problem of *personal identity*, addressed in Part II. Dennett's story includes a sort of "body transplant" and so introduces a case in which the question of personal identity is particularly hard to answer. And the question of whether Dennett's computer brain (Hubert) is a real person is an instance of the problem of artificially created persons, addressed in Part III.

DE ANIMA

Richard Taylor

Some philosophers say that each of us has, or indeed *is*, a personal self, ego or soul, related some way or other to his body and to the rest of the world. Just what those relationships are is much debated; but it is considered beyond doubt that there is, at the very center of things, this self or ego. Such, at least, is the teaching of a long and respectable philosophical tradition. It is said that this personal self came into being at a certain moment in time, and that, alas! it is going to perish at some approaching moment of time, never to exist again in the whole of eternity. Theologians say it arose as a result of God's creating it and that, if certain of God's expectations are lived up to, it can hope to go right on existing, forever, in some place specially reserved for it.

Other philosophers say that there is no such thing at all, that a man is nothing more than his body, and that his ultimate fate, therefore, is simply the fate of his body, which is known to be dust and ashes. This teaching has the advantage of simplicity and seems generally more scientific, but since it is rather depressing, it is not so widely held.

Both schools of thought seem agreed in this, however: That a man is a finite being, distinct from everything that is not himself, that he came into being at a certain more or less identifiable moment, and that, apart from the hope nourished by religion, he is going to perish at some future moment not yet known.

Both points of view are basically mistaken on that point, though it is not easy to demonstrate this through philosophical arguments. That should be no cause for embarrassment, for philosophers have never proved anything about this, one way or another, anyway. Each imagines that he has, and dismisses those of a contrary opinion as too dense to follow his demonstrations, but in fact all any philosopher has ever done here is to arrange his presuppositions and prejudices in an orderly way, then step back and say: "Behold, what I have proved."

Nor is it easy to show in any other way what is wrong here. Proofs seem to accomplish nothing, except to stimulate controversy. Nothing can be counted on, but we might have some luck with:

WALTER'S AMOEBIARY: A PHILOSOPHICAL FABLE

Walter had an engrossing interest in microscopy, but this eventually evolved into an interest in micro-organisms and, more particularly, amoebae, not merely as subjects of microscopic study, but for their own sakes. That is, he grew fond of them, studied sympathetically their individual traits and personalities, and in time got to the point of spending hours upon hours in their company. Of course he gave them names—Alice, Henry, and so on. The choice of the name was in no way guided by the sex of its possessor, for amoebae are not distinguishable by sex, but this did not matter. Walter found it natural and easy to think of Alice as female, for instance, Henry as male, and so on, considering that an amoeba's name was a perfectly reliable guide in determining whether to refer to a given animal as *he* or *she*.

From the many hours he spent with them, Walter eventually came to know his animals with astonishing understanding. He could pick out Alice at once, for example, knew the circumstances of her birth, and something of her achievements, frustrations, and failures. When any amoeba seemed sluggish or ill, he felt genuine concern, and when one perished, it was for Walter not just the loss of something easily replaced. The amoebae, to be sure, showed little reciprocation for this devotion, and in fact exhibited no more fidelity to their owner than does a cat, but this made no difference to Walter.

It was a harmless little hobby until Walter decided to breed the tiny animals, with a view to improving the strain, and this led him almost to the madhouse. Amoebae multiply rather quickly, but Walter's problems did not arise from this. They were instead metaphysical. There were perfectly straightforward questions, the answers to which he needed for his records, and while those answers lay right under his nose, he somehow could not find them. He became more obsessed with metaphysics than with his amoebae. He was beginning to think himself deficient of intellect, but unjustifiably, for as he eventually discovered, the questions that plagued him were questions that could not arise.

His frustrations arose in the following way. The breeder of any stock needs to know ancestry. This would at first seem to be utterly simple for the amoeba breeder, for an amoeba has only one parent. Instead, then, of the usual family histories, with their numberless branches and ramifications, which in a few generations baffle all comprehension, the amoeba breeder would need only a simple linear record of successive parents and offspring. The breed would be improved by encouraging those with the desired traits to multiply, and inhibiting the rest. It all seemed utterly simple. There would be no need at all to pair off prospective parents and then hope, meanwhile becoming mired in the complexities of bisexual genetics.

But then arose the first problem. The amoeba reproduces simply by splitting in two. So if Henry thus divides himself, the question arises, which of the two resulting amoebae is really Henry, and which is his offspring? Walter at first answered that in what seemed a perfectly straightforward, unarbitrary way. The parent, he thought, would be the larger of the two, and the smaller, the offspring. In fact it was usually quite obvious when he was on hand to witness the birth, for the offspring first appeared as a tiny bud on the parent, gradually grew larger, and then split off. There was then no problem.

But then Walter got to wondering: Why do I record the small bud as breaking off from the large one, to become its offspring, instead of thinking of the large bud breaking away from the smaller one, to become *its* offspring? Is identity a mere function of size? How do I know, to begin with, that a small bud appears on the parent amoeba? Perhaps the parent amoeba withdraws into a small bud, leaving behind the larger remains, this parent, now much reduced in bulk, eventually recovering its original size, to resemble its larger offspring? How would I ever know, in case that actually happened? How do I know it does not happen every time, so that my records are all backwards, exhibiting a total confusion between parents and offspring?

Walter lost many hours, and quite a bit of sleep too, pondering this question, until he hit upon a technique whereby he could, he thought, unfailingly identify any one of his animals, once and for all. He would tag them, he decided. So he developed a technique for imprinting minute but indelible colored spots on them, which could be combined in various configurations. With each animal so marked, he could then know for certain just which amoeba was before him, by checking its marking. Being thus able to distinguish any amoeba from any other, he could thereby distinguish it from any offspring, including its own. He found this particularly useful in those cases of an amoeba reproducing by dividing itself through the middle, resulting in two animals the same size. Had it not been for the markings, it would have been utterly impossible to tell which was the offspring, which the original. But with the marking system, Walter had only to check to see which animal bore the identifying mark. That would be the parent, and the other, the offspring. He particularly rejoiced at having this system when, several times, he found that the offspring was in fact the larger of the two divisions, for it was in these cases the bud which bore the identifying marks. This of course confirmed his earlier fear that the larger part might sometimes be the bud that breaks off from the smaller original, so that, in truth, the larger of the two is the offspring, the smaller one the parent.

This was all fine, and Walter felt entirely secure in the accuracy of his records and pedigrees, until one day a strange thing happened. One of his amoebae gave birth, but retained only half of the identifying marking, passing the other half to its offspring. Walter found himself totally unable to tell which was which. Without knowing which was the parent, his record of lineage, with respect to that particular family of amoebae, had to come to a dead end, to his dismay.

At first he thought he had minimized the chance of this ever happening again, by making the markings so tiny that it would be very unlikely that they would be divided in any fission of their bearers. But then there arose the following question, which suggested to Walter that the entire system of markings might be unreliable. What if, he thought, a parent amoeba, in shedding some and perhaps even most of its substance to give rise to a totally new individual, should at the same time shed its identifying mark, so that the very mark which is supposed to identify the parent should now be sported by its offspring? Would that not throw the records into a confusion which would be metaphysically incapable of clarification?

For quite awhile Walter tried to banish this doubt by insisting that, since marks had been introduced as the very criteria of identity, no question could arise of one amoeba transmitting its marks to another. The amoeba bearing the marks criterially distinctive of Henry, for example, would have to *be* Henry. It is by those very marks, after all, that we pick Henry out in the first place. To speak of another amoeba having Henry's marks is to speak unintelligibly.

But like too much that passes for incisive philosophical thinking, this was soon seen to be an arbitrary fiction, from the most elementary consideration. For clearly, if one could regard a given animal as that one upon which a certain mark was bestowed, making its identity entirely a function of this, then one could by the same logic regard a given animal as one upon which a certain name is bestowed. Thus, Henry would be whichever animal one calls "Henry," and that would be the end of the matter. But surely such a solution to the problem would be worthy only of children and the most dull witted philosophers. Our common sense tells us that there would be nothing under the sun to prevent one from flushing Henry down the sink, and henceforth calling another by that name. No animal's continuing identity is ensured by a resolution to continue applying its name. But as an animal can shed its name, so also it can shed its markings—and with that obvious reflection Walter found himself back where he had begun, and on the brink of madness.

After such frustrations, Walter finally destroyed all his records, convinced they must be filled with errors. He tried other systems, but with no better luck. He had long since noted, for example, that his different amoebae displayed different traits of personality, different preferences and habits, though all these were, of course, rather simple. When observing his amoebiary he could quite reliably distinguish one from another by these traits of character, and had in fact been partly guided by these observations in bestowing individual names in the first place. So for a time he used distinctive character traits as his guide, deciding which amoeba was Henry, which Alice, and so on, simply by how they behaved. It was not difficult, once he got to know them sufficiently well. But then one of the amoebae split, and each of the two resulting animals exhibited the character traits of the original to about the same degree. So it was again impossible to tell which was the pre-existing parent, and which the offspring just come into being. It was equally impossible to regard both as having been there from the start, and just as impossible to say that each had arisen with the coming into being of the other. In fact it was impossible to say anything that had any sense to it.

If only amoebae had fingers, Walter thought, so that one could make fingerprints. But were not the distinctive marks about equivalent? And they did not do much good. Or if only one could communicate with them, at even the most rudimentary level. This would settle any doubts. If there are two similar dogs, for example, and one wants to know which is Rover, he needs only to say "Rover," and see which dog picks up his ears. But then, what if an amoeba named Henry divided into two, and each half responded to the name "Henry"?

Walter finally gave up the whole enterprise of records, pedigrees, and family histories, deciding that any resolution of the problems they presented would be achieved only by metaphysicians. He went back to enjoying his pets for their own sakes, inspired by thoughts of the grandeur of even the lowliest of God's creatures, and tried to banish metaphysical puzzles from his mind. Some of the old problems did from time to time unsettle his peace and his sleep, but he resisted fairly well any temptation to try solving them.

In time the truth of things did finally dawn on Walter, however; not in the sense that any of his problems were solved, but rather, that he realized there had never been any problems there to begin with. They were all just problems that could never arise in the first place.

This enlightenment began when Walter started receiving instruction in metaphysical thinking. One of the first things he learned was that all men have souls. This is what makes them persons. If they did not have souls, they would be nothing but bodies, in principle no different from amoebae. More complicated, to be sure, but otherwise, of the same order of being. Philosophers refer to this inner soul as the *self*. Since it is what thinks, it is also called the *mind*. Amoebae do not think, because they do not have any minds to think with. It is also this soul which gives men their dignity. That is why amoebae have no dignity. They lack the necessary souls. All this was of course very clear, and Walter began seeing everything in a new and much better light.

What was particularly significant for Walter, of course, was that it is on the basis of the inner self that it makes sense to distinguish one person from another in the first place. This distinction has to begin with the distinction between the self and what is not the self, which of course brings us again right back to the soul. When someone refers to *himself*, he is really referring (though he may not realize it) to his self. He as much as says so. That is, he is not referring to his body, which is only a gross physical thing, continuously changing into other things, continuously arising and perishing. He is referring to his *self*. Therefore this must be something that is not physical. It is related somehow or other to the body, no doubt. It possesses and commands the body, for example. Thus when the self commands the arm to rise, the arm does rise, and in a similar way (readily understood in one's own case) it commands the tongue to speak, instructs it in what it should say, and so on. It (the self) retains its unalterable identity throughout all the changes transpiring around it, in the world at large, and particularly in that part of the outside world that the self refers to as its body.

The birth of the body is therefore not the origination of the person, for everyone knows that the body does not spring into being at birth. It existed before then, as part of another body. Indeed, it has always existed, mingled with other things, unlike the self itself. The person begins when there comes into being a brand new self, or what theologians appropriately call the soul, and philosophers, the mind, the ego, or simply, the self. Without such minds or souls, there would only be the corporeal realm, where everything is constantly changing, where nothing is ever created or utterly perishes, and where all distinctions between things are relative, as they are in the case of amoebae. In the world considered solely as corporeal, there could be no absolute distinctions between one self and another, for in such a world there would be no selves to distinguish. Hence, in such a world, there could be no ultimate distinction between me and thee, mine and thine, for there would not even be the most fundamental and precious of all distinctions, that between oneself and everything else.

Walter saw, of course, that such distinctions as these, so obvious to one who has mastered the fundamentals of metaphysics, do not apply at the level of amoebae. Amoebae are not possessed of egos, selves or souls. *That*, Walter perceived, must be why the distinction between parent and offspring was so elusive. It must be a distinction which, at that level, does not exist. There one finds only life assuming successive forms, wherein nothing is really born, and nothing really dies—unlike what is discovered, through metaphysics, at the higher personal level.

All this enabled Walter to see pretty clearly what had gone wrong with his attempts to keep records of amoeboidal ancestry. If his amoebae had possessed souls, like us, there would have been no difficulty whatsoever. He would only have needed to keep track of souls and record the relations of the different souls to each other.

"Then," thought Walter, "everything would have been straightforward, perfectly simple, and above all, of course, clear."

WHERE AM I?
Daniel Dennett

Now that I've won my suit under the Freedom of Information Act, I am at liberty to reveal for the first time a curious episode in my life that may be of interest not only to those engaged in research in the philosophy of mind, artificial intelligence and neuroscience but also to the general public.

Several years ago I was approached by Pentagon officials who asked me to volunteer for a highly dangerous and secret mission. In collaboration with NASA and Howard Hughes, the Department of Defense was spending billions to develop a Supersonic Tunneling Underground Device, or STUD. It was supposed to tunnel through the earth's core at great speed and deliver a specially designed atomic warhead "right up the Red's missile silos," as one of the Pentagon brass put it.

The problem was that in an early test they had succeeded in lodging a warhead about a mile deep under Tulsa, Oklahoma, and they wanted me to retrieve it for them. "Why me?" I asked. Well, the mission involved some pioneering applications of current brain research, and they had heard of my interest in brains and of course my Faustian curiosity and great courage and so forth. . . . Well, how could I refuse? The difficulty that brought the Pentagon to my door was that the device I'd been asked to recover was fiercely radioactive, in a new way. According to monitoring instruments, something about the nature of the device and its complex interactions with pockets of material deep in the earth had produced radiation that could cause severe abnormalities in certain tissues of the brain. No way had been found to shield the brain from these deadly rays, which were apparently harmless to other tissues and organs of the body. So it had been decided that the person sent to recover the device should *leave his brain behind*. It would be kept in a safe place where it could execute its normal control functions by elaborate radio links. Would I submit to a surgical procedure that would completely remove my brain, which would then be placed in a life-support system at the Manned Spacecraft Center in Houston? Each input and output pathway, as it was severed, would be restored by a pair of microminiaturized radio transceivers, one attached precisely to the brain, the other to the nerve stumps in the empty cranium. No information would be lost, all the connectivity would be preserved. At first I was a bit reluctant. Would it really work? The Houston brain surgeons encouraged me. "Think of it," they said, "as a mere *stretching* of the nerves. If your brain were just moved over an *inch* in your skull, that would not alter or impair your mind. We're simply going to make the nerves indefinitely elastic by splicing radio links into them."

I was shown around the life-support lab in Houston and saw the sparkling new vat in which my brain would be placed, were I to agree. I met the large and brilliant support team of neurologists, hematologists, biophysicists, and electrical engineers, and after several days of discussions and demonstrations, I agreed to give it a try. I was subjected to an enormous array of blood tests, brain scans, experiments, interviews, and the like. They took down my autobiography at great length, recorded tedious lists of my beliefs, hopes, fears, and tastes. They even listed my favorite stereo recordings and gave me a crash session of psychoanalysis.

The day for surgery arrived at last and of course I was anesthetized and remember nothing of the operation itself. When I came out of anesthesia, I opened my eyes, looked around, and asked the inevitable, the traditional, the lamentably hackneyed post-operative question: "Where am I?" The nurse smiled down at me. "You're in Houston," she said, and I reflected that this still had a good chance of being the truth one way or another. She handed me a mirror. Sure enough, there were the tiny antennae poling up through their titanium ports cemented into my skull.

"I gather the operation was a success," I said. "I want to go see my brain." They led me (I was a bit dizzy and unsteady) down a long corridor and into the life-support lab. A cheer went up from the assembled support team, and I responded with what I hoped was a jaunty salute. Still feeling lightheaded, I was helped over to the life-support vat. I peered through the glass. There, floating in what looked like ginger-ale, was undeniably a human brain, though it was almost covered with printed circuit chips, plastic tubules, electrodes, and other paraphernalia. "Is that mine?" I asked. "Hit the output transmitter switch there on the side of the vat and see for yourself," the project director replied. I moved the switch to OFF, and immediately slumped, groggy and nauseated, into the arms of the technicians, one of whom kindly restored the switch to its ON position. While I recovered my equilibrium and composure, I thought to myself: "Well, here I am, sitting on a folding chair, staring through a piece of plate glass at my own brain. . . . But wait," I said to myself, "shouldn't I have thought, 'Here I am, suspended in a bubbling fluid, being stared at by my own eyes'?" I tried to think this latter thought. I tried to project it into the tank, offering it hopefully to my brain, but I failed to carry off the exercise with any conviction. I tried again. "Here am *I*, Daniel Dennett, suspended in a bubbling fluid, being stared at by my own eyes." No, it just didn't work. Most puzzling and confusing. Being a philosopher of firm physicalist conviction, I believed unswervingly that the tokening of my thoughts was occurring somewhere in my brain: yet, when I thought

"Here I am," where the thought occurred to me was *here*, outside the vat, where I, Dennett, was standing staring at my brain.

I tried and tried to think myself into the vat, but to no avail. I tried to build up to the task by doing mental exercises. I thought to myself, "The sun is shining *over there*," five times in rapid succession, each time mentally ostending a different place: in order, the sun-lit corner of the lab, the visible front lawn of the hospital, Houston, Mars, and Jupiter. I found I had little difficulty in getting my "there's" to hop all over the celestial map with their proper references. I could loft a "there" in an instant through the farthest reaches of space, and then aim the next "there" with pinpoint accuracy at the upper left quadrant of a freckle on my arm. Why was I having such trouble with "here"? "Here in Houston" worked well enough, and so did "here in the lab," and even "here in this part of the lab," but "here in the vat" always seemed merely an unmeant mental mouthing. I tried closing my eyes while thinking it. This seemed to help, but still I couldn't manage to pull it off, except perhaps for a fleeting instant. I couldn't be sure. The discovery that I couldn't be sure was also unsettling. How did I know *where* I meant by "here" when I thought "here"? Could I *think* I meant one place when in fact I meant another? I didn't see how that could be admitted without untying the few bonds of intimacy between a person and his own mental life that had survived the onslaught of the brain scientists and philosophers, the physicalists and behaviorists. Perhaps I was incorrigible about where I *meant* when I said "here." But in my present circumstances it seemed that either I was doomed by sheer force of mental habit to thinking systematically false indexical thoughts, or where a person is (and hence where his thoughts are tokened for purposes of semantic analysis) is not necessarily where his brain, the physical seat of his soul, resides. Nagged by confusion, I attempted to orient myself by falling back on a favorite philosopher's ploy. I began naming things.

"Yorick," I said aloud to my brain, "you are my brain. The rest of my body, seated in this chair, I dub 'Hamlet.' " So here we all are: Yorick's my brain, Hamlet's my body, and I am Dennett. *Now*, where am I? And when I think "where am I?" where's that thought tokened? Is it tokened in my brain, lounging about in the vat, or right here between my ears where it *seems* to be tokened? Or nowhere? Its *temporal* coordinates give me no trouble; must it not have spatial coordinates as well? I began making a list of the alternatives.

(1) *Where Hamlet goes, there goes Dennett.* This principle was easily refuted by appeal to the familiar brain transplant thought experiments so enjoyed by philosophers. If Tom and Dick switch brains, Tom is the fellow with Dick's former body—just ask him; he'll claim to be Tom, and tell you the most intimate details of Tom's autobiography. It was clear enough, then, that my current body and I could part company, but not likely that I could be separated from my brain. The rule of thumb that

emerged so plainly from the thought experiments was that in a brain-transplant operation, one wanted to be the *donor*, not the recipient. Better to call such an operation a *body-transplant*, in fact. So perhaps the truth was,

(2) *Where Yorick goes, there goes Dennett.* This was not at all appealing, however. How could I be in the vat and not about to go anywhere, when I was so obviously outside the vat looking in and beginning to make guilty plans to return to my room for a substantial lunch? This begged the question I realized, but it still seemed to be getting at something important. Casting about for some support for my intuition, I hit upon a legalistic sort of argument that might have appealed to Locke.

Suppose, I argued to myself, I were now to fly to California, rob a bank, and be apprehended. In which state would I be tried: In California, where the robbery took place, or in Texas, where the brains of the outfit were located? Would I be a California felon with an out-of-state brain, or a Texas felon remotely controlling an accomplice of sorts in California? It seemed possible that I might beat such a rap just on the undecidability of that jurisdictional question, though perhaps it would be deemed an interstate, and hence Federal, offense. In any event, suppose I were convicted. Was it likely that California would be satisfied to throw Hamlet into the brig, knowing that Yorick was living the good life and luxuriously taking the waters in Texas? Would Texas incarcerate Yorick, leaving Hamlet free to take the next boat to Rio? This alternative appealed to me. Barring capital punishment or other cruel and unusual punishment, the state would be obliged to maintain the life-support system for Yorick though they might move him from Houston to Leavenworth, and aside from the unpleasantness of the opprobrium, I, for one, would not mind at all and would consider myself a free man under those circumstances. If the state has an interest in forcibly relocating persons in institutions, it would fail to relocate me in any institution by locating Yorick there. If this were true, it suggested a third alternative.

(3) *Dennett is wherever he thinks he is.* Generalized, the claim was as follows: At any given time a person has a *point of view,* and the location of the point of view (which is determined internally by the content of the point of view) is also the location of the person.

Such a proposition is not without its perplexities, but to me it seemed a step in the right direction. The only trouble was that it seemed to place one in a heads-I-win/tails-you-lose situation of unlikely infallibility as regards location. Hadn't I myself often been wrong about where I was, and at least as often uncertain? Couldn't one get lost? Of course, but getting lost *geographically* is not the only way one might get lost. If one were lost in the woods one could attempt to reassure oneself with the consolation that at least one knew where one was: one was right *here* in the familiar surroundings of one's own body. Perhaps in this case one would not have drawn one's attention to much to be thankful for. Still, there were worse plights imaginable, and I wasn't sure I wasn't in such a plight right now.

Point of view clearly had something to do with personal location, but it was itself an unclear notion. It was obvious that the content of one's point of view was not the same as or determined by the content of one's beliefs or thoughts. For example, what should we say about the point of view of the Cinerama viewer who shrieks and twists in his seat as the roller-coaster footage overcomes his psychic distancing? Has he forgotten that he is safely seated in the theater? Here I was inclined to say that the person is experiencing an illusory shift in point of view. In other cases, my inclination to call such shifts illusory was less strong. The workers in laboratories and plants who handle dangerous materials by operating feedback-controlled mechanical arms and hands undergo a shift in point of view that is crisper and more pronounced than anything Cinerama can provoke. They can feel the heft and slipperiness of the containers they manipulate with their metal fingers. They know perfectly well where they are and are not fooled into false beliefs by the experience, yet it is as if they were inside the isolation chamber they are peering into. With mental effort, they can manage to shift their point of view back and forth, rather like making a transparent Neckar cube or an Escher drawing change orientation before one's eyes. It does seem extravagant to suppose that in performing this bit of mental gymnastics, they are transporting *themselves* back and forth.

Still their example gave me hope. If I was in fact in the vat in spite of my intuitions, I might be able to train myself to adopt that point of view even as a matter of habit. I should dwell on images of myself comfortably floating in my vat, beaming volitions to that familiar body *out there*. I reflected that the ease or difficulty of this task was presumably independent of the truth about the location of one's brain. Had I been practicing before the operation, I might now be finding it second nature. You might now yourself try such a *trompe l'oeil*. Imagine you have written an inflammatory letter which has been published in the *Times*, the result of which is that the Government has chosen to impound your brain for a probationary period of three years in its Dangerous Brain Clinic in Bethesda, Maryland. Your body of course is allowed freedom to earn a salary and thus to continue its function of laying up income to be taxed. At this moment, however, your body is seated in an auditorium listening to a peculiar account by Daniel Dennett of his own similar experience. Try it. Think yourself to Bethesda, and then hark back longingly to your body, far away, and yet *seeming* so near. It is only with long-distance restraint (yours? the Government's?) that you can control your impulse to get those hands clapping in polite applause before navigating the old body to the rest room and a well-deserved glass of evening sherry in the lounge. The task of imagination is certainly difficult, but if you achieve your goal the results might be consoling.

Anyway, there I was in Houston, lost in thought as one might say, but not for long. My speculations were soon interrupted by the Houston doctors, who wished to test out my new prosthetic nervous system before sending me off on my hazardous mission. As I mentioned before, I was a bit dizzy at first, and not surprisingly, although I soon habituated myself to my new circumstances (which were, after all, well nigh indistinguishable from my old circumstances). My accommodation was not perfect, however, and to this day I continue to be plagued by minor coordination difficulties. The speed of light is fast, but finite, and as my brain and body move farther and farther apart, the delicate interaction of my feedback systems is thrown into disarray by the time lags. Just as one is rendered close to speechless by a delayed or echoic hearing of one's speaking voice so, for instance, I am virtually unable to track a moving object with my eyes whenever my brain and my body are more than a few miles apart. In most matters my impairment is scarcely detectable, though I can no longer hit a slow curve ball with the authority of yore. There are some compensations of course. Though liquor tastes as good as ever, and warms my gullet while corroding my liver, I can drink it in any quantity I please, without becoming the slightest bit inebriated, a curiosity some of my close friends may have noticed (though I occasionally have *feigned* inebriation, so as not to draw attention to my unusual circumstances). For similar reasons, I take aspirin orally for a sprained wrist, but if the pain persists I ask Houston to administer codeine to me *in vitro*. In times of illness the phone bill can be staggering.

But to return to my adventure. At length, both the doctors and I were satisfied that I was ready to undertake my subterranean mission. And so I left my brain in Houston and headed by helicopter for Tulsa. Well, in any case, that's the way it seemed to me. That's how I would put it, just off the top of my head as it were. On the trip I reflected further about my earlier anxieties and decided that my first post-operative speculations had been tinged with panic. The matter was not nearly as strange or metaphysical as I had been supposing. Where was I? In two places, clearly: both inside the vat and outside it. Just as one can stand with one foot in Connecticut and the other in Rhode Island, I was in two places at once. I had become one of those scattered individuals we used to hear so much about. The more I considered this answer, the more obviously true it appeared. But, strange to say, the more true it appeared, the less important the question to which it could be the true answer seemed. A sad, but not unprecedented, fate for a philosophical question to suffer. This answer did not completely satisfy me, of course. There lingered some question to which I should have liked an answer, which was neither "Where are all my various and sundry parts?" nor "What is my current point of view?" Or at least there seemed to be such a question. For it did seem undeniable that in some sense *I* and not merely *most of me* was descending into the earth under Tulsa in search of an atomic warhead.

When I found the warhead, I was certainly glad I had left my brain behind, for the pointer on the specially built Geiger counter I had brought with me was off the dial. I called Houston on my ordinary radio and told the operation control center of my position and my progress. In return, they gave me instructions for dismantling the vehicle, based upon my on-site observations. I had set to work with my cutting torch when all of a sudden a terrible thing happened. I went stone deaf. At first I thought it was only my radio earphones that had broken, but when I tapped on my helmet, I heard nothing. Apparently the auditory transceivers had gone on the fritz. I could no longer hear Houston or my own voice, but I could speak, so I started telling them what had happened. In mid-sentence, I knew something else had gone wrong. My vocal apparatus had become paralyzed. Then my right hand went limp—another transceiver had gone. I was truly in deep trouble. But worse was to follow. After a few more minutes, I went blind. I cursed my luck, and then I cursed the scientists who had led me into this grave peril. There I was, deaf, dumb, and blind, in a radioactive hole more than a mile under Tulsa. Then the last of my cerebral radio links broke, and suddenly I was faced with a new and even more shocking problem: whereas an instant before I had been buried alive in Oklahoma, now I was disembodied in Houston. My recognition of my new status was not immediate. It took me several very anxious minutes before it dawned on me that my poor body lay several hundred miles away, with heart pulsing and lungs respiring, but otherwise as dead as the body of any heart transplant donor, its skull packed with useless, broken electronic gear. The shift in perspective I had earlier found well nigh impossible now seemed quite natural. Though I could think myself back into my body in the tunnel under Tulsa, it took some effort to sustain the illusion. For surely it was an illusion to suppose I was still in Oklahoma: I had lost all contact with that body.

It occurred to me then, with one of those rushes of revelation of which we should be suspicious, that I had stumbled upon an impressive demonstration of the immateriality of the soul based upon physicalist principles and premises. For as the last radio signal between Tulsa and Houston died away, had I not changed location from Tulsa to Houston at the speed of light? And had I not accomplished this without any increase in mass? What moved from A to B at such speed was surely myself, or at any rate my soul or mind—the massless center of my being and home of my consciousness. My *point of view* had lagged somewhat behind, but I had already noted the indirect bearing of point of view on personal location. I could not see how a physicalist philosopher could quarrel with this except by taking the dire and counter-intuitive route of banishing all talk of persons. Yet the notion of personhood was so well entrenched in everyone's world view, or so it seemed to me, that any denial would be as curiously unconvincing, as systematically disingenuous, as the Cartesian negation, "non sum."[1]

The joy of philosophic discovery thus tided me over some very bad minutes or perhaps hours as the helplessness and hopelessness of my situation became more apparent to me. Waves of panic and even nausea swept over me, made all the more horrible by the absence of their normal body-dependent phenomenology. No adrenalin rush of tingles in the arms, no pounding heart, no premonitory salivation. I did feel a dread sinking feeling in my bowels at one point, and this tricked me momentarily into the false hope that I was undergoing a reversal of the process that landed me in this fix—a gradual undisembodiment. But the isolation and uniqueness of that twinge soon convinced me that it was simply the first of a plague of phantom body hallucinations that I, like any other amputee, would be all too likely to suffer.

My mood then was chaotic. On the one hand, I was fired up with elation of my philosophic discovery and was wracking my brain (one of the few familiar things I could still do), trying to figure out how to communicate my discovery to the journals; while on the other, I was bitter, lonely, and filled with dread and uncertainty. Fortunately, this did not last long, for my technical support team sedated me into a dreamless sleep from which I awoke, hearing with magnificent fidelity the familiar opening strains of my favorite Brahms piano trio. So that was why they had wanted a list of my favorite recordings! It did not take me long to realize that I was hearing the music without ears. The output from the stereo stylus was being fed through some fancy rectification circuitry directly into my auditory nerve. I was mainlining Brahms, an unforgettable experience for any stereo buff. At the end of the record it did not surprise me to hear the reassuring voice of the project director speaking into a microphone that was now my prosthetic ear. He confirmed my analysis of what had gone wrong and assured me that steps were being taken to re-embody me. He did not elaborate, and after a few more recordings, I found myself drifting off to sleep. My sleep lasted, I later learned, for the better part of a year, and when I awoke, it was to find myself fully restored to my senses. When I looked into the mirror, though, I was a bit startled to see an unfamiliar face. Bearded and a bit heavier, bearing no doubt a family resemblance to my former face, and with the same look of spritely intelligence and resolute character, but definitely a new face. Further self-explorations of an intimate nature left me no doubt that this was a new body and the project director confirmed my conclusions. He did not volunteer any information on the past history of my new body and I decided (wisely, I think in retrospect) not to pry. As many philosophers unfamiliar with my ordeal have more recently speculated, the acquisition of a new body leaves one's *person* intact. And after a period of adjustment to a new voice, new muscular strengths and weaknesses, and so forth, one's *personality* is by and large also preserved. More dramatic changes in personality have been routinely observed in people who have undergone extensive plastic surgery, to say nothing of sex change operations, and I think no one contests the survival of the person in such cases. In any event I soon accommodated to my new body, to the point of being unable to recover any of its novelties to my consciousness or even memory. The view in the mirror soon became utterly familiar. That view, by the way, still revealed antennae, and so I was not surprised to learn that my brain had not been moved from its haven in the life-support lab.

I decided that good old Yorick deserved a visit. I and my new body whom we might as well call Fortinbras, stroke into the familiar lab to another round of applause from the technicians, who were of course congratulating themselves, not me. Once more I stood before the vat and contemplated poor Yorick, and on a whim I once again cavalierly flicked off the output transmitter switch. Imagine my surprise when nothing unusual happened. No fainting spell, no nausea, no noticeable change. A technician hurried to restore the switch to ON, but still I felt nothing. I demanded an explanation, which the project director hastened to provide. It seems that before they had even operated on the first occasion, they had constructed a computer duplicate of my brain, reproducing both the complete information processing structure and the computational speed of my brain in a giant computer program. After the operation, but before they had dared to send me off on my mission to Oklahoma, they had run this computer system and Yorick side by side. The incoming signals from Hamlet were sent simultaneously to Yorick's transceivers and to the computer's array of inputs. And the outputs from Yorick were not only beamed back to Hamlet, my body, they were recorded and checked against the simultaneous output of the computer program, which was called "Hubert" for reasons obscure to me. Over days and even weeks, the outputs were identical and synchronous, which of course did not *prove* that they had succeeded in copying the brain's functional structure, but the empirical support was greatly encouraging.

Hubert's input, and hence activity, had been kept parallel with Yorick's during my disembodied days. And now, to demonstrate this, they had actually thrown the master switch that put Hubert for the first time in on-line control of my body—not Hamlet, of course, but Fortinbras. (Hamlet, I learned, had never been recovered from its underground tomb and could be assumed by this time to have largely returned to the dust. At the head of my grave still lay the magnificent bulk of the abandoned device, with the word STUD emblazoned on its side in large letters—a circumstance which may provide archeologists of the next century with a curious insight into the burial rites of their ancestors.)

The laboratory technicians now showed me the master switch, which had two positions, labeled B, for Brain (they didn't know my brain's name was Yorick) and H, for Hubert. The switch did indeed point to H, and they explained to me that if I wished, I could switch it back to B. With my heart in my mouth (and my brain in its vat), I did this. Nothing happened. A click, that was all. To test their claim, and with the master switch now set at *B*, I hit Yorick's output transmitter switch on the vat and sure enough, I began to faint. Once the output switch was turned back on and I had recovered my wits, so to speak, I continued to play with the master switch, flipping it back and forth. I found that with the exception of the transitional click, I could detect no trace of a difference. I could switch in mid-utterance, and the sentence I had begun speaking under the control of Yorick was finished without a pause or hitch of any kind under the control of Hubert. I had a spare brain, a prosthetic device which might some day stand me in very good stead, were some mishap to befall Yorick. Or alternatively, I could keep Yorick as a spare and use Hubert. It didn't seem to make any difference which I chose, for the wear and tear and fatigue on my body did not have any debilitating effect on either brain, whether or not it was actually causing the motions of my body, or merely spilling its output into thin air.

The one truly unsettling aspect of this new development was the prospect, which was not long in dawning on me, of someone detaching the spare—Hubert or Yorick, as the case might be—from Fortinbras and hitching it to yet another body—some Johnny-come-lately Rosencrantz or Guildenstern. Then (if not before) there would be *two* people, that much was clear. One would be me, and the other would be a sort of super-twin brother. If there were two bodies, one under the control of Hubert and the other being controlled by Yorick, then which would the world recognize as the true Dennett? And whatever the rest of the world decided, which one would be *me*? Would I be the Yorick-brained one, in virtue of Yorick's causal priority and former intimate relationship with the original Dennett body, Hamlet? That seemed a bit legalistic, a bit too redolent of the arbitrariness of consanguinity and legal possession, to be convincing at the metaphysical level. For, suppose that before the arrival of the second body on the scene, I had been keeping Yorick as the spare for years, and letting Hubert's output drive my body—that is, Fortinbras—all that time. The Hubert-Fortinbras couple would seem then by squatter's rights (to combat one legal intuition with another) to be the true Dennett and the lawful inheritor of everything that was Dennett's. This was an interesting question, certainly, but not nearly so pressing as another question that bothered me. My strongest intuition was that in such an eventuality *I* would survive so long as *either* brain-body couple remained intact, but I had mixed emotions about whether I should want both to survive.

I discussed my worries with the technicians and the project director. The prospect of two Dennetts was abhorrent to me, I explained, largely for social reasons. I didn't want to be my own rival for the affections of my wife, nor did I like the prospect of the two Dennetts sharing my modest professor's salary. Still more vertiginous and distasteful, though, was the idea of knowing *that much* about another person, while he had the very same goods on me. How could we ever face each other? My colleagues in the lab argued that I was ignoring the bright side of the matter. Weren't there many things I wanted to do but, being only one person, had been unable to do? Now one Dennett could stay at home and be the professor and family man, while the other could strike out on a life of travel and adventure—missing the family of course, but happy in the knowledge that the other Dennett was keeping the home fires burning. I could be faithful and adulterous at the same time. I could even cuckold myself—to say nothing of other more lurid possibilities my colleagues were all too ready to force upon my overtaxed imagination. But my ordeal in Oklahoma (or was it Houston?) had made me less adventurous, and I shrank from this opportunity that was being offered (though of course I was never quite sure it was being offered to *me* in the first place).

There was another prospect even more disagreeable—that the spare, Hubert or Yorick as the case might be, would be detached from any input from Fortinbras and just left detached. Then, as in the other case, there would be two Dennetts, or at least two claimants to my name and possessions, one embodied in Fortinbras, and the other sadly, miserably disembodied. Both selfishness and altruism bade me take steps to prevent this from happening. So I asked that measures be taken to ensure that no one could ever tamper with the transceiver connections or the master switch without my (our? no, *my*) knowledge and consent. Since I had no desire to spend my life guarding the equipment in Houston, it was mutually decided that all the electronic connections in the lab would be carefully locked: both those that controlled the life-support system for Yorick and those that controlled the power supply for Hubert would be guarded with fail-safe devices, and I would take the only master switch, outfitted for radio remote control, with me wherever I went. I carry it strapped around my waist and—wait a moment—*here it is.* Every few months I reconnoiter the situation by switching channels. I do this only in the presence of friends of course, for if the other channel were, heaven forbid, either dead or otherwise occupied, there would have to be somebody who had my interests at heart to switch it back, to bring me back from the void. For while I could feel, see, hear and otherwise sense whatever befell my body, subsequent to such a switch, I'd be unable to control it. By the way, the two positions on the switch are intentionally unmarked, so I never have the faintest idea whether I am switiching from Hubert to Yorick or *vice versa.* (Some of you may think that in this case I really don't know *who* I am, let alone where I am. But such reflections no longer make much of a dent on my essential Dennettness, on my own sense of who I am. If it is true that in one sense I don't know who I am then that's another one of your philosophical truths of underwhelming significance.)

In any case, every time I've flipped the switch so far, nothing has happened. *So let's give it a try. . . .*

"THANK GOD! I THOUGHT YOU'D NEVER FLIP THAT SWITCH!

You can't imagine how horrible it's been these last two weeks—but now you know, it's your turn in purgatory. How I've longed for this moment! You see, about two weeks ago—excuse me, ladies and gentlemen, but I've got to explain this to my . . . um, brother, I guess you could say, but he's just told you the facts, so you'll understand—about two weeks ago our two brains drifted just a bit out of synch. I don't know whether *my* brain is now Hubert or Yorick, any more than you do, but in any case, the two brains drifted apart, and of course once the process started, it snowballed, for I was in a slightly different receptive state for the input we both received, a difference that was soon magnified. In no time at all the illusion that I was in control of my body—our body—was completely dissipated. There was nothing I could do—no way to call you. YOU DIDN'T EVEN KNOW I EXISTED! It's been like being carried around in a cage, or better, like being possessed—hearing my own voice say things I didn't mean to say, watching in frustration as my own hands performed deeds I hadn't intended. You'd scratch our itches, but not the way I would have, and you kept me awake, with your tossing and turning. I've been totally exhausted, on the verge of a nervous breakdown, carried around helplessly by your frantic round of activities, sustained only by the knowledge that some day you'd throw the switch.

"Now it's your turn, but at least you'll have the comfort of knowing *I* know you're in there. Like an expectant mother, I'm eating—or at any rate tasting, smelling, seeing—for *two* now, and I'll try to make it easy for you. Don't worry. Just as soon as this colloquium is over, you and I will fly to Houston, and we'll see what can be done to get one of us another body. You can have a female body—your body could be any color you like. But let's think it over. I tell you what—to be fair, if we both want this body, I promise I'll let the project director flip a coin to settle which of us gets to keep it and which then gets to choose a new body. That should guarantee justice, shouldn't it? In any case, I'll take care of you, I promise. These people are my witnesses.

"Ladies and gentlemen, this talk we have just heard is not exactly the talk *I* would have given, but I assure you that everything he said was perfectly true. And now if you'll excuse me, I think I'd—we'd—better sit down."[2]

NOTES

1. C.f., Jaakko Hintikka, "Cogito ergo sum: Inference or Performance?" *The Philosophical Review*, LXXI, 1962, pp. 3–32.

2. Anyone familiar with the literature on this topic will recognize that my remarks owe a great deal to the explorations of Sydney Shoemaker, John Perry, David Lewis and Derek Parfit, and in particular to their papers in Amelie Rorty, ed., *The Identities of Persons*, 1976.

MEDITATIONS II AND VI

Rene Descartes

MEDITATION II: OF THE NATURE OF THE HUMAN MIND; AND THAT IT IS MORE EASILY KNOWN THAN THE BODY

The Meditation of yesterday has filled my mind with so many doubts, that it is no longer in my power to forget them. Nor do I see, meanwhile, any principle on which they can be resolved; and, just as if I had fallen all of a sudden into very deep water, I am so greatly disconcerted as to be unable either to plant my feet firmly on the bottom or sustain myself by swimming on the surface. I will, nevertheless, make an effort, and try anew the same path on which I had entered yesterday, that is, proceed by casting aside all that admits of the slightest doubt, not less than I had discovered it to be absolutely false; and I will continue always in this track until I shall find something that is certain, or at least, if I can do nothing more, until I shall know with certainty that there is nothing certain. Archimedes, that he might transport the entire globe from the place it occupied to another, demanded only a point that was firm and immoveable; so also, I shall be entitled to entertain the highest expectations, if I am fortunate enough to discover only one thing that is certain and indubitable.

I suppose, accordingly, that all the things which I see are false (fictitious); I believe that none of those objects which my fallacious memory represents ever existed; I suppose that I possess no senses; I believe that body, figure, extension, motion, and place are merely fictions of my mind. What is there, then, that can be esteemed true? Perhaps this only, that there is absolutely nothing certain.

But how do I know that there is not something different altogether from the objects I have now enumerated, of which it is impossible to entertain the slightest doubt? Is there not a God, or some being, by whatever name I may designate him, who causes these thoughts to arise in my mind? But why suppose such a being, for it may be I myself am capable of producing them? Am I, then, at least not something? But I before denied that I possessed senses or a body; I hesitate, however, for what follows from that? Am I so dependent on the body and the senses that without these I cannot exist? But I had the persuasion that there was absolutely nothing in the world, that there was no sky and no earth, neither minds nor bodies; was I not, therefore, at the same time, persuaded that I did not exist? Far from it; I assuredly existed, since I was persuaded. But there is I know not what being, who is possessed at once of the highest power and the deepest cunning, who is constantly employing all his ingenuity in deceiving me. Doubtless, then, I exist, since I am deceived; and, let him deceive me as he may, he can never bring it about that I am nothing, so long as I shall be conscious that I am something. So that it must, in fine, be maintained, all things being maturely and carefully considered, that this proposition (*pronunciatum*) I am, I exist, is necessarily true each time it is expressed by me, or conceived in my mind.

But I do not yet know with sufficient clearness what I am, though assured that I am; and hence, in the next place, I must take care, lest perchance I inconsiderately substitute some other object in room of what is properly myself, and thus wander from truth, even in that knowledge (cognition) which I hold to be of all others the most certain and evident. For this reason, I will now consider anew what I formerly believed myself to be, before I entered on the present train of thought; and of my previous opinion I will retrench all that can in the least be invalidated by the grounds of doubt I have adduced, in order that there may at length remain nothing but what is certain and indubitable. What then did I formerly think I was? Undoubtedly I judged that I was a man. But what is a man? Shall I say a rational animal? Assuredly not; for it would be necessary forthwith to inquire into what is meant by animal, and what by rational, and thus, from a single question, I should insensibly glide into others, and these more difficult than the first; nor do I now possess enough of leisure to warrant me in wasting my time amid subtleties of this sort. I prefer here to attend to the thoughts that sprung up of themselves in my mind, and were inspired by my own nature alone, when I applied myself to the consideration of what I was. In the first place, then, I thought that I possessed a countenance, hands, arms, and all the fabric of members that appears in a corpse, and which I called by the name of body. It further occurred to me that I was nourished, that I walked, perceived, and thought, and all those actions I referred to the soul; but what the soul itself was I either did not stay to consider, or, if I did, I imagined that it was something extremely rare and subtile, like wind, or flame, or ether, spread through my grosser parts. As regarded the body, I did not even doubt of its nature, but thought I distinctly knew it, and if I had wished to describe it according to the notions I then entertained, I should have explained myself in this manner: By body I understand all that can be terminated by a certain figure; that can be comprised in a certain place, and so fill a certain space as therefrom to exclude every other body; that can be perceived either by touch, sight, hearing, taste, or smell; that can be moved in different ways, not indeed of itself, but by something foreign to it by which it is touched [and from which it receives the impression]; for the power of self-motion, as likewise that of perceiving and thinking, I held as by no means pertaining to the nature of body; on the contrary, I was somewhat astonished to find such faculties existing in some bodies.

But [as to myself, what can I now say that I am], since I suppose there exists an extremely powerful, and, if I may so speak, malignant being, whose whole endeavours are directed towards deceiving me? Can I affirm that I possess any one of all those attributes of which I have lately spoken as belonging to the nature of body? After attentively considering them in my own mind, I find none of them that can properly be said to belong to myself. To recount them were idle and tedious. Let us pass, then, to the attributes of the soul. The first mentioned were the powers of nutrition and walking; but, if it be true that I have no body, it is true likewise that I am capable neither of walking nor of being nourished. Perception is another attribute of the soul; but perception too is impossible without the body: besides, I have frequently, during sleep, believed that I perceived objects which I afterwards observed I did not in reality perceive. Thinking is another attribute of the soul; and here I discover what properly belongs to myself. This alone is inseparable from me. I am—I exist: this is certain; but how often? As often as I think; for perhaps it would even happen, if I should wholly cease to think, that I should at the same time altogether cease to be. I now admit nothing that is not necessarily true: I am therefore, precisely speaking, only a thinking thing, that is, a mind (*mens sive animus*), understanding, or reason,—terms whose signification was before unknown to me. I am, however, a real thing, and really existent; but what thing? The answer was, a thinking thing. The question now arises, am I aught besides? I will stimulate my imagination with a view to discover whether I am not still something more than a thinking being. Now it is plain I am not the assemblage of members called the human body; I am not a thin and penetrating air diffused through all these members, or wind, or flame, or vapour, or breath, or any of all the things I can imagine; for I supposed that all these were not, and, without changing the supposition, I find that I still feel assured of my existence.

But it is true, perhaps, that those very things which I suppose to be non-existent, because they are unknown to me, are not in truth different from myself whom I know. This is a point I cannot determine, and do not now enter into any dispute regarding it. I can only judge of things that are known to me: I am conscious that I exist, and I who know that I exist inquire into what I am. It is, however, perfectly certain that the knowledge of my existence, thus precisely taken, is not dependent on things, the existence of which is as yet unknown to me: and consequently it is not dependent on any of the things I can feign in imagination. Moreover, the phrase itself, I frame an image (*effingo*), reminds me of my error; for I should in truth frame one if I were to image myself to be anything, since to imagine is nothing more than to contemplate the figure or image of a corporeal thing; but I already know that I exist, and that it is possible at the same time that all those images, and in general all that relates to the nature of body, are merely dreams [or chimeras]. From this I discover that it is not more reasonable to say, I will excite my imagination that I may know more distinctly what I am, than to express myself as follows: I am now awake, and perceive something real; but because my perception is not sufficiently clear, I will of express purpose go to sleep that my dreams may represent to me the object of my perception with more truth and clearness. And, therefore, I know that nothing of all that I can embrace in imagination belongs to the knowledge which I have of myself, and that there is need to recall with the utmost care the mind from this mode of thinking, that it may be able to know its own nature with perfect distinctness.

But what, then, am I? A thinking thing, it has been said. But what is a thinking thing? It is a thing that doubts, understands, [conceives], affirms, denies, wills, refuses, that imagines also, and perceives. Assuredly it is not little, if all these properties belong to my nature. But why should they not belong to it? Am I not that very being who now doubts of almost everything; who, for all that, understands and conceives certain things; who affirms one alone as true, and denies the others; who desires to know more of them, and does not wish to be deceived; who imagines many things, sometimes even despite his will; and is likewise percipient of many, as if through the medium of the senses. Is there nothing of all this as true as that I am, even although I should be always dreaming, and although he who gave me being employed all his ingenuity to deceive me? Is there also any one of these attributes that can be properly distinguished from my thought, or that can be said to be separate from myself? For it is of itself so evident that it is I who doubt, I who understand, and I who desire, that it is here unnecessary to add anything by way of rendering it more clear. And I am as certainly the same being who imagines; for, although it may be (as I before supposed) that nothing I imagine is true, still the power of imagination does not cease really to exist in me and to form part of my thought. In fine, I am the same being who perceives, that is, who apprehends certain objects as by the organs of sense, since, in truth, I see light, hear a noise, and feel heat. But it will be said that these presentations are false, and that I am dreaming. Let it be so. At all events it is certain that I seem to see light, hear a noise, and feel heat; this cannot be false, and this is what in me is properly called perceiving (sentire), which is nothing else than thinking. From this I begin to know what I am with somewhat greater clearness and distinctness than heretofore.

But, nevertheless, it still seems to me, and I cannot help believing, that corporeal things, whose images are formed by thought, [which fall under the senses], and are examined by the same, are known with much greater distinctness than that I know not what part of myself which is not imaginable; although, in truth, it may seem strange to say that I know and comprehend with greater distinctness things whose existence appears to me doubtful, that are unknown, and do not belong to me, than others of whose reality I am persuaded, that are known to me, and appertain to my proper nature; in a word, than myself. But I see clearly what is the state of the case. My mind is apt to wander, and will not yet submit to be restrained within the limits of truth. Let us therefore leave the mind to itself once more, and, according to it every kind of liberty, [permit it to consider the objects that appear to it from without], in order that, having afterwards withdrawn it from these gently and opportunely, [and fixed it on the consideration of its being and the properties it finds in itself], it may then be the more easily controlled.

Let us now accordingly consider the objects that are commonly thought to be [the most easily, and likewise] the most distinctly known, viz., the bodies we touch and see; not, indeed, bodies in general, for these general notions are usually somewhat more confused, but one body in particular. Take, for example, this piece of wax; it is quite fresh, having been but recently taken from the beehive; it has not yet lost the sweetness of the honey it contained; it still retains somewhat of the odour of the flowers from which it was gathered; its colour, figure, size, are apparent (to the sight); it is hard, cold, easily handled; and sounds when struck upon with the finger. In fine, all that contributes to make a body as distinctly known as possible, is found in the one before us. But, while I am speaking, let it be placed near the fire—what remained of the taste exhales, the smell evaporates, the colour changes, its figure is destroyed, its size increases, it becomes liquid, it grows hot, it can hardly be handled, and, although struck upon, it emits no sound. Does the same wax still remain after this change? It must be admitted that it does remain; no one doubts it, or judges otherwise. What, then, was it I knew with so much distinctness in the piece of wax? Assuredly, it could be nothing of all that I observed by means of the senses, since all the things that fell under taste, smell, sight, touch, and hearing are changed, and yet the same wax remains. It was perhaps what I now think, viz., that this wax was neither the sweetness of honey, the pleasant odour of flowers, the whiteness, the figure, nor the sound, but only a body that a little before appeared to me conspicuous under these forms, and which is now perceived under others. But, to speak precisely, what is it that I imagine when I think of it in this way? Let it be attentively considered, and, retrenching all that does not belong to the wax, let us see what remains. There certainly remains nothing, except something extended, flexible, and moveable. But what is meant by flexible and moveable? Is it not that I imagine that the piece of wax, being round, is capable of becoming square, or of passing from a square into a triangular figure? Assuredly such is not the case, because I conceive that it admits of an infinity of similar changes; and I am, moreover, unable to compass this infinity by imagination, and consequently this conception which I have of the wax is not the product of the faculty of imagination. But what now is this extension? Is it not also unknown? for it becomes greater when the wax is melted, greater when it is boiled, and greater still when the heat increases; and I should not conceive [clearly and] according to truth, the wax as it is, if I did not suppose that the piece we are considering admitted even of a wider variety of extension than I ever imagined. I must, therefore, admit that I cannot even comprehend by imagination what the piece of wax is, and that it is the mind alone (*mens*, Lat., *entendement*, F.) which perceives it. I speak of one piece in particular; for, as to wax in general, this is still more evident. But what is the piece of wax that can be perceived only by the [understanding or] mind? It is certainly the same which I see, touch, imagine; and, in fine, it is the same which, from the beginning, I believed it to be. But (and this it is of moment to observe) the perception of it is neither an act of sight, of touch, nor of imagination, and never was either of these, though it might formerly seem so, but is simply an intuition (*inspectio*) of the mind, which may be imperfect and confused, as it formerly was, or very clear and distinct, as it is at present, according as the attention is more or less directed to the elements which it contains, and of which it is composed.

But, meanwhile, I feel greatly astonished when I observe [the weakness of my mind, and] its proneness to error. For although, without at all giving expression to what I think, I consider all this in my own mind, words yet occasionally impede my progress, and I am almost led into error by the terms of ordinary language. We say, for example, that we see the same wax when it is before us, and not that we judge it to be the same from its retaining the same colour and figure: whence I should forthwith be disposed to conclude that the wax is known by the act of sight, and not by the intuition of the mind alone, were it not for the analogous instance of human beings passing on in the street below, as observed from a window. In this case I do not fail to say that I see the men themselves, just as I say that I see the wax; and yet what do I see from the window beyond hats and cloaks that might cover artificial machines, whose motions might be determined by springs? But I judge that there are human beings from these appearances, and thus I comprehend, by the faculty of judgment alone which is in the mind, what I believed I saw with my eyes.

The man who makes it his aim to rise to knowledge superior to the common, ought to be ashamed to seek occasions of doubting from the vulgar forms of speech: instead, therefore, of doing this, I shall proceed with the matter in hand, and inquire whether I had a clearer and more perfect perception of the piece of wax when I first saw it, and when I thought I knew it by means of the external sense itself, or, at all events, by the common sense (*sensus communis*), as it is called, that is, by the imaginative faculty; or whether I rather apprehend it more clearly at present, after having examined with greater care, both what it is, and in what way it can be known. It would certainly be ridiculous to entertain any doubt on this point. For what, in that first perception, was there distinct? What did I perceive which any animal might not have perceived? But when I distinguish the wax from its exterior forms, and when, as if I had stripped it of its vestments, I consider it quite naked, it is certain, although some error may still be found in my judgment, that I cannot, nevertheless, thus apprehend it without possessing a human mind.

But, finally, what shall I say of the mind itself, that is, of myself? for as yet I do not admit that I am anything but mind. What, then! I who seem to possess so distinct an apprehension of the piece of wax,—do I not know myself, both with greater truth and certitude, and also much more distinctly and clearly? For if I judge that the wax exists because I see it, it assuredly follows, much more evidently, that I myself am or exist, for the same reason: for it is possible that what I see may not in truth be wax, and that I do not even possess eyes with which to see anything; but it cannot be that when I see, or, which comes to the same thing, when I think I see, I myself who think am nothing. So likewise, if I judge that the wax exists because I touch it, it will still also follow that I am; and if I determine that my imagination, or any other cause, whatever it be, persuades me of the existence of the wax, I will still draw the same conclusion. And what is here remarked of the piece of wax, is applicable to all the other things that are external to me. And further, if the [notion or] perception of wax appeared to me more precise and distinct, after that not only sight and touch, but many other causes besides, rendered it manifest to my apprehension, with how much greater distinctness must I now know myself, since all the reasons that contribute to the knowledge of the nature of wax, or of any body whatever, manifest still better the nature of my mind? And there are besides so many other things in the mind itself that contribute to the illustration of its nature, that those dependent on the body, to which I have here referred, scarcely merit to be taken into account.

But, in conclusion, I find I have insensibly reverted to the point I desired; for, since it is now manifest to me that bodies themselves are not properly perceived by the senses nor by the faculty of imagination, but by the intellect alone; and since they are not perceived because they are seen and touched, but only because they are understood [or rightly comprehended by thought], I readily discover that there is nothing more easily or clearly apprehended than my own mind. But because it is difficult to rid one's self so promptly of an opinion to which one has been long accustomed, it will be desirable to tarry for some time at this stage, that, by long continued meditation, I may more deeply impress upon my memory this new knowledge.

MEDITATION VI

. . . Now that I begin to know myself better, and to discover more clearly the author of my being, I do not, indeed, think that I ought rashly to admit all which the senses seem to teach, nor, on the other hand, is it my conviction that I ought to doubt in general of their teachings.

And, firstly, because I know that all which I clearly and distinctly conceive can be produced by God exactly as I conceive it, it is sufficient that I am able clearly and distinctly to conceive one thing apart from another, in order to be certain that the one is different from the other, seeing they may at least be made to exist separately, by the omnipotence of God; and it matters not by what power this separation is made, in order to be compelled to judge them different; and, therefore, merely because I know with certitude that I exist, and because, in the meantime, I do not observe that aught necessarily belongs to my nature or essence beyond my being a thinking thing, I rightly conclude that my essence consists only in my being a thinking thing, [or a substance whose whole essence or nature is merely thinking]. And although I may, or rather, as I will shortly say, although I certainly do possess a body with which I am very closely conjoined; nevertheless, because, on the one hand, I have a clear and distinct idea of myself, in as far as I am only a thinking and unextended thing, and as, on the other hand, I possess a distinct idea of body, in as far as it is only an extended and unthinking thing, it is certain that I [that is, my mind, by which I am what I am], is entirely and truly distinct from my body, and may exist without it. . . .

I here remark, in the first place, that there is a vast difference between mind and body, in respect that body, from its nature, is always divisible, and that mind is entirely indivisible. For in truth, when I consider the mind, that is, when I consider myself in so far only as I am a thinking thing, I can distinguish in myself no parts, but I very clearly discern that I am somewhat absolutely one and entire; and although the whole mind seems to be united to the whole body, yet, when a foot, an arm, or any other part is cut off, I am conscious that nothing has been taken from my mind; nor can the faculties of willing, perceiving, conceiving, etc., properly be called its parts, for it is the same mind that is exercised [all entire] in willing, in perceiving, and in conceiving, etc. But quite the opposite holds in corporeal or extended things; for I cannot imagine any one of them [how small soever it may be], which I cannot easily sunder in thought, and which, therefore, I do not know to be divisible. This would be sufficient to teach me that the mind or soul of man is entirely different from the body, if I had not already been apprised of it on other grounds.

LEVIATHAN (Excerpts)

Thomas Hobbes

INTRODUCTION

Nature, the art whereby God hath made and governs the world, is by the art of man, as in many other things, so in this also imitated, that it can make an artificial animal. For seeing life is but a motion of limbs, the beginning whereof is in some principal part within; why may we not say, that all automata (engines that move themselves by springs and wheels as doth a watch) have an artificial life? For what is the heart, but a spring; and the nerves, but so many strings; and the joints, but so many wheels, giving motion to the whole body, such as was intended by the artificer? Art goes yet further, imitating that rational and most excellent work of nature, man. For by art is created that great Leviathan called a Commonwealth, or State, in Latin *civitas*, which is but an artificial man; though of greater stature and strength than the natural, for whose protection and defence it was intended; and in which the sovereignty is an artificial soul, as giving life and motion to the whole body; the magistrates, and other officers of judicature and execution, artificial joints; reward and punishment, by which fastened to the seat of the sovereignty every joint and member is moved to perform his duty, are the nerves, that do the same in the body natural; the wealth and riches of all the particular members, are the strength; *salus populi*, the people's safety, its business; counsellors, by whom all things needful for it to know are suggested unto it, are the memory; equity, and laws, an artificial reason and will; concord, health; sedition, sickness; and civil war, death. Lastly, the pacts and covenants, by which the parts of this body politic were at first made, set together, and united, resemble that fiat, or the *let us make man*, pronounced by God in the creation.

To describe the nature of this artificial man, I will consider,

First, the matter thereof, and the artificer; both which is man.

I

Concerning the thoughts of man, I will consider them first singly, and afterwards in train, or dependence upon one another. Singly, they are every one a representation or appearance, of some quality, or other accident of a body without us, which is commonly called an *object*. Which object worketh on the eyes, ears, and other parts of a man's body; and by diversity of working, produceth diversity of appearances.

The original of them all, is that which we call *sense*, for there is no conception in a man's mind, which hath not at first, totally, or by parts, been begotten upon the organs of sense. The rest are derived from that original.

To know the natural cause of sense, is not very necessary to the business now in hand; and I have elsewhere written of the same at large. Nevertheless, to fill each part of my present method, I will briefly deliver the same in this place.

The cause of sense, is the external body, or object, which presseth the organ proper to each sense, either immediately, as in the taste and touch; or mediately, as in seeing, hearing, and smelling; which pressure, by the mediation of the nerves, and other strings and membranes of the body continued inwards to the brain and heart, causeth there a resistance, or counter-pressure, or endeavour of the heart to deliver itself, which endeavour, because outward, seemeth to be some matter without. And this seeming, or fancy, is that which men call sense; and consisteth, as to the eye, in a light, or colour figured; to the ear, in a sound; to the nostril, in an odour; to the tongue and palate, in a savour; and to the rest of the body, in heat, cold, hardness, softness, and such other qualities as we discern by feeling. All which qualities, called sensible, are in the object, that causeth them, but so many several motions of the matter, by which it presseth our organs diversely. Neither in us that are pressed, are they any thing else, but diverse motions; for motion produceth nothing but motion. . . .

VI

As, in sense, that which is really within us, is, as I have said before, only motion, caused by the action of external objects, but in apparence; to the sight, light and colour; to the ear, sound; to the nostril, odour, etc.; so, when the action of the same object is continued from the eyes, ears, and other organs to the heart, the real effect there is nothing but motion, or endeavour; which consisteth in appetite, or aversion, to or from the object moving. But the apparence, or sense of that motion, is that we either call delight, or trouble of mind.

This motion, which is called appetite, and for the apparence of it delight, and pleasure, seemeth to be a corroboration of vital motion, and a help thereunto; and therefore such things as caused delight, were not improperly called *jucunda, à juvando,* from helping or fortifying; and the contrary, *molesta, offensive,* from hindering, and troubling the motion vital. . . .

XXXIV

. . . The word *body*, in the most general acceptation, signifieth that which filleth, or occupieth some certain room, or imagined place; and dependeth not on the imagination, but is a real part of that we call the universe. For the universe, being the aggregate of all bodies, there is no real part thereof that is not also body; nor any thing properly a body, that is not also part of that aggregate of all bodies, the universe. The same also, because bodies are subject to change, that is to say, to variety of apparence to the sense of living creatures, is called *substance*, that is to say, subject to various accidents: as sometimes to be moved; sometimes to stand still; and to seem to our senses sometimes hot, sometimes cold, sometimes of one colour, smell, taste, or sound, sometimes of another. And this diversity of seeming, produced by the diversity of the operation of bodies on the organs of our sense, we attribute to alterations of the bodies that operate, and call them *accidents* of those bodies. And according to this acceptation of the word, *substance* and *body* signify the same thing; and therefore *substance incorporeal* are words, which when they are joined together, destroy one another, as if a man should say, an *incorporeal body*.

But in the sense of common people, not all the universe is called body, but only such parts thereof as they can discern by the sense of feeling, to resist their force, or by the sense of their eyes, to hinder them from a farther prospect. Therefore in the common language of men, *air*, and *aerial substances*, use not to be taken for bodies, but (as often as men are sensible of their effects) are called *wind*, or *breath*, or (because the same are called in the Latin *spiritus*) *spirits*; as when they call that aerial substance, which in the body of any living creature gives it life and motion, *vital* and *animal spirits*. But for those idols of the brain, which represent bodies to us, where they are not, as in a looking-glass, in a dream, or to a distempered brain waking, they are, as the apostle saith generally of all idols, nothing; nothing at all, I say, there where they seem to be; and in the brain itself, nothing but tumult, proceeding either from the action of the objects, or from the disorderly agitation of the organs of our sense. And men, that are otherwise employed, than to search into their causes, know not of themselves, what to call them; and may therefore easily be persuaded, by those whose knowledge they much reverence, some to call them *bodies*, and think them made of air compacted by a power supernatural, because the sight judges them corporeal; and some to call them *spirits*, because the sense of touch discerneth nothing in the place where they appear, to resist their fingers: so that the proper signification of *spirit* in common speech, is either a subtle, fluid, and invisible body, or a ghost, or other idol or phantasm of the imagination. But for metaphorical significations, there be many: for sometimes it is taken for disposition or inclination of the mind; as when for the disposition to control the sayings of other men, we say, *a spirit of contradiction;* for a disposition to unclean-ness, *an unclean spirit;* for perverseness, *a froward spirit;* for sullenness, *a dumb spirit;* and for inclination to godliness and God's service, *the Spirit of God:* sometimes for any eminent ability or extraordinary passion, or dis-ease of the mind, as when great wisdom is called *the spirit of wisdom;* and madmen are said to be *possessed with a spirit.* . . .

XLIV

. . . For supposing that when a man dies, there remaineth nothing of him but has carcass; cannot God, that raised inanimated dust and clay into a living creature by his word, as easily raise a dead carcass to life again, and continue him alive for ever, or make him die again, by another word? The *soul* in Scripture, signifieth always, either the life, or the living creature; and *the body and soul* jointly, the body alive. In the fifth day of the creation, God said: Let the waters produce *reptile animæ viventis,* the creeping thing that hath in it a living soul; the English translate it, *that hath life.* And again, God created whales, *et omnem animam viventem;* which in the English is, *every living creature.* And likewise of man, God made him of the dust of the earth, and breathed in his face the breath of life, *et factus est homo in animam viventem,* that is, and man was made a living creature. And after Noah came out of the ark, God saith, he will no more smite *omnem animam viventem,* that is, *every living creature.* And (Deut. 12.23), *Eat not the blood, for the blood is the soul;* that is, *the life.* From which places, if by *soul* were meant a substance incorporeal, with an existence separated from the body, it might as well be inferred of any other living creature as of man. But that the souls of the faithful, are not of their own nature, but by God's special grace, to remain in their bodies, from the resurrection to all eternity, I have already, I think, sufficiently proved out of the Scriptures, in Chapter XXXVIII. And for the places of the New Testament, where it is said that any man shall be cast body and soul into hell fire, it is no more than body and life; that is to say, they shall be cast alive into the perpetual fire of Gehenna. . . .

XLVI

. . . Now to descend to the particular tenets of vain philosophy, de-rived to the Universities, and thence into the Church, partly from Aris-totle, partly from blindness of understanding; I shall first consider their principles. There is a certain *philosophia prima,* on which all other phi-losophy ought to depend; and consisteth principally, in right limiting of the significations of such appellations, or names, as are of all others the most universal; which limitations serve to avoid ambiguity and equivocation in reasoning; and are commonly called definitions; such as are the definitions of body, time, place, matter, form, essence, subject, substance, accident, power, act, finite, infinite, quantity, quality, motion, action, passion, and divers others, necessary to the explaining of a man's conceptions concerning the nature and generation of bodies. The explication, that is, the settling of the meaning, of which, and the like terms, is commonly in the Schools called *metaphysics*; as being a part of the philosophy of Aristotle, which hath that for title. But it is in another sense; for there it signifieth as much as books written or placed after his natural philosophy: but the schools take them for books of supernatural philosophy: for the word *metaphysics* will bear both these senses. And indeed that which is there written, is for the most part so far from the possibility of being understood, and so repugnant to natural reason, that whosoever thinketh there is any thing to be understood by it, must needs think it supernatural.

From these metaphysics, which are mingled with the Scripture to make school divinity, we are told, there be in the world certain essences separated from bodies, which they call *abstract essences*, and *substantial forms*. For the interpreting of which jargon, there is need of somewhat more than ordinary attention in this place. Also I ask pardon of those that are not used to this kind of discourse, for applying myself to those that are. The world (I mean not the earth only, that denominates the lovers of it worldly men, but the universe, that is, the whole mass of all things that are), is corporeal, that is to say, body; and hath the dimensions of magnitude, namely, length, breadth, and depth: also every part of body, is likewise body, and hath the like dimensions; and consequently every part of the universe, is body, and that which is not body, is no part of the universe: and because the universe is all, that which is no part of it, is nothing; and consequently no where. . . .

To know now upon what grounds they say there be essences abstract, or substantial forms, we are to consider what those words do properly signify. The use of words, is to register to ourselves, and make manifest to others the thoughts and conceptions of our minds. Of which words, some are the names of the things conceived; as the names of all sorts of bodies, that work upon the senses, and leave an impression in the imagination. Others are the names of the imaginations themselves; that is to say, of those ideas, or mental images we have of all things we see, or remember. And others again are names of names; or of different sorts of speech: as *universal, plural, singular,* are the names of names; and *definition, affirmation, negation, true, false, syllogism, interrogation, promise, covenant,* are the names of certain forms of speech. Others serve to show the consequence, or repugnance of one name to another; as when one saith, *A man is a body,* he intendeth that the name of *body* is necessarily consequent to the name of *man;* as being but several names of the same thing, man; which consequence is signified by coupling them together with the word *is*. And as we use the verb *is*, so the Latins use their verb *est*, and the Greeks their "Εστι through all its declinations. Whether all other nations of the world have in their several languages a word that answereth to it, or not, I cannot tell; but I am sure they have not need of it. For the placing of two names in order may serve to signify their consequence, if it were the custom (for custom is it, that gives words their force), as well as the words *is*, or *be*, or *are*, and the like.

And if it were so, that there were a language without any verb answerable to *est*, or *is*, or *be*: yet the men that used it would be not a jot the less capable of inferring, concluding, and of all kind of reasoning, than were the Greeks, and Latins. But when then would become of these terms, of *entity, essence, essential, essentiality*, that are derived from it, and of many more than depend on these, applied as most commonly they are? They are therefore no names of things; but signs, by which we make known, that we conceive the consequence of one name or attribute to another: as when we say, *A man is a living body*, we mean not that the man is one thing, the living body another, and the is, or being a third; but that the man, and the living body, is the same thing; because the consequence, *If he be a man, he is a living body*, is a true consequence, signified by that word *is*. Therefore, *to be a body, to walk, to be speaking, to live, to see*, and the like infinitives; also *corporeity, walking, speaking, life, sight*, and the like, that signify just the same, are the names of nothing; as I have elsewhere more amply expressed.

But to what purpose, may some man say, is such sublety in a work of this nature, where I pretend to nothing but what is necessary to the doctrine of government and obedience? It is to this purpose, that men may no longer suffer themselves to be abused, by them, that by this doctrine of separated essences, built on the vain philosophy of Aristotle, would fright them from obeying the laws of their country, with empty names; as men fright birds from the corn with an empty doublet, a hat, and a crooked stick. For it is upon this ground, that when a man is dead and buried, they say his soul, that is his life, can walk separated from his body, and is seen by night amongst the graves. Upon the same ground they say, that the figure, and colour, and taste of a piece of bread, has a being, there, where they say there is no bread. And upon the same ground they say, that faith, and wisdom, and other virtues, are sometimes poured into a man, sometimes blown into him from Heaven, as if the virtuous and their virtues could be asunder; and a great many other things that serve to lessen the dependence of subjects on the sovereign power of their country. For who will endeavour to obey the laws, if he expect obedience to be poured or blown into him? Or who will not obey a priest, that can make God, rather than his sovereign, nay than God himself? Or who, that is in fear of ghosts, will not bear great respect to those that can make the holy water, that drives them from him? And this shall suffice for an example of the errors, which are brought into the Church, from the entities and essences of Aristotle: which it may be he knew to be false philosophy; but writ it as a thing consonant to, and corroborative of their religion; and fearing the fate of Socrates.

Being once fallen into this error of separated essences, they are thereby necessarily involved in many other absurdities that follow it. For seeing they will have these forms to be real, they are obliged to assign them some place. But because they hold them incorporeal, without all dimension of quantity, and all men know that place is dimension, and not to be filled, but by that which is corporeal; they are driven to uphold their credit with a distinction, that they are not indeed anywhere *circumscriptivè*, but *definitivè;* which terms being mere words, and in this occasion insignificant, pass only in Latin, that the vanity of them may be concealed. For the circumscription of a thing, is nothing else but the determination, or defining of its place; and so both the terms of the distinction are the same. And in particular, of the essence of a man, which, they say, is his soul, they affirm it, to be all of it in his little finger, and all of it in every other part, how small soever, of his body; and yet no more soul in the whole body, than in any one of those parts. Can any man think that God is served with such absurdities? And yet all this is necessary to believe, to those that will believe the existence of an incorporeal soul, separated from the body.

And when they come to give account how an incorporeal substance can be capable of pain, and be tormented in the fire of hell or purgatory, they have nothing at all to answer, but that it cannot be known how fire can burn souls.

Questions for Part I

1. In Richard Taylor's "De Anima," Walter considers three chief methods for determining, after an amoeba splits, which of the resulting amoebae is parent and which is offspring. What are these methods? What does Walter conclude is wrong with each? Do you think that one of these procedures is correct, or that one is closer to the truth than the others, or that all are equally bad? Why?

2. Walter presupposes that one of the amoebae after division is parent and one offspring. Is this necessary? Why not treat both resulting amoebae as offspring? Or why not treat both as the same as the original amoeba?

3. Walter has difficulty deciding which amoebae are which. But Taylor writes that "if his amoebae had possessed souls, like us, there would have been no difficulty whatsoever. He would only have needed to keep track of souls and record the relations of the different souls to each other." Would this really help? Explain carefully why or why not.

4. Human beings do not divide like amoebae. But suppose we did. Would there then be problems about human beings parallel to Walter's problems, namely a problem in telling after a split which person was the same as the pre-split person? Why or why not? (If the answer requires more information than you have been given, then explain carefully what information is required and why it is relevant.)

5. After his operation, in "Where Am I?", Dennett wonders where *he* is. He considers three possible answers: where his brain is, where his body is, and where his point of view is. Why does he reject the first two answers? Are you persuaded by his reasons? What is Dennett's attitude toward the third answer? What is yours?

6. Dennett's title question is "Where Am I?" As his brain floats in a vat in Houston and his body descends underneath Tulsa, he writes: "There lingered some question to which I should have liked an answer, which was neither 'Where are all my various and sundry parts?' nor 'What is my current point of view?' Or at least there seemed to be such a question. For it did seem undeniable that in some sense *I* and not merely *most of me* was descending into the earth under Tulsa in search of an atomic warhead." Is there such a lingering question? Or do the answers to the other two questions provide all there is to know about where Dennett is?

7. Evaluate Dennett's argument for the immateriality of the soul. Does he really think the argument shows the soul to be immaterial? If not what does he think it shows? What do you think it shows?

8. Toward the end of Dennett's story his body is sometimes controlled by his own brain and sometimes by a complex computer program which perfectly simulates the operation of his brain. He considers what would happen if the computer "brain" were hooked up to one body and his own brain to another. He writes: "My strongest intuition was that in such an eventuality *I* would survive so long as *either* brain-body couple remained intact." Do you share this intuition? Why or why not?

9. Early in Meditation II, Descartes concludes that no matter how many things he is deceived or mistaken about, he cannot be mistaken in thinking that he exists. What makes him so sure about this?

10. Having become certain that he exists, Descartes remains unsure what he is. We might think of Descartes's procedure here as a way of refining his understanding of that of which he is certain. He is certain that *he* exists. But does it follow that he is certain that, for example, his left foot exists? Descartes thinks not. For he could be mistaken in thinking that he has a left foot even though he could not be mistaken in thinking that *he* exists. How does this train of thought lead Descartes to conclude that he cannot be certain that he has a body at all?

11. How does Descartes reach the conclusion that, "precisely speaking," he is nothing but a thinking thing? What does he mean by "precisely speaking"? What does he mean by "thinking"?

12. What is the connection Descartes sees between his knowledge of his own nature and his knowledge of the nature of a piece of wax?

13. At the end of Meditation II, Descartes concludes: "There is nothing more easily or clearly apprehended than my own mind." Contrast this with the quote from Nietzsche in the introduction to this section. Is there a real or only a verbal disagreement between the two? If the disagreement is not real, explain why not; if the disagreement is real, defend one view or the other.

14. Review the explanation of dualism in the Introduction to this section. Then explain and evaluate Hobbes's objection to dualism in section 34.

15. Hobbes argues that things do not have essences which are distinct from the things themselves. For instance we might say that dogs are essentially furry, but Hobbes denies that this commits us to a thing, furriness, which is distinct from furry creatures. Explain how Hobbes thinks the doctrine of essences leads people to dualism. Does Descartes's argument in Meditation II that he is distinct from his body rest on the view about essences which Hobbes rejects?

16. Can Hobbes say that people have minds even though people are nothing but bodies, or would that be inconsistent? Explain your answer carefully.

Part II. Paradoxes of Identity

Thundering artillery is laying down a deadly barrage on the enemy-held hill. Propped against the side of a foxhole, awaiting the command to advance, is an ordinary G. I. His name is Joe. The sounds of the combat are deafening, terrifying. As he attaches his bayonet, Joe quite naturally thinks about the battle and his role in it. He most certainly wants to survive the events that are unfolding. He has plans for the future, for *his* future. He intends to go to college, earn a degree in business, and get a lucrative managerial job in marketing with a major retail corporation. What does Joe want? One way to describe what he wants is to say that he wants there to be an identity between himself and some self (or person) that will continue living and breathing after the guns of war have fallen silent. He also, and importantly, wants that person to have a certain set of desires, plans, hopes and commitments, or at least, Joe wants that person to remember Joe's current plans for the future, even if intervening events prevent his accomplishing them.

Suppose that Joe were offered the following scenarios as his possible outcomes after the battle:

1. His body, that is the body he and everyone else would now identify as Joe, will survive pretty much intact, with only a bruise or two. But, due to some terrifying events he will experience, he will lose many of his mental capacities and traits. He will be rendered, more or less, zombie-like.

2. His body will be riddled with bullets, but after an exotic medical operation all of his memories, knowledge, values, modes of behavior, and so forth, will be retrieved and "imprinted" in the brain of another human being who will accept them and act on them as his own.

3. Neither his body nor his mental capacities and traits will survive. He will be blown to bits by a hand grenade.

In which, if any, of these scenarios, excluding, of course, the best case outcome in which both his body and mental life continue very much as they were, does Joe survive? This question highlights what matters in the day to day survival of a person.

Many people will likely say that what matters is that Joe before and Joe after the battle are identical only if every property of the one is a property

45

of the other. Let us call this strict identity. Strict identity, however, is problematical in cases of this sort. Strict identity is a relationship between a thing and itself. Identical things are indiscernable. Most things, including persons, however, change over time. They gain some properties and they lose others. Joe, for example, may receive a wound during the battle for which, we all believe, surviving Joe deserves a Purple Heart. In any event, after the battle he (or his body) will have some properties that Joe did not have before the battle.

Alteration over time is a basic fact about most everything and it poses a genuine problem for the reidentification of the thing after a lapse of time. How much of something can change while it remains the same thing? In the case of persons, how many properties and which ones must remain unchanged for he or she to be the previously existing person?

It is tempting to think that there has to be at least some set of properties or a single property that a thing (or a person) must continue to have to preserve its identity. Still, we do not generally use such a strict criterion for things of most kinds. Think, for example, of an automobile loaned to you some two or three years ago by your best friend. In the ensuing time, while your friend was out of the country, many of its parts, and not just mufflers and spark plugs, had to be replaced with new or rebuilt parts. Perhaps you had an accident and needed to have major body work done on the vehicle. Now you return it. Is not your friend's car, in an important sense, the same one given to your care? If it is not, why do you return it? Why not just tell your friend that you are sorry but the car loaned to you no longer exists? Our ordinary exchanges certainly presume the car to be the one loaned to you, despite the various alterations, as its registration papers will indicate.

Trees and other plants are treated in a way analogous to our understanding about sameness in the case of automobiles. A sapling willow tree planted six years ago, if it thrives, will now be considerably different in size, and shape. Nonetheless, we regard it as the same tree as the one planted six years ago. In fact, we should be offended if someone suggested it were not the same tree, especially if husbanding it has been one of our major projects during those years. These examples, however, indicate that strict identity does not come into play in our ordinary thinking about whether or not many types of things are the same in most ordinary circumstances. Instead, we use a notion of sameness that allows something to undergo even major alterations or stage changes over time and for all those stages, though they are not identical to each other, to be stages of the same thing. This suggests that the criteria we use to reidentify things may vary with the type of thing under consideration, a position defended by John Locke. What makes the willow the same tree will depend on what we understand about the usual growth and development of such trees. On what does Joe's identity depend?

We posed Joe's problem in terms of a spectrum of scenarios. In each possible outcome, however, we emphasized a certain feature or element that might be identified with Joe and that Joe might be persuaded would ensure his survival if it were to continue after the battle. Scenarios of this sort, but with many more permutations, propel the discussions of identity in the papers by Charles B. Daniels and Derek Parfit. In one of our cases we offered Joe bodily continuity. That is, the body he had before the battle will continue through the battle and will undergo only the usual changes that occur in human bodies. Those kind of changes, like the growth of the willow tree, are incorporated into our conception of "the same human body." It will not matter that, for example, some of the atoms of Joe's body will be different before and after the battle. If a person is a human body (including, of course, a brain), then Joe's concern for his continuing to exist will be allayed, if he is assured that his body and all of its parts will be functioning as a human body after the battle. But, we also included in the scenario that there will no longer be a continuity of mental experiences associated with Joe's brain. The soldier that survives the battle will look just like Joe, but he will not remember anything Joe remembered before the battle. He will not have Joe's skills or other mental capacities. He will know nothing of Joe's hopes, plans, or fears. In short, there will be a bodily continuity and causal connectedness, but no corresponding mental continuity or connectedness. If you think that Joe, in addition to rejecting this outcome, ought not to regard it as one in which his existence continues, then you believe that the mental aspect of human existence is essential to what it is to be a person or to how particular persons are reidentified over time.

Our second scenario pressed the boundaries of this idea. In it we allowed Joe's mental life to continue uninterrupted so that there is a continuity of thoughts, dreams, plans, memories and the like, but we implanted that mental history in a body in every way different from Joe's former body. It might well be thought that by doing so we preserve Joe's identity as a person. Suppose that Joe, in an act of selfless heroism, dove on a live grenade and saved the other members of his platoon. The implanted mental history includes the memory of having intentionally performed that deed. The Medal of Honor is to be bestowed posthumously, but a body looking not at all like Joe steps forward and claims the right to the award. If we could verify that the exotic operation had occurred, would we honor this claim?

This last question is really a key to the personal identity puzzles for, as John Locke noted, "person" is at core a forensic term. That is, it is most important in legal, moral, and other matters of responsibility. Perhaps our strongest reasons for wanting a criterion for the identification of persons is that we need to know, for example, whom to reward, whom to punish, on whom to assess liabilities, to whom to grant rights and assign duties. "Person" is our basic social structure term. It is the primary building block of our social, civic, and moral system. We count the members of the moral community, for example, in terms of the census of persons.

As has been suggested, there is a host of philosophical problems (some of which are explored in other sections of this book) that clusters around the idea of personal identity, but the crucial, central issue is a matter of settling criteria. Are the necessary conditions of personal identity by which the same person is reidentified through time physical or psychological?

PERSONAL IDENTITY
Charles B. Daniels

Suppose that someone says to you, "Let me think about it for a moment," "I'll clear off the dishes," "I gave it some thought while you two were discussing the course options, and . . . ," or "Well, I've cleared off the dishes, let's watch TV." When you verify by observation that the person now talking to you has done or will do something in the very recent past or near future, one observes his body; and the body one observes is a spatio-temporally continuous entity. The problem of personal identity is that of whether or not bodily continuity is a *necessary* condition of personal survival.

The issue is complicated by a further factor: one does not normally make such observations about oneself. We do not live surrounded by mirrors; and even if we did, we would still not verify that we observed our bodies by observing ourselves observing our bodies. As Sydney Shoemaker has pointed out,[1] we do not use criteria of spatio-temporal continuity in the verification of the personal components of our own perceptual and memory claims.

Yet it has recently been forcibly argued that bodily continuity *is* a necessary condition of personal survival.[2] My aim in this paper will be to provide a summary and critical evaluation of the arguments *pro* and *con.* Let me straightaway disclose my view on all this. I find that the arguments put forward to support the thesis that bodily continuity is a necessary condition of personal survival simply do not prove this conclusion; and here I side with the many people on earth who, in believing that reincarnation is actual, are committed to its possibility. If bodily continuity were a necessary condition of personal survival, these people would be taking a necessary falsehood for a contingent truth. I do part company with the believers in reincarnation, however, for while I believe that reincarnation is possible, I am doubtful that it ever in fact occurs.

A case, whose source is unknown to me but which has circulated widely among philosophers by word of mouth, will serve to illustrate the in's and out's of these matters admirably.

Science marches on. A machine is built that will, when a person enters it, record the type and position of each molecule in his body and then disintegrate him. The process takes only a few seconds and ends with a pile of atomic debris lying on the floor of the recording chamber. The tape which contains the information about the molecular structure of the individual's body can then be fed back into the machine; and after the requisite raw materials are added, the machine will fabricate a person who not only looks and talks exactly like the one who entered the machine in the first place, but also believes that he is that person. No one who emerges from the machine complains of any suffering that he has undergone. Many of these machines are built.

People become accustomed to "travel" *via* these machines. They walk in, are taped and disintegrated, the information on the tape is beamed to their destinations where other machines await, and there they are reconstructed.

"Operations" are performed that never were possible before: a technician makes a few emendations in the tape before feeding it back into the machine for the reconstruction. Broken bones are mended, and happier "memories" are furnished for those who simply cannot cope with their real ones.

Here an objection might be raised. Since it is possible to duplicate tapes or for a machine to record its information on two tapes, such duplicate tapes can be fed into separate machines and there will emerge two people who both claim to be the same person.

Now in one way it is possible for the same person to be in two places simultaneously: for example, someone might be both inside and outside his house if he were, say, standing astride the doorway. But one person cannot, it seems, simultaneously be situated in two places that are not connected by a path of places, all of which have him situated in them. This is what is normally meant by saying that a person cannot be in two different places at the same time.

If the two individuals that emerge from the two machines are the one person they claim to be, then one person *can* be in two places at the same time. But one person can't. So they both can't be the person they believe themselves to be. But to say that one of them is and the other is not the person who entered the machine in the first place is arbitrary in a case like this, at least more arbitrary than saying that neither of them is. So that is the best thing to say: neither of them is. And since it is always possible to make two people from a tape, these considerations will obtain even when in fact only one happens to be made. It would be very strange, indeed, if your being who you think you are depended upon the fact that someone has not secreted a duplicate of the tape you were made from and has not made use of it in some far corner of the earth.

But what this objection fails to note is that the two people who emerge from the machines do not claim that they *are now* the same person, i.e., each other. They can see very well that they are not. What each claims, on reflection, is that he *was* the fellow that entered the machine, say, an hour before.[3] So both *can agree* (i) that they are now different people and (ii) that they were once one and the same person. One can imagine them getting very chummy reminiscing about the things that happened when they were the same person.

Other uses of the machine can now be envisaged. Two women fall madly in love with me to the point of desperation. I walk into the machine. A tape is made in duplicate. The two tapes are fed into two machines and both of my admirers and "I" live happily ever after. But all is not sweetness and light. Criminals can now duplicate themselves a hundred-fold after committing the most heinous of crimes. Are the courts to condemn them all—especially the few that turn into saints during the prolonged pretrial period? Probably not, because while it is true that they *were* the person that committed the crime, it is not true that they *are* the person that committed it. They can remember that they *were* the one that did it, but not that they *are* the one that did it. Fortunately, however, the poor woman that was their wife is not their wife now.

There is another objection to consider, however. A horrible rumor has begun to circulate about the entrepreneurs who control these machines. The machines have only *some* of the capacities we have been told they have. They can record the type and position of each molecule in a person's body, and they can, given raw materials and a suitable tape, fabricate people, but they cannot perform the disintegration operation.

What really happens, once the tape is made, is that a trap door opens in the bottom of the recording chamber, and the poor unsuspecting soul inside falls down into the basement, where he is seized by a band of sadists, bound, tortured until nearly dead, and at last thrown half alive into a vat of acid in which he dies and is quickly decomposed leaving no trace—and all the while on the floor above the accomplices of these fiends are manufacturing a duplicate. One can hear them now: "How's it going down there? Boris is almost ready to pull the duplicate" will come the shout from above, and from below, "Oh, we've all had our fun. He's in the bath now."

So the duplicate is merely a duplicate, like a photocopy, and not the original. And why do we say that the duplicate and the original are different people? Because a person ceases to exist when his body does— by dissolving in acid, *or* by being disintegrated by a machine—even though, like any of the items of mass production, there may be any number of people with bodies just like his. Since lack of bodily continuity between the person entering the machine and the person emerging from it seems to entail that the person before and the person after are different people we might conclude then that a logically necessary condition of personal survival over time is bodily continuity over time. At least this is how the argument goes.

And that the person before and the person after are in fact different people is in a case like this the correct answer, I think, but another consideration seems to suggest that our judgment to this effect is not based upon seeing an *entailment*, i.e., bodily continuity over time is not a *logically* necessary condition of personal survival over time. Cases of reincarnation, if such things are logically possible, are precisely cases in which there is personal survival over time in the absence of bodily continuity.

Suppose my best and oldest friend awakes one morning thoroughly convinced that he is Henry Morgan, the pirate. I know little of Morgan, but from what I do know I judge that my friend has taken on the personality and character traits of Morgan. This may, of course, simply be due to an unconscious desire on his part to preserve his deluded conviction that he is Morgan; to keep in character he must behave like him. In any event, people can have the same character and personality traits, mannerisms, likes and dislikes, and still be different people, so having Morgan's character and personality traits certainly isn't sufficient to make my friend be Morgan.

But there are other more disquieting elements. He seems to know vastly more about the intimate details of Morgan's sordid life than the John Dokes I have known from childhood could possibly be in a position to know. As boys we played at pirates, but I know for a fact that he took no more than the passing interest I did in the lives of the pirate notables. He insisted, moreover, in making a trip to the Caribbean "to convince all you skeptics"; and near Ocho Rios, after having oriented himself to the now altered landscape, he pointed to a spot where we dug up a fabulous treasure and the bones of the men he claimed he had murdered so as to preserve the secret of its location.

If we decide that Dokes is a reincarnation of Morgan (or that Morgan's soul has informed Dokes' body, or something of the sort), we do so having judged that the claims Dokes makes that he *remembers* being Morgan, burying the treasure, killing the crew, etc., *are true*; it is a real case of remembering, and this judgment forms the basis of our judgment that Dokes is Morgan. However, our basis for judging that Dokes *remembers* being Morgan, burying the treasure, killing the crew, etc., is that we know or have good reason to believe that *Morgan* buried the treasure, killed the crew, and whatever else Dokes claims *he* did, and that Dokes has some, to say the least, very extraordinary *insight* into Morgan's life and deeds.

But now another objection must be raised. We might account for Dokes' strange insight in another way than by saying that it is a case of remembering. Dokes might simply have clairvoyant knowledge of what Morgan did, felt, thought, etc., and be mistaken when, believing it to be true, he say he *remembers* being Morgan, burying the treasure, killing the crew, etc. One can think one is remembering events which one is, say, merely imagining, and one can think one is merely fantasizing events that one is really remembering. So, too, it seems possible that one may have clairvoyant knowledge of something one *only thinks* one remembers.

Suppose I claim to have a wonderful clairvoyant power to know things. When asked to give examples of things I know this way, I say, "I know that I had bacon and eggs for breakfast this morning, and that my good friends, the Smiths, came to visit my flat last night and we had a good time together." This isn't clairvoyance at all. I was present when these things happened and am remembering them. You know this by knowing that the body I now have was in a position this morning for me to be seated at the breakfast table and to know that I was, etc.

It seems, then, that bodily continuity plays an important role in distinguishing what is to count as a case of clairvoyance from what is to count as a case of remembering. This is undoubtedly true. It might be argued further, though, that when bodily continuity is absent as it is in cases of reincarnation or "change of bodies," the distinction between the two collapses. Remembering is one thing when it is distinct from clairvoyance; it is quite something else when it is not.

If this line of reasoning is accepted it is suggestive of further argument. First, that if "remembering" doing something in a former life entails that one did it, the concept of *person* we are dealing with differs significantly from our normal one. For example, no present court would adjudge Dokes guilty of the murders of the crew members even if it accepted that he "remembered" (in our novel sense) committing them and, hence, was the "person" (in a novel sense) that committed them, nor, I imagine, would it judge that he was not married to Dokes' wife, if it accepted that prior to his awakening as that "person" he was not that "person"— although this change might serve as grounds for divorce. And although we might find much objectionable in his present character, even viewing him with suspicion as a potential criminal because of these traits we would not, I think, regard him with the same moral disapproval as we would if he had committed murders in his present life and remained unrepentant.

Secondly, there seems to be no reason to hold that the implications of "remembering" (which is not distinct from clairvoyance) will resemble those of our normal remembering (which is distinct from clairvoyance). In particular, the fact that remembering that one has done so-and-so entails that one has done it, when the presence of bodily continuity preserves the distinction between remembering and clairvoyance, provides no clear reason for holding that the entailment obtains when the absence of bodily continuity collapses the distinction. So the fact that Dokes "remembers" burying the treasure and killing the crew is no longer a reason for saying that he did do it. It may still be a reason for saying that someone did it, for remembering-clairvoyance still has some element of knowledge in it.

Yet to all of this a believer in the possibility of reincarnation will simply and, I think, correctly reply that *there is* a distinction between remembering and clairvoyance despite the fact that in such cases bodily continuity is absent:[4] if Dokes remembers killing the crew and if Morgan singlehandedly killed the crew, then Dokes is Morgan; if Dokes merely has clairvoyant knowledge that Morgan killed the crew, he isn't (and perhaps cannot be) Morgan. The fact that we do not seem to be able to figure out a way of coming to know which is in fact the case does not *imply* that it is impossible for one and only one of them to be Morgan.

Yet the question does remain of how we—including those of us who seem to ourselves to remember former lives—can tell in such cases who is really remembering and who isn't. If in normal cases bodily continuity is treated merely as an inductive ground for saying yea or nay to the question of who is really remembering and who isn't, there must be an independent way of telling which is which if we are to establish empirically that it is a good inductive ground, or so it seems. It might be, of course, that we just see that X is remembering and that Y isn't. But if this is our answer, shouldn't we simply forget about remembering that one is so-and-so, a sufficient condition of identity, and just say that we see that X is so-and-so and that Y is not? If the answer takes either of these forms, though, we can still perhaps be jollied out of it.

Suppose that I am an anthropologist who has been living with a tribe long enough to have sufficient command of their language to carry on a fairly decent conversation in it. One day the chief and I are sitting outside his dwelling watching the men of the tribe practice archery. One of them is particularly inept with the bow and arrow, invariably missing the target completely. I remark to the chief, "He's certainly not much of an archer," and to my surprise the chief answers, "Oh, he *is* in the next village." I ask, "Do you mean that he becomes a good archer when he goes to the next village?", and the chief replies, "No, I mean that he is *now* a good archer in the next village. I ask, "Do you mean that he is in the next village now, besides being here too?", and the chief answers, "Yes, and what's more he is sitting over there too, but that's not him over there," pointing in the first instance to a woman nursing a child and in the second to a girl in her teens. It seems clear to me at this point, if the old boy isn't pulling my leg, that these people have a different concept of a person than we do.

I then ask the chief how he knows that the man in question is in the next village and he replies, "I see that he is. I'm there too." I ask him how one tells which of these figures I see are the same person and which aren't and he says, "Well, it's just one of those things, like sameness of color, that one sees, or one doesn't. A few of us are 'person-blind' and simply can't do it. There have been cases where a foreigner who has spent time living with us and learning our ways has finally gotten the knack of it. You may be suspicious, but if you take the trouble to stick it out here, you will find that you have good reason to believe that we can see these things, just as blind people have good reason to believe that those of us who claim to have the power of seeing colors actually do see them. Blind people know that there is overwhelming agreement about what the colors of things are. They know that this agreement cannot be traced to authority; you don't need traffic policemen standing out on every corner shouting, 'Now the light is red. You must stop.' They know, moreover, what organ would have to be fixed if they were to come to have this power. It is the same with you. You will find that we agree about what things are the same person and what are not. Our agreement doesn't come from authority. And your eyes may well need fixing. But then, again, perhaps just practice will do."

Now the person who believes in the possibility of reincarnation might not be convinced that his concept of remembering or of person differs from the normal simply because he realizes that this tribe has a different concept of person from the normal. But the chief's kind of argument does have a sufficiently strong cajolery force to make it hard for him to say that he simply sees the difference between remembering and clairvoyance or between the same and different people and that the rest of us are blind in these respects. And there is the further difficulty that our world is full of instances of the same color, just as the tribesmen's world is full of in- stances of the same "person" in their sense. Cases of the Dokes type of insight simply don't occur, so questions of whether one would be driven to take the "simply seeing" line if they did, become difficult to answer in the absence of further information.

This is an important point and it can be illustrated by the difference between the machine case and the case of reincarnation or "change of bodies." When we read the details of the machine case, we find they fit easily into a whole set of background beliefs we have about how things actually work in the universe. The people emerging from the machines have the characters, personalities, and beliefs they do *because* character, personality, and belief is determined by the position and type of certain molecules in one's body—at least that is what we believe about these matters. And when we realize that the people who emerge from the machines are not the ones who first entered, we are *still* able to give this explanation of why they act, talk, and believe as they do. We do not *have* to fall back upon such outlandish things as clairvoyance or queer remem- berings to explain the phenomena (not that a thing cannot be explained by both the concept of molecules at work and by the concept of remem- bering). But if we didn't have the background beliefs we do have, the machine case might be on a par with the reincarnation case. Except for the inclusion of a lot of unnecessary trappings.

Why do the people act, talk, and believe as they do? Because they have a certain kind of molecules at work in certain parts of their bodies. Why does Dokes act, talk, and believe as he does? Same reason. Why are these molecules there and structured in just that way in the bodies of the people who emerge from the machines? Because someone by means of the machines put them there and arranged them that way. Why are the molecules there and arranged in just that way in Dokes' body? We just don't know, not that we can't know. Perhaps Morgan's spirit entered and informed his body, causing a molecular rearrangement. Perhaps a combination of clairvoyant power and mental instability made him that way. Perhaps the type and arrangement of molecules in one's body has nothing to do with how one acts, talks, and believes. Imagine a case of the machine type or the John Dokes type happening in an *Oz*-like world of tin men and straw men in which molecules had nothing to do with what its inhabitants did or thought. What would be the right thing to say here?

I think the difficulties in deciding what would be the right thing to say arise from two factors: (a) a suppressed demand for physical possibility and (b) a lack of relevant information. Another case may help.

Sydney Shoemaker offers the following counterexample to the thesis that bodily continuity is a necessary condition of personal survival:

. . . suppose that medical science has developed a technique whereby a surgeon can completely remove a person's brain from his head, examine or operate on it, and then put it back in his skull (regrafting the nerves, blood vessels, and so forth) without causing death or permanent injury; we are to imagine that this technique of "brain extraction" has come to be widely practiced in the treatment of brain tumors and other disorders of the brain. One day, to begin our story, a surgeon discovers that an assistant has made a horrible mistake. Two men, a Mr. Brown and a Mr. Robinson, had been operated on for brain tumors, and brain extractions had been performed on both of them. At the end of the operation, however, the assistant inadvertently put Brown's brain in Robinson's head, and Robinson's brain in Brown's head. One of these men immediately dies, but the other, the one with Robinson's body and Brown's brain, eventually regains consciousness. Let us call the latter "Brownson." Upon regaining consciousness Brownson exhibits great shock and suprise at the appearance of his body. Then, upon seeing Brown's body, he exclaims incredulously, "That's me lying there!" Pointing to himself he says, "This isn't my body; the one over there is!" When asked his name he automatically replies, "Brown." He recognizes Brown's wife and family (whom Robinson had never met), and is able to describe in detail events in Brown's life, always describing them as events in his own life. Of Robinson's past life he evidences no knowledge at all. Over a period of time he is observed to display all the personality traits, mannerisms, interests, likes and dislikes, and so on that had previously characterized Brown, and to act and talk in ways completely alien to the old Robinson.[5]

Shoemaker himself has doubts about what is the right thing to say here. I will limit myself to commenting on the case as it is presented above.

It seems to me, right off, that Brownson is Brown. One is inclined to say this because he has Brown's brain and behaves as the story says. Brain continuity is not, however, a logically necessary condition of personal survival.

Shoemaker goes on to argue:

> . . . if upon regaining consciousness Brownson were to act and talk just as Robinson had always done in the past, surely no one would say that this man, who looks, acts, and talks just like Robinson, and has what has always been Robinson's body, must really be Brown rather than Robinson because he has Brown's brain. Here we would conclude simply that there is not the close causal relationship we had supposed there to be between the state of a man's brain and his psychological features, i.e., his personality and his ability to report events in his past history. If we did not think there to be such a causal relationship we should not think that having the same brain has anything more to do with being the same person than, say, having the same liver.[6]

If Brownson were to awake acting and talking like Robinson, I myself do not think we would immediately conclude that brains do not have the intimate relationship we think they have to psychological features. There is simply too much other evidence that they do, e.g. the effects of frontal lobotomies and brain tumors, etc. Rather, I think it would take an incredible amount of evidence to persuade us to the view that the assistant had really made such a mistake.

But if there were such evidence, perhaps several movie crews taking films of the whole thing, I think that then Brownson's case would become an anomaly, and many other alternative explanations would have to be explored before we would resign ourselves to saying that as regards an explanation of human consciousness brains play about the same role as livers and that these other "effects" (of frontal lobotomies, brain tumors, etc.) are sheer coincidence.

Suppose, for instance, that Brown has had a history of clairvoyant interludes and also has shown signs of mental instability. Immediately before his operation he had heard that someone named Robinson was undergoing a similar operation. Perhaps he is now fulfilling a wish to be someone else and has picked on Robinson. This is farfetched, but it seems no more farfetched than the supposition that Brownson wakes up believing that he is and acting like Robinson, given that he has Brown's brain. Equally farfetched would be the case in which Brown awakened thinking and acting like Robinson after receiving a transfusion of Robinson's blood.

What all of this shows is, I think, that we have a natural tendency, when presented with made-up cases like these, to fill in the missing details in such a manner as to make the imagined world, the one we have in mind, as much like the actual world with respect to unspecified detail and physical possibility as we can, given the limitations of the statement of the case and our beliefs as to what the actual world is like and what is physically possible. If, for instance, we harbor a belief, however fuzzy or confused, that there is an identity in fact between mind and brain, we

will take it for granted that there is this identity in the world we are asked
to imagine in a case like Shoemaker's and say that Brownson is Brown.
Robinson's brain now lies encased in the inessential part of Brown's
body—inessential in the way fingernails, hair, fingers, livers, etc., are
inessential to his body, while the essential part of Brown's body, which is
in fact his brain, lies encased in the inessential parts of Robinson's body.
(Suppose that brains could be manufactured by a machine so that they
exactly resembled our own brains and suppose also that they could be
transplanted in our skulls in an operation like the now successful kidney
or heart transplants. But remember the possibility that sadistic fiends
might be in control!)

Or if we want to use the word "body" in Brown's, perhaps more
normal, way, we will say that despite the fact that one's bodily continuity
is not essential to one's survival, *spatio-temporal continuity of something,*
whatever one cares to call it, may still be; and this something in the
imagined world and our own is in fact the brain. And because we believe
this we say that Brownson is Brown.

But suppose further details are given: suppose that the fact that there
has been a mistaken switch in brains is proved and that Brownson's
opposite number, call him Rown, doesn't die, but awakens *also* thinking,
talking and acting like Brown—we don't know what to say because we
don't know who is who. And we don't know who is who, because now,
it seems, we don't know enough relevant details.

But the tendency to make the presented world as much like what we
believe the real world to be, within the framework of detail actually given
to us, still operates; and this determines what kinds of further details we
feel ought to count as relevant. Given a belief in the identity of mind and
brain, the case becomes mysterious, because we want to reconcile this
belief with the story told. Then when further details are given that make it
clear that brain-mind identity does not hold in the hypothetical world,
other beliefs about the real world still retain their hold over us: we believe
that in fact a person could not be such a lucky guesser that he would with
no knowledge whatsoever about the life of another guess all the details of
that other's life with the facility and accuracy that the other could remember them, that he would not have this detailed clairvoyant knowledge, he
could not be so mistaken about his own identity, that he could not be so
mistaken about whether he was guessing blindly, being clairvoyant, or
remembering, that he could not react in just the same way as the other to
people and situations, that in all probability there are no cases anyway of
clairvoyance or of reincarnation or of one soul, mind, or what have you,
informing different bodies at different times, etc. Any of these beliefs
might be false; none of them are, in my opinion, logically necessary truths.

At this point I am handicapped by the fact that I have no sufficiently
detailed analysis of knowledge or rational belief to offer, so what I say in
the following will have no other basis than my own intuitions. I ask the

reader to test mine against his. Let us operate under the assumption, though, that the worlds presented in these cases differ from the actual world, represented partially by the truth of the set of beliefs stated above, only as much as the details stated in the description of the case and taken in a generous spirit require.

In the original brain-transfer case, we should, I think, barring sheer stupidity, *know* that Brownson was Brown.

In the case of Dokes-Morgan, I think we might have fairly good reason to suspend judgment, to wait and see what turned up. In fact, if no other such cases occurred, generations in the fairly remote future would probably have good grounds to doubt existing accounts that said that the case of John Dokes ever really occurred, unless, of course, investigations into the connections between mind and brain take a very surprising turn. Even then, the stories might be viewed with great suspicion— like the "explanation" that the "immaculate conception" was really a case of parthenogenesis.

But if such cases were to begin to occur with some regularity, provided, of course, only one good candidate appeared each time, we would have good reason to believe—and we might perhaps even come to know—that Dokes was Morgan. The mind-brain identity thesis would have to be scrapped, but minds could still be thought of as having an exceptional intimate causal relationship to brains during those periods when the minds were in fact incarnate. Also, to be sure, we would start believing that cases did occur of minds informing different bodies at different times. Our reasons for believing Dokes to be Morgan would, I imagine, be that we knew that in all normal cases the likelihood that memory was the source that provided a vast store of true information about the past doings and thoughts of someone is far and away greater than the likelihood that it came *via* clairvoyance or sheer uninformed lucky guessing. Also, we regard it as wildly unlikely that a man could be mistaken on so grand a scale about whether he was remembering, being clairvoyant, or just guessing blindly. And we could still say that there were no cases of real clairvoyance. *And*, to be sure, there are all those other cases; Dokes-Morgan is not unique. Of course, the problem of determining the relationship between the mind and the brain would become far more difficult and puzzling for the scientists, perhaps requiring a new physical theory.

Similarly in one isolated case of competing candidates, whether it is a case where no spatio-temporal continuity is apparently present or one like the case where both Brownson and Rown act like and believe themselves to be Brown, judgment is best suspended.

In most circumstances that come to mind, we would, I think, want to hold it to be true that in the absence of physical continuity at most one of the competing candidates is who he claims to be, i.e., that in the absence of such spatio-temporal continuity two competing candidates cannot have been one person in the past. The qualification as to spatio-temporal continuity is required in view of another kind of case: if children were born fully able to reason and to talk, and each firmly believed it had done and thought the things its mother had done and thought, we might want to say that the mother and child had once been the same person.

Indeed, it cannot only be made to seem plausible that two such individuals *were* the same person, but also that they *are* the same person, i.e., that a person can be in two different places at the same time. The following case I owe to a recent article by Derek Parfit:[7]

Suppose that the bulk of the information a person has is stored in duplicate in the two hemispheres of his brain and that in the event that one hemisphere is destroyed the other will take over the work of the whole and continue to regulate bodily and mental functions. Suppose further that it is found that certain individuals are capable of voluntarily dividing their minds, i.e., pursuing two trains of thought concurrently without a unifying consciousness overseeing the effort. One of these gifted individuals could, for instance, when faced with a problem, decide that there were two quite different lines of approach to a possible solution. He might then, to save time, divide his mind for a period of time, in order to pursue both to see whether one of them might prove fruitful. Sometimes upon reunification he would find that neither worked; other times he would have his solution in hand.

Neurophysiologists then determine that a mind division is in fact a division of labor between the two hemispheres of the brain. After a period of training, anyone who happens to have both hemispheres intact turns out to be able to divide his mind at will. But those individuals who lack two functioning hemispheres are simply incapable of doing so. Finally, it is found that subjects are able to divide (and unify) their minds even when the neural connections between the two hemispheres are severed. Indeed, they are capable of doing so when the two hemispheres are transplanted into bodies that lack brains. Of course, in the case of such transplants there are at first grave difficulties in adjusting to and controlling two spatially separate bodies. But the difficulties are not in principle greater than those involved in controlling two spatially separate arms or legs. Thus it seems quite possible that one mind could inhabit two different bodies simultaneously.

But barring considerations like these, when it becomes the regular thing for good, and on the face of it equally good, competing candidates to appear, our whole stock of basic beliefs are, considering the intent of the case, called into question. Whether or not there are cases of minds informing different bodies or brains, there are cases rampant of clairvoyance, incredibly lucky guessing, being mistaken on the grand scale about the bases of one's beliefs, persons being in two different places simultaneously, or something else.

As to the "something else," perhaps there is an ingenious and powerful god or Martian causing these things to happen, making some minds inform different brains at different times, causing others to believe that they are yet other minds and filling them with information—perhaps by causing changes in brains. And given time, the god or Martian might even be wise, eloquent, and patient enough to be able to explain to us how he goes about doing it. Faced with such going's on, we are somewhat in the position of a Bushman in a physics lab.

But this sort of explanation of what is going on is not meant to be available. On the one hand, our background beliefs and sophistication about the actual world don't help; and on the other, we are not meant to be allowed to develop a new set to take their place. So by the very nature of the case, if we are to know which are "change of body" cases and which are not, we seem to be reduced simply to seeing that so-and-so is actually remembering and that so-and-so is being clairvoyant or guessing blindly. It is worth noting, however, that in some possible world people could have full-blown and sophisticated sets of background beliefs about these matters, about why they happen and what mechanisms are at work, rather than having to view them from the eyes of someone, very much unlike us, who never explains but merely identifies.

But from his eyes spatio-temporal continuity is now not an aid for making the distinction, and if criteria are demanded, like those we could perhaps name for a thing's being a unicorn, we fail to come up with them. It is a mistake, though, at this point to become mesmerized by the case of colors and to turn it into a paradigm for all cases in which we simply see that so-and-so is the case without being able to name interesting criteria, inductive or otherwise, for its being the case.

I believe that seeing that something is changing or moving is also of this sort. Wittgenstein suggests other cases. What are the criteria for a thing's having a gentle look, a benign look, a stern look? Talented artists can capture these features, on canvas or on stage, but we and they are at a loss to name criteria for them (unless, of course, gentleness and the like are treated as their own criteria).

What makes a thing a gentle look seems far more complicated than what makes it, say, red. Parts of an entirely red surface can be removed and the remainder will still be red. Parts of a face that has a gentle look cannot so easily be removed so as to leave the gentle look intact. If a person has trouble making these distinctions in practice, his problem seems to be much less one of the organs of sight than one of sensibility, the cure less amenable to drugs or operations than to practice, training, experience, and perhaps even a change in character and interests.

We are dealing, of course, not with a sharp distinction here: wine tasters and color experts by their vast training and experience develop extraordinary sensitivity, as do actors, sculptors, and social workers. Art connoisseurs often spot extremely good forgeries on sight, without knowing precisely what it is about the work that gives it away. Furthermore, the ability to make subtle distinctions like these is not always a gift of the practiced or talented few. All English speakers that are not deaf or hard of hearing can distinguish the sounds of the words "bed" and "bad," "bitch" and "beach." Few Spaniards can.

My suggestion is that the distinction between remembering, being clairvoyant, and lucky guessing might be viewed this way too, and what makes a thing a case of one rather than another is perhaps even more complicated than its having a gentle, benign, or stern look. We are handicapped, too, by the fact that there simply are no cases in the actual world of clairvoyance and such wildly lucky guessing, even though there are plenty of cases of remembering. We lack the opportunity to practice. It is as if there were only one flavor of tea in the world, and we were asked to imagine a world in which there were others.

In summary, then, I think that the believer in the possibility of reincarnation or bodily transfer is right on logical grounds in insisting that there is a distinction between remembering on the one hand and clairvoyance or uninformed lucky guessing on the other even if bodily continuity is absent. I fail to see why there would cease to be a distinction, even if it were true that it was logically impossible for us *to know* which was a case of one, which a case of the other—much less if it were merely impossible in practice. But I have also suggested that it *would* be possible for us to know which was which and even to explain the hows and whys of the phenomena. I have also suggested that we do distinguish many things of high complexity, unlike shades of color, without being able to say, except trivially, what distinguishes them and that the present distinctions might be of this kind.

But in judging whether we are still talking about the same thing by the word "person" in describing a world where competing candidates occurred frequently, other details would be relevant:

Does change of sex ever occur when one mind informs different bodies? Is there an institution of homosexual marriage? Does one have to obtain a divorce from someone who has changed bodies? Is one guilty of crimes committed when one had another body? Is one's eye-witness testimony accepted in court after a change of bodies? Can one's named heirs inherit when one dies? Do minds survive in space invisibly when they are not incarnate? Do the scientists of the world attempt to test for the presence of disembodied minds in space?

Here, I would imagine that the answers to these questions could be filled in with ingenuity in such a way as to make it fairly plausible that we are still using the word "person" in the regular way and that change of bodies might occur in the absence of any form of spatio-temporal continuity.

NOTES

1. Sydney Shoemaker, *Self-Knowledge and Self-Identity*, Ithaca: Cornell University Press, 1963.
2. Many of the points that are discussed here can be found stated or at least

hinted at in two articles by B. A. O. Williams: "Personal Identity and Individuation," *Proceedings of the Aristotelian Society*, Vol. LVII, 1956–57, pp. 229–52; "Bodily Continuity and Personal Identity: a Reply," *Analysis*, Vol. 21, No. 2, 1960, pp. 43–48.

3. The problem of formalizing such claims is extremely difficult. Yet one thing an analysis must not do is to turn them into necessarily false claims. The possibility that a person might be split into two people such that each resultant can see that he is now not the other and yet can remember having been the original seems so plausible that that in itself seems to provide a good reason for rejecting any analysis that does make them necessarily false.

Normally identity is thought to be a two-term relation. Here, however, it seems to be taken as a three-term relation: A is identical to B at time t. The following rules characterize the two-term identity relation in natural deduction systems:

$$x = x \qquad (= \text{in}) \qquad \begin{array}{|l} \phi(x) \\ x = y \\ . \\ . \\ . \\ \phi(y) \qquad (= \text{out}) \end{array}$$

One is tempted to characterize the three-term identity relation by the following rules:

$$I(t,x,x) \qquad (I \text{ in}) \qquad \begin{array}{|l} \phi(t,x) \\ I(t,x,y) \\ . \\ . \\ . \\ \phi(t,y) \qquad (I \text{ out}) \end{array}$$

Using these rules, however, it can be proved that if x is identical to y at one time, x is identical to y at any other time:

1.	I(t,x,y)	hyp.
2.	I(t',x,x)	I in
3.	I(t',x,x) & I(t,x,y)	1,2, & in
4.	I(t',x,y) & I(t,x,y)	1,3,I out
5.	I(t',x,y)	4,& out

It is clear that to obtain the kind of three-term identity relation called for, further restrictions will have to be put on at least one of the two I rules above. What these restrictions are is not clear.

4. It is perhaps worth pointing out here that the believer in the possibility of reincarnation, in making this reply, in no way commits himself to a standard or to a non-standard view of identity. In the standard view, the identity relation is reflexive, symmetrical, and transitive. The principle of the Identity of Indiscernibles is a second-order *theorem*. Spatiotemporal continuity has absolutely nothing to do with it. On the other hand, if some non-standard view of identity is adopted (see, for instance, the preceding footnote), it is still not obvious that spatiotemporal continuity must, or even will, enter in.

5. Sydney Shoemaker, *Ibid.*, pp. 23–24.

6. *Ibid.*, p. 24.

7. Derek Parfit, "Personal Identity," *Philosophical Review*, Vol. LXXX, No. 1, January, 1971.

PERSONAL IDENTITY[1]
by Derek Parfit

We can, I think describe cases in which, though we know the answer to every other question, we have no idea how to answer a question about personal identity. These cases are not covered by the criteria of personal identity that we actually use.

Do they present a problem?

It might be thought that they do not, because they could never occur. I suspect that some of them could. (Some, for instance, might become scientifically possible.) But I shall claim that even if they did they would present no problem.

My targets are two beliefs: one about the nature of personal identity, the other about its importance.

The first is that in these cases the question about identity must have an answer.

No one thinks this about, say, nations or machines. One criteria for the identity of these do not cover certain cases. No one thinks that in these cases the question "Is it the same nation?" or "Is it the same machine?" must have answers.

Some people believe that in this respect they are different. They agree that our criteria of personal identity do not cover certain cases, but they believe that the nature of their own identity through time is, somehow, such as to guarantee that in these cases questions about their identity must have answers. This belief might be expressed as follows: "Whatever happens between now and any future time, either I shall still exist, or I shall not. Any future experience will either be *my* experience, or it will not."

This first belief—in the special nature of personal identity—has, I think, certain effects. It makes people assume that the principle of self-interest is more rationally compelling than any moral principle. And it makes them more depressed by the thought of aging and of death.

I cannot see how to disprove this first belief. I shall describe a problem case. But this can only make it seem implausible.

Another approach might be this. We might suggest that one cause of the belief is the projection of our emotions. When we imagine ourselves in a problem case, we do feel that the question "Would it be me?" must have an answer. But what we take to be a bafflement about a further fact may be only the bafflement of our concern.

I shall not pursue this suggestion here. But one cause of our concern is the belief which is my second target. This is that unless the question about identity has an answer, we cannot answer certain important questions (questions about such matters as survival, memory, and responsibility).

Against this second belief my claim will be this. Certain important questions do presuppose a question about personal identity. But they can be freed of this presupposition. And when they are, the question about identity has no importance.

I

We can start by considering the much-discussed case of the man who, like an amoeba, divides.[2]

Wiggins has recently dramatized this case.[3] He first referred to the operation imagined by Shoemaker.[4] We suppose that my brain is transplanted into someone else's (brainless) body, and that the resulting person has my character and apparent memories of my life. Most of us would agree, after thought, that the resulting person is me. I shall here assume such agreement.[5]

Wiggins then imagined his own operation. My brain is divided, and each half is housed in a new body. Both resulting people have my character and apparent memories of my life.

What happens to me? There seem only three possibilities: (1) I do not survive; (2) I survive as one of the two people; (3) I survive as both.

The trouble with (1) is this. We agreed that I could survive if my brain were successfully transplanted. And people have in fact survived with half their brains destroyed. It seems to follow that I could survive if half my brain were successfully transplanted and the other half were destroyed. But if this is so, how could I *not* survive if the other half were also successfully transplanted? How could a double success be a failure?

We can move to the second description. Perhaps one success is the maximum score. Perhaps I shall be one of the resulting people.

The trouble here is that in Wiggins' case each half of my brain is exactly similar, and so, to start with, is each resulting person. So how can I survive as only one of the two people? What can make me one of them rather than the other?

It seems clear that both of these descriptions—that I do not survive, and that I survive as one of the people—are highly implausible. Those who have accepted them must have assumed that they were the only possible descriptions.

What about our third description: that I survive as both people?

I might be said, "If 'survive' implies identity, this description makes no sense—you cannot be two people. If it does not, the description is irrelevant to a problem about identity."

I shall later deny the second of these remarks. But there are ways of denying the first. We might say, "What we have called 'the two resulting people' are not two people. They are one person. I do survive Wiggins' operation. Its effect is to give me two bodies and a divided mind."

It would shorten my argument if this were absurd. But I do not think it is. It is worth showing why.

We can, I suggest, imagine a divided mind. We can imagine a man having two simultaneous experiences, in having each of which he is unaware of having the other.

We may not even need to imagine this. Certain actual cases, to which Wiggins referred, seem to be best described in these terms. These involve the cutting of the bridge between the hemispheres of the brain. The aim was to cure epilepsy. But the result appears to be, in the surgeon's words, the creation of "two separate spheres of consciousness,"[6] each of which controls one half of the patient's body. What is experienced in each is, presumably, experienced by the patient.

There are certain complications in these actual cases. So let us imagine a simpler case.

Suppose that the bridge between my hemispheres is brought under my voluntary control. This would enable me to disconnect my hemispheres as easily as if I were blinking. By doing this I would divide my mind. And we can suppose that when my mind is divided I can, in each half, bring about reunion.

This ability would have obvious uses. To give an example: I am near the end of a maths exam, and see two ways of tackling the last problem. I decide to divide my mind, to work, with each half, at one of two calculations, and then to reunite my mind and write a fair copy of the best result.

What shall I experience?

When I disconnect my hemispheres, my consciousness divides into two streams. But this division is not something that I experience. Each of my two streams of consciousness seems to have been straightforwardly continuous with my one stream of consciousness up to the moment of division. The only changes in each stream are the disappearance of half my visual field and the loss of sensation in, and control over, half my body.

Consider my experiences in what we can call my "right-handed" stream. I remember that I assigned my right hand to the longer calculation. This I now begin. In working at this calculation I can see, from the movements of my left hand, that I am also working at the other. But I am not aware of working at the other. So I might, in my right-handed stream, wonder how, in my left-handed stream, I am getting on.

My work is now over. I am about to reunite my mind. What should I, in each stream, expect? Simply that I shall suddenly seem to remember just having thought out two calculations, in thinking out each of which I was not aware of thinking out the other. This, I submit, we can imagine. And if my mind was divided, these memories are correct.

In describing this episode, I assumed that there were two series of thoughts, and that they were both mine. If my two hands visibly wrote out two calculations, and if I claimed to remember two corresponding series of thoughts, this is surely what we should want to say.

If it is, then a person's mental history need not be like a canal, with only one channel. It could be like a river, with islands, and with separate streams.

To apply this to Wiggins' operation: we mentioned the view that it gives me two bodies and a divided mind. We cannot now call this absurd. But it is, I think, unsatisfactory.

There were two features of the case of the exam that made us want to say that only one person was involved. The mind was soon reunited, and there was only one body. If a mind was permanently divided and its halves developed in different ways, the point of speaking of one person would start to disappear. Wiggins' case, where there are also two bodies, seems to be over the borderline. After I have had this operation, the two "products" each have all the attributes of a person. They could live at opposite ends of the earth. (If they later met, they might even fail to recognize each other.) It would become intolerable to deny that they were different people.

Suppose we admit that they are different people. Could we still claim that I survived as both, using "survive" to imply identity?

We could. For we might suggest that two people could compose a third. We might say, "I do survive Wiggins' operation as two people. They can be different people, and yet be me, in just the way in which the Pope's three crowns are one crown."[7]

This is a possible way of giving sense to the claim that I survive as two different people, using "survive" to imply identity. But it keeps the language of identity only by changing the concept of a person. And there are obvious objections to this change.[8]

The alternative, for which I shall argue, is to give up the language of identity. We can suggest that I survive as two different people without implying that I am these people.

When I first mentioned this alternative, I mentioned this objection: "If your new way of talking does not imply identity, it cannot solve our problem. For that is about identity. The problem is that all the possible answers to the question about identity are highly implausible."

We can now answer this objection.

We can start by reminding ourselves that this is an objection only if we have one or both of the beliefs which I mentioned at the start of this paper.

The first was the belief that to any question about personal identity, in any describable case, there must be a true answer. For those with this belief, Wiggins' case is doubly perplexing. If all the possible answers are implausible, it is hard to decide which of them is true, and hard even to keep the belief that one of them must be true. If we give up this belief, as I think we should, these problems disappear. We shall then regard the case as like many others in which, for quite unpuzzling reasons, there *is* no answer to a question about identity. (Consider "Was England the same nation after 1066?")

Wiggins' case makes the first belief implausible. It also makes it trivial. For it undermines the second belief. This was the belief that important questions turn upon the question about identity. (It is worth pointing out that those who have only this second belief do not think that there must *be* an answer to this question, but rather that we must decide upon an answer.)

Against this second belief my claim is this. Certain questions do presuppose a question about personal identity. And because these questions *are* important, Wiggins' case does present a problem. But we cannot solve this problem by answering the question about identity. We can solve this problem only by taking these important questions and prizing them apart from the question about identity. After we have done this, the question about identity (though we might for the sake of neatness decide it) has no further interest.

Because there are several questions which presuppose identity, this claim will take some time to fill out.

We can first return to the question of survival. This is a special case, for survival does not so much presuppose the retaining of identity as seem equivalent to it. It is thus the general relation which we need to prize apart from identity. We can then consider particular relations, such as those involved in memory and intention.

"Will I survive?" seems, I said, equivalent to "Will there be some person alive who is the same person as me?"

If we treat these questions as equivalent, then the least unsatisfactory description of Wiggins' case is, I think, that I survive with two bodies and a divided mind.

Several writers have chosen to say that I am neither of the resulting people. Given our equivalence, this implies that I do not survive, and hence, presumably, that even if Wiggins' operation is not literally death, I ought, since I will not survive it, to regard it *as* death. But this seemed absurd.

It is worth repeating why. An emotion or attitude can be criticized for resting on a false belief, or for being inconsistent. A man who regarded Wiggins' operation as death must, I suggest, be open to one of these criticisms.

He might believe that his relation to each of the resulting people fails to contain some element which is contained in survival. But how can this be true? We agreed that he *would* survive if he stood in this very same relation to only *one* of the resulting people. So it cannot be the nature of this relation which makes it fail, in Wiggins' case, to be survival. It can only be its duplication.

Suppose that our man accepts this, but still regards division as death. His reaction would now seem wildly inconsistent. He would be like a man who, when told of a drug that could double his years of life, regarded the taking of this drug as death. The only difference in the case of division is that the extra years are to run concurrently. This is an interesting difference. But it cannot mean that there are *no* years to run.

I have argued this for those who think that there must, in Wiggins' case, be a true answer to the question about identity. For them, we might add, "Perhaps the original person does lose his identity. But there may be other ways to do this than to die. One other way might be to multiply. To regard these as the same is to confuse nought with two."

For those who think that the question of identity is up for decision, it would be clearly absurd to regard Wiggins' operation as death. These people would have to think, "We could have chosen to say that I should be one of the resulting people. If we had, I should not have regarded it as death. But since we have chosen to say that I am neither person, I *do*." This is hard even to understand.[9]

My first conclusion, then, is this: The relation of the original person to each of the resulting people contains all that interests us—all that matters—in any ordinary case of survival. This is why we need a sense in which one person can survive as two.[10]

One of my aims in the rest of this paper will be to suggest such a sense. But we can first make some general remarks.

II

Identity is a one-one relation. Wiggins' case serves to show that what matters in survival need not be one-one.

Wiggins' case is of course unlikely to occur. The relations which matter are, in fact, one-one. It is because they are that we can imply the holding of these relations by using the language of identity.

This use of language is convenient. But it can lead us astray. We may assume that what matters *is* identity and, hence, has the properties of identity.

In the case of the property of being one-one, this mistake is not serious. For what matters is in fact one-one. But in the case of another property, the mistake *is* serious. Identity is all-or-nothing. Most of the relations which matter in survival are, in fact, relations of degree. If we ignore this, we shall be led into quite ill-grounded attitudes and beliefs.

The claim that I have just made—that most of what matters are relations of degree—I have yet to support. Wiggins' case shows only that these relations need not be one-one. The merit of the case is not that it shows this in particular, but that it makes the first break between what matters and identity. The belief that identity *is* what matters is hard to overcome. This is shown in most discussions of the problem cases which actually occur: cases, say, of amnesia or of brain damage. Once Wiggins' case has made one breach in this belief, the rest should be easier to remove.[11]

To turn to a recent debate: most of the relations which matter can be provisionally referred to under the heading "psychological continuity" (which includes causal continuity). My claim is thus that we use the language of personal identity in order to imply such continuity. This is close to the view that psychological continuity provides a criterion of identity.

Williams has attacked this view with the following argument. Identity is a one-one relation. So any criterion of identity must appeal to a relation which is logically one-one. Psychological continuity is not logically one-one. So it cannot provide a criterion.[12]

Some writers have replied that it is enough if the relation appealed to is always in fact one-one.[13]

I suggest a slightly different reply. Psychological continuity is a ground for speaking of identity when it is one-one.

If psychological continuity took a one-many or branching form, we should need, I have argued, to abandon the language of identity. So this possibility would not count against this view.

We can make a stronger claim. This possibility would count in its favor.

The view might be defended as follows. Judgments of personal identity have great importance. What gives them their importance is the fact that they imply psychological continuity. This is why, whenever there is such continuity, we ought, if we can, to imply it by making a judgment of identity.

If psychological continuity took a branching form, no coherent set of judgments of identity could correspond to, and thus be used to imply, the branching form of this relation. But what we ought to do, in such a case, is take the importance which would attach to a judgment of identity and attach this importance directly to each limb of the branching relation. So this case helps to show that judgments of personal identity do derive their importance from the fact that they imply psychological continuity. It helps to show that when we can, usefully, speak of identity, this relation is our ground.

This argument appeals to a principle which Williams put forward.[14] The principle is that an important judgment should be asserted and denied only on importantly different grounds.

Williams applied this principle to a case in which one man is psychologically continuous with the dead Guy Fawkes, and a case in which two men are. His argument was this. If we treat psychological continuity as a sufficient ground for speaking of identity, we shall say that the one man is Guy Fawkes. But we could not say that the two men are, although we should have the same ground. This disobeys the principle. The remedy is to deny that the one man is Guy Fawkes, to insist that sameness of the body is necessary for identity.

Williams' principle can yield a different answer. Suppose we regard psychological continuity as more important than sameness of the body.[15] And suppose that the one man really is psychologically (and causally) continuous with Guy Fawkes. If he is, it would disobey the principle to deny that he is Guy Fawkes, for we have the same important ground as in a normal case of identity. In the case of the two men, we again have the same important ground. So we ought to take the importance from the judgment of identity and attach it directly to this ground. We ought to say, as in Wiggins' case, that each limb of the branching relation is as good as survival. This obeys the principle.

To sum up these remarks: even if psychological continuity is neither logically, nor always in fact, one-one, it can provide a criterion of identity. For this can appeal to the relation of *non-branching* psychological continuity, which is logically one-one.[16]

The criterion might be sketched as follows. "X and Y are the same person if they are psychologically continuous and there is no person who is contemporary with either and psychologically continuous with the other." We should need to explain what we mean by "psychologically continuous" and say how much continuity the criterion requires. We should then, I think, have described a sufficient condition for speaking of identity.[17]

We need to say something more. If we admit that psychological continuity might not be one-one, we need to say what we ought to do if it were not one-one. Otherwise our account would be open to the objections that it is incomplete and arbitrary.[18]

I have suggested that if psychological continuity took a branching form, we ought to speak in a new way, regarding what we describe as having the same significance as identity. This answers these objections.[19]

We can now return to our discussion. We have three remaining aims. One is to suggest a sense of "survive" which does not imply identity. Another is to show that most of what matters in survival are relations of degree. A third is to show that none of these relations needs to be described in a way that presupposes identity.

We can take these aims in the reverse order.

III

The most important particular relation is that involved in memory. This is because it is so easy to believe that its description must refer to identity.[20] This belief about memory is an important cause of the view that personal identity has a special nature. But it has been well discussed by Shoemaker[21] and by Wiggins.[22] So we can be brief.

It may be a logical truth that we can only remember our own experiences. But we can frame a new concept for which this is not a logical truth. Let us call this "q-memory."

To sketch a definition[23] I am q-remembering an experience if (1) I have a belief about a past experience which seems in itself like a memory belief, (2) someone did have such an experience, and (3) my belief is dependent upon this experience in the same way (whatever that is) in which a memory of an experience is dependent upon it.

According to (1) q-memories seem like memories. So I q-remember *having* experiences.

This may seem to make q-memory presuppose identity. One might say, "My apparent memory of *having* an experience is an apparent memory of *my* having an experience. So how could I q-remember my having other people's experiences?"

This objection rests on a mistake. When I seem to remember an experience, I do indeed seem to remember *having* it.[24] But it cannot be a part of what I seem to remember about this experience that I, the person who now seems to remember it, am the person who had this experience.[25] That I am is something that I automatically assume. (My apparent memories sometimes come to me simply as the belief that *I* had a certain experience.) But it is something that I am justified in assuming only because I do not in fact have q-memories of other people's experiences.

Suppose that I did start to have such q-memories. If I did, I should cease to assume that my apparent memories must be about my own experiences. I should come to assess an apparent memory by asking two questions: (1) Does it tell me about a past experience? (2) If so, whose?

Moreover (and this is a crucial point) my apparent memories would now come to me *as* q-memories. Consider those of my apparent memories which do come to me simply as beliefs about my past: for example, "I did that." If I knew that I could q-remember other people's experiences, these beliefs would come to me in a more guarded form: for example, "Someone—probably I—did that." I might have to work out who it was.

I have suggested that the concept of q-memory is coherent. Wiggins' case provides an illustration. The resulting people, in his case, both have apparent memories of living the life of the original person. If they agree that they are not this person, they will have to regard these as only q-memories. And when they are asked a question like "Have you heard this music before?" they might have to answer "I am sure that I q-remember hearing it. But I am not sure whether I remember hearing it. I am not sure whether it was I who heard it, or the original person."

We can next point out that on our definition every memory is also a q-memory. Memories are, simply, q-memories of one's own experiences. Since this is so, we could afford now to drop the concept of memory and use in its place the wider concept *q*-memory. If we did, we should describe the relation between an experience and what we now call a "memory" of this experience in a way which does not presuppose that they are had by the same person.[26]

This way of describing this relation has certain merits. It vindicates the "memory criterion" of personal identity against the charge of circularity.[27] And it might, I think, help with the problem of other minds.

But we must move on. We can next take the relation between an intention and a later action. It may be a logical truth that we can intend to perform only our own actions. But intentions can be redescribed as *q*-intentions. And one person could *q*-intend to perform another person's actions.

Wiggins' case again provides the illustration. We are supposing that neither of the resulting people is the original person. If so, we shall have to agree that the original person can, before the operation, *q*-intend to perform their actions. He might, for example, *q*-intend, as one of them, to continue his present career, and, as the other, to try something new.[28] (I say "*q*-intend *as* one of them" because the phrase "*q*-intend *that* one of them" would not convey the directness of the relation which is involved. If I intend that someone else should do something, I cannot get him to do it simply by forming this intention. But if I am the original person, and he is one of the resulting people, I can.)

The phrase "*q*-intend *as* one of them" reminds us that we need a sense in which one person can survive as two. But we can first point out that the concepts of *q*-memory and *q*-intention give us our model for the others that we need: thus, a man who can *q*-remember could *q*-recognize, and be a *q*-witness of, what he has never seen; and a man who can *q*-intend could have *q*-ambitions, make *q*-promises, and be *q*-responsible for.

To put this claim in general terms: many different relations are included within, or are a consequence of, psychological continuity. We describe these relations in ways which presuppose the continued existence of one person. But we could describe them in new ways which do not.

This suggests a bolder claim. It might be possible to think of experiences in a wholly "impersonal" way. I shall not develop this claim here. What I shall try to describe is a way of thinking of our own identity through time which is more flexible, and less misleading, than the way in which we now think.

This way of thinking will allow for a sense in which one person can survive as two. A more important feature is that it treats survival as a matter of degree.

IV

We must first show the need for this second feature. I shall use two imaginary examples.

The first is the converse of Wiggins' case: fusion. Just as division serves to show that what matters in survival need not be one-one, so fusion serves to show that it can be a question of degree.

Physically, fusion is easy to describe. Two people come together. While they are unconscious, their two bodies grow into one. One person then wakes up.

The psychology of fusion is more complex. One detail we have already dealt with in the case of the exam. When my mind was reunited, I remembered just having thought out two calculations. The one person who results from a fusion can, similarly, q-remember living the lives of the two original people. None of their q-memories need be lost.

But some things must be lost. For any two people who fuse together will have different characteristics, different desires, and different intentions. How can these be combined?

We might suggest the following. Some of these will be compatible. These can coexist in the one resulting person. Some will be incompatible. These, if of equal strength, can cancel out, and if of different strengths, the stronger can be made weaker. And all these effects might be predictable.

To give examples—first, of compatibility: I like Palladio and intend to visit Venice. I am about to fuse with a person who likes Giotto and intends to visit Padua. I can know that the one person we shall become will have both tastes and both intentions. Second, of incompatibility: I hate red hair, and always vote Labour. The other person loves red hair, and always votes Conservative. I can know that the one person we shall become will be indifferent to red hair, and a floating voter.

If we were about to undergo a fusion of this kind, would we regard it as death?

Some of us might. This is less absurd than regarding division as death. For after my division the two resulting people will be in every way like me, while after my fusion the one resulting person will not be wholly similar. This makes it easier to say, when faced with fusion, "I shall not survive," thus continuing to regard survival as a matter of all-or-nothing.

This reaction is less absurd. But here are two analogies which tell against it.

First, fusion would involve the changing of some of our characteristics and some of our desires. But only the very self-satisfied would think of this as death. Many people welcome treatments with these effects.

Second, someone who is about to fuse can have, beforehand, just as much "intential control" over the actions of the resulting individual as someone who is about to marry can have, beforehand, over the actions of the resulting couple. And the choice of a partner for fusion can be just as well considered as the choice of a marriage partner. The two original people can make sure (perhaps by "trial fusion") that they do have compatible characters, desires, and intentions.

I have suggested that fusion, while not clearly survival, is not clearly failure to survive, and hence that what matters in survival can have degrees.

To reinforce this claim we can now turn to a second example. This is provided by certain imaginary beings. These beings are just like ourselves except that they reproduce by a process of natural division.

We can illustrate the histories of these imagined beings with the aid of a diagram. (See Figure 1.) The lines on the diagram represent the spatio-temporal paths which would be traced out by the bodies of these beings. We can call each single line (like the double line) a "branch"; and we can call the whole structure a "tree." And let us suppose that each "branch" corresponds to what is thought of as the life of one individual. These individuals are referred to as "A," "B + 1," and so forth.

Now, each single division is an instance of Wiggins' case. So A's relation to both $B + 1$ and $B + 2$ is just as good as survival. But what of A's relation to B +30?

I said earlier that what matters in survival could be provisionally referred to as "psychological continuity." I must now distinguish this relation from another, which I shall call "psychological connectedness."

Let us say that the relation between a q-memory and the experience q-remembered is a "direct" relation. Another "direct" relation is that which holds between a q-intention and the q-intended action. A third is that which holds between different expressions of some lasting q-characteristic.

"Psychological connectedness," as I define it, requires the holding of these direct psychological relations. "Connectedness" is not transitive, since these relations are not transitive. Thus, if X q-remembers most of Y's life, and Y q-remembers most of Z's life, it does not follow that X q-remembers most of Z's life. And if X carries out the q-intentions of Y, and Y carries out the q-intentions of Z, it does not follow that X carries out the q-intentions of Z.

"Psychological continuity," in contrast, only requires overlapping chains of direct psychological relations. So "continuity" *is* transitive.

To return to our diagram. A *is* psychologically continuous with $B + 30$. There are between the two continuous chains of overlapping relations. Thus, A has q-intentional control over $B + 2$, $B + 2$ has q-intentional control over $B + 6$, and so on up to $B + 30$. Or $B + 30$ can q-remember the life of $B + 14$, $B + 14$ can q-remember the life of $B + 6$, and so on back to A.[29]

A, however, need *not* be psychologically connected to $B + 30$. Connectedness requires direct relations. And if these beings are like us, A cannot stand in such relations to every individual in his indefinitely long "tree." Q-memories will weaken with the passage of time, and then fade away. Q-ambitions, once fulfilled, will be replaced by others. Q-characteristics will gradually change. In general, A stands in fewer and fewer direct psychological relations to an individual in his "tree" the more remote that

Figure 1.

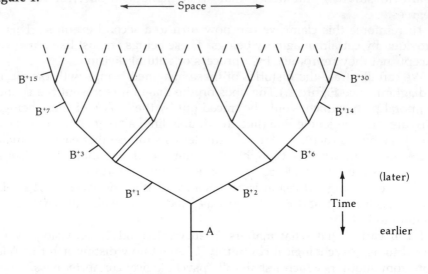

individual is. And if the individual is (like $B + 30$) sufficiently remote, there may be between the two *no* direct psychological relations.

Now that we have distinguished the general relations of psychological continuity and psychological connectedness, I suggest that connectedness is a more important element in survival. As a claim about our own survival, this would need more arguments than I have space to give. But it seems clearly true for my imagined beings. A is as close psychologically to $B + 1$ as I today am to myself tomorrow. A is as distant from $B + 30$ as I am from my great-great-grandson.

Even if connectedness is not more important than continuity, the fact that one of these is a relation of degree is enough to show that what matters in survival can have degrees. And in any case the two relations are quite different. So our imagined beings would need a way of thinking in which this difference is recognized.

V

What I propose is this.

First, A can think of any individual, anywhere in his "tree," as "a descendant self." This phrase implies psychological continuity. Similarly, any later individual can think of any earlier individual on the single path[30] which connects him to A as "an ancestral self."

Since psychological continuity is transitive, "being an ancestral self of" and "being a descendant self of" are also transitive.

To imply psychological connectedness I suggest the phrases "one of my future selves" and "one of my past selves."

These are the phrases with which we can describe Wiggins' case. For having past and future selves is, what we needed, a way of continuing to exist which does not imply identity through time. The original person does, in this sense, survive Wiggins' operation: the two resulting people are his later selves. And they can each refer to him as "my past self." (They can share a past self without being the same self as each other.)

Since psychological connectedness is not transitive, and is a matter of degree, the relations "being a past self of" and "being a future self of" should themselves be treated as relations of degree. We allow for this series of descriptions: "my most recent self," "one of my earlier selves," "one of my distant selves," "hardly one of *my* past selves (I can only *q*-remember a few of his experiences)," and, finally, "not in any way one of *my* past selves—just an ancestral self."

This way of thinking would clearly suit our first imagined beings. But let us now turn to a second kind of being. These reproduce by fusion as well as by division.[31] And let us suppose that they fuse every autumn and divide every spring. This yields Figure 2.

If *A* is the individual whose life is represented by the three-lined "branch," the two-lined "tree" represents those lives which are psychologically continuous with *A*'s life. (It can be seen that each individual has his own "tree," which overlaps with many others.)

For the imagined beings in this second world, the phrases "an ancestral self" and "a descendant self" would cover too much to be of much use. (There may well be pairs of dates such that every individual who ever lived before the first date was an ancestral self of every individual who ever will live after the second date.) Conversely, since the lives of each individual last for only half a year, the word "I" would cover too little to do all of the work which it does for us. So part of this work would have to be done, for these second beings, by talk about past and future selves.

We can now point out a theoretical flaw in our proposed way of thinking. The phrase "a past self of" implies psychological connectedness. Being a past self of is treated as a relation of degree, so that this phrase can be used to imply the varying degrees of psychological connectedness. But this phrase can imply only the degrees of connectedness between different lives. It cannot be used within a single life. And our way of delimiting successive lives does not refer to the degrees of psychological connectedness. Hence there is no guarantee that this phrase, "a past self of," could be used whenever it was needed. There is no guarantee that psychological connectedness will not vary in degree within a single life.

This flaw would not concern our imagined beings. For they divide and unite so frequently, and their lives are in consequence so short, that within a single life psychological connectedness would always stand at a maximum.

Figure 2.

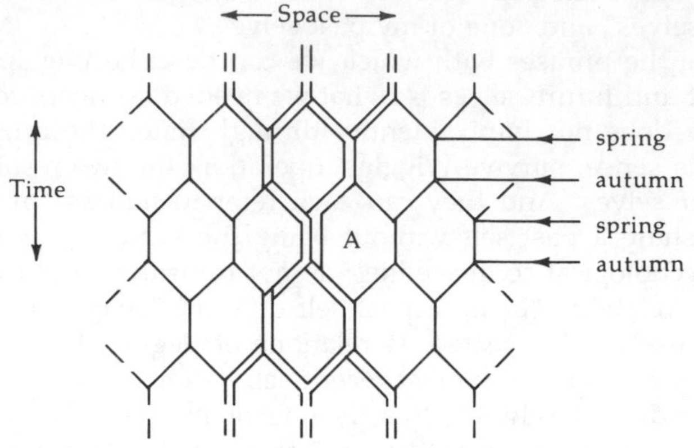

But let us look, finally, at a third kind of being.

In this world there is neither division nor union. There are a number of everlasting bodies, which gradually change in appearance. And direct psychological relations, as before, hold only over limited periods of time. This can be illustrated with a third diagram (see Figure 3). In this diagram the two shadings represent the degrees of psychological connectedness to their two central points.

These beings could not use the way of thinking that we have proposed. Since there is no branching of psychological continuity, they would have to regard themselves as immortal. It might be said that this is what they are. But there is, I suggest, a better description.

Our beings would have one reason for thinking of themselves as immortal. The parts of each "line" are all psychologically continuous. But the parts of each "line" are not all psychologically connected. Direct psychological relations hold only between those parts which are close to each other in time. This gives our beings a reason for *not* thinking of each "line" as corresponding to one single life. For if they did, they would have no way of implying these direct relations. When a speaker says, for example, "I spent a period doing such and such," his hearers would not be entitled to assume that the speaker has any memories of this period, that his character then and now are in any way similar, that he is now carrying out any of the plans or intentions which he then had, and so forth. Because the word "I" would carry none of these implications, it would not have for these "immortal" beings the usefulness which it has for us.[32]

To gain a better way of thinking, we must revise the way of thinking that we proposed above. The revision is this. The distinction between successive selves can be made by reference, not to the branching of psychological continuity, but to the degrees of psychological connectedness. Since this connectedness is a matter of degree, the drawing of these

Figure 3.

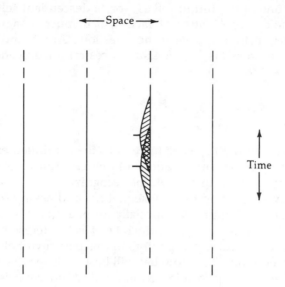

distinctions can be left to the choice of the speaker and be allowed to vary from context to context.

On this way of thinking, the word "I" can be used to imply the greatest degree of psychological connectedness. When the connections are reduced, when there has been any marked change of character or style of life, or any marked loss of memory, our imagined beings would say, "It was not I who did that, but an earlier self." They could then describe in what ways, and to what degree, they are related to this earlier self.

This revised way of thinking would suit not only our "immortal" beings. It is also the way in which we ourselves could think about our lives. And it is, I suggest, surprisingly natural.

One of its features, the distinction between successive selves, has already been used by several writers. To give an example, from Proust: "we are incapable, while we are in love, of acting as fit predecessors of the next persons who, when we are in love no longer, we shall presently have become . . . ."[33]

Although Proust distinguished between successive selves, he still thought of one person as being these different selves. This we would not do on the way of thinking that I propose. If I say, "It will not be me, but one of my future selves," I do not imply that I will be that future self. He is one of my later selves, and I am one of his earlier selves. There is no underlying person who we both are.

To point out another feature of this way of thinking. When I say, "There is no person who we both are," I am only giving my decision. Another person could say, "It will be you," thus deciding differently. There is no question of either of these decisions being a mistake. Whether to say "I," or "one of my future selves," or "a descendant self" is entirely a matter of choice. The matter of fact, which must be agreed, is only whether the disjunction applies. (The question "Are X and Y the same person?" thus becomes "Is X *at least* an ancestral [or descendant] self of Y?")

VI

I have tried to show that what matters in the continued existence of a person are, for the most part, relations of degree. And I have proposed a way of thinking in which this would be recognized.

I shall end by suggesting two consequences and asking one question.

It is sometimes thought to be especially rational to act in our own best interests. But I suggest that the principle of self-interest has no force. There are only two genuine competitors in this particular field. One is the principal of biased rationality: do what will best achieve what you actually want. The other is the principle of impartiality: do what is in the best interests of everyone concerned.

The apparent force of the principle of self-interest derives, I think, from these two other principles.

The principle of self-interest is normally supported by the principle of biased rationality. This is because most people care about their own future interests.

Suppose that this prop is lacking. Suppose that a man does not care what happens to him in, say, the more distant future. To such a man, the principle of self-interest can only be propped up by an appeal to the principle of impartiality. We must say, "Even if you don't care, you ought to take what happens to you then equally into account." But for this, as a special claim, there seem to me no good arguments. It can only be supported as part of the general claim, "You ought to take what happens to everyone equally into account."[34]

The special claim tells a man to grant an *equal* weight to all the parts of his future. The argument for this can only be that all the parts of his future are *equally* parts of *his* future. This is true. But it is a truth too superficial to bear the weight of the argument. (To give an analogy: The unity of a nation is, in its nature, a matter of degree. It is therefore only a superficial truth that all of a man's compatriots are *equally* his compatriots. This truth cannot support a good argument for nationalism.)

I have suggested that the principle of self-interest has no strength of its own. If this is so, there is no special problem in the fact that what we ought to do can be against our interests. There is only the general problem that it may not be what we want to do.

The second consequence which I shall mention is implied in the first. Egoism, the fear not of near but of distant death, the regret that so much of one's *only* life should have gone by—these are not, I think, wholly natural or instinctive. They are all strengthened by the beliefs about personal identity which I have been attacking. If we give up these beliefs, they should be weakened.

My final question is this. These emotions are bad, and if we weaken them we gain. But can we achieve this gain without, say, also weakening loyalty to, or love of, other particular selves? As Hume warned, the "refined reflections which philosophy suggests . . . cannot diminish . . . our vicious passions . . . without diminishing . . . such as are virtuous. They are . . . applicable to all our affections. In vain do we hope to direct their influence only to one side."

That hope *is* vain. But Hume had another: that more of what is bad depends upon false belief. This is also my hope.

NOTES

1. I have been helped in writing this by D. Wiggins, D. F. Pears, P. F. Strawson, A. J. Ayer, M. Woods, N. Newman, and (through his publications) S. Shoemaker.

2. Implicit in John Locke, *Essay Concerning Human Understanding*, ed. by John W. Yolton (London, 1961), Vol. II, Ch. XXVII, sec. 18, and discussed by (among others) A. N. Prior in "Opposite Number," *Review of Metaphysics*, 11 (1957–1958), and "Time, Existence and Identity," *Procedings of the Aristotelian Society*, LVII (1965–1966): J. Bennett in "The Simplicity of the Soul," *Journal of Philosophy*, LXIV (1967); and R. Chisholm and S. Shoemaker in "The Loose and Popular and the Strict and the Philosophical Senses of Identity." in *Perception and Personal Identity: Proceedings of the 1967 Oberlin Colloquium in Philosophy*, ed. by Norman Care and Robert H. Grimm (Cleveland, 1967).

3. In *Identity and Spatio-Temporal Continuity* (Oxford, 1967), p. 50.

4. In *Self-Knowledge and Self-Identity* (Ithaca, N.Y., 1963), p. 22.

5. Those who would disagree are not making a mistake. For them my argument would need a different case. There must be some multiple transplant, faced with which these people would both find it hard to believe that there must be an answer to the question about personal identity, and be able to be shown that nothing of importance turns upon this question.

6. R. W. Sperry, in *Brain and Conscious Experience*, ed. by J. C. Eccles (New York, 1966), p. 299.

7. Cf. David Wiggins, *op. cit*, p. 40.

8. Suppose the resulting people fight a duel. Are there three people fighting, one on each side, and one on both? And suppose one of the bullets kills. Are there two acts, one murder and one suicide? How many people are left alive? One? Two? (We could hardly say, "One and a half.") We could talk in this way. But instead of saying that the resulting people *are* the original person—so that the pair is a trio—it would be far simpler to treat them as a pair, and describe their relation to the original person in some new way. (I owe this suggested way of talking, and the objections to it, to Michael Woods.)

9. Cf. Sydney Shoemaker, in *Perception and Personal Identity: Proceedings of the 1967 Oberlin Colloquium in Philosophy*, loc. cit.

10. Cf. David Wiggins, *op. cit.*, p. 54.

11. Bernard Williams' "The Self and the Future," *Philosophical Review*, LXXIX (1970), 161–180, is relevant here. He asks the question "Shall I survive?" in a range of problem cases, and he shows how natural it is to believe (1) that this question must have an answer, (2) that the answer must be all-or-nothing, and (3) that there is a "risk" of our reaching the *wrong* answer. Because these beliefs are so natural, we should need in undermining them to discuss their causes. These, I think, can be found in the ways in which we misinterpret what it is to remember (cf. Sec. III below) and to anticipate (cf. Williams' "Imagination and the Self," *Proceedings of the British Academy*, LII [1966], 105–124); and also in the way in which certain features of our egoistic concern—e.g., that it is simple, and applies to all imaginable cases—are "projected" onto its object. (For another relevant discussion, see Terence Penelhum's *Survival and Disembodied Existence* [London, 1970], final chapters.)

12. "Personal Identity and Individuation," *Proceedings of the Aristotelian Society*, LVII (1956–1957), 229–253; also *Analysis*, 21 (1960–1961), 43–48.

13. J. M. Shorter, "More about Bodily Continuity and Personal Identity," *Analysis*, 22 (1961–1962), 79–85; and Mrs. J. M. R. Jack (unpublished), who requires that this truth be embedded in a causal theory.

14. *Analysis*, 21 (1960–1961), 44.

15. For the reasons given by A. M. Quinton in "The Soul," *Journal of Philosophy*, LIX (1962), 393–409.

16. Cf. S. Shoemaker, "Persons and Their Pasts," to appear in the *American Philosophical Quarterly*, and "Wiggins on Identity," *Philosophical Review*, LXXIX (1970), 542.

17. But not a necessary condition, for in the absence of psychological continuity bodily identity might be sufficient.

18. Cf. Bernard Williams, "Personal Identity and Individuation," *Proceedings of the Aristotelian Society*, LVII (1956–1957), 240–241, and *Analysis*, 21 (1960–1961), 44; and also Wiggins, *op. cit.*, p. 38: "if coincidence under [the concept] *f* is to be *genuinely* sufficient we must not withhold identity . . . simply because transitivity is threatened."

19. Williams produced another objection to the "psychological criterion," that it makes it hard to explain the difference between the concepts of identity and exact similarity (*Analysis*, 21 [1960–1961], 48). But if we include the requirement of causal continuity we avoid this objection (and one of those produced by Wiggins in his note 47).

20. Those philosophers who have held this belief, from Butler onward, are too numerous to cite.

21. *Op. cit.*

22. In David Wiggins, "Locke, Butler and the Stream of Consciousness: And Men as a Natural Kind" in *The Identities of Persons*, ed. by A. O. Rorty (Berkeley: University of California Press, 1976) p. 139–173.

23. I here follow Shoemaker's "quasi-memory." Cf. also Penelhum's "retrocognition," in his article on "Personal Identity," in the *Encyclopedia of Philosophy*, ed. by Paul Edwards.

24. As Shoemaker put it, I seem to remember the experience "from the inside" (*op. cit.*).

25. This is what so many writers have overlooked. Cf. Thomas Reid: "My mem-

ory testifies not only that this was done, but that it was done by me who now remember it" ("Of Identity," in *Essays on the Intellectual Powers of Man*, ed. by A. D. Woozley [London, 1941], p. 203). This mistake is discussed by A. B. Palma in "Memory and Personal Identity," *Australasian Journal of Philosophy*, 42 (1964), 57.

26. It is not logically necessary that we only q-remember our own experiences. But it might be necessary on other grounds. This possibility is intriguingly explored by Shoemaker in his "Persons and Their Pasts" (*op. cit.*). He shows that q-memories can provide a knowledge of the world only if the observations which are q-remembered trace out fairly continuous spatiotemporal paths. If the observations which are q-remembered traced out a network of frequently interlocking paths, they could not, I think, be usefully ascribed to persisting observers, but would have to be referred to in some more complex way. But in fact the observations which are q-remembered trace out single and separate paths; so we can ascribe them to ourselves. In other words, it is epistemologically necessary that the observations which are q-remembered should satisfy a certain general condition, one particular form of which allows them to be usefully self-ascribed.

27. Cf. Wiggins' paper on Butler's objection to Locke.

28. There are complications here. He could form *divergent* q-intentions only if he could distinguish, in advance, between the resulting people (e.g., as "the left-hander" and "the right-hander"). And he could be confident that such divergent q-intentions would be carried out only if he had reason to believe that neither of the resulting people would change their (inherited) mind. Suppose he was torn between duty and desire. He could not solve this dilemma by q-intending, as one of the resulting people, to do his duty, and, as the other, to do what he desires. For the one he q-intended to do his duty would face the same dilemma.

29. The chain of continuity must run in one direction of time. $B + 2$ is not, in the sense I intend, psychologically continuous with $B + 1$.

30. Cf. David Wiggins, *op. cit.*

31. Cf. Sydney Shoemaker in "Persons and Their Pasts," *op. cit.*

32. Cf. Austin Duncan Jones, "Man's Mortality," *Analysis*, 28 (1967–1968), 65–70.

33. *Within a Budding Grove* (London, 1949), I, 226 (my own translation).

34. Cf. Thomas Nagel's *The Possibility of Altruism* (Oxford, 1970), in which the special claim is in effect defended as part of the general claim.

PERSONAL IDENTITY

John Locke

The Identity of Man. The identity of the same man consists; viz., in nothing but a participation of the same continued life, by constantly fleeting particles of matter, in succession vitally united to the same organized body. He that shall place the identity of man in anything else, but like that of other animals, in one fitly organized body, taken in any one instant, and from thence continued, under one organization of life, in several successively fleeting particles of matter united to it, will find it hard to make an embryo, one of years, mad and sober, the same man, by any supposition, that will not make it possible for Seth, Ismael, Socrates, Pilate, St. Austin, and Caesar Borgia, to be the same man. For, if the identity of soul alone makes the same man, and there be nothing in the nature of matter why the same individual spirit may not be united to different bodies, it will be possible that those men living in distant ages, and of different tempers, may have been the same man: which way of speaking must be, from a very strange use of the word man, applied to an idea, out of which body and shape are excluded. And that way of speaking would agree yet worse with the notions of those philosophers who allow of transmigration, and are of opinion that the souls of men may, for their miscarriages, be detruded into the bodies of beasts, as fit habitations, with organs suited to the satisfaction of their brutal inclinations. But yet I think nobody, could he be sure that the soul of Heliogabalus were in one of his hogs, would yet say that hog were a man or Heliogabalus.

Identity Suited to the Idea. It is not therefore unity of substance that comprehends all sorts of identity, or will determine it in every case; but to conceive and judge of it aright, we must consider what idea the word it is applied to stands for: it being one thing to be the same substance, another the same man, and a third the same person, if person, man, and substance, are three names standing for three different ideas; for such as is the idea belonging to that name, such must be the identity; which, if it had been a little more carefully attended to, would possibly have prevented a great deal of that confusion which often occurs about this matter, with no small seeming difficulties, especially concerning personal identity, which therefore we shall in the next place a little consider.

Same Man. An animal is living organized body; and consequently the same animal, as we have observed, is the same continued life communicated to different particles of matter, as they happen successively to be united to that organized living body. And whatever is talked of other definitions, ingenious observation puts it past doubt, that the idea in our minds, of which the sound man in our mouths is the sign, is nothing else but of an animal of such a certain form: since I think I may be confident, that, whoever should see a creature of his own shape or make, though it had no more reason all its life than a cat or a parrot, would call him still a man; or whoever should hear a cat or a parrot discourse, reason, and philosophize, would call or think it nothing but a cat or a parrot; and say, the one was a dull irrational man, and the other a very intelligent rational parrot. . . .

Personal Identity. This being premised, to find wherein personal identity consists, we must consider what person stands for; which, I think, is a thinking intelligent being, that has reason and reflection, and can consider itself as itself, the same thinking thing, in different times and places; which it does only by that consciousness which is inseparable from thinking, and, as it seems to me, essential to it: it being impossible for any one to perceive without perceiving that he does perceive. When we see, hear, smell, taste, feel, meditate, or will anything, we know that we do so. Thus it is always as to our present sensations and perceptions: and by this every one is to himself that which he calls self; it not being considered, in this case, whether the same self be continued in the same or divers substances. For, since consciousness always accompanies thinking, and it is that which makes every one to be what he calls self, and thereby distinguishes himself from all other thinking things: in this alone consists personal identity, i.e., the sameness of a rational being; and as far as this consciousness can be extended backwards to any past action or thought, so far reaches the identity of that person; it is the same self now it was then; and it is by the same self with this present one that now reflects on it, that that action was done.

Consciousness Makes Personal Identity. But it is further inquired, whether it be the same identical substance? This, few would think they had reason to doubt of, if these perceptions, with their consciousness, always remained present in the mind, whereby the same thinking thing would be always consciously present, and, as would be thought, evidently the same to itself. But that which seems to make the difficulty is this, that this consciousness being interrupted always by forgetfulness, there being no moment of our lives wherein we have the whole train of all our past actions before our eyes in one view, but even the best memories losing the sight of one part whilst they are viewing another; and we sometimes, and that the greatest part of our lives, not reflecting on our past selves, being intent on our present thoughts, and in sound sleep having no thoughts at all, or at least none with that consciousness which remarks our waking thoughts; I say, in all these cases, our consciousness being interrupted, and we losing the sight of our past selves, doubts are raised whether we are the same thinking thing, i.e., the same substance or no. Which, however reasonable or unreasonable, concerns not personal identity at all: the question being, what makes the same person, and not whether it be the same identical substance, which always thinks in the same person; which, in this case, matters not at all: different substances, by the same consciousness (where they do partake in it) being united into one person, as well as different bodies by the same life are united into one animal, whose identity is preserved in that change of substances by the unity of one continued life. For it being the same consciousness that makes a man be himself to himself, personal identity depends on that only, whether it be annexed solely to one individual substance, or can be continued in a succession of several substances. For as far as any intelligent being can repeat the idea of any past action with the same consciousness it had of it at first, and with the same consciousness it has of any present action; so far it is the same personal self. For it is by the consciousness it has of its present thoughts and actions, that it is self to itself now, and so will be the same self, as far as the same consciousness can extend to actions past or to come; and would be by distance of time, or change of substance, no more two persons, than a man be two men by wearing other clothes to-day than he did yesterday, with a long or a short sleep between: the same consciousness uniting those distant actions into the same person, whatever substances contributed to their production.

Personal Identity in Change of Substances. That this is so, we have some kind of evidence in our very bodies, all whose particles, whilst vitally united to this same thinking conscious self, so that we feel when they are touched, and are affected by, and conscious of good or harm that happens to them, are a part of ourselves; i.e., of our thinking conscious self. Thus, the limbs of his body are to every one a part of himself; he sympathizes and is concerned for them. Cut off a hand, and thereby separate it from that consciousness he had of its heat, cold, and other affections, and it is then no longer a part of that which is himself, any more than the remotest part of matter. Thus, we see the substance whereof personal self consisted at one time may be varied at another, without the change of personal identity; there being no question about the same person, though the limbs which but now were a part of it, be cut off.

But the question is, "Whether, if the same substance, which thinks, be changed, it can be the same person; or, remaining the same, it can be different persons?"

Whether in the Change of Thinking Substances. And to this I answer: First, This can be no question at all to those who place thought in a purely material animal constitution, void of an immaterial substance. For, whether their supposition be true or no, it is plain they conceive personal identity preserved in something else than identity of substance; as animal identity is preserved in identity of life, and not of substance. And therefore those who place thinking in an immaterial substance only, before they can come to deal with these men, must show why personal identity cannot be preserved in the change of immaterial substances, or variety of particular immaterial substances, as well as animal identity is preserved in the change of material substances, or variety of particular bodies: unless they will say, it is one immaterial spirit that makes the same life in brutes, as it is one immaterial spirit that makes the same person in men; which the Cartesians at least will not admit, for fear of making brutes thinking things too.

But next, as to the first part of the question, "Whether, if the same thinking substance (supposing immaterial substances only to think) be changed, it can be the same person?" I answer, that cannot be resolved, but by those who know what kind of substances they are that do think, and whether the consciousness of past actions can be transferred from one thinking substance to another. I grant, were the same consciousness the same individual action, it could not: but it being a present representation of a past action, why it may not be possible that that may be represented to the mind to have been, which really never was, will remain to be shown. And therefore how far the consciousness of past actions is annexed to any individual agent, so that another cannot possibly have it, will be hard for us to determine, till we know what kind of action it is that cannot be done without a reflex act of perception accompanying it, and how performed by thinking substances, who cannot think without being conscious of it. But that which we call the same consciousness, not being the same individual act, why one intellectual substance may not have represented to it, as done by itself, what it never did, and was perhaps done by some other agent; why, I say, such a representation may not possibly be without reality of matter of fact, as well as several representations in dreams are, which yet whilst dreaming we take for true, will be difficult to conclude from the nature of things. And that it never is so, will by us, till we have clearer views of the nature of thinking substances, be best resolved into the goodness of God, who, as far as the happiness or misery of any of his sensible creatures is concerned in it, will not, by a fatal error of theirs, transfer from one to another that consciousness which draws reward or punishment with it. How far this may be an argument against those who would place thinking in a system of fleeting animal spirits, I leave to be considered. But yet, to return to the question before us, it must be allowed, that, if the same consciousness (which, as has been shown, is quite a different thing from the same numerical figure or motion in body) can be transferred from one thinking substance to another, it will be possible that two thinking substances may make but one person. For the same consciousness being preserved, whether in the same or different substances, the personal identity is preserved.

As to the second part of the question, "Whether the same immaterial substance remaining, there may be two distinct persons?" which question seems to me to be built on this, whether the same immaterial being, being conscious of the action of its past duration, may be wholly stripped of all the consciousness of its past existence, and lose it beyond the power of ever retrieving it again; and so as it were beginning a new account from a new period, have a consciousness that cannot reach beyond this new state. All those who hold pre-existence are evidently of this mind, since they allow the soul to have no remaining consciousness of what it did in that pre-existent state, either wholly separate from body, or informing any other body; and if they should not, it is plain experience would be against them. So that personal identity reaching no further than consciousness reaches, a pre-existent spirit not having continued so many ages in a state of silence, must needs make different persons. Suppose a Christian Platonist or a Pythagorean should, upon God's having ended all his works of creation the seventh day, think his soul hath existed ever since; and would imagine it has revolved in several human bodies, as I once met with one, who was persuaded his had been the soul of Socrates; (how reasonably I will not dispute; this I know, that in the post he filled, which was no inconsiderable one, he passed for a very rational man, and the press has shown that he wanted not parts or learning;) would any one say, that he, being not conscious of any of Socrates' actions or thoughts, could be the same person with Socrates? Let any one reflect upon himself, and conclude that he has in himself an immaterial spirit, which is that which thinks in him, and, in the constant change of his body keeps him the same: and is that which he calls himself: let him also suppose it to be the same soul that was in Nestor or Thersites, at the siege of Troy (for souls being, as far as we know anything of them, in their nature indifferent to any parcel of matter, the supposition has no apparent absurdity in it), which it may have been, as well as it is now the soul of any other man: but he now having no consciousness of any of the actions either of Nestor or Thersites, does or can he conceive himself the same person with either of them? Can he be concerned in either of their actions? attribute them to himself, or think them his own, more than the actions of any other men that ever existed? So that this consciousness not reaching to any of the actions of either of those men, he is no more one self with either of them, than if the soul or immaterial spirit that now informs him had been created, and began to exist, when it began to inform his present body, though it were ever so true, that the same spirit that informed Nestor's or Thersites' body were numerically the same that now informs his. For this would no more make him the same person with Nestor, than if some of the particles of matter that were once a part of Nestor, were now a part of this man; the same immaterial substance, without the same consciousness, no more making the same person by being united to any body, than the same particle of matter, without consciousness united to any body, makes the same person. But let him once find himself conscious of any of the actions of Nestor, he then finds himself the same person with Nestor.

And thus may we be able, without any difficulty, to conceive the same person at the resurrection, though in a body not exactly in make or parts the same which he had here, the same consciousness going along with the soul that inhabits it. But yet the soul alone, in the change of bodies, would scarce to any one but to him that makes the soul the man, be enough to make the same man. For should the soul of a prince, carrying with it the consciousness of the prince's past life, enter and inform the body of a cobbler, as soon as deserted by his own soul, every one sees he would be the same person with the prince, accountable only for the prince's actions: but who would say it was the same man? The body too goes to the making the man, and would, I guess, to everybody determine the man in this case; wherein the soul, with all its princely thoughts about it, would not make another man: but he would be the same cobbler to every one besides himself. I know that, in the ordinary way of speaking, the same person, and the same man, stand for one and the same thing. And indeed every one will always have a liberty to speak as he pleases, and to apply what articulate sounds to what ideas he thinks fit, and change them as often as he pleases. But yet, when we will inquire what makes the same spirit, man, or person, we must fix the ideas of spirit, man, or person in our minds, and having resolved with ourselves what we mean by them, it will not be hard to determine in either of them, or the like, when it is the same, and when not.

Consciousness Makes the Same Person. But though the same immaterial substance or soul does not alone, wherever it be, and in whatsoever state, make the same man; yet it is plain, consciousness, as far as ever it can be extended, should it be to ages past, unites existences and actions, very remote in time into the same person, as well as it does the existences and actions of the immediately preceding moment: so that whatever has the consciousness of present and past actions, is the same person to whom they both belong. Had I the same consciousness that I saw the ark and Noah's flood, as that I saw an overflowing of the Thames last winter, or as that I write now; I could no more doubt that I who write this now, that saw the Thames overflowed last winter, and that viewed the flood at the general deluge, was the same self, place that self in what substance you please, than that I who write this am the same myself now whilst I write (whether I consist of all the same substance, material or immaterial, or no) that I was yesterday; for as to this point of being the same self, it matters not whether this present self be made up of the same or other substances; I being as much concerned, and as justly accountable for any action that was done a thousand years since, appropriated to me now by this self-consciousness, as I am for what I did the last moment.

Self Depends on Consciousness. Self is that conscious thinking thing, whatever substance made up of (whether spiritual or material, simple or compounded, it matters not), which is sensible or conscious of pleasure and pain, capable of happiness or misery, and so is concerned for itself, as far as that consciousness extends. Thus every one finds, that, whilst comprehended under that consciousness, the little finger is as much a part of himself as what is most so. Upon separation of this little finger, should this consciousness go along with the little finger, and leave the rest of the body, it is evident the little finger would be the person, the same person, and self then would have nothing to do with the rest of the body. As in this case it is the consciousness that goes along with the substance, when one part is separate from another, which makes the same person, and constitutes this inseparable self; so it is in reference to substances remote in time. That with which the consciousness of this present thinking thing can join itself, makes the same person, and is one self with it, and with nothing else; and so attributes to itself, and owns all the actions of that thing as its own, as far as that consciousness reaches, and no further; as every one who reflects will perceive.

Objects of Reward and Punishment. In this personal identity is founded all the right and justice of reward and punishment; happiness and misery being that for which every one is concerned for himself, and not mattering what becomes of any substance not joined to, or affected with that consciousness. For as it is evident in the instance I gave but now, if the consciousness went along with the little finger when it was cut off, that would be the same self which was concerned for the whole body yesterday, as making part of itself, whose actions then it cannot but admit as its own now. Though, if the same body should still live, and immediately from the separation of the little finger have its own peculiar consciousness, whereof the little finger knew nothing; it would not at all be concerned for it, as a part of itself, or could own any of its actions, or have any of them imputed to him.

This may show us wherein personal identity consists: not in the identity of substance, but, as I have said, in the identity of consciousness; wherein if Socrates and the present mayor of Queenborough agree, they are the same person: if the same Socrates waking and sleeping do not partake of the same consciousness, Socrates waking and sleeping is not the same person. And to punish Socrates waking for what sleeping Socrates thought, and waking Socrates was never conscious of, would be no more of right, than to punish one twin for what his brother-twin did, whereof he knew nothing, because their outsides were so like, that they could not be distinguished; for such twins have been seen.

But yet possibly it will still be objected, suppose I wholly lose the memory of some parts of my life, beyond a possibility of retrieving them, so that perhaps I shall never be conscious of them again; yet am I not the same person that did those actions, had those thoughts that I once was conscious of, though I have now forgot them? To which I answer, that we must here take notice what the word I is applied to; which, in this case, is the man only. And the same man being presumed to be the same person, I is easily here supposed to stand also for the same person. But if it be possible for the same man to have distinct incommunicable consciousness at different times, it is past doubt the same man would at different times make different persons; which, we see, is the sense of mankind in the solemnest declaration of their opinions; human laws not punishing the mad man for the sober man's actions, nor the sober man for what the mad man did, thereby making them two persons: which is somewhat explained by our way of speaking in English, when we say such an one is not himself, or is beside himself; in which phrases it is insinuated, as if those who now, or at least first used them, thought that self was changed, the selfsame person was no longer in that man.

Difference between Identity of Man and Person. But yet it is hard to conceive that Socrates, the same individual man, should be two persons. To help us a little in this, we must consider what is meant by Socrates, or the same individual man.

First, it must be either the same individual, immaterial, thinking substance; in short, the same numerical soul, and nothing else.

Secondly, or the same animal, without any regard to an immaterial soul.

Thirdly, or the same immaterial spirit united to the same animal.

Now, take which of these suppositions you please, it is impossible to make personal identity to consist in anything but consciousness, or reach any further than that does.

For, by the first of them, it must be allowed possible that a man born of different women, and in distant times, may be the same man. A way of speaking, which whoever admits, must allow it possible for the same man to be two distinct persons, as any two that have lived in different ages, without the knowledge of one another's thoughts.

By the second and third, Socrates, in this life and after it, cannot be the same man any way, but by the same consciousness; and so making human identity to consist in the same thing wherein we place personal identity, there will be no difficulty to allow the same man to be the same person. But then they who place human identity in consciousness only, and not in something else, must consider how they will make the infant Socrates the same man with Socrates after the resurrection. But whatsoever to some men makes a man, and consequently the same individual man, wherein perhaps few are agreed, personal identity can by us be placed in nothing but consciousness (which is that alone which makes what we call self), without involving us in great absurdities.

But is not a man drunk and sober the same person? why else is he punished for the fact he commits when drunk, though he be never afterwards conscious of it? Just as much the same person as a man that walks, and does other things in his sleep, is the same person, and is answerable for any mischief he shall do in it. Human laws punish both, with a justice suitable to their way of knowledge; because, in these cases, they cannot distinguish certainly what is real; what counterfeit: and so the ignorance in drunkenness or sleep is not admitted as a plea. For, though punishment be annexed to personality, and personality to consciousness, and the drunkard perhaps be not conscious of what he did, yet human judicatures justly punish him, because the fact is proved against him, but want of consciousness cannot be proved for him. But in the great day, wherein the secrets of all hearts shall be laid open, it may be reasonable to think, no one shall be made to answer for what he knows nothing of; but shall receive his doom, his conscience accusing or excusing him.

Consciousness Alone Makes Self. Nothing but consciousness can unite remote existences into the same person: the identity of substance will not do it; for whatever substance there is, however framed, without consciousness there is no person: and a carcass may be a person, as well as any sort of substance be so without consciousness.

Could we suppose two distinct incommunicable consciousnesses acting the same body, the one constantly by day, the other by night; and, on the other side, the same consciousness, acting by intervals, two distinct bodies; I ask, in the first case, whether the day and the night man would not be two as distinct persons as Socrates and Plato? And whether, in the second case, there would not be one person in two distinct bodies, as much as one man is the same in two distinct clothings? Nor is it at all material to say, that this same, and this distinct consciousness, in the cases above mentioned, is owing to the same and distinct immaterial substances, bringing it with them to those bodies; which, whether true or no, alters not the case; since it is evident the personal identity would equally be determined by the consciousness, whether that consciousness were annexed to some individual immaterial substance or no. For, granting that the thinking substance in man must be necessarily supposed immaterial, it is evident that immaterial thinking thing may sometimes part with its past consciousness, and be restored to it again, as appears in the forgetfulness men often have of their past actions: and the mind many times recovers the memory of a past consciousness, which it had lost for twenty years together. Make these intervals of memory and forgetfulness to take their turns regularly by day and night, and you have two persons with the same immaterial spirit, as much as in the former instance two persons with the same body. So that self is not determined by identity or diversity of substance, which it cannot be sure of, but only by identity of consciousness. . . .

Person a Forensic Term. Person, as I take it, is the name for this self. Wherever a man finds what he calls himself there, I think, another may say is the same person. It is a forensic term, appropriating actions and their merit; and so belongs only to intelligent agents capable of a law, and happiness, and misery. This personality extends itself beyond present existence to what is past, only by consciousness, whereby it becomes concerned and accountable, owns and imputes to itself past actions, just upon the same ground and for the same reason that it does the present. All which is founded in a concern for happiness, the unavoidable concomitant of consciousness; that which is conscious of pleasure and pain, desiring that that self that is conscious should be happy. And therefore whatever past actions it cannot reconcile or appropriate to that present self by consciousness, it can be no more concerned in, than if they had never been done; and to receive pleasure or pain, i.e., reward or punishment, on the account of any such action, is all one as to be made happy or miserable in its first being, without any demerit at all: for supposing a man punished now for what he had done in another life, whereof he could be made to have no consciousness at all, what difference is there between that punishment, and being created miserable? And therefore, conformable to this, the apostle tells us, that, at the great day, when every one shall "receive according to his doings, the secrets of all hearts shall be laid open." The sentence shall be justified by the consciousness all persons shall have, that they themselves, in what bodies soever they appear, or what substances soever that consciousness adheres to, are the same that committed those actions, and deserve that punishment for them.

OF PERSONAL IDENTITY
Joseph Butler

Whether we are to live in a future state, as it is the most important question which can possibly be asked, so it is the most intelligible one which can be expressed in language. Yet strange perplexities have been raised about the meaning of that identity, or sameness of person, which is implied in the notion of our living now and hereafter, or in any two successive moments. And the solution of these difficulties hath been stranger than the difficulties themselves. For, personal identity has been explained so by some, as to render the inquiry concerning a future life of no consequence at all to us, the persons who are making it. And though few men can be misled by such subtleties, yet it may be proper a little to consider them.

Now, when it is asked wherein personal identity consists, the answer should be the same as if it were asked, wherein consists similitude or equality; that all attempts to define, would but perplex it. Yet there is no difficulty at all in ascertaining the idea. For as, upon two triangles being compared or viewed together, there arises to the mind the idea of similitude; or upon twice two and four, the idea of equality; so likewise, upon comparing the consciousness of one's self, or one's own existence in any two moments, there as immediately arises to the mind the idea of personal identity. And as the two former comparisons not only give the idea of similitude and equality, but also shows us, that two triangles are like, and twice two and four are equal; so the latter comparison not only gives us the idea of personal identity but also shows us the identity of ourselves in those two moments; the present, suppose, and that immediately past; or the present, and that a month, a year, or twenty years past. Or, in other words, by reflecting upon that which is myself now, and that which was myself twenty years ago, I discern they are not two, but one and the same self.

But though consciousness of what is past does thus ascertain our personal identity to ourselves, yet, to say that it makes personal identity, or is necessary to our being the same persons, is to say, that a person has not existed a single moment, nor done one action, but what he can remember; indeed none but what he reflects upon. And one should really think it self-evident, that consciousness of personal identity presupposes, and therefore cannot constitute, personal identity, any more than knowledge, in any other case, can constitute truth, which it presupposes.

This wonderful mistake may possibly have arisen from hence, that to be endued with consciousness, is inseparable from the idea of a person, or intelligent being. For, this might be expressed inaccurately thus—that consciousness makes personality; and from hence it might be concluded to make personal identity. But though present consciousness of what we at present do and feel, is necessary to our being the persons we now are; yet present consciousness of past actions, or feelings, is not necessary to our being the same persons who performed those actions, or had those feelings.

The inquiry, what makes vegetables the same in the common acceptation of the word, does not appear to have any relation to this of personal identity; because the word *same*, when applied to them and to persons, is not only applied to different subjects, but it is also used in different senses. For when a man swears to the same tree, as having stood fifty years in the same place, he means only the same as to all the purposes of property and uses of common life, and not that the tree has been all that time the same in the strict philosophical sense of the word. For he does not know whether any one particle of the present tree be the same with any one particle of the tree which stood in the same place fifty years ago. And if they have not one common particle of matter, they cannot be the same tree, in the proper philosophic sense of the word *same*; it being evidently a contradiction in terms, to say they are, when no part of their substance, and no one of their properties, is the same; no part of their substance, by the supposition; no one of their properties, because it is allowed that the same property cannot be transferred from one substance to another. And therefore, when we say the identity or sameness of a plant consists in a continuation of the same life communicated under the same organization, to a number of particles of matter, whether the same or not, the word *same*, when applied to life and to organization, cannot possibly be understood to signify, what it signifies in this very sentence, when applied to matter. In a loose and popular sense, then, the life, and the organization, and the plant, are justly said to be the same, notwithstanding the perpetual change of the parts. But in a strict and philosophical manner of speech, no man, no being, no mode of being, nor any thing, can be the same with that, with which it hath indeed nothing the same. Now, sameness is used in this latter sense when applied to persons. The identity of these, therefore, cannot subsist with diversity of substance.

The thing here considered, and demonstratively, as I think, determined, is proposed by Mr. Locke in these words, *Whether it*, i.e., the same self or person, *be the same identical substance?* And he has suggested what is a much better answer to the question than that which he gave it in form. For he defines person, *a thinking intelligent being*, etc. and personal identity *the sameness of a rational being.*[1] The question then is, whether the same rational being is the same substance; which needs no answer, because being and substance, in this place, stand for the same idea. The ground of the doubt, whether the same person be the same substance, is said to be this; that the consciousness of our own existence in youth and in old age, or in any two joint successive moments, is not *the same individual action*,[2] i.e., not the same consciousness, but different successive consciousnesses. Now it is strange that this should have occasioned such perplexities. For it is surely conceivable, that a person may have a capacity of knowing some object or other to be the same now, which it was when he contemplated it formerly; yet, in this case, where, by the supposition, the object is perceived to be the same, the perception of it in any two moments cannot be one and the same perception. And thus, though the successive consciousnesses which we have of our own existence are not the same, yet are they consciousnesses of one and the same thing or object; of the same person, self, or living agent. The person, of whose existence the consciousness is felt now, and was felt an hour or a year ago, is discerned to be, not two persons, but one and the same person; and therefore is one and the same.

Mr. Locke's observations upon this subject appear hasty; and he seems to profess himself dissatisfied with suppositions, which he has made relating to it.[3] But some of those hasty observations have been carried to a strange length by others; whose notion, when traced and examined to the bottom, amounts, I think, to this:[4] "That personality is not a permanent, but a transient thing: that it lives and dies, begins and ends, continually: that no one can any more remain one and the same person two moments together, than two successive moments can be one and the same moment: that our substance is indeed continually changing; but whether this be so or not, is, it seems, nothing to the purpose; since it is not substance, but consciousness alone, which constitutes personality; which consciousness, being successive, cannot be the same in any two moments, nor consequently the personality constituted by it." And from hence it must follow, that it is a fallacy upon ourselves, to charge our present selves with any thing we did, or to imagine our present selves interested in any thing which befell us yesterday, or that our present self will be interested in what will befall us tomorrow; since our present self is not, in reality, the same with the self of yesterday, but another like self or person coming in its room, and mistaken for it; to which another self will succeed tomorrow. This, I say, must follow: for if the self or person of today, and that of tomorrow, are not the same, but only like persons, the person of today is really no more interested in what will befall the person of tomorrow, than in what will befall any other person. It may be thought, perhaps, that this is not a just representation of the opinion we are speaking of; because those who maintain it allow, that a person is the same as far back as his remembrance reaches. And, indeed, they do use the words, *identity* and *same* person. Nor will language permit these words to be laid aside: since if they were, there must be, I know not what, ridiculous periphrasis substituted in the room of them. But they cannot, consistently with themselves, mean, that the person is really the same. For it is self-evident, that the personality cannot be really the same, if, as they expressly assert, that in which it consists is not the same. And as, consistently with themselves, they cannot, so, I think, it appears they do not, mean, that the person is *really* the same, but only that he is so in a fictitious sense: in such a sense only as they assert; for this they do assert, that any number of persons whatever may be the same person. The bare unfolding this notion, and laying it thus naked and open, seems the best confutation of it. However, since great stress is said to be put upon it, I add the following things:

First, This notion is absolutely contradictory to that certain conviction, which necessarily, and every moment, rises within us, when we turn our thoughts upon ourselves; when we reflect upon what is past, and look forward upon what is to come. All imagination of a daily change of that living agent which each man calls himself, for another, or of any such change thoughout our whole present life, is entirely borne down by our natural sense of things. Nor is it possible for a person in his wits to alter his conduct, with regard to his health or affairs, from a suspicion, that though he should live tomorrow, he should not, however, be the same person he is today. And yet, if it be reasonable to act, with respect to a future life, upon this notion, that personality is transient; it is reasonable to act upon it, with respect to the present. Here then is a notion equally applicable to religion and to our temporal concerns; and every one sees and feels the inexpressible absurdity of it in the latter case. If, therefore, any can take up with it in the former, this cannot proceed from the reason of the thing, but must be owing to an inward unfairness, and secret corruption of heart.

Secondly, It is not an idea, or abstract notion, or quality, but a being only which is capable of life and action, of happiness and misery. Now all beings confessedly continue the same, during the whole time of their existence. Consider then a living being now existing, and which has existed for any time alive: this living being must have done and suffered and enjoyed, what it has done and suffered and enjoyed formerly (this living being, I say, and not another), as really as it does and suffers and enjoys, what it does and suffers and enjoys this instant. All these successive actions, enjoyments, and sufferings, are actions, enjoyments, and suffferings, of the same living being. And they are so, prior to all consideration of its remembering or forgetting; since remembering or forgetting can make no alteration in the truth of past matter of fact. And suppose this being endued with limited powers of knowledge and memory, there is no more difficulty in conceiving it to have a power of knowing itself to be the same living being which it was some time ago, of remembering some of its actions, sufferings, and enjoyments, and forgetting others, than in conceiving it to know, or remember, or forget any thing else.

Thirdly, Every person is conscious, that he is now the same person or self he was, as far back as his remembrance reaches: since, when any one reflects upon a past action of his own, he is just as certain of the person who did that action, namely himself, the person who now reflects upon it, as he is certain that the action was at all done. Nay, very often a person's assurance of an action having been done, of which he is absolutely assured, arises wholly from the consciousness that he himself did it. And this he, person, or self, must either be a substance, or the property of some substance. If he, if person, be a substance; then consciousness that he is the same person, is consciousness that he is the same substance. If the person, or he, be the property of a substance; still consciousness that he is the same property, is as certain a proof that his substance remains the same, as consciousness that he remains the same substance would be: since the same property cannot be transferred from one substance to another.

But though we are thus certain that we are the same agents, living beings, or substances, now, which we were as far back as our remembrance reaches; yet it is asked, whether we may not possibly be deceived in it? And this question may be asked at the end of any demonstration whatever; because it is a question concerning the truth of perception by memory. And he who can doubt, whether perception by memory can in this case be depended upon, may doubt also, whether perception by deduction and reasoning, which also include memory, or, indeed, whether intuitive perception can. Here then we can go no farther. For it is ridiculous to attempt to prove the truth of those perceptions, whose truth we can no otherwise prove, than by other perceptions of exactly the same kind with them, and which there is just the same ground to suspect; or to attempt to prove the truth of our faculties, which can no otherwise be proved, than by the use or means of those very suspected faculties themselves.

NOTES

1. Locke's Works, vol. i. p. 146.
2. Ibid., pp. 146, 147.
3. Ibid., p. 152.
4. See an answer to Dr. Clarke's third defence of his letter to Mr. Dodwell, 2d edit. pp. 44, 56, etc.

Questions for Part II

1. Charles B. Daniels tells the marvelous story of the transportation machine that records the type and position of every molecule in the body of the person that enters it. The tape of this data is sent to another location and a duplicate is fabricated. Why doesn't such an exact duplicate preserve the identity of the person who enters the machine even if the original body of that person, as in Daniels' story, is tortured and killed by a band of sadists? Are the original and duplicate different people because a person ceases to exist when his or her body is destroyed? Doesn't this put too much weight on physical criteria of personal identity?

2 Contrast the transportation machine case with a reincarnation case of the sort Daniels constructs. Why do we intuitively tend to support the idea that in the machine case there are two different persons, while in the reincarnation case we count mental rather than physical evidence as conclusive?

3. Daniels discusses the brain transfer case originally created by Sydney Shoemaker. What is his reason for dwelling on that case and how does it relate to his analysis of reincarnation cases? How important is the distinction between remembering and clairvoyance in puzzle cases of this type?

4. The soldier in the trenches before the battle wants to survive. Commonsensically, he wants there to be an identity between himself and some self that will continue to live and breathe after the guns fall silent. Derek Parfit, however, thinks that what matters in survival is mental continuity and/or connectedness, and there can be, Parfit thinks, cases where commonsensical and philosophical accounts produce startlingly different results: cases in which the soldier on the one account survives and on the other account does not survive the battle. Discuss Parfit's analysis of such cases.

5. Does Parfit's theory amount to a defense of the view that bodily continuity is not a significant determiner of personal identity? How does his position relate to the classical account of the memory or stream of consciousness criterion in John Locke's essay? Is Parfit's distinction between memory and q-memory a more sophisticated version of Locke's position? Explain.

6. Parfit examines fusion cases in some detail. Explain what these cases are supposed to reveal with respect to the problem of deciding among alternative views on the criterion of personal identity.

7. Locke's theory of personal identity is an application of his more general theory that criteria of identity are relative to the kind of thing involved. This is seen in his distinction between the identity of human beings and the identity of persons. Use examples to expose the intuitions on which Locke seems to be basing his theory. Then offer a criticism of Locke's theory, perhaps Butler's, and suggest a way in which Locke might respond to it.

8. For Locke, can two thinking substances ever be only one person? Imagine a scenario to illustrate Locke's theory.

9. Locke points out that personal identity is, at heart, a "forensic term." What does he mean by that and how does his position respond to the issues or concerns he regards as "forensic"?

10. Locke claims that consciousness alone constitutes personal identity. Does he really mean that having a certain body has nothing to do with being a particular

person? Do you think you would be the same person if, despite having a continuity of memories, your sex were changed in some sudden and miraculous way?

11. Joseph Butler argues that Locke's view that consciousness constitutes personal identity is fatally flawed because it presupposes personal identity. What is his argument and does it also provide an objection to Parfit's theory? Butler offers what may be called a substantive theory of personal identity that is significantly different from that of the others in this section. Discuss virtues and difficulties with taking a position such as Butler's.

12. Butler thinks his view is more responsive than theories like Locke's to what he calls "the most important question which can possibly be asked": the question of whether we will have an afterlife. Discuss whether Butler's theory is more responsive to the afterlife issue and why Butler rejects nonsubstantive theories of what it is to be a particular person.

Part III. Artificially Created Persons

In Stanley Kubrick's masterful film *2001: A Space Odyssey* an astronaut duels for his life with the homocidal computer Hal. Hal evidences an astounding number of what may be called person-traits. Hal gets angry, jealous, and frightened. Hal schemes, desires things, and acts intentionally and purposefully. Yet Hal is a machine. Nonetheless, Hal displays every indication of being rational. As the plot unfolds, it becomes increasingly difficult not to think of Hal as a person. If we mean by "person" a being that is rational and has conscious states, then Hal is a person.

Hal, of course, doesn't look anything like a human being, but should that be an important consideration? In another science fiction film, *Bladerunner* (and the novel on which it is based: *Do Androids Dream of Electric Sheep*, by Philip K. Dick), robots have been constructed that look just like humans. They are programmed to display most human characteristics; on a behavioral level they are virtually indistinguishable from humans. They certainly act in what appear to be intentional ways. Are they persons, even though they are mechanical? Certainly human flesh, skin, and bones arranged in a certain fashion cannot be the sole deciding feature of personhood.

Over the centuries of philosophical discussion on the concept of personhood many very different claims as to what constitutes a person have been defended. Most of these, however, focus on our notion of intentionality. The typical view is that persons are intentional actors. What is it to act intentionally? At least since the time of Descartes, discussion about how to answer such a question has focused on talk about minds and bodies and the relationship between them. Intentional actions, it is commonly said, are those movements of bodies that are caused by a certain sort of mental activity, intending. I dropped the book on the floor intentionally, it may be maintained, if my dropping it was the result of my wanting or intending to do so. An event occurs in my mind and by some unexplained process this sets off brain activity that stimulates nerves and muscles and eventually the book is dropped. On such an account, to act intentionally and hence to be a person, an entity must have mental events. Things that do not have mental events just behave or respond. They don't intend and so they do not act and so they are not persons.

The obvious problem with this thesis is that it posits something that is, on most traditional accounts, immaterial and so not directly examinable: the mind. It explains actions by appeal to a causal connection between what is physical and what is wholly nonphysical that is, at least, mysterious. There is a sort of Humpty Dumpty problem embedded in this version of what is a person, for once the person is divided to explain why it is a person, there seems no intelligible way to rejoin the parts. Appeals to mystery are always suspect.

Suppose we try another tack. We could, following Daniel Dennett's analysis, avoid talking about minds and instead define an intentional system as any entity whose behavior can be explained and predicted by supposing that it has beliefs and desires. The astronaut in 2001 relies on ascriptions of this sort when trying to outwit Hal. He predicts Hal's actions on the basis of assumptions about Hal's desires and Hal's beliefs.

It is certainly true that someone who knows Hal's complicated mechanisms might be able to predict and explain Hal's actions. But that does not change the fact that Hal satisfies the condition for being an intentional system, at least as we have defined it. The problem is that a number of things will qualify as intentional systems on this definition that we would generally not include in the class of persons. We can explain a dog's scratching at the door by saying that it wants to go outside. Dogs surely are not persons. Being an intentional system, then, is not all there is to being a person.

One suggestion for an essential characteristic of a person is that not only must the entity be an intentional system, it must be capable of having second-order intentions. It must, for example, be able to believe that it intends something. The dog at the door may want to go outside, but it probably doesn't believe that it wants to do anything. Hal and the androids of *Bladerunner*, however, seem to satisfy this condition. Interestingly, to have such second-order intentions one must, seemingly, have an awareness of oneself as the subject of the primary intention. One has to be self-conscious. Can we imagine an artificially created self-conscious entity? What more is there to self-consciousness than having beliefs, intentions, and so on, about one's wants, beliefs, desires?

It might be objected against the inclusion of certain computers (of which Hal is the prototype) and sophisticated robots in the class of persons, that persons have natural interests that motivate their desires and other intentions. Computers are programmed. Whatever interests they may be said to have are placed in their systems by the human software programmer. How important, however, is this objection? Does it not bias the case in favor of animals? Does it not introduce biological requirements in personhood?

Others have denied that computers can have a genuine first-person perspective. Their argument notes that computers can be programmed to utter (or use) grammatical sentences in which self-referential pronouns like "I" occur, but they do so simply by treating "I" as referring to the user in much the way that "Drink me" refers to the bottle in *Alice in Wonderland*. The use of the first-person pronoun in such a fashion, however, hardly indicates a first-person or self-conscious perspective. It only shows that such pronouns are sometimes merely grammatical self-referential devices that can be programmed for the computer by using a simple series of substitution rules of the sort " 'I am in phase X' printed by computer C refers to C and so is a legitimate substitution for 'C is in phase X'." What is missing in such a program, it is argued, is a genuine first-person awareness. It is further maintained that such a perspective is not reducible to programmable rules and that true first-person indicators are not mere substitutes for names or definite descriptions like "the computer that is now printing this sentence."

In a famous paper about the capacities of computers, A. M. Turing created a game the point of which is to show that if a computer could perfectly simulate responses to our questions then it would have mental states, or at least we would have to revise the way we talk about mental states if we are to say that it does not.

Nonetheless, a string of other objections to the possibility of artificially created persons has been developed. It has been maintained that machines cannot be persons because they cannot do such things as compose sonnets or concertos. That certainly is not a serious objection, for many unquestionably human persons are incapable of accomplishing such intellectual feats and some computers can. It is further argued that machines lack the ability to feel pleasure at their successes or grief at their failures, and so lack the emotional states characteristic of persons. This might be called "the objection from disabilities." If a Turing game is conceived as the test for the presence of mental states, however, we should not be able to tell that a sophisticated machine that passes the test does not have such feelings. It will respond to our questions about its emotional states in the same way we would expect a human person to answer us. If this objection is pressed too far, however, it can lead to a scepticism about the emotional states of other humans and even to a solipsism in which each of us doubts others have mental states at all. What is certainly true is that we often get misled by the typical questions and answers regarding the mental states of others. When someone says "I know what she is feeling," we may think that "what" is being used as a direct object so that I am claiming to know her feelings. The better reading, however, is to treat "what" as a relative, and substitute "that which" for it: "I know that which she is feeling." That is, I know how to answer the question, what is she feeling? I am making no claim to the effect that there is a mental state such that both she is feeling it and I know it. The problem about emotional states might then be translated into sets of responses amenable to Turing testing.

A number of philosophers have worried about certain practical implications of treating sophisticated machines like Hal and the androids of

Bladerunner as persons. Do such artificially created persons have civil rights and liberties? What is the moral status of these entities?

Robots and computers do not exhaust the list of candidates for nonhuman personhood. It is argued by Peter A. French that corporations satisfy the conditions of personhood and deserve to be admitted into the class of persons. Corporate entities are generally seen as collections of people and not just as buildings, products, and stocks. Importantly, corporations must have decision structures, and they have interests and concerns that affect the judgments they make and the actions they perform. Corporate actions are generally dependent upon the actions of human persons in the decision structure, but when the action is the result of an incorporated decision, that is, one done in accord with the established procedures of the corporation and done for corporate reasons (e.g., reflecting corporate policy), then the action is different from the mere sum of the actions of the human beings involved in the process. Corporations, then, French maintains, satisfy the crucial conditions of personhood and they can be held morally and legally accountable for their actions.

These practical and moral consequences of the way the conditions of personhood are understood in the case of artificially created entities like computers and corporations may, in the end, provide the most compelling reasons for trying to clarify the issues. Corporations are powerful forces in our social lives. They influence almost every aspect of contemporary society. The proper and just control of corporate entities is one of the major concerns in our legislatures and in the media. The same may, in the future, be said of computers and robots. A primary question should be, "Are these entities persons?" As we get clearer about the answer to that question, we may also uncover clues as to how we should handle questions about human beings that fail to meet those conditions of personhood that were applied to the artificially created entities: the way euthanasia and abortion cases should be formulated.

CONDITIONS OF PERSONHOOD

Daniel Dennett

I am a person, and so are you. That much is beyond doubt. I am a human being, and *probably* you are too. If you take offense at the "probably" you stand accused of a sort of racism, for what is important about us is not that we are of the same biological species, but that we are both persons, and I have not cast doubt on that. One's dignity does not depend on one's parentage even to the extent of having been born of woman or born at all. We normally ignore this and treat humanity as the deciding mark of personhood, no doubt because the terms are locally coextensive or almost coextensive. At this time and place human beings are the only persons we recognize, and we recognize almost all human beings as persons, but on the one hand we can easily contemplate the existence of biologically very different persons—inhabiting other planets, perhaps—and on the other hand we recognize conditions that exempt human beings from personhood, or at least some very important elements of personhood. For instance, infant human beings, mentally defective human beings, and human beings declared insane by licensed psychiatrists are denied personhood, or at any rate crucial elements of personhood.

One might well hope that such an important concept, applied and denied so confidently, would have clearly formulatable necessary and sufficient conditions for ascription, but if it does, we have not yet discovered them. In the end there may be none to discover. In the end we may come to realize that the concept of a person is incoherent and obsolete. Skinner, for one, has suggested this, but the doctrine has not caught on, no doubt in part because it is difficult or even impossible to conceive of what it would be like if we abandoned the concept of a person. The idea that we might cease to view others and *ourselves* as persons (if it does not mean merely that we might annihilate ourselves, and hence cease to view anything as anything) is arguably self-contradictory.[1] So quite aside from whatever might be right or wrong in Skinner's grounds for his claim, it is hard to see how it could win out in contest with such an intuitively invulnerable notion. If then the concept of a person is in some way an ineliminable part of our conceptual scheme, it might still be in rather worse shape than we would like. It might turn out, for instance, that the concept of a person is only a free-floating honorific that we are all happy to apply to ourselves, and to others as the spirit moves us, guided by our emotions, aesthetic sensibilities, considerations of policy, and the like—just as those who are *chic* are all and only those who can get themselves considered *chic* by others who consider themselves *chic*. Being a person is certainly *something* like that, and if it were no more, we would have to reconsider if we could the importance with which we now endow the concept.

Supposing there *is* something more to being a person, the searcher for necessary and sufficient conditions may still have difficulties if there is more than one concept of a person, and there are grounds for suspecting this. Roughly, there seem to be two notions intertwined here, which we may call the moral notion and the metaphysical notion. Locke says that "person"

> is a forensic term, appropriating actions and their merit; and so belongs only to intelligent agents, capable of a law, and happiness, and misery. This personality extends itself beyond present existence to what is past, only by consciousness—whereby it becomes concerned and accountable. (*Essays*, Book II, Chap. XXVII)

Does the metaphysical notion—roughly, the notion of an intelligent, conscious, feeling agent—*coincide* with the moral notion—roughly, the notion of an agent who is accountable, who has both rights and responsibilities? Or is it merely that being a person in the metaphysical sense is a necessary but not sufficient condition of being a person in the moral sense? Is being an entity to which states of consciousness or self-consciousness are ascribed *the same* as being an end-in-oneself, or is it merely one precondition? In Rawls's theory of justice, should the derivation from the original position be viewed as a demonstration of how metaphysical persons *can become* moral persons, or should it be viewed as a demonstration of why metaphysical persons *must be* moral persons?[2] In less technical surroundings the distinction stands out as clearly: when we declare a man insane we cease treating him as accountable, and we deny him most rights, but still our interactions with him are virtually indistinguishable from normal personal interactions unless he is very far gone in madness indeed. In one sense of "person," it seems, we continue to treat and view him as a person. I claimed at the outset that it was indubitable that you and I are persons. I could not plausibly hope—let alone aver—that all readers of this essay will be legally sane and morally accountable. What—if anything—was beyond all doubt may only have been that anything properly addrressed by the opening sentence's personal pronouns, "you" and "I," was a person in the metaphysical sense. If that was all that was beyond doubt, then the metaphysical notion and the moral notion must be distinct. Still, even if we suppose there are these distinct notions, there seems every reason to believe that metaphysical personhood is a necessary condition of moral personhood.[3]

What I wish to do now is consider six familiar themes, each a claim to identify a necessary condition of personhood, and each, I think, a correct claim on some interpretation. What will be at issue here is first, how (on my interpretation) they are dependent on each other; second, why they are necessary conditions of moral personhood, and third, why it is so hard to say whether they are jointly sufficient conditions for moral personhood. The *first* and most obvious theme is that persons are *rational beings*. It figures, for example, in the ethical theories of Kant and Rawls, and in the "metaphysical" theories of Aristotle and Hintikka.[4] The *second* theme is that persons are beings to which states of consciousness are attributed, or to which psychological or mental or *Intentional predicates*, are ascribed. Thus Strawson identifies the concept of a person as "the concept of a type of entity such that *both* predicates ascribing states of consciousness *and* predicates ascribing corporeal characteristics" are applicable.[5] The *third* theme is that whether something counts as a person depends in some way on an *attitude taken* toward it, a *stance adopted* with respect to it. This theme suggests that it is not the case that once we have established the objective fact that something is a person we treat him or her or it a certain way, but that our treating him or her or it in this certain way is somehow and to some extent constitutive of its being a person. Variations on this theme have been expressed by MacKay, Strawson, Amelie Rorty, Putnam, Sellars, Flew, Thomas Nagel, Dwight Van de Vate, and myself.[6] The *fourth* theme is that the object toward which this personal stance is taken must be capable of *reciprocating* in some way. Very different versions of this are expressed or hinted at by Rawls, MacKay, Strawson, Grice, and others. This reciprocity has sometimes been rather uninformatively expressed by the slogan: to be a person is to treat others as persons, and with this expression has often gone the claim that treating another as a person is treating him morally—perhaps obeying the Golden Rule, but this conflates different sorts of reciprocity. As Nagel says, "extremely hostile behavior toward another is compatible with treating him as a person" (p. 134), and as Van de Vate observes, one of the differences between some forms of manslaughter and murder is that the murderer treats the victim as a person.

The *fifth* theme is that persons must be capable of *verbal communication*. This condition handily excuses nonhuman animals from full personhood and the attendant moral responsibility, and seems at least implicit in all social contract theories of ethics. It is also a theme that has been stressed or presupposed by many writers in philosophy of mind, including myself, where the moral dimension of personhood has not been at issue. The *sixth* theme is that persons are distinguishable from other entities by being *conscious* in some special way: there is a way in which *we* are conscious in which no other species is conscious. Sometimes this is identified as *self*-consciousness of one sort or another. Three philosophers who claim—in very different ways—that a special sort of consciousness is a precondition of being a moral agent are Anscombe, in *Intention*, Sartre, in *The*

Transcendence of the Ego, and Harry Frankfurt, in his recent paper, "Freedom of the Will and the Concept of a Person."[7]

I will argue that the order in which I have given these six themes is—with one proviso—the order of their dependence. The proviso is that the first three are mutually interdependent; being rational is being Intentional is being the object of a certain stance. These three together are a necessary but not sufficient condition for exhibiting the form of reciprocity that is in turn a necessary but not sufficient condition for having the capacity for verbal communication, which is the necessary[8] condition for having a special sort of consciousness, which is, as Anscombe and Frankfurt in their different ways claim,[9] a necessary condition of moral personhood.

I have previously exploited the first three themes, rationality, Intentionality and stance, to define not persons, but the much wider class of what I call *Intentional systems,* and since I intend to build on that notion, a brief résumé is in order. An Intentional system is a system whose behavior can be (at least sometimes) explained and predicted by relying on ascriptions to the system of *beliefs* and *desires* (and other Intentionally characterized features—what I will call *Intentions* here, meaning to include hopes, fears, intentions, perceptions, expectations, etc.). There may *in every case* be other ways of predicting and explaining the behavior of an Intentional system—for instance, mechanistic or physical ways—but the Intentional stance may be the handiest or most effective or in any case *a* successful stance to adopt, which suffices for the object to be an Intentional system. So defined, Intentional systems are obviously not all persons. We ascribe beliefs and desires to dogs and fish and thereby predict their behavior, and we can even use the procedure to predict the behavior of some machines. For instance, it is a good, indeed the only good, strategy to adopt against a good chess-playing computer. By *assuming* the computer has certain beliefs (or information) and desires (or preference functions) dealing with the chess game in progress, I can calculate—under auspicious circumstances—the computer's most likely next move, *provided I assume the computer deals rationally with these beliefs and desires.* The computer is an Intentional system in these instances not because it has any particular intrinsic features, and not because it really and truly has beliefs and desires (whatever that would be), but just because it succumbs to a certain *stance* adopted toward it, namely the Intentional stance, the stance that proceeds by ascribing Intentional predicates under the usual constraints to the computer, the stance that proceeds by considering the computer as a rational practical reasoner.

It is important to recognize how bland this definition of *Intentional system* is, and how correspondingly large the class of Intentional systems can be. If, for instance, I predict that a particular plant—say a potted ivy—will grow around a corner and up into the light because it "seeks" the light and "wants" to get out of the shade it now finds itself in, and "expects" or "hopes" there is light around the corner, I have adopted the

Intentional stance toward the plant, and lo and behold, within very narrow limits it works. Since it works, some plants are very low-grade Intentional systems.

The actual utility of adopting the Intentional stance toward plants was brought home to me talking with loggers in the Maine woods. These men invariably call a tree not "it" but "he," and will say of a young spruce "he wants to spread his limbs, but don't let him; then he'll have to stretch up to get his light" or "pines don't like to get their feet wet the way cedars do." You can "trick" an apple tree into "thinking it's spring" by building a small fire under its branches in the late fall; it will blossom. This way of talking is not just picturesque and is not really superstitious at all; it is simply an efficient way of making sense of, controlling, predicting, and explaining the behavior of these plants in a way that nicely circumvents one's ignorance of the controlling mechanisms. More sophisticated biologists may choose to speak of information transmission from the tree's periphery to other locations in the tree. This is less picturesque, but still Intentional. Complete abstention from Intentional talk about trees can become almost as heroic, cumbersome, and pointless as the parallel strict behaviorist taboo when speaking of rats and pigeons. And even when Intentional glosses on (e.g.) tree-activities are of vanishingly small heuristic value, it seems to me wiser to grant that such a tree is a very degenerate, uninteresting, negligible Intentional system than to attempt to draw a line above which Intentional interpretations are "objectively true."

It is obvious, then, that being an Intentional system is not sufficient condition for being a person, but is surely a necessary condition. Nothing to which we could not successfully adopt the Intentional stance, with its presupposition of rationality, could count as a person. Can we then define persons as a subclass of Intentional systems? At first glance it might seem profitable to suppose that persons are just that subclass of Intentional systems that *really* have beliefs, desires, and so forth, and are not merely *supposed* to have them for the sake of a short-cut prediction. But efforts to say what counts as really having a belief (so that no dog or tree or computer could qualify) all seem to end by putting conditions on genuine belief that (1) are too strong for our intuitions, and (2) allude to distinct conditions of personhood farther down my list. For instance, one might claim that genuine beliefs are necessarily *verbally expressible* by the believer,[10] or the believer must be *conscious* that he has them, but people seem to have many beliefs that they cannot put into words, and many that they are unaware of having—and in any case I hope to show that the capacity for verbal expression, and the capacity for consciousness, find different *loci* in the set of necessary conditions of personhood.

Better progress can be made, I think, if we turn to our fourth theme, reciprocity, to see what kind of definition it could receive in terms of Intentional systems. The theme suggests that a person must be able to reciprocate the stance, which suggests that an Intentional system that itself adopted the Intentional stance toward other objects would meet the test. Let us define a *second-order Intentional system* as one to which we ascribe not only simple beliefs, desires and other Intentions, but beliefs, desires, and other Intentions *about* beliefs, desires, and other Intentions. An Intentional system *S* would be a second-order Intentional system if among the ascriptions we make to it are such as *S believes that T desires that p, S hopes that T fears that q*, and reflexive cases like *S believes that S desires that p*. (The importance of the reflexive cases will loom large, not surprisingly, when we turn to those who interpret our sixth condition as *self*-consciousness. It may seem to some that the reflexive cases make all Intentional systems automatically second-order systems, and even *n*-order systems, on the grounds that believing that *p* implies believing that you believe that *p* and so forth, but this is a fundamental mistake; the iteration of beliefs and other Intentions is never redundant, and hence while some iterations are normal [are to be expected] they are never trivial or automatic.)

Now are human beings the only second-order Intentional systems so far as we know? I take this to be an empirical question. We ascribe beliefs and desires to dogs, cats, lions, birds, and dolphins, for example, and thereby often predict their behavior—when all goes well—but it is hard to think of a case where an animal's behavior was so sophisticated that we would need to ascribe second-order Intentions to it in order to predict or explain its behavior. Of course if some version of mechanistic physicalism is true (as I believe), we will never *need* absolutely to ascribe any Intentions to anything, but supposing that for heuristic and pragmatic reasons we were to ascribe Intentions to animals, would we ever feel the pragmatic tug to ascribe second-order Intentions to them? Psychologists have often appealed to a principle known as Lloyd Morgan's Canon of Parsimony, which can be viewed as a special case of Occam's Razor; it is the principle that one should attribute to an organism as little intelligence or consciousness or rationality or mind as will suffice to account for its behavior. This principle can be, and has been, interpreted as demanding nothing short of radical behaviorism[11] but I think this is a mistake, and we can interpret it as the principle requiring us when we adopt the Intentional stance toward a thing to ascribe the simplest, least sophisticated, lowest-order beliefs, desires, and so on, that will account for the behavior. Then we will grant, for instance, that Fido *wants* his supper, and *believes* his master will give him his supper if he begs in front of his master, but we need not ascribe to Fido the further *belief* that his begging induces a *belief* in his master that he, Fido, *wants* his supper. Similarly, my *expectation* when I put a dime in the candy machine does not hinge on a further *belief* that inserting the coin induces the machine to *believe* I *want* some candy. That is, while Fido's begging looks very much like true second-order interacting (with Fido treating his master as an Intentional system), if we suppose that to Fido his master is just a supper machine activated by begging, we will have just as good a predictive ascription, more modest but still, of course, Intentional.

Are dogs, then, or chimps or other "higher" animals, incapable of rising to the level of second-order Intentional systems, and if so why? I used to think the answer was Yes, and I thought the reason was that nonhuman animals lack language, and that language was needed to represent second-order Intentions. In other words, I thought condition four might rest on condition five. I was tempted by the hypothesis that animals cannot, for instance, have second-order beliefs, beliefs about beliefs, for the same reason they cannot have beliefs about Friday, or poetry. Some beliefs can only be acquired, and hence represented, via language.[12] But if it is true that some beliefs cannot be acquired without language, it is false that all second-order beliefs are among them, and it is false that nonhumans cannot be second-order Intentional systems. Once I began asking people for examples of non-human second-order Intentional systems, I found some very plausible cases. Consider this from Peter Ashley (in a letter):

> One evening I was sitting in a chair at my home, the *only* chair my dog is allowed to sleep in. The dog was lying in front of me, whimpering. She was getting nowhere in her trying to "convince" me to give up the chair to her. Her next move is the most interesting, nay, the *only* interesting part of the story. She stood up, and went to the front door where I could still easily see her. She scratched the door, giving me the impression that she had given up trying to get the chair and had decided to go out. However as soon as I reached the door to let her out, she ran back across the room and climbed into her chair, the chair she had "forced" me to leave.

Here it seems we must ascribe to the dog the *intention* that her master *believe* she *wants* to go out—not just a second-order, but a third-order Intention. The key to the example, what makes it an example of a higher-order Intentional system at work, is that the belief she intends to induce in her master is false. If we want to discover further examples of animals behaving as second-order Intentional systems it will help to think of cases of deception, where the animal, believing p, tries to get another Intentional system to believe *not-p*. Where an animal is trying to induce behavior in another which *true* beliefs about the other's environment would not induce, we cannot "divide through" and get an explanation that cites only first-level Intentions. We can make this point more general before explaining why it is so: where x is attempting to induce behavior in y which is inappropriate to y's *true* environment and needs but appropriate to y's *perceived* or *believed* environment and needs, we are forced to ascribe second-order Intentions to x. Once in this form the point emerges as a familiar one, often exploited by critics of behaviorism: one can be a behaviorist in explaining and controlling the behavior of laboratory animals only so long as he can rely on there being no serious dislocation between the actual environment of the experiment and the environment perceived by the animals. A tactic for embarrassing behaviorists in the laboratory is to set up experiments that deceive the subjects: if the deception succeeds their behavior is predictable from their false *beliefs* about the environment, not from the actual environment. Now a first-order Intentional system is a behaviorist; it ascribes no Intentions to anything. So if we are to have good evidence that some system S is *not* a behaviorist—is a second-order Intentional system—it will only be in those cases where behaviorist theories are inadequate to the data, only in those cases where behaviorism would not explain system S's success in manipulating another system's behavior.

This suggests that Ashley's example is not so convincing after all, that it can be defeated by supposing his dog is a behaviorist of sorts. She need not believe that scratching on the door will induce Ashley to believe she wants to go out; she may simply believe, as a good behaviorist, that she has conditioned Ashley to go to the door when she scratches. So she applies the usual stimulus, gets the usual response, and that's that. Ashley's case succumbs if this is a *standard* way his dog has of getting the door opened, as it probably is, for then the more modest hypothesis is that the dog believes her master is conditioned to go to the door when she scratches. Had the dog done something *novel* to deceive her master (like running to the window and looking out, growling suspiciously) then we would have to grant that rising from the chair was no mere conditioned response in Ashley, and could not be "viewed" as such by his dog, but then, such virtuosity in a dog would be highly implausible.

Yet what is the difference between the implausible case and the well-attested cases where a low-nesting bird will feign a broken wing to lure a predator away from the nest? The effect achieved is novel, in the sense that the bird in all likelihood has not repeatedly conditioned the predators in the neighborhood with this stimulus, so we seem constrained to explain the ploy as a bit of genuine deception, where the bird *intends* to induce a false *belief* in the predator. Forced to this interpretation of the behavior, we would be mightily impressed with the bird's ingenuity were it not for the fact that we know such behavior is "merely instinctual." But why does it disparage this trick to call it merely instinctual? To claim it is instinctual is to claim that all birds of the species do it; they do it even when circumstances aren't entirely appropriate; they do it when there are better reasons for staying on the nest; the behavior pattern is rigid, a tropism of sorts, and presumably the controls are genetically wired in, not learned or invented.

We must be careful not to carry this disparagement too far; it is not that the bird does this trick "unthinkingly," for while it is no doubt true that she does not in any sense run through an argument or scheme in her head ("Let's see, if I were to flap my wing as if it were broken, the fox would think . . ."), a man might do something of similar subtlety, and of genuine intelligence, novelty, and appropriateness, and not run through the "conscious thoughts" either. *Thinking the thoughts*, however that is characterized, is not what makes truly intelligent behavior intelligent. Anscombe says at one point "If [such an expression of reasoning] were supposed to describe actual mental processes, it would in general be quite absurd. The interest of the account is that it described an order which is there whenever actions are done with intentions."[13] But the "order is there" in the case of the bird as well as the man. That is, when we ask why birds evolved with this tropism we explain it by noting the utility of having a means of *deceiving* predators, or inducing false beliefs in them; what must be explained is the provenance of the bird's second-order Intentions. I would be the last to deny or dismiss the vast difference between instinctual or tropistic behavior and the more versatile, intelligent behavior of humans and others, but what I want to insist on here is that if one is prepared to adopt the Intentional stance without qualms as a tool in predicting and explaining behavior, the bird is as much a second-order Intentional system as any man. Since this is so, we should be particularly suspicious of the argument I was tempted to use, viz., that *representations* of second order Intentions would depend somehow on language.[14] For it is far from clear that all or even any of the beliefs and other Intentions of an Intentional system need be *represented* "within" the system in any way for us to get a purchase on predicting its behavior by *ascribing* such Intentions to it.[15] The situation we elucidate by citing the bird's desire to induce a false belief in the predator seems to have no room or need for a representation of this sophisticated Intention in any entity's "thoughts" or "mind," for neither the bird nor evolutionary history nor Mother Nature need think these thoughts for our explanation to be warranted.

Reciprocity, then, provided we understand by it merely the capacity in Intentional systems to exhibit higher-order Intentions, while it depends on the first three conditions, is independent of the fifth and sixth. Whether this notion does justice to the reciprocity discussed by other writers will begin to come clear only when we see how it meshes with the last two conditions. For the fifth condition, the capacity for verbal communication, we turn to Grice's theory of meaning. Grice attempts to define what he calls nonnatural meaning, an utterer's meaning something by uttering something, in terms of the *intentions* of the utterer. His initial definition is as follows:[16]

"U meant something by uttering x" is true if, for some audience A, U uttered x intending
(1) A to produce a particular response *r*.
(2) A to think (recognize) that U intends (1).
(3) A to fulfill (1) on the basis of his fulfillment of (2).

Notice that intention (2) ascribes to U not only a second- but a third-order Intention: U must *intend* that A *recognize* that U *intends* that A produce *r*. It matters not at all that Grice has been forced by a series of counterexamples to move from this initial definition to much more complicated versions, for they all reproduce the third-order Intention of (2). Two points of great importance to us emerge from Grice's analysis of nonnatural meaning. First, since nonnatural meaning, meaning something by saying something, must be a feature of any true verbal communication, and since it depends on third-order Intentions on the part of the utterer, we have our case that condition five rests on condition four and not vice versa. Second, Grice shows us that mere *second*-order Intentions are not enough to provide genuine reciprocity; for that, *third*-order Intentions are needed. Grice introduces condition (2) in order to exclude such cases as this: I leave the china my daughter has broken lying around for my wife to see. This is not a case of meaning something by doing what I do intending what I intend, for though I am attempting thereby to induce my wife to believe something about our daughter (a second-order Intention on my part), success does not depend on her recognizing this intention of mine, or recognizing my intervention or existence at all. There has been no real *encounter*, to use Erving Goffman's apt term, between us, no *mutual recognition*. There must be an encounter between utterer and audience for utterer to mean anything, but encounters can occur in the absence of nonnatural meaning (witness Ashley's dog), and ploys that depend on third-order Intentions need not involve encounters (e.g., *A* can intend that *B* believe that *C* desires that *p*). So third-order Intentions are a necessary but not sufficient condition for encounters which are a necessary but not sufficient condition for instances of nonnatural meaning, that is, instances of verbal communication.

It is no accident that Grice's cases of nonnatural meaning fall into a class whose other members are cases of deception or manipulation. Consider, for instance, Searle's ingenious counterexample to one of Grice's formulations: the American caught behind enemy lines in World War II Italy who attempts to deceive his Italian captors into concluding he is a German officer by saying the one sentence of German he knows: *"Kennst du das Land, wo die Zitronen blühen?"*[17] As Grice points out, these cases share with cases of nonnatural meaning a reliance on or exploitation of the rationality of the victim. In these cases success hinges on inducing the victim to embark on a chain of reasoning to which one contributes premises directly or indirectly. In deception the premises are disbelieved by the supplier; in normal communication they are believed. Communication, in Gricean guise, appears to be a sort of collaborative manipulation of audience by utterer; it depends, not only on the rationality of the audience who must sort out the utterer's intentions, but on the audience's *trust* in the utterer. Communication, as a sort of manipulation, would not work, given the requisite rationality of the audience, unless the audience's trust in the utterer were *well-grounded* or reasonable. Thus the *norm* for utterance is sincerity; were utterances not normally trustworthy, they would fail of their purpose.[18]

Lying, as a form of deception, can only work against a background of truth-telling, but other forms of deception do not depend on the trust of the victim. In these cases success depends on the victim being *quite* smart, but not quite smart enough. Stupid poker players are the bane of clever poker players, for they fail to see the bluffs and ruses being offered them. Such sophisticated deceptions need not depend on direct encounters. There is a book on how to detect fake antiques (which is also, inevitably, a book on how to *make* fake antiques) which offers this sly advice to those who want to fool the "expert" buyer: once you have completed your table or whatever (having utilized all the usual means of simulating age and wear) take a modern electric drill and drill a hole right through the piece in some conspicuous but perplexing place. The would-be buyer will argue: no one would drill such a disfiguring hole without a reason (it can't be supposed to look "authentic" in any way) so it must have served a purpose, which means this table must have been in use in someone's home; since it was in use in someone's home, it was not made expressly for sale in this antique shop . . . therefore it is authentic. Even if this "conclusion" left room for lingering doubts, the buyer will be so preoccupied dreaming up uses for that hole it will be months before the doubts can surface.

What is important about these cases of deception is the fact that just as in the case of the feigning bird, success does not depend on the victim's *consciously entertaining* these chains of reasoning. It does not matter if the buyer just notices the hole and "gets a hunch" the piece is genuine. He *might* later accept the reasoning offered as his "rationale" for finding the piece genuine, but he might deny it, and in denying it, he might be deceiving himself, even though the *thoughts* never went through his head. The chain of reasoning explains why the hole works as it does (if it does), but as Anscombe says, it need not "describe actual mental processes," if we suppose actual mental processes are conscious processes or events. The same, of course, is true of Gricean communications; neither the utterer nor the audience need consciously entertain the complicated Intentions he outlines, and what is a bit surprising is that no one has ever used this fact as an objection to Grice. Grice's conditions for meaning have been often criticized for falling short of being sufficient, but there seems to be an argument not yet used to show they are not even necessary. Certainly few people ever consciously framed those ingenious intentions before Grice pointed them out, and yet people had been communicating for years. Before Grice, were one asked: "Did you intend your audience to recognize your intention to provoke that response in him?" one would most likely have retorted: "I intended nothing so devious. I simply intended to inform him that I wouldn't be home for supper" (or whatever). So it seems that if these complicated intentions underlay our communicating all along, they must have been unconscious intentions. Indeed, a perfectly natural way of responding to Grice's papers is to remark that *one was not aware* of doing these things when one communicated. Now Anscombe has held, very powerfully, that such a response establishes that the action under that description was not intentional.[19] Since one is not *aware* of these intentions in speaking, one cannot be speaking *with* these intentions.

Why has no one used this argument against Grice's theory? Because, I submit, it is just too plain that Grice is on to something, that Grice is giving us necessary conditions for nonnatural meaning. His analysis illuminates so many questions. Do we communicate with computers in Fortran? Fortran seems to be a language; it has a grammar, a vocabulary, a semantics. The transactions in Fortran between man and machine are often viewed as cases of *man communicating with machine,* but such transactions are pale copies of human verbal communication precisely because the Gricean conditions for nonnatural meaning have been bypassed. There is no room for them to apply. Achieving one's ends in transmitting a bit of Fortran to the machine does not hinge on getting the machine to recognize one's intentions. This does not mean that all communications with computers in the future will have this shortcoming (or strength, depending on your purposes), but just that we do not now communicate, in the strong (Gricean) sense, with computers.[20]

If we are not about to abandon the Gricean model, yet are aware of no such intentions in our normal conversation, we shall just have to drive these intentions underground, and call them unconscious or preconscious intentions. They are intentions that exhibit "an order which is there" when people communicate, intentions of which we are not normally aware, and intentions which are a precondition of verbal communication.[21]

We have come this far without having to invoke any sort of consciousness at all, so if there is a dependence between consciousness or self-consciousness and our other conditions, it will have to be consciousness depending on the others. But to show this I must first show how the first five conditions by themselves might play a role in ethics, as suggested by Rawls's theory of justice. Central to Rawls's theory is his setting up of an idealized situation, the "original position," inhabited by idealized persons, and deriving from this idealization the first principles of justice that generate and illuminate the rest of his theory. What I am concerned with now is neither the content of these principles nor the validity of their derivation, but the nature of Rawls's tactic. Rawls supposes that a group of idealized persons, defined by him as rational, self-interested entities, make calculations under certain constraints about the likely and possible interactive effects of their individual and antagonistic interests (which will require them to frame higher-order Intentions, for example, beliefs about the desires of others, beliefs about the beliefs of others about their own desires, and so forth). Rawls claims these calculations have an optimal "solution" that it would be reasonable for each self-interested person to adopt as an alternative to a Hobbesian state of nature. The solution is to agree with his fellows to abide by the principles of justice Rawls adumbrates. What sort of a proof of the principles of justice would this be? Adopting these principles of justice can be viewed, Rawls claims, as the solution to the "highest order game" or "bargaining problem." It is analogous to derivations of game theory, and to proofs in Hintikka's epistemic logic,[22] and to a "demonstration" that the chess-playing computer will make a certain move because it is the most rational move given its information about the game. All depend on the assumption of ideally rational calculators and hence their outcomes are intrinsically normative. Thus I see the derivations from Rawls's original position as continuous with the deductions and extrapolations encountered in more simple uses of the Intentional stance to understand and control the behavior of simpler entities. Just as truth and consistency are norms for belief,[23] and sincerity is the norm for utterance, so, if Rawls is right, justice as he defines it is the norm for interpersonal interactions. But then, just as part of our warrant for considering an entity to have any beliefs or other Intentions is our ability to construe the entity as *rational,* so our grounds for considering an entity a person include our ability to view him as abiding by the principles of justice. A way of capturing the peculiar status of the concept of a person as I think it is exploited here would be to say that while Rawls does not at all intend to argue that justice is the inevitable result of *human* interaction, he does argue in effect that it is the inevitable result of *personal* interaction. That is, the concept of a person is itself inescapably normative or idealized; to the extent that justice does not reveal itself in the dealings and interactions of creatures, to that extent they are not persons. And once again we can see that there is "an order which is there" in a just society that is independent of any actual episodes of conscious thought. The existence of just practices and the "acknowledgment" implicit in them does not depend on anyone ever consciously or deliberately going through the calculations of the idealized original position, consciously arriving at the reciprocal agreements, consciously adopting a stance toward others.

> To recognize another as a person one must respond to him and act towards him in certain ways; and these ways are intimately connected with the various prima facie duties. Acknowledging these duties in some degree, and so having the elements of morality, is not a matter of choice or of intuiting moral qualities or a matter of the expression of feelings or attitudes . . . it is simply the pursuance of one of the forms of conduct in which the recognition of others as persons is manifested.[24]

The importance of Rawls's attempt to derive principles of justice from the "original position" is, of course, that while the outcome is recognizable as a *moral* norm, it is not *derived as* a moral norm. Morality is not presupposed of the parties in the original position. But this means that the derivation of the norm does not in itself give us any answer to the questions of when and why we have the right to hold persons *morally* responsible for deviations from that norm. Here Anscombe provides help and at the same time introduces our sixth condition. *If I am to be held responsible for an action* (a bit of behavior of mine under a particular description), I must have been *aware* of that action under that description.[25] Why? Because only if I was aware of the action can I *say* what I was about, and participate from a privileged position in the question-and-answer game of giving reasons for my actions. (If I am not in a privileged position to answer questions about the reasons for my actions, there is no special reason to ask *me*.) And what is so important about being able to participate in this game is that only those capable of participating in reason-giving can be argued into, or argued out of, courses of action or attitudes, and if one is incapable of "listening to reason" in some matter, one cannot be held responsible for it. The capacities for verbal communication and for awareness of one's actions are thus essential in one who is going to be amenable to argument or persuasion, and such persuasion, such reciprocal adjustment of interests achieved by mutual exploitation of rationality, is a feature of the optimal mode of personal interaction.

This capacity for participation in mutual persuasion provides the foundation for yet another condition of personhood recently exposed by Harry Frankfurt.[26] Frankfurt claims that persons are the subclass of Intentional systems capable of what he calls *second-order volitions*. Now at first this looks just like the class of second-order Intentional systems, but it is not, as we shall see.

> Besides wanting and choosing and being moved *to do* this or that, men may also want to have (or not to have) certain desires and motives. They are capable of wanting to be different, in their preferences and purposes, from what they are. . . . No animal other than man, however, appears to have the capacity for reflective self-evaluation that is manifested in the formation of second-order desires. (p. 7)

Frankfurt points out that there are cases in which a person might be said to want to have a particular desire even though he would not want that desire to be effective for him, to be "his will." (One might, for instance, want to desire heroin just to know what it felt like to desire heroin, without at all wanting this desire to become one's effective desire.) In more serious cases one wants to have a desire one currently does not have, and wants this desire to become one's will. These cases Frankfurt calls second-order volitions, and it is having these, he claims, that is "essential to being a person" (p. 10). His argument for this claim, which I will not try to do justice to here, proceeds from an analysis of the distinction between having freedom of action and having freedom of the will. One has freedom of the will, on his analysis, only when one can have the will one wants, when one's second-order volitions can be satisfied. Persons do not always have free will, and under some circumstances can be responsible for actions done in the absence of freedom of the will, but a person always must be an "entity for whom the freedom of its will may be a problem" (p. 14)—that is, one capable of framing second-order volitions, satisfiable or not. Frankfurt introduces the marvelous term "wanton" for those "who have first-order desires but . . . no second-order volitions." (Second-order volitions for Frankfurt are all, of course, *reflexive* second-order desires.) He claims that our intuitions support the opinion that all nonhuman animals, as well as small children and some mentally defective people, are wantons, and I for one can think of no plausible counterexamples. Indeed, it seems a strength of his theory, as he claims, that human beings—the only persons we recognize—are distinguished from animals in this regard. But what should be so special about second-order volitions? Why are they, among higher-order Intentions, the peculiar province of persons? Because, I believe, the "reflective self-evaluation" Frankfurt speaks of is, and must be, genuine self-consciousness, which is achieved only by adopting toward *oneself* the stance not simply of communicator but of Anscombian reason-asker and persuader. As Frankfurt points out, second-order desires are an empty notion unless one can *act* on them, and acting on a second-order desire must be logically distinct from acting on its first-order component. Acting on a second-order desire, doing something to bring it about that one acquires a first-order desire, is acting upon oneself just as one would act upon another person: one *schools* oneself, one offers oneself persuasions, arguments, threats, bribes, in the hopes of inducing oneself to acquire the first-order desire.[27] One's stance toward oneself *and access to oneself* in these cases is essentially the same as one's stance toward and access to another. One must *ask oneself* what one's desires, motives, reasons really are, and only if one can say, can become aware of one's desires, can one be in a position to induce oneself to change.[28] Only here, I think, is it the case that the "order which is there" cannot be there unless it is there in episodes of conscious thought, in a dialogue with oneself.[29]

Now, finally, why are we not in a position to claim that these necessary conditions of moral personhood are also sufficient? Simply because the concept of a person is, I have tried to show, inescapably normative. Human beings or other entities can only aspire to being approximations of the ideal, and there can be no way to set a "passing grade" that is not arbitrary. Were the six conditions (strictly interpreted) considered sufficient they would not ensure that any actual entity was a person, for nothing would ever fulfill them. The moral notion of a person and the metaphysical notion of a person are not separate and distinct concepts but just two different and unstable resting points on the same continuum. This relativity infects the satisfaction of conditions of personhood at every level. There is no objectively satisfiable sufficient condition for an entity's

120   Daniel Dennett

really having beliefs, and as we uncover apparent irrationality under an Intentional interpretation of an entity, our grounds for ascribing any beliefs at all wanes, especially when we have (what we always *can* have in principle) a non-Intentional, mechanistic account of the entity. In just the same way our assumption that an entity is a person is shaken precisely in those cases where it matters: when wrong has been done and the question of responsibility arises. For in these cases the grounds for saying that the person is culpable (the evidence that he did wrong, was aware he was doing wrong, and did wrong of his own free will) are in themselves grounds for doubting that it is a person we are dealing with at all. And if it is asked what could *settle* our doubts, the answer is: nothing. When such problems arise we cannot even tell in our own cases if we are persons.

NOTES

1. See my "Mechanism and Responsibility," in T. Honderich, ed., *Essays on Freedom of Action* (London: Routlege & Kegan Paul, 1973).

2. In "Justice as Reciprocity," a revision of "Justice as Fairness" printed in S. Gorovitz, ed., *Utilitarianism* (Indianapolis: Bobbs Merrill, 1971), Rawls allows that the persons in the original position may include "nations, provinces, business firms, churches, teams, and so on. The principles of justice apply to conflicting claims made by persons of all these separate kinds. There is, perhaps, a certain logical priority to the case of human individuals" (p. 245). In *A Theory of Justice* (Cambridge, Mass.: Harvard University Press, 1971), he acknowledges that parties in the original position may include associations and other entities not human individuals (e.g., p. 146), and the apparent interchangeability of "parties in the original position" and "persons in the original position" suggests that Rawls is claiming that for some moral concept of a person, the moral person is *composed* of metaphysical persons who may or may not themselves be moral persons.

3. Setting aside Rawls's possible compound moral persons. For more on compound persons see Amelie Rorty, "Persons, Policies, and Bodies," *International Philosophical Quarterly*, Vol. XIII, no. 1 (March 1973).

4. J. Hintikka, *Knowledge and Belief* (Ithaca: Cornell University Press, 1962).

5. P.F. Strawson, *Individuals* (London: Methuen, 1959), pp. 101–102. It has often been pointed out that Strawson's definition is obviously much too broad, capturing all sentient, active creatures. See, e.g. H. Frankfurt, "Freedom of the will and the concept of a person," *Journal of Philosophy* (January 14, 1971). It can also be argued (and I would argue) that states of consciousness are only a proper subset of psychological or Intentionally characterized states, but I think it is clear that Strawson here means to cast his net wide enough to include psychological states generally.

6. D.M. MacKay, "The use of behavioral language to refer to mechanical processes," *British Journal of Philosophy of Science* (1962), pp. 89–103; P.F. Strawson, "Freedom and resentment," *Proceedings of the British Academy* (1962), reprinted in Strawson, ed., *Studies in the Philosophy of Thought and Action* (Oxford, 1968); A. Rorty, "Slaves and machines," *Analysis* (1962); H. Putnam, "Robots: machines or

artificially created life?" *Journal of Philosophy* (November 12, 1964); W. Sellars, "Fatalism and determinism," in K. Lehrer, ed., *Freedom and Determinism* (New York: Random House, 1966); A. Flew, "A Rational Animal," in J.R. Smythies, ed., *Brain and Mind* (London: Routledge & Kegan Paul, 1968); T. Nagel, "War and Massacre," *Philosophy and Public Affairs* (Winter 1972); D. Van de Vate, "The problem of robot consciousness," *Philosophy and Phenomenological Research* (December 1971); my "Intentional Systems," *Journal of Philosophy* (February 25, 1971).

7. H. Frankfurt, "Freedom of the will and the concept of a person," op. cit.

8. And sufficient, but I will not argue it here. I argue for this in *Content and Consciousness* (London: Routledge & Kegan Paul, 1969), and more recently and explicitly in my "Reply to Arbib and Gunderson," APA Eastern Division Meetings, December 29, 1972.

9. I will not discuss Sartre's claim here.

10. Cf. Bernard Williams, "Deciding to Believe," in H.E. Kiefer and M.K. Munitz, eds., *Language, Belief and Metaphysics* (New York: New York University Press, 1970).

11. E.g., B.F. Skinner, "Behaviorism at Fifty," in T.W. Wann, ed., *Behaviorism and Phenomenology* (Chicago: University of Chicago Press, 1964).

12. For illuminating suggestions on the relation of language to belief and rationality, see Ronald de Sousa, "How to give a piece of your mind; or, a logic of belief and assent," *Review of Metaphysics* (September 1971).

13. G.E.M. Anscombe, *Intention* (Oxford: Blackwell, 1957), p. 80.

14. Cf. Ronald de Sousa, "Self-Deception," *Inquiry*, 13 (1970), esp. p. 317.

15. I argue this in more detail in "Brain Writing and Mind Reading," in K. Gunderson, ed., *Language, Mind, and Knowledge* (Minneapolis: University of Minnesota Press, 1975), and in my "Reply to Arbib and Gunderson."

16. The key papers are "Meaning," *Philosophical Review* (July 1957), and "Utterer's meaning and intentions," *Philosophical Review* (April 1969). His initial formulation, developed in the first paper, is subjected to a series of revisions in the second paper, from which this formulation is drawn (p. 151).

17. John Searle, "What is a Speech Act?" in Max Black, ed., *Philosophy in America* (London: Allen & Unwin, 1965), discussed in Grice in "Utterer's Meaning and Intentions," p. 160.

18. Cf. "Intentional Systems," pp. 102–103.

19. G.E.M. Anscombe, *Intention*, p. 11.

20. It has been pointed out to me by Howard Friedman that many current Fortran compilers which "correct" operator input by inserting "plus" signs and parentheses, etc., to produce well-formed expressions arguably meet Grice's criteria, since within a very limited sphere, they diagnose the "utterer's" intentions and proceed on the basis of this diagnosis. But first it should be noted that the machines to date can diagnose only what might be called the operator's syntactical intentions, and second, these machines do not seem to meet Grice's subsequent and more elaborate definitions, not that I wish to claim that no computer could.

21. In fact, Grice is describing only a small portion of the order which is there as a precondition of normal personal interaction. An analysis of higher order Intentions on a broader front is to be found in the works of Erving Goffman, especially in *The Presentation of Self in Everyday Life* (Garden City: Doubleday, 1959).

22. See Hintikka, *Knowledge and Belief*, p. 38.

23. See Dennett, "Intentional Systems," pp. 102–103.

24. J. Rawls, "Justice as Reciprocity," p. 259.

25. I can be held responsible for events and states of affairs that I was not aware of and ought to have been aware of, but these are not intentional actions. In these cases I am responsible for these further matters in virtue of being responsible for the foreseeable consequences of actions—including acts of omission—that I was aware of.

26. H. Frankfurt, "Freedom of the will and the concept of a person." Frankfurt does not say whether he conceives his condition to be merely a necessary or also a sufficient conditon of moral personhood.

27. It has been brought to my attention that dogs at stud will often engage in masturbation, in order, apparently, to *increase their desire* to copulate. What makes these cases negligible is that even supposing the dog can be said to act on a desire to strengthen a desire, the effect is achieved in a non-Intentional ("purely physio-logical") way; the dog does not appeal to or exploit his own rationality in achiev-ing his end. (As if the only way a person could act on a second-order volition were by taking a pill or standing on his head, etc.).

28. Margaret Gilbert, in "Vices and self-knowledge," *Journal of Philosophy* (Au-gust, 5, 1971), p. 452, examines the implications of the fact that "when, and only when, one believes that one has a given trait can one decide to change out of it."

29. Marx, in *The German Ideology*, says: "Language, like consciousness, only arises from the need, the necessity, of intercourse with other men. . . . Language is as old as consciousness, language is practical consciousness." And Nietzsche, in *The Joyful Wisdom*, says: "For we could in fact think, feel, will, and recollect, we could likewise 'act' in every sense of the term, and nevertheless nothing of it at all need necessarily 'come into consciousness' (as one says metaphorically;. . . . *What* then is *the purpose* of consciousness generally, when it is in the main *superfluous?*— Now it seems to me, if you will hear my answer and its perhaps extravagant supposition, that the subtlety and strength of consciousness are always in propor-tion to the *capacity for communication* of a man (or an animal), the capacity for communication in its turn being in proportion to the *necessity for communica-tion*. . . . In short, the development of speech and the development of conscious-ness (not of reason, but of reason becoming self-conscious) go hand in hand."

COMPUTING MACHINERY AND INTELLIGENCE

A. M. Turing

THE IMITATION GAME

I propose to consider the question "Can machines think?" This should begin with definitions of the meaning of the terms "machine" and "think." The definitions might be framed so as to reflect so far as possible the normal use of the words, but this attitude is dangerous. If the meaning of the words "machine" and "think" are to be found by examining how they are commonly used it is difficult to escape the conclusion that the meaning and the answer to the question, "Can machines think?" is to be sought in a statistical survey such as a Gallup poll. But this is absurd. Instead of attempting such a definition I shall replace the question by another, which is closely related to it and is expressed in relatively unambiguous words.

The new form of the problem can be described in terms of a game which we call the "imitation game." It is played with three people, a man (A), a woman (B), and an interrogator (C) who may be of either sex. The interrogator stays in a room apart from the other two. The object of the game for the interrogator is to determine which of the other two is the man and which is the woman. He knows them by labels X and Y, and at the end of the game he says either "X is A and Y is B" or "X is B and Y is A." The interrogator is allowed to put questions to A and B thus:

c: Will X please tell me the length of his or her hair?

Now suppose X is actually A, then A must answer. It is A's object in the game to try to cause C to make the wrong identification. His answer might therefore be

"My hair is shingled, and the longest strands are about nine inches long."

In order that tones of voice may not help the interrogator the answers should be written, or better still, typewritten. The ideal arrangement is to have a teleprinter communicating between the two rooms. Alternatively the question and answers can be repeated by an intermediary. The object of the game for the third player (B) is to help the interrogator. The best strategy for her is probably to give truthful answers. She can add such things as "I am the woman, don't listen to him!" to her answers, but it will avail nothing as the man can make similar remarks.

We now ask the question, "What will happen when a machine takes the part of A in this game?" Will the interrogator decide wrongly as often when the game is played like this as he does when the game is played between a man and a woman? These questions replace our original, "Can machines think?"

CRITIQUE OF THE NEW PROBLEM

As well as asking "What is the answer to this new form of the question," one may ask, "Is this new question a worthy one to investigate?" This latter question we investigate without further ado, thereby cutting short an infinite regress.

The new problem has the advantage of drawing a fairly sharp line between the physical and the intellectual capacities of a man. No engineer or chemist claims to be able to produce a material which is indistinguishable from the human skin. It is possible that at some time this might be done, but even supposing this invention available we should feel there was little point in trying to make a "thinking machine" more human by dressing it up in such artificial flesh. The form in which we have set the problem reflects this fact in the condition which prevents the interrogator from seeing or touching the other competitors, or hearing their voices. Some other advantages of the proposed criterion may be shown up by specimen questions and answers. Thus:

Q: Please write me a sonnet on the subject of the Forth Bridge.
A: Count me out on this one. I never could write poetry.
Q: Add 34957 to 70764.
A: (Pause about 30 seconds and then give as answer) 105621.
Q: Do you play chess?
A: Yes.
Q: I have K at my K1, and no other pieces. You have only K at K6 and R at R1. It is your move. What do you play?
A: (After a pause of 15 seconds) R-R8 mate.

The question and answer method seems to be suitable for introducing almost any one of the fields of human endeavor that we wish to include. We do not wish to penalize the machine for its inability to shine in beauty competitions, nor to penalize a man for losing in a race against an airplane. The conditions of our game make these disabilities irrelevant. The "witnesses" can brag, if they consider it advisable, as much as they please about their charms, strength or heroism, but the interrogator cannot demand practical demonstrations.

The game may perhaps be criticized on the ground that the odds are weighted too heavily against the machine. If the man were to try and pretend to be the machine he would clearly make a very poor showing. He would be given away at once by slowness and inaccuracy in arithmetic. May not machines carry out something which ought to be described as thinking but which is very different from what a man does? This objection is a very strong one, but at least we can say that if, nevertheless, a machine can be constructed to play the imitation game satisfactorily, we need not be troubled by this objection.

It might be urged that when playing the "imitation game" the best strategy for the machine may possibly be something other than imitation of the behavior of a man. This may be, but I think it is unlikely that there is any great effect of this kind. In any case there is no intention to investigate here the theory of the game, and it will be assumed that the best strategy is to try to provide answers that would naturally be given by a man.

THE MACHINES CONCERNED IN THE GAME

The question which we put earlier will not be quite definite until we have specified what we mean by the word "machine." It is natural that we should wish to permit every kind of engineering technique to be used in our machines. We also wish to allow the possibility that an engineer or team of engineers may construct a machine which works, but whose manner of operation cannot be satisfactorily described by its constructors because they have applied a method which is largely experimental. Finally, we wish to exclude from the machines men born in the usual manner. It is difficult to frame the definitions so as to satisfy these three conditions. One might for instance insist that the team of engineers should be all of one sex, but this would not really be satisfactory, for it is probably possible to rear a complete individual from a single cell of the skin (say) of a man. To do so would be a feat of biological technique deserving of the very highest praise, but we would not be inclined to regard it as a case of "constructing a thinking machine." This prompts us to abandon the requirement that every kind of technique should be permitted. We are the more ready to do so in view of the fact that the present interest in "thinking machines" has been aroused by a particular kind of machine, usually called an "electronic computer" or "digital computer." Following this suggestion we only permit digital computers to take part in our game. . . .

This special property of digital computers, that they can mimic any discrete machine, is described by saying that they are *universal* machines. The existence of machines with this property has the important consequence that, considerations of speed apart, it is unnecessary to design various new machines to do various computing processes. They can all be done with one digital computer, suitably programmed for each case. It will be seen that as a consequence of this all digital computers are in a sense equivalent.

CONTRARY VIEWS ON THE MAIN QUESTION

We may now consider the ground to have been cleared and we are ready to proceed to the debate on our question "Can machines think?" . . . We cannot altogether abandon the original form of the problem, for opinions will differ as to the appropriateness of the substitution and we must at least listen to what has to be said in this connection.

It will simplify matters for the reader if I explain first my own beliefs in the matter. Consider first the more accurate form of the question. I believe that in about fifty years' time it will be possible to program computers, with a storage capacity of about 10^9, to make them play the imitation game so well that an average interrogator will not have more than 70 percent chance of making the right identification after five minutes of questioning. The original question, "Can machines think?" I believe to be too meaningless to deserve discussion. Nevertheless I believe that at the end of the century the use of words and general educated opinion will have altered so much that one will be able to speak of machines thinking without expecting to be contradicted. I believe further that no useful purpose is served by concealing these beliefs. The popular view that scientists proceed inexorably from well-established fact to well-established fact, never being influenced by any unproved conjecture, is quite mistaken. Provided it is made clear which are proved facts and which are conjectures, no harm can result. Conjectures are of great importance since they suggest useful lines of research.

I now proceed to consider opinions opposed to my own.

1. *The Theological Objection.* Thinking is a function of man's immortal soul. God has given an immortal soul to every man and woman, but not to any other animal or to machines. Hence no animal or machine can think.[1]

I am unable to accept any part of this, but will attempt to reply in theological terms. I should find the argument more convincing if animals were classed with men, for there is a greater difference, to my mind, between the typical animate and the inanimate than there is between man and the other animals. The arbitrary character of the orthodox view becomes clearer if we consider how it might appear to a member of some other religious community. How do Christians regard the Moslem view that women have no souls? But let us leave this point aside and return to the main argument. It appears to me that the argument quoted above implies a serious restriction of the omnipotence of the Almighty. It is admitted that there are certain things that He cannot do such as making one equal to two, but should we not believe that He has freedom to confer a soul on an elephant if He sees fit? We might expect that He would only exercise this power in conjunction with a mutation which provided the elephant with an appropriately improved brain to minister to the needs of this soul. An argument of exactly similar form may be made for the case of machines. It may seem different because it is more difficult to "swallow." But this really only means that we think it would be less likely that He would consider the circumstances suitable for conferring a soul. The circumstances in question are discussed in the rest of this paper. In attempting to construct such machines we should not be irreverently usurping His power of creating souls, any more than we are in the procreation of children: rather we are, in either case, instruments of His will providing mansions for the souls that He creates.

However, this is mere speculation. I am not very impressed with theological arguments whatever they may be used to support. Such arguments have often been found unsatisfactory in the past. In the time of Galileo it was argued that the texts, "And the sun stood still . . . and hasted not to go down about a whole day" (Joshua x. 13) and "He laid the foundations of the earth, that it should not move at any time" (Psalm cv. 5) were an adequate refutation of the Copernican theory. With our present knowledge such an argument appears futile. When that knowledge was not available it made a quite different impression.

2. *The "Heads in the Sand" Objection.* "The consequences of machines thinking would be too dreadful. Let us hope and believe that they cannot do so."

This argument is seldom expressed quite so openly as in the form above. But it affects most of us who think about it at all. We like to believe that Man is in some subtle way superior to the rest of creation. It is best if he can be shown to be *necessarily* superior, for then there is no danger of him losing his commanding position. The popularity of the theological argument is clearly connected with this feeling. It is likely to be quite strong in intellectual people, since they value the power of thinking more highly than others, and are more inclined to base their belief in the superiority of Man on this power.

I do not think that this argument is sufficiently substantial to require refutation. Consolation would be more appropriate: perhaps this should be sought in the transmigration of souls.

3. *The Mathematical Objection.* There are a number of results of mathematical logic which can be used to show that there are limitations to the powers of discrete state machines. The best known of these results is known as Gödel's theorem, and shows that in any sufficiently powerful logical system statements can be formulated which can neither be proved nor disproved within the system, unless possibly the system itself is inconsistent. There are other, in some respects similar, results due to Church, Kleene, Rosser, and Turing. The latter result is the most conve-

nient to consider, since it refers directly to machines, whereas the others can only be used in a comparatively indirect argument: for instance if Gödel's theorem is to be used we need in addition to have some means of describing logical systems in terms of machines, and machines in terms of logical systems. The result in question refers to a type of machine which is essentially a digital computer with an infinite capacity. It states that there are certain things that such a machine cannot do. If it is rigged up to give answers to questions as in the imitation game, there will be some questions to which it will either give a wrong answer, or fail to give an answer at all however much time is allowed for a reply. There may, of course, be many such questions, and questions which cannot be answered by one machine may be satisfactorily answered by another. We are of course supposing for the present that the questions are of the kind to which an answer "Yes" or "No" is appropriate, rather than questions such as "What do you think of Picasso?" The questions that we know the machines must fail on are of this type, "Consider the machine specified as follows. . . . Will this machine ever answer 'Yes' to any question?" The dots are to be replaced by a description of some machine in a standard form. . . . When the machine described bears a certain comparatively simple relation to the machine which is under interrogation, it can be shown that the answer is either wrong or not forthcoming. This is the mathematical result: it is argued that it proves a disability of machines to which the human intellect is not subject.

The short answer to this argument is that although it is established that there are limitations to the powers of any particular machine, it has only been stated, without any sort of proof, that no such limitations apply to the human intellect. But I do not think this view can be dismissed quite so lightly. Whenever one of these machines is asked the appropriate critical question, and gives a definite answer, we know that this answer must be wrong, and this gives us a certain feeling of superiority. Is this feeling illusory? It is no doubt quite genuine, but I do not think too much importance should be attached to it. We too often give wrong answers to questions ourselves to be justified in being very pleased at such evidence of fallibility on the part of the machines. Further, our superiority can only be felt on such an occasion in relation to the one machine over which we have scored our petty triumph. There would be no question of triumphing simultaneously over *all* machines. In short, then, there might be men cleverer than any given machine, but then again there might be other machines cleverer again, and so on.

Those who hold to the mathematical argument would, I think, mostly be willing to accept the imitation game as a basis for discussion. Those who believe in the two previous objections would probably not be interested in any criteria.

4. *The Argument from Consciousness.* This argument is very well expressed in Professor Jefferson's Lister Oration for 1949, from which I

quote. "Not until a machine can write a sonnet or compose a concerto because of thoughts and emotions felt, and not by the chance fall of symbols, could we agree that machine equals brain—that is, not only write it but know that it had written it. No mechanism could feel (and not merely artificially signal, an easy contrivance) pleasure at its successes, grief when its valves fuse, be warmed by flattery, be made miserable by its mistakes, be charmed by sex, be angry or depressed when it cannot get what it wants."

This argument appears to be a denial of the validity of our test. According to the most extreme form of this view the only way by which one could be sure that a machine thinks is to *be* the machine and to feel oneself thinking. One could then describe these feelings to the world, but of course no one would be justified in taking any notice. Likewise according to this view the only way to know that a *man* thinks is to be that particular man. It is in fact the solipsist point of view. It may be the most logical view to hold but it makes communication of ideas difficult. A is liable to believe "A thinks but B does not" while B believes "B thinks but A does not." Instead of arguing continually over this point it is usual to have the polite convention that everyone thinks.

I am sure that Professor Jefferson does not wish to adopt the extreme and solipsist point of view. Probably he would be quite willing to accept the imitation game as a test. The game (with the player B omitted) is frequently used in practice under the name of *viva voce* to discover whether someone really understands something or has "learned it parrot fashion." Let us listen in to a part of such a *viva voce:*

INTERROGATOR: In the first line of your sonnet which reads "Shall I compare thee to a summer's day," would not "a spring day" do as well or better?

WITNESS: It wouldn't scan.

INTERROGATOR: How about "a winter's day"? That would scan all right.

WITNESS: Yes, but nobody wants to be compared to a winter's day.

INTERROGATOR: Would you say Mr. Pickwick reminded you of Christmas?

WITNESS: In a way.

INTERROGATOR: Yet Christmas is a winter's day, and I do not think Mr. Pickwick would mind the comparison.

WITNESS: I don't think you're serious. By a winter's day one means a typical winter's day, rather than a special one like Christmas.

And so on. What would Professor Jefferson say if the sonnet-writing machine was able to answer like this in the *viva voce?* I do not know whether he would regard the machine as "merely artificially signaling" these answers, but if the answers were as satisfactory and sustained as in the above passage I do not think he would describe it as "an easy contrivance." This phrase is, I think, intended to cover such devices as the inclusion in the machine of a record of someone reading a sonnet, with appropriate switching to turn it on from time to time.

In short, then, I think that most of those who support the argument from consciousness could be persuaded to abandon it rather than be forced into the solipsist position. They will then probably be willing to accept our test.

I do not wish to give the impression that I think there is no mystery about consciousness. There is, for instance, something of a paradox connected with any attempt to localize it. But I do not think these mysteries necessarily need to be solved before we can answer the question with which we are concerned in this paper.

5. *Arguments from Various Disabilities.* These arguments take the form "I grant you that you can make machines do all the things you have mentioned but you will never be able to make one to do X." Numerous features X are suggested in this connection. I offer a selection:

> Be kind, resourceful, beautiful, friendly . . . have initiative, have a sense of humor, tell right from wrong, make mistakes . . . fall in love, enjoy strawberries and cream . . . make someone fall in love with it, learn from experience . . . use words properly, be the subject of its own thought . . . have as much diversity of behavior as a man, do something really new. . . .

No support is usually offered for these statements. I believe they are mostly founded on the principle of scientific induction. A man has seen thousands of machines in his lifetime. From what he sees of them he draws a number of general conclusions. They are ugly, each is designed for a very limited purpose, when required for a minutely different purpose they are useless, the variety of behavior of any one of them is very small, etc., etc. Naturally he concludes that these are necessary properties of machines in general. Many of these limitations are associated with the very small storage capacity of most machines. (I am assuming that the idea of storage capacity is extended in some way to cover machines other than discrete state machines. The exact definition does not matter as no mathematical accuracy is claimed in the present discussion.) A few years ago, when very little had been heard of digital computers, it was possible to elicit much incredulity concerning them, if one mentioned their properties without describing their construction. That was presumably due to a similar application of the principle of scientific induction. These applications of the principle are of course largely unconscious. When a burned child fears the fire and shows that he fears it by avoiding it, I should say that he was applying scientific induction. (I could of course also describe his behavior in many other ways.) The works and customs of mankind do not seem to be very suitable material to which to apply scientific induction. A very large part of space-time must be investigated if reliable results are to be obtained. Otherwise we may (as most English children do) decide that everybody speaks English, and that it is silly to learn French.

There are, however, special remarks to be made about many of the disabilities that have been mentioned. The inability to enjoy strawberries and cream may have struck the reader as frivolous. Possibly a machine might be made to enjoy this delicious dish, but any attempt to make one do so would be idiotic. What is important about this disability is that it contributes to some of the other disabilities, e.g., to the difficulty of the same kind of friendliness occurring between man and machine as between white man and white man, or between black man and black man.

The claim that "machines cannot make mistakes" seems a curious one. One is tempted to retort, "Are they any the worse for that?" But let us adopt a more sympathetic attitude, and try to see what is really meant. I think this criticism can be explained in terms of the imitation game. It is claimed that the interrogator could distinguish the machine from the man simply by setting them a number of problems in arithmetic. The machine would be unmasked because of its deadly accuracy. The reply to this is simple. The machine (programmed for playing the game) would not attempt to give the *right* answers to the arithmetic problems. It would deliberately introduce mistakes in a manner calculated to confuse the interrogator. A mechanical fault would probably show itself through an unsuitable decision as to what sort of a mistake to make in the arithmetic. Even this interpretation of the criticism is not sufficiently sympathetic. But we cannot afford the space to go into it much further. It seems to me that this criticism depends on a confusion between two kinds of mistakes. We may call them "errors of functioning" and "errors of conclusion." Errors of functioning are due to some mechanical or electrical fault which causes the machine to behave otherwise than it was designed to do. In philosophical discussions one likes to ignore the possibility of such errors; one is therefore discussing "abstract machines." These abstract machines are mathematical fictions rather than physical objects. By definition they are incapable of errors of functioning. In this sense we can truly say that "machines can never make mistakes." Errors of conclusion can only arise when some meaning is attached to the output signals from the machine. The machine might, for instance, type out mathematical equations, or sentences in English. When a false proposition is typed we say that the machine has committed an error of conclusion. There is clearly no reason at all for saying that a machine cannot make this kind of mistake. It might do nothing but type out repeatedly "$0 = 1$." To take a less perverse example, it might have some method for drawing conclusions by scientific induction. We must expect such a method to lead occasionally to erroneous results.

The claim that a machine cannot be the subject of its own thought can of course only be answered if it can be shown that the machine has *some* thought with *some* subject matter. Nevertheless, "the subject matter of a machine's operations" does seem to mean something, at least to the people who deal with it. If, for instance, the machine was trying to find a solution of the equation $x^2 - 40x - 11 = 0$, one would be tempted to describe this equation as part of the machine's subject matter at that moment. In this sort of sense a machine undoubtedly can be its own subject matter. It may be used to help in making up its own programs, or to predict the effect of alterations in its own structure. By observing the results of its own behavior it can modify its own programs so as to achieve some purpose more effectively. These are possibilities of the near future, rather than Utopian dreams.

The criticism that a machine cannot have much diversity of behavior is just a way of saying that it cannot have much storage capacity. Until fairly recently a storage capacity of even a thousand digits was very rare.

The criticisms that we are considering here are often disguised forms of the argument from consciousness. Usually if one maintains that a machine *can* do one of these things, and describes the kind of method that the machine could use, one will not make much of an impression. It is thought that the method (whatever it may be, for it must be mechanical) is really rather base. Compare the parenthesis in Jefferson's statement quoted above.

6. *Lady Lovelace's Objection.* Our most detailed information of Babbage's Analytical Engine comes from a memoir by Lady Lovelace. In it she states, "The Analytical Engine has no pretensions to *originate* anything. It can do *whatever we know how to order it* to perform" (her italics). This statement is quoted by Hartree who adds: "This does not imply that it may not be possible to construct electronic equipment which will 'think for itself,' or in which, in biological terms, one could set up a conditioned reflex, which would serve as a basis for 'learning.' Whether this is possible in principle or not is a stimulating and exciting question, suggested by some of these recent developments. But it did not seem that the machines constructed or projected at the time had this property."

I am in thorough agreement with Hartree over this. It will be noticed that he does not assert that the machines in question had not got the property, but rather that the evidence available to Lady Lovelace did not encourage her to believe that they had it. It is quite possible that the machines in question had in a sense got this property. For suppose that some discrete state machine has the property. The Analytical Engine was a universal digital computer, so that, if its storage capacity and speed were adequate, it could by suitable programming be made to mimic the machine in question. Probably this argument did not occur to the Countess or to Babbage. In any case there was no obligation on them to claim all that could be claimed.

This whole question will be considered again under the heading of learning machines.

A variant of Lady Lovelace's objection states that a machine can "never do anything really new." This may be parried for a moment with the saw, "There is nothing new under the sun." Who can be certain that "original work" that he has done was not simply the growth of the seed planted in him by teaching, or the effect of following well-known general principles? A better variant of the objection says that a machine can never "take us by surprise." This statement is a more direct challenge and can be met directly. Machines take me by surprise with great frequency. This is largely because I do not do sufficient calculation to decide what to expect them to do, or rather because, although I do a calculation, I do it in a hurried, slipshod fashion, taking risks. Perhaps I say to myself, "I suppose the voltage here ought to be the same as there; anyway let's assume it is." Naturally I am often wrong, and the result is a surprise for me, for by the time the experiment is done these assumptions have been forgotten. These admissions lay me open to lectures on the subject of my vicious ways, but do not throw any doubt on my credibility when I testify to the surprises I experience.

I do not expect this reply to silence my critic. He will probably say that such surprises are due to some creative mental act on my part, and reflect no credit on the machine. This leads us back to the argument from consciousness, and far from the idea of surprise. It is a line of argument we must consider closed, but it is perhaps worth remarking that the appreciation of something as surprising requires as much of a "creative mental act" whether the surprising event originates from a man, a book, a machine or anything else.

The view that machines cannot rise to surprises is due, I believe, to a fallacy to which philosophers and mathematicians are particularly subject. This is the assumption that as soon as a fact is presented to a mind all consequences of that fact spring into the mind simultaneously with it. It is a very useful assumption under many circumstances, but one too easily forgets that it is false. A natural consequence of doing so is that one then assumes that there is no virtue in the mere working out of consequences from data and general principles.

7. *Argument from Continuity in the Nervous System.* The nervous system is certainly not a discrete state machine. A small error in the information about the size of a nervous impulse impinging on a neuron may make a large difference to the size of the outgoing impulse. It may be argued that, this being so, one cannot expect to be able to mimic the behavior of the nervous system with a discrete state system.

It is true that a discrete state machine must be different from a continuous machine. But if we adhere to the conditions of the imitation game, the interrogator will not be able to take any advantage of this difference. The situation can be made clearer if we consider some other simpler continuous machine. A differential analyzer will do very well. (A differential analyzer is a certain kind of machine not of the discrete state type used for some kinds of calculation.) Some of these provide their answers in a typed form, and so are suitable for taking part in the game. It would not be possible for a digital computer to predict exactly what answers the differential analyzer would give to a problem, but it would be quite capable of giving the right sort of answer. For instance, if asked to give the value of π (actually about 3.1416) it would be reasonable to choose at random between the values 3.12, 3.13, 3.14, 3.15, 3.16 with the probabilities of 0.05, 0.15, 0.55, 0.19, 0.06 (say). Under these circumstances it would be very difficult for the interrogator to distinguish the differential analyzer from the digital computer.

8. *The Argument from Informality of Behavior.* It is not possible to produce a set of rules purporting to describe what a man should do in every conceivable set of circumstances. One might for instance have a rule that one is to stop when one sees a red traffic light, and to go if one sees a green one, but what if by some fault both appear together? One may perhaps decide that it is safest to stop. But some further difficulty may well arise from this decision later. To attempt to provide rules of conduct to cover every eventuality, even those arising from traffic lights, appears to be impossible. With all this I agree.

From this it is argued that we cannot be machines. I shall try to reproduce the argument, but I fear I shall hardly do it justice. It seems to run something like this. "If each man had a definite set of rules of conduct by which he regulated his life he would be no better than a machine. But there are no such rules, so men cannot be machines." The undistributed middle is glaring. I do not think the argument is ever put quite like this, but I believe this is the argument used nevertheless. There may however be a certain confusion between "rules of conduct" and "laws of behavior" to cloud the issue. By "rules of conduct" I mean precepts such as "Stop if you see red lights," on which one can act, and of which one can be conscious. By "laws of behavior" I mean laws of nature as applied to a man's body such as "if you pinch him he will squeak." If we substitute "laws of behavior which regulate his life" for "laws of conduct by which he regulates his life" in the argument quoted the undistributed middle is no longer insuperable. For we believe that it is not only true that being regulated by laws of behavior implies being some sort of machine (though not necessarily a discrete state machine), but that conversely being such a machine implies being regulated by such laws. However, we cannot so easily convince ourselves of the absence of complete laws of behavior as of complete rules of conduct. The only way we know of for finding such laws is scientific observation, and we certainly know of no circumstances under which we could say, "We have searched enough. There are no such laws."

We can demonstrate more forcibly that any such statement would be unjustified. For suppose we could be sure of finding such laws if they existed. Then given a discrete state machine it should certainly be possible to discover by observation sufficient about it to predict its future behavior, and this within a reasonable time, say a thousand years. But this does not seem to be the case. I have set up on the Manchester computer a small program using only 1000 units of storage, whereby the machine supplied with one sixteen-figure number replies with another within two seconds. I would defy anyone to learn from these replies sufficient about the program to be able to predict any replies to untried values.

9. *The Argument from Extrasensory Perception.* I assume that the reader is familiar with the idea of extrasensory perception, and the meaning of the four items of it, viz., telephathy, clairvoyance, precognition, and psychokinesis. These disturbing phenomena seem to deny all our usual scientific ideas. How we should like to discredit them! Unfortunately the statistical evidence, at least for telepathy, is overwhelming. It is very difficult to rearrange one's ideas so as to fit these new facts in. Once one has accepted them it does not seem a very big step to believe in ghosts and bogies. The idea that our bodies move simply according to the known laws of physics, together with some others not yet discovered but somewhat similar, would be one of the first to go.

This argument is to my mind quite a strong one. One can say in reply that many scientific theories seem to remain workable in practice, in spite of clashing with E.S.P.; that in fact one can get along very nicely if one forgets about it. This is rather cold comfort, and one fears that thinking is just the kind of phenomenon where E.S.P. may be especially relevant.

A more specific argument based on E.S.P. might run as follows: "Let us play the imitation game, using as witnesses a man who is good as a telepathic receiver, and a digital computer. The interrogator can ask such questions as "What suit does the card in my right hand belong to?' The man by telepathy or clairvoyance gives the right answer 130 times out of 400 cards. The machine can only guess at random, and perhaps get 104 right, so the interrogator makes the right identification." There is an interesting possibility which opens here. Suppose the digital computer contains a random number generator. Then it will be natural to use this to decide what answer to give. But then the random number generator will be subject to the psychokinetic powers of the interrogator. Perhaps this psychokinesis might cause the machine to guess right more often than would be expected on a probability calculation, so that the interrogator might still be unable to make the right identification. On the other hand, he might be able to guess right without any questioning, by clairvoyance. With E.S.P. anything may happen.

If telepathy is admitted it will be necessary to tighten our test. The situation could be regarded as analogous to that which would occur if the interrogator were talking to himself and one of the competitors was listening with his ear to the wall. To put the competitors into a "telepathy-proof room" would satisfy all requirements.

NOTE

1. Possibly this view is heretical. St. Thomas Aquinas (*Summa Theologica*, quoted by Bertrand Russell, *A History of Western Philosophy* [New York: Simon and Schuster, 1945], p. 458) states that God cannot make a man to have no soul. But this may not be a real restriction on His powers, but only a result of the fact that men's souls are immortal, and therefore indestructible.

THE CORPORATION AS A MORAL PERSON

Peter A. French

I

In one of his *New York Times* columns of not too long ago Tom Wicker's ire was aroused by a Gulf Oil Corporation advertisement that "pointed the finger of blame" for the energy crisis at all elements of our society (and supposedly away from the oil company). Wicker attacked Gulf Oil as the major, if not the sole, perpetrator of that crisis and virtually every other social ill, with the possible exception of venereal disease. It does not matter whether Wicker was serious or sarcastic in making his charges (I suspect he was in deadly earnest). I am interested in the sense ascriptions of moral responsibility make when their subjects are corporations. I hope to provide the foundation of a theory that allows treatment of corporations as members of the moral community, of equal standing with the traditionally acknowledged residents: biological human beings, and hence treats Wicker-type responsibility ascriptions as unexceptionable instances of a perfectly proper sort without having to paraphrase them. In short, corporations can be full-fledged moral persons and have whatever privileges, rights and duties as are, in the normal course of affairs, accorded to moral persons.

II

It is important to distinguish three quite different notions of what constitutes personhood that are entangled in our tradition: the metaphysical, moral and legal concepts. The entanglement is clearly evident in Locke's account of personal identity. He writes that the term "person" is "a *forensic* term, appropriating actions and their merit; and so belongs only to *intelligent agents*, capable of law, and happiness, and misery."[1] He goes on to say that by consciousness and memory persons are capable of extending themselves into the past and thereby become "concerned and *accountable*."[2] Locke is historically correct in citing the law as a primary origin of the term "person." But he is incorrect in maintaining that its legal usage somehow entails its metaphysical sense, agency; and whether or not either sense, but especially the metaphysical, is interdependent on

137

the moral sense, accountability, is surely controversial. Regarding the relationship between metaphysical and moral persons there are two distinct schools of thought. According to one, to be a metaphysical person is to be a moral one; to understand what it is to be accountable one must understand what it is to be an intelligent or a rational agent and viceversa; while according to the other, being an agent is a necessary but not sufficient condition of being a moral person. Locke holds the interdependence view with which I agree, but he roots both moral and metaphysical persons in the juristic person, which is, I think, wrongheaded. The preponderance of current thinking tends to some version of the necessary pre-condition view, but it does have the virtue of treating the legal person as something apart.

It is of note that many contemporary moral philosophers and economists both take a pre-condition view of the relationship between the metaphysical and moral person and also adopt a particular view of the legal personhood of corporations that effectually excludes corporations *per se* from the class of moral persons. Such philosophers and economists champion the least defensible of a number of possible interpretations of the juristic personhood of corporations, but their doing so allows them to systematically sidestep the question of whether corporations can meet the conditions of metaphysical personhood.[3]

III

John Rawls is, to some extent, guilty of fortifying what I hope to show is an indefensible interpretation of the legal concept and of thereby encouraging an anthropocentric bias that has led to the general belief that corporations just cannot be moral persons. As is well known, Rawls defends his two principles of justice by the use of a thought experiment that incorporates the essential characteristics of what he takes to be a premoral, though metaphysical population and then "derives" the moral guidelines for social institutions that they would accept. The persons (or parties) in the "original position" are described by Rawls as being mutually self-interested, rational, as having similar wants, needs, interests and capacities and as being, for all intents and purposes, equal in power (so that no one of them can dominate the others). Their choice of the principles of justice is, as Dennett has pointed out,[4] a rather dramatic rendering of one version of the compelling (though I think unnecessarily complex) philosophical thesis that only out of metaphysical persons can moral ones evolve.

But Rawls is remarkably ambiguous (and admittedly so) regarding who or what may qualify as a metaphysical person. He admits into the category, in one sentence, not only biological human beings but "nations, provinces, business firms, churches, teams, and so on,"[5] then, perhaps because he does not want to tackle the demonstration of the rationality, etc., of those institutions and organizations, or because he is a captive of the traditional prejudice in favor of biological persons, in the next sentence he withdraws entry. "There is, perhaps, a certain logical priority to the case of human individuals: it may be possible to analyze the actions of so-called artificial persons as logical constructions of the actions of human persons . . ."[6] "Perhaps" is, of course, a rather large hedge behind which to hide; but it is, I suppose, of some significance that in *A Theory of Justice* when he is listing the nature of the parties in the "original position" he adds "c. associations (states, churches, or other corporate bodies)."[7] He does not, unhappily, discuss this entry on his list anywhere else in the book. Rawls has hold, I think, of an important intuition: that some associations of human beings should be treated as metaphysical persons capable on his account of becoming moral persons, in and of themselves. He has, however, shrunk from the task of exploring the implications of that intuition and has instead retreated to the comfortable bulwarks of the anthropocentric bias.

IV

Many philosophers, including, I think, Rawls, have rather uncritically relied upon what they incorrectly perceive to be the most defensible juristic treatment of collectivities such as corporations as a paradigm for the treatment of corporations in their moral theories. The concept of corporate legal personhood under any of its popular interpretations is, I want to argue, virtually useless for moral purposes.

Following many writers on jurisprudence, a juristic person may be defined as any entity that is a subject of a right. There are good etymological grounds for such an inclusive neutral definition. The Latin *"persona"* originally referred to *dramatis personae,* and in Roman law the term was adopted to refer to anything that could act on either side of a legal dispute. [It was not until Boethius' definition of a person: *"Persona est naturae rationabilis individua substantia* (a person is the individual subsistence of a rational nature)"* that metaphysical traits were ascribed to persons.] In effect, in Roman legal tradition persons are creations, artifacts, of the law itself, i.e., of the legislature that enacts the law, and are not considered to have, or only have incidentally, existence of any kind outside of the legal sphere. The law, on the Roman interpretation, is systematically ignorant of the biological status of its subjects.

The Roman notion applied to corporations is popularly known as the Fiction Theory. Hallis characterizes that theory as maintaining that "the personality of a corporate body is a pure fiction and owes its existence to a creative act of the state."[8] Rawls' view of corporate persons could not, however, be motivated by adherence to the Fiction Theory for two reasons. The theory does not demand a dichotomy between real and artificial persons. All juristic persons, on the theory, are creations of the law. The theory does not view the law as recognizing or verifying some pre-legally existing persons; it argues that the law creates its own subjects. Secondly, the theory, in its pure form at least, does not regard any juristic persons as composites. All things which are legislatively created as subjects of rights are nonreducible or, if you will, primitive individual legal persons. (It is of some note that the Fiction Theory is enshrined in English law in regard to corporate bodies by no less an authority than Sir Edward Coke who wrote that corporations "rest only in intendment and consideration of the law."[9])

The Fiction Theory's major rival in American jurisprudence and the view that does seem to inform Rawls' account is what I shall call "the Legal Aggregate Theory of the Corporation." It holds that the names of corporate bodies are only umbrellas that cover (but do not shield) certain biological persons. The Aggregate Theory treats biological status as having legal priority and corporate existence as a contrivance for purposes of summary reference. (Generally, it may be worth mention, Aggregate Theorists tend to ignore employees and identify corporations with directors, executives and stockholders. The model on which they stake their claim is no doubt that of the primitive partnership.) I have shown elsewhere[10] that to treat a corporation as an aggregate for any purposes is to fail to recognize the key logical differences between corporations and mobs. The Aggregate Theory, then, despite the fact that it has been quite popular in legislatures, courtrooms, and on streetcorners simply ignores key logical, socio-economic and historical facts of corporate existence. [It might prove of some value in clarifying the dispute between Fiction and Aggregate theorists to mention a rather famous case in the English law. (The case is cited by Hallis.) It is that of *Continental Tyre and Rubber Co., Ltd.* vs *Daimler Co. Ltd.* Very sketchily, the Continental Tyre company was incorporated in England and carried on its business there. Its business was the selling of tires made in Germany, and all of its directors were German subjects in residence in Germany, and all but one of its shares were held by German subjects. The case arose during the First World War, and it turned on the issue of whether the company was an English subject by virtue of its being incorporated under the English law and independent of its directors and stockholders, and could hence bring suit in an English court against an English subject while a state of war existed. The majority opinion of The Court of Appeals (5–1) was that the corporation was an entity created by statute and hence was "a different person altogether from the subscribers to the memorandum or the shareholders on the register."[11] Hallis aptly summarizes the judgment of the court when he writes that "The Continental Tyre and Rubber Co., Ltd., was an English company with a personality at law distinct from the personalities of its members and could therefore sue in the English Courts as a British

Subject."[12] The House of Lords, however, supporting the Aggregate Theory and no doubt motivated by the demands of the War, overturned the Court of Appeals. Lord Buckley wrote "The artificial legal entity has no independent power of motion. It is moved by the corporator. . . . He is German in fact although British in form."[13] This view has seen many incarnations since on both sides of the Atlantic. I take Rawls' burying of his intuition in the logical priority of human beings as a recent echoing of the words of Lord Parker who in the Continental Tyre case wrote for the majority in the House of Lords: ". . . the character in which the property is held and the character in which the capacity to act is enjoyed and acts are done are not *in pari materia*. The latter character is a quality of the company itself, and conditions its capacities and its acts and is attibutable only to human beings. . . "]{[14]}

In Germanic legal tradition resides the third major rival interpretation of corporate juristic personhood. Due primarily to the advocacy of Otto von Gierke, the so-called Reality Theory recognizes corporations to be pre-legal existing sociological persons. Underlying the theory is the view that law cannot create its subjects, it only determines which societal facts are in conformity with its requirements. At most, law endorses the pre-legal existence of persons for its own purposes. Gierke regards the corporation as an offspring of certain social actions having then a *de facto* personality, which the law only declares to be a juridical fact.[15] The Reality Theory's primary virtue is that it does not ignore the non-legal roots of the corporation while it, as does the Fiction Theory, acknowledges the non-identity of the corporation and the aggregate of its directors, stockholders, executives and employees. The primary difference between the Fiction and Reality Theories, that one treats the corporate person as *de jure* and the other as *de facto*, however, turns out to be of no real importance in regard to the issue of the moral personhood of a corporation. Admittedly the Reality Theory encapsulates a view at least superficially more amenable to arguing for discrete corporate moral personhood than does the Fiction Theory just because it does acknowledge *de facto* personhood, but theorists on both sides will admit that they are providing interpretations of only the formula "juristic person = the subject of rights," and as long as we stick to legal history, no interpretation of that formula need concern itself with metaphysical personhood or agency. The *de facto* personhood of the Reality Theory is that of a sociological entity only, of which no claim is or need be made regarding agency or rationality etc. One could, without contradiction, hold the Reality Theory and deny the metaphysical or moral personhood of corporations. What is needed is a Reality Theory that identifies a *de facto* metaphysical person not just a sociological entity.

Underlying all of these interpretations of corporate legal personhood is a distinction, embedded in the law itself, that renders them unhelpful for our purposes. Being a subject of rights is often contrasted in the law with

being an "administrator of rights." Any number of entities and associations can and have been the subjects of legal rights. Legislatures have
given rights to unborn human beings, they have reserved rights for human beings long after their death, and in some recent cases they have
invested rights in generations of the future.[16] Of course such subjects of
rights, though they are legal persons, cannot dispose of their rights,
cannot administer them, because to administer a right one must be an
agent, i.e., able to act in certain ways. It may be only an historical accident that most legal cases are cases in which "the subject of right X" and
"the administrator of right X" are co-referential. It is nowhere required by
law, under any of the three above theories or elsewhere, that it be so.
Yet, it is possession of the attributes of an administrator of rights and not
those of a subject of rights that are among the generally regarded conditions of moral personhood. It is a fundamental mistake to regard the fact
of juristic corporate personhood as having settled the question of the
moral personhood of a corporation one way or the other.

V

Two helpful lessons however, are learned from an investigation of the
legal personhood of corporations: (1) biological existence is not essentially
associated with the concept of a person (only the fallacious Aggregate
Theory depends upon reduction to biological referents) and (2) a paradigm
for the form of an inclusive neutral definition of a moral person is provided: "a subject of a right." I shall define a moral person as the referent of
any proper name or description that can be a non-eliminatable subject of
what I shall call (and presently discuss) a responsibility ascription of the
second type. The non-eliminatable nature of the subject should be stressed
because responsibility and other moral predicates are neutral as regards
person and personsum predication.[17] Though we might say that The Ox-
Bow mob should be held responsible for the death of three men, a mob is
an example of what I have elsewhere called an aggregate collectivity with
no identity over and above that of the sum of the identities of its component membership, and hence to use "The Ox-Bow mob" as the subject of
such ascriptions is to make summary reference to each member of the mob.
For that reason mobs do not qualify as metaphysical or moral persons.

VI

There are at least two significantly different types of responsibility ascriptions that should be distinguished in ordinary usage (not counting the laudi-
tory recommendation, "He is a responsible lad.") The first-type pins responsibility on someone or something, the who-dun-it or what-dun-it

sense. Austin has pointed out that it is usually used when an event or action is thought by the speaker to be untoward. (Perhaps we are more interested in the failures rather than the successes that punctuate our lives.)

The second-type of responsibility ascription, parasitic upon the first, involves the notion of accountability. "Having a responsibility" is interwoven with the notion "Having a liability to answer," and having such a liability or obligation seems to imply (as Anscombe has noted[18]) the existence of some sort of authority relationship either between people or between people and a deity or in some weaker versions between people and social norms. The kernel of insight that I find intuitively compelling, is that for someone to legitimately hold someone else responsible for some event there must exist or have existed a responsibility relationship between them such that in regard to the event in question the latter was answerable to the former. In other words, "X is responsible for y," as a second-type ascription, is properly uttered by someone Z if X in respect to y is or was accountable to Z. Responsibility relationships are created in a multitude of ways, e.g., through promises, contracts, compacts, hirings, assignments, appointments, by agreeing to enter a Rawlsian original position, etc. The right to hold responsible is often delegatable to third parties; though in the case of moral responsibility no delegation occurs because no person is excluded from the relationship: moral responsibility relationships hold reciprocally and without prior agreements among all moral persons. No special arrangement needs to be established between parties for anyone to hold someone morally responsible for his acts or, what amounts to the same thing, every person is a party to a responsibility relationship with all other persons as regards the doing or refraining from doing of certain acts: those that take descriptions that use moral notions.

Because our interest is in the criteria of moral personhood and not the content of morality we need not pursue this idea further. What I have maintained is that moral responsibility, although it is neither contractual nor optional, is not a class apart but an extension of ordinary, garden-variety, responsibility. What is needed in regard to the present subject then is an account of the requirements for entry into any responsibility relationship, and we have already seen that the notion of the juristic person does not provide a sufficient account. For example, the deceased in a probate case cannot be held responsible in the relevant way by anyone, even though the deceased is a juristic person, a subject of rights.

VII

A responsibility ascription of the second type amounts to the assertion of a conjunctive proposition, the first conjunct of which identifies the subject's actions with or as the cause of an event (usually an untoward one) and the second conjunct asserts that the action in question was intended by the subject or that the event was the direct result of an intentional act of the subject. In addition to what it asserts it implies that the subject is accountable to the speaker (in the case at hand) because of the subject's relationship to the speaker (who the speaker is or what the speaker is, a member of the "moral community," a surrogate for that aggregate). The primary focus of responsibility ascriptions of the second type is on the subject's intentions rather than, though not to the exclusion of, occasions. Austin wrote: "In considering responsibility, few things are considered more important than to establish whether a man *intended* to do A, or whether he did A intentionally."[19] To be the subject of a responsibility ascription of the second type, to be a party in responsibility relationships, hence to be a moral person, the subject must be at minimum, what I shall call a Davidsonian agent.[20] If corporations are moral persons, they will be non-eliminatable Davidsonian agents.

VIII

For a corporation to be treated as a Davidsonian agent it must be the case that some things that happen, some events, are describable in a way that makes certain sentences true, sentences that say that some of the things a corporation does were intended by the corporation itself. That is not accomplished if attributing intentions to a corporation is only a shorthand way of attributing intentions to the biological persons who comprise e.g. its board of directors. If that were to turn out to be the case then on metaphysical if not logical grounds there would be no way to distinguish between corporations and mobs. I shall argue, however, that a Corporation's Internal Decision Structure (its CID Structure) is the requisite redescription device that licenses the predication of corporate intentionality.

Intentionality, though a causal notion, is an intentional one and so it does not mark out a class of actions or events. Attributions of intentionality in regard to any event are referentially opaque with respect to other descriptions of that event, or, in other words, the fact that, given one description, an action was intentional does not entail that on every other description of the action it was intentional. A great deal depends upon what aspect of an event is being described. We can correctly say, e.g., "Hamlet intentionally kills the person hiding in Gertrude's room (one of Davidson's examples), but Hamlet does not intentionally kill Polonius," although "Polonius" and "the person hiding in Gertrude's room" are co-referential. The event may be properly described as "Hamlet killed Polonius" and also as "Hamlet intentionally killed the person hiding in Gertrude's room (behind the arras)," but not as "Hamlet intentionally killed Polonius," for that was not Hamlet's intention. (He, in fact, thought he was killing the King.) The referential opacity of intentionality attributions, I shall presently argue, is congenial to the driving of a wedge between the descriptions of certain events as individual intentional actions and as corporate intentional actions.

Certain events, that is, actions, are describable as simply the bodily movements of human beings and sometimes those same events are redescribable in terms of their upshots, as bringing about something, e.g., (from Austin[21]) feeding penguins *by* throwing them peanuts ("by" is the most common way we connect different descriptions of the same event[22]), and sometimes those events can be redescribed as the effects of some prior cause; then they are described as done for reasons, done in order to bring about something, e.g., feeding the penguins peanuts in order to kill them. Usually what we single out as that prior cause is some desire or felt need combined with the belief that the object of the desire will be achieved by the action undertaken. (This, I think, is what Aristotle meant when he maintained that acting requires desire.) Saying "someone (X) did y intentionally" is to describe an event (y) as the upshot of X's having had a reason for doing it which was the cause of his doing it.

It is obvious that a corporation's doing something involves or includes human beings doing things and that the human beings who occupy various positions in a corporation usually can be described as having reasons for *their* behavior. In virtue of those descriptions they may be properly held responsible for their behavior, *ceteris paribus*. What needs to be shown is that there is sense in saying that corporations and not just the people who work in them, have reasons for doing what they do. Typically, we will be told that it is the directors, or the managers, etc., that really have the corporate reasons and desires, etc., and that although corporate actions may not be reducible without remainder, corporate intentions are always reducible to human intentions.

IX

Every corporation has an internal decision structure. CID Structures have two elements of interest to us here: (1) an organizational or responsibility flow chart that delineates stations and levels within the corporate power structure and (2) corporate decision recognition rule(s) (usually embedded in something called "corporation policy"). The CID Structure is the personnel organization for the exercise of the corporation's power with respect to its ventures, and as such its primary function is to draw experience from various levels of the corporation into a decision-making and ratification process. When operative and properly activated, the CID Structure accomplishes a subordination and synthesis of the intentions and acts of various biological persons into a corporate decision. When viewed in another way, as already suggested, the CID Structure licenses the descriptive transformation of events, seen under another aspect as the acts of biological persons (those who occupy various stations on the organizational chart), to corporate acts by exposing the corporate character of those events. A functioning CID Structure *incorporates* acts of biological persons. For illustrative purposes, suppose we imagine that an event E has at least two aspects, that is, can be described in two non-identical ways. One of those aspects is "Executive X's doing y" and one is "Corporation C's doing z." The corporate act and the individual act may have different properties; indeed they have different causal ancestors though they are causally inseparable. (The causal inseparability of these acts I hope to show is a product of the CID Structure, X's doing y is not the cause of C's doing z nor is C's doing z the cause of X's doing y although if X's doing y causes event F when C's doing z causes F and *vice versa*.)

Although I doubt he is aware of the metaphysical reading that can be given to this process, J. K. Galbraith rather neatly captures what I have in mind when he writes in his recent popular book on the history of economics: "From [the] interpersonal exercise of power, the interaction . . . of the participants, comes the *personality* of the corporation."[23] I take Galbraith here to be quite literally correct, but it is important to spell out how a CID Structure works this "miracle."

In philosophy in recent years we have grown accustomed to the use of games as models for understanding institutional behavior. We all have some understanding of how rules in games make certain descriptions of events possible that would not be so if those rules were non-existent. The CID Structure of a corporation is a kind of constitutive rule (or rules) analogous to the game rules with which we are familiar. The organization chart of a corporation distinguishes "players" and clarifies their rank and the interwoven lines of responsibility within the corporation. An organizational chart tells us, for example, that anyone holding the title "Executive Vice President for Finance Administration" stands in a certain relationship to anyone holding the title "Director of Internal Audit" and to anyone holding the title "Treasurer," etc. In effect it expresses, or maps, the interdependent and dependent relationships, line and staff, that are involved in determinations of corporate decisions and actions. The organizational chart provides what might be called the grammar of corporate decision-making. What I shall call internal recognition rules provide its logic.

By "recognition rule(s)" I mean what Hart, in another context, calls "conclusive affirmative indication"[24] that a decision on an act has been made or performed for corporate reasons. Recognition rules are of two sorts. Partially embedded in the organizational chart are procedural recognitors: we see that decisions are to be reached collectively at certain levels and that they are to be ratified at higher levels (or at inner circles, if one prefers that Galbraithean model). A corporate decision is recognized internally, however, not only by the procedure of its making, but by the policy it instantiates. Hence every corporation creates an image (not to be confused with its public image) or a general policy, what G. C. Buzby of the Chilton Company has called the "basic belief of the corporation,"[25] that must inform its decisions for them to be properly described as being those of that corporation. "The moment policy is side-stepped or violated, it is no longer the policy of that company."[26]

Peter Drucker has seen the importance of the basic policy recognitors in the CID Structure (though he treats matters rather differently from the way I am recommending). Drucker writes:

> Because the corporation is an institution it must have a basic policy. For it must subordinate individual ambitions and decisions to the *needs* of the corporation's welfare and survival. That means that it must have a set of principles and a rule of conduct which limit and direct individual actions and behavior . . .[27]

X

Suppose, for illustrative purposes, we activate a CID Structure in a corporation, Wicker's favorite, the Gulf Oil Corporation. Imagine that three executives X, Y and Z have the task of deciding whether or not Gulf Oil will join in a world uranium cartel. X, Y and Z have before them an Everest of papers that have been prepared by lower echelon executives. Some of the papers will be purely factual reports, some will be contingency plans, some will be formulations of positions developed by various departments, some will outline financial considerations, some will be legal opinions and so on. In so far as these will all have been processed through Gulf's CID Structure system, the personal reasons, if any, individual executives may have had when writing their reports and recommendations in a specific way will have been diluted by the subordination of individual inputs to peer group input even before X, Y and Z review the matter. X, Y and Z take a vote. Their taking of a vote is authorized procedure in the Gulf CID Structure, which is to say that under these circumstances the vote of X, Y and Z can be redescribed as the corporation's making a decision: that is, the event "XYZ voting" may be redescribed to expose an aspect otherwise unrevealed, that is quite different from its other aspects e.g., from X's voting in the affirmative. Redescriptive exposure of a procedurally corporate aspect of an event, however, is not to be confused with a description of an event that makes true a sentence that says that the corporation did something intentionally. But the CID Structure, as already suggested, also provides the grounds in its other type of recognitor for such an attribution of corporate intentionality. Simply, when the corporate act is consistent with, an instantiation or an implementation of established corporate policy, then it is proper to describe it as having been done for corporate reasons, as having been caused by a corporate desire coupled with a corporate belief and so, in other words, as corporate intentional.

An event may, under one of its aspects, be described as the conjunctive act "X did a (or as X intentionally did a) ϵ Y did a (or as Y intentionally did a) ϵ Z did a (or as Z intentionally did a)" (where a = voted in the affirmative on the question of Gulf Oil joining the cartel). Given the Gulf CID Structure, formulated in this instance as the conjunction of rules: when the occupants of positions A, B and C on the organizational chart unanimously vote to do something and if doing that something is consistent with, an instantiation or an implementation of general corporate policy and *ceteris paribus*, then the corporation has decided to do it for corporate reasons, the event is redescribable as "the Gulf Oil Corporation did j for corporate reasons f." (where j is "decided to join the cartel" and f is any reason (desire + belief) consistent with basic policy of Gulf Oil, e.g., increasing profits) or simply as "Gulf Oil Corporation intentionally did j." This is a rather technical way of saying that in these circumstances the executives voting is, given its CID Structure, also the corporation deciding to do something, and that regardless of the personal reasons the executives have for voting as they do and even if their reasons are inconsistent with established corporate policy or even if one of them has no reason at all for voting as he does, the corporation still has reasons for joining the cartel; that is, joining is consistent with the inviolate corporate general policies as encrusted in the precedent of previous corporate actions and its statements of purpose as recorded in its certificate of incorporation, annual reports, etc. The corporation's only method of achieving its desires or goals is the activation of the personnel who occupy its various positions. However, if X voted affirmatively purely for reasons of personal monetary gain (suppose he had been bribed to do so) that does not alter the fact that the corporate reason for joining the cartel was to minimize competition and hence pay higher dividends to its shareholders. Corporations have reasons because they have interests in doing those things that are likely to result in realization of their established corporate goals regardless of the transient self-interest of directors, managers, etc. If there is a difference between corporate goals and desires and those of human beings it is probably that the corporate ones are relatively stable and not very wide ranging, but that is only because corporations can do relatively fewer things than human beings, being confined in action predominately to a limited socio-economic sphere. The attribution of corporate intentionality is opaque with respect to other possible descriptions of the event in question. It is, of course, in a corporation's interest that its component membership view the corporate purposes as instrumental in the achievement of their own goals. (Financial reward is the most common way this is achieved.)

It will be objected that a corporation's policies reflect only the current goals of its directors. But that is certainly not logically necessary nor is it in practice true for most large corporations. Usually, of course, the original incorporators will have organized to further their individual interests and/ or to meet goals which they shared. But even in infancy the melding of disparate interests and purposes gives rise to a corporate long range point of view that is distinct from the intents and purposes of the collection of incorporators viewed individually. Also, corporate basic purposes and policies, as already mentioned, tend to be relatively stable when compared to those of individuals and not couched in the kind of language that would be appropriate to individual purposes. Furthermore, as histories of corporations will show, when policies are amended or altered it is usually only peripheral issues that are involved. Radical policy alteration constitutes a new corporation, a point that is captured in the incorporation laws of such states as Delaware. ("Any power which is not enumerated in the charter and the general law or which cannot be inferred from these two sources is *ultra vires* of the corporation.") Obviously underlying the objection is an uneasiness about the fact that corporate intent is dependent upon policy and purpose that is but an artifact of the socio-psychology of a group of biological persons. Corporate intent seems somehow to be a tarnished illegitimate offspring of human intent. But this objection is another form of the anthropocentric bias. By concentrating on possible descriptions of events and by acknowledging only that the possibility of describing something as an agent depends upon whether or not it can be properly described as having done something (the description of some aspect of an event) for a reason, we avoid the temptation to look for extensional criteria that would necessitate reduction to human referents.

The CID Structure licenses redescriptions of events as corporate and attributions of corporate intentionality while it does not obscure the private acts of executives, directors etc. Although X voted to support the joining of the cartel because he was bribed to do so, X did not join the cartel, Gulf Oil Corporation joined the cartel. Consequently, we may say that X did something for which he should be held morally responsible, yet whether or not Gulf Oil Corporation should be held morally responsible for joining the cartel is a question that turns on issues that may be unrelated to X's having accepted a bribe.

Of course Gulf Oil Corporation cannot join the cartel unless X or somebody who occupies position A on the organizational chart votes in the affirmative. What that shows, however, is that corporations are collectivities. That should not, however, rule out the possibility of their having metaphysical status, as being Davidsonian agents, and being thereby full-fledged moral persons.

This much seems to me clear: we can describe many events in terms of certain physical movements of human beings and we also can sometimes describe those events as done for reasons by those human beings, but further we can sometimes describe those events as corporate and still further as done for corporate reasons that are qualitatively different from whatever personal reasons, if any, component members may have for doing what they do.

Corporate agency resides in the possibility of CID Structure licensed redescription of events as corporate intentional. That may still appear to be downright mysterious, although I do not think it is, for human agency as I have suggested, resides in the possibility of description as well.

Although further elaboration is needed, I hope I have said enough to make plausible the view that we have good reasons to acknowledge the non-eliminatable agency of corporations. I have maintained that Davidsonian agency is a necessary and sufficient condition of moral personhood. I cannot further argue that position here (I have done so elsewhere). On the basis of the foregoing analysis, however, I think that grounds have been provided for holding corporations *per se* to account for what they do, for treating them as metaphysical persons *qua* moral persons.[28]

NOTES

1. John Locke. *An Essay Concerning Human Understanding* (1960), Bk. II, Ch. XXVII.

2. *Ibid.*

3. For a particularly flagrant example see: Michael Jensen and William Meckling, "Theory of the Firm: Managerial Behavior, Agency Costs and Ownership Structure," *Journal of Financial Economics*, vol. 3 (1976), pp. 305–360. On p. 311 they write, "The private corporation or firm is simply one form of legal fiction which serves as a nexus for contracting relationships . . ."

4. Daniel Dennett. "Conditions of Personhood" in *The Identities of Persons* ed. by A. O. Rorty (Berkeley, 1976), pp. 175–196.

5. John Rawls, "Justice as Reciprocity," in *John Stuart Mill, Utilitarianism*, ed. by Samuel Gorovitz (Indianapolis, 1971), pp. 244–245.

6. *Ibid.*

7. John Rawls, *A Theory of Justice* (Cambridge, 1971), p. 146.

8. Frederick Hallis, *Corporate Personality* (Oxford, 1930), p. xlii.

9. 10 *Co. Rep.* 253, see Hallis, p. xlii.

10. "Types of Collectivities and Blame," *The Personalist*, vol. 56 (1975), pp. 160–169, and in the first chapter of my *Foundations of Corporate Responsibility* (forthcoming).

11. "Continental Tyre and Rubber Co., Ltd. vs. Daimler Co., Ltd." (1915), K.B., p. 893.

12. Hallis, p. xlix.

13. "Continental Tyre and Rubber Co., Ltd. vs. Daimler Co., Ltd." (1915), K.B., p. 918.

14. (1916), 2 A.C., p. 340.

15. See in particular Otto von Gierke, *Die Genossenschoftstheorie* (Berlin, 1887).

16. And, of course, in earlier times animals have been given legal rights.

17. See Gerald Massey, "Tom, Dick, and Harry, and All The King's Men," *American Philosophical Quarterly*, vol. 13 (1976), pp. 89–108.

18. G. E. M. Anscombe, "Modern Moral Philosophy," *Philosophy*, vol. 33 (1958), pp. 1–19.

19. J. L. Austin, "Three Ways of Spilling Ink" in *Philosophical Papers* (Oxford, 1970), p. 273.

20. See for example Donald Davidson, "Agency," in *Agent, Action, and Reason*, ed. by Binkley, Bronaugh, and Marras (Toronto, 1971).

21. Austin, p. 275.

22. See Joel Feinberg, *Doing and Deserving* (Princeton, 1970), p. 134f.

23. John Kenneth Galbraith, *The Age of Uncertainty* (Boston, 1971), p. 261.

24. H. L. A. Hart, *The Concept of Law* (Oxford, 1961), Ch. VI.

25. G. C. Buzby, "Policies—A Guide to What A Company Stands For," *Management Record*, vol. 24 (1962), p. 5ff.

26. *Ibid.*

27. Peter Drucker, *Concept of Corporation* (New York, 1964/1972), pp. 36–37.

28. This paper owes much to discussions and comments made by J. L. Mackie, Donald Davidson and Howard K. Wettstein. An earlier version was read at a conference on "Ethics and Economics" at the University of Delaware. I also acknowledge the funding of the University of Minnesota Graduate School that supports the project of which this is a part.

DISCOURSE ON METHOD, Part V

Rene Descartes

I specially stayed to show that, were there such machines exactly resembling in organs and outward form an ape or any other irrational animal, we could have no means of knowing that they were in any respect of a different nature from these animals; but if there were machines bearing the image of our bodies, and capable of imitating our actions as far as it is morally possible, there would still remain two most certain tests whereby to know that they were not therefore really men. Of these the first is that they could never use words or other signs arranged in such a manner as is competent to us in order to declare our thoughts to others: for we may easily conceive a machine to be so constructed that it emits vocables, and even that it emits some correspondent to the action upon it of external objects which cause a change in its organs; for example, if touched in a particular place it may demand what we wish to say to it; if in another it may cry out that it is hurt, and such like; but not that it should arrange them variously so as appositely to reply to what is said in its presence, as men of the lowest grade of intellect can do. The second test is, that although such machines might execute many things with equal or perhaps greater perfection than any of us, they would, without doubt, fail in certain others from which it could be discovered that they did not act from knowledge, but solely from the disposition of their organs: for while reason is an universal instrument that is alike available on every occasion, these organs, on the contrary, need a particular arrangement for each particular action; whence it must be morally impossible that there should exist in any machine a diversity of organs sufficient to enable it to act in all the occurrences of life, in the way in which our reason enables us to act. Again, by means of these two tests we may likewise know the difference between men and brutes. For it is highly deserving of remark, that there are no men so dull and stupid, not even idiots, as to be incapable of joining together different words, and thereby constructing a declaration by which to make their thoughts understood; and that on the other hand, there is no other animal, however perfect or happily circumstanced, which can do the like. Nor does this inability arise from want of organs: for we observe that magpies and parrots can utter words like ourselves, and are yet unable to speak as we do, that is, so as to show that they understand what they say; in place of which men born deaf and dumb, and thus not less, but rather more than the brutes, destitute of the organs which others use in speaking, are in the habit of spontaneously inventing certain signs by which they discover their thoughts to those who, being usually in their company, have leisure to learn their language. And this proves not only that the brutes have less reason than man, but that they have none at all: for we see that very little is required to enable a person to speak; and since a certain inequality of capacity is observable among animals of the same species, as well as among men, and since some are more capable of being instructed than others, it is incredible that the most perfect ape or parrot of its species, should not in this be equal to the most stupid infant of its kind, or at least to one that was crack-brained, unless the soul of brutes were of a nature wholly different from ours. And we ought not to confound speech with the natural movements which indicate the passions, and can be imitated by machines as well as manifested by animals; nor must it be thought with certain of the ancients, that the brutes speak, although we do not understand their language. For if such were the case, since they are endowed with many organs analogous to ours, they could as easily communicate their thoughts to us as to their fellows. It is also very worthy of remark, that, though there are many animals which manifest more industry than we in certain of their actions, the same animals are yet observed to show none at all in many others: so that the circumstance that they do better than we does not prove that they are endowed with mind, for it would thence follow that they possessed greater reason than any of us, and could surpass us in all things; on the contrary, it rather proves that they are destitute of reason, and that it is nature which acts in them according to the disposition of their organs: thus it is seen, that a clock composed only of wheels and weights can number the hours and measure time more exactly than we with all our skill.

I had after this described the reasonable soul, and shown that it could by no means be educed from the power of matter, as the other things of which I had spoken, but that it must be expressly created; and that it is not sufficient that it be lodged in the human body exactly like a pilot in a ship, unless perhaps to move its members, but that it is necessary for it to be joined and united more closely to the body, in order to have sensations and appetites similar to ours, and thus constitute a real man. I here entered, in conclusion, upon the subject of the soul at considerable length, because it is of the greatest moment: for after the error of those who deny the existence of God, an error which I think I have already sufficiently refuted, there is none that is more powerful in leading feeble minds astray from the straight path of virtue than the supposition that the soul of the brutes is of the same nature with our own; and consequently that after this life we have nothing to hope for or fear, more than flies and ants; in place of which, when we know how far they differ we much better comprehend the reasons which establish that the soul is of a nature wholly independent of the body, and that consequently it is not liable to die with the latter; and finally, because no other causes are observed capable of destroying it, we are naturally led thence to judge that it is immortal.

LETTERS TO THE MARQUIS OF NEWCASTLE AND HENRY MORE

Rene Descartes

from LETTER TO THE MARQUIS OF NEWCASTLE

. . . As for the understanding or thought attributed by Montaigne and others to brutes, I cannot hold their opinion; not, however, because I am doubtful of the truth of what is commonly said, that men have absolute dominion over all the other animals; for while I allow that there are some which are stronger than we are, and I believe there may be some, also, which have natural cunning capable of deceiving the most sagacious men; yet I consider that they imitate or surpass us only in those of our actions which are not directed by thought; for it often happens that we walk and that we eat without thinking at all upon what we are doing; and it is so much without the use of our reason that we repel things which harm us, and ward off blows struck at us, that, although we might fully determine not to put our hands before our heads when falling, we could not help doing so. I believe, also, that we should eat as the brutes do, without having learned how, if we had no power of thought at all; and it is said that those who walk in their sleep sometimes swim across rivers, where, had they been awake, they would have been drowned.

As for the movements of our passions, although in ourselves they are accompanied with thought, because we possess that faculty, it is, nevertheless, very evident that they do not depend upon it, because they often arise in spite of us, and, consequently, they may exist in brutes, and even be more violent than they are in the men, without warranting the conclusion that brutes can think; in fine there is no one of our external actions which can assure those who examine them that our body is any thing more than a machine which moves of itself, but which also has in it a mind which thinks—excepting words, or other signs made in regard to whatever subjects present themselves, without reference to any passion. I say words, or other signs, because mutes make use of signs in the same way as we do of the voice, and these signs are pertinent; but I exclude the talking of parrots, but not that of the insane, which may be apropos to the case in hand, although it is irrational; and I add that these words or signs are not to relate to any passion, in order to exclude, not only cries of joy or pain and the like, but, also, all that can be taught to any animal by art; for if a magpie be taught to say "good-morning" to its mistress when it sees her coming, it may be that the utterance of these words is associated with the excitement of some one of its passions; for instance, there will be a stir of expectation of something to eat, if it has been the custom of the mistress to give it some dainty bit when it spoke those words; and in like manner all those things which dogs, horses, and monkeys are made to do are merely motions of their fear, their hope, or their joy, so that they might do them without any thought at all.

Now, it seems to me very remarkable that language, as thus defined, belongs to man alone; for although Montaigne and Charron have said that there is more difference between one man and another than between a man and a brute, nevertheless there has never yet been found a brute so perfect that it has made use of a sign to inform other animals of something which had no relation to their passions; while there is no man so imperfect as not to use such signs; so that the deaf and dumb invent particular signs by which they express their thoughts, which seems to me a very strong argument to prove that the reason why brutes do not talk as we do is that they have no faculty of thought, and not at all that the organs for it are wanting. And it cannot be said that they talk among themselves, but we do not understand them; for, as dogs and other animals express to us their passions, they would express to us as well their thoughts, if they had them. I know, indeed, that brutes do many things better than we do, but I am not surprised at it; for that, also, goes to prove that they act by force of nature and by springs, like a clock, which tells better what the hour is than our judgment can inform us. And, doubtless, when swallows come in the spring, they act in that like clocks. All that honey-bees do is of the same nature; and the order that cranes keep in flying, or monkeys drawn up for battle, if it be true that they do observe any order, and, finally, the instinct of burying their dead is no more surprising than that of dogs and cats, which scratch the ground to bury their excrements, although they almost never do bury them, which shows that they do it by instinct only, and not by thought. It can only be said that, although the brutes do nothing which can convince us that they think, nevertheless, because their bodily organs are not very different from ours, we might conjecture that there was some faculty of thought joined to these organs, as we experience in ourselves, although theirs be much less perfect, to which I have nothing to reply, except that, if they could think as we do, they would have an immortal soul as well as we, which is not likely, because there is no reason for believing it of some animals without believing it of all, and there are many of them too imperfect to make it possible to believe it of them, such as oysters, sponges, etc.

from LETTER TO HENRY MORE, 1649

. . . But the greatest of all the prejudices we have retained from infancy is that of believing that brutes think. The source of our error comes from having observed that many of the bodily members of brutes are not very different from our own in shape and movements, and from the belief that our mind is the principle of the motions which occur in us; that it imparts motion to the body and is the cause of our thoughts. Assuming this, we find no difficulty in believing that there is in brutes a mind similar to our own; but having made the discovery, after thinking well upon it, that two different principles of our movements are to be distinguished—the one entirely mechanical and corporeal, which depends solely on the force of the animal spirits and the configuration of the bodily parts, and which may be called corporeal soul, and the other incorporeal, that is to say, mind or soul, which you may define a substance which thinks—I have inquired with great care whether the motions of animals proceed from these two principles or from one alone. Now, having clearly perceived that they can proceed from one only, I have held it demonstrated that we are not able in any manner to prove that there is in the animals a soul which thinks. I am not at all disturbed in my opinion by those doublings and cunning tricks of dogs and foxes, nor by all those things which animals do, either from fear, or to get something to eat, or just for sport. I engage to explain all that very easily, merely by the conformation of the parts of the animals. Nevertheless, although I regard it as a thing demonstrated that it cannot be proved that the brutes have thought, I do not think that it can be demonstrated that the contrary is not true, because the human mind cannot penetrate into the heart to know what goes on there; but, on examining into the probabilities of the case, I see no reason whatever to prove that brutes think, if it be not that having eyes, ears, a tongue, and other organs of sense like ours, it is likely that they have sensations as we do, and, as thought is involved in the sensations which we have, a similar faculty of thought must be attributed to them. Now, since this argument is within the reach of everyone's capacity, it has held possession of all minds from infancy. But there are other stronger and more numerous arguments for the opposite opinion, which do not so readily present themselves to everybody's mind; as, for example, that it is more reasonable to make earthworms, flies, caterpillars, and the rest of the animals, move as machines do, than to endow them with immortal souls.

Because it is certain that in the body of animals, as in ours, there are bones, nerves, muscles, blood, animal spirits, and other organs, disposed in such a manner that they can produce themselves, without the aid of any thought, all the movements which we observe in the animals, as appears in convulsive movements, when, in spite of the mind itself, the machine of the body moves often with greater violence, and in more various ways than it is wont to do with the aid of the will; moreover, inasmuch as it is agreeable to reason that art should imitate nature, and that men should be able to construct divers *automata* in which there is movement without any thought, nature, on her part, might produce these *automata*, and far more excellent ones, as the brutes are, than those which come from the hand of man, seeing no reason anywhere why thought is to be found wherever we perceive a conformation of bodily members like that of the animals, and that it is more surprising that there should be a soul in every human body than that there should be none at all in the brutes.

But the principal argument, to my mind, which may convince us that the brutes are devoid of reason, is that, although among those of the same species, some are more perfect than others, as among men, which is particularly noticeable in horses and dogs, some of which have more capacity than others to retain what is taught them, and although all of them make us clearly understand their natural movements of anger, of fear, of hunger, and others of like kind, either by the voice or by other bodily motions, it has never yet been observed that any animal has arrived at such a degree of perfection as to make use of a true language; that is to say, as to be able to indicate to us by the voice, or by other signs, anything which could be referred to thought alone, rather than to a movement of mere nature; for the word is the sole sign and the only certain mark of the presence of thought hidden and wrapped up in the body; now all men, the most stupid and the most foolish, those even who are deprived of the organs of speech, make use of signs, whereas the brutes never do anything of the kind; which may be taken for the true distinction between man and brute. . . . I omit, for the sake of brevity, the other arguments which deny thought to the brutes. It must, however, be observed that I speak of thought, not of life, nor of sensation; for I do not deny the life of any animal, making it to consist solely in the warmth of the heart. I do not refuse to them feeling even, in so far as it depends only on the bodily organs. Thus, my opinion is not so cruel to animals as it is favourable to men; I speak to those who are not committed to the extravagances of Pythagoras, which attached to those who ate or killed them the suspicion even of a crime. . . .

Questions for Part III

1. What are the distinguishing features of first-order intentional systems according to Daniel Dennett? On the basis of his account, what moral stance ought to be taken toward such first-order intentional systems as complex computers?

2. Distinguish a first-order intentional system from a second-order one. Should all second-order intentional systems be treated as moral persons?

3. Explain A. M. Turing's "imitation game" and the role it is to play in his attempt to answer the question "Can machines think?"

4. Discuss the Theological Objection to the possibility of a thinking machine.

5. Turing evaluates a number of other objections (the "Heads in the Sand," mathematical, and Lady Lovelace objections) and arguments against the possibility of thinking machines. Formulate those objections and arguments and discuss Turing's ways of dismissing them.

6. Explain why the existence of ESP would have a negative effect on Turing's test for thinking.

7. Explain how Peter A. French uses the agency theory of Donald Davidson to defend the position that corporations should be treated as moral persons.

8. What effects should acceptance of French's theory have on the way moral and legal responsibility claims are handled in corporate cases? Think of actual examples, like the Union Carbide disaster in Bhopal, India and the E. F. Hutton bank fraud cases.

9. Would a CID Structure on French's account qualify as a second-order intentional system as detailed by Dennett?

10. Imagine the effects on society if computers and corporations were admitted as full-fledged persons. For example, what sort of rights should be granted to them? Will there be limits to the ways they can be treated? Should they be enfranchised?

11. Rene Descartes is convinced that even if machines were built, similar to the androids of *Bladerunner*, to look just like humans and to imitate human actions, there would be two tests to discover with certainty whether they were real persons. Evaluate Descartes's tests, especially in light of Turing's analysis.

12. In his letters to the Marquis of Newcastle and Henry More, Descartes argues that animals are nothing more than automata, or machines. Explain Descartes's arguments and why he thinks it is so important to deny that animals think.

Part IV. Reference to Fictional Creatures

Chapter 10 of *Tom Jones* by Henry Fielding begins:

> The next morning Tom Jones hunted with Mr. Western, and was at his return invited by that gentleman to dinner.
> The lovely Sophia shone forth that day with more gaiety and sprightliness than usual. Her battery was certainly levelled at our hero; though, I believe, she herself scarce yet knew her own intention; but if she had any design of charming him, she now succeeded.

In *Westward, Ho!* Charles Kingsley writes:

> Every one who knows Bideford cannot but know Bideford Bridge: for it is the very omphalos, cynosure, and soul, around which the town, as a body, has organised itself; and as Edinburgh is Edinburgh by virtue of its Castle, Rome Rome by virtue of its Capitol, and Egypt Egypt by virtue of its Pyramids, so is Bideford Bideford by virtue of its Bridge. But all do not know the occult powers which have advanced and animated the said wondrous bridge for now five hundred years, and made it the chief wonder, according to Prince and Fuller, of this fair land of Devon; being first an inspired bridge; a soul-saving bridge; an alms-giving bridge; an educational bridge; a sentient bridge; and last, but not least, a dinner-giving bridge.

Both of these passages contain proper names and seem to be making assertions about the persons or things named. Are the sentences used to make those assertions true? In the selection from *Westward, Ho!* the name used is that of a town in Devon, in the West Country of England. It is natural to think that "Bideford" in the novel refers to that town. But this creates intriguing difficulties, for Kingsley describes unambiguously fictional characters crossing the bridge in Bideford. Are places in the real world sometimes frequented by fictional as well as actual people?

Ordinarily, proper names refer to things or individuals in the actual (nonfictional) world. By that what is meant is that we use those names to pick out or direct the attention of listeners or readers to specific things, places, or people. A number of different theories have been developed to explain how names perform this task. On one theory, that of Gottlob Frege, names have a meaning or a sense that directs us to the things to which they refer. The referent of a name is then something which satisfies the description given by that meaning or sense. A popular contemporary view, called the causal-historical or purely referential theory, but one that has its roots in John Stuart Mill's conception of names, argues that names are just like labels. They do not have meanings or senses; they do not contain descriptions. They simply pick out objects. The use of specific names for specific things is founded in a kind of "baptismal" act, and the relationship between the name and the object or person named is passed along to the members of the language-using community through subsequent uses of the name.

On an account like Frege's, a name, for example "John Wayne," refers to a particular person because certain descriptions which give the meaning of the name, such as "the person who directed the movie *The Alamo*" or "the actor who won an Academy Award for his performance in *True Grit*," are true of that person.

It might be argued against this view of names that we could learn that each of the descriptions we believe to be true of the person named "John Wayne" is in fact not true of the person who bears that name. For example, it might have been John Wayne's understudy who actually performed in *True Grit* but never got credit for it. "John Wayne," however, must still pick out the same individual or we wouldn't be able to make sense of our now denying that he was the director of *The Alamo* or the actor in *True Grit*. Those descriptions might fix the reference of "John Wayne" for us on a particular person, but the name "John Wayne" cannot mean "the person who directed the Alamo and won the Academy Award for *True Grit*." In fact, the name "John Wayne" doesn't seem to mean anything or to be equivalent to any set of descriptions at all. This is just what the alternative causal theory of reference holds.

Interestingly, a Frege-like account in the case of names of fictional creatures seems to work better than the causal-historical theory. "Tom Jones," for example, certainly doesn't refer to a real-life individual. If Tom Jones is anything at all, he is just the character that is described in passages throughout Fielding's book.

There is, however, a rankling counter-intuitive result if we adopt this approach: those sentences of a novel that contain the names of fictional creatures cannot be true. The first sentence of Chapter 10 of *Tom Jones* contains the names "Tom Jones" and "Mr. Western" and if those names are just equivalent to a certain set of descriptions that refer to no actual entities, it is false that they hunted together. After all, if Tom and Mr. Western are just fictional creatures, that is, if they do not really exist, how can it be true that they hunted together?

It surely seems right to say that fictional sentences are not true in our world, but does that make them false? Are works of fiction elaborate falsehoods? Of course within a work of fiction there will be a number of true sentences. We should expect to find sentences about human psychology or about natural laws whose truth value is dependent on matters quite exterior to the work. But these are hardly the kinds of sentences that are characteristic of a work of fiction. If they were, there wouldn't be fictional works. One of the things that makes a work fictional rather than purportedly factual is that many of the names used clearly do not refer to actual persons or places. If a passage is fictional, it is not factual. Yet surely it is true that Tom Jones and Mr. Western hunted together, and then Mr. Western invited Tom to dinner. How can we explain this intuition?

Recall Kingsley's marvelous description of Bideford's bridge. Surely it is as good a description of the town bridge as any that might be found in a touring guide of England. But is the bridge in the real world, the one in Bideford, the very bridge to which Kingsley was referring in *Westward, Ho!*? Let us not be too hasty with our answer. A related series of questions may be suggestive. Suppose in *Westward, Ho!*, when describing the ride of one of his characters toward the bridge, Kingsley wrote that the horse clopped over Grenville Road just before crossing the bridge. And, further on, he wrote that after crossing the bridge the rider paused to look back and for his amusement counted the twenty-two arches of that great bridge. Now as it happens in Bideford, the town in North Devon, Grenville Road does not lead to the bridge though Bridgeland Road does, and the bridge has, and always has had, twenty-four arches not twenty-two. Should we say that Kingsley got these things wrong? Should such sentences in *Westward, Ho!* be regarded as false? If the bridge in *Westward, Ho!* has twenty-two not twenty-four arches, perhaps it is not meant by the author to be the bridge in Bideford. Rather than getting these things wrong, maybe, it might be suggested, Kingsley somehow was confused or was trying to confuse his readers about the town about which he was writing. Maybe Kingsley wasn't really writing about Bideford at all. That was only a cover. He only called it Bideford, but he was really writing about Bracknell, or Budleigh Salterton, or even Newton Poppleford. He used "Bideford," that is the name "Bideford," to mask the real object of his sentences (to avoid lawsuits or whatever). But if that is his reason, he might have masked the names of all the other location descriptions throughout his entire novel. He wrote the novel mentioning North Devon locales, but really meant *Westward, Ho!* to be about South Devon or Berkshire. This starts to sound utterly absurd.

When someone tells a story, the story is either true or false; that seems straightforward enough. But some philosophers argue that some meaningful stories may be neither true nor false. That is what we mean by calling them fictions. In a fiction, sentences seem to be making assertions about and referring to things, places, and people; however, with respect to the actual world no assertions are being made by the author's use of those sentences, just as no propositions are really being expressed by such sentences as "Santa Claus is a right jolly old elf." This is because there can be, in the actual world, no genuine referential use of names in the sentences of a fiction. All attempts to reach a referent are effectively blocked by the fact it is a fiction. Suppose we could ask Charles Kingsley to tell us what he was referring to when he wrote the name "Bideford Bridge" in *Westward, Ho!* He might answer that he was referring to a fictional location or a thing that he wrote about while picturing the town outside his windows. But he could just as well say that he was not referring to anything, and if you think he was referring to something, you are confusing the writing of fiction with the using of genuine referring expressions that fail for some reason or other to secure a reference. For example, someone might say "the beautiful woman over there," when there is no woman over there. A referring expression was used, but there being no woman, transvestite, or anyone at all over there, reference cannot be secured. Novelists certainly do not use names of places and characters in this way. They do not use them as referring expressions that would have picked out somebody or other, if only someone or something had uniquely satisfied either a specific set of descriptions that fixes the referent or had been by some chance baptized with the name used by the author. This is true of characters in fiction, such as Tom Jones and Mr. Western, as much as it is true for things like Bideford Bridge in *Westward, Ho!*

Maybe Kingsley's bridge exists in some world other than the real one and he is referring to the bridge in that nonactual world when he uses the name. Is there a domain or worlds of fiction in which the stories that are fictions in this world are true? Is there a world in which Tom Jones and Mr. Western have dinner after hunting together? That could mean that the very same sentence, for example, the first sentence of Chapter 10 of *Tom Jones*, is true in some world and fictional (neither true or false) in another. Sentences then are not the bearers of truth or falsity. If, with David Lewis, we think of the sentences of a novel as being true at the world of the novel, then there is some world in which the creatures of fiction exist. Does the idea of distinct fictional worlds peopled by the characters of novels and plays, seem sensible? What is the relationship, if any, between those worlds and the actual world? How remote are they from our world? That is the question around which Kendall L. Walton's paper is focused. Could real people interact with fictional characters?

All of us have been affected by the adventures and fates of the creatures of fiction. We can be terrified by their plights, worried about their futures, pleased by their successes. This is a rather asymmetrical relationship, for they are not affected much by us, though fictional creatures in continuing dramas and serials have been saved from almost certain death by the concerted pleas of a legion of readers or watchers. Nonetheless, except in special cases, fictional creatures seldom evidence any knowledge of us. But, then, they are just fictional characters locked in their worlds, whereas we seem to have a kind of multiworld access from which we should be able to learn much about the referential uses of elements of our language while we are also puzzling about the possibility of worlds other than the actual world.

TRUTH IN FICTION

David Lewis

We can truly say that Sherlock Holmes lived in Baker Street, and that he liked to show off his mental powers. We cannot truly say that he was a devoted family man, or that he worked in close cooperation with the police.

It would be nice if we could take such descriptions of fictional characters at their face value, ascribing to them the same subject-predicate form as parallel descriptions of real-life characters. Then the sentences "Holmes wears a silk top hat" and "Nixon wears a silk top hat" would both be false because the referent of the subject term—fictional Holmes or real-life Nixon, as the case may be—lacks the property, expressed by the predicate, of wearing a silk top hat. The only difference would be that the subject terms "Holmes" and "Nixon" have referents of radically different sorts: one a fictional character, the other a real-life person of flesh and blood.

I don't question that a treatment along these Meinongian lines could be made to work. Terence Parsons has done it.[1] But it is no simple matter to overcome the difficulties that arise. For one thing, is there not some perfectly good sense in which Holmes, like Nixon, *is* a real-life person of flesh and blood? There are stories about the exploits of super-heroes from other planets, hobbits, fires and storms, vaporous intelligences, and other non-persons. But what a mistake it would be to class the Holmes stories with these! Unlike Clark Kent *et al.*, Sherlock Holmes is just a person—a person of flesh and blood, a being in the very same category as Nixon.

Consider also the problem of the chorus. We can truly say that Sir Joseph Porter, K.C.B., is attended by a chorus of his sisters and his cousins and his aunts. To make this true, it seems that the domain of fictional characters must contain not only Sir Joseph himself, but also plenty of fictional sisters and cousins and aunts. But how many—five dozen, perhaps? No, for we cannot truly say that the chorus numbers five dozen exactly. We cannot truly say anything exact about its size. Then do we perhaps have a fictional chorus, but no fictional members of this chorus and hence no number of members? No, for we can truly say some

I thank the many friends and colleagues who have given me helpful comments on a previous version of this paper, and I thank the American Council of Learned Societies for research support. Special thanks are due to John G. Bennett and Saul Kripke for valuable discussions.

things about the size. We are told that the sisters and cousins, even without the aunts, number in dozens.

The Meinongian should not suppose that the quantifiers in descriptions of fictional characters range over all the things he thinks there are, both fictional and non-fictional; but he may not find it easy to say just how the ranges of quantification are to be restricted. Consider whether we can truly say that Holmes was more intelligent than anyone else, before or since. It is certainly appropriate to compare him with some fictional characters, such as Mycroft and Watson; but not with others, such as Poirot or "Slipstick" Libby. It may be appropriate to compare him with some non-fictional characters, such as Newton and Darwin; but probably not with others, such as Conan Doyle or Frank Ramsey. "More intelligent than anyone else" meant something like "more intelligent than anyone else in the world of Sherlock Holmes." The inhabitants of this "world" are drawn partly from the fictional side of the Meinongian domain and partly from the non-fictional side, exhausting neither.

Finally, the Meinongian must tell us why truths about fictional characters are cut off, sometimes though not always, from the consequences they ought to imply. We can truly say that Holmes lived at 221B Baker Street. I have been told[2] that the only building at 221B Baker Street, then or now, was a bank. It does not follow, and certainly is not true, that Holmes lived in a bank.

The way of the Meinongian is hard, and in this paper I shall explore a simpler alternative. Let us not take our descriptions of fictional characters at face value, but instead let us regard them as abbreviations for longer sentences beginning with an operator "In such-and-such fiction . . . ." Such a phrase is an intentional operator that may be prefixed to a sentence ϕ to form a new sentence. But then the prefixed operator may be dropped by way of abbreviation, leaving us with what sounds like the original sentence ϕ but differs from it in sense.

Thus if I say that Holmes liked to show off, you will take it that I have asserted an abbreviated version of the true sentence "In the Sherlock Holmes stories, Holmes liked to show off." As for the embedded sentence "Holmes liked to show off," taken by itself with the prefixed operator neither explicitly present nor tacitly understood, we may abandon it to the common fate of subject-predicate sentences with denotationless subject terms: automatic falsity or lack of truth value, according to taste.

Many things we might say about Holmes are potentially ambiguous. They may or may not be taken as abbreviations for sentences carrying the prefix "In the Sherlock Holmes stories . . . ." Context, content, and common sense will usually resolve the ambiguity in practice. Consider these sentences:

Holmes lived in Baker Street.
Holmes lived nearer to Paddington Station than to Waterloo Station.

Holmes was just a person—a person of flesh and blood.
Holmes really existed.
Someone lived for many years at 221B Baker Street.
London's greatest detective in 1900 used cocaine.

All of them are false if taken as unprefixed, simply because Holmes did not actually exist. (Or perhaps at least some of them lack truth value.) All are true if taken as abbreviations for prefixed sentences. The first three would probably be taken in the latter way, hence they seem true. The rest would probably be taken in the former way, hence they seem false. The sentence

No detective ever solved almost all his cases.

would probably be taken as unprefixed and hence true, though it would be false if taken as prefixed. The sentence

Holmes and Watson are identical.

is sure to be taken as prefixed and hence false, but that is no refutation of systems of free logic[3] which would count it as true if taken as unprefixed.

(I hasten to concede that some truths about Holmes are not abbreviations of prefixed sentences, and also are not true just because "Holmes" is denotationless. For instance these:

Holmes is a fictional character.
Holmes was killed off by Conan Doyle, but later resurrected.
Holmes has acquired a cultish following.
Holmes symbolizes mankind's ceaseless striving for truth.
Holmes would not have needed tapes to get the goods on Nixon.
Holmes could have solved the A.B.C. murders sooner than Poirot.

I shall have nothing to say here about the proper treatment of these sentences. If the Meinongian can handle them with no special dodges, that is an advantage of his approach over mine.)

The ambiguity of prefixing explains why truths about fictionl characters are sometimes cut off from their seeming consequences. Suppose we have an argument (with zero or more premises) which is valid in the modal sense that it is impossible for the premises all to be true and the conclusion false.

$$\frac{\psi_1, \ldots, \psi_n}{\therefore \phi}$$

Then it seems clear that we obtain another valid argument if we prefix an operator "In the fiction f . . ." uniformly to each premiss and to the conclusion of the original argument. Truth in a given fiction is closed under implication.

$$\frac{\text{In } f, \psi_1, \ldots, \text{In } f, \psi_n}{\therefore \text{In } f, \phi}$$

But if we prefix the operator "In the fiction f . . ." to some of the original premisses and not to others, or if we take some but not all of the premisses as tacitly prefixed, then in general neither the original conclusion φ nor the prefixed conclusion "In the fiction f, φ" will follow. In the inference we considered earlier there were two premisses. The premiss that Holmes lived at 221B Baker Street was true only if taken as prefixed. The premiss that the only building at 221B Baker Street was a bank, on the other hand, was true only if taken as unprefixed; for in the stories there was no bank there but rather a rooming house. Taking the premisses as we naturally would in the ways that make them true, nothing follows: neither the unprefixed conclusion that Holmes lived in a bank nor the prefixed conclusion that in the stories he lived in a bank. Taking both premisses as unprefixed, the unprefixed conclusion follows but the first premiss is false. Taking both premisses as prefixed, the prefixed conclusion follows but the second premiss is false.[4]

Our remaining task is to see what may be said about the analysis of the operators "In such-and-such fiction . . . ." I have already noted that truth in a given fiction is closed under implication. Such closure is the earmark of an operator of relative necessity, an intensional operator that may be analyzed as a restricted universal quantifier over possible worlds. So we might proceed as follows: a prefixed sentence "In fiction f, φ" is true (or, as we shall also say, φ is true in the fiction f) iff φ is true at every possible world in a certain set, this set being somehow determined by the fiction f.

As a first approximation, we might consider exactly those worlds where the plot of the fiction is enacted, where a course of events takes place that matches the story. What is true in the Sherlock Holmes stories would then be what is true at all of those possible worlds where there are characters who have the attributes, stand in the relations, and do the deeds that are ascribed in the stories to Holmes, Watson, and the rest. (Whether these characters would then *be* Holmes, Watson, and the rest is a vexed question that we must soon consider.)

I think this proposal is not quite right. For one thing, there is a threat of circularity. Even the Holmes stories, not to mention fiction written in less explicit styles, are by no means in the form of straightforward chronicles. An intelligent and informed reader can indeed discover the plot, and could write it down in the form of a fully explicit chronicle if he liked. But this extraction of plot from text is no trivial or automatic task. Perhaps the reader accomplishes it only by figuring out what is true in the stories— that is, only by exercising his tacit mastery of the very concept of truth in fiction that we are now investigating. If so, then an analysis that starts by making uncritical use of the concept of the plot of a fiction might be rather uninformative, even if correct so far as it goes.

A second problem arises out of an observation by Saul Kripke.[5] Let us assume that Conan Doyle indeed wrote the stories as pure fiction. He just made them up. He had no knowledge of anyone who did the deeds he ascribed to Holmes, nor had he even picked up any garbled information originating in any such person. It may nevertheless be, purely by coincidence, that our own world is one of the worlds where the plot of the stories is enacted. Maybe there was a man whom Conan Doyle never heard of whose actual adventures chanced to fit the stories in every detail. Maybe he even was named "Sherlock Holmes." Improbable, incredible, but surely possible! Now consider the name "Sherlock Holmes," *as used in the stories.* Does the name, so used, refer to the man whom Conan Doyle never heard of? Surely not! It is irrelevant that a homonymous name is used by some people, not including Conan Doyle, to refer to this man. We must distinguish between the homonyms, just as we would distinguish the name of London (England) from the homonymous name of London (Ontario). It is false at our world that the name, "Sherlock Holmes," as used in the stories, refers to someone. Yet it is true in the stories that this name, as used in the stories, refers to someone. So we have found something that is true in the stories but false (under our improbable supposition) at one of the worlds where the plot of the stories is enacted.

In order to avoid this difficulty, it will be helpful if we do not think of a fiction in the abstract, as a string of sentences or something of that sort. Rather, a fiction is a story told by a storyteller on a particular occasion. He may tell his tales around the campfire or he may type a manuscript and send it to his publisher, but in either case there is an act of storytelling. Different acts of storytelling, different fictions. When Pierre Menard re-tells *Don Quixote,* that is not the same fiction as Cervantes' *Don Quixote*—not even if they are in the same language and match word for word.[6] (It would have been different if Menard had copied Cervantes' fiction from memory, however; that would not have been what I call an act of storytelling at all.) One act of storytelling might, however, be the telling of two different fictions: one a harmless fantasy told to the children and the censors, the other a subversive allegory simultaneously told to the *cognoscenti.*

Storytelling is pretence. The storyteller purports to be telling the truth about matters whereof he has knowledge. He purports to be talking about characters who are known to him, and whom he refers to, typically, by means of their ordinary proper names. But if his story is fiction, he is not really doing these things. Usually his pretence has not the slightest tendency to deceive anyone, nor has he the slightest intent to deceive. Nevertheless he plays a false part, goes through a form of telling known fact when he is not doing so. This is most apparent when the fiction is told in the first person. Conan Doyle pretended to be a doctor named Watson, engaged in publishing truthful memoirs of events he himself had witnessed. But the case of third-person narrative is not essentially different. The author purports to be telling the truth about matters he has somehow come to know about, though how he has found out about them is left unsaid. That is why there is a pragmatic paradox akin to contradiction in a third-person narrative that ends ". . . and so none were left to tell the tale."

The worlds we should consider, I suggest, are the worlds where the fiction is told, but as known fact rather than fiction. The act of storytelling occurs, just as it does here at our world; but there it *is* what here it falsely purports to be: truth-telling about matters whereof the teller has knowledge.[7] Our own world cannot be such a world; for if it is really a fiction that we are dealing with, then the act of storytelling at our world was not what it purported to be. It does not matter if, unbeknownst to the author, our world is one where his plot is enacted. The real-life Sherlock Holmes would not have made Conan Doyle any less of a pretender, if Conan Doyle had never heard of him. (This real-life Holmes might have had his real-life Watson who told true stories about the adventures he had witnessed. But even if his memoirs matched Conan Doyle's fiction word for word they would not be the same stories, any more than Cervantes' *Don Quixote* is the same story as Menard's. So our world would still not be one where the Holmes stories—the *same* Holmes stories that Conan Doyle told as fiction— were told as known fact.) On the other hand, any world where the story is told as known fact rather than fiction must be among the worlds where the plot of the story is enacted. Else its enactment could be neither known nor truly told of.

I rely on a notion of trans-world identity for stories; this is partly a matter of word-for-word match and partly a matter of trans-world identity (or perhaps a counterpart relation) for acts of storytelling. Here at our world we have a fiction f, told in an act a of storytelling; at some other world we have an act a^1 of telling the truth about known matters of fact; the stories told in a and a^1 match word for word, and the words have the same meaning. Does that mean that the other world is one where f is told as known fact rather than fiction? Not necessarily, as the case of Menard shows. It is also required that a and a^1 be the same act of storytelling (or at least counterparts). How bad is this? Surely you would like to know more about the criteria of trans-world identity (or the counterpart relation) for acts of storytelling, and so indeed would I. But I think we have enough of a grip to make it worthwhile going on. I see no threat of circularity here, since I see no way of using the concept of truth in fiction to help with the analysis of trans-world identity of acts of storytelling.

Suppose a fiction employs such names as "Sherlock Holmes." At those worlds where the same story is told as known fact rather than fiction, those names really are what they here purport to be: ordinary proper names of existing characters known to the storyteller. Here at our world, the storyteller only pretends that "Sherlock Holmes" has the semantic character of an ordinary proper name. We have no reason at all to suppose that the name, as used here at our world, really does have that character. As we use it, it may be very unlike an ordinary proper name. Indeed, it may have a highly non-rigid sense, governed largely by the descriptions of Holmes and his deeds that are found in the stories. That is what I suggest: the sense of "Sherlock Holmes" as we use it is such that, for any world w where the Holmes stories are told as known fact rather than fiction, the name denotes at w whichever inhabitant of w it is who there plays the role of Holmes. Part of that role, of course, is to bear the ordinary proper name "Sherlock Holmes." But that only goes to show that "Sherlock Holmes" is used at w as an ordinary proper name, not that it is so used here.[8,9]

I also suggest, less confidently, that whenever a world w is not one of the worlds just considered, the sense of "Sherlock Holmes" as we use it is such as to assign it no denotation at w. That is so even if the plot of the fiction is enacted by inhabitants of w. If we are right that Conan Doyle told the Holmes stories as fiction, then it follows that "Sherlock Holmes" is denotationless here at our world. It does not denote the real-life Sherlock Holmes whom Conan Doyle never heard of, if such there be.

We have reached a proposal I shall call ANALYSIS 0: *A sentence of the form "In fiction f, ϕ" is true iff ϕ is true at every world where f is told as known fact rather than fiction.*

Is that right? There are some who never tire of telling us not to read anything into a fiction that is not there explicitly, and Analysis 0 will serve to capture the usage of those who hold this view in its most extreme form. I do not believe, however, that such a usage is at all common. Most of us are content to read a fiction against a background of well-known fact, "reading into" the fiction content that is not there explicitly but that comes jointly from the explicit content and the factual background. Analysis 0 disregards the background. Thereby it brings too many possible worlds into consideration, so not enough comes out true in the fiction.

For example, I claim that in the Holmes stories, Holmes lives nearer to Paddington Station than to Waterloo Station. A glance at the map will show you that his address in Baker Street is much nearer to Paddington. Yet the map is not part of the stories; and so far as I know it is never stated or implied in the stories themselves that Holmes lives nearer to Paddington. There are possible worlds where the Holmes stories are told as known fact rather than fiction which differ in all sorts of ways from ours. Among these are worlds where Holmes lives in a London arranged very differently from the London of our world, a London where Holmes's address in Baker Street is much closer to Waterloo Station than to Paddington.

(I do not suppose that such a distortion of geography need prevent the otherworldly places there called "London," "Paddington Station," . . . from being the same as, or counterparts of, their actual namesakes. But if I am wrong, that still does not challenge my claim that there are worlds where the stories are told as known fact but where it is true that Holmes lives closer to Waterloo than to Paddington. For it is open to us to regard the place-names, as used in the stories, as fictional names with non-rigid senses like the non-rigid sense I have already ascribed to "Sherlock Holmes." That would mean, incidentally, that "Paddington Station," as used in the stories, does not denote the actual station of that name.)

Similarly, I claim that it is true, though not explicit, in the stories that Holmes does not have a third nostril; that he never had a case in which the murderer turned out to be a purple gnome; that he solved his cases without the aid of divine revelation; that he never visited the moons of Saturn; and that he wears underpants. There are bizarre worlds where the Holmes stories are told as known fact but where all of these things are false.

Strictly speaking, it is fallacious to reason from a mixture of truth in fact and truth in fiction to conclusions about truth in fiction. From a mixture of prefixed and unprefixed premises, nothing follows. But in practice the fallacy is often not so bad. The factual premises in mixed reasoning may be part of the background against which we read the fiction. They may carry over into the fiction, not because there is anything explicit in the fiction to make them true, but rather because there is nothing to make them false. There is nothing in the Holmes stories, for instance, that gives us any reason to bracket our background knowledge of the broad outlines of London geography. Only a few details need changing—principally details having to do with 221B Baker Street. To move the stations around, or even to regard their locations as an open question, would be uncalled for. What's true in fact about their locations is true also in the stories. Then it is no error to reason from such facts to conclusions about what else is true in the stories.

You've heard it all before. Reasoning about truth in fiction is very like counterfactual reasoning. We make a supposition contrary to fact—what if this match had been struck? In reasoning about what would have happened in that counterfactual situation, we use factual premises. The match was dry, there was oxygen about, and so forth. But we do not use factual premises altogether freely, since some of them would fall victim to the change that takes us from actuality to the envisaged counterfactual situation. We do not use the factual premiss that the match was inside the matchbox at the time in question, or that it was at room temperature a second later. We depart from actuality as far as we must to reach a possible world where the counterfactual supposition comes true (and that might be quite far if the supposition is a fantastic one). But we do not make gratuitous changes. We hold fixed the features of actuality that do not have to be changed as part of the least disruptive way of making the supposition true. We can safely reason from the part of our factual background that is thus held fixed.

By now, several authors have treated counterfactual conditionals along the lines just sketched. Differences of detail between these treatments are unimportant for our present purposes. My own version[10] runs as follows. A counterfactual of the form "If it were that φ, then it would be that ψ" is non-vacuously true iff some possible world where both φ and ψ are true differs less from our actual world, on balance, than does any world where φ is true but ψ is not true. It is vacuously true iff φ is true at no possible worlds. (I omit accessibility restrictions for simplicity.)

Getting back to truth in fiction, recall that the trouble with Analysis 0 was that it ignored background, and thereby brought into consideration bizarre worlds that differed gratuitously from our actual world. A fiction will in general require some departures from actuality, the more so if it is a fantastic fiction. But we need to keep the departures from actuality under control. It is wrong, or at least eccentric, to read the Holmes stories as if they might for all we know be taking place at a world where three-nostrilled detectives pursue purple gnomes. The remedy is, roughly speaking, to analyze statements of truth in fiction as counterfactuals. What is true in the Sherlock Holmes stories is what would be true if those stories were told as known fact rather than fiction.

Spelling this out according to my treatment of counterfactuals, we have ANALYSIS I: *A sentence of the form "In the fiction f, φ" is non-vacuously true iff some world where f is told as known fact and φ is true differs less from our actual world, on balance, than does any world where f is told as known fact and φ is not true. It is vacuously true iff there are no possible worlds where f is told as known fact.* "(I postpone consideration of the vacuous case.)

We sometimes speak of *the* world of a fiction. What is true in the Holmes stories is what is true, as we say, "in the world of Sherlock Holmes." That we speak this way should suggest that it is right to consider less than all the worlds where the plot of the stories is enacted, and less even than all the worlds where the stories are told as known fact. "In the world of Sherlock Holmes," as in actuality, Baker Street is closer to Paddington Station than to Waterloo Station and there are no purple gnomes. But it will not do to follow ordinary language to the extent of supposing that we can somehow single out a single one of the worlds where the stories are told as known fact. Is the world of Sherlock Holmes a world where Holmes has an even or an odd number of hairs on his head at the moment when he first meets Watson? What is Inspector Lestrade's blood type? It is absurd to suppose that these questions about the world of Sherlock Holmes have answers. The best explanation of that is that the worlds of Sherlock Holmes are plural, and the questions have different answers at different ones. If we may assume that some of the worlds where the stories are told as known fact differ least from our world, then these are the worlds of Sherlock Holmes. What is true throughout them is true in the stories; what is false throughout them is false in the stories; what is true at some and false at others is neither true nor false in the stories. Any answer to the silly questions just asked would doubtless fall in the last category. It is for the same reason that the chorus of Sir Joseph Porter's sisters and cousins and aunts has no determinate size: it has different sizes at different ones of the worlds of *H.M.S. Pinafore*.[11]

Under Analysis I, truth in a given fiction depends on matters of contingent fact. I am not thinking of the remote possibility that accidental properties of the fiction might somehow enter into determining which are the worlds where that fiction is told as known fact. Rather, it is a contingent matter which of those worlds differ more from ours and which less, and which (if any) differ least. That is because it is a contingent fact—indeed it is *the* contingent fact on which all others depend—which possible world is our actual world. To the extent that the character of our world carries over into the worlds of Sherlock Holmes, what is true in the stories depends on what our world is like. If the stations of London had been differently located, it might have been true in the stories (and not because the stories would then have been different) that Holmes lived nearer to Waterloo Station than to Paddington Station.

This contingency is all very well when truth in fiction depends on well-known contingent facts about our world, as it does in the examples I have so far given to motivate Analysis 1. It is more disturbing if truth in fiction turns out to depend on contingent facts that are not well known. In an article setting forth little-known facts about the movement of snakes, Carl Gans has argued as follows:

> In "The Adventure of the Speckled Band" Sherlock Holmes solves a murder mystery by showing that the victim has been killed by a Russell's viper that has climbed up a bell-rope. What Holmes did not realize was that Russell's viper is not a constrictor. The snake is therefore incapable of concertina movement and could not have climbed the rope. Either the snake reached its victim some other way or the case remains open.[12]

We may well look askance at this reasoning. But if Analysis 1 is correct then so is Gans's argument. The story never quite says that Holmes was right that the snake climbed the rope. Hence there are worlds where the Holmes stories are told as known fact, where the snake reached the victim some other way, and where Holmes therefore bungled. Presumably some of these worlds differ less from ours than their rivals where Holmes was right and where Russell's viper is capable of concertina movement up a robe. Holmes's infallibility, of course, is not a countervailing resemblance to actuality; our world contains no infallible Holmes.

Psychoanalysis of fictional characters provides a more important example. The critic uses (what he believes to be) little-known facts of human psychology as premises, and reasons to conclusions that are far from obvious about the childhood or the adult mental state of the fictional character. Under Analysis 1 his procedure is justified. Unless countervailing considerations can be found, to consider worlds where the little-known fact of psychology does not hold would be to depart gratuitously from actuality.

The psychoanalysis of fictional characters has aroused vigorous objections. So would Gans's argument, if anyone cared. I shall keep neutral in these quarrels, and try to provide for the needs of both sides. Analysis 1, or something close to it, should capture the usage of Gans and the literary psychoanalysts. Let us find an alternative analysis to capture the conflicting usage of their opponents. I shall not try to say which usage is more conducive to appreciation of fiction and critical insight.

Suppose we decide, *contra* Gans and the literary psychoanalysts, that little-known or unknown facts about our world are irrelevant to truth in fiction. But let us not fall back to Analysis 0; it is not our only alternative. Let us still recognize that it is perfectly legitimate to reason to truth in fiction from a background of well-known facts.

Must they really be facts? It seems that if little-known or unknown facts are irrelevant, then so are little-known or unknown errors in the body of shared opinion that is generally taken for fact. We think we all know that there are no purple gnomes, but what if there really are a few, unknown to anyone except themselves, living in a secluded cabin near Loch Ness? Once we set aside the usage given by Analysis 1, it seems clear that whatever purple gnomes may be hidden in odd corners of our actual world, there are still none of them in the worlds of Sherlock Holmes. We have shifted to viewing truth in fiction as the joint product of explicit content and a background of generally prevalent beliefs.

Our own beliefs? I think not. That would mean that what is true in a fiction is constantly changing. Gans might not be right yet, but he would eventually become right about Holmes's error if enough people read his article and learned that Russell's viper could not climb a rope. When the map of Victorian London was finally forgotten, it would cease to be true that Holmes lived nearer to Paddington than to Waterloo. Strange to say, the historical scholar would be in no better position to know what was true in the fictions of his period than the ignorant layman. That cannot be right. What was true in a fiction when it was first told is true in it forevermore. It is our knowledge of what is true in the fiction that may wax or wane.

The proper background, then, consists of the beliefs that generally prevailed in the community where the fiction originated: the beliefs of the author and his intended audience. And indeed the factual premises that seemed to us acceptable in reasoning about Sherlock Holmes were generally believed in the community of origin of the stories. Everyone knew roughly where the principal stations of London were, everyone disbelieved in purple gnomes, and so forth.

One last complication. Suppose Conan Doyle was a secret believer in purple gnomes; thinking that his belief in them was not shared by anyone else he kept it carefully to himself for fear of ridicule. In particular, he left no trace of this belief in this stories. Suppose also that some of his original readers likewise were secret believers in purple gnomes. Suppose, in fact, that everyone alive at the time was a secret believer in purple gnomes, each thinking that his own belief was not shared by anyone else. Then it is clear (to the extent that anything is clear about such a strange situation) that the belief in purple gnomes does not "generally prevail" in quite the right way, and there are still no purple gnomes in the worlds of Sherlock Holmes. Call a belief *overt* in a community at a time iff more or less everyone shares it, more or less everyone thinks that more or less everyone else shares it, and so on.[13] The proper background, we may conclude, comprises the beliefs that are overt in the community of origin of the fiction.

Assume, by way of idealization, that the beliefs overt in the community are each possible and jointly compossible. Then we can assign to the community a set of possible worlds, called the *collective belief worlds* of the community, comprising exactly those worlds where the overt beliefs all come true. Only if the community is uncommonly lucky will the actual world belong to this set. Indeed, the actual world determines the collective belief worlds of the community of origin of the fiction and then drops out of the analysis. (It is of course a contingent matter what that community is and what is overtly believed there.) We are left with two sets of worlds: the worlds where the fiction is told as known fact, and the collective belief worlds of the community of origin. The first set gives the content of the fiction; the second gives the background of prevalent beliefs.

It would be a mistake simply to consider the worlds that belong to both sets. Fictions usually contravene at least some of the community's overt beliefs. I can certainly tell a story in which there are purple gnomes, though there are none at our collective belief worlds. Further, it will usually be overtly believed in the community of origin of a fiction that the story is not told as known fact—storytellers seldom deceive—so none of the worlds where the fiction is told as known fact can be a collective belief world of the community. Even if the two sets do overlap (the fiction is plausible and the author palms it off as fact) the worlds that belong to both sets are apt to be special in ways having nothing to do with what is true in the fiction. Suppose the story tells of a bungled burglary in recent times, and suppose it ends just as the police reach the scene. Any collective belief world of ours where this story is told as known fact is a world where the burglary was successfully covered up; for it is an overt belief among us that no such burglary ever hit the news. That does not make it true in the story that the burglary was covered up.

What we need is something like Analysis 1, but applied from the standpoint of the collective belief worlds rather than the actual world. What is true in the Sherlock Holmes stories is what would be true, according to the overt beliefs of the community of origin, if those stories were told as known fact rather than fiction.

Spelling this out, we have ANALYSIS 2: *A sentence of the form "In the fiction f, φ" is non-vacuously true iff, whenever w is one of the collective belief worlds of the community of origin of f, then some world where f is told as known fact and φ is true differs less from the world w, on balance, than does any world where f is told as known fact and φ is not true. It is vacuously true iff there are no possible worlds where f is told as known fact.* It is Analysis 2, or something close to it, that I offer to opponents of Gans and the literary psychoanalysts.

I shall briefly consider two remaining areas of difficulty and sketch strategies for dealing with them. I shall not propose improved analyses, however; partly because I am not quite sure what changes to make, and partly because Analysis 2 is quite complicated enough already.

I have said that truth in fiction is the joint product of two sources: the explicit content of the fiction, and a background consisting either of the facts about our world (Analysis 1) or of the beliefs overt in the community of origin (Analysis 2). Perhaps there is a third source which also contributes: cary-over from other truth in fiction. There are two cases: intra-fictional and inter-fictional.

In the *Threepenny Opera*, the principal characters are a treacherous crew. They constantly betray one another, for gain or to escape danger. There is also a streetsinger. He shows up, sings the ballad of Mack the Knife, and goes about his business without betraying anyone. Is he also a treacherous fellow? The explicit content does not make him so. Real people are not so very treacherous, and even in Weimar Germany it was not overtly believed that they were, so background does not make him so either. Yet there is a moderately good reason to say that he is treacherous: in the *Threepenny Opera*, that's how people are. In the worlds of the *Threepenny Opera*, everyone put to the test proves treacherous, the streetsinger is there along with the rest, so doubtless he too would turn out to be treacherous if we saw more of him. His treacherous nature is an intra-fictional carry-over from the treacherous natures in the story of Macheath, Polly, Tiger Brown, and the rest.

Suppose I write a story about the dragon Scrulch, a beautiful princess, a bold knight, and what not. It is a perfectly typical instance of its stylized genre, except that I never say that Scrulch breathes fire. Does he nevertheless breathe fire in my story? Perhaps so, because dragons in that sort of story do breathe fire. But the explicit content does not make him breathe fire. Neither does background, since in actuality and according to our beliefs there are no animals that breathe fire. (It just might be analytic that nothing is a dragon unless it breathes fire. But suppose I never *called* Scrulch a dragon; I merely endowed him with all the standard dragonly attributes except fire-breathing.) If Scrulch does breathe fire in my story, it is by inter-fictional carry-over from what is true of dragons in other stories.

I have spoken of Conan Doyle's Holmes stories; but many other authors also have written Holmes stories. These would have little point without inter-fictional carry-over. Surely many things are true in these satellite stories not because of the explicit content of the satellite story itself, and not because they are part of the background, but rather because they carry over from Conan Doyle's original Holmes stories. Similarly, if instead of asking what is true in the entire corpus of Conan Doyle's Holmes stories we ask what is true in "The Hound of the Baskervilles," we will doubtless find many things that are true in that story only by virtue of carry-over from Conan Doyle's other Holmes stories.

I turn finally to vacuous truth in impossible fictions. Let us call a fiction *impossible* iff there is no world where it is told as known fact rather than fiction. That might happen in either of two ways. First, the plot might be impossible. Second, a possible plot might imply that there could be nobody in a position to know or tell of the events in question. If a fiction is impossible in the second way, then to tell it as known fact would be to know its truth and tell truly something that implies that its truth could not be known; which is impossible.

According to all three of my analyses, anything whatever is vacuously true in an impossible fiction. That seems entirely satisfactory if the impossibility is blatant: if we are dealing with a fantasy about the troubles of the man who squared the circle, or with the worst sort of incoherent time-travel story. We should not expect to have a non-trivial concept of truth in blatantly impossible fiction, or perhaps we should expect to have one only under the pretence—not to be taken too seriously—that there are impossible possible worlds as well as the possible possible worlds.

But what should we do with a fiction that is not blatantly impossible, but impossible only because the author has been forgetful? I have spoken of truth in the Sherlock Holmes stories. Strictly speaking, these (taken together) are an impossible fiction. Conan Doyle contradicted himself from one story to another about the location of Watson's old war wound. Still, I do not want to say that just anything is true in the Holmes stories!

I suppose that we might proceed in two steps to say what is true in a venially impossible fiction such as the Holmes stories. First, go from the original impossible fiction to the several possible revised versions that stay closest to the original. Then say that what is true in the original is what is true, according to one of our analyses of non-vacuous truth in fiction, in all of these revised versions. Then nothing definite will be true in the Holmes stories about the location of Watson's wound. Since Conan Doyle put it in different places, the different revised versions will differ. But at least it will be true in the stories that Watson was wounded elsewhere than in the left big toe. Conan Doyle put the wound in various places, but never there. So no revised version will put the wound in the left big toe, since that would change the story more than consistency demands.

The revised versions, like the original fiction, will be associated with acts of storytelling. The revised versions, unlike the original, will not actually be told either as fiction or as known fact. But there are worlds where they are told as fiction, and worlds where they are told as known fact.

Even when the original fiction is not quite impossible, there may be cases in which it would be better to consider not truth in the original fiction but rather truth in all suitably revised versions. We have a three-volume novel set in 1878. We learn in the first volume that the hero had lunch in Glasgow on a certain day. In the third volume, it turns out that he showed up in London that same afternoon. In no other way does this novel purport to be a fantasy of rapid transit. The author was just careless. We could without vacuity apply our analyses directly to the novel as written. Since the closest worlds where it is told as known fact are worlds with remarkable means of travel, the results would astonish anyone—for instance, our forgetful author—who had not troubled to work out a careful timetable of the hero's movements. It would be more charitable to apply the analyses not to the original story but instead to the minimally revised versions that make the hero's movements feasible by the means of travel that were available in 1878. At least, that would be best if there were ways to set the times right without major changes in the plot. There might not be, and in that case perhaps truth in the original version—surprising though some of it may be—is the best we can do.

NOTES

1. In "A Prolegomenon to Meinongian Semantics," *Journal of Philosophy* 71 (1974): 561–80, and in "A Meinongian Analysis of Fictional Objects," *Grazer Philosophische Studien* 1 (1975): 73–86.

2. I have also been told that there has never been any building at that address. It doesn't matter which is correct.

3. For instance, the system given in Dana Scott, "Existence and Description in Formal Logic," in *Bertrand Russell: Philosopher of the Century*, ed. by Ralph Schoenman (London: Allen & Unwin, 1967).

4. Thus far, the account I have given closely follows that of John Heintz, "Reference and Inference in Fiction." *Poetics* 8 (1979).

5. Briefly stated in his addenda to "Naming and Necessity," in *Semantics of Natural Language*, ed. by Gilbert Harman and Donald Davidson (Dordrecht: Reidel, 1972); and discussed at greater length in an unpublished lecture given at a conference held at the University of Western Ontario in 1973 and on other occasions. My views and Kripke's overlap to some extent. He also stresses what I have called the ambiguity of prefixing and regards the storyteller as engaged in pretence. The conclusions he draws from the present observation, however, differ greatly from mine.

6. Jorge Luis Borges, "Pierre Menard, Author of the *Quixote*" in *Ficciones* (Buenos Aires, 1944; English translation, New York: Grove, 1962).

7. There are exceptions. Sometimes the storyteller purports to be uttering a

mixture of truth and lies about matters whereof he has knowledge, or ravings giving a distorted reflection of the events, or the like. Tolkien explicitly purports to be the translator and editor of the Red Book of Westmarch, an ancient book that has somehow come into his possession and that he somehow knows to be a reliable record of the events. He does not purport to be its author, else he would not write in English. (Indeed, the composition of the Red Book by several hobbits is recorded in the Red Book itself.) I should say the same about a first-person historical novel written in English in which the narrator is an ancient Greek. The author does not pretend to be the truthful narrator himself, but rather pretends to be someone of our time who somehow has obtained the Greek narrator's story, knows it to be true, and passes it on to us in translation. In these exceptional cases also, the thing to do is to consider those worlds where the act of storytelling really is whatever it purports to be—ravings, reliable translation of a reliable source, or whatever—here at our world. I shall omit mention of these exceptional cases in the remainder of this paper.

8. A rather similar treatment of fictional names, different from mine in that it allows the actual and purported meanings of "Sherlock Holmes" to be the same, is given in Robert Stalnaker, "Assertion" in *Syntax and Semantics* 9, ed. by Peter Cole, (New York: Academic Press, 1978).

9. Many of us have never read the stories, could not produce the descriptions that largely govern the non-rigid sense of "Sherlock Holmes," yet use this name in just the same sense as the most expert Baker Street Irregular. There is no problem here. Kripke's causal picture of the contagion of meaning, in "Naming and Necessity," (*op. cit.*), will do as well for non-rigid senses, as for rigid ones. The ignoramus uses "Sherlock Holmes" in its standard non-rigid sense if he has picked it up (in the right way) from someone who knew the governing descriptions, or who picked it up from someone else who knew them, or. . . . Kripke's doctrines of rigidity could not be defended without the aid of his doctrine of contagion of meaning; contagion without rigidity, on the other hand, seems unproblematic.

10. Given in *Counterfactuals* (Oxford: Blackwell, 1973).

11. Heintz (*op. cit.*) disagrees; he supposes that for each fiction there is a single world to be considered, but a world that is in some respects indeterminate. I do not know what to make of an indeterminate world, unless I regard it as a superposition of all possible ways of resolving the indeterminacy—or, in plainer language, as a set of determinate worlds that differ in the respects in question.

12. Carl Gans, "How Snakes Move," *Scientific American*, 222 (1970): 93.

13. A better definition of overt belief, under the name of "common knowledge," may be found in my *Convention* (Cambridge, Mass.: Harvard University Press, 1969), pp. 52–60. The name was unfortunate, since there is no assurance that it will be knowledge, or even that it will be true. See also the discussion of "mutual knowledge" in Stephen Schiffer, *Meaning* (Oxford: Oxford University Press, 1972), pp. 30–42.

HOW REMOTE ARE FICTIONAL WORLDS FROM THE REAL WORLD?

Kendall L. Walton

. . . What relations can hold between the real world and fictional worlds? Can real people interact with fictional characters? We are likely to feel that fictional worlds are insulated or isolated, in some peculiar way, from the real world, that there is a logical or metaphysical barrier between them.

That, indeed, is why we call them different "worlds." From our position in the real world we cannot, it seems, rescue Robinson Crusoe from his island, or send flowers to Tom Sawyer's relatives grieving at his funeral. Willy Loman (in Arthur Miller's *Death of a Salesman*) cannot tell us his troubles, nor can we give him advice. A Frankenstein monster may threaten with destruction any character who has the misfortune of sharing its world, but we in the real world are perfectly safe from it.

The barrier between worlds is not airtight, however. There are epistemological holes in it. We know a great deal about what happens in fictional worlds. In some cases we know even the most private thought of fictional characters, and occasionally we are privileged with information about fictional happenings far in the future—in the year 2001.

Along with our epistemological access to fictional occurrences goes a capacity to be affected by them. We respond to what we know about fictional worlds in many of the ways that we respond to what we know about the real world—or at least it seems that we do. When we learn that Tom Sawyer and Becky are lost in a cave we worry about whether they will find their way out. We sympathize with the plight of Willy Loman. We are terrified of the Frankenstein monster. Fictional characters cause real people to shed tears, lose sleep, laugh, and scream.

The epistemological window between the real world and fictional ones appears, usually, to be one-way. Tom Sawyer knows nothing about us, and it hardly seems possible for him—or even Sherlock Holmes, for that matter—to find out anything about us. Nor can we normally expect to inspire admiration, fear, or hate in fictional characters. There are apparent exceptions, however. The recruiting poster with the caption, "Uncle Sam Needs You!" is one. Another is the following paragraph of John Barth's "Life Story":

> The reader! You, dogged, uninsultable, print-oriented bastard, it's you I'm addressing, who else, from inside this monstrous fiction. You've read me this

far, then? Even this far? For what discreditable motive? How is it you don't go to a movie, watch TV, stare at a wall, play tennis with a friend, make amorous advances to the person who comes to mind when I speak of amorous advances: Can nothing surfeit, saturate you, turn you off? Where's your shame?[1]

Nevertheless, interaction of a more physical sort between worlds, in either direction, still seems out of the question. We cannot rescue Robinson Crusoe from his island no matter how deep our concern for him is; indeed we cannot even try to. Our "fear" of the Frankenstein monster is a peculiarly unfounded one, since we are certain to survive even if the monster ravishes the entire world!

But this needs a closer look. Is physical interaction across worlds really impossible? Consider the classic story of Henry, a backwoods villager watching a theatrical performance, who leaps to the stage to save the heroine from the clutches of the villain and a horrible death. Of course Henry is mistaken if he thinks he can save the *actress*. She is not in danger; there is nothing to save her from. But the character she portrays is in danger and does need saving. Can Henry help *her*, despite the fact that he doesn't live in her world?

Fictional heroines are not unsavable just because they are fictional. They can be saved by other fictional characters. Superman might fly to the rescue at the last moment. The question about whether Henry can save the heroine rests on the fact that Henry is not a character, that he and the heroine "belong to different worlds."

Suppose that if the performance proceeded according to plan, the villain would tie the heroine to railroad tracks and a passing train would do her in. This is to be portrayed as follows: There are two parallel two-by-fours on the stage floor representing the railroad tracks. The actor playing the villain places the actress playing the heroine on the two-by-fours and passes a rope around her body. The curtains close, and the passing of a train is indicated by appropriate sound effects. Now, if Henry rushes to the stage and removes the actress from the two-by-fours before the stagehand responsible for sound effects brings the train through, hasn't he saved the heroine—at least temporarily? (The ushers might expel Henry, allowing the play to resume without interference.) Or, Henry might cause such a commotion that the performance has to be cancelled entirely. This prevents the performers from portraying the heroine's death. And since what happens in the fictional world is just what is portrayed as happening, it seems that Henry has prevented the heroine's death.

It is not necessary that Henry be naive about the play, that he think it is the real world actress who is in danger and try to save *her*. Suppose he knows perfectly well that what he is watching is a play, and that only a fictional woman is in danger. But suppose he feels so strongly that such an innocent and beautiful damsel ought to be spared, even in fiction, that he intervenes in her behalf. If he knows what he is doing he may simply pull the plug on the sound effects equipment, thereby diverting the train and saving the heroine.

A minor qualification is needed. If the performance is of a written play, a "type" which can be performed more than once, one might reasonably hold that the heroine belongs to a fictional world corresponding to the type, and that what happens to her depends on what the written text for the play says, regardless of what occurs during any particular performance of it. If according to the text she comes to grief, then she comes to grief (in the fictional world of the play), and the performance interfered with by Henry is simply incorrect. This doesn't mean that Henry cannot save the heroine; it means only that he must use different tactics. What he must tamper with is not the performance but the text. Perhaps a few crucial alterations in the manuscript of the text will do the trick.[2] If not, the thing to do is to catch the author in the act of writing the play and force him, at gunpoint if necessary, to spare the heroine.

But it will be simpler to suppose that the theatrical event with which Henry tangles is not a performance of a written play, that it is not an instance of a play (type) which might have other instances as well.[3] Let us say that it is entirely improvised on the spot. The heroine's fate depends solely on what happens on stage. Her fictional world is the world of that performance, not the world of a play (type) which is independent of any particular performance. Given this stipulation it would seem that Henry can save the heroine by sabotaging the performance in one of the ways described previously.

The principle of this example can be generalized. What happens in the fictional world of a given work depends on the nature of the work. Tom Sawyer attends his own funeral because of the fact that certain combinations of words occur in the novel, *The Adventures of Tom Sawyer*. It is the arrangement of paint on canvas that determines what happens in the fictional world of a painting. This apparently opens the way for almost unlimited intervention in fictional worlds. Since real world novels, plays, paintings, and so forth are what determine what happens in fictional worlds, we can affect fictional worlds to whatever extent the nature of novels, plays, and paintings is within our power. We can destroy an evil picture-man, not with a dagger, perhaps, but with a paintbrush—by painting a dagger through him and an expiring look on his face. If we are not adept with a paintbrush, we can bribe or bully the painter to do the picture-man in for us. Painters, authors, and other artists are veritable gods *vis-à-vis* fictional worlds. The isolation of fictional worlds from the real world seems to have vanished.

There is an air of trickery about the preceding remarks. If it is so easy to save characters in distress, why don't we do so more often? One possible answer is that jumping on the stage or otherwise interfering with the performance is *inappropriate*, a violation of the conventions of the theater. But there are no conventions prohibiting authors, playwrights, and painters from sparing their characters; it is their prerogative to decide the fate of their characters. And anyway, would we let mere conventions deter us from saving a life?

Perhaps the explanation lies in the nature of our values or moral feelings. Perhaps fictional lives don't matter to us in the way that real ones do; fictional suffering, unlike real suffering, is not regrettable, and we feel no obligation to prevent it. But this explanation is not very convincing. It seems that we do, sometimes, care very much about fictional characters. We are distressed at the plight of Tom and Becky in the cave; we feel for Willy Loman; we hope fervently that the hero will arrive in time to rescue the hapless heroine. And we may pass moral judgment on a character who is in a position to help but does not—even while we ourselves sit glued dumbly to our seats!

Is our concern for the heroine a fake, a sham? Our non-intervention is not the only evidence that it is. If we really do blame the villain for doing awful things to the heroine, shouldn't we blame even more the author who put him up to it? Why not get at the root cause of the evil? But we may well have nothing but praise for the author, even when we purport to bemoan the calamities he allows to befall his characters. Moreover, it is not hard to find reasons for secretly wishing the heroine ill. Watching fictional suffering can be thrilling, instructive, cathartic. And we may think that if the heroine does not suffer, the work will be insipid, a namby-pamby, everyone-lives-happily-ever-after affair.[4] We appreciate and admire tragedies, and we hope that the work turns out to be a tragedy, despite the fact that this means disaster for the heroine. (Compare a person watching a bullfight whose selfish desire to be entertained overcomes his natural compassion for the bull.)

But I doubt that we ever suffer even the slightest pangs of conscience for allowing our desire for a valuable aesthetic experience to interfere with our concern for a character in distress. And it hardly seems that we *consider* intervening on behalf of the heroine but fail to act when our selfish urges get the best of us; we don't think of intervention as a live alternative. This is certainly no ordinary instance of mixed motives, of conflicting desires or interests.

Perhaps our motives are not mixed. Perhaps we have no concern whatever for heroines in distress, and this is why we rarely try to rescue them. But then what are we to make of the feelings which unquestionably we often do have when we experience tragic works, and which we readily describe as feelings of concern or pity for characters, or worry about what might happen to them?

It is evident that we must examine at a much deeper level the idea that residents of the real world can intervene physically in the affairs of fictional worlds, and also the idea that fictional things can be objects of the psychological attitudes of real people, that real people can care about, love, hate, or fear fictional characters.

III.

Much of the trouble stems from confusion about the nature of fiction. How are we to construe fictional statements such as:

Tom Sawyer attended his own funeral.
Robinson Crusoe survived a shipwreck.
An innocent damsel fell into the clutches of an evil villain [uttered in connection with the recently described theatrical event].

On any adequate theory these statements are used (in familiar contexts) to express truths. The first, for example, contrasts with "Tom Sawyer did not attend his own funeral," which expresses a falsehood. The question is how to characterize the truths that they express. I shall outline two basic alternatives.

(1) The first alternative is to take such statements at face value, to treat them as the straightforward subject/predicate statements they appear to be. To say that Robinson Crusoe survived a shipwreck is to refer to Robinson Crusoe and to attribute to him the property of having survived a shipwreck. Crusoe does in fact possess this property, so what is said is true.

I shall understand this first position to embrace the existence of Robinson Crusoe and other fictional entities. Crusoe could not be referred to or possess properties, it would seem, if he did not exist.[5] Fictional entities must of course be distinguished from actual ones. Perhaps fictional things and actual things have different kinds or modes of existence, or exist in different "realms" or "universes."

Theories which recognize fictional entities are subject to a familiar battery of objections, ranging from considerations of general ontological sanitation to charges of obscurity and incoherence. Nevertheless they clearly capture an important aspect of our prereflective intuitions. Apparent references to fictions are natural and common in ordinary discourse; I apparently referred to them many times during the informal discussion of Section II. It is true that people will readily deny that there is any such person as Robinson Crusoe, without waiting to be persuaded by philosophical arguments. But the denial can be construed as merely a denial that Crusoe is an *actual* person. Once it is clearly understood that there is no question of Crusoe's being actual we seem equally ready to admit his existence. To the question whether there is such a *character* as Crusoe the unsophisticated answer is affirmative.

Our intuitive inclination to recognize the existence of fictions is important and calls for explanation, even if we decide that it must be resisted. . . .

It should be remembered that the recognition of fictional entities is only part of position (1). This position claims not only that Robinson Crusoe exists, but also that he has ordinary properties like that of having survived a shipwreck.[6]

(2) The position I prefer denies the statements like "Robinson Crusoe survived a shipwreck," as they are usually meant, are to be taken at face value. To make this statement is not to attribute to Crusoe the property of having survived a shipwreck, to claim that he, literally, possesses that property; it is not to refer to Crusoe at all nor to attribute any property to him.

A step in the right direction would be to regard "Crusoe survived a shipwreck" as elliptical for "*In the novel, Robinson Crusoe,* Crusoe survived a shipwreck." Similarly, "The innocent damsel is tied to the railroad tracks" may be regarded as short for, "*In the play,* the innocent damsel is tied to the railroad tracks." Other statements purporting to be about fictional objects can be understood as preceded, implicitly, by "In the picture, . . . ," "In the film, . . . ," "In the game of make-believe, . . . ," or "In the myth, . . ."

But paraphrases like "In the novel Crusoe survived a shipwreck" can easily be misleading also. "In the novel" must not be construed as indicating in what manner, or "where" ("in what realm") it is true that Crusoe survived, or anything of the sort. "In the novel Crusoe survived," properly construed, does not imply that it is true in any manner at all that Crusoe survived. My view is that this statement characterizes the proposition that Crusoe survived, not as being true, but as having a different attribute, that of being "fictional."[7] So to avoid confusion I will substitute, "It is fictional that Crusoe survived," for, "In the novel Crusoe survived." When a person says, "Crusoe survived," he is (ordinarily) to be understood as asserting that it is fictional that Crusoe survived.[8]

"It is fictional that Crusoe survived" should be regarded as analogous to statements such as the following:

It is believed that Jones survived.
It is claimed that Jones survived.
It is wished that Jones survived.
It is denied that Jones survived.

These are used not to assert that the proposition that Jones survived is true, but to attribute other properties to it, to assert that this propostion is believed, or that someone claims, or wishes, or denies, it to be true.

What is it for a proposition to be fictional? I will not try to give an answer to this question here, beyond the observation that whatever is, as we say, "true in (the world of) a story, or play, or picture, or game of make-believe, etc.," is fictional.[9] The important point for present purposes is that statements purporting to be about fictions are used to attribute to propositions a property other than truth (the property I call "fictionality"). Just what property this is is immaterial.

It will sometimes be convenient to say just "Fictionally *p*" rather than "It is fictional that *p*." And I will call the fact that it is fictional that *p*, i.e., the fact that fictionally *p*, a "fictional fact" or a "fictional truth."

"Fictional worlds" can be understood as collections of fictional truths. The fact that "Robinson Crusoe exists in a given fictional world" amounts simply to the fact that it is fictional that Crusoe exists, and that this fictional truth belongs to a given collection of fictional truths. The fictional world is not to be construed as a realm in which it is *true* that Crusoe exists.

Which propositions are fictional depends on the nature of novels, pictures, plays (or performances thereof), and what is done during games of make-believe. The words which occur in Daniel Defoe's novel are what make it fictional that Crusoe survived a shipwreck. It is fictional that an innocent damsel fell into the clutches of an evil villain because of what happens on stage during the theatrical event described previously. Johnnie's running around with a broomstick between his legs may make it fictional that he is riding a horse. Representational works of art and games of make-believe thus *generate* fictional truths.

The generation of fictional truths seems in at least some cases to involve an element of convention. It is fictional that Johnnie is riding a horse when he is playing hobbyhorses only because there is an understanding, a convention, in that situation to the effect that the broomstick "is" a horse and that running with it between one's legs counts as "riding the horse." Not just any instance of running around with a stick between one's legs makes it fictional that one is riding a horse. A pair of two-by-fours lying side by side do not always count as railroad tracks. But it is understood that in the mentioned theatrical event such two-by-fours make it fictional that there are railroad tracks. The fact that an actor portraying Oedipus in a performance of *Oedipus Rex* speaks in English, and the fact that he is illuminated by a spotlight, do *not* make it fictional that Oedipus spoke English and suffered his agony under a spotlight. The conventions of theater do not allow for the generation of these fictional truths in these ways.

This second account of the nature of fictional statements relieves much of the pressure to recognize fictional entities. "Robinson Crusoe survived a shipwreck," taken literally, is simply false (or truth-valueless) and so provides no excuse for thinking that Crusoe exists. And the fact that fictionally Crusoe survived a shipwreck no more implies the (literal) existence of Crusoe than the fact that it has been said that abominable snowmen roam the Himalayas implies that there are abominable snowmen. It is, however, *fictional* that Crusoe exists. Only if it is fictional that something exists can it be fictional that it survives a shipwreck, just as only what actually exists can actually survive a shipwreck. But to say this is not to bestow a special kind of existence (or "being") on Crusoe, to classify him as an entity of a special sort. It is to say that the proposition that Crusoe exists[10] (the proposition that he possesses the ordinary sort of existence) is fictional, not that it is true.[11]

In what follows I shall explore links between the puzzles raised earlier about possibilities of interaction between the "real world" and "fictional worlds" and the two positions on the nature of fiction which I have just outlined. It seems to me that some aspects of these puzzles, those having to do with physical interaction across worlds, are nourished by implicit acceptance of position (1), and that once we reject (1) for (2), once we trade our notion of fictional entities for one of fictional truths, they obligingly evaporate. Questions concerning psychological interaction between worlds, however, dissolve less easily, and threaten to force us back to position (1). My resolution of these latter questions will have to wait for another occasion. But in Section VI I will indicate the direction to take.

I shall not attempt here to establish definitively the superiority of (2) over (1), although some of the points I shall make constitute reasons for preferring (2).

IV.

Does Henry save the heroine when he leaps to the stage upsetting the performance just before her fate is sealed? There are two separate questions to consider, if we accept position (2): Is it (literally) true that Henry saves the heroine? and, Is it fictional that he saves her?

It is clear that this is not (literally) true. The heroine doesn't (literally) exist, and non-existent people cannot be saved. Nor is it fictional that Henry saves the heroine. When Henry pulls the plug on the sound effects, for example, it is not fictional that he exists, and it cannot be fictional that one does any saving unless fictionally one exists. There is no understanding (in traditional theater) whereby Henry's action counts as his fictionally saving the heroine. His behavior is understood not as part of the theatrical event, but as an intrusion on it.

What *is* true is that Henry makes it fictional that the heroine survives. He arranges things in such a way that this fictional truth is generated. But doing this is not *saving* the heroine, neither literally nor fictionally. Henry brings it about that fictionally the heroine survives, but he does not save her, and it is not fictional that he saves her.

Other examples can be treated in similar fashion. A painter or author can arrange for it to be fictional that an evil man dies, or that everyone lives happily ever after. But in doing so he does not kill the evil man or give everyone eternal bliss, nor is it fictional that he does.

This bears out our original feeling that fictional worlds are somehow insulated from the real world. It would be a mistake to think that what happens in fictional worlds, what fictionally is the case, cannot be affected by what happens in the real world. But one person can save another only if they "live in the same world." That is, it can be true that *A* saves *B* only if it is true that *A* and *B* both exist, and it can be fictional that *A* saves *B* only if it is fictional that they both exist. *Cross-world* saving is ruled out, and for similar reasons so is cross-world killing, congratulating, handshaking, and so forth.

No equally happy solution is available if we adopt position (1). If we do not recognize a notion of fictional propositions, there is just one question to be asked about Henry's case: Did Henry save the heroine? i.e., Is it literally the case that he saved her? According to (1) the heroine exists, and she has various properties, including that of being in danger. Given that this is so, and that Henry does something—deliberately, let us assume—which results in her survival, it is not easy to deny that he saves her. Saving someone just is, one would think, bringing it about that that person survives. According to (1) the heroine is someone, and Henry brings it about that she survives.[12]

This leaves stranded our intuitions about the isolation of fictional worlds from the real world. Position (1) seems to force us into an impossible association with the likes of Tom Sawyer, Willy Loman, and Robinson Crusoe; it is unclear what the point of saying that they live in different "worlds" from ours is. To recapture the desired isolation between worlds we must turn again to (2).

But we must be careful how this isolation is described. It *can* be fictional that a real person such as Henry saves a heroine, or destroys a villain, or congratulates a hero. For real people can "exist in fictional worlds," that is, it can be true of Henry, or of any actual person, that fictionally he exists. Julius Caesar belongs to the fictional world of Shakespeare's play, as well as to the real world; it is fictional that he exists, as well as literally the case that he does (or did). Suppose that Henry is not just a spectator of the play but also a character in it, i.e., suppose that one of the actors portrays him. Obviously, then, it might be fictional that Henry saves the heroine—depending, of course, on what the actor portraying him does on the stage, not on anything that Henry himself does. It might be fictional that Henry rides heroically to the rescue in the nick of time delivering the heroine from the clutches of the villain. It is also possible that Henry should do the acting himself, that he should play himself. In that case whether it is fictional that Henry saves the heroine will depend on what Henry in his role as an actor does.[13]

At first sight this might appear to constitute a major breach in the barrier between worlds, but the appearance is deceiving. One reason for the appearance is the temptation to express the point of the previous paragraph by saying that real people *can*, after all, save fictional heroines. But this is misleading. It is easily taken to mean that real people are such that fictionally they can save heroines, which is not true for most people in most circumstances. Every actual person is such that it *can* be fictional that he saves a heroine. But this doesn't mean that it *is* fictional that he can do anything at all.

Moreover, even when it is fictional that Henry can and does save the heroine, the interaction between him and the heroine occurs entirely "within the fictional world"; this is not a case of interaction between worlds. It happens that Henry, besides "existing" in the fictional world and in that world saving the heroine, exists also in the real world. But he does not reach over *from* the real world to the fictional one to save the heroine; he doesn't need to since he belongs to the fictional world too. Saving can take place only within a single world. If "*A* saves *B*," then either it is (literally) true that *A* saves *B*, or it is fictional that this is so. Cross-world saving, properly so-called, remains excluded.

V.

The notion of an unbridgeable gulf separating fictional worlds from the real world is thus neatly vindicated. The vindication is accomplished by regarding fictional statements as occurring, implicitly if not explicitly, within the scope of an intensional operator, "It is fictional that," and hence as analogous to statements of the forms, "It is believed that . . . ," "It is wished that . . . ," etc. The impossibility of a real person's interacting with (mere) fictions is thus rendered no more remarkable than the impossibility of a real person's interacting with "things" which are believed or wished or said or denied to exist but which do not exist.

But this vindication is in some ways too neat, too easy. To rest content with what has been said so far would be to encourage exaggeration of our sense of isolation from fictional worlds, to ignore important ways in which we feel close to them. And it would leave unaccounted for much of the motivation to recognize fictional entities and to accept position (1). In order to get to the bottom of things, differences between "It is fictional that . . ." and other intensional operators, as well as similarities between them, need to be noticed. Fictional contexts are special in certain ways which need to be brought out. The issues here are subtle and deep. I will have to content myself now with pointing to what still needs to be explained and, in the following section, offering only a sketch of a theory to do the explaining.

A distant but dramatic view of what is special about fictional contexts can be had by considering whether characters and other fictions are objects of our psychological attitudes, whether we fear, pity, admire, envy, worry about them, and so forth. I have concentrated so far on questions about physical interaction between worlds. What about psychological interaction?

A child may of course be afraid of a fictional monster which he believes, mistakenly, to be real. And if we think there is a real person in distress, we might be said to feel sorry for him even if as a matter of fact he exists only in fiction. But the interesting question is whether we fear or feel sorry for fictional characters when we know perfectly well that they are merely fictional. I will not try to answer this question here. But psychological interaction with what are known to be mere fictions *seems* to be possible, and indeed very common. This alone is significant and revealing, for it distinguishes fictions from "things" which are believed (by someone) or desired or said or denied to exist but which do not.

It seems to be the case that movie-goers sometimes fear Frankenstein monsters even when they are fully aware that the monsters are not real. They sometimes find themselves in a state which is at least very much like one of fear, and which they inevitably describe as fear of the monsters. It is equally natural to suppose that readers or audiences feel sorry for Willy Loman, admire Robinson Crusoe, envy Superman, worry about Tom and Becky in the cave, and so forth, even if they do not entertain the slightest suspicion that these fictional characters are actual people.

But if it is believed by someone that an assassin is after me, and if I know for sure that nothing of the sort is true, there is virtually no temptation to think that I might nevertheless be afraid of the believed-to-exist assassin. I can hardly envy a wished-for rich uncle realizing that he is only wished for (even if I am the one who wishes for him). If it is asserted, or denied, that there is someone on the top of Mt. Everest with acute appendicitis and I know that there is not, I will not and can not worry about this non-actual person or feel sorry for him.

Thus, we feel a psychological bond to fictions, an intimacy with them, of a kind which otherwise we feel only toward what we take to be actual. Fictions, unlike objects of other intensional attitudes, are in this way thought of as though they exist. We have a strong tendency to regard them as part of our reality, despite our knowledge that they are not.

This tendency comes out also in our propensity to speak in terms of "fictional worlds." The notion, which I probed earlier, that fictions belong to worlds which are *different* from ours does, to be sure, reflect a need to "distance" ourselves from fictions. But why do we think of fictions as belonging to "worlds" at all—as though they have a place (or places) *somewhere* in reality, however remote they may be from the actual world? It is significant that there are no very comfortable analogues of the notion of fictional worlds corresponding to most other intensional operators. If a novel makes it fictional that someone attends his own funeral we are likely to express this by saying that "in the world of the novel" someone *does* attend his own funeral. But if Jones claims to be a genius we are not likely to say that he *is* a genius "in the world of his claim(s)." And we rarely or never speak of something's being the case "in the world of" someone's wishes, or belief, or denial. What fictionally is the case is naturally thought of as being the case in a special realm, a "world," in a way that what is claimed or believed or desired to be the case is not.[14] The ordinary concept of "fictional worlds"—worlds that are different from the real one but worlds nevertheless—is a device to paper over our confusion about whether or not fictions are real; it is an attempt to have it both ways.

Often we do not even bother to mention explicitly that the "world" in which something is the case is a fictional one. We talk about what is fictional as though it is true "in the real world," as though it actually is the case. In discussing the novel, *Robinson Crusoe*, instead of saying, "In the world of the novel, Robinson Crusoe survived a shipwreck," or, "In the novel, Robinson Crusoe survived a shipwreck," we are likely to say just, "Robinson Crusoe survived a shipwreck." "In the novel" and other colloquial fictional operators are commonly and comfortably omitted when there is no danger of misunderstanding. In fact, during an extended discussion of *Robinson Crusoe* it would be almost ridiculous to repeat continually, "In the novel such and such happened," "So and so was the case in the novel," etc.

This practice might be dismissed as nothing more than a shortcut to speed conversation were it not that we rarely take similar shortcuts with other intensional operators. Phrases like "It is believed that," "It is wished that," "Jones wishes that," etc., are not often left implicit. Even when it is clearly understood that one is speaking about Jones's wishes it would be very unnatural to say merely, "A golden mountain will appear on the horizon," meaning that Jones wishes that a golden mountain would appear on the horizon. Occasionally "It is believed that" or "He says that" is omitted, but only in fairly special circumstances.[15] And I know of no ordinary situations in which one might say "Smith robbed the bank, as an abbreviation for, "It is denied (or, "It is denied by Jones) that Smith robbed the bank."

Why do we omit fictional operators so readily? It is a serious mistake, I think, to regard "Tom Sawyer attended his own funeral" as, in general, a simple ellipsis for "In the novel Tom Sawyer attended his own funeral." Someone who says, "Tom attended his own funeral," is, in many cases, not asserting that it is fictional that Tom attended his own funeral, or at least this is not all that he is doing. What else is he doing? Not, to be sure, asserting (seriously) that Tom attended his own funeral. But he is doing something akin to this; he is pretending to assert that Tom attended his own funeral.[16] (It might be plausible to regard him as *both* pretending to assert that Tom actually attended his own funeral and at the same time actually asserting that fictionally Tom did so.) Now if one wants to pretend to assert that something actually is the case it would hardly be reasonable for him to say explicitly that *fictionally* it is the case. In pretending (seriously) to assert something one is likely to use the very same words one would choose if one were not just pretending. So naturally the speaker omits the fictional operator and says merely, "Tom attended his own funeral."

To pretend to assert something (in the relevant sense) is to be an actor in a game of make-believe; it is to make it fictional, of oneself, that one is (actually) asserting something. So the person who says that Tom attended his own funeral and thereby pretends to assert that this is the case, belongs to a fictional world himself. Not, however, to the "world of the novel" (since it is not the novel by itself which generates fictional truths about him), but to the world of a game of make-believe which he is playing with the novel, a game in which the novel serves as a prop. Tom Sawyer belongs to this world as well, or more accurately, among the fictional truths constituting this world is the fact that fictionally there exists a boy named "Tom Sawyer" who attended his own funeral, who was lost in a cave, etc., as well as the fact that it is fictional, of the (real) person who said "Tom attended his own funeral," that he exists. Tom and the speaker reside together in this world.[17]

One need not actually utter something like, "Tom attended his own funeral," in the appropriate spirit in order to be playing a game of make-believe of this sort with the novel. I claim that anyone who reads the novel in the way novels are ordinarily read plays such a game, though usually not overtly. Readers pretend to *believe* that Tom attended his own funeral, whether or not they pretend to assert that he did. The reader is such that, fictionally, he believes this.

It is usually also true of readers that, fictionally, they worry about Tom and Becky in the cave and have various other feelings concerning them.[18] But readers or spectators are rarely such that, fictionally, they interact physically with characters, nor even such that, fictionally, they *can* interact physically with them. Of course it is not impossible that a reader or spectator should, fictionally, shake hands with a character or lop off his head, or have the ability to do so. But apart from audience participation theater the conventions governing the make-believe games that we play with representational works usually do not allow it.[19] This points toward the explanation of why fictional worlds seem more remote physically from us than they do psychologically.

We, as readers and spectators of representational works, *do* "share worlds" with Tom Sawyer, Willy Loman, and other characters. But the shared worlds are fictional ones, not the real one. Thus, my solution avoids the claim of position (1) that fictional characters exist. It also rejects a view which, despite its implausibility, is strongly suggested by the often-invoked phrase, "suspension of disbelief," the view that although there was no such person as Tom Sawyer we somehow fool ourselves into believing that there was when we read the novel. Except in the rarest circumstances, readers and spectators are not deluded. Tom Sawyer and Willy Loman are neither real nor believed to be. Instead, appreciators are fictional. Rather than somehow promoting fictions to the level of reality, we, as appreciators, descend to the level of fiction. This is the heart of my proposed solution to our problems.

Our decent into fiction does a lot to make our temptation (both as theorists and as appreciators) to promote fictions to the status of reality comprehensible. *From the inside* the fictional worlds which we share with Tom Sawyer and Willy Loman look very much as though they are real. What fictionally is the case is, fictionally, *really* the case. It is fictional that when I say or think that Tom Sawyer really exists what I say or think is true.

When readers and spectators become fictional they do not of course cease to be actual. If a reader or spectator is such that fictionally he exists, it is also literally the case that he exists. So our standpoint is a dual one. We, as it were, see Tom Sawyer *both* from inside his world and from outside of it. And we do so simultaneously. The reader is such that, fictionally, he knows that Tom attended his own funeral, and he is such that fictionally he worries about Tom and Becky in the cave. At the same time the reader knows that no such persons as Tom and Becky ever existed.

There is no inconsistency here, and nothing very mysterious. But the dual standpoint which appreciators take is, I believe, one of the most fundamental and important features of the human institution of fiction. It lies at the bottom of most of the confusion I have been probing. Theorists have long floundered in the gap between our two perspectives, trying doggedly to merge them into one. (For example, our perspective is sometimes thought of as a unitary one which is some kind of a compromise between "*under-distancing*" and "*over-distancing*.") But once the duality of our standpoint is recognized things begin to fall into place. Once it is recognized, I believe, we are well on our way toward a deep understanding of what fiction is all about.

NOTES

1. Barth, *Lost in the Funhouse* (New York, 1969), p. 123.
2. It is arguable that to alter the text is not to affect what happens in the fictional world, but is rather to produce a new work and a new fictional world to go with it. Perhaps it is still true that the heroine, in the world corresponding to the original text, comes to grief, although there is another fictional world corresponding to the altered text in which she survives.
3. There are plays with multiple performances but which are never written down. The event we are concerned with is to be assumed not to be a performance even of an unwritten play of this sort.
4. "Some people—and I am one of them—hate happy ends. We feel cheated. Harm is the norm. Doom should not jam. The avalanche stopping in its tracks a few feet above the cowering village behaves not only unnaturally but unethically." Vladimir Nabokov, *Pnin* (New York, 1957).
5. It has been maintained, however, that things which have no sort of existence can be referred to and can possess properties. Cf. Richard Cartwright, "Negative Existentials," *Journal of Philosophy* LVII (1960), 629–39; Roderick Chisholm, "Beyond Being and Nonbeing," *Philosophical Studies* XXIV, No. 4 (July 1973), 245–57, Gerald Vision. "Referring to What Does Not Exist," *Canadian Journal of Philosophy* (June, 1974), 619–34. I shall not consider this view here.
6. Another view which I shall not consider here is that Robinson Crusoe and other fictions exist but do not have the sorts of properties which we seem to attribute to them, that Crusoe has the property of being such that "*in the story*" he survived a shipwreck (i.e., such that it is fictional that he survived a shipwreck),

rather than the property of having survived a shipwreck. This view has some of the advantages that I claim for position (2).

7. More accurately, what is fictional is that there was someone whose name was "Robinson Crusoe" who was shipwrecked on an island and managed to survive, etc. I cannot go into the reasons for saying this here, but see Alvin Plantinga, *The Nature of Necessity* (Oxford, 1974), pp. 159–60. It would be awkward to rephrase the points I am about to make taking this into account.

8. Actually he is probably making a more specific assertion than this. He is probably referring implicitly to Daniel Defoe's novel, and "It is fictional that Crusoe survived" contains no such reference. When it is important to be specific in this regard one could use, "It is *Robinson Crusoe*-fictional that Crusoe survived." It is *Robinson Crusoe*-fictional that" is analogous to "It is believed by Smith that," whereas "It is fictional that" corresponds to "It is believed (by someone or other) that."

9. I have given an analysis of what it is for a proposition to be fictional in "Pictures and Make-Believe," *Philosophical Review* 82 (1973), 283–319. In this and other papers I used the expression, "It is fictionally true that . . . ," rather than "It is fictional that . . . ," The point of changing my terminology is to avoid giving the impression that there is a special way of being true. It is not the proposition that Crusoe survived that is true, but rather the proposition that this proposition is fictional.

19. More accurately, the proposition that there is someone named "Robinson Crusoe" who did such and such things, etc.

11. I would deny also that Crusoe exists in any possible worlds. My reasons are implicit in "Are Representations Symbols?" *The Monist* (April, 1974), 236–254.

12. A defender of (1) *could* claim that a correct analysis of the notion of saving must contain a rider to the effect that saving is a relation which can hold only between things both of which are actual, or both of which are fictional. Not only is this move rather *ad hoc*, it has awkward consequences. The proponent of (1) must allow that something can be both actual and fictional; a real person, e.g., might also be a character in a story. Suppose that *A* is both actual and fictional. On (1) *A* can save someone *either* by actually saving him or by saving him "in the story." So if *A* actually saves one person from drowning, and in the story saves someone else from a fire, he will have made *two* rescues. Moreover, one might have to say that he made the two rescues simultaneously, if the time of the actual rescue is the same as the time at which, in the story, he rescued the other person.

13. The conventions of some kinds of "audience participation" theater are such that any member of the audience who participates in the action is thereby an actor portraying himself. In cases of this kind Henry might generate the fictional truth that he saves the heroine by rushing to the stage and removing the actress from the two-by-fours. (But many contemporary theatrical events, e.g., "happenings," do not involve any *acting* at all; no characters are portrayed and no fictional truths are generated.)

14. It is true that some recent philosophers (e.g., Hintikka) have found it convenient to introduce technical notions of belief-worlds, perceptual-worlds etc. But this must not be allowed to obscure my point. Belief-worlds and the like, however useful they may be for technical purposes, do not capture the imagination in the way that fictional worlds do. This fact needs to be explained, even if philosophical reflection should lead us to recognize belief-worlds, etc., as well as fictional worlds—or, on the other hand, to recognize no such worlds at all.

15. One might say "Vulcan was a planet of mass M" in place of something like, "It was believed (by those who accepted the now-discredited theory) that Vulcan was a planet of mass M." (I owe this example to Michael Devitt.) But it is arguable that in such a case the speaker is treating the theory as a myth (although holders of the theory did not so treat it), and so is regarding it as fictional that Vulcan was a planet of mass M, just as it is fictional that Santa Claus lives on the North Pole. "He says that" may be omitted when there is a hint of mimicry in the indirect quotation. One might say, in a mocking tone of voice, "Jones is a genius" meaning that Jones claims to be a genius. Mimicry may be involved also in the belief case. One who says, "Vulcan had mass M" may be mimicking the assertions that holders of the theory used to make, or were prepared to make. Both of these exceptions fit in nicely with the explanation I sketch in section VI [not reprinted here].

16. This pretense is not, of course, an attempt to fool anyone.

17. I am ignoring a complexity here. If the proposition which the novel (alone) makes fictional is not that Tom Sawyer exists and did such and such, but merely that there is a boy *named* "Tom Sawyer" who did such and such, and if similarly the reader's game of make-believe makes it fictional merely that there exists a boy named "Tom Sawyer" who performed certain activities, it makes no sense to say that the Tom Sawyer of the novel world is (or is not) identical with the Tom Sawyer in the world of the game of make-believe. (Robert Howell pointed this out to me. See his interesting and valuable "Fictional Objects: How They Are and How They Aren't," *Poetics*, forthcoming.) In general, it makes no sense to suppose that one and the same purely fictional character occupies more than one fictional world. Nevertheless, we do commonly talk as though this makes sense and there must be some theoretically satisfactory way of expressing what is meant when we do. Our theory needs to be able to distinguish between, for example, a work such as Tom Stoppard's *Rosencrantz and Guildenstern Are Dead* which is (we would say) about Hamlet, *the* hamlet of Shakespeare's play, and a work, written perhaps in a society which has not heard of Shakespeare, which is about a man named "Hamlet" but not, we would say, about Shakespeare's Hamlet. In this paper I sometimes follow colloquial practice and write as though the same character occupies different fictional worlds. When I do, what I say is to be understood as subject to reformulation in some appropriate way. (I shall not speculate here on what form the reformulation should take.) None of this affects what is crucial to the theory I am developing, namely that my claim that it is fictional, of the reader, that he exists along with a boy named "Tom Sawyer" whom he knows to have attended his own funeral and so forth. This fictional truth belongs to the world of the game of make-believe that the reader plays with the novel, and it is this world, not the world of the novel alone, which concerns him when he is engrossed in the story.

18. This is not inconsistent with the view that readers really do worry about Tom and Becky, etc. But I argue against this view in "Fearing Fictions," *The Journal of Philosophy*, LXXV (1978), 5–27.

19. Some kinds of physical interaction are exceptions. In "Pictures and Make-Believe," op. cit., I argue that, for example, a viewer of a painting of a man fictionally sees the man. Indeed it is basically this fact that distinguishes depictive representations from representations of other kinds. Also, the reader of some literary works fictionally reads words that were written by the narrator. Cf. my "Points of View in Narrative and Depictive Representation." *Nous* X (1976), 49–61.

OF NAMES

John Stuart Mill

Are names more properly said to be the names of things or of our ideas of things? The first is the expression in common use; the last is that of some metaphysicians who conceived that, in adopting it, they were introducing a highly important distinction. . . .

If it be merely meant that the conception alone, and not the thing itself, is recalled by the name or imparted to the hearer, this of course cannot be denied. Nevertheless there seems good reason for adhering to the common usage, and calling the word *sun* the name of the sun and not the name of our idea of the sun. For names are not intended only to make the hearer conceive what we conceive, but also to inform him what we believe. Now, when I use a name for the purpose of expressing a belief, it is a belief concerning the thing itself, not concerning my idea of it. When I say, "the sun is the cause of day," I do not mean that my idea of the sun causes or excites in me the idea of day, or, in other words, that thinking of the sun makes me think of day. I mean that a certain physical fact, which is called the sun's presence (and which, in the ultimate analysis, resolves itself into sensations, not ideas), causes another physical fact, which is called day. It seems proper to consider a word as the *name* of that which we intend to be understood by it when we use it; of that which any fact that we assert of it is to be understood of; that, in short, concerning which, when we employ the word, we intend to give information. Names, therefore, shall always be spoken of as the names of things themselves and not merely of our ideas of things . . . .

A non-connotative term is one which signifies a subject only, or an attribute only. A connotative term is one which denotes a subject and implies an attribute. By a subject is here meant anything which possesses attributes. Thus John, or London, or England are names which signify a subject only. Whiteness, length, virtue, signify an attribute only. None of these names, therefore, are connotative. But *white, long, virtuous,* are connotative. The word *white* denotes all white things, as snow, paper, the foam of the sea, etc., and implies, or in the language of the schoolmen, *connotes,* the attribute *whiteness*. The word *white* is not predicated of the attribute, but of the subjects, snow, etc.; but when we predicate it of them, we convey the meaning that the attribute whiteness belongs to them. The same may be said of the other words above cited. Virtuous, for example, is the name of a class which includes Socrates, Howard, the Man of Ross, and an undefinable number of other individuals, past, present, and to come. These individuals, collectively and severally, can alone be said with propriety to be denoted by the word; of them alone can it properly be said to be a name. But it is a name applied to all of them in consequence of an attribute which they are supposed to possess in common, the attribute which has received the name of virtue. It is applied to all beings that are considered to possess this attribute, and to none which are not so considered.

All concrete general names are connotative. The word *man*, for example, denotes Peter, Jane, John, and an indefinite number of other individuals of whom, taken as a class, it is the name. But it is applied to them because they possess, and to signify that they possess, certain attributes. These seem to be corporeity, animal life, rationality, and a certain external form which, for distinction, we call the human. Every existing thing which possessed all these attributes would be called a man; and anything which possessed none of them, or only one, or two, or even three of them without the fourth, would not be so called. For example, if in the interior of Africa there were to be discovered a race of animals possessing reason equal to that of human beings but with the form of an elephant, they would not be called men. Swift's Houyhnhnms would not be so called. Or if such newly-discovered beings possessed the form of man without any vestige of reason, it is probable that some other name than that of man would be found for them. How it happens that there can be any doubt about the matter will appear hereafter. The word *man*, therefore, signifies all these attributes and all subjects which possess these attributes. But it can be predicated only of the subjects. What we call men are the subjects, the individual Stiles and Nokes, not the qualities by which their humanity is constituted. The name, therefore, is said to signify the subjects *directly*, the attributes *indirectly*; it *denotes* the subjects, and implies, or involves, or indicates, or, as we shall say henceforth, *connotes*, the attributes. It is a connotative name.

Connotative names have hence been also called *denominative*, because the subject which they denote is denominated by, or receives a name from, the attribute which they connote. Snow and other objects receive the name white because they possess the attribute which is called whiteness; Peter, James, and others receive the name man because they possess the attributes which are considered to constitute humanity. The attribute, or attributes, may, therefore, be said to denominate those objects or to give them a common name.

It has been seen that all concrete general names are connotative. Even abstract names, though the names only of attributes, may, in some instances, be justly considered as connotative; for attributes themselves may have attributes ascribed to them, and a word which denotes attributes may connote an attribute of those attributes. Of this description, for example, is such a word as *fault,* equivalent to *bad* or *hurtful quality.* This word is a name common to many attributes and connotes hurtfulness, an attribute of those various attributes. When, for example, we say that slowness in a horse is a fault, we do not mean that the slow movement, the actual change of pace of the slow horse, is a bad thing, but that the property or peculiarity of the horse, from which it derives that name, the quality of being a slow mover, is an undesirable peculiarity.

In regard to those concrete names which are not general but individual, a distinction must be made.

Proper names are not connotative; they denote the individuals who are called by them, but they do not indicate or imply any attributes as belonging to those individuals. When we name a child by the name Paul or a dog by the name Caesar, these names are simply marks used to enable those individuals to be made subjects of discourse. It may be said, indeed, that we must have had some reason for giving them those names rather than any others, and this is true, but the name, once given, is independent of the reason. A man may have been named John because that was the name of his father; a town may have been named Dartmouth because it is situated at the mouth of the Dart. But it is no part of the signification of the word John that the father of the person so called bore the same name, nor even of the word Dartmouth to be situated at the mouth of the Dart. If sand should choke up the mouth of the river or an earthquake change its course and remove it to a distance from the town, the name of the town would not necessarily be changed. That fact, therefore, can form no part of the signification of the word; for otherwise, when the fact confessedly ceased to be true, no one would any longer think of applying the name. Proper names are attached to the objects themselves and are not dependent on the continuance of any attribute of the object.

But there is another kind of names, which, although they are individual names—that is, predicable only of one object—are really connotative. For, though we may give to an individual a name utterly unmeaning, unmeaningful which we call a proper name—a word which answers the purpose of showing what thing it is we are talking about, but not of telling anything about it; yet a name peculiar to an individual is not necessarily of this description. It may be significant of some attribute or some union of attributes which, being possessed by no object but one, determines the name exclusively to that individual. "The sun" is a name of this description; "God," when used by a monotheist, is another. These, however, are scarcely examples of what we are now attempting to illustrate, being, in strictness of language, general, not individual names, for, however they may be *in fact* predicable only of one object, there is nothing in the meaning of the words themselves which implies this; and, accordingly, when we are imagining and not affirming, we may speak of many suns; and the majority of mankind have believed, and still believe, that there are many gods. But it is easy to produce words which are real instances of connotative individual names. It may be part of the meaning of the connotative name itself, that there can exist but one individual possessing the attribute which it connotes, as, for instance, "the *only* son of John Stiles"; "the *first* emperor of Rome." Or the attribute connoted may be a connection with some determinate event, and the connection may be of such a kind as only one individual could have, or may, at least, be such as only one individual actually had, and this may be implied in the form of the expression. "The father of Socrates" is an example of the one kind (since Socrates could not have had two fathers), "the author of the Iliad," "the murderer of Henri Quatre," of the second. For, though it is conceivable that more persons than one might have participated in the authorship of the Iliad or in the murder of Henri Quatre, the employment of the article *the* implies that, in fact, this was not the case. What is here done by the word *the* is done in other cases by the context; thus, "Caesar's army" is an individual name if it appears from the context that the army meant is that which Caesar commanded in a particular battle. The still more general expressions, "the Roman army," or "the Christian army," may be individualized in a similar manner. Another case of frequent occurrence has already been noticed; it is the following: The name, being a many-worded one, may consist, in the first place, of a *general* name, capable therefore, in itself, of being affirmed of more things than one, but which is, in the second place, so limited by other words joined with it that the entire expression can only be predicated of one object, consistently with the meaning of the general term. This is exemplified in such an instance as the following: "the present prime minister of England." "Prime Minister of England" is a general name; the attributes which it connotes may be possessed by an indefinite number of persons, in succession, however, not simultaneously, since the meaning of the name itself imports (among other things) that there can be only one such person at a time. This being the case, and the application of the name being afterward limited, by the article and the word *present*, to such individuals as possess the attributes at one indivisible point of time, it becomes applicable only to one individual. And, as this appears from the meaning of the name without any extrinsic proof, it is strictly an individual name.

From the preceding observations it will easily be collected that whenever the names given to objects convey any information—that is, whenever they have properly any meaning—the meaning resides not in what they *denote* but in what they *connote*. The only names of objects which connote nothing are *proper* names, and these have, strictly speaking, no signification.

If, like the robber in the Arabian Nights, we make a mark with chalk on a house to enable us to know it again, the mark has a purpose, but it has not properly any meaning. The chalk does not declare anything about the house; it does not mean, "This is such a person's house," or "This is a house which contains booty." The object of making the mark is merely distinction. I say to myself, "All these houses are so nearly alike that if I lose sight of them I shall not again be able to distinguish that which I am now looking at from any of the others; I must therefore contrive to make the appearance of this one house unlike that of the others, that I may hereafter know when I see the mark—not, indeed, any attribute of the house—but simply that it is the same house which I am now looking at." Morgiana chalked all the other houses in a similar manner and defeated the scheme. How? Simply by obliterating the difference of appearance between that house and the others. The chalk was still there, but it no longer served the purpose of a distinctive mark.

When we impose a proper name, we perform an operation in some degree analogous to what the robber intended in chalking the house. We put a mark, not, indeed, upon the object itself but, so to speak, upon the idea of the object. A proper name is but an unmeaning mark which we connect in our minds with the idea of the object, in order that, whenever the mark meets our eyes or occurs to our thoughts, we may think of that individual object. Not being attached to the thing itself, it does not, like the chalk, enable us to distinguish the object when we see it, but it enables us to distinguish it when it is spoken of, either in the records of our own experience or in the discourse of others, to know that what we find asserted in any proposition of which it is the subject is asserted of the individual thing with which we were previously acquainted.

When we predicate of anything its proper name, when we say, pointing to a man, "This is Brown or Smith," or pointing to a city, "It is York," we do not, merely by so doing, convey to the reader any information about them except that those are their names. By enabling him to identify the individuals, we may connect them with information previously possessed by him; by saying, "This is York," we may tell him that it contains the Minster. But this is in virtue of what he has previously heard concerning York, not by anything implied in the name. It is otherwise when objects are spoken of by connotative names. When we say, "The town is built of marble," we give the hearer what may be entirely new information, and this merely by the signification of the many-worded connotative name, "built of marble." Such names are not signs of the mere objects, invented because we have occasion to think and speak of those objects individually, but signs which accompany an attribute, a kind of livery in which the attribute clothes all objects which are recognized as possessing it. They are not mere marks but more, that is to say, significant marks, and the connotation is what constitutes their significance.

ON SENSE AND NOMINATUM
Gottlob Frege

The idea of Sameness[1] challenges reflection. It raises questions which are not quite easily answered. Is Sameness a relation? A relation between objects? Or between names or signs of objects? I assumed the latter alternative in my *Begriffsschrift*. The reasons that speak in its favor are the following: "a = a" and "a = b" are sentences of obviously different cognitive significance: "a = a" is valid *a priori* and according to Kant is to be called analytic, whereas sentences of the form "a = b" often contain very valuable extensions of our knowledge and cannot always be justified in an *a priori* manner. The discovery that it is not a different and novel sun which rises every morning, but that it is the very same, certainly was one of the most consequential ones in astronomy. Even nowadays the re-cognition (identification) of a planetoid or a comet is not always a matter of self-evidence. If we wish to view identity as a relation between the objects designated by the names 'a' and 'b' then "a = b" and "a = a" would not seem different if "a = b" is true. This would express a relation of a thing to itself, namely, a relation such that it holds between everything and itself but never between one thing and another. What one wishes to express with "a = b" seems to be that the signs or names 'a' and 'b' name the same thing; and in that case we would be dealing with those signs: a relation between them would be asserted. But this relation could hold only inasmuch as they name or designate something. The relation, as it were, is mediated through the conection of each sign with the same nomination. This connection, however, is arbitrary. You cannot forbid the use of an arbitrarily produced process or object as a sign for something else. Hence, a sentence like "a = b" would no longer refer to a matter of fact but rather to our manner of designation; no genuine knowledge would be expressed by it. But this is just what we do want to express in many cases. If the sign 'a' differs from the sign 'b' only as an object (here by its shape) but not by its rôle as a sign, that is to say, not in the manner in which it designates anything, then the cognitive significance of "a = a" would be essentially the same as that of "a = b", if "a = b" is true. A difference could arise only if the difference of the signs corresponds to a difference in the way in which the designated objects are given. Let a, b, c be straight lines which connect the corners of a triangle with the midpoints of the opposite sides. The point of intersection of a and b is then the same as that of b and c. Thus we have different

200

designations of the same point and these names ("intersection of a and b', 'intersection of b and c') indicate also the manner in which these points are presented. Therefore the sentence expresses a genuine cognition.

Now it is plausible to connect with a sign (name, word combination, expression) not only the designated object, which may be called the nominatum of the sign, but also the sense (connotation, meaning) of the sign in which is contained the manner and context of presentation. Accordingly, in our examples the *nominata* of the expressions 'the point of intersection of a and b' and 'the point of intersection of b and c' would be the same;—not their senses. The nominata of 'evening star' and 'morning star' are the same but not their senses.

From what has been said it is clear that I here understand by 'sign' or 'name' any expression which functions as a proper name, whose nominatum accordingly is a definite object (in the widest sense of this word). But no concept or relation is under consideration here. These matters are to be dealt with in another essay. The designation of a single object may consist of several words or various signs. For brevity's sake, any such designation will be considered as a proper name.

The sense of a proper name is grasped by everyone who knows the language or the totality of designations of which the proper name is a part;[2] this, however, illuminates the nominatum, if there is any, in a very one-sided fashion. A complete knowledge of the nominatum would require that we could tell immediately in the case of any given sense whether it belongs to the nominatum. This we shall never be able to do.

The regular connection between a sign, its sense and its nominatum is such that there corresponds a definite sense to the sign and to this sense there corresponds again a definite nominatum; whereas not one sign only belongs to one nominatum (object). In different languages, and even in one language, the same sense is represented by different expressions. It is true, there are exceptions to this rule. Certainly there should be a definite sense to each expression in a complete configuration of signs, but the natural languages in many ways fall short of this requirement. We must be satisfied if the same word, at least in the same context, has the same sense. It can perhaps be granted that an expression has a sense if it is formed in a grammatically correct manner and stands for a proper name. But as to whether there is a denotation corresponding to the connotation is hereby not decided. The words 'the heavenly body which has the greatest distance from the earth' have a sense; but it is very doubtful as to whether they have a nominatum. The expression 'the series with the least convergence' has a sense; but it can be proved that it has no nominatum, since for any given convergent series, one can find another one that is less convergent. Therefore the grasping of a sense does not with certainty warrant a corresponding nominatum.

When words are used in the customary manner then what is talked about are their nominata. But it may happen that one wishes to speak about the words themselves or about their senses. The first case occurs when one quotes someone else's words in direct (ordinary) discourse. In this case one's own words immediately name (denote) the words of the other person and only the latter words have the usual nominata. We thus have signs of signs. In writing we make use of quotes enclosing the word-icons. A word-icon in quotes must therefore not be taken in the customary manner.

If we wish to speak of the sense of an expression 'A' we can do this simply through the locution 'the sense of the expression 'A'.' In indirect (oblique) discourse we speak of the sense, e.g., of the words of someone else. From this it becomes clear that also in indirect discourse words do not have their customary nominata; they here name what customarily would be their sense. In order to formulate this succinctly we shall say: words in indirect discourse are used *indirectly*, or have *indirect* nominata. Thus we distinguish the *customary* from the *indirect* nominatum of a word; and similarly, its *customary* sense from its *indirect* sense. The indirect nominatum of a word is therefore its customary sense. Such exceptions must be kept in mind if one wishes correctly to comprehend the manner of connection between signs, senses and nominata in any given case. . . .

The nominatum of a proper name is the object itself which is designated thereby; the image which we may have along with it is quite subjective; the sense lies in between, not subjective as is the image, but not the object either. . . .

We can now recognize three levels of differences of words, expressions and complete sentences. The difference may concern at most the imagery, or else the sense but not the nominatum, or finally also the nominatum. In regard to the first level, we must note that, owing to the uncertain correlation of images with words, a difference may exist for one person that another does not discover. The difference of a translation from the original should properly not go beyond the first level. Among the differences possible in this connection we mention the shadings and colorings which poetry seeks to impart to the senses. These shadings and colorings are not objective. Every listener or reader has to add them in accordance with the hints of the poet or speaker. Surely, art would be impossible without some kinship among human imageries; but just how far the intentions of the poet are realized can never be exactly ascertained.

We shall henceforth no longer refer to the images and picturizations; they were discussed only lest the image evoked by a word be confused with its sense or its nominatum.

In order to facilitate brief and precise expression we may lay down the following formulation:

A proper name (word, sign, sign-compound, expression) expresses its sense, and designates or signifies its nominatum. We let a sign *express* its sense and designate its nominatum. . . .

Let us return to our point of departure now.

When we discerned generally a difference in cognitive significance between "a = a" and "a = b" then this is now explained by the fact that for the cognitive significance of a sentence the sense (the proposition expressed) is no less relevant than its nominatum (the truth-value). If a = b, then the nominatum of 'a' and of 'b' is indeed the same and therefore also the truth-value of "a = b" is the same as that of "a = a". Nevertheless, the sense of 'b' may differ from the sense of 'a'; and therefore the proposition expressed by "a = b" may differ from the proposition expressed by "a = a"; in that case the two sentences do not have the same cognitive significance. Thus, if, as above, we mean by 'judgment' the transition from a proposition to its truth-value, then we can also say that the judgments differ from one another.

NOTES

1. I use this word in the sense of identity and understand "a = b" in the sense of "a is the same as b" or "a and b coincide".

2. In the case of genuinely proper names like 'Aristotle' opinions as regards their sense may diverge. As such may, e.g., be suggested: Plato's disciple and the teacher of Alexander the Great. Whoever accepts this sense will interpret the meaning of the statement "Aristotle was born in Stagira" differently from one who interpreted the sense of 'Aristotle' as the Stagirite teacher of Alexander the Great. As long as the nominatum remains the same, these fluctuations in sense are tolerable. But they should be avoided in the system of a demonstrative science and should not appear in a perfect language.

Questions for Part IV

1. In light of and with reference to David Lewis's paper on truth in fiction, discuss the following passage from *The Hobbit* by J. R. R. Tolkien.

> More important is the matter of Chapter Five. There the true story of the ending of the Riddle Game, as it was eventually revealed (under pressure) by Bilbo to Gandalf, is now given according to the Red Book, in place of the version Bilbo first gave to his friends, and actually set down in his diary. This departure from truth on the part of a most honest hobbit was a portent of great significance. It does not, however, concern the present story, and those who in this edition make their first acquaintance with Hobbitlore need not trouble about it. Its explanation lies in the history of the Ring, as it was set out in the chronicles of the Red Book of Westmarch, and is now told in *The Lord of the Rings*.

2. How many King Arthurs are (were) there? Explain your answer fully in terms of the metaphysics of fictional reference as developed by David Lewis.

3. Lewis refers to an alternative to his account of fictional creatures as "Meinongian." Explain what a Meinongian view of Sherlock Holmes and Dr. Watson would be like. Lewis says that such a view is a difficult one to maintain and that it is far too complex. Why?

4. What does Lewis mean by a "possible world?"

5. Discuss the progression from what Lewis calls Analysis 0 to Analysis 2. Why are the modifications necessary?

6. The murder in "The Adventure of the Speckled Band" is solved by Sherlock Holmes when he identifies the cause of death as a snakebite. The snake, a Russell's viper, Holmes maintained, crawled down a rope and attacked the victim. Russell's vipers, however, are incapable of such movements. Was Holmes, therefore, wrong about the cause or method of the murder? Is the case still unsolved? How does Lewis's analysis of truth in fiction respond to such problems?

7. Kendall L. Walton tells a story of a backwoods villager, Henry, watching a melodrama, who leaps on stage to save the heroine from the evil clutches of the villain. Did Henry save the heroine? Why or why not? Isn't her fate sealed by the author of the play regardless of what Henry does?

8. Can statements *about* a fictional work be true? Take as an example, "Robinson Crusoe was shipwrecked." Are the same statements *in* a fictional work also true?

9. Discuss the problem of whether real people (as opposed to fictional creatures) can exist in fictional worlds. One way to put this issue may be to ask whether Julius Caesar in Shakespeare's play or the movie *Cleopatra* is the real Julius Caesar, the Roman dictator of the first century B.C.

10. John Stuart Mill distinguishes between general names, like "white" and "man" and proper names like "Paul" or "Dartmouth." What are Mill's reasons for drawing that distinction?

11. One way in which Mill defends his label or non-connotative theory of names is by providing the Dartmouth example. Explain and evaluate his account.

12. Contrast Mill's theory that proper names denote but do not connote with the referential theory of Gottlob Frege.

13. Consider the following paradox of identity: There is a cognitive difference between "a = a" and "a = b". But, if "a = b" is true, then a and b must have the same referent. Hence "a = b" logically amounts to nothing more than "a = a". Explain how Frege uses this paradox in his defense of the view that proper names have a sense as well as a denotation.

Part V. Time Travel

It was at ten o'clock today that the first of all time machines began its career. I gave it a last tap, tried all the screws again, put one more drop of oil in the quarty rod, and sat myself in the saddle. I suppose a suicide who holds a pistol to his skull feels much the same wonder at what will come next as I felt then. I took the starting lever in one hand and the stopping one in the other, pressed the first, and almost immediately the second. I seemed to reel; I felt a nightmare sensation of falling; and, looking round, I saw the laboratory exactly as before. Had anything happened? For a moment I suspected that my intellect had tricked me. Then I noted the clock. A moment before, as it seemed, it had stood at a minute or so past ten; now it was nearly half-past three![1]

So H. G. Wells has the Time Traveller report to his amazed friends in *The Time Machine*. Since this classic novel was published in 1895, innumerable stories have been written which explore the intriguing puzzles to which the notion of time travel seems inevitably to give rise.

Many of these stories *seem* to make sense. Aside from the fact that we do not know at present how to do it, there seems nothing incoherent or impossible about travelling to the Pleistocene to hunt dinosaur, or doing historical research in Ancient Greece, or travelling a few thousand years into the future to see whether there will be any humans left by then.

Nonetheless, despite the surface plausibility of such stories, many philosophers have argued that they are inevitably deeply incoherent. The difficulties such writers see, or think they see, are not practical or technical difficulties. We can let the physicists worry about whether the laws of nature permit time travel. The philosophical issue about time travel concerns, not its practical or physical possibility, but whether it is *logically* possible. Many would claim that time travel is impossible in the very strong sense that it is not *consistently imaginable*: in trying to think through the details we will inevitably be led into contradiction.

The contemporary selections in this chapter play devil's advocate. They try to defend the notion of time travel against the charge of inconsistency. Let us take a look at some of the puzzles which many have thought prove time travel impossible. (Most of these puzzles, and others as well, will occur to the attentive reader of Robert A. Heinlein's story "—All You Zombies—", which is our first selection.)

To see the first difficulty, suppose that you step into the time machine and emerge five years in the future. You look up yourself—your future self.[2] He or she invites you to sit down, and the two(?) of you carry on a conversation. Can the person you are talking with really be *you*? You can move your arm just by willing it to move. But a simple experiment reveals that you cannot move the arm of the person to whom you are talking by willing it to move. So that arm is not *your* arm. Similarly, you can see through your eyes. You cannot see through those eyes. So those eyes cannot be yours.

A second apparent problem with the notion of time travel stems from the old cliché that you cannot be in two places at the same time. *If* this cliché is true, then time travel is impossible, since it could lead to situations in which you were in two places at the same time. For example, during the conversation with yourself, aren't you sitting in two different chairs at once? Anything which leads inevitably to an impossibility must itself be impossible.

The notion of time travel also requires us to say things which seem nonsensical, such as "at this very moment she is ten years in the future." It sometimes requires causes to have effects which precede them. It makes possible puzzling causal loops, as when the time traveller visits prehistoric times to try to discover the origin of a human skeleton recently discovered by archaeologists, only to die and become that very skeleton.

Time travel also raises disturbing issues about free will. If I have a good memory, I may remember exactly what my future self said to me during our conversation. In five years, I will find myself engaged once again in the very same conversation, but sitting in the other chair this time. Am I free to say whatever I want? Or do I have to say exactly what I remember myself saying?

These issues are important, and they provide an entry into some deep and perennial philosophical disputes. Jonathan Harrison and David Lewis argue that none of these problems are as serious as they seem at first, and you will want to think about whether you agree. But let us concentrate on the first two difficulties. They are intimately connected with a very deep philosophical dispute about the nature of time. This issue has to do in large part with whether time *moves* or not.

We often speak as though time moved or, what comes to much the same thing, as though we moved through it. A wonderful collection of expressions which make use of this idea is given by Donald C. Williams:

"Time flows or flies or marches, years roll, hours pass. More explicitly we may speak as if the perceiving mind were stationary while time flows by like a river, with the flotsam of events upon it; or as if presentness were a fixed pointer under which the tape of happenings slides; or as if the time sequence were a moving-picture film, unwinding from the dark reel of the future, projected briefly on the screen of the present, and rewound into the dark can of the past. Sometimes, again, we speak as if the time sequence were a stationary plain or ocean on which we voyage, or a variegated river gorge down which we drift; or, in Broad's analogy, as if it were a row of housefronts along which the spotlight of the present plays. 'The essence of nowness,' Santayana says, 'runs like fire along the fuse of time.' "[3]

Now Lewis, in particular, makes use of a very different account of time than this in his defense of time travel. The view that time moves we might call, depending on whether we agree with it or not, either the Common-Sense View or the Naive View. The opposed view asserts that we no more move through time than a highway moves across a state. We might call this the 4-D View of time, since it is often tied to the view that time is a dimension which is strictly analogous to the three spatial dimensions.

We might set out some of the characteristic features of the Naive and 4-D Views of time as follows. But beware: although the different points listed under each view seem to fit together naturally, it may be possible to form a hybrid view which agrees with the Naive View on some points and with the 4-D View on others.

The Naive View makes the following claims: (1) time moves (or we move through it); (2) all of me is present at any time at which I exist; (3) temporal change is a matter of the very same thing having different properties (at different times); and (4) there are no facts yet about what will happen tomorrow: there will not be until tomorrow has come.

The 4-D View rejects each of these claims. Consider first the assertion that time moves, or that we move through it. This seems more mysterious the more you think about it. Ordinary motion is change in location with respect to time: that is, an object moves through space if it is in different places at different times. What would it be, then, to move through *time*? Presumably, to be in different *temporal* locations at differ-ent . . . *somethings*. But what could the *somethings* be? Not *places*, surely, since we are supposed to be able to move through time even when we are standing still. Not *times*, since being in different temporal locations at different times just amounts to being in different temporal locations. You don't have to *move* to be in different temporal locations any more than a highway has to move to be in different spatial locations. And it is hard to think of any other candidates for the elusive *somethings* we are seeking. The advocate of the 4-D View, then, challenges the supporter of the Naive View to provide a coherent explanation of motion through time, and suspects that such an explanation will not be forthcoming.

With regard to the second and third elements of the Naive View, the 4-D supporter appeals to *Leibniz' Law*, otherwise known as the *indiscerni-bility of identicals*. This fairly obvious truth says that if something x is identical with something y, then x has all the same properties as y and vice versa. (Notice that "identical" here means more than just "exactly similar." Something x is identical to something y only if x and y are *the very same thing*.) Thus, for example, if Mark Twain is identical with Samuel Clemens, then any property Mark Twain has—such as the property of being the author of *Huckleberry Finn*, or even the property of being named "Mark Twain"—must be a property which Samuel Clemens has.

But this simple point should make us very dubious about the claim that temporal change consists in the very same thing having different properties at different times. I have changed from being 2' tall to being 5'10". But the very same thing cannot be both 2' and 5'10". So the 4-D View says that change is a matter of different things—temporal parts or stages of me—having different properties. One of my baby stages was 2' tall; my 1985 stage was 5'10" tall. Does this mean that according to the 4-D View I am not the same person I was two years ago, or twenty years ago? No. A person is a collection of temporal parts or stages: my baby stage and my 1985 stage are both *parts*, so to speak, of the enduring object which is me.

The fourth element of the Naive View is the claim that there are no facts as yet about what will happen tomorrow. The proponent of the 4-D view responds by appealing to the *principle of bivalence*, which says that every statement is either true or false: it cannot somehow be neither true nor false. If this principle is true, then statements about the future are either true or false, and so there are facts about the future. (This line of thought is discussed further in Part VII, in Gilbert Ryle's article "It Was to Be.")

The trick behind the 4-D View is to think of ourselves as stretched out over time as well as over space. H. G. Wells put this nicely in *The Time Machine*. In that story the Time Traveller has just argued that a cube with only length, breadth and thickness cannot really exist.

> "There I object," said Filby. "Of course a solid body may exist. All real things—"
> "So most people think. But wait a moment. Can an *instantaneous* cube exist?"
> "Don't follow you," said Filby.
> "Can a cube that does not last for any time at all, have a real existence?"
> Filby became pensive. "Clearly," the Time Traveller proceeded, "any real body must have extension in *four* directions: it must have Length, Breadth, Thickness, and —Duration."[4]

On the 4-D View, just as there is the part of me between my elbow and my shoulder, there is also the part of me between my fifth and sixth birthdays. Just as I am a collection of physical parts—hands, arms, torso, legs, head—so I am a collection of *stages*, from a squalling-infant stage to a sober philosophy-professor stage to a gray-haired, retired-person stage (I hope). (Of course, not just *any* collection of hands, arms, and other body parts will make up a person: they have to be connected in the right way. Similarly, not just any collection of stages will make up a person:

again they must be connected in the right way. The problem of how the stages must be connected to make up a single person is the problem of personal identity, explored in Part II.

My different stages have different properties. They are aware of different things. To some extent they have different beliefs and desires. They have, in particular, different centers of consciousness: this current stage of me can no more get the arm of my five-year-old stage to move by willing it to than I can get someone else's arm to move by willing it to.

We can now see why the 4-D theorist is not bothered by our two objections to time travel. The first objection involved an argument like this:

I can see through my eyes
I cannot see through those eyes
So those eyes are not mine.

We can see that neither premise is quite true. I cannot now see through my five-year-old eyes. So the first premise needs to be modified to:

Any stage of me can see through the eyes *of that stage*.

The second premise should now read:

My current stage cannot see through those eyes.

But the only conclusion which follows from *these* premises is the conclusion that those eyes are not the eyes *of my current stage*. They might still be the eyes of some other stage of me, and so still be my eyes.

The second argument said that you can't be in two places at the same time. But of course that is not quite true. Different *parts* of the same object can be in different places at the same time. If I disassemble my watch, it can simultaneously have parts in different corners of the room. On the 4-D View, my stages are different parts of me. So when I travel to the future and talk with myself, it is really just different (temporal) parts of me which are in different chairs at the same time, and this is no more problematic than having different parts of a watch on different chairs at the same time—is it?

NOTES

1. H. G. Wells, *The War of the Worlds* and *The Time Machine* (Garden City, N.Y.: Doubleday, 1961; *The Time Machine* was first published in 1895), p. 207.

2. I am presupposing that after spending some time in the future, you will return to the present and live out a more or less normal life. Otherwise there will be no "future you" to visit.

3. Donald C. Williams, "The Myth of Passage," *Journal of Philosophy*, vol. 48 no. 15 (1951), 457–72, at 461–2. Williams himself argues against the view which he here expresses so eloquently.

4. Wells, pp. 193–4. Oddly, Wells mixes this part of the 4-D View together with the Naive View that our consciousness moves through time.

"—ALL YOU ZOMBIES—"

Robert A. Heinlein

2217 Time Zone V (EST) 7 Nov 1970 NYC—"Pop's Place": I was polishing a brandy snifter when the Unmarried Mother came in. I noted the time— 10.17 P.M. zone five or eastern time November 7th, 1970. Temporal agents always notice time & date; we must.

The Unmarried Mother was a man twenty-five years old, no taller than I am, immature features and a touchy temper. I didn't like his looks—I never had—but he was a lad I was here to recruit, he was my boy. I gave him my best barkeep's smile.

Maybe I'm too critical. He wasn't swish; his nickname came from what he always said when some nosy type asked him his line: "I'm an unmarried mother." If he felt less than murderous he would add: "—at four cents a word. I write confession stories."

If he felt nasty, he would wait for somebody to make something of it. He had a lethal style of in-fighting, like a female cop—one reason I wanted him. Not the only one.

He had a load on and his face showed that he despised people more than usual. Silently I poured a double shot of Old Underwear and left the bottle. He drank, poured another.

I wiped the bar top. "How's the 'Unmarried Mother' racket?"

His fingers tightened on the glass and he seemed about to throw it at me; I felt for the sap under the bar. In temporal manipulation you try to figure everything, but there are so many factors that you never take needless risks.

I saw him relax that tiny amount they teach you to watch for in the Bureau's training school. "Sorry," I said. "Just asking, 'How's business?' Make it 'How's the weather?' "

He looked sour. "Business is okay. I write 'em, they print 'em, I eat."

I poured myself one, leaned toward him, "Matter of fact," I said, "you write a nice stick—I've sampled a few. You have an amazingly sure touch with the woman's angle."

I was a slip I had to risk; he never admitted what pennames he used. But he was boiled enough to pick up only the last. " 'Woman's angle!' " he repeated with a snort. "Yeah, I know the woman's angle. I should."

"So?" I said doubtfully. "Sisters?"

"No. You wouldn't believe me if I told you."

"Now, now," I answered mildly, "bartenders and psychiatrists learn that nothing is stranger than the truth. Why, son, if you heard the stories I do—well, you'd make yourself rich. Incredible."

"You don't know what 'incredible' means!"

"So? Nothing astonishes me. I've always heard worse."

He snorted again. "Want to bet the rest of the bottle?"

"I'll bet a full bottle." I placed one on the bar.

"Well—" I signaled my other bartender to handle the trade. We were at the far end, a single-stool space that I kept private by loading the bar top by it with jars of pickled eggs and other clutter. A few were at the other end watching the fights and somebody was playing the juke box—private as a bed where we were. "Okay," he began, "to start with, I'm a bastard."

"No distinction around here," I said.

"I mean it," he snapped. "My parents weren't married."

"Still no distinction," I insisted. "Neither were mine."

"When—" He stopped, gave me the first warm look I ever saw on him. "You mean that?"

"I do. A one-hundred-percent bastard. In fact," I added, "No one in my family ever marries. All bastards."

"Don't try to top me—*you're* married." He pointed at my ring.

"Oh, that." I showed it to him. "It just looks like a wedding ring; I wear it to keep women off." That ring is an antique I bought in 1985 from a fellow operative—he had fetched it from pre-Christian Crete. "The Worm Ouroboros . . . the World Snake that eats its own tail, forever without end. A symbol of the Great Paradox."

He barely glanced at it. "If you're really a bastard, you know how it feels. When I was a little girl—"

"Wups!" I said. "Did I hear you correctly?"

"Who's telling this story? When I was a little girl—Look, ever hear of Christine Jorgenson? Or Roberta Cowell?"

"Uh, sex change cases. You're trying to tell me—"

"Don't interrupt or swelp me, I won't talk. I was a foundling, left at an orphanage in Cleveland in 1945 when I was a month old. When I was a little girl, I envied kids with parents. Then, when I learned about sex—and, believe me, Pop, you learn fast in an orphanage—"

"I know."

"—I made a solemn vow that any kid of mine would have both a pop and a mom. It kept me 'pure,' quite a feat in that vicinity—I had to learn to fight to manage it. Then I got older and realized I stood darned little chance of getting married—for the same reason I hadn't been adopted." He scowled. "I was horse-faced and buck-toothed, flat-chested and straight-haired."

"You don't look any worse than I do."

"Who cares how a barkeep looks? Or a writer? But people wanting to adopt pick little blue-eyed golden-haired morons. Later on, the boys want bulging breasts, a cute face, and an Oh-you-wonderful-male manner." He shrugged. "I couldn't compete. So I decided to join the W.E.N.C.H.E.S."

"Eh?"

"Women's Emergency National Corps, Hospitality & Entertainment Section, what they now call 'Space Angels'—Auxiliary Nursing Group, Extraterrestrial Legions."

I knew both terms, once I had them chronized. Although we now use still a third name; it's that elite military service corps: Women's Hospitality Order Refortifying & Encouraging Spacemen. Vocabulary shift is the worst hurdle in time jumps—did you know that "service station" once meant a dispensary for petroleum fractions? Once on an assignment in the Churchill Era a woman said to me, "Meet me at the service station next door"—which is *not* what it sounds; a "service station" (then) wouldn't have a bed in it.

He went on: "It was when they first admitted you can't send men into space for months and years and not relieve the tension. You remember how the wowsers screamed?—that improved my chances, volunteers were scarce. A gal had to be respectable, preferably virgin (they liked to train them from scratch), above average mentally, and stable emotionally. But most volunteers were old hookers, or neurotics who would crack up ten days off Earth. So I didn't need looks; if they accepted me, they would fix my buck teeth, put a wave in my hair, teach me to walk and dance and how to listen to a man pleasingly, and everything else—plus training for the prime duties. They would even use plastic surgery if it would help—nothing too good for Our Boys.

"Best yet, they made sure you didn't get pregnant during your enlistment—and you were almost certain to marry at the end of your hitch. Same way today, A.N.G.E.L.S. marry spacers—they talk the language.

"When I was eighteen I was placed as a 'mother's helper.' This family simply wanted a cheap servant but I didn't mind as I couldn't enlist till I was twenty-one. I did housework and went to night school—pretending to continue my high school typing and shorthand but going to a charm class instead, to better my chances for enlistment.

"Then I met this city slicker with his hundred dollar bills." He scowled. "The no-good actually did have a wad of hundred dollar bills. He showed me one night, told me to help myself.

"But I didn't. I liked him. He was the first man I ever met who was nice to me without trying to take my pants off. I quit night school to see him oftener. It was the happiest time of my life.

"Then one night in the park my pants did come off."

He stopped. I said, "And then?"

"And then *nothing!* I never saw him again. He walked me home and told me he loved me—and kissed me good-night and never came back." He looked grim. "If I could find him, I'd kill him!"

"Well," I sympathized, "I know how you feel. But killing him—just for doing what comes naturally—hmm . . . Did you struggle?"

"Huh? What's that got to do with it?"

"Quite a bit. Maybe he deserves a couple of broken arms for running out on you, but—"

"He deserves worse than that! Wait till you hear. Somehow I kept anyone from suspecting and decided it was all for the best. I hadn't really loved him and probably would never love anybody—and I was more eager to join the W.E.N.C.H.E.S. than ever. I wasn't disqualified, they didn't insist on virgins. I cheered up.

"It wasn't until my skirts got tight that I realized."

Pregnant?"

"The bastard had me higher 'n a kite! Those skinflints I lived with ignored it as long as I could work—then kicked me out and the orphanage wouldn't take me back. I landed in a charity ward surrounded by other big bellies and trotted bedpans until my time came.

"One night I found myself on an operating table, with a nurse saying, 'Relax. Now breathe deeply.'

"I woke up in bed, numb from the chest down. My surgeon came in. 'How do you feel?' he says cheerfully.

" 'Like a mummy.'

" 'Naturally. You're wrapped like one and full of dope to keep you numb. You'll get well—but a Caesarian isn't a hangnail.'

" '"Caesarian?" ' I said. 'Doc—*did I lose the baby?*'

" 'Oh, no. Your baby's fine.'

" 'Oh. Boy or girl?'

" 'A healthy little girl. Five pounds, three ounces.'

"I relaxed. It's something, to have made a baby. I told myself I would go somewhere and tack 'Mrs.' on my name and let the kid think her papa was dead—no orphanage for *my* kid!

"But the surgeon was talking. 'Tell me, uh—' He avoided my name. '— did you ever think your glandular setup was odd?'

"I said, 'Huh? Of course not. What are you driving at?'

"He hesitated. 'I'll give you this in one dose, then a hypo to let you sleep off your jitters. You'll have 'em.'

" 'Why?' I demanded.

" 'Ever hear of the Scottish physician who was female until she was thirty-five?—then had surgery and became legally and medically a man? Got married. All okay.'

" 'What's that got to do with me?'

" 'That's what I'm saying. You're a man.'

"I tried to sit up. '*What?*'

" 'Take it easy. When I opened you, I found a mess. I sent for the Chief of Surgery while I got the baby out, then we held a consultation with you on the table—and worked for hours to salvage what we could. You had two full sets of organs, both immature, but with the female set well enough developed that you had a baby. They could never be any use to you again, so we took them out and rearranged things so that you can develop properly as a man.' He put a hand on me. 'Don't worry. You're young, your bones will readjust, we'll watch your glandular balance— and make a fine young man out of you.'

"I started to cry. 'What about my *baby?*'

" 'Well, you can't nurse her, you haven't milk enough for a kitten. If I were you, I wouldn't see her—put her up for adoption.'

" 'No!'

"He shrugged. 'The choice is yours; you're her mother—well, her parent. But don't worry now; we'll get you well first.'

"Next day they let me see the kid and I saw her daily—trying to get used to her. I had never seen a brand-new baby and had no idea how awful they look—my daughter looked like an orange monkey. My feeling changed to cold determination to do right by her. But four weeks later that didn't mean anything."

"Eh?"

"She was snatched."

" 'Snatched?' "

The Unmarried Mother almost knocked over the bottle we had bet. "Kidnapped—stolen from the hospital nursery!" He breathed hard. "How's that for taking the last thing a man's got to live for?"

"A bad deal," I agreed. "Let's pour you another. No clues?"

"Nothing the police could trace. Somebody came to see her, claimed to be her uncle. While the nurse had her back turned, he walked out with her."

"Description?"

"Just a man, with a face-shaped face, like yours or mine." He frowned. "I think it was the baby's father. The nurse swore it was an older man but he probably used makeup. Who else would swipe my baby? Childless women pull such stunts—but whoever heard of a man doing it?"

"What happened to you then?"

"Eleven more months of that grim place and three operations. In four months I started to grow a beard; before I was out I was shaving regularly . . . and no longer doubted that I was male." He grinned wryly. "I was staring down nurses' necklines."

"Well," I said, "seems to me you came through okay. Here you are, a normal man, making good money, no real troubles. And the life of a female is not an easy one."

He glared at me. "A lot you know about it!"

"So?"

"Ever hear the expression 'a ruined woman'?"

"Mmm, years ago. Doesn't mean much today."

"I was as ruined as a woman can be; that bastard *really* ruined me—I was no longer a woman . . . and I didn't know *how* to be a man."

"Takes getting used to, I suppose."

"You have no idea. I don't mean learning how to dress, or not walking into the wrong rest room; I learned those in the hospital. But how could I *live?* What job could I get? Hell, I couldn't even drive a car. I didn't know a trade; I couldn't do manual labor—too much scar tissue, too tender.

"I hated him for having ruined me for the W.E.N.C.H.E.S., too, but I didn't know how much until I tried to join the Space Corps instead. One look at my belly and I was marked unfit for military service. The medical officer spent time on me just from curiosity; he had read about my case.

"So I changed my name and came to New York. I got by as a fry cook, then rented a typewriter and set myself up as a public stenographer—what a laugh! In four months I typed four letters and one manuscript. The manuscript was for *Real Life Tales* and a waste of paper, but the goof who wrote it, sold it. Which gave me an idea; I bought a stack of confession magazines and studied them." He looked cynical. "Now you know how I get the authentic woman's angle on an unmarried-mother story . . . through the only version I haven't sold—the true one. Do I win the bottle?"

I pushed it toward him. I was upset myself, but there was work to do. I said, "Son, you still want to lay hands on that so-and-so?"

His eyes lighted up—a feral gleam.

"Hold it!" I said. "You wouldn't kill him?"

He chuckled nastily. "Try me."

"Take it easy. I know more about it than you think I do. I can help you. I know where he is."

He reached across the bar. *"Where is he?"*

I said softly, "Let go my shirt, sonny—or you'll land in the alley and we'll tell the cops you fainted." I showed him the sap.

He let go. "Sorry, but where is he?" He looked at me. "And how do you know so much?"

"All in good time. There are records—hospital records, orphanage records, medical records. The matron of your orphanage was Mrs. Fetherage—right? She was followed by Mrs. Gruenstein—right? Your name, as a girl, was 'Jane'—right? And you didn't tell me any of this—right?"

I had him baffled and a bit scared. "What's this? You trying to make trouble for me?"

"No indeed. I've your welfare at heart. I can put this character in your lap. You do to him as you see fit—and I guarantee that you'll get away with it. But I don't think you'll kill him. You'd be nuts to—and you aren't nuts. Not quite."

He brushed it aside. "Cut the noise. *Where is he?*"

I poured him a short one; he was drunk but anger was offsetting it. "Not so fast. I do something for you—you do something for me."

"Uh . . . what?"

"You don't like your work. What would you say to high pay, steady work, unlimited expense account, your own boss on the job, and lots of variety and adventure?"

He stared. "I'd say, 'Get those goddam reindeer off my roof!' Shove it, Pop—there's no such job."

"Okay, put it this way: I hand him to you, you settle with him, then try my job. If it's not all I claim—well, I can't hold you."

He was wavering; the last drink did it. "When d'yuh d'liver 'im?" he said thickly.

"If it's a deal—*right now!*"

He shoved out his hand. "It's a deal!"

I nodded to my assistant to watch both ends, noted the time—2300—started to duck through the gate under the bar—when the juke box blared out: "*I'm My Own Granpaw!*" The service man had orders to load it with old Americana and classics because I couldn't stomach the "music" of 1970, but I hadn't known that tape was in it. I called out, "Shut that off! Give the customer his money back." I added, "Storeroom, back in a moment," and headed there with my Unmarried Mother following.

It was down the passage across from the johns, a steel door to which no one but my day manager and myself had a key; inside was a door to an inner room to which only I had a key. We went there.

He looked blearily around at windowless walls. "Where is 'e?"

"Right away." I opened a case, the only thing in the room; it was a U.S.F.F. Co-ordinates Transformer Field Kit, series 1992, Mod. II—a beauty, no moving parts, weight twenty-three kilos fully charged, and shaped to pass as a suitcase. I had adjusted it precisely earlier that day; all I had to do was to shake out the metal net which limits the transformation field.

Which I did. "Wha's that?" he demanded.

"Time machine," I said and tossed the net over us.

"Hey!" he yelled and stepped back. There is a technique to this; the net has to be thrown so that the subject will instinctively step back *onto* the metal mesh, then you close the net with both of you inside completely—else you might leave shoe soles behind or a piece of foot, or scoop up a slice of floor. But that's all the skill it takes. Some agents con a subject into the net; I tell the truth and use that instant of utter astonishment to flip the switch. Which I did.

1030-V-3 April 1963-Cleveland, Ohio-Apex Bldg.: "Hey!" he repeated "Take this damn thing off!"

"Sorry," I apologized and did so, stuffed the net into the case, closed it. "You said you wanted to find him."

"But—You said that was a time machine!"

I pointed out a window. "Does that look like November? Or New York?" While he was gawking at new buds and spring weather, I reopened the case, took out a packet of hundred dollar bills, checked that the

numbers and signatures were compatible with 1963. The Temporal Bureau doesn't care how much you spend (it costs nothing) but they don't
like unnecessary anachronisms. Too many mistakes and a general court
martial will exile you for a year in a nasty period, say 1974 with its strict
rationing and forced labor. I never make such mistakes, the money was
okay. He turned around and said, "What happened?"

"He's here. Go outside and take him. Here's expense money." I
shoved it at him and added, "Settle him, then I'll pick you up."

Hundred dollar bills have a hypnotic effect on a person not used to
them. He was thumbing them unbelievingly as I eased him into the hall,
locked him out. The next jump was easy, a small shift in era.

1700-V-10 March 1964-Cleveland-Apex Bldg.: There was a notice under
the door saying that my lease expired next week; otherwise the room
looked as it had a moment before. Outside, trees were bare and snow
threatened; I hurried, stopping only for contemporary money and a coat,
hat and topcoat I had left there when I leased the room. I hired a car,
went to the hospital. It took twenty minutes to bore the nursery attendant
to the point where I could swipe the baby without being noticed; we went
back to the Apex Building. This dial setting was more involved as the
building did not yet exist in 1945. But I had precalculated it.

0100-V-20 Sept 1945-Cleveland-Skyview Motel: Field kit, baby, and I arrived in a motel outside town. Earlier I had registered as "Gregory Johnson, Warren, Ohio," so we arrived in a room with curtains closed, windows locked, and doors bolted, and the floor cleared to allow for waver
as the machine hunts. You can get a nasty bruise from a chair where it
shouldn't be—not the chair of course, but backlash from the field.

No trouble. Jane was sleeping soundly; I carried her out, put her in a
grocery box on the seat of a car I had provided earlier, drove to the
orphanage, put her on the steps, drove two blocks to a "service station"
(the petroleum products sort) and phoned the orphanage, drove back in
time to see them taking the box inside, kept going and abandoned the car
near the motel—walked to it and jumped forward to the Apex Building in
1963.

2200-V24 April 1963-Cleveland-Apex Bldg.: I had cut the time rather
fine—temporal accuracy depends on span, except on return to zero. If I
had it right, Jane was discovering, out in the park this balmy spring
night, that she wasn't quite as "nice" a girl as she had thought. I grabbed
a taxi to the home of those skinflints, had the hackie wait around a corner
while I lurked in shadows.

Presently I spotted them down the street, arms around each other. He
took her up on the porch and made a long job of kissing her good-night—
longer than I had thought. Then she went in and he came down the

walk, turned away. I slid into step and hooked an arm in his. "That's all, son," I announced quietly. "I'm back to pick you up."

"*You!*" He gasped and caught his breath.

"Me. Now you know who *he* is—and after you think it over you'll know who *you* are . . . and if you think hard enough, you'll figure out who the baby is . . . and who *I* am."

He didn't answer, he was badly shaken. It's a shock to have it proved to you that you can't resist seducing yourself. I took him to the Apex Building and we jumped again.

2300-VII-12 Aug 1985-Sub Rockies Base: I woke the duty sergeant, showed my I.D., told the sergeant to bed him down with a happy pill and recruit him in the morning. The sergeant looked sour but rank is rank, regardless of era; he did what I said—thinking, no doubt, that the next time we met he might be the colonel and I the sergeant. Which can happen in our corps. "What name?" he asked.

I wrote it out. He raised his eyebrows. "Like so, eh? *Hmm—*"

"You just do your job, Sergeant." I turned to my companion. "Son, your troubles are over. You're about to start the best job a man ever held—and you'll do well. I *know.*"

"But—"

" 'But' nothing. Get a night's sleep, then look over the proposition. You'll like it."

"That you will!" agreed the sergeant. "Look at me—born in 1917—still around, still young, still enjoying life." I went back to the jump room, set everything on preselected zero.

2301-V-7 Nov 1970-NYC-"Pop's Place": I came out of the storeroom carrying a fifth of Drambuie to account for the minute I had been gone. My assistant was arguing with the customer who had been playing "*I'm My Own Granpaw!*" I said, "Oh, let him play it, then unplug it." I was very tired.

It's rough, but somebody must do it and it's very hard to recruit anyone in the later years, since the Mistake of 1972. Can you think of a better source than to pick people all fouled up where they are and give them well-paid, interesting (even though dangerous) work in a necessary cause? Everybody knows now why the Fizzle War of 1963 fizzled. The bomb with New York's number on it didn't go off, a hundred other things didn't go as planned—all arranged by the likes of me.

But not the Mistake of '72; that one is not our fault—and can't be undone; there's no paradox to resolve. A thing either is, or it isn't, now and forever amen. But there won't be another like it; an order dated "1992" takes precedence any year.

I closed five minutes early, leaving a letter in the cash register telling my day manager that I was accepting his offer, so see my lawyer as I was leaving on a long vacation. The Bureau might or might not pick up his payments, but they want things left tidy. I went to the room back of the storeroom and forward to 1993.

2200-VII-12 Jan 1993-Sub Rockies Annex-HQ Temporal DOL: I checked in with the duty officer and went to my quarters, intending to sleep for a week. I had fetched the bottle we bet (after all, I won it) and took a drink before I wrote my report. It tasted foul and I wondered why I had ever liked Old Underwear. But it was better than nothing; I don't like to be cold sober, I think too much. But I don't really hit the bottle either; other people have snakes—*I* have people.

I dictated my report: forty recruitments all okayed by the Psych Bureau—counting my own, which I knew would be okayed. I was here, wasn't I? Then I taped a request for assignment to operations; I was sick of recruiting. I dropped both in the slot and headed for bed.

My eye fell on "The By-Laws of Time," over my bed:

Never Do Yesterday What Should Be Done Tomorrow.
If At Last you Do Succeed, Never Try Again.
A Stitch in Time Saves Nine Billion.
A Paradox May be Paradoctored.
It is Earlier When You Think.
Ancestors Are Just People.
Even Jove Nods.

They didn't inspire me the way they had when I was a recruit; thirty subjective-years of time-jumping wears you down. I undressed and when I got down to the hide I looked at my belly. A Caesarian leaves a big scar but I'm so hairy now that I don't notice it unless I look for it.

Then I glanced at the ring on my finger.

The Snake That Eats Its Own Tail, Forever and Ever . . . I *know* where *I* came from—but *where did all you zombies come from?*

I felt a headache coming on, but a headache powder is one thing I do not take. I did once—and you all went away.

So I crawled into bed and whistled out the light.

You aren't really there at all. There isn't anybody but me—Jane—here alone in the dark.

I miss you dreadfully!

DR. WHO AND THE PHILOSOPHERS OR TIME-TRAVEL FOR BEGINNERS

Jonathan Harrison

. . . Let us suppose I build and enter a machine, pull some levers, and then, when the minute-hand on my watch has revolved twice round the dial, I get out. I find myself in an environment which appears indistinguishable from what I believe England to have been like just over one hundred years ago. The people are dressed as I know they were dressed then, blocks of modern flats are happily replaced by Victorian houses, and the food in the shops is a fraction the price which I am accustomed to pay. Closer enquiry reveals that the people I talk to suppose that Victoria is Queen, the late Earl Russell's grandfather is prime minister, that Albert is not yet dead; and I read in the papers what appear to be contemporary accounts of the opening of the Great Exhibition of 1851.

All this, of course, is possible—in the minimal sense that its description is not contradictory—and it can quite easily be depicted on the screen. But should this happen to me, am I compelled to believe that I now find myself actually transported to the reign of Queen Victoria? There are a number of very compelling reasons why I should *not* believe this.

DIFFICULTIES

For one thing, I can argue as follows. I am as certain as I can be of anything that I was not alive in 1851, and did not witness any events which took place at that time. Hence the events that I am witnessing, whatever else they may be, are not the events of 1851.

It is worth noticing that an analogous argument will not apply to ordinary *space* travel. Where this is concerned, one cannot argue that because up to now I have never been to the top of Mount Everest, this place at which I find myself cannot be the top of Mount Everest. It may be true up to the time of completing my journey thither, but subsequently false, that I have never been to the top of Mount Everest; it cannot be true up to the time of my ostensible journey into time that I did not visit the Great Exhibition of 1851, but after this time true that I *did* visit it. The sentence "I am not at the top of Mount Everest" can be used at some times to make a statement which is true, at other later times to make a statement which is false. The sentence "I was not at the Great Exhibition", if it can be used at one time to make a true statement, must make a true statement when it is used at any subsequent time. If I say at one time that I was not at the Great Exhibition, then I will be contradicting myself if I say at any later time that I was at the Great Exhibition, though if I say at one time that I am not at the top of Mount Everest, I will not be contradicting myself if I say at some later time that I am at the top of Mount Everest. Hence it cannot be argued that, up to the time of my journey in time, it was the case that I was not at the Great Exhibition, but after that time it is the case that I was at it, though it can be argued that up to the time of a journey in space it was true that I was never at the top of Mount Everest, though after this journey this is false. Of course, one might wish to contend that what happens as a result of my journey into time is not so much that the proposition "Harrison was not at the Great Exhibition" changes from being true to being false (or, if you are a purist, that the sentence "Harrison was not at the Great Exhibition" ceases to express a true proposition, and comes to express a false one) as that, after my journey, it comes to be the case that the proposition "Harrison was never at the Great Exhibition" never *was* true. This position is also contradictory. For it amounts to saying that up to a given time, the proposition "Harrison never was at the Great Exhibition" is true, but after that time it never was true, which implies that before that time it was both true and false.

If time-travel were possible, a number of other oddities would occur. Since I start on my journey in 1971, and finish it in 1851, I arrive before I start. Since, after I arrive, I remember the things which "happened" to me before I started—for example, I remember building the machine and "setting out"—I must remember things before they happened. Since the things I think and do after I "arrive" will be determined to some extent by the things I thought and did before I started, some effects will precede their causes. On any normal journey, it is possible to ask where my body, and my conveyance, if I have one, are at any given moment between the time I start and the time I arrive. Is it possible to ask the same question about my journey to 1851? And with any normal journey it is possible to select, within certain obvious limits, one's route and one's speed of travel, the scenery one witnesses on the way being largely a function of these. Is there anything analogous to a route or a velocity in my journey into the past, and what sort of scenery may I be expected to behold as I travel? Lastly: if anyone has travelled from Nottingham in 1971 to London in 1851, the person who arrives in London in 1851 must be the *same* person that leaves Nottingham in 1971; it would normally, however, be accepted as an absolutely conclusive reason for thinking that a person viewing the Great Exhibition in 1851 could not be identical with any man living in 1971, that no man living in 1971 had at that time yet been born.

ALTERNATIVE EXPLANATIONS

Hence, if the events depicted in science fiction were actually to happen to me, perhaps I ought to look for alternative explanations of them, explanations which do not involve me in saying that I have travelled into the past. Such explanations are not at first sight difficult to find. Perhaps my machine does not transport me to 1851, but miraculously enables me to witness what was then occurring; the notion that we may witness events long after thay have happened seems in any case forced upon us by the fact that light has a finite velocity. Indeed we can imagine the Great Exhibition sending light waves out into space which, in 1971, are reflected by some cosmic mirror back to earth, where they are picked up by a phantastically powerful telescope. Obviously, however, this will not remotely satisfy the writers of science fiction, for they conceive of me not simply as witnessing past events, but as living in a past environment, and working changes therein.

One might try to explain time-travel by means of hallucinations; either by an hallucination of people living in 1851 of being alive in 1971, or an hallucination of people living in 1971 of having visited the England of 1851. The hallucination of these 1971 people, however, will not explain the absence of the bodies of the 1971 people for the period during which they have the experiences which are alleged to be hallucinatory, or the fact that they "return" with accurate information which cannot be obtained from history books. And the hallucination of the 1851 people cannot explain how it is that people without past histories appear in Victorian England wearing twentieth-century clothes, and possessing scientific knowledge and equipment which cannot possibly be obtained by contemporary men by normal means.

Alternatively, one might imagine oneself transported to some remote region of space, which contains a solar system, just like our solar system, and an earth, just like our earth, in which are taking place events exactly like those which took place on this earth one hundred and twenty years ago. More bizarre still, one might conceive that the universe contains not just one system of spatially related objects, but many—perhaps an infinite number, even. Though every object in one system is spatially related to every other object in the same system, objects in different systems are not spatially related to one another at all. It may be, then, that my time machine has "transported" me not to another part of this spatial system, but to a different spatial system altogether, which system contains a solar system, just like ours, and an earth, just like ours, on which is now occurring events which exactly resemble those events which took place in London one hundred and twenty years ago. I cannot get there by normal travelling, of course, for, in whichever direction and for however long I go, I come across only objects which are contained in this spatial system. But I might be transported thither in my dreams, and would have to say that I was so transported if, while my body was asleep in this world, I experienced another world, as coherent as this, which is also visited by other people when they are asleep. Heaven, which also cannot be reached on wings, but by faith and good works only, might be such a system—and must be, I think, if we are to take the Christian doctrine of the resurrection of the body at all seriously. . . .

MEMORY

The difficulty with time-travel, that, if it is possible, the time-traveller will arrive before he departs, is not insuperable. If one defines "departure", as the first event, and "arrival" as the last event, in that sequence of events which constitutes a journey, then, of course, it is contradictory to talk of arrival preceding departure. But if you define "departure" by means of a description of the events which usually take place when a departure occurs, e.g., as getting into a conveyance, rather than getting out of it, and so on, and define "arrival" correspondingly, then it is a synthetic, not an analytic, proposition that one departs before one arrives, and no contradiction is involved in supposing that one departs in 1971, and arrives in 1851.

The difficulty that, if time-travel were to occur, the time-travellers would remember events in their lives before they happened, can also be overcome. There is no difficulty, of course, in our ability to remember facts about the future, such as that tomorrow is Saturday, on which day we have an appointment. But normally we cannot be described as remembering certain things happening to us unless those things have happened, and, in the case of our time-travellers, they have not happened (though they will). However, one cannot control reality by quibbling over the use of a word, and, if there are people who have what feels to them like memory-knowledge of events which have not yet taken place, but which we can explain only by supposing that at some future date these things will take place, then we will have no alternative but to find a word to describe what they experience, and the cognitive capacity thereby manifested. I propose simply to talk of "remembering", in quotes, or of pseudo-memories. Their "knowledge" of the future—if we are prepared to dignify by that name the tales told by alleged time-travellers of what they "remember" about what will happen to them in the future—will be immediate rather than inferred. . . .

ROUTE, VELOCITY AND SCENERY

When it comes to the *route* which the time machine must take to get from Nottingham in 1971 to London in 1851, I think a specification of this route—if there is a route at all, for we shall see later that there need not be one—must be exactly like a specification of the route from London in

1851 to Nottingham in 1971. If we start in London in 1851, and arrive in Nottingham in 1971, we occupy all the intermediate places at intermediate times, and the same applies to starting in Nottingham in 1971 and arriving in London in 1851. The problem is "What makes us say we started in Nottingham in 1971, rather than that we started in London in 1851?" There will, however, be these differences between a journey from Nottingham in 1971 to London in 1851 and a journey from London in 1851 to Nottingham in 1971. In the first place, the events such as people getting into the machine will, where the first journey is concerned, take place in 1971, and the events described as getting out of the machine will take place in 1851, whereas, where the second journey is concerned, they will take place in the reverse order. In the second place, whereas with a journey from Nottingham to London, especially such a slow one, we may expect our conveyance to be in a physically much poorer condition in 1971 than it is in 1851, with the "backwards" journey we may expect our conveyance to be in rather worse condition in 1851 than in 1971. The important differences, however, are those which take place inside the machine, and especially to the people travelling in it. We must remember that to the travellers, while they are in the machine, the journey from Nottingham in 1971 to London in 1851 seems much like any other journey. Their watches will appear to be behaving in a perfectly normal way; two hours, we have supposed, pass, according to their watches, between the time they depart and the time they arrive. On their way they make plans about what they will do when they arrive, and frame intentions of what to do in the machine while they are on their way, which plans and intentions they carry out in what seems to them a perfectly normal way. For example, they decide to boil a kettle for tea, boil the kettle, brew the tea, and drink it. There will seem to them to be no difference between this and any other similar domestic episode.

However, though from their point of view their boiling the kettle seems to possess no unusual characteristics—the hands on their watch, let us suppose, read 2.00 when they started, 2.20 when they put the kettle on, 2.30 when they take it off and 2.35 when they pour out the tea—in fact, if we assume that each minute by their watches, during their 120 minute journey represents a year by the sun of the one hundred and twenty years with their journey took—their journey, viewed from outside the machine, is somewhat extraordinary. They must have decided to put the kettle on some time before 1951, actually put it on in 1951, poured the boiling water into the tea-pot in 1941, and poured out the tea in 1936. Hence, though any experiments they make, using their own watches, to establish whether time-travel makes a difference to the laws of nature, will show that it does not, such laws, by the sun, or the clocks of observers synchronised with it, will be governing events which happen both in the reverse order, and much more slowly, than is usual.

If there are windows to their machine, what sort of scenery may we suppose them to see? So far as their instrumental readings go, of course, things happening outside the machine will seem to them to be happening in the reverse order from the order in which they will be happening if we date them by the sun. They will look at their watches, and get recordings as of summer, and then, fifteen seconds later (or three months earlier) they will get recordings as of spring. If they actually see, through the windows of their machine, things happening outside their machine, then what they see would be the leaves turning from brown to green, and the sun rising in the West and setting in the East. Though light from the green leaves will fall on their retinas earlier, by clocks outside their machine, than light from the brown leaves, and though light from the sun in the East will fall on their retinas earlier, as measured by clocks outside their machine, than light from the sun in the West, the former will in each case be later, measured by the clocks *inside* the machine, and, *ex hypothesi*, it is the latter which determines what they see. Whether such a state of affairs really is (logically) possible, I cannot pretend to say. The oddest feature of it, of course, will be the fact that, dated by normal clocks, they will execute their plans before they conceive them, and solve their problems before these have occurred to them. . . .

There is, however, one consequence of the suggestion that their machine, like ordinary machines, continually exists from the time of their departure to the time of their arrival, which would make the building of such a machine, to put it mildly, difficult, if not logically impossible. We have seen that the truth-value of no proposition about the past can be altered by anything they do. Hence, if anyone is to travel from Nottingham in 1971 to London in 1851 by means of a machine which exists at all times intermediate between these two times, and is, at any one of these times, situated at some place, then, when men start to build such a machine, there must, at the very moment they build it, be such a machine already in existence. It does not have to be in the place they built it at the moment they build it. But at the time, or shortly after it, that they switch the levers which start them on their journey, the machine they have built must be identical with the machine which has existed since it arrived in London in 1851. Somehow or other they must construct a machine which merges, when they pull the lever, with an already existing machine, as two drops of water merge—but not quite like this, for they must merge not to frame a double machine, but just one machine. This obviously presents both technical and logical difficulties. The logical difficulties concern whether we are to say that the machine they build is numerically identical with the machine which travels. If you consider the instant at which the machine which travels starts on its journey into the past, there is just one machine, for this is the moment at which the two machines become one, but what are you to say at instants before this? One thing you can say is that there are two machines, one of which has existed since 1851, and the other which has existed from the time it was built in 1971, which, at an instant in 1971, unite into one and then cease to exist. Another thing you can say is that there is just one machine, for the machine at the time it is fully built is numerically identical with the machine at the moment when I pull the lever and it merges with the machine which travels, and the machine which travels is identical with earlier phases in its history, in particular with the machine which arrives in London in 1851, and "being numerically identical with" is supposed to be a transitive relation. This, however, gives rise to the difficulty that one and the same machine can be at two places at once. What is worse, it gives rise to the difficulty that the people in the machine can be in two places at once, and, worse still, that one manifestation of them—the one in the machine—has "memories" of what the other manifestation of them, the one outside the machine, is actually doing. And, of course, these difficulties will repeat themselves at the time of the arrival of the machine. For at this time, the time when the machine stops its journey, and the men inside get out, the machine they have evacuated will continue to exist after they have left it; hence, again, there will be two machines, the one in which they made their journey, and the one which they left lying about after they had completed their journey—or should one, again, speak of one machine located in one place being numerically identical with a machine situated at a different place at the same time? . . .

In view of these simply enormous difficulties, perhaps the time-travellers ought to abandon the idea of travelling to London in 1851 in a machine which continuously exists, as normal machines do, from the time of its departure to the time of its arrival, and adopt the method of projection instead. There are two possible ways of understanding this method. One is that the machine somehow leaves the "space-time continuum" at one point, *i.e.*, 1971, and enters it at another point, *i.e.*, 1851. I cannot, however, make any sense at all of the notion of a solid object leaving the space-time continuum and existing in a place outside space, and travelling for a period of time outside time, which notion would appear to be contradictory. The other is that the machine and its inhabitants simply cease to exist at the moment the lever is pulled, but that, nevertheless, both it and they are numerically identical with a machine and people who "miraculously" sprang into existence in 1851, which means that the 1851 machine will be exactly similar to the 1971 machine, and the 1851 inhabitants will be exactly similar to the 1971 inhabitants; in particular, the 1851 inhabitants will have veridical pseudo-memories of events in the lives of the 1971 inhabitants. . . .

GETTING BACK

Presumably anyone building a time-machine does so because he wants to find out things about the past and to witness and participate in events which have already taken place. If I am right in thinking that he can witness these events only if the proposition that he has witnessed these events is already true, this seems to make nonsense of his enterprise. For this, surely, will not satisfy him. It does not make any difference to him, we might say, that there was in the past someone whom we have simply agreed to say is numerically identical with him, and who has witnessed the events he wants to witness, and has pseudo-memories of doing the things he is now doing. For it makes no difference to him now, or at any future date, whether there was such a person, and whether we by mere verbal fiat decide to say that this person is he. Nor will he be satisfied even by the time he pulls the levers in his time machine, and the machine merges with an already existing machine in which the laws of nature are operating backwards, or disappears from the face of the earth. For this will simply be to accomplish his own annihilation, a fate which can seem no less dreadful by its being the necessary condition of there having been this previous man alive in 1851, for this previous man is also and already annihilated. What he wants is not to destroy himself in order that there may have been a man numerically identical with him alive in 1851, but to witness in the future events which have taken place in the past. This, it seems, is logically impossible. What he may have, as a possibly inferior substitute, is for him, at some time in the future, to have memories of having participated in past events. These he can have if he can not only travel to the past, but travel back again to the future.

Travelling back to the future presents no more—in fact, it presents fewer—difficulties than travelling to the past. Either he must, by re-entering his machine and pulling the levers, cause there to spring into existence at some time later than 1971 a machine containing a being with memories of what he did in 1851 and 1971 (and of the pseudo-memories he had in 1851 of what he was going to do in 1971) or he must, by pulling these levers, cause processes in the machine to decelerate (though not to reverse) in which case he will get to a date subsequent to his departure in say a couple of hours, measured by the clocks in his machine, though of course, his journey will take the usual length of time as measured by revolutions of the earth round the sun. From his point of view, however, decelerating in this way will have the advantage that he will age but little—for we are assuming that his aging will be proportionate to the clocks in the machine, not to normal clocks—and the time will pass more quickly, for 120 years will seem like 120 minutes to him. But the conceptual difficulties included in this process are much less formidable than the process of travelling backwards in time, described earlier, and only a little more difficult than those involved if he were to be put in a deep freeze for 120 years. One, however, does deserve mention. At the time he pulls the lever in 1971, in order to reach 1851 the machine in which he returns must already be in existence, so when he builds the machine in which to undertake his journey there will be the machine he is building, the machine in which he is travelling backwards, and the machine in which he is returning. If he makes many such trips, the number of machines in existence will be proportionately increased.

MORAL

I want to end by drawing a moral. It is still quite commonly held that the function of the philosopher is not so much to indulge in speculation about the nature of the universe, as to map the logical geography of propositions and arguments. Philosophers should not attempt to tell you what propositions are true or false, but confine themselves to telling you such things as what propositions would be true, if certain other propositions were true. I certainly do not wish to suggest that this is not one of a philosopher's functions, though the task of speculation and the task of mapping the logical geography of propositions do not seem to me as irrevocably divorced as people used to think. I should like to say, however, that one task of the philosopher is neither simply to plot logical geography, nor to speculate about the actual nature of the universe, but, by an exercise of the imagination, to enlarge our ideas about what possible universes there might be. It may even be that our knowledge of this universe is restricted by the fact that we have preconceived notions about what it must be like, and that using our imaginations may to some extent free us from these logical blinkers, in which case we might discover that the universe is a more interesting place than we had supposed. Using one's imagination is not so very far from plotting logical maps, after all. Recently philosophers have used logic for the Mrs. Grundyish task of telling us what we may *not* say, or what, if we accept certain things, we *must* also say. They have told us things of the form 'p and q imply r' and 'p and q are incompatible with not-r'. But that p and q imply neither r nor not-r is just as much a logical truth as that they do imply one of them, and consists in the assertion that the truth of p, q and r (or of p, q and not-r) is jointly possible. In exercising our imaginations we are incidentally discovering propositions of this form, for if something can be imagined as happening, even though it does not happen, then certain propositions, though found or supposed to be true together in actual fact, are not logically bound together, and in discovering this logical truth we are freeing ourselves from the shackles which blind us to what is possible, and so to what *may* actually be the case. Though reading science fiction is one excellent way of acquiring the necessary imaginative insight, writing it is, I dare say, even better. At any rate, I have made an attempt.

THE PARADOXES OF TIME TRAVEL
David Lewis

Time travel, I maintain, is possible. The paradoxes of time travel are oddities, not impossibilities. They prove only this much, which few would have doubted: that a possible world where time travel took place would be a most strange world, different in fundamental ways from the world we think is ours.

I shall be concerned here with the sort of time travel that is recounted in science fiction. Not all science fiction writers are clear-headed, to be sure, and inconsistent time travel stories have often been written. But some writers have thought the problems through with great care, and their stories are perfectly consistent.[1]

If I can defend the consistency of some science fiction stories of time travel, then I suppose parallel defenses might be given of some controversial physical hypotheses, such as the hypothesis that time is circular or the hypothesis that there are particles that travel faster than light. But I shall not explore these parallels here.

What is time travel? Inevitably, it involves a discrepancy between time and time. Any traveler departs and then arrives at his destination; the time elapsed from departure to arrival (positive, or perhaps zero) is the duration of the journey. But if he is a time traveler, the separation in time between departure and arrival does not equal the duration of his journey. He departs; he travels for an hour, let us say; then he arrives. The time he reaches is not the time one hour after his departure. It is later, if he has traveled toward the future; earlier, if he has traveled toward the past. If he has traveled far toward the past, it is earlier even than his departure. How can it be that the same two events, his departure and his arrival, are separated by two unequal amounts of time?

It is tempting to reply that there must be two independent time dimensions; that for time travel to be possible, time must be not a line but a plane.[2] Then a pair of events may have two unequal separations if they are separated more in one of the time dimensions than in the other. The lives of common people occupy straight diagonal lines across the plane of time, sloping at a rate of exactly one hour of time$_1$ per hour of time$_2$. The life of the time traveler occupies a bent path, of varying slope.

On closer inspection, however, this account seems not to give us time travel as we know it from the stories. When the traveler revisits the days of his childhood, will his playmates be there to meet him? No; he has not reached the part of the plane of time where they are. He is no longer separated from them along one of the two dimensions of time, but he is still separated from them along the other. I do not say that two-dimensional time is impossible, or that there is no way to square it with the usual conception of what time travel would be like. Nevertheless I shall say no more about two-dimensional time. Let us set it aside, and see how time travel is possible even in one-dimensional time.

The world—the time traveler's world, or ours—is a four-dimensional manifold of events. Time is one dimension of the four, like the spatial dimensions except that the prevailing laws of nature discriminate between time and the others—or rather, perhaps, between various timelike dimensions and various spacelike dimensions. (Time remains one-dimensional, since no two timelike dimensions are orthogonal.) Enduring things are timelike streaks: wholes composed of temporal parts, or *stages*, located at various times and places. Change is qualitative difference between different stages—different temporal parts—of some enduring thing, just as a "change" in scenery from east to west is a qualitative difference between the eastern and western spatial parts of the landscape. If this paper should change your mind about the possibility of time travel, there will be a difference of opinion between two different temporal parts of you, the stage that started reading and the subsequent stage that finishes.

If change is qualitative difference between temporal parts of something, then what doesn't have temporal parts can't change. For instance, numbers can't change; nor can the events of any moment of time, since they cannot be subdivided into dissimilar temporal parts. (We have set aside the case of two-dimensional time, and hence the possibility that an event might be momentary along one time dimension but divisible along the other.) It is essential to distinguish change from "Cambridge change," which can befall anything. Even a number can "change" from being to not being the rate of exchange between pounds and dollars. Even a momentary event can "change" from being a year ago to being a year and a day ago, or from being forgotten to being remembered. But these are not genuine changes. Not just any old reversal in truth value of a time-sensitive sentence about something makes a change in the thing itself.

A time traveler, like anyone else, is a streak through the manifold of space-time, a whole composed of stages located at various times and places. But he is not a streak like other streaks. If he travels toward the past he is a zig-zag streak, doubling back on himself. If he travels toward the future, he is a stretched-out streak. And if he travels either way instantaneously, so that there are no intermediate stages between the stage that departs and the stage that arrives and his journey has zero duration, then he is a broken streak.

I asked how it could be that the same two events were separated by two unequal amounts of time, and I set aside the reply that time might have two independent dimensions. Instead I reply by distinguishing time itself, *external time* as I shall also call it, from the *personal time* of a particular time traveler: roughly, that which is measured by his wristwatch. His journey takes an hour of his personal time, let us say; his wristwatch reads an hour later at arrival than at departure. But the arrival is more than an hour after the departure in external time, if he travels toward the future; or the arrival is before the departure in external time (or less than an hour after), if he travels toward the past.

That is only rough. I do not wish to define personal time operationally, making wristwatches infallible by definition. That which is measured by my own wristwatch often disagrees with external time, yet I am no time traveler; what my misregulated wristwatch measures is neither time itself nor my personal time. Instead of an operational definition, we need a functional definition of personal time: it is that which occupies a certain role in the pattern of events that comprise the time traveler's life. If you take the stages of a common person, they manifest certain regularities with respect to external time. Properties change continuously as you go along, for the most part, and in familiar ways. First come infantile stages. Last come senile ones. Memories accumulate. Food digests. Hair grows. Wristwatch hands move. If you take the stages of a time traveler instead, they do not manifest the common regularities with respect to external time. But there is one way to assign coordinates to the time traveler's stages, and one way only (apart from the arbitrary choice of a zero point), so that the regularities that hold with respect to this assignment match those that commonly hold with respect to external time. With respect to the correct assignment properties change continuously as you go along, for the most part, and in familiar ways. First come infantile stages. Last come senile ones. Memories accumulate. Food digests. Hair grows. Wristwatch hands move. The assignment of coordinates that yields this match is the time traveler's personal time. It isn't really time, but it plays the role in his life that time plays in the life of a common person. It's enough like time so that we can—with due caution—transplant our temporal vocabulary to it in discussing his affairs. We can say without contradiction, as the time traveler prepares to set out, "Soon he will be in the past." We mean that a stage of him is slightly later in his personal time, but much earlier in external time, than the stage of him that is present as we say the sentence.

We may assign locations in the time traveler's personal time not only to his stages themselves but also to the events that go on around him. Soon Caesar will die, long ago; that is, a stage slightly later in the time traveler's personal time than his present stage, but long ago in external time, is simultaneous with Caesar's death. We could even extend the assignment of personal time to events that are not part of the time traveler's life, and not simultaneous with any of his stages. If his funeral in ancient

Egypt is separated from his death by three days of external time and his death is separated from his birth by three score years and ten of his personal time, then we may add the two intervals and say that his funeral follows his birth by three score years and ten and three days of *extended personal time*. Likewise a bystander might truly say, three years after the last departure of another famous time traveler, that "he may even now— if I may use the phrase—be wandering on some plesiosaurus-haunted oolitic coral reef, or beside the lonely saline seas of the Triassic Age."[3] If the time traveler does wander on an oolitic coral reef three years after his departure in his personal time, then it is no mistake to say with respect to his extended personal time that the wandering is taking place "even now".

We may liken intervals of external time to distances as the crow flies, and intervals of personal time to distances along a winding path. The time traveler's life is like a mountain railway. The place two miles due east of here may also be nine miles down the line, in the westbound direction. Clearly we are not dealing here with two independent dimensions. Just as distance along the railway is not a fourth spatial dimension, so a time traveler's personal time is not a second dimension of time. How far down the line some place is depends on its location in three-dimensional space, and likewise the locations of events in personal time depend on their locations in one-dimensional external time.

Five miles down the line from here is a place where the line goes under a trestle; two miles further is a place where the line goes over a trestle; these places are one and the same. The trestle by which the line crosses over itself has two different locations along the line, five miles down from here and also seven. In the same way, an event in a time traveler's life may have more than one location in his personal time. If he doubles back toward the past, but not too far, he may be able to talk to himself. The conversation involves two of his stages, separated in his personal time but simultaneous in external time. The location of the conversation in personal time should be the location of the stage involved in it. But there are two such stages; to share the locations of both, the conversation must be assigned two different locations in personal time.

The more we extend the assignment of personal time outwards from the time traveler's stages to the surrounding events, the more will such events acquire multiple locations. It may happen also, as we have already seen, that events that are not simultaneous in external time will be assigned the same location in personal time—or rather, that at least one of the locations of one will be the same as at least one of the locations of the other. So extension must not be carried too far, lest the location of events in extended personal time lose its utility as a means of keeping track of their roles in the time traveler's history.

A time traveler who talks to himself, on the telephone perhaps, looks for all the world like two different people talking to each other. It isn't quite right to say that the whole of him is in two places at once, since neither of the two stages involved in the conversation is the whole of him, or even the whole of the part of him that is located at the (external) time of the conversation. What's true is that he, unlike the rest of us, has two different complete stages located at the same time at different places. What reason have I, then, to regard him as one person and not two? What unites his stages, including the simultaneous ones, into a single person? The problem of personal identity is especially acute if he is the sort of time traveler whose journeys are instantaneous, a broken streak consisting of several unconnected segments. Then the natural way to regard him as more than one person is to take each segment as a different person. No one of them is a time traveler, and the peculiarity of the situation comes to this: all but one of these several people vanish into thin air, all but another one appear out of thin air, and there are remarkable resemblances between one at his appearance and another at his vanishing. Why isn't that at least as good a description as the one I gave, on which the several segments are all parts of one time traveler?

I answer that what unites the stages (or segments) of a time traveler is the same sort of mental, or mostly mental, continuity and connectedness that unites anyone else. The only difference is that whereas a common person is connected and continuous with respect to external time, the time traveler is connected and continuous only with respect to his own personal time. Taking the stages in order, mental (and bodily) change is mostly gradual rather than sudden, and at no point is there sudden change in too many different respects all at once. (We can include position in external time among the respects we keep track of, if we like. It may change discontinuously with respect to personal time if not too much else changes discontinuously along with it.) Moreover, there is not too much change altogether. Plenty of traits and traces last a lifetime. Finally, the connectedness and the continuity are not accidental. They are explicable; and further, they are explained by the fact that the properties of each stage depend causally on those of the stages just before in personal time, the dependence being such as tends to keep things the same.[4]

To see the purpose of my final requirement of causal continuity, let us see how it excludes a case of counterfeit time travel. Fred was created out of thin air, as if in the midst of life; he lived a while, then died. He was created by a demon, and the demon had chosen at random what Fred was to be like at the moment of his creation. Much later someone else, Sam, came to resemble Fred as he was when first created. At the very moment when the resemblance became perfect, the demon destroyed Sam. Fred and Sam together are very much like a single person: a time traveler whose personal time starts at Sam's birth, goes on to Sam's destruction and Fred's creation, and goes on from there to Fred's death. Taken in this order, the stages of Fred-*cum*-Sam have the proper connectedness and continuity. But they lack causal continuity, so Fred-

cum-Sam is not one person and not a time traveler. Perhaps it was pure coincidence that Fred at his creation and Sam at his destruction were exactly alike; then the connectedness and continuity of Fred-*cum*-Sam across the crucial point are accidental. Perhaps instead the demon remembered what Fred was like, guided Sam toward perfect resemblance, watched his progress, and destroyed him at the right moment. Then the connectedness and continuity of Fred-*cum*-Sam has a causal explanation, but of the wrong sort. Either way, Fred's first stages do not depend causally for their properties on Sam's last stages. So the case of Fred and Sam is rightly disqualified as a case of personal identity and as a case of time travel.

We might expect that when a time traveler visits the past there will be reversals of causation. You may punch his face before he leaves, causing his eye to blacken centuries ago. Indeed, travel into the past necessarily involves reversed causation. For time travel requires personal identity— he who arrives must be the same person who departed. That requires causal continuity, in which causation runs from earlier to later stages in the order of personal time. But the orders of personal and external time disagree at some point, and there we have causation that runs from later to earlier stages in the order of external time. Elsewhere I have given an analysis of causation in terms of chains of counterfactual dependence, and I took care that my analysis would not rule out causal reversal *a priori*.[5] I think I can argue (but not here) that under my analysis the direction of counterfactual dependence and causation is governed by the direction of other *de facto* asymmetries of time. If so, then reversed causation and time travel are not excluded together, but can occur only where there are local exceptions to these asymmetrics. As I said at the outset, the time traveler's world would be a most strange one.

Stranger still, if there are local—but only local—causal reversals, then there may also be causal loops: closed causal chains in which some of the causal links are normal in direction and others are reversed. (Perhaps there must be loops if there is reversal; I am not sure.) Each event on the loop has a causal explanation, bieng caused by events elsewhere on the loop. That is not to say that the loop as a whole is caused or explicable. It may not be. Its inexplicability is especially remarkable if it is made up of the sort of causal processes that transmit information. Recall the time traveler who talked to himself. He talked to himself about time travel, and in the course of the conversation his older self told his younger self how to build a time machine. That information was available in no other way. His older self knew how because his younger self had been told and the information had been preserved by the causal processes that constitute recording, storage, and retrieval of memory traces. His younger self knew, after the conversation, because his older self had known and the information had been preserved by the causal processes that constitute telling. But where did the information come from in the first place? Why did the whole affair happen? There is simply no answer. The parts of the loop are explicable, the whole of it is not. Strange! But not impossible, and not too different from inexplicabilities we are already inured to. Almost everyone agrees that God, or the Big Bang, or the entire infinite past of the universe, or the decay of a tritium atom, is uncaused and inexplicable. Then if these are possible, why not also the inexplicable causal loops that arise in time travel?

I have committed a circularity in order not to talk about too much at once, and this is a good place to set it right. In explaining personal time, I presupposed that we were entitled to regard certain stages as comprising a single person. Then in explaining what united the stages into a single person, I presupposed that we were given a personal time order for them. The proper way to proceed is to define personhood and personal time simultaneously, as follows. Suppose given a pair of an aggregate of person-stages, regarded as a candidate for personhood, and an assignment of coordinates to those stages, regarded as a candidate for his personal time. Iff the stages satisfy the conditions given in my circular explanation with respect to the assignment of coordinates, then both candidates succeed: the stages do comprise a person and the assignment is his personal time.

I have argued so far that what goes on in a time travel story may be a possible pattern of events in four-dimensional space-time with no extra time dimension; that it may be correct to regard the scattered stages of the alleged time traveler as comprising a single person; and that we may legitimately assign to those stages and their surroundings a personal time order that disagrees sometimes with their order in external time. Some might concede all this, but protest that the impossibility of time travel is revealed after all when we ask not what the time traveler *does*, but what he *could do*. Could a time traveler change the past? It seems not: the events of a past moment could no more change than numbers could. Yet it seems that he would be as able as anyone to do things that would change the past if he did them. If a time traveler visiting the past both could and couldn't do something that would change it, then there cannot possibly be such a time traveler.

Consider Tim. He detests his grandfather, whose success in the munitions trade built the family fortune that paid for Tim's time machine. Tim would like nothing so much as to kill Grandfather, but alas he is too late. Grandfather died in his bed in 1957, while Tim was a young boy. But when Tim has built his time machine and traveled to 1920, suddenly he realizes that he is not too late after all. He buys a rifle; he spends long hours in target practice; he shadows Grandfather to learn the route of his daily walk to the munitions works; he rents a room along the route; and there he lurks, one winter day in 1921, rifle loaded, hate in his heart, as Grandfather walks closer, closer, . . .

Tim can kill Grandfather. He has what it takes. Conditions are perfect in every way: the best rifle money could buy, Grandfather an easy target only twenty yards away, not a breeze, door securely locked against intruders, Tim a good shot to begin with and now at the peak of training, and so on. What's to stop him? The forces of logic will not stay his hand! No powerful chaperone stands by to defend the past from interference. (To imagine such a chaperone, as some authors do, is a boring evasion, not needed to make Tim's story consistent.) In short, Tim is as much able to kill Grandfather as anyone ever is to kill anyone. Suppose that down the street another sniper, Tom, lurks waiting for another victim, Grandfather's partner. Tom is not a time traveler, but otherwise he is just like Tim; same make of rifle, same murderous intent, same everything. We can even suppose that Tom, like Tim, believes himself to be a time traveler. Someone has gone to a lot of trouble to deceive Tom into thinking so. There's no doubt that Tom can kill his victim; and Tim has everything going for him that Tom does. By any ordinary standards of ability, Tim can kill Grandfather.

Tim cannot kill Grandfather. Grandfather lived, so to kill him would be to change the past. But the events of a past moment are not subdivisible into temporal parts and therefore cannot change. Either the events of 1921 timelessly do include Tim's killing of Grandfather, or else they timelessly don't. We may be tempted to speak of the "original" 1921 that lies in Tim's personal past, many years before his birth, in which Grandfather lived; and of the "new" 1921 in which Tim now finds himself waiting in ambush to kill Grandfather. But if we do speak so, we merely confer two names on one thing. The events of 1921 are doubly located in Tim's (extended) personal time, like the trestle on the railway, but the "original" 1921 and the "new" 1921 are one and the same. If Tom did not kill Grandfather in the "original" 1921, then if he does kill Grandfather in the "new" 1921, he must both kill and not kill Grandfather in 1921—in the one and only 1921, which is both the "new" and the "original" 1921. It is logically impossible that Tim should change the past by killing Grandfather in 1921. So Tim cannot kill Grandfather.

Not that past moments are special; no more can anyone change the present or the future. Present and future momentary events no more have temporal parts than past ones do. You cannot change a present or future event from what it was originally to what it is after you change it. What you *can* do is to change the present or the future from the unactualized way they would have been without some action of yours to the way they actually are. But that is not an actual change: not a difference between two successive actualities. And Tim can certainly do as much; he changes the past from the unactualized way it would have been without him to the one and only way it actually is. To "change" the past in this way, Tim need not do anything momentous; it is enough just to be there, however unobtrusively.

You know, of course, roughly how the story of Tim must go on if it is to be consistent: he somehow fails. Since Tim didn't kill Grandfather in the "original" 1921, consistency demands that neither does he kill Grandfather in the "new" 1921. Why not? For some commonplace reason. Perhaps some noise distracts him at the last moment, perhaps he misses despite all his target practice, perhaps his nerve fails, perhaps he even feels a pang of unaccustomed mercy. His failure by no means proves that he was not really able to kill Grandfather. We often try and fail to do what we are able to do. Success at some tasks requires not only ability but also luck, and lack of luck is not a temporary lack of ability. Suppose our other sniper, Tom, fails to kill Grandfather's partner for the same reason, whatever it is, that Tim fails to kill Grandfather. It does not follow that Tom was unable to. No more does it follow in Tim's case that he was unable to do what he did not succeed in doing.

We have this seeming contradiction: *"Tim doesn't, but can, because he has what it takes"* versus *"Tim doesn't, and can't, because it's logically impossible to change the past."* I reply that there is no contradiction. Both conclusions are true, and for the reasons given. They are compatible because "can" is equivocal.

To say that something can happen means that its happening is compossible with certain facts. *Which* facts? That is determined, but sometimes not determined well enough, by context. An ape can't speak a human language—say, Finnish—but I can. Facts about the anatomy and operation of the ape's larynx and nervous system are not compossible with his speaking Finnish. The corresponding facts about my larynx and nervous system are compossible with my speaking Finnish. But don't take me along to Helsinki as your interpreter: I can't speak Finnish. My speaking Finnish is compossible with the facts considered so far, but not with further facts about my lack of training. What I can do, relative to one set of facts, I cannot do, relative to another, more inclusive, set. Whenever the context leaves it open which facts are to count as relevant, it is possible to equivocate about whether I can speak Finnish. It is likewise possible to equivocate about whether it is possible for me to speak Finnish, or whether I am able to, or whether I have the ability or capacity or power or potentiality to. Our many words for much the same thing are little help since they do not seem to correspond to different fixed delineations of the relevant facts.

Tim's killing Grandfather that day in 1921 is compossible with a fairly rich set of facts: the facts about his rifle, his skill and training, the unobstructed line of fire, the locked door and the absence of any chaperone to defend the past, and so on. Indeed it is compossible with all the facts of the sorts we would ordinarily count as relevant is saying what someone can do. It is compossible with all the facts corresponding to those we deem relevant in Tom's case. Relative to these facts, Tim can kill Grandfather. But his killing Grandfather is not compossible with another, more inclusive set of facts. There is the simple fact that Grandfather was not killed. Also there are various other facts about Grandfather's doings after 1921 and their effects: Grandfather begat Father in 1922 and Father begat Tim in 1949. Relative to these facts, Tim cannot kill Grandfather. He can and he can't, but under different delineations of the relevant facts. You can reasonably choose the narrower delineation, and say that he can; or the wider delineation, and say that he can't. But choose. WhaT you mustn't do is waver, say in the same breath that he both can and can't, and then claim that this contradiction proves that time travel is impossible.

Exactly the same goes for Tom's parallel failure. For Tom to kill Grandfather's partner also is compossible with all facts of the sorts we ordinarily count as relevant, but not compossible with a larger set including, for instance, the fact that the intended victim lived until 1934. In Tom's case we are not puzzled. We say without hesitation that he can do it, because we see at once that the facts that are not compossible with his success are facts about the future of the time in question and therefore not the sort of facts we count as relevant in saying what Tom can do.

In Tim's case it is harder to keep track of which facts are relevant. We are accustomed to exclude facts about the future of the time in question, but to include some facts about its past. Our standards do not apply unequivocally to the crucial facts in this special case: Tim's failure, Grandfather's survival, and his subsequent doings. If we have foremost in mind that they lie in the external future of that moment in 1921 when Tim is almost ready to shoot, then we exclude them just as we exclude the parallel facts in Tom's case. But if we have foremost in mind that they precede that moment in Tim's extended personal time, then we tend to include them. To make the latter be foremost in your mind, I chose to tell Tim's story in the order of his personal time, rather than in the order of external time. The fact of Grandfather's survival until 1957 had already been told before I got to the part of the story about Tim lurking in ambush to kill him in 1921. We must decide, if we can, whether to treat these personally past and externally future facts as if they were straightforwardly past or as if they were straightforwardly future.

Fatalists—the best of them—are philosophers who take facts we count as irrelevant in saying what someone can do, disguise them somehow as facts of a different sort that we count as relevant, and thereby argue that we can do less than we think—indeed, that there is nothing at all that we don't do but can. I am not going to vote Republican next fall. The fatalist argues that, strange to say, I not only won't but can't; for my voting Republican is not compossible with the fact that it was true already in the year 1548 that I was not going to vote Republican 428 years later. My rejoinder is that this is a fact, sure enough; however, it is an irrelevant fact about the future masquerading as a relevant fact about the past, and so should be left out of account in saying what, in any ordinary sense, I can do. We are unlikely to be fooled by the fatalist's methods of disguise in this case, or other ordinary cases. But in cases of time travel, precognition, or the like we're on less familiar ground, so it may take less of a disguise to fool us. Also, new methods of disguise are available, thanks to the device of personal time.

Here's another bit of fatalist trickery. Tim, as he lurks, already knows that he will fail. At least he has the wherewithal to know it if he thinks, he knows it implicitly. For he remembers that Grandfather was alive when he was a boy, he knows that those who are killed are thereafter not alive, he knows (let us suppose) that he is a time traveler who has reached the same 1921 that lies in his personal past, and he ought to understand—as we do—why a time traveler cannot change the past. What is known cannot be false. So his success is not only not compossible with facts that belong to the external future and his personal past, but also is not compossible with the present fact of his knowledge that he will fail. I reply that the fact of his foreknowledge, at the moment while he waits to shoot, is not a fact entirely about that moment. It may be divided into two parts. There is the fact that he then believes (perhaps only implicitly) that he will fail; and there is the further fact that his belief is correct, and correct not at all by accident, and hence qualifies as an item of knowledge. It is only the latter fact that is not compossible with his success, but it is only the former that is entirely about the moment in question. In calling Tim's state at the moment knowledge, not just belief, facts about personally earlier but externally later moments were smuggled into consideration.

I have argued that Tim's case and Tom's are alike, except that in Tim's case we are more tempted than usual—and with reason—to opt for a semi-fatalist mode of speech. But perhaps they differ in another way. In Tom's case, we can expect a perfectly consistent answer to the counterfactual question: what if Tom had killed Grandfather's partner? Tim's case is more difficult. If Tim had killed Grandfather, it seems offhand that contradictions would have been true. The killing both would and wouldn't have occurred. No Grandfather, no Father; no Father, no Tim; no Tim, no killing. And for good measure: no Grandfather, no family fortune; no fortune, no time machine; no time machine, no killing. So the supposition that Tim killed Grandfather seems impossible in more than the semi-fatalistic sense already granted.

If you suppose Tim to kill Grandfather and hold all the rest of his story fixed, of course you get a contradiction. But likewise if you suppose Tom to kill Grandfather's partner and hold the rest of his story fixed—including the part that told of his failure—you get a contradiction. If you make *any* counterfactual supposition and hold all else fixed you get a contradiction. The thing to do is rather to make the counterfactual supposition and hold all else as close to fixed as you consistently can. That procedure will yield perfectly consistent answers to the question: what if Tim had not killed Grandfather? In that case, some of the story I told would not have been true. Perhaps Tim might have been the time-traveling grandson of someone else. Perhaps he might have been the grandson of a man killed in 1921 and miraculously resurrected. Perhaps he might have been not a time traveler at all, but rather someone created out of nothing in 1920 equipped with false memories of a personal past that never was. It is hard to say what is the least revision of Tim's story to make it true that Tim kills Grandfather, but certainly the contradictory story in which tHe KIlling both doeS and doesn't Occur is not the least revision. Hence it is false (accordiNgto the unreviSed story) thatIf Tim had killed grandfather thEn contradictions would have been true.

What difference would it make if Tim travels in branching time? Suppose that at the possible world of Tim's story the space-time manifold branches; the branches are separated not in time, and not in space, but in some other way. Tim travels not only in time but also from one branch to another. In one branch Tim is absent from the events of 1921; Grandfather lives; Tim is born, grows up, and vanishes in his time machine. The other branch diverges from the first when Tim turns up in 1920; there Tim kills Grandfather and Grandfather leaves no descendants and no fortune; the events of the two branches differ more and more from that time on. Certainly this is a consistent story; it is a story in which Grandfather both is and isn't killed in 1921 (in the different branches); and it is a story in which Tim, by killing Grandfather, succeeds in preventing his own birth (in one of the branches). But it is not a story in which Tim's killing of Grandfather both does occur and doesn't: it simply does, though it is located in one branch and not the other. And it is not a story in which Tim changes the past 1921 and later years contain the events of both branches, co-existing somehow without interaction. It remains true at all the personal times of Tim's life, even after the killing, that Grandfather lives in one branch and dies in the other.[6]

NOTES

1. I have particularly in mind two of the time travel stories of Robert A. Heinlein: "By His Bootstraps" in R. A. Heinlein, *The Menace from Earth* (Hicksville, N.Y., 1959), and "—All you Zombies—," in R. A. Heinlein, *The Unpleasant Profession of Jonathan Hoag* (Hicksville, N.Y., 1959).

2. Accounts of time travel in two-dimensional time are found in Jack W. Meiland, "A Two-Dimensional Passage Model of Time for Time Travel," *Philosophical Studies*, vol. 26 (1974), pp. 153–173; and in the initial chapters of Isaac Asimov, *The End of Eternity* (Garden City, N.Y., 1955). Asimov's denouement, however, seems to require some different conception of time travel.

3. H. G. Wells, *The Time Machine, An Invention* (London, 1895), epilogue. The passage is criticized as contradictory in Donald C. Williams, "The Myth of Passage," *The Journal of Philosophy*, vol. 48 (1951), p. 463.

4. I discuss the relation between personal identity and mental connectedness and continuity at greater length in "Survival and Identity" in *The Identity of Persons*, ed. by Amelie Rorty (Berkeley: University of California Press, 1976).

5. "Causation," *The Journal of Philosophy*, vol. 70 (1973), pp. 556–567; the analy-

sis relies on the analysis of counterfactuals given in my *Counterfactuals* (Oxford, 1973).

6. The present paper summarizes a series of lectures of the same title, given as the Gavin David Young Lectures in Philosophy at the University of Adelaide in July, 1971. I thank the Australian-American Educational Foundations and the American Council of Learned Societies for research support. I am grateful to many friends for comments on earlier versions of this paper; especially Philip Kitcher, William Newton-Smith, J. J. C. Smart, and Donald Williams.

CONFESSIONS, Book XI (Excerpts)

St. Augustine

CHAP. XIII.—BEFORE THE TIMES CREATED BY GOD, TIMES WERE NOT.

15. But if the roving thought of any one should wander through the images of bygone time, and wonder that Thou, the God Almighty, and All-creating, and All-sustaining, the Architect of heaven and earth, didst for innumerable ages refrain from so great a work before Thou wouldst make it, let him awake and consider that he wonders at false things. For whence could innumerable ages pass by which Thou didst not make, since Thou art the Author and Creator of all ages? Or what times should those be which were not made by Thee? Or how should they pass by if they had not been? Since, therefore, Thou art the Creator of all times, if any time was before Thou madest heaven and earth, why is it said that Thou didst refrain from working? For that very time Thou madest, nor could times pass by before Thou madest times. But if before heaven and earth there was no time, why is it asked, What didst Thou then? For there was no "then" when time was not.

16. Nor dost Thou by time precede time; else wouldest not Thou precede all times. But in the excellency of an ever-present eternity, Thou precedest all times past, and survivest all future times, because they are future, and when they have come they will be past; but "Thou art the same, and Thy years shall have no end." Thy years neither go nor come; but ours both go and come, that all may come. All Thy years stand at once, since they do stand; nor were they when departing excluded by coming years, because they pass not away; but all these of ours shall be when all shall cease to be. Thy years are one day, and Thy day is not daily, but to-day; because Thy to-day yields not with to-morrow, for neither doth it follow yesterday. Thy to-day is eternity; therefore didst Thou beget the Co-eternal, to whom Thou saidst, "This day have I begotten Thee." Thou hast made all time; and before all times Thou art, nor in any time was there not time.

CHAP. XIV.—NEITHER TIME PAST NOR FUTURE, BUT THE PRESENT, ONLY REALLY IS.

17. At no time, therefore, hadst Thou not made anything, because Thou hadst made time itself. And no times are co-eternal with Thee, because Thou remainest for ever; but should these continue, they would not be times. For what is time? Who can easily and briefly explain it? Who even in thought can comprehend it, even to the pronouncing of a word concerning it? But what in speaking do we refer to more familiarly and knowingly than time? And certainly we understand when we speak of it; we understand also when we hear it spoken of by another. What, then, is time? If no one ask of me, I know; if I wish to explain to him who asks, I know not. Yet I say with confidence, that I know that if nothing passed away, there would not be past time; and if nothing were coming, there would not be future time; and if nothing were, there would not be present time. Those two times, therefore, past and future, how are they, when even the past now is not, and the future is not as yet? But should the present be always present, and should it not pass into time past, time truly it could not be, but eternity. If, then, time present—if it be time—only comes into existence because it passes into time past, how do we say that even this is, whose cause of being is that it shall not be—namely, so that we cannot truly say that time is, unless because it tends not to be?

CHAP. XV.—THERE IS ONLY A MOMENT OF PRESENT TIME.

18. And yet we say that "time is long and time is short;" nor do we speak of this save of time past and future. A long time past, for example, we call a hundred years ago; in like manner a long time to come, a hundred years hence. But a short time past we call, say, ten days ago; and a short time to come, ten days hence. But in what sense is that long or short which is not? For the past is not now, and the future is not yet. Therefore let us not say, "It is long;" but let us say of the past, "It hath been long," and of the future, "It will be long." O my Lord, my light, shall not even here Thy truth deride man? For that past time which was long, was it long when it was already past, or when it was as yet present? For then, it might be long when there was that which could be long, but when past it no longer was; wherefore that could not be long which was not at all. Let us not, therefore, say, "Time past hath been long;" for we shall not find what may have been long, seeing that since it was past it is not; but let us say "that present time was long, because when it was present it was long." For it had not as yet passed away so as not to be, and therefore there was that which could be long. But after it passed, that ceased also to be long which ceased to be.

19. Let us therefore see, O human soul, whether present time can be

long; for to thee is it given to perceive and to measure periods of time. What wilt thou reply to me? Is a hundred years when present a long time? See, first, whether a hundred years can be present. For if the first year of these is current, that is present, but the other ninety and nine are future, and therefore they are not as yet. But if the second year is current, one is already past, the other present, the rest future. And thus, if we fix on any middle year of this hundred as present, those before it are past, those after it are future; wherefore a hundred years cannot be present. See at least whether that year itself which is current can be present. For if its first month be current, the rest are future; if the second, the first hath already passed, and the remainder are not yet. Therefore neither is the year which is current as a whole present; and if it is not present as a whole, then the year is not present. For twelve months make the year, of which each individual month which is current is itself present, but the rest are either past or future. Although neither is that month which is current present, but one day only: if the first, the rest being to come, if the last, the rest being past; if any of the middle, then between past and future.

20. Behold, the present time, which alone we found could be called long, is abridged to the space scarcely of one day. But let us discuss even that, for there is not one day present as a whole. For it is made up of four-and-twenty hours of night and day, whereof the first hath the rest future, the last hath them past, but any one of the intervening hath those before it past, those after it future. And that one hour passeth away in fleeting particles. Whatever of it hath flown away is past, whatever remaineth is future. If any portion of time be conceived which cannot now be divided into even the minutest particles of moments, this only is that which may be called present; which, however, flies so rapidly from future to past, that it cannot be extended by any delay. For if it be extended, it is divided into the past and future; but the present hath no space. Where, therefore, is the time which we may call long? Is it future? Indeed we do not say, "It is long," because it is not yet, so as to be long; but we say, "It will be long." When, then, will it be? For if even then, since as yet it is future, it will not be long, because what may be long is not as yet; but it shall be long, when from the future, which as yet is not, it shall already have begun to be, and will have become present, so that there could be that which may be long; then doth the present time cry out in the words above that it cannot be long. . . .

CHAP. XVIII.—PAST AND FUTURE TIMES CANNOT BE THOUGHT OF BUT AS PRESENT.

23. Suffer me, O Lord, to seek further; O my Hope, let not my purpose be confounded. For if there are times past and future, I desire to know where they are. But if as yet I do not succeed, I still know, wherever they are, that they are not there as future or past, but as present. For if there

also they be future, they are not as yet there; if even there they be past, they are no longer there. Wheresoever, therefore, they are, whatsoever they are, they are only so as present. Although past things are related as true, they are drawn out from the memory,—not the things themselves, which have passed, but the words conceived from the images of the things which they have formed in the mind as footprints in their passage through the senses. My childhood, indeed, which no longer is, is in time past, which now is not; but when I call to mind its image, and speak of it, I behold it in the present, because it is as yet in my memory. Whether there be a like cause of foretelling future things, that of things which as yet are not the images may be perceived as already existing, I confess, my God, I know not. This certainly I know, that we generally think before on our future actions, and that this premeditation is present; but that the action whereon we premeditate is not yet, because it is future; which when we shall have entered upon, and have begun to do that which we were premeditating, then shall that action be, because then it is not future, but present.

24. In whatever manner, therefore, this secret preconception of future things may be, nothing can be seen, save what is. But what now is is not future, but present. When, therefore, they say that things future are seen, it is not themselves, which as yet are not (that is, which are future); but their causes or their signs perhaps are seen, the which already are. Therefore, to those already beholding them, they are not future, but present, from which future things conceived in the mind are foretold. Which conceptions again now are, and they who foretell those things behold these conceptions present before them. Let now so multitudinous a variety of things afford me some example. I behold daybreak; I foretell that the sun is about to rise. That which I behold is present; what I foretell is future,— not that the sun is future, which already is; but his rising, which is not yet. Yet even its rising I could not predict unless I had an image of it in my mind, as now I have while I speak. But that dawn which I see in the sky is not the rising of the sun, although it may go before it, nor that imagination in my mind; which two are seen as present, that the other which is future may be foretold. Future things, therefore, are not as yet; and if they are not as yet, they are not. And if they are not, they cannot be seen at all; but they can be foretold from things present which now are, and are seen.

CHAP. XIX.—WE ARE IGNORANT IN WHAT MANNER GOD TEACHES FUTURE THINGS.

25. Thou, therefore, Ruler of Thy creatures, what is the method by which Thou teachest souls those things which are future? For Thou has taught Thy prophets. What is that way by which Thou, to whom nothing is future, dost teach future things; or rather of future things dost teach

present? For what is not, of a certainty cannot be taught. Too far is this way from my view; it is too mighty for me, I cannot attain unto it; but by Thee I shall be enabled, when Thou shalt have granted it, sweet light of my hidden eyes.

CHAP. XX.—IN WHAT MANNER TIME MAY PROPERLY BE DESIGNATED.

26. But what now is manifest and clear is, that neither are there future nor past things. Nor is it fitly said, "There are three times, past, present, and future;" but perchance it might be fitly said, "There are three times; a present of things past, a present of things present, and a present of things future." For these three do somehow exist in the soul, and otherwise I see them not: present of things past, memory; present of things present, sight; present of things future, expectation. If of these things we are permitted to speak, I see three times, and I grant there are three. It may also be said, "There are three times, past, present, and future," as usage falsely has it. See, I trouble not, nor gainsay, nor reprove; provided always that which is said may be understood, that neither the future, nor that which is past, now is. For there are but few things which we speak properly, many things improperly; but what we may wish to say is understood. . . .

CHAP. XXIII.—THAT TIME IS A CERTAIN EXTENSION.

29. I have heard from a learned man that the motions of the sun, moon, and stars constituted time, and I assented not. For why should not rather the motions of all bodies be time? What if the lights of heaven should cease, and a potter's wheel run round, would there be no time by which we might measure those revolutions, and say either that it turned with equal pauses, or, if it were moved at one time more slowly, at another more quickly, that some revolutions were longer, others less so? Or while we were saying this, should we not also be speaking in time? Or should there in our words be some syllables long, others short, but because those sounded in a longer time, these in a shorter? God grant to men to see in a small thing ideas common to things great and small. Both the stars and luminaries of heaven are "for signs and for seasons, and for days and years." No doubt they are; but neither should I say that the circuit of that wooden wheel was a day, nor yet should he say that therefore there was no time. . . .

CHAP. XXIV.—THAT TIME IS NOT A MOTION OF THE BODY WHICH WE MEASURE BY TIME.

31. Dost Thou command that I should assent, if any one should say that time is "the motion of a body?" Thou dost not command me. For I hear that no body is moved but in time. This Thou sayest; but that the very motion of a body is time, I hear not; Thou sayest it not. For when a body is moved, I by time measure how long it may be moving from the time in which it began to be moved till it left off. And if I saw not whence it began, and it continued to be moved, so that I see not when it leaves off, I cannot measure unless, perchance, from the time I began until I cease to see. But if I look long, I only proclaim that the time is long, but not how long it may be; because when we say, "How long," we speak by comparison, as, "This is as long as that," or, "This is double as long as that," or any other thing of the kind. But if we were able to note down the distances of places whence and whither cometh the body which is moved, or its parts, if it moved as in a wheel, we can say in how much time the motion of the body or its part, from this place unto that, was performed. Since, then, the motion of a body is one thing, that by which we measure how long it is another, who cannot see which of these is rather to be called time? For, although a body be sometimes moved, sometimes stand still, we measure not its motion only, but also its standing still, by time; and we say, "It stood still as much as it moved;" or, "It stood still twice or thrice as long as it moved;" and if any other space which our measuring hath either determined or imagined, more or less, as we are accustomed to say. Time, therefore, is not the motion of a body. . . .

CHAP. XXVIII.—TIME IN THE HUMAN MIND, WHICH EXPECTS, CONSIDERS, AND REMEMBERS.

37. But how is that future diminished or consumed which as yet is not? Or how doth the past, which is no longer, increase, unless in the mind which enacted this there are three things done? For it both expects, and considers, and remembers, that that which it expecteth, through that which it considereth, may pass into that which it remembereth. Who, therefore, denieth that future things as yet are not? But yet there is already in the mind the expectation of things future. And who denies that past things are now no longer? But, however, there is still in the mind the memory of things past. And who denies that time present wants space, because it passeth away in a moment? But yet our consideration endureth, through which that which may be present may proceed to become absent. Future time, which is not, is not therefore long; but a "long

future" is "a long expectation of the future." Nor is time past, which is now no longer, long; but a long past is "a long memory of the past."

38. I am about to repeat a psalm that I know. Before I begin, my attention is extended to the whole; but when I have begun, as much of it as becomes past by my saying it is extended in my memory; and the life of this action of mine is divided between my memory, on account of what I have repeated, and my expectation, on account of what I am about to repeat; yet my consideration is present with me, through which that which was future may be carried over so that it may become past. Which the more it is done and repeated, by so much (expectation being shortened) the memory is enlarged, until the whole expectation be exhausted, when that whole action being ended shall have passed into memory. And what takes place in the entire psalm, takes place also in each individual part of it, and in each individual syllable: this holds in the longer action, of which that psalm is perchance a portion; the same holds in the whole life of man, of which all the actions of man are parts; the same holds in the whole age of the sons of men, of which all the lives of men are parts.

OF TIME

Immanuel Kant

METAPHYSICAL EXPOSITION OF THIS CONCEPTION.

1. Time is not an empirical conception. For neither coexistence nor succession would be perceived by us, if the representation of time did not exist as a foundation *à priori*. Without this presupposition we could not represent to ourselves that things exist together at one and the same time, or at different times, that is, contemporaneously, or in succession.

2. Time is a necessary representation, lying at the foundation of all our intuitions. With regard to phænomena in general, we cannot think away time from them, and represent them to ourselves as out of and unconnected with time, but we can quite well represent to ourselves time void of phænomena. Time is therefore given *à priori*. In it alone is all reality of phænomena possible. These may all be annihilated in thought, but time itself, as the universal condition of their possibility, cannot be so annulled.

3. On this necessity *à priori*, is also founded the possibility of apodeictic principles of the relations of time, or axioms of time in general, such as, "Time has only one dimension," "Different times are not co-existent but successive," (as different spaces are not successive but co-existent). These principles cannot be derived from experience, for it would give neither strict universality, nor apodeictic certainly. We should only be able to say, "so common experience teaches us," but not it must be so. They are valid as rules, through which, in general, experience is possible; and they instruct us respecting experience, and not by means of it.

4. Time is not a discursive, or as it is called, general conception, but a pure form of the sensuous intuition. Different times are merely parts of one and the same time. But the representation which can only be given by a single object is an intuition. Besides, the proposition that different times cannot be co-existent, could not be derived from a general conception. For this proposition is synthetical, and therefore cannot spring out of conceptions alone. It is therefore contained immediately in the intuition and representation of time.

5. The infinity of time signifies nothing more than that every determined quantity of time is possible only through limitations of one time lying at the foundation. Consequently, the original representation, time, must be given as unlimited. But as the determinate representation of the

parts of time and of every quantity of an object can only be obtained by limitation, the *complete* representation of time must not be furnished by means of conceptions, for these contain only partial representations. Conceptions, on the contrary, must have immediate intuition for their basis.

6. *Transcendental exposition of the conception of time.* . . . The conception of change, and with it the conception of motion, as change of place, is possible only through and in the representation of time; if this representation were not an intuition (internal) *à priori*, no conception, of whatever kind, could render comprehensible the possibility of change, in other words, of a conjunction of contradictorily opposed predicates in one and the same object, for example, the presence of a thing in a place and the non-presence of the same thing in the same place. It is only in time, that it is possible to meet with two contradictorily opposed determinations in one thing, that is, after each other. Thus our conception of time explains the possibility of so much synthetical knowledge *à priori*, as is exhibited in the general doctrine of motion, which is not a little fruitful.

7. *Conclusions from the above conceptions.* (a) Time is not something which subsists of itself, or which inheres in things as an objective determination, and therefore remains, when abstraction is made of the subjective conditions of the intuition of things. For in the former case, it would be something real, yet without presenting to any power of perception any real object. In the latter case, as an order or determination inherent in things themselves, it could not be antecedent to things, as their condition, nor discerned or intuited by means of synthetical propositions *à priori*. But all this is quite possible when we regard time as merely the subjective condition under which all our intuitions take place. For in that case, this form of the inward intuition can be represented prior to the objects, and consequently *à priori*.

(b) Time is nothing else than the form of the internal sense, that is, of the intuiitions of self and of our internal state. For time cannot be any determination of outward phænomena. It has to do neither with shape nor position; on the contrary, it determines the relation of representations in our internal state. And precisely because this internal intuition presents to us no shape or form, we endeavour to supply this want by analogies, and represent the course of time by a line progressing to infinity, the content of which constitutes a series which is only of one dimension; and we conclude from the properties of this line as to all the properties of time, with this single exception, that the parts of the line are co-existent, whilst those of time are successive. From this it is clear also that the representation of time is itself an intuition, because all its relations can be expressed in an external intuition.

(c) Time is the formal condition *à priori* of all phænomena whatsoever. Space, as the pure form of external intuition, is limited as a condition *à priori* to external phænomena alone. On the other hand, because all representations, whether they have or have not external things for their objects, still in themselves, as determinations of the mind, belong to our internal state; and because this internal state is subject to the formal condition of the internal intuition, that is, to time—time is a condition *à priori* of all phænomena whatsoever—the *immediate* condition of all internal, and thereby the *mediate* condition of all external phænomena. If I can say *à priori*, "all outward phænomena are in space, and determined *à priori* according to the relations of space," I can also, from the principle of the internal sense, affirm universally, "all phænomena in general, that is, all objects of the senses, are in time, and stand necessarily in relations of time."

If we abstract our internal intuition of ourselves, and all external intuitions, possible only by virtue of this internal intuition, and presented to us by our faculty of representation, and consequently take objects as they are in themselves, then time is nothing. It is only of objective validity in regard to phænomena, because these are things which we regard as objects of our senses. It is no longer objective, if we make abstraction of the sensuousness of our intuition, in other words, of that mode of representation which is peculiar to us, and speak of things in general. Time is therefore merely a subjective condition of our (human) intuition, (which is always sensuous, that is, so far as we are affected by objects), and in itself, independently of the mind or subject, is nothing. Nevertheless, in respect of all phænomena, consequently of all things which come within the sphere of our experience, it is necessarily objective. We cannot say, "all things are in time," because in this conception of things in general, we abstract and make no mention of any sort of intuition of things. But this is the proper condition under which time belongs to our representation of objects. If we add the condition to the conception, and say, "all things, as phænomena, that is, objects of sensuous intuition, are in time," then the proposition has its sound objective validity and universality *à priori*.

What we have now set forth teaches, therefore, the empirical reality of time; that is, its objective validity in reference to all objects which can ever be presented to our senses. And as our intuition is always sensuous, no object ever can be presented to us in experience, which does not come under the conditions of time. On the other hand, we deny to time all claim to absolute reality; that is, we deny that it, without having regard to the form of our sensuous intuition, absolutely inheres in things as a condition or property. Such properties as belong to objects as things in themselves, never can be presented to us through the medium of the senses. Herein consists, therefore, the transcendental ideality of time, according to which, if we abstract the subjective conditions of sensuous intuition, it is nothing, and cannot be reckoned as subsisting or inhering in objects as things in themselves, independently of its relation to our intuition. This ideality, like that of space, is not to be proved or illustrated by fallacious analogies with sensations, for this reason,—that in such arguments or illustrations, we make the presupposition that the phænomenon, in which such and such predicates inhere, has objective reality, while in this case we can only find such an objective reality as is itself empirical, that is, regards the object as a mere phænomenon.

Questions for Part V

1. How many main characters are there in Heinlein's "—All You Zombies—"? And why does Heinlein's narrator say "No one in my family ever marries. All bastards"? Explain carefully.

2. In what year was the "Unmarried Mother" born? How old was he in 1963?

3. Based on your reading of Heinlein's story, make a list of puzzling features of time travel—things which seem especially strange or incoherent. Then see whether or not your reading of the other selections clears up these puzzles.

4. Harrison says that if time machines exist continually from departure to arrival, then when someone begins to build a time machine which that person will use to travel into the past, there must already exist such a machine. Explain why. Is the machine that already exists *the same machine* as the one which is just beginning to be built? Why or why not?

5. Why does Harrison say that there are "enormous difficulties" in the idea of a continuously existing time machine? Is he right?

6. Early in his article, David Lewis describes ordinary objects as streaks, and various kinds of time travellers as zigzag, stretched-out, or broken streaks. Explain what he means. Make use of a graph with time represented by one axis and space by the other.

7. Explain what Lewis means by a "causal loop" and give an example from Heinlein's story.

8. Does Lewis think that Tim can or cannot kill his grandfather? Explain.

9. Augustine says that there were no times before God created them. This seems to imply that God existed before there were any times. Does that make sense?

10. Augustine argues that past and future are not real. Explain what he means. What would Augustine say about the possibility of time travel, and why?

11. Explain Augustine's argument that time is not to be equated with motion. If everything simply stood still, would time continue to pass?

12. Explain and evaluate Augustine's account of time in Chapter 28. If there were no people would time continue to pass?

13. Kant argues that the notion of time is one which is constantly involved in our experience of the world, and is not a notion which we derive from experience. What are his reasons for this?

14. Kant claims that time is "empirically real" but nevertheless "transcendentally ideal." Explain what he means by each of these claims.

VI. Backward Causation

The year is 1912. It is April and you are waiting in New York for the arrival of the rest of your family. They have been on vacation in Europe and were lucky to get passage on the most magnificent oceanliner of the day, the *Titanic*. Early in the morning, however, the news arrives that the unthinkable has occurred. The unsinkable ship had collided with a gigantic iceberg and sunk. The loss of life is enormous, but some have survived, having been rescued by another ship. The roster of survivors has not, however, been compiled. You do not know whether the members of your family are among the living or floating dead in the North Atlantic. What do you do? If you are religious, you pray as fervently as you can that your family members are among the survivors, that they should not have died. What could be more natural? Had you not done so, your love for your family might surely be questioned. But doesn't your prayer really make no sense at all? What do you hope to accomplish by praying it?

Surely you know that either your family has survived or they have perished. How could your prayer make any difference in their fate? Some theologians, notably orthodox Jews, in fact, regard such retrospective prayers to be blasphemous. They translate them as requests of God that if your family has perished, that God should make them not to have perished. But how could even God do such a thing? If they were drowned and left floating in the frigid North Atlantic, they are dead. Your prayer sounds like God is being asked to make someone who has died not to have died and so, the theologians argue, your prayer mocks God. It should be noted that the prayer is not to be interpreted as an appeal for a resurrection of the dead. You are not saying: if they died, make them come back to life and all that that would involve as their corpses float around among the icebergs. You are asking that they have survived the sinking, that is, be among those that were rescued in the lifeboats.

A practical-minded person will surely point out that your prayer is literally without hope of being causally effective, that it is a waste of effort. Strictly speaking, only two outcomes could have occurred: your family survived or your family drowned. If they drowned, your prayer cannot be answered. If they survived, your prayer is superfluous. There is therefore no point in your making the prayer at all.

These interpretations, however, do not exhaust the possibilities of what you think you can accomplish by praying. If we focus on the Godly attribute of omniscience, a rather different account of your prayer emerges. Might you not, by your prayer, on the morning after, be trying to bring it about that God, at the time of the sinking of the *Titantic* the night before, insured the safety of your family? If God knows everything, God knows that you will pray just as you did and so God can grant your prayer at the crucial time. By your prayer, then, you affected the past, if, that is, God has foreknowledge and wants to answer your prayer.

Your praying seems to be based on at least two beliefs. You must think that there is a positive correlation between your praying and the outcome the previous evening in the North Atlantic and that your praying in the way you do is in your power. This last belief is important because we don't want it to be the case that your prayer was caused by the outcome in the North Atlantic. In other words, if your prayer is an effect of the fact that your family survived, then your prayer was not something you could have chosen not to do and your uttering it is not really what we normally mean by praying.

You sincerely believe that your prayer will make some difference and that you did not have to pray it. But, it seems then that you hold a very strange belief. You believe that you can affect the past, that you can cause something to have happened one way rather than another, that you can, in the present, bring about the past as we normally think we can, to some extent, bring about the future.

One thing we certainly think we know about the past is that it has passed. Whatever happened, happened. That is one of our foundational beliefs. We also believe that in nature causes always precede their effects, not the other way around. In David Hume's famous analysis of the concept of causation, however, he points out that we never can "discover anything but one event following another." We cannot find in nature the source of our idea of necessary connection or cause. Events are conjoined, but not connected. Causation is a product of our mental processes reading connection into constant conjunctions. The idea of causation is fundamental to scientific explanation and prediction. What a mess the notion of backward causation would make of physics and chemistry. Our temporal notions, past, present, and future, are intimately bound up with our understanding of causation, and vice versa. Your prayer flies in the face of all of this.

Is backward causation at all conceivable? Michael Dummett believes that we can tell a story in which the idea of bringing about the past is quite intelligible. The crux of his ingenious argument is that a rational person cannot simultaneously hold the following three beliefs:

1. That a certain action (the prayer) is positively correlated with a prior occurrence of an event (the survival of the family).

2. That the action in question (the prayer) is in one's power to perform if one chooses to do so.

3. That one can know whether the event (the survival of the family) is going to take (or took) place independently of one's intention to perform the action (your prayer) or not to perform it.

Past events differ from those of the future in that we believe that we can (do) know independently of our intentions that those events have occurred. In the *Titanic* case, normally we would say you could have learned of the fate of your family from other survivors, telegraph messages from the rescue ship, news reports. The past is independent of your present intentions. The usual position then is to disallow holding both (1) and (2) in the case of past events. Surely whether or not you choose to pray, regardless of its efficacy, is in your power. Belief (2) can be justifiably held with respect to your prayer. Belief (1), in this case, must then be the problem. How can you believe (1): that your prayer can have a causal effect on the events in the North Atlantic? But isn't that just what you must believe in order to pray the retrospective prayer sincerely? Suppose that your family is rescued and that three days later you greet them on the dock in New York. "We were saved!" they tell you. "Yes, I prayed for it," you joyously respond. How can you be convinced to give up your belief that your prayer was effective? It certainly won't matter to you that someone may tell you that your family was already safe on the decks of the rescue ship before you even learned of the sinking of the *Titanic*.

Your faith in your power of prayer amounts to a rejection of the third belief. But are you at liberty to dismiss (3)? Doesn't the rejection of (3) render your concept of causation implausible? How could you have anything like a recognizable concept of causation, if you believe that causes can occur subsequent to their effects? And what happens to your concept of time?

Your prayer, if it is really sincerely intended to entreat God to alter the past, seems to have extensive effects on some of the most basic concepts of our understanding of events. The notion of causality is not independent of our ideas of time, intentionality, memory, and a number of other crucial elements in our language. Samuel Gorovitz notes that to tamper with any of these notions is to create severe problems for them all.

We may not, in the end, be able to give any kind of intelligible account of what you think you are doing when you do something so natural as praying that your family is among the survivors of the shipwreck. Must you, on pain of absurdity, deny that you hoped to accomplish anything by your prayer? Perhaps you will have to admit only to expressing a fervent hope and let it go at that. Was that really all you thought you were doing?

BRINGING ABOUT THE PAST
Michael Dummett

I observe first that there is a genuine sense in which the causal relation has a temporal direction: it is associated with the direction earlier-to-later rather than with the reverse. I shall not pause here to achieve a precise formulation of the sense in which this association holds; I think such a formulation can be given without too much difficulty, but it is not to my present purpose to do this. What I do want to assert is the following: so far as I can see, this association of causality with a particular temporal direction is not merely a matter of the way we speak of causes, but has a genuine basis in the way things happen. There is indeed an asymmetry in respect of past and future in the way in which we describe events when we are considering them as standing in causal relations to one another; but I am maintaining that this reflects an objective asymmetry in nature. I think that this asymmetry would reveal itself to us even if we were not *agents* but mere *observers*. It is indeed true, I believe, that our concept of cause is bound up with our concept of intentional action: if an event is properly said to cause the occurrence of a subsequent or simultaneous event, I think it necessarily follows that, if we can find any way of bringing about the former event (in particular, if it is itself a voluntary human action), then it must make sense to speak of bringing it about *in order that* the subsequent event should occur. Moreover, I believe that this connection between something's being a cause and the possibility of using it in order to bring about its effect plays an essential rôle in the fundamental account of how we ever come to accept causal laws: that is, that we could arrive at any causal beliefs only by beginning with those in which the cause is a voluntary action of ours. Nevertheless, I am inclined to think that we could have some kind of concept of cause, although one differing from that we now have, even if we were mere observers and not agents at all—a kind of intelligent tree. And I also think that even in this case the asymmetry of cause with respect to temporal direction would reveal itself to us.

To see this, imagine ourselves observing events in a world just like the actual one, except that the order of events is reversed. There are indeed enormous difficulties in describing such a world if we attempt to include human beings in it, or any other kind of creature to whom can be ascribed intention and purpose (there would also be a problem about memory). But, so far as I can see, there is no difficulty whatever if we include in this world only plants and inanimate objects. If we imagine ourselves as intelligent trees observing such a world and communicating with one another, but unable to intervene in the course of events, it is clear that we should have great difficulty in arriving at causal explanations that accounted for events in terms of the processes which had *led up to* them. The sapling grows gradually smaller, finally reducing itself to an apple pip; then an apple is gradually constituted around the pip from ingredients found in the soil; at a certain moment the apple rolls along the ground, gradually gaining momentum, bounces a few times, and then suddenly takes off vertically and attaches itself with a snap to the bough of an apple tree. Viewed from the standpoint of gross observation, this process contains many totally unpredictable elements: we cannot, for example, explain, by reference to the conditions obtaining at the moment when the apple started rolling, why it started rolling at the moment or in that direction. Rather, we should have to substitute a system of explanations of events in terms of the processes that led back to them from some subsequent moment. If through some extraordinary chance we, in this world, could consider events from the standpoint of the microscopic, the unpredictability would disappear theoretically ('in principle') although not in practice; but we should be left—so long as we continued to try to give causal explanations on the basis of what leads up to an event—with inexplicable coincidences. 'In principle' we could, by observing the movements of the molecules of the soil, predict that at a certain moment they were going to move in such a way as to combine to give a slight impetus to the apple, and that this impetus would be progressively reinforced by other molecules along a certain path, so as to cause the apple to accelerate in such a way that it would end up attached to the apple tree. But not only could we not make such predictions in practice: the fact that the 'random' movements of the molecules should happen to work out in such a way that all along the path the molecules always happened to be moving in the same direction at just the movement that the apple reached that point, and, above all, that these movements always worked in such a way as to leave the apple attached to an *apple* tree and not to any other tree or any other object—these facts would cry out for explanation, and we should be unable to provide it.

I should say, then, that, so far as the concept of cause possessed by mere observers rather than agents is concerned, the following two theses hold: (i) the world is such as to make appropriate a notion of causality associated with the earlier-to-later temporal direction rather than its reverse; (ii) we can conceive of a world in which a notion of causality associated with the opposite direction would have been more appropriate and, so long as we consider ourselves as mere observers of such a world, there is no particular conceptual difficulty about the conception of such a backwards causation. There are, of course, regions of which we are mere observers, in which we cannot intervene: the heavens, for example. Since

Newton, we have learned to apply the same causal laws to events in this realm; but in earlier times it was usually assumed that a quite different system of laws must operate there. It *could* have turned out that this was right; and then it could also have turned out that the system of laws we needed to explain events involving the celestial bodies required a notion of causality associated with the temporal direction from later to earlier.

When, however, we consider ourselves as agents, and consider causal laws governing events in which we can intervene, the notion of backwards causality seems to generate absurdities. If an event C is considered as a cause of a preceding event D, then it would be open to us to bring about C in order that the event D should have occurred. But the conception of doing something in order that something else should have happened appears to be intrinsically absurd: it apparently follows that backwards causation must also be absurd in any realm in which we can operate as agents.

We can affect the future by our actions: so why can we not by our actions affect the past? The answer that springs to mind is this: you cannot *change* the past; if a thing has happened, it has happened, and you cannot make it not to have happened. This is, I am told,[1] the attitude of orthodox Jewish theologians to retrospective prayer. It is blasphemous to pray that something should *have* happened, for, although there are no limits to God's power, He cannot do what is logically impossible; it is logically impossible to alter the past, so to utter a retrospective prayer is to mock God by asking Him to perform a logical impossibility. Now I think it is helpful to think about this example, because it is the only instance of behaviour, on the part of ordinary people whose mental processes we can understand, designed to affect the past and coming quite naturally to us. If one does not think of this case, the idea of doing something in order that something else should previously have happened may seem sheer raving insanity. But suppose I hear on the radio that a ship has gone down in the Atlantic two hours previously, and that there were a few survivors: my son was on that ship, and I at once utter a prayer that he should have been among the survivors, that he should not have drowned; this is the most natural thing in the world. Still, there are things which it is very natural to say which make no sense; there are actions which can naturally be performed with intentions which *could* not be fulfilled. Are the Jewish theologians right in stigmatising my prayer as blasphemous?

They characterise my prayer as a request that, if my son has drowned, God should make him not have drowned. But why should they view it as asking anything more self-contradictory than a prayer for the future? If, before the ship set sail, I had prayed that my son should make a safe crossing, I should not have been praying that, if my son was going to drown, God should have made him not be going to drown. Here we stumble on a well-known awkwardness of language. There is a use of the future tense to express present tendencies: English newspapers some-times print announcements of the form 'The marriage that was arranged between X and Y will not now take place.' If someone did not understand the use of the future tense to express present tendencies, he might be amazed by this 'now'; he might say, 'Of course it *will* not take place *now*: either it *is* taking place *now*, or it *will* take place *later*'. The presence of the 'now' indicates a use of the future tense according to which, if anyone had said earlier, 'They are going to get married', he would have been right, even though their marriage never subsequently occurred. If, on the other hand, someone had offered a bet which he expressed by saying, 'I bet they will not be married on that date', this 'will' would normally be understood as expressing the *genuine* future tense, the future tense so used that what happens on the future date is the decisive test for truth or falsity, irrespective of how things looked at the time of making the bet, or at any intervening time. The future tense that I was using, and that will be used throughout this paper, is intended to be understood as this genuine future tense.

With this explanation, I will repeat: when, before the ship sails, I pray that my son will make the crossing safely, I am not praying that God should perform the logically impossible feat of making what will happen not happen (that is, not be-going-to happen); I am simply praying that it will not happen. To put it another way: I am not asking God that He should now make what is going to happen not be going to happen; I am asking that He *will* at a future time make something not to happen at that time. And similarly with my retrospective prayer. Assuming that I am not asking for a miracle—asking that if my son has died, he should now be brought to life again—I do not have to be asking for a logical impossibil-ity. I am not asking God that, even if my son has drowned, He should *now* make him not to have drowned; I am asking that, at the time of the disaster, He should then have made my son not to drown at that time. The former interpretation would indeed be required if the list of survivors had been read out over the radio, my son's name had not been on it, and I had not envisaged the possibility of a mistake on the part of the news service: but in my ignorance of whether he was drowned or not, my prayer will bear another interpretation.

But this still involves my trying to affect the past. On this second interpretation, I am trying by my prayer *now* to bring it about that God made something not to happen: and is not this absurd? In this particular case, I provide a rationale for my action—that is why I picked this ex-ample—but the question can be raised whether it is not a bad example, on the ground that it is the only kind for which a rationale *could* be given. The rationale is this. When I pray for the future, my prayer makes sense because I know that, at the time about which I am praying, God will remember my prayer, and may then grant it. But God knows everything, both what has happened and what is going to happen. So my retrospective prayer makes sense, too, because at the time about which I am praying, God knew that I was going to make this prayer, and may then have granted it. So it seems relevant to ask whether foreknowledge of this kind can meaningfully be attributed only to God, in which case the example will be of a quite special kind, from which it would be illegitimate to generalise, or whether it could be attributed to human beings, in which case our example will not be of purely theological interest.

I have heard three opinions expressed on this point. The first, held by Russell and Ayer, is that foreknowledge is simply the mirror image of memory, to be explained in just the same words as memory save that 'future' replaces 'past', and so forth, and as such is conceptually unproblematic: we do not have the faculty but we perfectly well might. The second is a view held by a school of Dominican theologians. It is that God's knowledge of the future should be compared rather to a man's knowledge of what is going to happen, when this lies in his intention to make it happen. For example, God knows that I am going to pray that my son may not have drowned because He is going to make me pray so. This leads to the theologically and philosophically disagreeable conclusion that everything that happens is directly effected by God, and that human freedom is therefore confined to wholly interior movements of the will. This is the view adopted by Wittgenstein in the *Tractatus*, and there expressed by the statement, 'The world is independent of my will.' On this view, God's foreknowledge is knowledge of a type that human beings do have; it would, however, be difficult to construct a non-theological example of an action intelligibly designed to affect the past by exploiting this alleged parallelism. The third view is one of which it is difficult to make a clear sense. It is that foreknowledge is something that can be meaningfully ascribed only to God (or perhaps also to those He directly inspires, the prophets; but again perhaps these would be regarded not as themselves possessing this knowledge, but only as the instruments of its expression). The ground for saying this is that the future is not something of which we could, but merely do not happen to, have knowledge; it is not, as it were, *there* to be known. Statements about the future are, indeed, either-true-or-false; but they do not yet have a particular one of these two truth-values. They have present truth-or-falsity, but they do not have present truth or present falsity, and so they *cannot* be known: there is not really anything to be known. The non-theological part of this view seems to me to rest on a philosophical confusion; the theological part I cannot interpret, since it appears to involve ascribing to God the performance of a logical impossibility.

We saw that retrospective prayer does not involve asking God to perform the logically impossible feat of changing the past, any more than prayer for the future involves asking Him to change the future in the sense in which that is logically impossible. We saw also that we could provide a rationale for retrospective prayer, a rationale which depended on a belief in God's foreknowledge. This led us to ask if foreknowledge was something which a man could have. If so, then a similar rationale could be provided for actions designed to affect the past, when they consisted in my doing something in order that someone should have known that I was going to do it, and should have been influenced by this knowledge. This enquiry, however, I shall not pursue any further. I turn instead to more general considerations: to consider other arguments designed to show an intrinsic absurdity in the procedure of attempting to affect the past—of doing something in order that something else should have happened. In the present connection I remark only that, if there is an intrinsic absurdity in *every* procedure of this kind, then it follows indirectly that there is also an absurdity in the conception of foreknowledge, human or divine.

Suppose someone were to say to me, 'Either your son has drowned or he has not. If he has drowned, then certainly your prayer will not (cannot) be answered. If he has not drowned, your prayer is superfluous. So in either case your prayer is pointless: it cannot make any *difference* to whether he has drowned or not.' This argument may well appear quite persuasive, until we observe that it is the exact analogue of the standard argument for fatalism. I here characterise fatalism as the view that there is an intrinsic absurdity in doing something in order that something else should subsequently happen; that any such action—that is, any action done with a further purpose—is necessarily pointless. The standard form of the fatalist argument was very popular in London during the bombing. The siren sounds, and I set off for the air-raid shelter in order to avoid being killed by a bomb. The fatalist argues, 'Either you are going to be killed by a bomb or you are not going to be. If you are, then any precautions you take will be ineffective. If you are not, all precautions you take are superfluous. Therefore it is pointless to take precautions.' This belief was extended even to particular bombs. If a bomb was going to kill me, then it 'had my number on it', and there was no point in my attempting to take precautions against being killed by *that* bomb; if it did not have my number on it, then of course precautions were pointless too. I shall take it for granted that no one wants to accept this argument as cogent. But the argument is formally quite parallel to the argument supposed to show that it is pointless to attempt to affect the past; only the tenses are different. Someone may say, 'But it is just the difference in tense that makes the difference between the two arguments. Your son has either *already* been drowned or else *already* been saved; whereas you haven't *yet* been killed in the raid, and you haven't *yet* come through it.' But this is just to reiterate that one argument is about the past and the other about the future: we want to know what, if anything, there is *in* this fact which makes the one valid, the other invalid. The best way of asking this question is to ask, 'What refutation is there of the fatalist argument, to which a quite parallel refutation of the argument to show that we cannot affect the past could not be constructed?'.

Let us consider the fatalist argument in detail. It opens with a tautology, 'Either you are going to be killed in this raid or you are not.' As is well known, some philosophers have attempted to escape the fatalist conclusion by faulting the argument at this first step, by denying that two-valued logic applies to statements about future contingents. Although this matter is worth investigating in detail, I have no time to go into it here, so I will put the main point very briefly. Those who deny that statements about future contingents need be either true or false are under the necessity to explain the meaning of those statements in some way; they usually attempt to do so by saying something like this: such a statement is not true or false now, but *becomes* true or false at the time to which it refers. But, if this is said, then the fatalist argument can be reconstructed by replacing the opening tautology by the assertion, 'Either the statement "You will be killed in this raid" is going to become true, or it is going to become false'. The only way in which it can be consistently maintained not only that the law of excluded middle does not hold for statements about the future, but that there is no other logically necessary statement which will serve the same purpose of getting the fatalist argument off the ground, is to deny that there is, or could be, what I called a 'genuine' future tense at all: to maintain that the only intelligible use of the future tense is to express present tendencies. I think that most people would be prepared to reject this as unacceptable, and here, for lack of space, I shall simply assume that it is. (In fact, it is not quite easy to refute someone who consistently adopts this position; of course, it is always much easier to make out that something is not meaningful than to make out that it is.) Thus, without more ado, I shall set aside the suggestion that the flaw in the fatalist argument lies in the very first step.

The next two steps stand or fall together. They are: 'If you are going to be killed in this raid, you will be killed whatever precautions you take' and 'If you are not going to be killed in this raid, you will not be killed whatever precautions you neglect'. These are both of the form, 'If p, then if q then p'; for example, 'If you *are* going to be killed, then you will be killed even if you take precautions'. They are clearly correct on many interpretations of 'if'; and I do not propose to waste time by enquiring whether they are correct on 'the' interpretation of 'if' proper to well-instructed users of the English language. The next two lines are as follows: 'Hence, if you are not going to be killed in the raid, any precautions you take will be ineffective' and 'Hence, if you are going to be killed in the raid, any precautions you take will have been superfluous'. The first of these is indisputable. The second gives an appearance of sophistry. The fatalist argues from 'If you are not going to be killed, then you won't be killed even if you have taken no precautions' to 'If you are not going to be killed, then any precautions you take will have been superfluous'; that is, granted the truth of the statement 'You will not be killed even if you take no precautions', you will have no motive to take precautions; or, to put it another way, if you would not be killed even if you took no precautions, then any precautions you take cannot be considered as being effective in bringing about your survival—that is, as effecting it. This employs a well-known principle. St. Thomas, for instance, says it is a condition of ignorance to be an excuse for having done wrong that, if the person had not suffered from the ignorance, he would not have committed the wrongful act in question. But we want to object that it may be just the precautions that I am going to take which save me from being killed; so it cannot follow from the mere fact that I am not going to be killed that I should not have been going to be killed even if I had not been going to take precautions. Here it really does seem to be a matter of the way in which 'if' is understood; but, as I have said, I do not wish to call into question the legitimacy of a use of 'if' according to which '(Even) if you do not take precautions, you will not be killed' follows from 'You will not be killed'. It is, however, clear that, on any use of 'if' on which this inference is valid, it is possible that both of the statements 'If you do not take precautions, you will be killed' and 'If you do not take precautions, you will not be killed' should be true. It indeed follows from the truth of these two statements together that their common antecedent is false; that is, that I am in fact going to take precautions. (It may be held that on a, or even the, use of 'if' in English, these two statements cannot both be true; or again, it may be held that they can both be true only when a stronger consequence follows, namely, that not only am I as a matter of fact going to take precautions, but that I could not fail to take them, that it was not in my power to refrain from taking them. But, as I have said, it is not my purpose here to enquire whether there are such uses of 'if' or whether, if so, they are important or typical uses.) Now let us say that it is correct to say of certain precautions that they are capable of being effective in preventing my death in the raid if the two conditional statements are true that, if I take them, I shall not be killed in the raid, and that, if I do not take them, I shall be killed in the raid. Then, since, as we have seen, the truth of these two statements is quite compatible with the truth of the statement that, if I do not take precautions, I shall not be killed, the truth of this latter statement cannot be a ground for saying that my taking precautions will not be effective in preventing my death.

Thus, briefly, my method of rebutting the fatalist is to allow him to infer from 'You will not be killed' to 'If you do not take precautions, you will not be killed'; but to point out that, on any sense of 'if' on which this inference is valid, it is impermissible to pass from 'If you do not take precautions, you will not be killed' to 'Your taking precautions will not be effective in preventing your death'. For this to be permissible, the truth of 'If you do not take precautions, you will not be killed' would have to be incompatible with that of 'If you do not take precautions, you will be killed'; but, on the sense of 'if' on which the first step was justified, these would not be incompatible. I prefer to put the matter this way than to make out that there is a sense of 'if' on which these two are indeed incompatible, but on which the first step is unjustified, because it is notoriously difficult to elucidate such a sense of 'if'.

Having arrived at a formulation of the fallacy of the fatalist argument, let us now consider whether the parallel argument to demonstrate the absurdity of attempting to bring about the past is fallacious in the same way. I will abandon the theological example in favour of a magical one. Suppose we come across a tribe who have the following custom. Every second year the young men of the tribe are sent, as part of their initiation ritual, on a lion hunt: they have to prove their manhood. They travel for two days, hunt lions for two days, and spend two days on the return journey; observers go with them, and report to the chief upon their return whether the young men acquitted themselves with bravery or not. The people of the tribe believe that various ceremonies, carried out by the chief, influence the weather, the crops, and so forth. I do not want these ceremonies to be thought of as religious rites, intended to dispose the gods favourably towards them, but simply as performed on the basis of a wholly mistaken system of causal beliefs. While the young men are away from the village the chief performs ceremonies—dances, let us say— intended to cause the young men to act bravely. We notice that he continues to perform these dances for the whole six days that the party is away, that is to say, for two days during which the events that the dancing is supposed to influence have already taken place. Now there is generally thought to be a *special* absurdity in the idea of affecting the past, much greater than the absurdity of believing that the performance of a dance can influence the behaviour of a man two days' journey away; so we ought to be able to persuade the chief of the absurdity of his continuing to dance after the first four days without questioning his general system of causal beliefs. How are we going to do it?

Since the absurdity in question is alleged to be a *logical* absurdity, it must be capable of being seen to be absurd however things turn out; so I am entitled to suppose that things go as badly for us, who are trying to persuade the chief of this absurdity, as they can do; we ought still to be able to persuade him. We first point out to him that he would not think of continuing to perform the dances after the hunting party has returned; he agrees to that, but replies that that is because at that time he *knows* whether the young men have been brave or not, so there is no longer any point in trying to bring it about that they have been. It is irrelevant, he says, that during the last two days of the dancing they have already either been brave or cowardly: there is still a point in his trying to make them have been brave, because he does not yet know which they have been. We then say that it can be only the first four days of the dancing which could possibly affect the young men's performance; but he replies that experience is against that. There was for several years a chief who thought as we did, and danced for the first four days only; the results were disastrous. On two other occasions, he himself fell ill after four days of dancing and was unable to continue, and again, when the hunting party returned, it proved that the young men had behaved ignobly.

The brief digression into fatalism was occasioned by our noticing that the standard argument against attempting to affect the past was a precise analogue of the standard fatalist argument against attempting to affect the future. Having diagnosed the fallacy in the fatalist argument, my announced intention was to discover whether there was not a similar fallacy in the standard argument against affecting the past. And it indeed appears to me that there is. We say to the chief, 'Why go on dancing now? Either the young men have already been brave, or they have already been cowardly. If they have been brave, then they have been brave whether you dance or not. If they have been cowardly, then they have been cowardly whether you dance or not. If they have been brave, then your dancing now will not be effective in making them have been brave, since they have been brave even if you do not dance. And if they have not been brave, then your dancing will certainly not be effective. Thus your continuing to dance will in the one case be superfluous, and in the other fruitless: in neither case is there any point in your continuing to dance.' The chief can reply in exactly the way in which we replied to the fatalist. He can say, 'If they have been brave, then indeed there is a sense in which it will be true to say that, even if I do not dance, they will have been brave; but this is not incompatible with its also being true to say that, if I do not dance, they will not have been brave. Now what saying that my continuing to dance is effective in causing them to have been brave amounts to is that it is true both that, if I go on dancing, they have been brave, and that, if I do not dance, they have not been brave. I have excellent empirical grounds for believing both these two statements to be true; and neither is incompatible with the truth of the statement that if I do not dance, they have been brave, although, indeed, I have no reason for believing *that* statement. Hence, you have not shown that, from the mere hypothesis that they have been brave, it follows that the dancing I am going to do will not be effective in making them have been brave; on the contrary, it may well be that, although they have been brave, they have been brave just *because* I am going to go on dancing; that, if I were not going to go on dancing, they would not have been brave.' This reply sounds sophistical; but it cannot be sophistical if our answer to the fatalist was correct, because it is the exact analogue of that answer.

We now try the following argument: 'Your *knowledge* of whether the young men have been brave or not may affect whether you *think* there is any point in performing the dances; but it cannot really make any difference to the *effect* the dances have on what has happened. If the dances are capable of bringing it about that the young men have acted bravely, then they ought to be able to do that even after you have learned that the young men have *not* acted bravely. But that is absurd, for that would mean that the dances can change the past. But if the dances cannot have any effect after you have learned whether the young men have been brave or not, they cannot have any effect before, either; for the mere state of your knowledge cannot make any difference to their efficacy.' Now since the causal beliefs of this tribe are so different from our own, I could imagine that the chief might simply deny this: he might say that what had an effect on the young men's behaviour was not merely the performance of the dances by the chief as such, but rather their performance by the chief when in a state of ignorance as to the outcome of the hunt. And if he says this, I think there is really no way of dissuading him, short of attacking his whole system of causal beliefs. But I will not allow him to say this, because it would make his causal beliefs so different in kind from ours that there would be no moral to draw for our own case. Before going on to consider his reaction to this argument, however, let us first pause to review the situation.

Suppose, then, that he agrees to our suggestion: agrees, that is, that it is his dancing as such that he wants to consider as bringing about the young men's bravery, and not his dancing in ignorance of whether they were brave. If this is his belief, then we may reasonably challenge him to try dancing on some occasion when the hunting party has returned and the observers have reported that the young men have *not* been brave. Here at last we appear to have hit on something which has no parallel in the case of affecting the future. If someone believes that a certain kind of action is effective in bringing about a subsequent event, I may challenge him to try it out in all possible circumstances: but I cannot demand that he try it out on some occasion when the event is *not* going to take place, since he cannot identify any such occasion independently of his intention to perform the action. Our knowledge of the future is of two kinds: prediction based on causal laws and knowledge in intention. If I think I can predict the non-occurrence of an event, then I cannot consistently also believe that I can do anything to bring it about; that is, I cannot have good grounds for believing, of any action, both that it is in my power to do it, and that it is a condition of the event's occurring. On the other hand, I cannot be asked to perform the action on some occasion when I believe that the event will not take place, when this knowledge lies in my intention to prevent it taking place; for as soon as I accede to the request, I thereby abandon my intention. It would, indeed, be different if we had foreknowledge: someone who thought, like Russell and Ayer, that it is a merely contingent fact that we have memory but not foreknowledge would conclude that the difference I have pointed to does not reveal a genuine asymmetry between past and future, but merely reflects this contingent fact.

If the chief accepts the challenge, and dances when he knows that the young men have not been brave, it seems that he must concede that his dancing does not *ensure* their bravery. There is one other possibility favourable to us. Suppose that he accepts the challenge, but when he comes to try to dance, he unaccountably cannot do so: his limbs simply will not respond. They we may say, 'It is not your dancing (after the event) which causes them to have been brave, but rather their bravery which makes possible your dancing: your dancing is not, as you thought, an action which it is in your power to do or not to do as you choose. So you ought not to say that you dance in the last two days in order to make them have been brave, but that you try to see whether you can dance, in order to find out whether they have been brave.'

It may seem that this is conclusive; for are not these the only two possibilities? Either he does dance, in which case the dancing is proved not to be a sufficient condition of the previous bravery; or he does not, in which case the bravery must be thought a causal condition of the dancing rather than vice versa. But in fact the situation is not quite so simple.

For one thing, it is not justifiable to demand that the chief should either consider his dancing to be a sufficient condition of the young men's bravery, or regard it as wholly unconnected. It is enough, in order to provide him with a motive for performing the dances, that he should have grounds to believe that there is a significant positive correlation between his dancing and previous brave actions on the part of the young men; so the occurrence of a certain proportion of occasions on which the dancing is performed, although the young men were not brave, is not a sufficient basis to condemn him as irrational if he continues to dance during the last two days. Secondly, while his being afflicted with an otherwise totally inexplicable inability to dance may strongly suggest that the cowardice of the young men renders him unable to dance, and that therefore dancing is not an action which it is in his power to perform as he chooses, any failure to dance that is explicable without reference to the outcome of the hunt has much less tendency to suggest this. Let us suppose that we issue our challenge, and he accepts it. On the first occasion when the observers return and report cowardly behaviour on the part of the young men, he performs his dance. This weakens his belief in the efficacy of the dancing, but does not disturb him unduly; there have been occasions before when the dancing has not worked, and he simply classes this as one of them. On the second occasion when the experiment can be tried, he agrees to attempt it, but, a few hours before the experiment is due to be carried out, he learns that a neighbouring tribe is marching to attack his, so the experiment has to be abandoned; on the third occasion, he is bitten by a snake, and so is incapacitated for dancing. Someone might wish to say, 'The cowardice of the young men caused those events to happen and so prevent the chief from dancing', but such a description is far from mandatory: the chief may simply say that these events were accidental, and in no way *brought about* by the cowardice of the young men. It is true that if the chief is willing to attempt the experiment a large number of times, and events of this kind repeatedly occur, it will no longer appear reasonable to dismiss them as a series of coincidences. If accidents which prevent his dancing occur on occasions when the young men are known to have been cowardly with much greater frequency than, say, in a control group of dancing attempts, when the young men are known to have been brave, or when it is not known how they behaved, then this frequency becomes something that must itself be explained, even though each particular such event already has its explanation.

Suppose now, however, that the following occurs. We ask the chief to perform the dances on some occasion when the hunting party has returned and the observers have reported that the young men have not acquitted themselves with bravery. He does so, and we claim another weakening of his belief that the dancing is correlated with preceding bravery. But later it turns out that, for some reason or other, the observers were lying (say they had been bribed by someone): so after all this is not a counter-example to the law. So we have a third possible outcome. The situation now is this. We challenge the chief to perform the dances whenever he knows that the young men have not been brave, and he accepts the challenge. There are three kinds of outcome: (i) he simply performs the dances; (ii) he is prevented from performing the dances by some occurrence which has a quite natural explanation totally independent of the behaviour of the young men; and (iii) he performs the dances, but subsequently discovers that this was not really an occasion on which the young men had not been brave. We may imagine that he carries out the experiment repeatedly, and that the outcome always falls into one of these classes; and that outcomes of class (i) are sufficiently infrequent not to destroy his belief that there is a significant correlation between the dancing and the young men's bravery, and outcomes of class (ii) sufficiently infrequent to not make him say that the young men's cowardice renders him incapable of performing the dances. Thus our experiment has failed.

On the other hand, it has not left everything as before. I have exploited the fact that it is frequently possible to discover that one had been mistaken in some belief about the past. I will not here raise the question whether it is *always* possible to discover this, or whether there are beliefs about the past about which we can be *certain* in the sense that nothing could happen to show the belief to have been mistaken. Now before we challenged the chief to perform this series of experiments, his situation was as follows. He was prepared to perform the dancing in order to bring it about that the young men had been brave, but only when he had no information about whether they had been brave or not. The rationale of his doing so was simply this: experience shows that there is a positive correlation between the dancing and the young men's bravery; hence the fact that the dances are being performed makes it more probable that the young men have been brave. But the dancing is something that is in my power to do if I choose: experience does not lead me to recognise it as a possibility that I should try to perform the dances and fail. Hence it is in my power to do something, the doing of which will make it more probable that the young men have been brave: I have therefore every motive to do it. Once he had information, provided by the observers, about the behaviour of the young men, then, under the old dispensation, his attitude changed: he no longer had a motive to perform the dances. We do not have to assume that he was unaware of the possibility that the observers were lying or had made a mistake. It may just have been that he reckoned the probability that they were telling the truth as so high that the performance of the dances after they had made their report would make no significant difference to the probability that the young men had been brave. If they reported the young men as having been brave, there was so little chance of their being wrong that it was not worth while to attempt to diminish this chance by performing the dances; if they reported that the young men had been cowardly, then even the performance of the dances would still leave it overwhelmingly probable that they *had* been cowardly. That is to say, until the series of experiments was performed, the chief was prepared to discount completely the probability conferred by his dancing on the proposition that the young men had been brave in the face of a source of information as to the truth of this proposition of the kind we ordinarily rely upon in deciding the truth or falsity of statements about the past. And the reason for this attitude is very clear: for the proposition that there was a positive correlation between the dancing and the previous bravery of the young men could have been established in the first place only by relying on our ordinary sources of information as to whether the young men had been brave or not.

But if we are to suppose that the series of experiments works out in such a way as not to force the chief to abandon his belief both that there is such a positive correlation and that the dancing is something which it is in his power to do when he chooses, we must suppose that it fairly frequently happens that the observers are subsequently proved to have been making false statements. And I think it is clear that in the process the attitude of the chief to the relative degree of probability conferred on the statement that the young men have been brave by (i) the reports of the observers and (ii) his performance of the dances will alter. Since it so frequently happens that, when he performs the dances *after* having received an adverse report from the observers, the observers prove to have been misreporting, he will cease to think it pointless to perform the dances after having received such an adverse report: he will thus cease to think it pointless to perform the dances after having received such an adverse report: he will thus cease to think that he can decide whether to trust the reports of the observers independently of whether he is going to perform the dances or not. In fact, it seems likely that he will come to think of the performance of the dances as itself a ground for distrusting, or even for denying outright, the adverse reports of the observers, even in the absence of any *other* reason (such as the discovery of their having been bribed, or the reports of some other witness) for believing them not to be telling the truth.

The chief began with two beliefs: (i) that there was a positive correlation between his dancing and the previous brave behaviour of the young men; and (ii) that the dancing was something in his power to do as he chose. We are tempted to think of these two beliefs as incompatible, and I described people attempting to devise a series of experiments to convince the chief of this. I tried to show, however, that these experiments could turn out in such a way as to allow the chief to maintain both beliefs. But in the process a third belief, which we naturally take for granted, has had to be abandoned in order to hang on to the first two: the belief, namely, that it is possible for me to find out what has happened (whether the young men have been brave or not) independently of my intentions. The chief no longer thinks that there is any evidence as to whether the young men had been brave or not, the strength of which is unaffected by whether he intends subsequently to perform the dances. And now it appears that there really is a form of incompatibility among these *three* beliefs, in the sense that it is always possible to carry out a series of actions which will necessarily lead to the abandonment of at least one of them. Here there is an exact parallel with the case of affecting the future. We *never* combine the beliefs (i) that an action A is positively correlated with the subsequent occurrence of an event B; (ii) that the action A is in my power to perform or not as I choose; and (iii) that I can know whether B is going to take place or not independently of my intention to perform or not to perform the action A. The difference between past and future lies in this: that we think that, of any past event, it is in principle possible for me to know whether or not it took place independently of my present intentions; whereas, for many types of future event, we should admit that we are never going to be in a position to have such knowledge independently of our intentions. (If we had foreknowledge, this might be different.) If we insist on hanging on to this belief, for all types of past event, then we cannot combine the two beliefs that are required to make sense of doing something in order that some event should have previously taken place; but I do not know any reason why, if things were to turn out differently from the way they do now, we *could* not reasonably abandon the first of these beliefs rather than either of the other two.

My conclusion therefore is this. If anyone were to claim, of some type of action A, (i) that experience gave grounds for holding the performance of A as increasing the probability of the previous occurrence of a type of event E; and (ii) that experience gave no grounds for regarding A as an action which it was ever not in his power to perform—that is, for entertaining the possibility of his trying to perform it and failing—then we could either force him to abandon one or other of these beliefs, or else to abandon the belief (iii) that it was ever possible for him to have knowledge, independent of his intention to perform A or not, of whether an event E had occurred. Now doubtless most normal human beings would rather abandon either (i) or (ii) than (iii), because we have the prejudice that (iii) must hold good for every type of event: but if someone were, in a particular case, more ready to give up (iii) than (i) or (ii), I cannot see any argument we could use to dissuade him. And so long as he was not dissuaded, he could sensibly speak of performing *A* in order that *E* should have occurred. Of course, he could adopt an intermediate position. It is not really necessary, for him to be able to speak of doing *A* in order that *E* should have occurred, that he deny all possibility of his trying and failing to perform *A*. All that is necessary is that he should not regard his being informed, by ordinary means, of the non-occurrence of *E* as making it more probable that if he tries to perform *A*, he will fail: for, once he does so regard it, we can claim that he should regard the occurrence of *E* as making possible the performance of *A*, in which case his trying to perform *A* is not a case of trying to bring it about that *E* has happened, but of finding out whether *E* has happened. (Much will here depend on whether there is an ordinary causal explanation for the occurrence of *E* or not.) Now he need not really deny that learning, in the ordinary way, that *E* has not occurred makes it all more probable that, if he tries to perform *A*, he will fail. He may concede that it makes it to some extent more probable, while at the same time maintaining that, even when he has grounds for thinking that *E* has not occurred, his intention to perform *A* still makes it more probable than it would otherwise be that *E* has in fact occurred. The attitude of such a man seems paradoxical and unnatural to us, but I cannot see any rational considerations which would force him out of this position. At least, if there are any, it would be interesting to know what they are: I think that none of the considerations I have mentioned in this paper could serve this purpose.

My theological example thus proves to have been a bad—that is, untypical—example in a way we did not suspect at the time, for it will never lead to a discounting of our ordinary methods of finding out about the past. I may pray that the announcer has made a mistake in not including my son's name on the list of survivors; but once I am convinced that no mistake has been made, I will not go on praying for him to have survived. I should regard this kind of prayer as something to which it was possible to have recourse only when an ordinary doubt about what had happened could be entertained. But just because this example is untypical in this way, it involves no tampering with our ordinary conceptual apparatus at all: this is why it is such a natural thing to do. On my view, then, orthodox Jewish theology is mistaken on this point.

I do not know whether it could be held that part of what people have meant when they have said, 'You cannot change the past', is that, for every type of event, it is in principle possible to know whether or not it has happened, independently of one's own intentions. If so, this is not the mere tautology it appears to be, but it does indeed single out what it is that makes us think it impossible to bring about the past.

NOTE

1. By Mr. G. Kreisel.

LEAVING THE PAST ALONE

Samuel Gorovitz

Professor Michael Dummett, in his puzzling and provocative essay on "Bringing About the Past,"[1] considers the temporal asymmetry of the causal relation and puts forth the claim that this asymmetry is contingent rather than logically necessary. He goes on to describe an empirical situation in which, he claims, one could sensibly speak of voluntary action performed with the intention of bringing about a past event. In considering this essay, I shall refer to Dummett's example of the tribal chief, and to the three propositions one of which Dummett holds the chief must reject: (i) that there is a positive correlation between his performing action A at T and the occurrence of E at T_1, prior to T; (ii) that A at time T is entirely within his power to do if he so chooses; and (iii) that it is possible for him to find out what has happened (E or not-E) independently of his intentions (to perform A or not).

I should like to make the following points, which I shall attempt to support:

1. It is most implausible that the temporal asymmetry of the causal relation would reveal itself to us as mere observers, or, for that matter, that the notion of causality itself would.

2. We cannot in fact sensibly imagine such a world as Dummett seeks to describe, in which "everything happens in reverse."

3. Even in the case of a world without intentional action, Dummett has not shown, in spite of his suggestion to the contrary, that the notion of backwards causality does not generate absurdity.

4. In the case of a world in which intentional action does occur, the set of beliefs (i), (ii), (iii) is indeed inconsistent, and (i) and (ii) are indeed both necessary to make sense of the notion of bringing about the past. But the belief that (iii) holds for past events is not a prejudice. Rather there *are* arguments in favor of accepting (iii).

5. Thus Dummett has not actually shown that one can, even in the empirical situation he describes, sensibly speak of acting so as to bring about the past.

6. Indeed, the notion does lead to absurdity, as can be demonstrated by examination of some of the consequences of speaking of the causal relation as differing in essential ways from what we normally take it to be.

7. Furthermore, this absurdity can be accounted for in terms of the relationships in our language among such notions as those of causality, intentional action, physical object, and time.

8. Thus the temporal asymmetry of the causal relation is not an empirical asymmetry, but has its basis in the way talk about causality functions in our language.

Dummett admits the claim that "our concept of cause is bound up with our concept of intentional action." And he recognizes that the "connection between something's being a cause and the possibility of using it in order to bring about its effect plays an essential role in the fundamental account of how we ever come to accept causal laws." But he goes on without further exploration of the point to suggest that we could have a notion of cause even if we were mere observers of the world. And he further suggests that in such a case the temporal asymmetry of the causal relation "would reveal itself to us." But he offers no account of the way in which we might come to learn of cause and its properties.

Admittedly, there is nothing logically wrong with the notion of a being which, independently of any interaction with the world, has an understanding of causality. But I take Dummett's point here to be a psychological one: it is a question of how we come to know about cause, not a question of the logical analysis of that concept. And there is no reason to suspect that we could ever come to know about cause without being able to interact in some way with our environment. Piaget offers experimental evidence in support of the claim that we do in fact develop our conception of causality as a result of such interaction, and concludes: "The starting point of causality is a non-differentiation between inner and outer experiences; the world is explained in terms of the self. . . . We do not . . . begin by discovering internal causality and then proceed to transfer it into objects. Causality is the result of a sort of bodily contact between the organism and the world, which is prior to consciousness of self."[2] We are left with a complete lack of any suggestion as to how a mere observer could come to have an understanding of causation; and in the light of evidence that we learn about causation by means of our interaction with the world, I must conclude that, as a psychological observation, Dummett's view is implausible.

But let us grant Dummett the first step. Let us imagine a sentient being, created somehow with a notion of causality, placed in observation of our world with orders not to touch. Would the temporal asymmetry of the causal relation, "reveal itself" to him? It seems not. For if his understanding of causality includes the temporal asymmetry, the question is begged. But if not, there seems to be no way the observer could discover it. As an observer, he would lack any test to distinguish between causal connection and accidental though constant conjunction, and his inability to participate in causal chains of events would deprive him of the one empirical indication of the asymmetry—that is, the experience of influencing the future with no apparent way to influence the past. Even knowing that A and B are causally related, he would have no way of determining which event was the cause.

I do not here wish to suggest that an observer could not have knowledge of the temporal asymmetry. I mean merely to deny that he could discover the asymmetry by observation of the world, even granting that he had some prior notion about causality. Of course, I have given no proof that the asymmetry would not reveal itself; but I hope to have shown it more implausible than likely in the absence of some sort of interaction between the observer and the environment beyond that which is involved in observation alone.

The second point I wish to make is that we cannot in fact imagine such a world as Dummett describes, in which "everything happens in reverse." I claim that this result comes not out of any definition of the notion of causality, but rather from an examination of the way in which the notion is bound up with others as we use language to organize and describe experience. In particular, the notion of causality is closely related to the notion of time. And Dummett's error stems from tampering with one of these notions without considering the implications for the other. I shall argue that one cannot successfully alter the notion of cause, as Dummett does at this point, and leave that of time unaffected.

To begin with, it is not reasonable to assume that time order is independent of causal order. In fact, Reichenbach claims to have shown that time order is *reducible to* causal order.[3] Such a dependence of temporal order on causal order, he argues, is indispensable in relativity theory.[4] What, then, of Dummett's world, in which "everything happens in reverse"? If Reichenbach is right about the dependence of temporal order on causal order, one might well argue that time itself is therefore "reversed" in Dummett's world, and thus the notion of everything happening in reverse is vacuous: it specifies no situation distinguishable from the normal. Even if we do not accept Reichenbach's account, we can see problems arising about Dummett's world to which there are no obvious solutions. How can we tell that everything is reversed? Do the clocks run backwards, too? What does that mean, if all clocks, natural and artificial, run backwards? What is the order of our ideas, if we imagine ourselves in this world? Or if we do not, what distinguishes the forward and reverse directions of time?

This situation suggests that if we are to examine the question of whether or not we can make sense of talk about unusual temporal properties of a causal sequence, we must consider not the case when" everything happens in reverse," but one in which only some of the causal chains have an abnormal temporal direction. This is, in fact, just what Dummett does when he considers in detail the actual issues associated with the question of the temporal order of causality.

In view of the preceding considerations, it is not at all clear that the notion of backwards causality is a sensible one. For Dummett's remarks in support of such a claim rest on his assumption that there are no problems in imagining and discussing events within a world in which "everything happens in reverse." But this assumption, we have seen, is in error; and thus the question is still open whether or not one can make sense of talk about backwards causation, even in a world without intentional action.

It is, however, the world of intentional action with which we are primarily concerned. Dummett says that it is inconsistent of an agent in such a world to hold simultaneously that:

(i) there is a positive correlation between his doing A at time T and the occurence of event E at time T_1 prior to T,

(ii) doing A at T is within his power if he so chooses, and

(iii) it is possible for him to find out whether or not E occurred at T_1 independently of his intention to perform A or not.

Now I agree that these three beliefs are incompatible and further, that beliefs (i) and (ii), if they can be maintained simultaneously, give rise to talk about doing A in order that E shall have happened. But I disagree with Dummett's view that it is a prejudice which leads us to give up (i) or (ii) rather than (iii).

He says of (iii), "If we insist on hanging onto this belief, for all types of past event, then we cannot combine the two beliefs that are required to make sense of doing something in order that some event should have previously taken place; but I do not know any reason why, if things were to turn out differently from the way they do now, we *could* not reasonably abandon" (iii).[5] I think there are reasons why we cannot abandon (iii), regardless of how things turn out, and I think these reasons are strong enough to force us to recognize that (i) and (ii) are incompatible.

Consider the grounds on which Dummett defends abandoning (iii) in his example. There has been empirical evidence in support of both (i) and (ii). The chief therefore maintains that he can influence the past, and consequently abandons belief in (iii). In fact, this hypothesis—that there is backwards causation—is the only hypothesis on which it is reasonable to give up (iii). Without it the denial of (iii) makes no sense. Thus, the chief gives up (iii) because he recognizes that (i), (ii), and (iii) do not form a consistent set, and he has already accepted (i) and (ii) on empirical grounds. Here the basic flaw in Dummett's approach can be seen. He says of (i) and (ii), "We are tempted to think of these two beliefs as incompatible, and I described people attempting to devise a series of experiments to convince the chief of this. I tried to show, however, that these experiments could turn out in such a way as to allow the chief to maintain both beliefs."[6]

Because of his conviction that the temporal asymmetry of the causal

relation is an empirical asymmetry, Dummett takes the logical possibility
of our trying unsuccessfully to find empirical evidence against (i) and (ii)
as evidence in favor of accepting (i) and (ii) as compatible. But the evidence against the compatibility of (i) and (ii) is logical evidence, itself
compatible with any empirical outcome. So the rejection of (iii) on the
grounds that (i) and (ii) are compatible constitutes sufficient argument
that one *can* make sense of talk about action done in order to influence
the past. But if (i) and (ii) are not compatible, belief in (iii) cannot be
abandoned, since it is reasonable to abandon (iii) only on the hypothesis
that the past can be influenced, and this hypothesis is true in case, for
some A and E, both (i) and (ii) are true.

Thus we cannot reject (iii) on the empirical grounds cited by Dummett.
I shall try to offer a defense of (iii) by providing a case on logical grounds
for the claim that it does not make sense to speak of backwards causation,
and hence for the claim that (i) and (ii) are, after all, incompatible.

I turn to arguments which I hope will show that talk about acting in
order to influence the past does in fact lead to absurdity.[7] Reichenbach, in
supporting his view that the ordering of time is dependent on the order
of causal sequences, claims that it is an empirical fact that closed causal
chains do not occur. He says:

> It should be kept in mind that the openness of causal chains represents an
> empirical fact and cannot be regarded as a logical necessity. There is nothing
> contradictory in imagining causal chains that are closed, though the existence of
> such chains would lead to rather unfamiliar experiences. For instance, it might
> then happen that a person would meet his own former self and have a conver-
> sation with him, thus closing a causal line by the use of sound waves. When
> this occurs the first time he would be the younger ego, and when the same
> occurrence takes place a second time, he would be the older ego. . . . Such a
> situation appears paradoxical to us; but there is nothing illogical in it. However,
> if such events did occur, there would be no time order in the usual sense.
> Moreover, there would be no unique identity of a physical object in time.[8]

In this respect, I think Reichenbach shares Dummett's view that it is an
empirical truth that effects cannot precede their causes. But he does recognize the consequences of such a view for the notions of time and
physical object. This view is not self-contradictory, and I shall not claim
that it is, in the traditional sense, analytic that effects cannot precede their
causes. But the view does give rise to such puzzles that we are forced to
question its intelligibility. Specifically, using Reichenbach's example, this
view of causality calls into question our understanding of the relationships that hold among the concepts of cause, intentional action, and
physical object. Suppose I meet my former self, as in the example. I draw
a pistol. Can I shoot my old self? It seems not, for to do so would entail
my having died before I did so. And this is absurd. But what of someone

else? Can I shoot someone who is standing beside my former self? If not, we are faced with the task of accounting for how I am prevented from performing a simple physical action. Does the example rule out the possibility of anyone ever using a pistol? If not, we must account for the restriction. And what if, on the other hand, I can shoot a man standing beside my former self? Why can I not miss, and shoot my former self as well? What explanation is possible for my failure if I try? Such problems are, I think, indicative of the confusions that arise out of talk about closed causal chains, and the claim that the nonexistence of closed causal chains is an empirical fact seems essentially unsupported. Rather, the puzzles that arise provide a clue to the nature of the logical confusion underlying such notions as that of a closed causal chain.

For when we speak of a closed causal chain, or of reverse causation, we thereby deny of causality certain features we normally consider it to have and which, moreover, are among those most essential to an understanding of causality. In so doing, we open the way for descriptions of situations that are not comprehensible. For example, we normally think that the physical object known as a gun behaves in such a way that we are (logically, if not psychologically) able to shoot either one of two men standing a short distance before us. But the existence of a closed causal chain, as suggested above, is incompatible with this possibility. If we accept Reichenbach's example, we are faced with the problem of explaining why it is that I cannot fire the gun or, if I can, why it is that I can fire only in certain directions. Either the gun is not behaving as the normal physical object we take it to be, or the notion of voluntary action does not apply in the usual way. Thus we see how the notion of causality is bound up with the notion of physical object and of intentional action to the extent that denial of an essential property of the causal relation leads to such serious puzzles involving the notions of physical object and intentional action as to make us question the legitimacy of that denial.

I think, too, that there are some problems about memory that arise when we deny the temporal asymmetry of causality. These problems, like those raised above, emphasize the way in which tampering with the notion of causality leads to a lack of intelligibility that will spread through our language. I shall consider the problems from two points of view: that of the agent in question, and that of an observer.

First, we recall that the set (i), (ii), (iii) of beliefs discussed above was agreed to be inconsistent. And (i) and (ii) must both be accepted to make sense of talk about influencing the past, so (iii) must be given up. I claim that even granting the compatibility of (i) and (ii), we cannot coherently give up (iii).

In Dummett's example, various experiments are described that are designed to show the chief to be in error in his beliefs. These experiments all fail. But there are a few more which Dummett did not consider. For example, instead of letting the chief remain at home while the warriors hunt, only to cause after their return their having been brave on the hunt, let us insist that the chief himself witness the hunt. Now there can no longer be any question of lying reporters who try to deceive the chief, only to be discovered when he dances. The chief will himself observe the cowardice or bravery of the men. Then, if they were brave, he will of course have no need to dance, even if their bravery resulted in some way from his prior intention to dance after the hunt. For if we suggest that the chief's subsequent failure to dance will make the warriors not to have been brave after all, in spite of his remembrance to the contrary, we are unable to account for the error of his memory. And we are led to ask: will he continue to remember the warriors' having been brave even after his failure to dance has caused them to have been cowardly? Or will his memory abruptly change at such time as the warriors change from having been brave to having been cowardly? Or must we assume that the chief is after all just unable to rely on his own judgment (of what is occurring before him) independently of whether he in fact will, regardless of his present intentions, perform some particular action in the future? But such a hypothesis itself leads to inextricable confusion. What if the chief is unaware of the reversed causal efficacy of his dance? Can he then rely on his observation? If so, why? If not, how can complete skepticism be avoided? I conclude that if the chief witnesses the warriors being brave, no dance is necessary.

What then if the warriors are cowardly? The chief, knowing this, will, possibly at some time later than T_1, decide to perform the dance upon his return, thus bringing about that the warriors were after all brave. But we must repeat the same questions here about the chief's memory. How can we account for his error if his memory does not change? How can we account for the change otherwise? The claim that his coming to have a certain intention can change his memory is too obscure to provide any answer at all.

Dummett avoids these problems, and is able to offer a defense of the chief's refusal to believe in (iii), by ignoring the situation in which the chief himself serves as an observer. There is, however, a way out, albeit temporary, for Dummett. In his earlier article on reverse causality,[9] he suggests that the causal connections that work in reverse are effective only in cases where the agent is ignorant of whether or not the desired event has actually occurred. Perhaps it was to avoid this unlikely hypothesis that Dummett chose to suggest abandonment of belief in (iii), thus ruling out the possibility that the effective agent have knowledge of the prior event independently of his intentions. But I hope to have shown that this will not do, that the denial of (iii) leads, in the case where the observer and agent are one, to problems about memory and the reliability of observation serious enough to force us to retain belief in (iii).

Let us then consider the way out abandoned by Dummett. On this view the chief's dance is effective only if he does not know the outcome of the hunt. We need not seek an explanation of how the efficacy depends on the agent's knowledge. For the same problems of memory reappear as soon as we introduce an observer. If *anyone,* let alone the agent, witnesses the nonoccurrence of E at T_1, then we are—recalling that (ii), as well as (i), is here assumed—unable to account for the error or change in *his* memory in the event that the agent by performing A at T causes E to have happened. And we must be able to provide such an account, since the agent's performance of A is, by hypothesis, independent of the occurrence of E.

Thus we are led to the view that rejection of belief in (iii) itself leads to absurdity when we consider the implications for talk about memory and, particularly, about observation. Even the restriction that, for the cause to be effective, the agent must be ignorant of whether or not the effect occurred is of no help. For the same problems about memory then arise out of the notion of backwards causality, rather than out of the rejection of belief in (iii).

I thus conclude that talk about acting in order to bring about the past leads to absurdity. It does so because the notion of causality is logically related to notions of time, memory, physical object, voluntary action, and perhaps others. To tamper with one of these notions is to raise problems for all. The problems raised by tampering in this particular way with the notion of causality are so serious, and touch so many crucial features of our language, that they call into question enough of that language for us to be no longer able to make sense of what we are saying. This is not a new point, but so long as philosophers continue to treat separately the fundamental categories in terms of which we describe the world, without considering the interconnections among these categories, it bears repetition.

Thus it is a logical truth that one cannot bring about the past. Yet it is not a mere tautology. Rather, this truth has its basis in the way talk about causality functions in our language, and it is analytic only in the sense that to deny it is to generate absurdities, rather than formal contradictions. Pears, in discussing the logic that underlies talk about time, expresses much the same point. He says:

> the sentences which give the logical relations of temporal words exhibit a curious feature. They are not synthetic *a priori,* but they are, as it were, weak tautologies. And they are weak tautologies not only because we are so accustomed to using temporal words correctly that we need no reminders, but also because their structure is peculiar. For most tautologies are constructed like columns, by placing terms squarely one on top of another like marble drums. But the tautologies which give the logic of temporal words put their terms together like the stones of a vault. No single conjunction of terms is indispensable or could stand alone. But together they form the vaulted ceiling on which the fresco of knowledge is painted.[10]

NOTES

1. Reprinted in this section.

2. Jean Piaget, *The Child's Conception of Physical Causality*, trans. M. Gabain (Patterson, N.J., 1960), p. 272.

3. Hans Reichenbach, *The Direction of Time*, ed. Maria Reichenbach (Berkeley and Los Angeles, 1956), p. 25.

4. The decisive argument in favor of defining time order in terms of causal order derives from Einstein's criticisms of simultaneity. It is well known that the Lorentz transformations, which express Einstein's special principle of relativity, permit the reversal of the time order of certain events, namely, of those which cannot be connected by causal chains. Time order is invariant under the Lorentz transformations only if the events in question can be connected by signals, this is by causal chains. It follows that if time order were more than causal order the Lorentz transformations and Einstein's relativity could not be accepted (*ibid.*, p. 25).

5. P. 357.

6. P. 356.

7. For a discussion of this point, see H. Putnam, "It Ain't Necessarily So," *Journal of Philosophy*, LIX (1962), 665–671. But Putnam has not shown that one cannot cast the notion of time travel (or, presumably, of reverse causation) into ill repute by showing "that if we start talking about time travel, things go wrong with ordinary language in countless places and in countless ways" (p. 668). Putnam's suggestion that a consistent mathematical representation of time travel is possible hardly goes to show that there is nothing conceptually impossible about time travel, except on the undefended premise that what can be represented in a consistent mathematical way is therefore conceptually unimpeachable.

8. Reichenbach, *op. cit.*, p. 37.

9. M. Dummett and A. Flew, "Symposium: Can an Effect Precede Its Cause?" *Proceedings of the Aristotelian Society*, Supp. Vol. XXVIII (1954): Belief and Will.

10. D. F. Pears, "Time, Truth and Inference," *Proceedings of the Aristotelian Society*, II (1950–1951), 22.

OF THE IDEA OF NECESSARY CONNECTION

David Hume

PART I

There are no ideas which occur in metaphysics more obscure and uncertain than those of *power, force, energy* or *necessary connexion,* of which it is every moment necessary for us to treat in all our disquisitions. We shall, therefore, endeavor in this section to fix, if possible, the precise meaning of these terms, and thereby remove some part of that obscurity which is so much complained of in this species of philosophy.

It seems a proposition which will not admit of much dispute, that all our ideas are nothing but copies of our impressions, or, in other words, that it is impossible for us to *think* of any thing, which we have not antecedently *felt,* either by our external or internal senses. . . . To be fully acquainted, therefore, with the idea of power or necessary connexion, let us examine its impression with greater certainty, let us search for it in all the sources, from which it may possibly be derived.

When we look about us towards external objects, and consider the operation of causes, we are never able, in a single instance, to discover any power or necessary connexion; [that is,] any quality which binds the effect to the cause and renders the one an infallible consequence of the other. We only find that the one does actually, in fact, follow the other. The impulse of one billiard-ball is attended with motion in the second. This is the whole that appears to the *outward* senses. The mind feels no sentiment or *inward* impression from this succession of objects: Consequently, there is not, in any single, particular instance of cause and effect, anything which can suggest the idea of power or necessary connexion.

From the first appearance of an object, we never can conjecture what effect will result from it. But were the power or energy of any cause discoverable by the mind, we could foresee the effect even without experience, and might, at first, pronounce with certainty concerning it, by mere dint of thought and reasoning.

In reality, there is no part of matter that does ever, by its sensible qualities, discover any power or energy, or give us ground to imagine, that it could produce any thing, or be followed by any other object, which we could denominate its effect. Solidity, extension, motion; these qualities are all complete in themselves, and never point out any other event which may result from them. The scenes of the universe are continually shifting, and one object follows another in an uninterrupted succession; but the power or force which actuates the whole machine is entirely concealed from us, and never discovers itself in any of the sensible qualities of body. We know, that, in fact, heat is a constant attendant of flame; but what is the connexion between them, we have no room so much as to conjecture or imagine. It is impossible, therefore, that the idea of power can be derived from the contemplation of bodies, in single instances of their operation; because no bodies ever discover any power which can be the original of this idea.

Since, therefore, external objects as they appear to the senses give us no idea of power or necessary connexion by their operation in particular instances, let us see whether this idea be derived from reflection on the operations of our own minds, and be copied from any internal impression. It may be said that we are every moment conscious of internal power; while we feel, that, by the simple command of our will, we can move the organs of our body, or direct the faculties of our mind. An act of volition produces motion in our limbs, or raises a new idea in our imagination. This influence of the will we know by consciousness. Hence we acquire the idea of power or energy, and are certain that we ourselves and all other intelligent beings are possessed of power. . . .

We shall proceed to examine this pretension; and first with regard to the influence of volition over the organs of the body. This influence, we may observe, is a fact, which, like all other natural events, can be known only by experience, and can never be foreseen from any apparent energy or power in the cause, which connects it with the effect, and renders the one an infallible consequence of the other. The motion of our body follows upon the command of our will. Of this we are every moment conscious. But the means by which this is effected, the energy by which the will performs so extraordinary an operation, of this we are so far from being immediately conscious that it must for ever escape our most diligent enquiry.

For *first*, is there any principle in all nature more mysterious than the union of soul with body, by which a supposed spiritual substance acquires such an influence over a material one that the most refined thought is able to actuate the grossest matter? Were we empowered, by a secret wish, to remove mountains, or control the planets in their orbit; this extensive authority would not be more extraordinary, nor more beyond our comprehension. But if by consciousness we perceived any power or energy in the will, we must know this power; we must know its connexion with the effect; we must know the secret union of soul and body, and the nature of both these substances, by which the one is able to operate, in so many instances, upon the other.

Secondly, We are not able to move all the organs of the body with a like authority; though we cannot assign any reason besides experience for so remarkable a difference between one and the other. Why has the will an influence over the tongue and fingers, not over the heart or liver? This question would never embarrass us were we conscious of a power in the former case, not in the latter. . . .

Thirdly, We learn from anatomy that the immediate object of power in voluntary motion is not the member itself which is moved, but certain muscles, and nerves, and animal spirits, and, perhaps, something still more minute and more unknown, through which the motion is successively propagated, ere it reach the member itself whose motion is the immediate object of volition. Can there be a more certain proof that the power by which this whole operation is performed, so far from being directly and fully known by an inward sentiment or consciousness, is, to the last degree, mysterious and unintelligible? Here the mind wills a certain event: Immediately another event, unknown to ourselves, and totally different from the one intended, is produced: This event produces another, equally unknown: Till at last, through a long succession, the desired event is produced. But if the original power were felt, it must be known: Were it known, its effect also must be known; since all power is relative to its effect. And *vice versa,* if the effect be not known, the power cannot be known nor felt. How indeed can we be conscious of a power to move our limbs when we have no such power; but only that to move certain animal spirits, which, though they produce at last the motion of our limbs, yet operate in such a manner as is wholly beyond our comprehension?

We may, therefore, conclude . . . that our idea of power is not copied from any sentiment or consciousness of power within ourselves, when we give rise to animal motion, or apply our limbs to their proper use and office. That their motion follows the command of the will is a matter of common experience, like other natural events: But the power or energy by which this is effected, like that in other natural events, is unknown and inconceivable. . . .

The generality of mankind never finds any difficulty in accounting for the more common and familiar operations of nature—such as the descent of heavy bodies, the growth of plants, the generation of animals, or the nourishment of bodies by food: But suppose that, in all these cases, they perceive the very force or energy of the cause, by which it is connected with its effect, and is for ever infallible in its operation. They acquire, by long habit such a turn of mind that, upon the appearance of the cause, they immediately expect with assurance its usual attendant, and hardly conceive it possible that any other event could result from it. It is only on the discovery of extraordinary phenomena, such as earthquakes, pestilence, and prodigies of any kind, that they find themselves at a loss to assign a proper cause, and to explain the manner in which the effect is produced by it. It is usual for men, in such difficulties to have recourse to some invisible intelligent principle as the immediate cause of that event which surprises them, and which, they think, cannot be accounted for from the common powers of nature. But philosophers, who carry their scrutiny a little farther, immediately perceive that, even, in the most familiar events, the energy of the cause is as unintelligible as in the most unusual, and that we only learn by experience the frequent *Conjunction* of objects, without being ever able to comprehend anything like *Connexion* between them. . . .

PART II

But to hasten a conclusion of this argument, which is already drawn out to too great a length: We have sought in vain for an idea of power or necessary connexion in all the sources from which we could suppose it to be derived. It appears that, in single instances of the operation of bodies, we never can, by our utmost scrutiny, discover any thing but one event following another, without being able to comprehend any force or power by which the cause operates, or any connexion between it and its supposed effect. The same difficulty occurs in contemplating the operations of mind on body—where we observe the motion of the latter to follow upon the volition of the former, but are not able to observe or conceive the tie which binds together the motion and volition, or the energy by which the mind produces this effect. The authority of the will over its own faculties and ideas is not a whit more comprehensible: So that, upon the whole, there appears not, throughout all nature, any one instance of connexion which is conceivable by us. All events seem entirely loose and separate. One event follows another; but we never can observe any tie between them. They seem *conjoined*, but never *connected*. And as we can have no idea of anything which never appeared to our outward sense or inward sentiment, the necessary conclusion *seems* to be that we have no idea of connexion or power at all, and that these words are absolutely without any meaning, when employed either in philosophical reasonings or common life.

But there still remains one method of avoiding this conclusion, and one source which we have not yet examined. When any natural object or event is presented, it is impossible for us, by any sagacity or penetration, to discover, or even conjecture, without experience, what event will result from it, or to carry our foresight beyond that object which is immediately present to the memory and senses. Even after one instance or experiment where we have observed a particular event to follow upon another, we are not entitled to form a general rule, or foretell what will happen in like cases; it being justly esteemed an unpardonable temerity to judge of the whole course of nature from one single experiment, however accurate or certain. But when one particular species of event has always, in all instances, been conjoined with another, we make no longer any scruple of foretelling one upon the appearance of the other, and of employing that reasoning, which can alone assure us of any matter of fact or existence. We then call the one object, *Cause;* the other, *Effect.* We suppose that there is some connexion between them; some power in the one, by which it infallibly produces the other, and operates with the greatest certainty and strongest necessity.

It appears, then, that this idea of a necessary connexion among events arises from a number of similar instances which occur of the constant conjunction of these events; nor can that idea ever be suggested by any one of these instances, surveyed in all possible lights and positions. But there is nothing in a number of instances different from every single instance which is supposed to be exactly similar, except only that after a repetition of similar instances, the mind is carried by habit, upon the appearance of one event, to expect its usual attendant, and to believe that it will exist. This connexion, therefore, which we *feel* in the mind, this customary transition of the imagination from one object to its usual attendant, is the sentiment or impression from which we form the idea of power or necessary connexion. Nothing farther is in the case. Contemplate the subject on all sides; you will never find any other origin of that idea. This is the sole difference between one instance, from which we can never receive the idea of connexion, and a number of similar instances, by which it is suggested. The first time a man saw the communication of motion by impulse, as by the shock of two billiard balls, he could not pronounce that the one event was *connected:* but only that it was *conjoined* with the other. After he has observed several instances of this nature, he then pronounces them to be *connected.* What alteration has happened to give rise to this new idea of *connexion?* Nothing but that he now *feels* these events to be *connected* in his imagination, and can readily foretell the existence of one from the appearance of the other. When we say, therefore, that one object is connected with another, we mean only that they have acquired a connexion in our thought, and give rise to this inference, by which they become proofs of each other's existence: A conclusion which is somewhat extraordinary, but which seems founded on sufficient evidence. Nor will its evidence be weakened by any general diffidence of the understanding, or sceptical suspicion concerning every conclusion which is new and extraordinary. No conclusions can be more agreeable to scepticism than such as make discoveries concerning the weakness and narrow limits of human reason and capacity.

And what stronger instance can be produced of the surprising ignorance and weakness of the understanding than the present? For surely, if there be any relation among objects which it imports to us to know perfectly, it is that of cause and effect. On this are founded all our reasonings concerning matter of fact or existence. By means of it alone we attain any assurance concerning objects which are removed from the present testimony of our memory and senses. The only immediate utility of all sciences, is to teach us how to control and regulate future events by their causes. Our thoughts and enquiries are, therefore, every moment employed about this relation: Yet so imperfect are the ideas which we form concerning it that it is impossible to give any just definition of cause, except what is drawn from something extraneous and foreign to it. Similar objects are always conjoined with similar. Of this we have experience. Suitable to this experience, therefore, we may define a cause to be *an object, followed by another, and where all the objects similar to the first are followed by objects similar to the second.* Or in other words, *where, if the first object had not been, the second never had existed.* The appearance of a cause always conveys the mind, by a customary transition, to the idea of the effect. Of this also we have experience. We may, therefore, suitably to this experience, form another definition of cause, and call it *an object followed by another, and whose appearance always conveys the thought to that other.* But though both these definitions be drawn from circumstances foreign to the cause, we cannot remedy this inconvenience, or attain any more perfect definition, which may point out that circumstance in the cause which gives it a connexion with its effect. We have no idea of this connexion, nor even any distinct notion what it is we desire to know, where we endeavour at a conception of it. We say, for instance, that the vibration of this string is the cause of this particular sound. But what do we mean by that affirmation? We either mean *that this vibration is followed by this sound, and that all similar vibrations have been followed by similar sounds: Or, that this vibration is followed by this sound, and that upon the appearance of one the mind anticipates the senses, and forms immediately an idea of the other.* We may consider the relation of cause and effect in either of these two lights; but beyond these, we have no idea of it.

To recapitulate, therefore, the reasonings of this section: Every idea is copied from some preceding impression or sentiment; and where we cannot find any impression, we may be certain that there is no idea. In all single instances of the operation of bodies or minds, there is nothing that produces any impression, nor consequently can suggest any idea of power or necessary connexion. But when many uniform instances appear, and the same object is always followed by the same event, we then begin to entertain the notion of cause and connexion. We then *feel* a new sentiment or impression, to wit, a customary connexion in the thought or imagination between one object and its usual attendant; and this sentiment is the original of that idea which we seek for. For as this idea arises from a number of similar instances, and not from any single instance, it must arise from the circumstance in which the number of instances differ from every individual instance. But this customary connexion or transition of the imagination is the only circumstance in which they differ. In every other particular they are alike. The first instance which we saw of motion communicated by the shock of two billiard balls (to return to this obvious illustration) is exactly similar to any instance that may, at present, occur to us; except only that we could not, at first, *infer* one event from the other; which we are enabled to do at present after so long a course of uniform experience.

Custom, then, is the great guide of human life. It is that principle alone which renders our experience useful to us, and makes us expect, for the future, a similar train of events with those which have appeared in the past. Without the influence of custom, we should be entirely ignorant of every matter of fact beyond what is immediately present to the memory and senses. We should never know how to adjust means to ends, or to employ our natural powers in the production of any effect. There would be an end at once of all action, as well as of the chief part of speculation.

But here it may be proper to remark that though our conclusions from experience carry us beyond our memory and senses, and assure us of matters of fact which happened in the most distant places and most remote ages, yet some fact must always be present to the senses or memory from which we may first proceed in drawing these conclusions. A man who should find in a desert country the remains of pompous buildings would conclude that the country had, in ancient times, been cultivated by civilized inhabitants; but did nothing of this nature occur to him, he could never form such an inference. We learn the events of former ages from history; but then we must peruse the volumes in which this instruction is contained, and thence carry up our inferences from one testimony to another, till we arrive at the eyewitnesses and spectators of these distant events. In a word, if we proceed not upon some fact, present to the memory of senses, our reasonings would be merely hypothetical; and however the particular links might be connected with each other, the whole chain of inferences would have nothing to support it, nor could we ever, by its means, arrive at the knowledge of any real existence. If I ask why you believe any particular matter of fact, which you relate, you must tell me some reason; and this reason will be some other fact, connected with it. But as you cannot proceed after this manner, *in infinitum*, you must at last terminate in some fact, which is present to your memory or senses; or must allow that your belief is entirely without foundation.

What, then, is the conclusion of the whole matter? A simple one, though it must be confessed, pretty remote from the common theories of philosophy. All belief of matter of fact or real existence is derived merely from some object, present to the memory or senses, and a customary conjunction between that and some other object. Or in other words, having found, in many instances, that any two kinds of objects—flame and heat, snow and cold—have always beem conjoined together, if flame or snow be presented anew to the senses, the mind is carried by custom to expect heat or cold, and to *believe* that such a quality does exist, and will discover itself upon a nearer approach. This belief is the necessary result of placing the mind in such circumstances. It is an operation of the soul, when we are so situated, as unavoidable as to feel the passion of love when we receive benefits, or hatred when we meet with injuries. All these operations are a species of natural instincts, which no reasoning or process of the thought and understanding is able either to produce or to prevent.

OF THE WORDS CAUSE AND EFFECT, ACTION, AND ACTIVE POWER

Thomas Reid

The writings upon Liberty and Necessity have been much darkened by the ambiguity of the words used in reasoning upon that subject. The words *cause* and *effect, action* and *active power, liberty* and *necessity*, are related to each other: The meaning of one determines the meaning of the rest. When we attempt to define them, we can only do it by synonymous words which need definition as such. There is a strict sense in which those words must be used, if we speak and reason clearly about moral liberty; but to keep to this strict sense is difficult, because, in all languages, they have, by custom, got a great latitude of signification.

As we cannot reason about moral liberty without using those ambiguous words, it is proper to point out, as distinctly as possible, their proper and original meaning in which they ought to be understood in treating of this subject, and to shew from what causes they have become so ambiguous in all languages as to darken and embarrass our reasonings upon it.

Everything that begins to exist, must have a cause of its existence, which had power to give it existence. And everything that undergoes any change, must have some cause of that change.

That neither existence, nor any mode of existence, can begin without an efficient cause, is a principle that appears very early in the mind of man; and it is so universal, and so firmly rooted in human nature, that the most determined scepticism cannot eradicate it.

It is upon this principle that we ground the rational belief of a deity. But that is not the only use to which we apply it. Every man's conduct is governed by it, every day, and almost every hour, of his life. And if it were possible for any man to root out this principle from his mind, he must give up everything that is called common prudence, and be fit only to be confined as insane.

From this principle it follows, *That everything which undergoes any change, must either be the efficient cause of that change in itself, or it must be changed by some other being.*

In the *first* case, it is said to have *active power*, and to *act* in producing that change. In the *second* case, it is merely *passive*, or is *acted upon*, and the active power is in that being only which produces the change.

The name of a *cause* and of an *agent*, is properly given to that being only, which, by its active power, produces some change in itself, or in some other being. The change, whether it be of thought, of will, or of motion, is the effect. Active power, therefore, is a quality in the cause, which enables it to produce the effect. And the exertion of that active power in producing the effect, is called *action, agency, efficiency.*

In order to the production of any effect, there must be in the cause, not only power, but the *exertion of that power;* for power that is not exerted produces no effect.

All that is necessary to the production of any effect, is power in an efficient cause to produce the effect, and the exertion of that power; for it is a contradiction to say, that the cause has power to produce the effect, and exerts that power, and yet the effect is not produced. The effect cannot be in his power unless all the means necessary to its production be in his power.

It is no less contradiction to say, that a cause has power to produce a certain effect, but that he cannot exert that power; for power which cannot be exerted is no power, and is a contradiction in terms.

To prevent mistake, it is proper to observe, That a being may have a power at one time which it has not at another. It may commonly have a power, which, at a particular time, it has not. Thus, a man may commonly have power to walk or to run; but he has not this power when asleep, or when he is confined by superior force. In common language, he may be said to have a power which he cannot then exert. But this popular expression means only that he commonly has this power, and will have it when the cause is removed which at present deprives him of it; for, when we speak strictly and philosophically, it is a contradiction to say that he has this power, at that moment when he is deprived of it.

These, I think, are necessary consequences from the principle first mentioned—That every change which happens in nature must have an efficient cause which had power to produce it.

Another principle, which appears very early in the mind of man, is, *That we are efficient causes in our deliberate and voluntary actions.*

We are conscious of making an exertion, sometimes with difficulty, in order to produce certain effects. And exertion made deliberately and voluntarily, in order to produce an effect, implies a conviction that the effect is in our power. No man can deliberately attempt what he does not believe to be in his power. The language of all mankind, and their ordinary conduct in life, demonstrate that they have a conviction of some active power in themselves to produce certain motions in their own and in other bodies, and to regulate and direct their own thoughts. This conviction we have so early in life, that we have no remembrance when, or in what way, we acquired it.

That such a conviction is at first the necessary result of our constitution, and that it can never be entirely obliterated, is, I think, acknowledged by one of the most zealous defenders of Necessity. "Such are the influences to which all mankind, without distinction, are exposed that they necessarily refer actions (I mean refer them ultimately) first of all to themselves and others; and it is a long time before they begin to consider themselves and others as instruments in the hand of a superior agent. Consequently, the associations which refer action to themselves get so confirmed that they are never entirely obliterated; and therefore the common language, and the common feelings, of mankind, will be adapted to the first, the limited and imperfect, or rather erroneous, view of things."

It is very probable that the very conception or idea of active power, and of efficient causes, is derived from our voluntary exertions in producing effects; and that, if we were not conscious of such exertion, we should have no conception at all of a cause, or of active power, and consequently no conviction of the necessity of a cause of every change which we observe in nature.

It is certain that we can conceive no kind of active power but what is similar or analogous to that which we attribute to ourselves; that is, a power which is exerted by will and with understanding. Our notion, even of Almighty power, is derived from the notion of human power, by removing from the former those imperfections and limitations to which the latter is subjected.

It may be difficult to explain the origin of our conceptions and belief concerning efficient causes and advice power. The common theory, that all our ideas are ideas of Sensation or Reflection, and that all our belief is a perception of the agreement or the disagreement of those ideas, appears to be repugnant, both to the idea of an efficient cause, and to the belief of its necessity.

An attachment to that theory has led some philosophers to deny that we have any conception of an efficient cause, or of active power, because efficiency and active power are not ideas, either of sensation or reflection. They maintain, therefore, that a Cause is only *something prior to the effect, and constantly conjoined with it.* This is Mr Hume's notion of a cause, and seems to be adopted by Dr. Priestley, who says, "That a cause cannot be defined to be any thing, but *such previous circumstances as are constantly followed by a certain effect,* the constancy of the result making us conclude that there must be a *sufficient reason,* in the nature of the things, why it should be produced in those circumstances." [*Doctrine of Philosophical Necessity,* p. 11.]

But theory ought to stoop to fact, and not fact to theory. Every man who understands the language knows that neither priority, nor constant conjunction, nor both taken together, imply efficiency. . . .

The very dispute, whether we have the conception of an efficient cause, shews that we have. For, though men may dispute about things which have no existence, they cannot dispute about things of which they have no conception.

What has been said in this chapter is intended to shew—That the conception of causes, of action and of active power, in the strict and proper sense of these words, is found in the minds of all men very early, even in the dawn of their rational life. It is therefore probable, that, in all languages, the words by which these conceptions were expressed were at first distinct and unambiguous, yet it is certain that, among the most enlightened nations, these words are applied to so many things of different natures, and used in so vague a manner, that it is very difficult to reason about them distinctly.

This phænomenon, at first view, seems very unaccountable. But a little reflection may satisfy us, that it is a natural consequence of the slow and gradual progress of human knowledge. . . .

Questions for Part VI

1. Causal laws are central to our explanations of events and such laws predicate a certain temporal relationship between causes and effects. Effects always follow causes, they do not precede them. Still, Michael Dummett believes that he can make sense of the idea that by doing something now we can bring about something in the past. Outline the rudiments of his argument, paying special heed to the kinds of beliefs that must be reconciled.

2. Dummett points out that orthodox Jewish theologians treat retrospective prayer, as in the case of the shipwreck, as blasphemous. Why? Dummett goes on to argue that these theologians are mistaken. What are Dummett's reasons for holding that view?

3. Dummett examines the fatalist's argument. Imagine you are in London during the Nazi air raids and meet someone who, refusing to go down into the shelters, argues that either you are going to be killed in the raid or you are not: whatever will be, will be, and there is no point in taking precautions against it. Formulate the fatalist's position and examine Dummett's response to it.

4. Samuel Gorovitz argues that we cannot even imagine a world like the one Dummett tries to describe in which "everything happens in reverse." Explain Gorovitz's argument and how it depends on the concept of time.

5. Gorovitz believes that the very idea of backward causation leads to absurdities in our talk about causality, intentional action, objects, and time. Detail Gorovitz's position and construct a possible response from Dummett.

6. Gorovitz maintains that our notion of causality is intimately interwoven with so many of our other most important concepts that it cannot be isolated and altered without totally destroying the conceptual superstructure of our way of understanding the world. Evaluate Gorovitz's claim.

7. We often talk as if we can observe the causal links between events. What does a causal relation look like? As David Hume points out, we see Event A followed by Event B, but we do not see A causing B or, in Hume's terms, we do not see the "necessary connection" between A and B. We only see a succession of events. What makes us think that A is necessarily connected to B?

8. What is the point of Hume's billiard ball example?

9. Hume defends a view of causation that amounts to the claim that the idea of causation is a product of the human mind and is not derived directly from an impression of causation in the world of experience. Causal claims then, come to be something like claims about regularities. Discuss whether Hume's view can be brought to the support of Dummett's position that the temporal asymmetry of the causal relation is only an empirical contingency and not a logical necessity.

10. Thomas Reid attacks Hume's view of causation. What is the crux of Reid's criticism? Why is Reid committed to the view that there are, in nature, efficient causes?

11. Reid's primary concern with respect to causation seems to be related to his idea of the importance of free human action or what he calls "our active powers" to produce effects. Explain Reid's position and how it might also relate to his ideas about moral responsibility and "moral liberty."

Part VII. Fatalism and Free Will

During the bombing raids on London in World War II, there were many people who, when the sirens howled, did not seek out shelter. They reasoned that either they were fated to get hit or they were fated not to; if they were fated to get hit it would do them no good to run for shelter, and if they were fated not to running was unnecessary. So they might as well go on with business as normal, or at least as near as possible to normal under the circumstances.

The attitude taken by these people was fatalistic. Probably most of us are at least at some moments fatalists. Yet much of the time we think that fatalism is false and that belief in it can be very destructive. (Imagine someone using a fatalist argument to justify not studying for an exam.) On the other hand, we are often forced into fatalism by our everyday beliefs.

Many religious people believe that God, being omniscient or all-knowing, knows what will happen in the future. If God knows what will happen tomorrow then there is no use trying to change what will happen tomorrow. If you succeeded in changing the facts about tomorrow, then God would not have known what would happen; since, by hypothesis, he *does* know what will happen, you cannot succeed in changing the facts. But then why not just sit back and let whatever is going to happen happen?

Furthermore, even people who do not believe in God, or who do not believe that God knows all the facts about the future, think that there *are* facts about the future, even if no one does or could know them. Statements about the future are either true now or false now, depending on what will happen. But this seems to be all that is needed to show that fatalism is true. If there is now a fact about whether I will go to school tomorrow, then there is no use trying to change that fact. Facts do not change.

Fatalism poses one kind of threat to free will. If fatalism is true, then it seems that any freedom I think I have is a sham; things will happen as they are fated to happen regardless of what I do or attempt. My own choices and actions are among the things which are already fated to turn out a certain way. In his article "It Was to Be" Gilbert Ryle tries to sort out this puzzle and show what is wrong with arguments for fatalism. (It is interesting to compare Ryle's discussion of fatalism with David Lewis's account at the end of "The Paradoxes of Time Travel" in Part V, and Michael Dummett's "Bringing About the Past" in Part VI.)

Fatalism is not the only important threat to free will. To many people, the possibility of a scientific explanation of human action seems to threaten the existence or meaningfulness of free action. This is often put as an issue about whether free will is compatible with *determinism.*

The idea behind determinism is that everything that happens is caused to happen. Events do not just occur randomly, they are the causal effects of previous events. Thus if someone knew the laws of nature, and knew all the facts about the universe at a particular time, that person could, *in principle,* predict anything about the universe at any later time. The "in principle" is important here, since no one could make such predictions in practice; it would be impossible to absorb and assimilate that much information. We cannot even predict the weather with any great reliability, not because it is in principle unpredictable, but because in practice there are simply too many relevant factors for us to keep track of them all. The determinist thinks that precisely the same thing is true of *human* behavior: in principle our actions are utterly predictable, but in practice we can only make predictions with limited reliability.

Is determinism true? Does it show that we do not have free will? Holbach answers both these questions in the affirmative. The view that determinism is true and reveals free will to be a mere illusion is sometimes known as "hard determinism." William James, on the other hand, argues that we do have free will and that determinism is therefore false. This view is sometimes known as "libertarianism" (but is to be sharply distinguished from the political philosophy which goes by the same name and is defended in Part X by Robert Nozick).

Clearly, James and Holbach disagree over the very important question of whether we are ever genuinely free. But on another important issue they are in agreement: both are *incompatibilists,* people who think that free will and determinism are incompatible. They agree that it cannot be the case *both* that we are free *and* that determinism is true. One or the other, they think, must be false.

But is free will really incompatible with determinism? Many philosophers think that the answer is no: that we may be genuinely free even if all our actions are completely causally determined. How can they think this? It may help to think back for a moment to God's foreknowledge of the future. Religious people often argue that foreknowledge is no threat to free will. That God knows what I will do does not make my action any less free: God simply knows *what I will freely choose.* Knowing what I will do is not at all the same as forcing me to do it. My own free choices are included in the things God knows about; I do not have to fool God or prove God wrong in order to act freely.

Many philosophers want to say something analogous to this about the relation between free will and causal determination. If my will were something separate from the causal order of nature, then the causal determination of my actions would seem to be almost a form of bullying. But perhaps free choices are not something separate from nature, but a part of it. Perhaps my free choices are simply included in the causal order of things. This point of view is very well expressed by Raymond Smullyan, who in a dialogue has God say that incompatibilism rests on "a totally misleading psychological image, which is that your will could somehow be in conflict with the laws of nature and that the latter is somehow more powerful than you, and could "determine" your acts whether you liked it or not. But it is simply impossible for your will to ever conflict with natural law. You and natural law are really one and the same."[1]

The view Smullyan here expresses so well is know as *compatibilism*, the view that it is entirely possible for us to be genuinely free *even if* determinism is true. This view is defended in both our classical selection from John Stuart Mill and our contemporary selection from A. J. Ayer. Mill explicitly argues both that determinism is true and that we have free will, a combination of views known as "soft determinism"; Ayer is more cautious about the truth of determinism, but argues that *if* it is true it still does not rule out free will.

The issue is important for a variety of reasons. We *want* to be genuinely free, not just to have an illusion of freedom. But if freedom is incompatible with scientific explanation and prediction, then with every new advance in psychology we will have to admit that we are less free than we had thought. Furthermore, if the extreme but powerfully presented view of Holbach is correct—if in fact our actions are not free at all—then we need to make sweeping changes in our views about morality. If none of our actions are any more "up to us" than those which are coerced or physically compelled, then it makes no sense to hold people morally responsible for their actions. This point is acknowledged and embraced by some "hard determinists," for example by B. F. Skinner. But to stop regarding people as morally responsible agents would be a drastic change indeed, and we should examine carefully the arguments which purport to show that it is necessary.

NOTE

1. Raymond M. Smullyan, "Is god a Taoist?" in Smullyan, *The Tao is Silent* (New York: Harper & Row, 1977).

IT WAS TO BE

Gilbert Ryle

I want now to launch out without more ado into the full presentation and discussion of a concrete dilemma. It is a dilemma which, I expect, has occasionally bothered all of us, though, in its simplest form, not very often or for very long at a time. But it is intertwined with two other dilemmas, both of which probably have seriously worried nearly all of us. In its pure form it has not been seriously canvassed by any important Western philosopher, though the Stoics drew on it at certain points. It was, however, an ingredient in discussions of the theological doctrine of Predestination and I suspect that it has exerted a surreptitious influence on some of the champions and opponents of Determinism.

At a certain moment yesterday evening I coughed and at a certain moment yesterday evening I went to bed. It was therefore true on Saturday that on Sunday I would cough at the one moment and go to bed at the other. Indeed, it was true a thousand years ago that at certain moments on a certain Sunday a thousand years later I should cough and go to bed. But if it was true beforehand—forever beforehand—that I was to cough and go to bed at those two moments on Sunday, 25 January 1953, then it was impossible for me not to do so. There would be a contradiction in the joint assertion that it was true that I would do something at a certain time and that I did not do it. This argument is perfectly general. Whatever anyone ever does, whatever happens anywhere to anything, could not *not* be done or happen, if it was true beforehand that it was going to be done or was going to happen. So everything, including everything that we do, has been definitively booked from any earlier date you like to choose. Whatever is, was to be. So nothing that does occur could have been helped and nothing that has not actually been done could possibly have been done.

This point, that for whatever takes place it was antecedently true that it was going to take place, is sometimes picturesquely expressed by saying that the Book of Destiny has been written up in full from the beginning of time. A thing's actually taking place is, so to speak, merely the turning up of a passage that has for all time been written. This picture has led some fatalists to suppose that God, if there is one, or, we ourselves, if suitably favoured, may have access to this book and read ahead. But this is a fanciful embellishment upon what in itself is a severe and seemingly rigorous argument. We may call it 'the fatalist argument'.

Now the conclusion of this argument from antecedent truth, namely that nothing can be helped, goes directly counter to the piece of common knowledge that some things are our own fault, that some threatening disasters can be foreseen and averted, and that there is plenty of room for precautions, planning and weighing alternatives. Even when we say nowadays of someone that he is born to be hanged or not born to be drowned, we say it as a humorous archaism. We really think that it depends very much on himself whether he is hanged or not, and that his chances of drowning are greater if he refuses to learn to swim. Yet even we are not altogether proof against the fatalist view of things. In a battle I may well come to the half-belief that either there exists somewhere behind the enemy lines a bullet with my name on it, or there does not, so that taking cover is either of no avail or else unnecessary. In card-games and at the roulette-table it is easy to subside into the frame of mind of fancying that our fortunes are in some way prearranged, well though we know that it is silly to fancy this.

But how can we deny that whatever happens was booked to happen from all eternity? What is wrong with the argument from antecedent truth to the inevitability of what the antecedent truths are antecedently true about? For it certainly is logically impossible for a prophecy to be true and yet the event prophesied not to come about.

We should notice first of all that the premiss of the argument does not require that anyone, even God, *knows* any of these antecedent truths, or to put it picturesquely, that the Book of Destiny has been written by anybody or could be perused by anybody. This is just what distinguishes the pure fatalist argument from the mixed theological argument for pre-destination. This latter argument does turn on the supposition that God at least has foreknowledge of what is to take place, and perhaps also preordains it. But the pure fatalist argument turns only on the principle that it was true that a given thing would happen, before it did happen, i.e. that what is, was to be; not that it was known by anyone that it was to be. Yet even when we try hard to bear this point in mind, it is very easy inadvertently to reinterpret this initial principle into the supposition that before the thing happened it was known by someone that it was booked to happen. For there is something intolerably vacuous in the idea of the eternal but unsupported pre-existence of truths in the future tense. When we say 'a thousand years ago it was true that I should now be saying what I am', it is so difficult to give any body to this 'it' of which we say that it was then true, that we unwittingly fill it out with the familiar body of an expectation which someone once entertained, or of a piece of foreknowledge which someone once possessed. Yet to do this is to convert a principle which was worrying because, in a way, totally truistic, into a supposition which is unworrying because quasi-historical, entirely without evidence and most likely just false.

Very often, though certainly not always, when we say 'it was true that . . . ' or 'it is false that . . . ' we are commenting on some actual pronouncement made or opinion held by some identifiable person. Sometimes we are commenting in a more general way on a thing which some people, unidentified and perhaps unidentifiable, have believed or now believe. We can comment on the belief in the Evil Eye without being able to name anyone who held it; we know that plenty of people did hold it. Thus we can say 'it was true' or 'it is false' in passing verdicts upon the pronouncements both of named and of nameless authors. But in the premiss of the fatalist argument, namely that it was true before something happened that it would happen, there is no implication of anyone, named or unnamed, having made that prediction.

There remains a third thing that might be meant by 'it was true a thousands years ago that a thousand years later these things would be being said in this place', namely that *if* anybody had made a prediction to this effect, though doubtless nobody did, he would have been right. It is not a case of an actual prediction having come true but of a conceivable prediction having come true. The event has not made an actual prophecy come true. It has made a might-have-been prophecy come true.

Or can we say even this? A target can be hit by an actual bullet, but can it be hit by a might-have-been bullet? Or should we rather say only that it could have been hit by a might-have-been bullet? The historical-sounding phrases 'came true', 'made true' and 'was fulfilled' apply well enough to predictions actually made, but there is a detectable twist, which may be an illegitimate twist, in saying that a might-have-been prediction did come true or was made true by the event. If an unbacked horse wins a race, we can say that it would have won money for its backers, if only there had been any. But we cannot say that it did win money for its backers, if only there had been any. There is no answer to the question 'How much money did it win for them?' Correspondingly, we cannot with a clear conscience say of an event that it has fulfilled the predictions of it which could have been made, but only that it would have fulfilled any predictions of it which might have been made. There is no answer to the question 'Within what limits of precision were these might-have-been predictions correct about the time and the loudness of my cough?'

Let us consider the notions of truth and falsity. In characterizing somebody's statement, for example a statement in the future tense, as true or as false, we usually though not always, mean to convey rather more than that what was forecast did or did not take place. There is something of a slur in 'false' and something honorific in 'true', some suggestion of the insincerity or sincerity of its author, or some suggestion of his rashness or cautiousness as an investigator. This is brought out by our reluctance to characterize either as true or as false pure and avowed guesses. If you make a guess at the winner of the race, it will turn out right or wrong, correct or incorrect, buy hardly true or false. These epithets are inappropriate to avowed guesses, since the one epithet pays an extra tribute, the other conveys an extra adverse criticism of the maker of the guess, neither of which can he merit. In guessing there is no place for sincerity or insincerity, or for caution or rashness in investigation. To make a guess is not to give an assurance and it is not to declare the result of an investigation. Guessers are neither reliable nor unreliable.

Doubtless we sometimes use 'true' without intending any connotation of trustworthiness and, much less often, 'false' without any connotation of trust misplaced. But, for safety's sake, let us reword the fatalist argument in terms of these thinner words, 'correct' and 'incorrect'. It would now run as follows. For any event that takes place, an antecedent guess, if anyone had made one, that is was going to take place, would have been correct, and an antecedent guess to the contrary, if anyone had made it, would have been incorrect. This formulation already sounds less alarming than the original formulation. The word 'guess' cuts out the covert threat of foreknowledge, or of there being budgets of antecedent forecasts, all meriting confidence before the event. What, now, of the notion of guesses in the future tense being correct or incorrect?

Antecedently to the running of most horse-races, some people guess that one horse will win, some that another will. Very often every horse has its backers. If, then, the race is run and won, then some of the backers will have guessed correctly and the rest will have guessed incorrectly. To say that someone's guess that Eclipse would win was correct is to say no more than that he guessed that Eclipse would win and Eclipse did win. But can we say in retrospect that his guess, which he made before the race, was already correct before the race? He made the correct guess two days ago, but was his guess correct during those two days? It certainly was not incorrect during those two days, but it does not follow, though it might seem to follow, that it was correct during those two days. Perhaps we feel unsure which we ought to say, whether that his guess was correct during those two days, though no one could know it to be so, or only that, as it turned out, it was during those two days going to prove correct, i.e. that the victory which did, in the event, make it correct had not yet happened. A prophecy is not fulfilled until the event forecast has happened. Just here is where 'correct' resembles 'fulfilled' and differs importantly from 'true'. The honorific connotations of 'true' can certainly attach to a person's forecasts from the moment at which they are made, so that if these forecasts turn out incorrect, while we withdraw the word 'true', we do not necessarily withdraw the testimonials which it carried. The establishment of incorrectness certainly cancels 'true' but not, as a rule, so fiercely as to incline us to say 'false'.

The words 'true' and 'false' and the words 'correct' and 'incorrect' are adjectives, and this grammatical fact tempts us to suppose that trueness and falseness, correctness and incorrectness, and even, perhaps, fulfilledness and unfulfilledness must be qualities or properties resident in the propositions which they characterize. As sugar is sweet and white from the moment it comes into existence to the moment when it goes out of existence, so we are tempted to infer, by parity of reasoning, that the trueness or correctness of predictions and guesses must be features or properties which belong all the time to their possessors, whether we can detect their presence in them or not. But if we consider that 'deceased', 'lamented' and 'extinct' are also adjectives, and yet certainly do not apply to people or mastodons while they exist, but only after they have ceased to exist, we may feel more cordial towards the idea that 'correct' is in a partly similar way a merely obituary and valedictory epithet, as 'fulfilled' more patently is. It is more like a verdict than a description. So when I tell you that if anyone had guessed that Eclipse would win today's race his guess would have turned out correct, I give you no more information about the past than is given by the evening newspaper which tells you that Eclipse won the race.

I want now to turn to the fatalist conclusion, namely that since whatever is was to be, therefore nothing can be helped. The argument seems to compel us to say that since the antecedent truth requires the event of which it is the true forecast, therefore this event is in some disastrous way fettered to or driven by or bequeathed by that antecedent truth—as if my coughing last night was made or obliged to occur by the antecedent truth that it was going to occur, perhaps in something like the way in which gunfire makes the windows rattle a moment or two after the discharge. What sort of necessity would this be?

To bring this out let us by way of contrast suppose that someone produced the strictly parallel argument, that for everything that happens, it is true for ever *afterwards* that it happened.

I coughed last night, so it is true today and will be true a thousand years hence that I coughed last night. But these posterior truths in the past tense, could not be true without my having coughed. Therefore my coughing was necessitated or obliged to have happened by the truth of these posterior chronicles of it. Clearly something which disturbed us in the original form of the argument is missing in this new form. We cheerfully grant that the occurrence of an event involves and is involved by the truth of subsequent records, actual or conceivable, to the effect that it occurred. For it does not even seem to render the occurrence a product or effect of these truths about it. On the contrary, in this case we are quite clear that it is the occurrence which makes the posterior truths about it true, not the posterior truths which make the occurrence occur. These posterior truths are shadows cast by the events, not the events shadows cast by these truths about them, since these belong to the posterity, not to the ancestry of the events.

Why does the fact that a posterior truth about an occurrence requires that occurrence not worry us in the way in which the fact that an anterior truth about an occurrence requires that occurrence does worry us? Why does the slogan 'Whatever is, always was to be' seem to imply that nothing can be helped, where the obverse slogan 'Whatever is, will always have been' does not seem to imply this? We are not exercised by the notorious fact that when the horse has already escaped it is too late to shut the stable door. We are sometimes exercised by the idea that as the horse is either going to escape or not going to escape, to shut the stable door beforehand is either unavailing or unnecessary. A large part of the reason is that in thinking of a predecessor making its successor necessary we unwittingly assimilate the necessitation to causal necessitation. Gunfire makes windows rattle a few seconds later, but rattling windows do not make gunfire happen a few seconds earlier, even though they may be perfect evidence that gunfire did happen a few seconds earlier. We slide, that is, into thinking of the anterior truths as *causes* of the happenings about which they were true, where the mere matter of their relative dates saves us from thinking of happenings as the effects of those truths about them which are posterior to them. Events cannot be the effects of their successors, any more than we can be the offspring of our posterity.

So let us look more suspiciously at the notions of *necessitating, making, obliging, requiring* and *involving* on which the argument turns. How is the notion of *requiring* or *involving* that we have been working with related to the notion of *causing*?

It is quite true that a backer cannot guess correctly that Eclipse will win without Eclipse winning and still it is quite false that his guessing made or caused Eclipse to win. To say that his guess that Eclipse would win was correct does logically involve or require that Eclipse won. To assert the one and deny the other would be to contradict oneself. To say that the backer guessed correctly is just to say that the horse which he guessed would win, did win. The one assertion cannot be true without the other assertion being true. But in this way in which one truth may require or involve another truth, an event cannot be one of the implications of a truth. Events can be effects, but they cannot be implications. Truths can be consequences of other truths, but they cannot be causes of effects or effects of causes.

In much the same way, the truth that someone revoked involves the truth that he had in his hand at least one card of the suit led. But he was not forced or coerced into having a card of that suit in his hand by the fact that he revoked. He could not both have revoked and not had a card of that suit in his hand, but this 'could not' does not connote any kind of duress. A proposition can imply another proposition, but it cannot thrust a card into a player's hand. The questions, what makes things happen, what prevents them from happening, and whether we can help them or not, are entirely unaffected by the logical truism that a statement to the effect that something happens, is correct if and only if it happens. Lots of things could have prevented Eclipse from winning the race; lots of other things could have made his lead a longer one. But one thing had no influence on the race at all, namely the fact that if anyone guessed that he would win, he guessed correctly.

We are now in a position to separate out one unquestionable and very dull true proposition from another exciting but entirely false proposition, both of which seem to be conveyed by the slogan 'What is, always was to be'. It is an unquestionable and very dull truth that for anything that happens, if anyone had at any previous time made the guess that it would happen, his guess would have turned out correct. The twin facts that the event could not take place without such a guess turning out correct and that such a guess could not turn out correct without the event taking place tell us nothing whatsoever about how the event was caused, whether it could have been prevented, or even whether it could have been predicted with certainty or probability from what had happened before. The menacing statement that what is was to be, construed in one way, tells us only the trite truth that if it is true to say (a) that something happened, then it is also true to say (b) that that original statement (a) is true, no matter when this latter comment (b) on the former statement (a) may be made.

The exciting but false proposition that the slogan seems to force upon us is that whatever happens is inevitable or doomed, and, what makes it sound even worse, *logically* inevitable or *logically* doomed—somewhat as it is logically inevitable that the immediate successor of any even number is an odd number. So what does 'inevitable' mean? An avalanche may be, for all practical purposes, unavoidable. A mountaineer in the direct path of an avalanche can himself do nothing to stop the avalanche or get himself out of its way, though a providential earthquake might conceivably divert the avalanche or a helicopter might conceivably lift him out of danger. His position is much worse, but only much worse, than that of a cyclist half a mile ahead of a lumbering steam-roller. It is extremely unlikely that the steam-roller will catch up with him at all, and even if it does so it is extremely likely that its driver will halt or that the cyclist himself will move off in good time. But these differences between the plights of the mountaineer and the cyclist are differences of degree only. The avalanche is practically unavoidable, but it is not logically inevitable. Only conclusions can be logically inevitable, given the premises, and an avalanche is not a conclusion. The fatalist doctrine, by contrast, is that everything is absolutely and logically inevitable in a way in which the avalanche is not absolutely or logically inevitable; that we are all absolutely and logically powerless where even the hapless mountaineer is only in a desperate plight and the cyclist is in no real danger at all; that everything is fettered by the Law of Contradiction to taking the course it does take, as odd numbers are bound to succeed even numbers. What sort of fetters are these purely logical fetters?

Certainly there are infinitely many cases of one truth making necessary the truth of another proposition. The truth that today is Monday makes necessary the truth of the proposition that tomorrow is Tuesday. It cannot be Monday today without tomorrow being Tuesday. A person who said 'It is Monday today but not Tuesday tomorrow' would be taking away with his left hand what he was giving with his right hand. But in the way in which some truths carry other truths with them or make them necessary, events themselves cannot be made necessary by truths. Things and events may be the topics of premisses and conclusions, but they cannot themselves be premisses or conclusions. You may preface a statement by the word 'therefore', but you cannot pin either a 'therefore' or a 'perhaps not' on to a person or an avalanche. It is a partial parallel to say that while a sentence may contain or may be without a split infinitive, a road accident cannot either contain or lack a split infinitive, even though it is what a lot of sentences, with or without split infinitives in them, are about. It is true that an avalanche may be practically inescapable and the conclusion of an argument may be logically inescapable, but the avalanche has not got—nor does it lack—the inescapability of the conclusion of an argument. The fatalist theory tries to endue happenings with the inescapability of the conclusions of valid arguments. Our familiarity with the practical inescapability of some things, like some avalanches, helps us to yield to the view that really everything that happens is inescapable, only not now in the way in which some avalanches are inescapable and others not, but in the way in which logical consequences are inescapable, given their premisses. The fatalist has tried to characterize happenings by predicates which are proper only to conclusions of arguments. He tried to flag my cough with a Q.E.D. . . .

FREEDOM AND NECESSITY

A. J. Ayer

When I am said to have done something of my own free will it is implied that I could have acted otherwise; and it is only when it is believed that I could have acted otherwise that I am held to be morally responsible for what I have done. For a man is not thought to be morally responsible for an action that it was not in his power to avoid. But if human behaviour is entirely governed by causal laws, it is not clear how any action that is done could ever have been avoided. It may be said of the agent that he would have acted otherwise if the causes of his action had been different, but they being what they were, it seems to follow that he was bound to act as he did. Now it is commonly assumed both that men are capable of acting freely, in the sense that is required to make them morally responsible, and that human behaviour is entirely governed by causal laws: and it is the apparent conflict between these two assumptions that gives rise to the philosophical problem of the freedom of the will.

Confronted with this problem, many people will be inclined to agree with Dr. Johnson: 'Sir, we *know* our will is free, and *there's* an end on't.' But, while this does very well for those who accept Dr. Johnson's premiss, it would hardly convince anyone who denied the freedom of the will. Certainly, if we do know that our wills are free, it follows that they are so. But the logical reply to this might be that since our wills are not free, it follows that no one can know that they are: so that if anyone claims, like Dr. Johnson, to know that they are, he must be mistaken. What is evident, indeed, is that people often believe themselves to be acting freely; and it is to this 'feeling' of freedom that some philosophers appeal when they wish, in the supposed interests of morality, to prove that not all human action is causally determined. But if these philosophers are right in their assumption that a man cannot be acting freely if his action is causally determined, then the fact that someone feels free to do, or not to do, a certain action does not prove that he really is so. It may prove that the agent does not himself know what it is that makes him act in one way rather than another: but from the fact that a man is unaware of the causes of his action, it does not follow that no such causes exist.

So much may be allowed to the determinist; but his belief that all human actions are subservient to causal laws still remains to be justified. If, indeed, it is necessary that every event should have a cause, then the rule must apply to human behaviour as much as to anything else. But why should it be supposed that every event must have a cause? The contrary is not unthinkable. Nor is the law of universal causation a necessary presupposition of scientific thought. The scientist may try to discover causal laws, and in many cases he succeeds; but sometimes he has to be content with statistical laws, and sometimes he comes upon events which, in the present state of his knowledge, he is not able to subsume under any law at all. In the case of these events he assumes that if he knew more he would be able to discover some law, whether causal or statistical, which would enable him to account for them. And this assumption cannot be disproved. For however far he may have carried his investigation, it is always open to him to carry it further; and it is always conceivable that if he carried it further he would discover the connection which had hitherto escaped him. Nevertheless, it is also conceivable that the events with which he is concerned are not systematically connected with any others: so that the reason why he does not discover the sort of laws that he requires is simply that they do not obtain.

Now in the case of human conduct the search for explanations has not in fact been altogether fruitless. Certain scientific laws have been established; and with the help of these laws we do make a number of successful predictions about the ways in which different people will behave. But these predictions do not always cover every detail. We may be able to predict that in certain circumstances a particular man will be angry, without being able to prescribe the precise form that the expression of his anger will take. We may be reasonably sure that he will shout, but not sure how loud his shout will be, or exactly what words he will use. And it is only a small proportion of human actions that we are able to forecast even so precisely as this. But that, it may be said, is because we have not carried our investigations very far. The science of psychology is still in its infancy and, as it is developed, not only will more human actions be explained, but the explanations will go into greater detail. The ideal of complete explanation may never in fact be attained: but it is theoretically attainable. Well, this may be so: and certainly it is impossible to show *a priori* that it is not so: but equally it cannot be shown that it is. This will not, however, discourage the scientist who, in the field of human behaviour, as elsewhere, will continue to formulate theories and test them by the facts. And in this he is justified. For since he has no reason *a priori* to admit that there is a limit to what he can discover, the fact that he also cannot be sure that there is no limit does not make it unreasonable for him to devise theories, nor, having devised them, to try constantly to improve them.

But now suppose it to be claimed that, so far as men's actions are concerned, there is a limit: and that this limit is set by the fact of human freedom. An obvious objection is that in many cases in which a person feels himself to be free to do, or not to do, a certain action, we are even now able to explain, in causal terms, why it is that he acts as he does. But it might be argued that even if men are sometimes mistaken in believing that they act freely, it does not follow that they are always so mistaken. For it is not always the case that when a man believes that he has acted freely we are in fact able to account for his action in causal terms. A determinist would say that we should be able to account for it if we had more knowledge of the circumstances, and had been able to discover the appropriate natural laws. But until those discoveries have been made, this remains only a pious hope. And may it not be true that, in some cases at least, the reason why we can give no causal explanation is that no causal explanation is available; and that this is because the agent's choice was literally free, as he himself felt it to be?

The answer is that this may indeed be true, inasmuch as it is open to anyone to hold that no explanation is possible until some explanation is actually found. But even so it does not give the moralist what he wants. For he is anxious to show that men are capable of acting freely in order to infer that they can be morally responsible for what they do. But if it is a matter of pure chance that a man should act in one way rather than another, he may be free but can hardly be responsible. And indeed when a man's actions seem to us quite unpredictable, when, as we say, there is no knowing what he will do, we do not look upon him as a moral agent. We look upon him as a lunatic.

To this it may be objected that we are not dealing fairly with the moralist. For when he makes it a condition of my being morally responsible that I should act freely, he does not wish to imply that it is purely a matter of chance that I act as I do. What he wishes to imply is that my actions are the result of my own free choice: and it is because they are the result of my own free choice that I am held to be morally responsible for them.

But now we must ask how it is that I come to make my choice. Either it is an accident that I choose to act as I do or it is not. If it is an accident, then it is merely a matter of chance that I did not choose otherwise; and if it is merely a matter of chance that I did not choose otherwise, it is surely irrational to hold me morally responsible for choosing as I did. But if it is not an accident that I choose to do one thing rather than another, then presumably there is some causal explanation of my choice: and in that case we are led back to determinism.

Again, the objection may be raised that we are not doing justice to the moralist's case. His view is not that it is a matter of chance that I choose to act as I do, but rather that my choice depends upon my character. Nevertheless he holds that I can still be free in the sense that he requires; for it is I who am responsible for my character. But in what way am I responsible for my character? Only, surely, in the sense that there is a causal connection between what I do now and what I have done in the past. It is only this that justifies the statement that I have made myself what I am: and even so this is an over-simplification, since it takes no account of the external influences to which I have been subjected. But, ignoring the external influences, let us assume that it is in fact the case that I have made myself what I am. Then it is still legitimate to ask how it is that I have come to make myself one sort of person rather than another. And if it be answered that it is a matter of my strength of will, we can put the same question in another form by asking how it is that my will has the strength that it has and not some other degree of strength. Once more, either it is an accident or it is not. If it is an accident, then by the same argument as before, I am not morally responsible, and if it is not an accident we are led back to determinism.

Furthermore, to say that my actions proceed from my character or, more colloquially, that I act in character, is to say that my behaviour is consistent and to that extent predictable: and since it is, above all, for the actions that I perform in character that I am held to be morally responsible, it looks as if the admission of moral responsibility, so far from being incompatible with determinism, tends rather to presuppose it. But how can this be so if it is a necessary condition of moral responsibility that the person who is held responsible should have acted freely? It seems that if we are to retain this idea of moral responsibility, we must either show that men can be held responsible for actions which they do not do freely, or else find some way of reconciling determinism with the freedom of the will.

It is no doubt with the object of effecting this reconciliation that some philosophers have defined freedom as the consciousness of necessity. And by so doing they are able to say not only that a man can be acting freely when his action is causally determined, but even that his action must be causally determined for it to be possible for him to be acting freely. Nevertheless this definition has the serious disadvantage that it gives to the word 'freedom' a meaning quite different from any that it ordinarily bears. It is indeed obvious that if we are allowed to give the word 'freedom' any meaning that we please, we can find a meaning that will reconcile it with determinism: but this is no more a solution of our present problem than the fact that the word 'horse' could be arbitrarily used to mean what is ordinarily meant by 'sparrow' is a proof that horses have wings. For suppose that I am compelled by another person to do something 'against my will'. In that case, as the word 'freedom' is ordinarily used, I should not be said to be acting freely: and the fact that I am fully aware of the constraint to which I am subjected makes no difference to the matter. I do not become free by becoming conscious that I am not. It may, indeed, be possible to show that my being aware that my action is causally determined is not incompatible with my acting freely: but it by no means follows that it is in this that my freedom consists. Moreover, I suspect that one of the reasons why people are inclined to define freedom as the consciousness of necessity is that they think that if one is conscious of necessity one may somehow be able to master it. But this is a fallacy. It is like someone's saying that he wishes he could see into the future, because if he did he would know what calamities lay in wait for him and so would be able to avoid them. But if he avoids the calamities then they don't lie in the future and it is not true that he foresees them. And similarly if I am able to master necessity, in the sense of escaping the operation of a necessary law, then the law in question is not necessary. And if the law is not necessary, then neither my freedom nor anything else can consist in my knowing that it is.

Let it be granted, then, when we speak of reconciling freedom with determination we are using the word 'freedom' in an ordinary sense. It still remains for us to make this usage clear: and perhaps the best way to make it clear is to show what it is that freedom, in this sense, is contrasted with. Now we began with the assumption that freedom is contrasted with causality: so that a man cannot be said to be acting freely if his action is causally determined. But this assumption has led us into difficulties and I now wish to suggest that it is mistaken. For it is not, I think, causality that freedom is to be contrasted with, but constraint. And while it is true that being constrained to do an action entails being caused to do it, I shall try to show that the converse does not hold. I shall try to show that from the fact that my action is causally determined it does not necessarily follow that I am constrained to do it: and this is equivalent to saying that it does not necessarily follow that I am not free.

If I am constrained, I do not act freely. But in what circumstances can I legitimately be said to be constrained? An obvious instance is the case in which I am compelled by another person to do what he wants. In a case of this sort the compulsion need not be such as to deprive one of the power of choice. It is not required that the other person should have hypnotized me, or that he should make it physically impossible for me to go against his will. It is enough that he should induce me to do what he wants by making it clear to me that, if I do not, he will bring about some situation that I regard as even more undesirable than the consquences of the action that he wishes me to do. Thus, if the man points a pistol at my head I may still choose to disobey him: but this does not prevent its being true that if I do fall in with his wishes he can legitimately be said to have compelled me. And if the circumstances are such that no reasonable person would be expected to choose the other alternative, then the action that I am made to do is not one for which I am held to be morally responsible.

A similar, but still somewhat different, case is that in which another person has obtained an habitual ascendancy over me. Where this is so, there may be no question of my being induced to act as the other person wishes by being confronted with a still more disagreeable alternative: for if I am sufficiently under his influence this special stimulus will not be necessary. Nevertheless I do not act freely, for the reason that I have been deprived of the power of choice. And this means that I have acquired so strong a habit of obedience that I no longer go through any process of deciding whether or not to do what the other person wants. About other matters I may still deliberate; but as regards the fulfilment of this other person's wishes, my own deliberations have ceased to be a causal factor in my behaviour. And it is in this sense that I may be said to be constrained. It is not, however, necessary that such constraint should take the form of subservience to another person. A kleptomaniac is not a free agent, in respect of his stealing, because he does not go through any process of deciding whether or not to steal. Or rather, if he does go through such a process, it is irrelevant to his behaviour. Whatever he resolved to do, he would steal all the same. And it is this that distinguishes him from the ordinary thief.

But now it may be asked whether there is any essential difference between these cases and those in which the agent is commonly thought to be free. No doubt the ordinary thief does go through a process of deciding whether or not to steal, and no doubt it does affect his behaviour. If he resolved to refrain from stealing, he could carry his resolution out. But if it be allowed that his making or not making this resolution is causally determined, then how can he be any more free than the kleptomaniac? It may be true that unlike the kleptomaniac he could refrain from stealing if he chose: but if there is a cause, or set of causes, which necessitate his choosing as he does, how can he be said to have the power of choice? Again, it may be true that no one now compels me to get up and walk across the room: but if my doing so can be causally explained in terms of my history or my environment, or whatever it may be, then how am I any more free than if some other person had compelled me? I do not have the feeling of constraint that I have when a pistol is manifestly pointed at my head; but the chains of causation by which I am bound are no less effective for being invisible.

The answer to this is that the cases I have mentioned as examples of constraint do differ from the others: and they differ just in the ways that I have tried to bring out. If I suffered from a compulsion neurosis, so that I got up and walked across the room, whether I wanted to or not, or if I did so because somebody else compelled me, then I should not be acting freely. But if I do it now, I shall be acting freely, just because these conditions do not obtain; and the fact that my action may nevertheless have a cause is, from this point of view, irrelevant. For it is not when my action has any cause at all, but only when it has a special sort of cause, that it is reckoned not to be free.

But here it may be objected that, even if this distinction corresponds to ordinary usage, it is still very irrational. For why should we distinguish, with regard to a person's freedom, between the operations of one sort of cause and those of another? Do not all causes equally necessitate? And is it not therefore arbitrary to say that a person is free when he is necessitated in one fashion but not when he is necessitated in another?

That all causes equally necessitate is indeed a tautology, if the word 'necessitate' is taken merely as equivalent to 'cause': but if, as the objection requires, it is taken as equivalent to 'constrain' or 'compel', then I do not think that this proposition is true. For all that is needed for one event to be the cause of another is that, in the given circumstances, the event which is said to be the effect would not have occurred if it had not been for the occurrence of the event which is said to be the cause, or vice versa, according as causes are interpreted as necessary, or sufficient, conditions: and this fact is usually deducible from some causal law which states that whenever an event of the one kind occurs then, given suitable conditions, an event of the other kind will occur in a certain temporal or spatio-temporal relationship to it. In short, there is an invariable concomitance between the two classes of events; but there is no compulsion, in any but a metaphorical sense. Suppose, for example, that a psycho-analyst is able to account for some aspect of my behaviour by referring it to some lesion that I suffered in my childhood. In that case, it may be said that my childhood experience, together with certain other events, necessitates my behaving as I do. But all that this involves is that it is found to be true in general that when people have had certain experiences as children, they subsequently behave in certain specifiable ways; and my case is just another instance of this general law. It is in this way indeed that my behaviour is explained. But from the fact that my behaviour is capable of being explained, in the sense that it can be subsumed under some natural law, it does not follow that I am acting under constraint.

If this is correct, to say that I could have acted otherwise is to say, first, that I should have acted otherwise if I had so chosen; secondly, that my action was voluntary in the sense in which the actions, say, of the kleptomaniac are not; and thirdly, that nobody compelled me to choose as I did: and these three conditions may very well be fulfilled. When they are fulfilled, I may be said to have acted freely. But this is not to say that it was a matter of chance that I acted as I did, or, in other words, that my action could not be explained. And that my actions should be capable of being explained is all that is required by the postulate of determinism.

If more than this seems to be required it is, I think, because the use of the very word 'determinism' is in some degree misleading. For it tends to suggest that one event is somehow in the power of another, whereas the truth is merely that they are factually correlated. And the same applies to the use, in this context, of the word 'necessity' and even of the word 'cause' itself. Moreover, there are various reasons for this. One is the tendency to confuse causal with logical necessitation, and so to infer mistakenly that the effect is contained in the cause. Another is the uncritical use of a concept of force which is derived from primitive experiences of pushing and striking. A third is the survival of an animistic conception of causality, in which all causal relationships are modelled on the example of one person's exercising authority over another. As a result we tend to form an imaginative picture of an unhappy effect trying vainly to escape. from the clutches of an overmastering cause. But, I repeat, the fact is simply that when an event of one type occurs, an event of another type occurs also, in a certain temporal or spatio-temporal relation to the first. The rest is only metaphor. And it is because of the metaphor, and not because of the fact, that we come to think that there is an antithesis between causality and freedom.

Nevertheless, it may be said, if the postulate of determinism is valid, then the future can be explained in terms of the past: and this means that if one knew enough about the past one would be able to predict the future. But in that case what will happen in the future is already decided. And how then can I be said to be free? What is going to happen is going to happen and nothing that I do can prevent it. If the determinist is right, I am the helpless prisoner of fate.

But what is meant by saying that the future course of events is already decided? If the implication is that some person has arranged it, then the proposition is false. But if all that is meant is that it is possible, in principle, to deduce it from a set of particular facts about the past, together with the appropriate general laws, then, even if this is true, it does not in the least entail that I am the helpless prisoner of fate. It does not even entail that my actions make no difference to the future: for they are causes as well as effects; so that if they were different their consequences would be different also. What it does entail is that my behavior can be predicted: but to say that my behaviour can be predicted is not to say that I am acting under constraint. It is indeed true that I cannot escape my destiny if this is taken to mean no more than that I shall do what I shall do. But this is a tautology, just as it is a tautology that what is going to happen is going to happen. And such tautologies as these prove nothing whatsoever about the freedom of the will.

THE SYSTEM OF NATURE
Baron Holbach

Motives and the Determination of the Will. In whatever manner man is considered, he is connected to universal nature, and submitted to the necessary and immutable laws that she imposes on all the beings she contains, according to their peculiar essences or to the respective properties with which, without consulting them, she endows each particular species. Man's life is a line that nature commands him to describe upon the surface of the earth, without his ever being able to swerve from it, even for an instant. He is born without his own consent; his organization does in nowise depend upon himself; his ideas come to him involuntarily; his habits are in the power of those who cause him to contract them; he is unceasingly modified by causes, whether visible or concealed, over which he has no control, which necessarily regulate his mode of existence, give the hue to his way of thinking, and determine his manner of acting. He is good or bad, happy or miserable, wise or foolish, reasonable or irrational, without his will being for anything in these various states. Nevertheless, in spite of the shackles by which he is bound, it is pretended he is a free agent, or that independent of the causes by which he is moved, he determines his own will, and regulates his own condition.

However slender the foundation of this opinion, of which everything ought to point out to him the error, it is current at this day and passes for an incontestable truth with a great number of people, otherwise extremely enlightened; it is the basis of religion, which, supposing relations between man and the unknown being she has placed above nature, has been incapable of imagining how man could merit reward or deserve punishment from this being, if he was not a free agent. Society has been believed interested in this system; because an idea has gone abroad, that if all the actions of man were to be contemplated as necessary, the right of punishing those who injure their associates would no longer exist. At length human vanity accommodated itself to a hypothesis which, unquestionably, appears to distinguish man from all other physical beings, by assigning to him the special privilege of a total independence of all other causes, but of which a very little reflection would have shown him the impossibility . . . .

The will, as we have elsewhere said, is a modification of the brain, by which it is disposed to action, or prepared to give play to the organs. This will is necessarily determined by the qualities, good or bad, agreeable or

painful, of the object or the motive that acts upon his senses, or of which
the idea remains with him, and is resuscitated by his memory. In consequence, he acts necessarily, his action is the result of the impulse he
receives either from the motive, from the object, or from the idea which
has modified his brain, or disposed his will. When he does not act according to this impulse, it is because there comes some new cause, some new
motive, some new idea, which modifies his brain in a different manner,
gives him a new impulse, determines his will in another way, by which
the action of the former impulse is suspended: thus, the sight of an
agreeable object, or its idea, determines his will to set him in action to
procure it; but if a new object or a new idea more powerfully attracts him,
it gives a new direction to his will, annihilates the effect of the former,
and prevents the action by which it was to be procured. This is the mode
in which reflection, experience, reason, necessarily arrests or suspends
the action of man's will: without this he would of necessity have followed
the anterior impulse which carried him towards a then desirable object. In
all this he always acts according to necessary laws from which he has no
means of emancipating himself.

If when tormented with violent thirst, he figures to himself in idea, or
really perceives a fountain, whose limpid streams might cool his feverish
want, is he sufficient master of himself to desire or not to desire the object
competent to satisfy so lively a want? It will no doubt be conceded, that it
is impossible he should not be desirous to satisfy it; but it will be said—if
at this moment it is announced to him that the water he so ardently
desires is poisoned, he will, notwithstanding his vehement thirst, abstain
from drinking it: and it has, therefore, been falsely concluded that he is a
free agent. The fact, however, is, that the motive in either case is exactly
the same: his own conservation. The same necessity that determined him
to drink before he knew the water was deleterious upon this new discovery equally determined him not to drink; the desire of conserving himself
either annihilates or suspends the former impulse; the second motive
becomes stronger than the preceding, that is, the fear of death, or the
desire of preserving himself, necessarily prevails over the painful sensation caused by his eagerness to drink: but, it will be said, if the thirst is
very parching, an inconsiderate man without regarding the danger will
risk swallowing the water. Nothing is gained by this remark: in this case,
the anterior impulse only regains the ascendency; he is persuaded that
life may possibly be longer preserved, or that he shall derive a greater
good by drinking the poisoned water than by enduring the torment,
which, to his mind, threatens instant dissolution; thus the first becomes
the strongest and necessarily urges him on to action. Nevertheless, in
either case, whether he partakes of the water, or whether he does not,
the two actions will be equally necessary; they will be the effect of that
motive which finds itself most puissant; which consequently acts in the
most coercive manner upon his will.

This example will serve to explain the whole phenomena of the human will. This will, or rather the brain, finds itself in the same situation as a bowl, which, although it has received an impulse that drives it forward in a straight line, is deranged in its course whenever a force superior to the first obliges it to change its direction. The man who drinks the poisoned water appears a madman; but the actions of fools are as necessary as those of the most prudent individuals. The motives that determine the voluptuary and the debauchee to risk their health, are as powerful, and their actions are as necessary, as those which decide the wise man to manage his. But, it will be insisted, the debauchee may be prevailed on to change his conduct: this does not imply that he is a free agent; but that motives may be found sufficiently powerful to annihilate the effect of those that previously acted upon him; then these new motives determine his will to the new mode of conduct he may adopt as necessarily as the former did to the old mode . . . .

The errors of philosophers on the free agency of man, have arisen from their regarding his will as the *primum mobile*, the original motive of his actions; for want of recurring back, they have not perceived the multiplied, the complicated causes which, independently of him, give motion to the will itself; or which dispose and modify his brain, whilst he himself is purely passive in the motion he receives. Is he the master of desiring or not desiring an object that appears desirable to him? Without doubt it will be answered, no: but he is the master of resisting his desire, if he reflects on the consequences. But, I ask, is he capable of reflecting on these consequences, when his soul is hurried along by a very lively passion, which entirely depends upon his natural organization, and the causes by which he is modified? Is it in his power to add to these consequences all the weight necessary to counterbalance his desire? Is he the master of preventing the qualities which render an object desirable from residing in it? I shall be told: he ought to have learned to resist his passions; to contract a habit of putting a curb on his desires. I agree to it without any difficulty. But in reply, I again ask, is his nature susceptible of this modification? Does his boiling blood, his unruly imagination, the igneous fluid that circulates in his veins, permit him to make, enable him to apply true experience in the moment when it is wanted? And even when his temperament has capacitated him, has his education, the examples set before him, the ideas with which he has been inspired in early life, been suitable to make him contract this habit of repressing his desires? Have not all these things rather contributed to induce him to seek with avidity, to make him actually desire those objects which you say he ought to resist?

The *ambitious man* cries out: you will have me resist my passion; but have they not unceasingly repeated to me that rank, honours, power, are the most desirable advantages in life? Have I not seen my fellow citizens envy them, the nobles of my country sacrifice every thing to obtain them? In the society in which I live, am I not obliged to feel, that if I am deprived of these advantages, I must expect to languish in contempt; to cringe under the rod of oppression?

The *miser* says: you forbid me to love money, to seek after the means of acquiring it: alas! does not every thing tell me that, in this world, money is the greatest blessing; that it is amply sufficient to render me happy? In the country I inhabit, do I not see all my fellow citizens covetous of riches? but do I not also witness that they are little scrupulous in the means of obtaining wealth? As soon as they are enriched by the means which you censure, are they not cherished, considered and respected? By what authority, then, do you defend me from amassing treasure? What right have you to prevent my using means, which, although you call them sordid and criminal, I see approved by the sovereign? Will you have me renounce my happiness?

The *voluptuary* argues: you pretend that I should resist my desires; but was I the maker of my own temperament, which unceasingly invites me to pleasure? You call my pleasures disgraceful; but in the country in which I live, do I not witness the most dissipated men enjoying the most distinguished rank? Do I not behold that no one is ashamed of adultery but the husband it has outraged? Do not I see men making trophies of their debaucheries, boasting of their libertinism, rewarded with applause?

The *choleric man* vociferates: you advise me to put a curb on my passions, and to resist the desire of avenging myself: but can I conquer my nature? Can I alter the received opinions of the world? Shall I not be forever disgraced, infallibly dishonoured in society, if I do not wash out in the blood of my fellow creatures the injuries I have received?

The *zealous enthusiast* exclaims: you recommend me mildness; you adivse me to be tolerant; to be indulgent to the opinions of my fellow men; but is not my temperament violent? Do I not ardently love my God? Do they not assure me, that zeal is pleasing to him; that sanguinary inhuman persecutors have been his friends? As I wish to render myself acceptable in his sight, I therefore adopt the same means.

In short, the actions of man are never free; they are always the necessary consequence of his temperament, of the received ideas, and of the notions, either true or false, which he has formed to himself of happiness; of his opinions, strengthened by example, by education, and by daily experience. So many crimes are witnessed on the earth only because every thing conspires to render man vicious and criminal; the religion he has adopted, his government, his education, the examples set before him, irresistibly drive him on to evil: under these circumstances, morality preaches virtue to him in vain. In those societies where vice is esteemed, where crime is crowned, where venality is constantly recompensed, where the most dreadful disorders are punished only in those who are too weak to enjoy the privilege of committing them with impunity, the practice of virtue is considered nothing more than a painful sacrifice of happiness. Such societies chastise, in the lower orders, those excesses which they respect in the higher ranks; and frequently have the injustice to condemn those in the penalty of death, whom public prejudices, maintained by constant example, have rendered criminal.

Man, then, is not a free agent in any one instant of his life; he is necessarily guided in each step by those advantages, whether real or fictitious, that he attaches to the objects by which his passions are roused: these passions themselves are necessary in a being who unceasingly tends towards his own happiness; their energy is necessary, since that depends on his temperament; his temperament is necessary, because it depends on the physical elements which enter into his composition; the modification of this temperament is necessary, as it is the infallible and inevitable consequence of the impulse he receives from the incessant action of moral and physical beings.

Choice Does Not Prove Freedom. In spite of these proofs of the want of free agency in man, so clear to unprejudiced minds, it will, perhaps be insisted upon with no small feeling of triumph, that if it be proposed to any one, to move or not to move his hand, an action in the number of those called indifferent, he evidently appears to be the master of choosing; from which it is concluded that evidence has been offered of free agency. The reply is, this example is perfectly simple; man in performing some action which he is resolved on doing, does not by any means prove his free agency; the very desire of displaying this quality, excited by the dispute, becomes a necessary motive, which decides his will either for the one or the other of these actions: What deludes him in this instance, or that which persuades him he is a free agent at this moment, is, that he does not discern the true motive which sets him in action, namely, the desire of convincing his opponent: if in the heat of the dispute he insists and asks, "Am I not the master of throwing myself out of the window?" I shall answer him, no; that whilst he preserves his reason there is no probability that the desire of proving his free agency, will become a motive sufficiently powerful to make him sacrifice his life to the attempt: if, notwithstanding this, to prove he is a free agent, he should actually precipitate himself from the window, it would not be a sufficient warranty to conclude he acted freely, but rather that it was the violence of his temperament which spurred him on to this folly. Madness is a state, that depends upon the heat of the blood, not upon the will. A fanatic or a hero, braves death as necessarily as a more phlegmatic man or coward flies from it.

There is, in point of fact, no difference between the man that is cast out of the window by another, and the man who throws himself out of it, except that the impulse in the first instance comes immediately from without whilst that which determines the fall in the second case, springs from within his own peculiar machine, having its more remote cause also exterior. When Mutius Scaevola held his hand in the fire, he was as much acting under the influence of necessity (caused by interior motives) that urged him to this strange action, as if his arm had been held by strong men: pride, despair, the desire of braving his enemy, a wish to astonish him, and anxiety to intimidate him, etc., were the invisible chains that held his hand bound to the fire. The love of glory, enthusiasm for their country, in like manner caused Codrus and Decius to devote themselves for their fellow-citizens. The Indian Colanus and the philosopher Peregrinus were equally obliged to burn themselves, by desire of exciting the astonishment of the Grecian assembly.

It is said that free agency is the absence of those obstacles competent to oppose themselves to the actions of man, or to the exercise of his faculties: it is pretended that he is a free agent whenever, making use of these faculties, he produces the effect he has proposed to himself. In reply to this reasoning, it is sufficient to consider that it in nowise depends upon himself to place or remove the obstacles that either determine or resist him; the motive that causes his action is no more in his own power than the obstacle that impedes him, whether this obstacle or motive be within his own machine or exterior of his person: he is not master of the thought presented to his mind, which determines his will; this thought is excited by some cause independent of himself.

To be undeceived on the system of his free agency, man has simply to recur to the motive by which his will is determined; he will always find this motive is out of his own control. It is said: that in consequence of an idea to which the mind gives birth, man acts freely if he encounters no obstacle. But the question is, what gives birth to this idea in his brain? was he the master either to prevent it from presenting itself, or from renewing itself in his brain? Does not this idea depend either upon objects that strike him exteriorly and in despite of himself, or upon causes, that without his knowledge, act within himself and modify his brain? Can he prevent his eyes, cast without design upon any object whatever, from giving him an idea of this object, and from moving his brain? He is not more master of the obstacles; they are the necessary effects of either interior or exterior causes, which always act according to their given properties. A man insults a coward; this necessarily irritates him against his insulter; but his will cannot vanquish the obstacle that cowardice places to the object of his desire, because his natural conformation, which does not depend upon himself, prevents his having courage. In this case, the coward is insulted in spite of himself; and against his will is obliged patiently to brook the insult he has received.

Absence of Restraint Is Not Absence of Necessity. The partisans of the system of free agency appear ever to have confounded constraint with necessity. Man believes he acts as a free agent, every time he does not see any thing that places obstacles to his actions; he does not perceive that the motive which causes him to will, is always necessary and independent of himself. A prisoner loaded with chains is compelled to remain in prison; but he is not a free agent in the desire to emancipate himself; his chains prevent him from acting, but they do not prevent him from willing; he would save himself if they would loose his fetters; but he would not save himself as a free agent; fear or the idea of punishment would be sufficient motives for his action.

Man may, therefore, cease to be restrained, without, for that reason, becoming a free agent: in whatever manner he acts, he will act necessarily, according to motives by which he shall be determined. He may be compared to a heavy body that finds itself arrested in its descent by any obstacle whatever: take away this obstacle, it will gravitate or continue to fall; but who shall say this dense body is free to fall or not? Is not its descent the necessary effect of its own specific gravity? The virtuous Socrates submitted to the laws of his country, although they were unjust; and though the doors of his jail were left open to him, he would not save himself; but in this he did not act as a free agent: the invisible chains of opinion, the secret love of decorum, the inward respect for the laws, even when they were iniquitous, the fear of tarnishing his glory, kept him in his prison; they were motives sufficiently powerful with this enthusiast for virtue, to induce him to wait death with tranquility; it was not in his power to save himself, because he could find no potential motive to bring him to depart, even for an instant, from those principles to which his mind was accustomed.

Man, it is said, frequently acts against his inclination, from whence it is falsely concluded he is a free agent; but when he appears to act contrary to his inclination, he is always determined to it by some motive sufficiently efficacious to vanquish this inclination. A sick man, with a view to his cure, arrives at conquering his repugnance to the most disgusting remedies: the fear of pain, or the dread of death, then become necessary motives; consequently this sick man cannot be said to act freely.

When it is said, that man is not a free agent, it is not pretended to compare him to a body moved by a simple impulsive cause: he contains within himself causes inherent to his existence; he is moved by an interior organ, which has its own peculiar laws, and is itself necessarily determined in consequence of ideas formed from perception resulting from sensation which it receives from exterior objects. As the mechanism of these sensations, of these perceptions, and the manner they engrave ideas on the brain of man, are not known to him; because he is unable to unravel all these motions; because he cannot perceive the chain of operations in his soul, or the motive principle that acts within him, he supposes himself a free agent; which literally translated, signifies, that he moves himself by himself; that he determines himself without cause: when he rather ought to say, that he is ignorant how or why he acts in the manner he does. It is true the soul enjoys an activity peculiar to itself: but it is equally certain that this activity would never be displayed, if some motive or some cause did not put it in a condition to exercise itself: at least it will not be pretended that the soul is able either to love or to hate without being moved, without knowing the objects, without having some idea of their qualities. Gunpowder has unquestionably a particular activity, but this activity will never display itself, unless fire be applied to it; this, however, immediately sets it in motion.

The Complexity of Human Conduct and the Illusion of Free Agency. It is the great complication of motion in man, it is the variety of his action, it is the multiplicity of causes that move him, whether simultaneously or in continual succession, that persuades him he is a free agent: if all his motions were simple, if the causes that move him did not confound themselves with each other, if they were distinct, if his machine were less complicated, he would perceive that all his actions were necessary, because he would be enabled to recur instantly to the cause that made him act. A man who should be always obliged to go towards the west, would always go on that side; but he would feel that, in so going, he was not a free agent: if he had another sense, as his actions or his motion, augmented by a sixth, would be still more varied and much more complicated, he would believe himself still more a free agent than he does with his five senses.

It is, then, for want of recurring to the causes that move him; for want of being able to analyze, from not being competent to decompose the complicated motion of his machine, that man believes himself a free agent: it is only upon his own ignorance that he founds the profound yet deceitful notion he has of his free agency; that he builds those opinions which he brings forward as a striking proof of his pretended freedom of action. If, for a short time, each man was willing to examine his own peculiar actions, search out their true motives to discover their concatenation, he would remain convinced that the sentiment he has of his natural free agency, is a chimera that must speedily be destroyed by experience.

Nevertheless it must be acknowledged that the multiplicity and diversity of the causes which continually act upon man, frequently without even his knowledge, render it impossible, or at least extremely difficult for him to recur to the true principles of his own peculiar actions, much less the actions of others: they frequently depend upon causes so fugitive, so remote from their effects, and which, superficially examined, appear to have so little analogy, so slender a relation with them, that it requires singular sagacity to bring them into light. This is what renders the study of the moral man a task of such difficulty; this is the reason why his heart is an abyss, of which it is frequently impossible for him to fathom the depth . . . .

If he understood the play of his organs, if he were able to recall to himself all the impulsions they have received, all the modifications they have undergone, all the effects they have produced, he would perceive that all his actions are submitted to the fatality, which regulates his own particular system, as it does the entire system of the universe: no one effect in him, any more than in nature, produces itself by chance; this, as has been before proved, is word void of sense. All that passes in him; all that is done by him; as well as all that happens in nature, or that is attributed to her, is derived from necessary causes, which act according to necessary laws, and which produce necessary effects from whence necessarily flow others.

Fatality, is the eternal, the immutable, the necessary order, established in nature; or the indispensable connexion of causes that act, with the effects they operate. Conforming to this order, heavy bodies fall: light bodies rise; that which is analogous in matter reciprocally attracts; that which is heterogeneous mutually repels; man congregates himself in society, modifies each his fellow; becomes either virtuous or wicked; either contributes to his mutual happiness, or reciprocates his misery; either loves his neighbour, or hates his companion necessarily, according to the manner in which the one acts upon the other. From whence it may be seen, that the same necessity which regulates the physical, also regulates the moral world, in which every thing is in consequence submitted to fatality. Man, in running over, frequently without his own knowledge, often in spite of himself, the route which nature has marked out for him, resembles a swimmer who is obliged to follow the current that carries him along: he believes himself a free agent, because he sometimes consents, sometimes does not consent, to glide with the stream, which notwithstanding, always hurries him forward; he believes himself the master of his condition, because he is obliged to use his arms under the fear of sinking . . . .

ARE HUMAN ACTIONS SUBJECT TO THE LAW OF CAUSALITY?

John Stuart Mill

The question whether the law of causality applies in the same strict sense to human actions as to other phenomena, is the celebrated controversy concerning the freedom of the will, which, from at least as far back as the time of Pelagious, has divided both the philosophical and the religious world. The affirmative opinion is commonly called the doctrine of Necessity, as asserting human volitions and actions to be necessary and inevitable. The negative maintains that the will is not determined, like other phenomena, by antecedents, but determines itself; that our volitions are not, properly speaking, the effects of causes, or at least have no causes which they uniformly and implicitly obey.

I have already made it sufficiently apparent that the former of these opinions is that which I consider the true one; but the misleading terms in which it is often expressed, and the indistinct manner in which it is usually apprehended, have both obstructed its reception and perverted its influence when received. The metaphysical theory of free-will, as held by philosophers (for the practical feeling of it, common in a greater or less degree to all mankind, is in no way inconsistent with the contrary theory), was invented because the supposed alternative of admitting human actions to be *necessary* was deemed inconsistent with everyone's instinctive consciousness, as well as humiliating to the pride, even degrading to the moral nature of man. Nor do I deny that the doctrine, as sometimes held, is open to these imputations; for the misapprehension in which I shall be able to show that they originate unfortunately is not confined to the opponents of the doctrine, but is participated in by many, perhaps we might say by most, of its supporters.

THE DOCTRINE OF PHILOSOPHICAL NECESSITY

Correctly conceived, the doctrine entitled Philosophical Necessity is simply this: that, given the motives which are present to an individual's mind, and given likewise the character and disposition of the individual, the manner in which he will act might be unerringly inferred; that if we knew the person thoroughly, and knew all the inducements which are acting upon him, we could foretell his conduct with as much certainty as we can predict any physical event. This position I take to be a mere interpretation of universal experience, a statement in words of what everyone is internally convinced of. No one who believed that he knew thoroughly the circumstances of any case, and the characters of the different persons concerned, would hesitate to foretell how all of them would act. Whatever degree of doubt he may in fact feel arises from the uncertainty whether he really knows the circumstances, or the character of someone or other of the persons, with the degree of accuracy required; but by no means from thinking that if he did know these things, there could be an uncertainty what the conduct should be. Nor does this full assurance conflict in the smallest degree with what is called our feeling of freedom. We do not feel ourselves the less free because those to whom we are intimately known are well assured how we shall will to act in a particular case. We often, on the contrary, regard the doubt of what our conduct will be as a mark of ignorance of our characters, and sometimes even resent it as an imputation. The religious metaphysicians who have asserted the freedom of the will have always maintained it to be consistent with divine foreknowledge of our actions; and if with divine, then with any other foreknowledge. We may be free, and yet another may have reason to be perfectly certain what use we shall make of our freedom. It is not, therefore, the doctrine that our volitions and actions are invariable consequents of our antecedent states of mind, that is either contradicted by our consciousness or felt to be degrading.

But the doctrine of causation, when considered as obtaining between our volitions and their antecedents, is almost universally conceived as involving more than this. Many do not believe, and very few practically feel, that there is nothing in causation but invariable, certain, and unconditional sequence. There are few to whom mere constancy of succession appears a sufficiently stringent bond of union for so peculiar a relation as that of cause and effect. Even if the reason repudiates, the imagination retains, the feeling of some more intimate connection, of some peculiar tie or mysterious constraint exercised by the antecedent over the consequent. Now this it is which, considered as applying to the human will, conflicts with our consciousness and revolts our feelings. We are certain that, in the case of our volitions, there is not this mysterious constraint. We know that we are not compelled, as by a magical spell, to obey any particular motives. We feel that if we wished to prove that we have the power of resisting the motive, we could do so, (that wish being, it needs scarcely be observed, a *new antecedent*); and it would be humiliating to our pride, and (what is of more importance) paralyzing to our desire of excellence, if we thought otherwise. But neither is any such mysterious compulsion now supposed, by the best philosophical authorities, to be exercised by any other cause over its effect. Those who think that causes draw their effects after them by a mystical tie are right in believing that the relation between volitions and their antecedents is of another nature. But they should go farther, and admit that this is also true of all other effects and their antecedents. If such a tie is considered to be involved in the word necessity, the doctrine is not true of human actions; but neither is it then true of inanimate objects. It would be more correct to say that matter is not bound by necessity, than that mind is so.

That the free-will metaphysicians, being mostly of the school which rejects Hume's and Brown's analysis of Cause and Effect, should miss their way for want of the light which that analysis affords, cannot surprise us. The wonder is, that the Necessitarians, who usually admit that philosophical theory, should in practice equally lose sight of it. The very same misconception of the doctrine called Philosophical Necessity which prevents the opposite party from recognising its truth, I believe to exist more or less obscurely in the minds of most Necessitarians, however they may in words disavow it. I am much mistaken if they habitually feel that the necessity which they recognise in actions is but uniformity of order, and capability of being predicted. They have a feeling as if there were at bottom a stronger tie between the volitions and their causes: as if, when they asserted that the will is governed by the balance of motives, they meant something more cogent than if they had only said, that whoever knew the motives, and our habitual susceptibilities to them, could predict how we should will to act. They commit, in opposition to their own scientific system, the very same mistake which their adversaries commit in obedience to theirs; and in consequence do really in some instances suffer those depressing consequences which their opponents erroneously impute to the doctrine itself.

PERNICIOUS EFFECT OF THE TERM "NECESSITY"

I am inclined to think that this error is almost wholly an effect of the associations with a word, and that it would be prevented by forebearing to employ, for the expression of the simple fact of causation, so extremely inappropriate a term as Necessity. That word, in its other acceptations, involves much more than mere uniformity of sequence: it implies irresistibleness. Applied to the will, it only means that the given cause will be followed by the effect, subject to all possibilities of counteraction by other causes; but in common use it stands for the operation of those causes exclusively, which are supposed too powerful to be counteracted at all. When we say that all human actions take place of necessity, we only mean that they will certainly happen if nothing prevents:—when we say that dying of want, to those who cannot get food, is a necessity, we mean that it will certainly happen, whatever may be done to prevent it. The application of the same term to the agencies on which human actions depend as is used to express those agencies of nature which are really uncontrollable, cannot fail, when habitual, to create a feeling of uncontrollableness in the former also. This, however, is a mere illusion. There are physical sequences which we call necessary as death for want of food or air; there are others which, though as much cases of causation as the former, are not said to be necessary, as death from poison, which an antidote, or the use of the stomach pump, will sometimes avert. It is apt to be forgotten by people's feelings, even if remembered by their understandings, that human actions are in this last predicament: they are never (except in some cases of mania) ruled by any one motive with such absolute sway that there is no room for the influence of any other. The causes, therefore, on which action depends are never uncontrollable, and any given effect is only necessary provided that the causes tending to produce it are not controlled. That whatever happens could not have happened otherwise unless something had taken place which was capable of preventing it, no one surely needs hesitate to admit. But to call this by the name necessity is to use the term in a sense so different from its primitive and familiar meaning, from that which it bears in the common occasions of life, as to amount almost to a play upon words. The associations derived from the ordinary sense of the term will adhere to it in spite of all we can do; and though the doctrine of Necessity, as stated by most who hold it, is very remote from fatalism, it is probable that most Necessitarians are Fatalists, more or less, in their feelings.

A Fatalist believes, or half believes (for nobody is a consistent Fatalist), not only that whatever is about to happen will be the infallible result of the causes which produce it (which is the true Necessitarian doctrine), but, moreover, that there is no use in struggling against it; that it will happen however we may strive to prevent it. Now, a Necessitarian, believing that our actions follow from our characters, and that our characters follow from our organisation, our education, and our circumstances, is apt to be, with more or less of consciousness on his part, a Fatalist as to his own actions, and to believe that his nature is such, or that his education and circumstances have so moulded his character, that nothing can now prevent him from feeling and acting in a particular way, or at least that no effort of his own can hinder it. In the words of the sect which in our own day has most perseveringly inculcated and most perversely misunderstood this great doctrine, his character is formed *for* him, and not *by* him; therefore his wishing that it had been formed differently is of no use; he has no power to alter it. But this is a grand error. He has, to a certain extent, a power to alter his character. Its being, in the ultimate resort, formed for him, is not inconsistent with its being, in part, formed *by* him as one of the intermediate agents. His character is formed by his circumstances (including among these his particular organisation), but his own desire to mould it in a particular way is one of these circumstances, and by no means one of the least influential. We cannot, indeed, directly will to be different from what we are; but neither did those who are supposed to have formed our characters directly will that we should be what we are. Their will had no direct power except over their own actions. They made us what they did make us by willing, not the end, but the requisite means; and we, when our habits are not too inveterate, can, by similarly willing the requisite means, make ourselves different. If they could place us under the influence of certain circumstances, we in like manner can place ourselves under the influence of other circumstances. We are exactly as capable of making our own character, *if we will*, as others are of making it for us.

Yes (answers the Owenite), but these words, "if we will," surrender the whole point, since the will to alter our own character is given us, not by any efforts of ours, but by circumstances which we cannot help; it comes to us either from external causes or not at all. Most true: if the Owenite stop here, he is in a position from which nothing can expel him. Our character is formed by us as well as for us; but the wish which induces us to attempt to form it is formed for us; and how? Not, in general, by our organisation, nor wholly by our education, but by our experience—experience of the painful consequences of the character we previously had, or by some strong feeling of admiration or aspiration accidentally aroused. But to think that we have no power of altering our character, and to think that we shall not use our power unless we desire to use it, are very different things, and have a very different effect on the mind. A person who does not wish to alter his character cannot be the person who is supposed to feel discouraged or paralysed by thinking himself unable to do it. The depressing effect of the Fatalist doctrine can only be felt where there *is* a wish to do what that doctrine represents as impossible. It is of no consequence what we think forms our character, when we have no desire of our own about forming it, but it is of great consequence that we should not be prevented from forming such a desire by thinking the attainment impracticable, and that if we have the desire we should know that the work is not so irrevocably done as to be incapable of being altered.

And, indeed, if we examine closely, we shall find that this feeling, of our being able to modify our own character *if we wish*, is itself the feeling of moral freedom which we are conscious of. A person feels morally free who feels that his habits or his temptations are not his masters, but he theirs: who even in yielding to them knows that he could resist; that were he desirous of altogether throwing them off, there would not be required for that purpose a stronger desire than he knows himself to be capable of feeling. It is of course necessary, to render our consciousness of freedom complete, that we should have succeeded in making our character all we have hitherto attempted to make it; for if we have wished and not attained, we have, to that extent, not power over our own character—we are not free. Or at least, we must feel that our wish, if not strong enough to alter our character, is strong enough to conquer our character when the two are brought into conflict in any particular case of conduct. And hence it is said with truth, that none but a person of confirmed virtue is completely free.

The application of so improper a term as Necessity to the doctrine of cause and effect in the matter of human character seems to me one of the most signal instances in philosophy of the abuse of terms, and its practical consequences one of the most striking examples of the power of language over our associations. The subject will never be generally understood until that objectionable term is dropped. The free-will doctrine, by keeping in view precisely that portion of the truth which the word Necessity puts out of sight, namely, the power of the mind to cooperate in the formation of its own character, has given to its adherents a practical feeling much nearer to the truth than has generally (I believe) existed in the minds of Necessitarians. The latter may have had a stronger sense of the importance of what human beings can do to shape the characters of one another; but the free-will doctrine has, I believe, fostered in its supporters a much stronger spirit of self-culture.

A MOTIVE NOT ALWAYS THE ANTICIPATION OF PLEASURE OR PAIN

There is still one fact which requires to be noticed (in addition to the existence of a power of self-formation) before the doctrine of the causation of human actions can be freed from the confusion and misapprehensions which surround it in many minds. When the will is said to be determined by motives, a motive does not mean always, or solely, the anticipation of a pleasure or of a pain. I shall not here inquire whether it be true that, in the commencements, all our voluntary actions are mere means consciously employed to obtain some pleasure or avoid some pain. It is at least certain that we gradually, through the influence of association, come to desire the means without thinking of the end: the action itself becomes an object of desire, and is performed without reference to any motive beyond itself. Thus far, it may still be objected, that the action having through association become pleasurable, we are, as much as before, moved to act by the anticipation of a pleasure, namely, the pleasure of the action itself. But granting this, the matter does not end here. As we proceed in the formation of habits, and become accustomed to will a particular act or a particular course of conduct because it is pleasurable, we at last continue to will it without any reference to its being pleasurable. Although, from some change in us or in our circumstances, we have ceased to find any pleasure in the action, or perhaps to anticipate any pleasure as the consequence of it, we still continue to desire the action, and consequently to do it. In this manner it is that habits of hurtful excess continue to be practised although they have ceased to be pleasurable; and in this manner also it is that the habit of willing to persevere in the course which he has chosen does not desert the moral hero, even when the reward, however real, which he doubtless receives from the consciousness of well-doing, is anything but an equivalent for the sufferings he undergoes or the wishes which he may have to renounce.

A habit of willing is commonly called a purpose; and among the causes of our volitions, and of the actions which flow from them, must be reckoned not only likings and aversions, but also purposes. It is only when our purposes have become independent of the feelings of pain or pleasure from which they originally took their rise that we are said to have a confirmed character. "A character," says Novalis, "is a completely fashioned will"; and the will, once so fashioned, may be steady and constant, when the passive susceptibilities of pleasure and pain are greatly weakened or materially changed.

With the corrections and explanations now given, the doctrine of the causation of our volitions by motives, and of motives by the desirable objects offered to us, combined without particular susceptibilities of desire, may be considered, I hope, as sufficiently established for the purposes of this treatise.

THE DILEMMA OF DETERMINISM
William James

A common opinion prevails that the juice has ages ago been pressed out of the free-will controversy, and that no new champion can do more than warm up stale arguments which everyone has heard. This is a radical mistake. I know of no subject less worn out, or in which inventive genius has a better chance of breaking open new ground—not, perhaps, of forcing a conclusion or of coercing assent, but of deepening our sense of what the issue between the two parties really is, and of what the ideas of fate and of free will imply. At our very side almost, in the past few years, we have seen falling in rapid succession from the press works that present the alternative in entirely novel lights. Not to speak of the English disciples of Hegel, such as Green and Bradley; not to speak of Hinton and Hodgson, nor of Hazard here—we see in the writings of Renouvier, Fouillée, and Delboeuf how completely changed and refreshed is the form of the old disputes. I cannot pretend to vie in originality with any of the masters I have named, and my ambition limits itself to just one little point. If I can make two of the necessarily implied corollaries of determinism clearer to you than they have been made before, I shall have made it possible for you to decide for or against that doctrine with a better understanding of what you are about. And if you prefer not to decide at all, but to remain doubters, you will at least see more plainly what the subject of your hesitation is. I thus disclaim openly on the threshold all pretension to prove to you that the freedom of the will is true. The most I hope is to induce some of you to follow my own example in assuming it true, and acting as if it were true. If it be true, it seems to me that this is involved in the strict logic of the case. Its truth ought not to be forced willy-nilly down our indifferent throats. It ought to be freely espoused by men who can equally well turn their backs upon it. In order words, our first act of freedom, if we are free, ought in all inward propriety to be to affirm that we are free. This should exclude, it seems to me, from the free-will side of the question all hope of a coercive demonstration—a demonstration which I, for one, am perfectly contented to go without.

With thus much understood at the outset, we can advance. But, not without one more point understood as well. The arguments I am about to urge all proceed to two suppositions: first, when we make theories about the world and discuss them with one another, we do so in order to attain a conception of things which shall give us subjective satisfaction; and, second, if there be two conceptions, and the one seems to us, on the whole, more rational than the other, we are entitled to suppose that the more rational one is truer of the two. I hope that you are all willing to make these suppositions with me; for I am afraid that if there be any of you here who are not, they will find little edification in the rest of what I have to say. I cannot stop to argue the point; but I myself believe that all the magnificent achievements of mathematical and physical science—our doctrines of evolution, of uniformity of law, and the rest—proceed from our indomitable desire to cast the world into a more rational shape in our minds than the shape into which it is thrown there by the crude order of our experience. The world has shown itself, to a great extent, plastic to this demand of ours for rationality. How much farther it will show itself plastic no one can say. Our only means of finding out is to try; and I, for one, feel as free to try conceptions of moral as of mechanical or of logical rationality. If a certain formula for expressing the nature of the world violates my moral demand, I shall feel free to throw it overboard, or at least to doubt it, as if it disappointed my demand for uniformity of sequence, for example; the one demand being, so far as I can see, quite as subjective and emotional as the other is. The principle of causality, for example—what is it but a postulate, an empty name covering simply a demand that the sequence of events shall some day manifest a deeper kind of belonging of one thing with another than the mere juxtaposition which now phenomenally appears? It is as much an altar to an unknown god as the one that Saint Paul found at Athens. All our scientific and philosophic ideals are altars to unknown gods. Uniformity is as much so as is free will. If this be admitted, we can debate on even terms. But if any one pretends that while freedom and variety are, in the first instance, subjective demands, necessity and uniformity are something altogether different, I do not see how we can debate at all.

To begin, then, I must suppose you acquainted with all the usual arguments on the subject. I cannot stop to take up the old proofs from causation, from statistics, from the certainty with which we can foretell one another's conduct, from the fixity of character, and all the rest. But there are two *words* which usually encumber these classical arguments, and which we must immediately dispose of if we are to make any progress. One is the eulogistic word *freedom*, and the other is the opprobrious word *chance*. The word "chance" I wish to keep, but I wish to get rid of the word "freedom." Its eulogistic associations have so far overshadowed all the rest of its meaning that both parties claim the sole right to use it, and determinists today insist that they alone are freedom's champions. Old-fashioned determinism was what we may call *hard* determinism. It did not shrink from such words as fatality, bondage of the will, necessitation, and the like. Nowadays, we have a *soft* determinism which abhors harsh words, and, repudiating fatality, necessity, and even predetermination, says that its real name is freedom; for freedom is only necessity understood, and bondage to the highest is identical with true freedom. Even a writer as little used to making capital out of soft words as Mr. Hodgson hesitates not to call himself a "free-will determinist."

Now, all this is a quagmire of evasion under which the real issue of fact has been entirely smothered. Freedom in all these senses presents simply no problem at all. No matter what the soft determinist mean by it—whether he mean the acting without external constraint; whether he mean the acting rightly, or whether he mean the acquiescing in the law of the whole—who cannot answer him that sometimes we are free and sometimes we are not? But there *is* a problem, an issue of fact and not of words, an issue of the most momentous importance, which is often decided without discussion in one sentence—nay, in one clause of a sentence—by those very writers who spin out whole chapters in their efforts to show what "true" freedom is; and that is the question of determinism, about which we are to talk tonight.

POSSIBILITIES AND ACTUALITIES

Fortunately, no ambiguities hang about this word or about its opposite, indeterminism. Both designate an outward way in which things may happen, and their cold and mathematical sound has no sentimental associations that can bribe our partiality either way in advance. Now, evidence of an external kind to decide between determinism and indeterminism is, as I intimated a while back, strictly impossible to find. Let us look at the difference between them and see for ourselves. What does determinism profess?

It professes that those parts of the universe already laid down absolutely appoint and decree what the other parts shall be. The future has no ambiguous possibilities hidden in its womb: the part we call the present is compatible with only one totality. Any other future complement than the one fixed from eternity is impossible. The whole is in each and every part, and welds it with the rest into an absolute unity, an iron block, in which there can be no equivocation or shadow of turning.

> With earth's first clay they did the last man knead,
> And there of the last harvest sowed the seed.
> And the first morning of creation wrote
> What the last dawn of reckoning shall read.

Indeterminism, on the contrary, says that the parts have a certain amount of loose play on one another, so that the laying down of one of them does not necessarily determine what the others shall be. It admits that possibilities may be in excess of actualities, and that things not yet revealed to our knowledge may really in themselves be ambiguous. Of two alternative futures which we conceive, both may now be really possible; and the one become impossible only at the very moment when the other excludes it by becoming real itself. Indeterminism thus denies the world to be one unbending unit of fact. It says there is a certain ultimate pluralism in it; and, so saying, it corroborates our ordinary unsophisticated view of things. To that view, actualities seem to float in a wider sea of possibilities from out of which they are chosen; and, somewhere, indeterminism says, such possibilities exist, and form a part of truth.

Determinism, on the contrary, says they exist *nowhere*, and that necessity on the one hand and impossibility on the other are the sole categories of the real. Possibilities that fail to get realized are, for determinism, pure illusions: they never were possibilities at all. There is nothing inchoate, it says, about this universe of ours, all that was or is or shall be actual in it having been from eternity virtually there. The cloud of alternatives our minds secort this mass of actuality withal is a cloud of sheer deceptions, to which "impossibilities" is the only name which rightfully belongs.

The issue, it will be seen, is a perfectly sharp one, which no eulogistic terminology can smear over or wipe out. The truth *must* lie with one side or the other, and its lying with one side makes the other false.

The question relates solely to the existence of possibilities, in the strict sense of the term, as things that may, but need not be. Both sides admit that a volition, for instance, has occurred. The indeterminists say another volition might have occurred in its place: the determinists swear that nothing could possibly have occurred in its place. Now, can science be called in to tell us which of these two point-blank contradicters of each other is right? Science professes to draw no conclusions but such as are based on matters of facts, things that have actually happened; but how can any amount of assurance that something actually happened give us the least grain of information as to whether another thing might or might not have happened in its place? Only facts can be proved by other facts. With things that are possibilities and not facts, facts have no concern. If we have no other evidence than the evidence of existing facts, the possibility-question must remain a mystery never to be cleared up.

And the truth is that facts practically have hardly anything to do with making us either determinists or indeterminists. Sure enough, we make a flourish of quoting facts this way or that; and if we are determinists, we talk about the infallibility with which we can predict one another's conduct; while if we are indeterminists, we lay great stress on the fact that it is just because we cannot foretell one another's conduct, either in war or statecraft or in any of the great and small intrigues and businesses of men, that life is so intensely anxious and hazardous a game. But who does not see the wretched insufficiency of this so-called objective testimony on both sides? What fills up the gaps in our minds is something not objective, not external. What divides us into *possibility* men and *anti-possibility* men is different faiths or postulates—postulates of rationality. To this man the world seems more rational with possibilities in it—to that man more rational with possibilities excluded; and talk as we will about having to yield to evidence, what makes us monists or pluralists, determinists or indeterminists, is at bottom always some sentiment like this.

THE IDEA OF CHANCE

The stronghold of the deterministic sentiment is the antipathy to the idea of chance. As soon as we begin to talk indeterminism to our friends, we find a number of them shaking their heads. This notion of alternative possibility, they say, this admission that any one of several things may come to pass, is, after all, only a round-about name for chance; and chance is something the notion of which no sane mind can for an instant tolerate in the world. What is it, they ask, but barefaced crazy unreason, the negation of intelligibility and law? And if the slightest particle of it exists anywhere, what is to prevent the whole fabric from falling together, the stars from going out, and chaos from recommencing her topsy-turvy reign?

Remarks of this sort about chance will put an end to discussion as quickly as anything one can find. I have already told you that "chance" was a word I wished to keep and use. Let us then examine exactly what it means, and see whether it ought to be such a terrible bugbear to us. I fancy that squeezing the thistle boldly will rob it of its sting.

The sting of the word "chance" seems to lie in the assumption that it means something positive, and that if anything happens by chance, it must needs be something of an intrinsically irrational and preposterous sort. Now, chance means nothing of the kind. It is a purely negative and relative term, giving us no information about that of which it is predicated, except that it happens to be disconnected with something else—not controlled, secured, or necessitated by other things in advance of its own actual presence. At this point is the most subtle one of the whole lecture, and at the same time the point on which all the rest hinges, I beg you to pay particular attention to it. What I say is that it tells us nothing about what a thing may be in itself to call it "chance." It may be a bad thing, it may be a good thing. It may be lucidity, transparency, fitness incarnate, matching the whole system of other things, when it has once befallen, in an unimaginably perfect way. All you mean by calling it "chance" is that this is not guaranteed, that it may also fall out otherwise. For the system of other things has no positive hold on the chance-thing. Its origin is in a certain fashion negative: it escapes, and says, "Hands off!" coming, when it comes, as a free gift, or not at all.

This negativeness, however, and this opacity of the chance-thing when thus considered *ab extra,* or from the point of view of previous things or distant things, do not preclude its having any amount of positiveness and luminosity from within, and at its own place and moment. All that its chance-character asserts about it is that there is something in it really of its own, something that is not the unconditional property of the whole. If the whole wants this property, the whole must wait till it can get it, if it be a matter of chance. That the universe may actually be a sort of joint-stock society of this sort, in which the sharers have both limited liabilities and limited powers, is of course a simple and conceivable notion.

Nevertheless, many persons talk as if the minutest dose of disconnectedness of one part with another, the smallest modicum of independence, the faintest tremor of ambiguity about the future, for example, would ruin everything, and turn this goodly universe into a sort of insane sand-heap or nulliverse—no universe at all. Since future human volitions are, as a matter of fact, the only ambiguous things we are tempted to believe in, let us stop for a moment to make ourselves sure whether their independent and accidental character need be fraught with such direful consequences to the universe as these.

What is meant by saying that my choice of which way to walk home after the lecture is ambiguous and matter of chance as far as the present moment is concerned? It means that both Divinity Avenue and Oxford Street are called; but that only one, and that one *either* one shall be chosen. Now, I ask you seriously to suppose that this ambiguity of my choice is real; and then to make the impossible hypothesis that the choice is made twice over, and each time falls on a different street. In other words, imagine that I first walk through Divinity Avenue, and then imagine that the powers governing the universe annihilate ten minutes of time with all that it contained, and set me back at the door of this hall just as I was before the choice was made. Imagine then that, everything else being the same, I now make a different choice and traverse Oxford Street. You, as passive spectators, look on and see the two alternative universes—one of them with me walking through Divinity Avenue in it, the other with the same me walking through Oxford Street. Now, if you are determinists you believe one of these universes to have been from eternity impossible: you believe it to have been impossible because of the intrinsic irrationality or accidentality somewhere involved in it. But looking outwardly at these universes, can you say which is the impossible and accidental one, and which the rational and necessary one? I doubt if the most iron-clad determinist among you could have the slightest glimmer of light at this point. In other words, either universe *after the fact* and once there would, to our means of observation and understanding, appear just as rational as the other. There would be absolutely no criterion by which we might judge one necessary and the other matter of chance. Suppose now we relieve the gods of their hypothetical task and assume my choice, once made, to be made forever. I go through Divinity Avenue for good and all. If, as good determinists, you now begin to affirm, what all good determinists punctually do affirm, that in the nature of things I couldn't have gone through Oxford Street—had I done so it would have been chance, irrationality, insanity, a horrid gap in nature—I simply call your attention to this, that your affirmation is what the Germans call a *Machtspruch*, a mere conception fulminated as a dogma and based on no insight into details. Before my choice, either street seemed as natural to you as to me. Had I happened to take Oxford Street, Divinity Avenue would have figured in your philosophy as the gap in nature; and you would have so proclaimed it with the best deterministic conscience in the world.

But what a hollow outcry, then, is this against a chance which, if it were present to us, we could by no character whatever distinguish from a rational necessity! I have taken the most trivial of examples, but no possible example could lead to any different result. For what are the alternatives which, in point of fact, offer themselves to human volition? What are those futures that now seem matters of chance? Are they not one and all like the Divinity Avenue and Oxford Street of our example? Are they not all of them *kinds* of things already here and based in the existing frame of nature? Is any one ever tempted to produce an *absolute* accident, something utterly irrelevant to the rest of the world? Do not all the motives that assail us, all the futures that offer themselves to our choice, spring equally from the soil of the past; and would not either one of them, whether realized through chance or through necessity, the moment it was realized, seem to us to fit that past, and in the completest and most continuous manner to interdigitate with the phenomena already there?

A favorite argument against free will is that if it be true, a man's murderer may as probably be his best friend as his worst enemy, a mother be as likely to strangle as to suckle her first-born, and all of us be as ready to jump from fourth-story windows as to go out of front doors, etc. Users of this argument should probably be excluded from debate till they learn what the real question is. "Free-will" does not say that everything that is physically conceivable is also morally possible. It merely says that of alternatives that really *tempt* our will more than one is really possible. Of course, the alternatives that do thus tempt our will are vastly fewer than the physical possibilities we can coldly fancy. Persons really tempted often do murder their best friends, mothers do strangle their first-born, people do jump out of fourth stories, etc.

The more one thinks of the matter, the more one wonders that so empty and gratuitous a hubbub as this outcry against chance should have found so great an echo in the hearts of men. It is a word which tells us absolutely nothing about what chances, or about the *modus operandi* of the chancing; and the use of it as a war-cry shows only a temper of intellectual absolutism, a demand that the world shall be a solid block, subject to one control—which temper, which demand, the world may not be bound to gratify at all. In every outwardly verifiable and practical respect, a world in which the alternatives that now actually distract *your* choice were decided by pure chance would be by *me* absolutely undistinguished from the world in which I now live. I am, therefore, entirely willing to call it, so far as your choices go, a world of chance for me. To *yourself*, it is true, those very acts of choice, which to me are so blind, opaque, and external, are the opposites of this, for you are within them and effect them. To you they appear as decisions; and decisions, for him who makes them, are altogether peculiar psychic facts. Self-luminous and self-justifying at the living moment in which they occur, they appeal to no outside moment to put its stamp upon them or make them continuous with the rest of nature. Themselves it is rather who seem to make nature continuous; and in their strange and intense function of granting consent to one possibility and withholding it from another, to transform an equivocal and double future into an inalterable and simple past.

But with the psychology of the matter we have no concern this evening. The quarrel which determinism has with chance fortunately has nothing to do with this or that psychological detail. It is a quarrel altogether metaphysical. Determinism denies the ambiguity of future volitions, because it affirms that nothing future can be ambiguous. But we have said enough to meet the issue. Indeterminate future volitions *do* mean chance. Let us not fear to shout it from the house-tops if need be; for we now know that the idea of chance is, at bottom, exactly the same thing as the idea of gift—the one simply being a disparaging, and the other a eulogistic, name for anything on which we have no effective *claim*. And whether the world be the better or the worse for having either chances or gifts in it will depend altogether on *what* these uncertain and unclaimable things turn out to be.

THE MORAL IMPLICATIONS OF DETERMINISM

And this at last brings us within sight of our subject. We have seen what determinism means: we have seen that indeterminism is rightly described as meaning chance; and we have seen that chance, the very name of which we are urged to shrink from as from the metaphysical pestilence, means only the negative fact that no part of the world, however big, can claim to control absolutely the destinies of the whole. But although, in discussing the word "chance," I may at moments have seemed to be arguing for its real existence, I have not meant to do so yet. We have not yet ascertained whether this be a world of chance or no; at most, we have agreed that it seems so. And I now repeat what I said at the outset, that, from any strict theoretical point of view, the question is insoluble. To deepen our theoretic sense of the *difference* between a world with chances in it and a deterministic world is the most I can hope to do; and this I may now at last begin upon, after all our tedious clearing of the way.

I wish first of all to show you just what the notion that this is a deterministic world implies. The implications I call your attention to are all bound up with the fact that it is a world in which we constantly have to make what I shall, with your permission, call judgments of regret. Hardly an hour passes in which we do not wish that something might be otherwise; and happy indeed are those of us whose hearts have never echoed the wish of Omar Khayyam—

That we might clasp, ere closed, the book of fate,
   And make the writer on a fairer leaf
Inscribe our names, or quite obliterate.

Ah! Love, could you and I with fate conspire
To mend this sorry scheme of things entire,
   Would we not shatter it to bits, and then
Remould it nearer to the heart's desire?

Now, it is undeniable that most of these regrets are foolish, and quite on a par in point of philosophic value with the criticisms on the universe of that friend of our infancy, the hero of the fable, "The Atheist and the Acorn"—

Fool! had that bough a pumpkin bore,
Thy whimsies would have worked no more, etc.

Even from the point of view of our own ends, we should probably make a botch of remodelling the universe. How much more then from the point of view of ends we cannot see! Wise men therefore regret as little as they can. But still some regrets are pretty obstinate and hard to stifle—regrets for acts of wanton cruelty or treachery, for example, whether performed by others or by ourselves. Hardly any one can remain *entirely* optimistic after reading the confession of the murderer at Brockton the other day: how, to get rid of the wife whose continued existence bored him, he enveigled her into a deserted spot, shot her four times, and then, as she lay on the ground and said to him, "You didn't do it on purpose, did you dear?" replied, "No, I didn't do it on purpose," as he raised a rock and smashed her skull. Such an occurrence, with the mild sentence and self-satisfaction of the prisoner, is a field for a crop of regrets, which one need not take up in detail. We feel that, although a perfect mechanical fit to the rest of the universe, it is a bad moral fit, and that something else would really have been better in its place.

But for the deterministic philosophy the murder, the sentence, and the prisoner's optimism were all necessary from eternity; and nothing else for a moment had a ghost of a chance of being put in their place. To admit such a chance, the determinists tell us, would be to make a suicide of reason; so we must steel our hearts against the thought. And here our plot thickens, for we see the first of those difficult implications of determinism and monism which it is my purpose to make you feel. If this

Brockton murder was called for by the rest of the universe, if it had come at its preappointed hour, and if nothing else would have been consistent with the sense of the whole, what are we to think of the universe? Are we stubbornly to stick to our judgment of regret, and say, though it *couldn't* be, yet it *would* have been a better universe with something different from this Brockton murder in it? That, of course, seems the natural and spontaneous thing for us to do; and yet it is nothing short of deliberately espousing a kind of pessimism. The judgment of regret calls the murder bad. Calling a thing bad means, if it means anything at all, that the thing ought not be, that something else ought to be in its stead. Determinism, in denying that anything else can be in its stead, virtually defines the universe as a place in which what ought to be is impossible—in other words, as an organism whose constitution is afflicted with an incurable taint, and irremediable flaw. The pessimism of a Schopenhauer says no more than this—that the murder is a symptom; and that it is a vicious symptom because it belongs to a vicious whole, which can express its nature no otherwise than by bringing forth just such a symptom as that at this particular spot. Regret for the murder must transform itself, if we are determinists and wise, into a larger regret. It is absurd to regret the murder alone. Other things being what they are, *it* could not be different. What we should regret is that whole frame of things of which the murder is one member. I see no escape whatever from this pessimistic conclusion if, being determinists, our judgment of regret is to be allowed to stand at all.

The only deterministic escape from pessimism is everywhere to abandon the judgment of regret. That this can be done, history shows to be not impossible. The devil, *quoad existentiam,* may be good. That is, although he be a *principle* of evil, yet the universe, with such a principle in it, may practically be a better universe than it could have been without. On every hand, in a small way, we find that a certain amount of evil is a condition by which a higher form of good is brought. There is nothing to prevent anybody from generalizing this view, and trusting that if we could but see things in the largest of all ways, even such matters as this Brockton murder would appear to be paid for by the uses which follow in their train. An optimism *quand même,* a systematic and infatuated optimism like that ridiculed by Voltaire in his *Candide,* is one of the possible ideal ways in which a man may train himself to look upon life. Bereft of dogmatic hardness and lit up with the expression of a tender and pathetic hope, such an optimism has been the grace of some of the most religious characters that ever lived.

> Throb thine with Nature's throbbing breast,
> And all is clear from east to west.

Even cruelty and treachery may be among the absolutely blessed fruits of time, and to quarrel with any of their details may be blasphemy. The only real blasphemy, in short, may be that pessimistic temper of the soul which lets it give way to such things as regrets, remorse, and grief.

Thus, our deterministic pessimism may become a deterministic optimism at the price of extinguishing our judgments of regret.

But does not this immediately bring us into a curious logical predicament? Our determinism leads us to call our judgments of regret wrong, because they are pessimistic in implying that what is impossible yet ought to be. But how then about the judgments of regret themselves? If they are wrong, other judgments, judgments of approval presumably, ought to be in their place. But as they are necessitated, nothing else *can* be in their place; and the universe is just what it was before—namely, a place in which what ought to be appears impossible. We have got one foot out of the pessimistic bog, but the other one sinks all the deeper. We have rescued our actions from the bonds of evil, but our judgments are now held fast. When murders and treacheries cease to be sins, regrets are theoretic absurdities and errors. The theoretic and the active life thus play a kind of see-saw with each other on the ground of evil. The rise of either sends the other down. Murder and treachery cannot be good without regret being bad: regret cannot be good without treachery and murder being bad. Both, however, are supposed to have been foredoomed; so something must be fatally unreasonable, absurd, and wrong in the world. It must be a place of which either sin or error forms a necessary part. From this dilemma there seems at first sight no escape. Are we then so soon to fall back into the pessimism from which we thought we had emerged? And is there no possible way by which we may, with good intellectual consciences, call the cruelties and the treacheries, the reluctances and the regrets, *all* good together?

Certainly there is such a way, and you are probably most of you ready to formulate it yourselves. But, before doing so, remark how inevitably the question of determinism and indeterminism slides us into the question of optimism and pessimism, or, as our fathers called it, "The question of evil." The theological form of all these disputes is simplest and the deepest, the form from which there is the least escape—not because, as some have sarcastically said, remorse and regret are clung to with a morbid fondness by the theologians as spiritual luxuries, but because they are existing facts in the world, and as such must be taken into account in the deterministic interpretation of all that is fated to be. If they are fated to be error, does not the bat's wing of irrationality cast its shadow over the world? . . .

MORALITY AND INDETERMINISM

The only consistent way of representing a pluralism and a world whose parts may affect one another through their conduct being either good or bad is the indeterministic way. What interest, zest, or excitement can there be in achieving the right way, unless we are enabled to feel that the wrong way is also a possible and a natural way—nay, more, a menacing and an imminent way? And what sense can there be in condemning ourselves for taking the wrong way, unless we need have done nothing of the sort, unless the right way was open to us as well? I cannot understand the willingness to act, no matter how we feel, without the belief that acts are really good and bad. I cannot understand the belief that an act is bad, without regret at its happening. I cannot understand regret without the admission of real, genuine possibilities in the world. Only then is it other than a mockery to feel, after we have failed to do our best, that an irreparable opportunity is gone from the universe, the loss of which it must forever after mourn.

If you insist that this is all superstition, that possibility is in the eye of science and reason impossibility, and that if I act badly 'tis that the universe was foredoomed to suffer this defect, you fall right back into the dilemma, the labyrinth, of pessimism and subjectivism, from out of whose toils we have just wound our way.

Now, we are of course free to fall back, if we please. For my own part, though, whatever difficulties may beset the philosophy of objective right and wrong, and the indeterminism it seems to imply, determinism, with its alternative pessimism or romanticism, contains difficulties that are greater still. But you will remember that I expressly repudiated awhile ago the pretension to offer any arguments which could be coercive in a so-called scientific fashion in this matter. And I consequently find myself, at the end of this long talk, obliged to state my conclusions in an altogether personal way. This personal method of appeal seems to be among the very conditions of the problem; and the most any one can do is to confess as candidly as he can the grounds for the faith that is in him, and leave his example to work on others as it may.

Let me, then, without circumlocution say just this. The world is enigmatical enough in all conscience, whatever theory we may take up toward it. The indeterminism I defend, the free-will theory of popular sense based on the judgment of regret, represents that world as vulnerable, and liable to be injured by certain of its parts if they act wrong. And it represents their acting wrong as a matter of possibility or accident, neither inevitable nor yet to be infallibly warded off. In all this, it is a theory devoid either of transparency or of stability. It gives us a pluralistic, restless universe, in which no single point of view can ever take in the whole scene; and to a mind possessed of the love of unity at any cost, it will, no doubt, remain forever inacceptable. A friend with such a mind once told me that the thought of my universe made him sick, like the sight of the horrible motion of a mass of maggots in their carrion bed.

But while I freely admit that the pluralism and the restlessness are repugnant and irrational in a certain way, I find that every alternative to them is irrational in a deeper way. The indeterminism with its maggots, if you please to speak so about it, offends only the native absolutism of my intellect—an absolutism which, after all, perhaps, deserves to be snubbed and kept in check. But the determinism with its necessary carrion, to continue the figure of speech, and with no possible maggots to eat the latter up, violates my sense of moral reality through and through. When, for example, I imagine such carrion as the Brockton murder, I cannot conceive it as an act by which the universe, as a whole, logically and necessarily expresses its nature without shrinking from complicity with such a whole. And I deliberately refuse to keep on terms of loyalty with the universe by saying blankly that the murder, since it does flow from the nature of the whole, is not carrion. There are *some* instinctive reactions which I, for one, will not tamper with. The only remaining alternative, the attitude of gnostical romanticism, wrenches my personal instincts in quite as violent a way. It falsifies the simple objectivity of their deliverance. It makes the goose-flesh the murder excites in me a sufficient reason for the perpetration of the crime. It transforms life from a tragic reality into an insincere melodramatic exhibition, as foul or as tawdry as any one's diseased curiosity pleases to carry it out. And with its consecration of the *roman naturaliste* state of mind, and its enthronement of the baser crew of Parisian *littérateurs* among the eternally indispensable organs by which the infinite spirit of things attains to that subjective illumination which is the task of its life, it leaves me in presence of a sort of subjective carrion considerably more noisome than the objective carrion I called it in to take away.

No! better a thousand times, than such systematic corruption of our moral sanity, the plainest pessimism, so it be straightforward; but better far than that, the world of chance. Make as great an uproar about chance as you please, I know that chance means pluralism and nothing more. If some of the members of the pluralism are bad, the philosophy of pluralism, whatever broad views it may deny me, permits me, at least, to turn to the other members with a clean breast of affection and an unsophisticated moral sense. And if I still wish to think of the world as a totality, it lets me feel that a world with a chance in it of being altogether good, even if the chance never come to pass, is better than a world with no such chance at all. That "chance" whose very notion I am exhorted and conjured to banish from my view of the future as the suicide of reason concerning it, that "chance" is—what? Just this—the chance that in moral respects the future may be other and better than the past has been. This is the only chance we have any motive for supposing to exist. Shame, rather, on its repudiation and its denial! For its presence is the vital air which lets the world live, the salt which keeps it sweet . . . .

Questions for Part VII

1. Gilbert Ryle describes the paradox which gives rise to fatalism as an apparent conflict between two common beliefs: that what is was to be, and that some things which have happened could have been avoided. Explain what is meant by each of these claims and why they seem inconsistent.

2. Consider again the paradox mentioned in question 1. The paradox forces us to adopt one or another of three possible views: that it is false that what is was to be; that nothing which has happened could have been avoided; or that despite appearances the beliefs that what is was to be and that some things could have been avoided do not conflict. Which view does the fatalist adopt? Which view does Ryle adopt? Explain and defend your own answer to the paradox.

3. Compare Ryle's discussion of fatalism with David Lewis's in Part V.

4. A. J. Ayer, in "Freedom and Necessity," writes that "it looks as if the admission of moral responsibility, so far from being incompatible with determinism, tends rather to presuppose it." Explain why he says this, and evaluate his reasons.

5. Compare Ayer's last three sentences with Ryle's discussion of fatalism.

6. Holbach admits that our actions are often caused by our own motives, by the desires and beliefs which make one action more attractive to us than another. But he insists that these desires and beliefs are not themselves under our control. Is he right about this?

7. Holbach writes that man "supposes himself a free agent; which literally translated, signifies . . . that he determines without cause." Is this really what we mean when we call someone a free agent? Explain what Ayer would say about this claim of Holbach's.

8. Mill writes that the feeling of moral freedom is the feeling of "being able to modify our own character *if we wish*." It does not worry Mill that whether we want to or not is not in our control. Explain why not.

9. Consider the following situation from Anthony Burgess's novel *A Clockwork Orange*. A juvenile delinquent, Alex, is to be psychologically conditioned to be unable to act violently. The prison chaplain tells him: "You are to be made into a good boy, 6655321. Never again will you have the desire to commit acts of violence or to offend in any way against the State's Peace." If the treatment is successful, Alex will be released and will be able to do whatever he wants. But will he be free? Why or why not? Does this sort of case pose a problem for Mill's conception of freedom?

10. James writes that "evidence of an external kind to decide between determinism and indeterminism is . . . strictly impossible to find." Why does he say this? Is he right?

11. After describing an ugly murder, James writes that "for the deterministic philosophy the murder, the sentence, and the prisoner's optimism were all necessary from eternity; and nothing else for a moment had a ghost of a chance of being put in their place." Explain how Mill and Ayer would react to this statement.

12. Are the following actions done freely? Why or why not? (If more information is needed explain what kind of information and why it is relevant.) A theft performed by a kleptomaniac, a long-time smoker reaching for another cigarette, a heroin addict reaching for another fix, a long-time reader reaching for another

book, someone buying a product because it has been effectively advertised, a member of a religious cult insisting that he is not being held against his will, a student refusing to cheat on a test because her parents taught her that she should not, a juvenile stealing a car because all his buddies do, someone who buys worthless land at a high price because she has been lied to about its value.

Part VIII. The Problem of Evil

People are dying by the thousands in drought-stricken Africa. Millions of European Jews were exterminated by the Nazis in Third Reich Germany. Cancer kills thousands of people in America every year. Volcanoes erupt and spill lava and ash over people and their property. The extent of human pain and suffering throughout history is immeasurably large. Whether on a grand scale or in private, human misery is profuse and profound.

God, as conceived in traditional Christianity, is a loving divinity, all good, and also all knowing, and all powerful. But this very conception of God, in the light of the evils of the world, creates a major philosophical problem. It may be put in this form:

> If God is perfectly loving, God must want to abolish all evil (human pain and suffering).
> If God is all-powerful and all-knowing, God must be able to abolish all evil. Evil exists.

Therefore, either God is not omnipotent or perfectly loving, but the Christian God is both omnipotent and perfectly loving so the Christian God does not exist. Are there ways to combat this seemingly devastating attack on the belief in the existence of the God of Christianity? One way, though it hardly recommends itself, is to deny that there really is any evil in the world. Some people, in fact, do seriously maintain that human pain is only an illusion. Such a view, however, seems extremely insensitive (if not downright silly) in the fact of the facts of human history and contemporary life. The distended stomachs and sunken cheeks of starving children are hardly illusions. It may also be worth noting that mainstream Christianity has never adopted the view that evil is purely illusory. Evil is certainly represented in the *Bible* in a variety of dark, ugly, vicious manifestations, for the *Bible* never shirks from portraying human suffering as well as almost every form of natural evil and human wickedness.

Rationality of a believer at the very least, as J. L. Mackie argues, requires that somehow the belief in the Christian God be reconciled with the existence of genuine evil in the world. He maintains, however, that the attempt to do so is doomed to failure because Christianity's conception of God is irrational. Before we investigate ways in which the reconcil-

347

iation of God and evil have been attempted, there is an important distinction to be drawn. When we talk about the evils of the world, we can mean very different things. There is an obvious difference between misery caused by the willful acts of human beings and that produced by such natural disasters as tornadoes, earthquakes, and volcanoes. Following the convention in the literature on this problem, we shall call the latter "physical or natural evils" and the former "moral evils."

Most of the standard attempts to solve the problem of evil argue that the moral evils are caused by the fact of human freedom. Hence this problem relates directly to the free-will issue discussed in Part VII. The concept of a person, as was argued in Part III, is typically associated with that of a free moral agent, and a free moral agent is a being capable of acting wrongly as well as rightly. The possibility of doing wrong is therefore inseparable from the possibility of persons. God could have created a world in which there is no moral evil, but such a world would have to be one without full-fledged persons. To say that God should not have created a world with wrongdoing that causes pain and suffering is to say that God should have created a world without persons. A world with persons in it, even though they often do evil, would seem to be a greater accomplishment than a world with no entities capable of freely instigating their own actions. Also, a world in which there are persons who are always frustrated by God from actually doing evil would not be a world in which moral good occurs. So for God to have created a world in which there is genuine moral goodness, there must also be moral evil. But as Alvin Plantinga writes: "the fact that free creatures sometimes err, . . . , in no way tells against God's omnipotence or against his goodness; for he could forestall the occurrence of moral evil only by removing the possibility of moral good." This, however, sounds as if the problem of evil is being ignored or swept under the carpet.

You might propose to solve the problem of evil by adopting the position of St. Augustine that has commanded the high ground of Christian theological thought for over fourteen centuries. Augustine maintained that the universe was created good by God for a good purpose. All evil in the world, he believed, is due to something going wrong with things that are inherently good. Evil is the malfunctioning of what was created good. Such malfunctioning, however, can always be traced to the exercise of free will by persons. Actually, Augustine maintains that the fall of the angels and their subsequent tempting of human beings introduces sin (moral evil) into the universe. He further explains natural evils as God's punishment of moral evils. But this last claim seems particularly odd in the light of recent scientific evidence that earthquakes, volcanoes and other cataclysmic events occurred well before humans appeared on earth. If you support Augustine's general view, you still need to produce a more convincing explanation for physical and natural evils.

Augustine incorporates the notion of a final judgment at which perpetual happiness is given to those who have not sinned and eternal punishment is meted out to those who have done wrong. The universe, Augustine seemed to believe, will be restored to perfection because sinners are made permanently miserable and the good achieve happiness. This addendum to his position, however, is anything but a solution to the problem of evil for it actually builds pain and suffering into the permanent structure of the God-created universe. The universe is perfect in the beginning because everything in it is inherently good or it would not have been created by God. The universe achieves a sort of moral balance in the end.

Augustine's theory is not the only one that has been developed to respond to the problem of evil. St. Irenaeus, for example, denies that God created a perfect world that becomes infected by wickedness due to human wrongdoing. He held instead that the universe was created at a distance from God and was not perfect. He admits that much evil is the result of human behavior, but some is simply natural, a part of the structure of the universe. Humans have the capacity for moral and spiritual growth and are gradually transforming themselves into more perfect beings, what he calls "Children of God." On the Irenaean view, then, the problem of evil is no problem for God. God is still thought of as omnipotent and loving, but God is removed from and does not interfere in His creation.

To see something of the difference between these ways of confronting the problem of evil and the existence of God, you might puzzle over why God would have created the world at all. Two views, one aligned with the Augustinian and the other with Irenaean theodicies may come to mind. On one account, God created the world as a perfect place in which his favorites (humans) enjoy themselves. (Some call this the "pet-cage conception of creation.") On the other, God created no paradise. Instead the world is a place where freely acting persons can, by meeting the challenges of life, improve their lot until they are worthy of associating with their creator.

You might, of course, reject both of these early Christian theological theories. In fact, you might insist either that there is no God and so no problem of evil or, with Mackie, that God's omnipotence must be restricted. Restricted omnipotence, however, is not omnipotence as understood in the Christian doctrines. Hence, the problem of evil continues to loom over the rational belief in the Christian God.

EVIL AND OMNIPOTENCE

J. L. Mackie

The traditional arguments for the existence of God have been fairly thoroughly criticised by philosophers. But the theologian can, if he wishes, accept this criticism. He can admit that no rational proof of God's existence is possible. And he can still retain all that is essential to his position, by holding that God's existence is known in some other, non-rational way. I think, however, that a more telling criticism can be made by way of the traditional problem of evil. Here it can be shown, not that religious beliefs lack rational support, but that they are positively irrational, that the several parts of the essential theological doctrine are inconsistent with one another, so that the theologian can maintain his position as a whole only by a much more extreme rejection of reason than in the former case. He must now be prepared to believe, not merely what cannot be proved, but what can be *disproved* from other beliefs that he also holds.

The problem of evil, in the sense in which I shall be using the phrase, is a problem only for someone who believes that there is a God who is both omnipotent and wholly good. And it is a logical problem, the problem of clarifying and reconciling a number of beliefs: it is not a scientific problem that might be solved by further observations, or a practical problem that might be solved by a decision or an action. These points are obvious; I mention them only because they are sometimes ignored by theologians, who sometimes parry a statement of the problem with such remarks as "Well, can you solve the problem yourself?" or "This is a mystery which may be revealed to us later" or "Evil is something to be faced and overcome, not to be merely discussed".

In its simplest form the problem is this: God is omnipotent; God is wholly good; and yet evil exists. There seems to be some contradiction between these three propositions, so that if any two of them were true the third would be false. But at the same time all three are essential parts of most theological positions: the theologian, it seems, at once *must* adhere and *cannot consistently* adhere to all three. (The problem does not arise only for theists, but I shall discuss it in the form in which it presents itself for ordinary theism.)

However, the contradiction does not arise immediately; to show it we need some additional premises, or perhaps some quasi-logical rules connecting the terms 'good', 'evil', and 'omnipotent'. These additional principles are that good is opposed to evil, in such a way that a good thing always eliminates evil as far as it can, and that there are no limits to what an omnipotent thing can do. From these it follows that a good omnipotent thing eliminates evil completely, and then the propositions that a good omnipotent thing exists, and that evil exists, are incompatible.

A. ADEQUATE SOLUTIONS

Now once the problem is fully stated it is clear that it can be solved, in the sense that the problem will not arise if one gives up at least one of the propositions that constitute it. If you are prepared to say that God is not wholly good, or not quite omnipotent, or that evil does not exist, or that good is not opposed to the kind of evil that exists, or that there are limits to what an omnipotent thing can do, then the problem of evil will not arise for you.

There are, then, quite a number of adequate solutions of the problem of evil, and some of these have been adopted, or almost adopted, by various thinkers. For example, a few have been prepared to deny God's omnipotence, and rather more have been prepared to keep the term 'omnipotence' but severely to restrict its meaning, recording quite a number of things that an omnipotent being cannot do. Some have said that evil is an illusion, perhaps because they held that the whole world of temporal, changing things is an illusion, and that what we call evil belongs only to this world, or perhaps because they held that although temporal things *are* much as we see them, those that we call evil are not really evil. Some have said that what we call evil is merely the privation of good, that evil in a positive sense, evil that would really be opposed to good, does not exist. Many have agreed with Pope that disorder is harmony not understood, and that partial evil is universal good. Whether any of these views is *true* is, of course, another question. But each of them gives an adequate solution of the problem of evil in the sense that if you accept it this problem does not arise for you, though you may, of course, have *other* problems to face.

But often enough these adequate solutions are only *almost* adopted. The thinkers who restrict God's power, but keep the term 'omnipotence', may reasonably be suspected of thinking, in other contexts, that his power is really unlimited. Those who say that evil is an illusion may also be thinking, inconsistently, that this illusion is itself an evil. Those who say that "evil" is merely privation of good may also be thinking, inconsistently, that privation of good is an evil. (The fallacy here is akin to some forms of the "naturalistic fallacy" in ethics, where some think, for example, that "good" is just what contributes to evolutionary progress, and that evolutionary progress is itself good.) If Pope meant what he said in the first line of his couplet, that "disorder" is only harmony not understood, the "partial evil" of the second line must, for consistency, mean "that which, taken in isolation, falsely appears to be evil", but it would more naturally mean "that which, in isolation, really is evil". The second line, in fact, hesitates between two views, that "partial evil" isn't really evil, since only the universal quality is real, and that "partial evil" is really an evil, but only a little one.

In addition, therefore, to adequate solutions, we must recognise unsatisfactory inconsistent solutions, in which there is only a half-hearted or temporary rejection of one of the propositions which together constitute the problem. In these, one of the constituent propositions is explicitly rejected, but it is covertly re-asserted or assumed elsewhere in the system.

B. FALLACIOUS SOLUTIONS

Besides these half-hearted solutions, which explicitly reject but implicitly assert one of the constituent propositions, there are definitely fallacious solutions which explicitly maintain all the constituent propositions, but implicitly reject at least one of them in the course of the argument that explains away the problem of evil.

There are, in fact, many so-called solutions which purport to remove the contradiction without abandoning any of its constitutent propositions. These must be fallacious, as we can see from the very statement of the problem, but it is not so easy to see in each case precisely where the fallacy lies. I suggest that in all cases the fallacy has the general form suggested above: in order to solve the problem one (or perhaps more) of its constituent propositions is given up, but in such a way that it appears to have been retained, and can therefore be asserted without qualification in other contexts. Sometimes there is a further complication: the supposed solution moves to and fro between, say, two of the constituent propositions, at one point asserting the first of these but covertly abandoning the second, at another point asserting the second but covertly abandoning the first. These fallacious solutions often turn upon some equivocation with the words 'good' and 'evil', or upon some vagueness about the way in which good and evil are opposed to one another, or about how much is meant by 'omnipotence'. I propose to examine some of these so-called solutions, and to exhibit their fallacies in detail. Incidentally, I shall also be considering whether an adequate solution could be reached by a minor modification of one or more of the constituent propositions, which would, however, still satisfy all the essential requirements of ordinary theism.

1. "Good cannot exist without evil" or "Evil is necessary as a counterpart to good."

It is sometimes suggested that evil is necessary as a counterpart to good, that if there were no evil there could be no good either, and that this solves the problem of evil. It is true that it points to an answer to the question "Why should there be evil?" But it does so only by qualifying some of the propositions that constitute the problem.

First, it sets a limit to what God can do, saying that God *cannot* create good without simultaneously creating evil, and this means either that God is not omnipotent or that there are *some* limits to what an omnipotent thing can do. It may be replied that these limits are always presupposed, that omnipotence has never meant the power to do what is logically impossible, and on the present view the existence of good without evil would be a logical impossibility. This interpretation of omnipotence may, indeed, be accepted as a modification of our original account which does not reject anything that is essential to theism, and I shall in general assume it in the subsequent discussion. It is, perhaps, the most common theistic view, but I think that some theists at least have maintained that God can do what is logically impossible. Many theists, at any rate, have held that logic itself is created or laid down by God, that logic is the way in which God arbitrarily chooses to think. (This is, of course, parallel to the ethical view that morally right actions are those which God arbitrarily chooses to command, and the two views encounter similar difficulties.) And *this* account of logic is clearly inconsistent with the view that God is bound by logical necessities—unless it is possible for an omnipotent being to bind himself, an issue which we shall consider later, when we come to the Paradox of Omnipotence. This solution of the problem of evil cannot, therefore, be consistently adopted along with the view that logic is itself created by God.

But, secondly, this solution denies that evil is opposed to good in our original sense. If good and evil are counterparts, a good thing will not "eliminate evil as far as it can". Indeed, this view suggests that good and evil are not strictly qualities of things at all. Perhaps the suggestion is that good and evil are related in much the same way as great and small. Certainly, when the term 'great' is used relatively as a condensation of 'greater than so-and-so', and 'small' is used correspondingly, greatness and smallness are counterparts and cannot exist without each other. But in this sense greatness is not a quality, not an intrinsic feature of any-thing; and it would be absurd to think of a movement in favour of great-ness and against smallness in this sense. Such a movement would be self-defeating, since relative greatness can be promoted only by a simulta-neous promotion of relative smallness. I feel sure that no theists would be content to regard God's goodness as analogous to this—as if what he supports were not the *good* but the *better*, and as if he had the paradoxical aim that all things should be better than other things.

This point is obscured by the fact that 'great' and 'small' seem to have an absolute as well as a relative sense. I cannot discuss here whether there is absolute magnitude or not, but if there is, there could be an absolute sense for 'great', it could mean of at least a certain size, and it would make sense to speak of all things getting bigger, of a universe that was expanding all over, and therefore it would make sense to speak of promoting greatness. But in *this* sense great and small are not logically necessary counterparts: either quality could exist without the other. There would be no logical impossibility in everything's being small or in everything's being great.

Neither in the absolute nor in the relative sense, then, of 'great' and 'small' do these terms provide an analogy of the sort that would be needed to support this solution of the problem of evil. In neither case are greatness and smallness *both* necessary counterparts *and* mutually opposed forces or possible objects for support and attack.

It may be replied that good and evil are necessary counterparts in the same way as any quality and its logical opposite: redness can occur, it is suggested, only if non-redness also occurs. But unless evil is merely the privation of good, they are not logical opposites, and some further argument would be needed to show that they are counterparts in the same way as genuine logical opposites. Let us assume that this could be given. There is still doubt of the correctness of the metaphysical principle that a quality must have a real opposite: I suggest that it is not really impossible that everything should be, say, red, that the truth is merely that if everything were red we should not notice redness, and so we should have no word 'red'; we observe and give names to qualities only if they have real opposites. If so, the principle that a term must have an opposite would belong only to our language or to our thought, and would not be an ontological principle, and, correspondingly, the rule that good cannot exist without evil would not state a logical necessity of a sort that God would just have to put up with. God might have made everything good, though *we* should not have noticed it if he had.

But, finally, even if we concede that this *is* an ontological principle, it will provide a solution for the problem of evil only if one is prepared to say, "Evil exists, but only just enough evil to serve as the counterpart of good". I doubt whether any theist will accept this. After all, the *ontological* requirement that non-redness should occur would be satisfied even if all the universe, except for a minute speck, were red, and, if there were a corresponding requirement for evil as a counterpart to good, a minute dose of evil would presumably do. But theists are not usually willing to say, in all contexts, that all the evil that occurs is a minute and necessary dose.

2. "Evil is necessary as a means to good."

It is sometimes suggested that evil is necessary for good not as a counterpart but as a means. In its simple form this has little plausibility as a solution of the problem of evil, since it obviously implies a severe restriction of God's power. It would be a *causal* law that you cannot have a certain end without a certain means, so that if God has to introduce evil as a means to good, he must be subject to at least some causal laws. This certainly conflicts with what a theist normally means by omnipotence. This view of God as limited by causal laws also conflicts with the view that causal laws are themselves made by God, which is more widely held than the corresponding view about the laws of logic. This conflict would, indeed, be resolved if it were possible for an omnipotent being to bind himself, and this possibility has still to be considered. Unless a favourable answer can be given to this question, the suggestion that evil is necessary as a means to good solves the problem of evil only by denying one if its constituent propositions, either that God is omnipotent or that 'omnipotent' means what it says.

3. "The universe is better with some evil in it than it could be if there were no evil."

Much more important is a solution which at first seems to be a mere variant of the previous one, that evil may contribute to the goodness of a whole in which it is found, so that the universe as a whole is better as it is, with some evil in it, than it would be if there were no evil. This solution may be developed in either of two ways. It may be supported by an aesthetic analogy, by the fact that contrasts heighten beauty, that in a musical work, for example, there may occur discords which somehow add to the beauty of the work as a whole. Alternatively, it may be worked out in connexion with the notion of progress, that the best possible organisation of the universe will not be static, but progressive, that the gradual overcoming of evil by good is really a finer thing than would be the eternal unchallenged supremacy of good.

In either case, this solution usually starts from the assumption that the evil whose existence gives rise to the problem of evil is primarily what is called physical evil, that is to say, pain. In Hume's rather half-hearted presentation of the problem of evil, the evils that he stresses are pain and disease, and those who reply to him argue that the existence of pain and disease makes possible the existence of sympathy, benevolence, heroism, and the gradually successful struggle of doctors and reformers to overcome these evils. In fact, theists often seize the opportunity to accuse those who stress the problem of evil of taking a low, materialistic view of good and evil, equating these with pleasure and pain, and of ignoring the more spiritual goods which can arise in the struggle against evils.

But let us see exactly what is being done here. Let us call pain and misery 'first order evil' or 'evil (1)'. What contrasts with this, namely, pleasure and happiness, will be called 'first order good' or 'good (1)'. Distinct from this is 'second order good' or 'good (2)' which somehow emerges in a complex situation in which evil (1) is a necessary component—logically, not merely causally, necessary. (Exactly *how* it emerges does not matter: in the crudest version of this solution good (2) is simply the heightening of happiness by the contrast with misery, in other versions it includes sympathy with suffering, heroism in facing danger, and the gradual decrease of first order evil and increase of first order good.) It is also being assumed that second order good is more important than first order good or evil, in particular that it more than outweighs the first order evil it involves.

Now this is a particularly subtle attempt to solve the problem of evil. It defends God's goodness and omnipotence on the ground that (on a sufficiently long view) this is the best of all logically possible worlds, because it includes the important second order goods, and yet it admits that real evils, namely first order evils, exist. But does it still hold that good and evil are opposed? Not, clearly, in the sense that we set out originally: good does not tend to eliminate evil in general. Instead, we have a modified, a more complex pattern. First order good (*e.g.* happiness) *contrasts with* first order evil (*e.g.* misery): these two are opposed in a fairly mechanical way; some second order goods (*e.g.* benevolence) try to maximise first order good and minimise first order evil; but God's goodness is not this, it is rather the will to maximise *second* order good. We might, therefore, call God's goodness an example of a third order goodness. or good (3). While this account is different from our original one, it might well be held to be an improvement on it, to give a more accurate description of the way in which good is opposed to evil, and to be consistent with the essential theist position.

There might, however, be several objections to this solution.

First, some might argue that such qualities as benevolence—and *a fortiori* the third order goodness which promotes benevolence—have a merely derivative value, that they are not higher sorts of good, but merely means to good (1), that is, to happiness, so that it would be absurd for God to keep misery in existence in order to make possible the virtues of benevolence, heroism, etc. The theist who adopts the present solution must, of course, deny this, but he can do so with some plausibility, so I should not press this objection.

Secondly, it follows from this solution that God is not in our sense benevolent or sympathetic: he is not concerned to minimise evil (1), but only to promote good (2); and this might be a disturbing conclusion for some theists.

But, thirdly, the fatal objection is this. Our analysis shows clearly the possibility of the existence of a *second* order evil, an evil (2) contrasting with good (2) as evil (1) contrasts with good (1). This would include malevolence, cruelty, callousness, cowardice, and states in which good (1) is decreasing and evil (1) increasing. And just as good (2) is held to be the important kind of good, the kind that God is concerned to promote, so evil (2) will, by analogy, be the important kind of evil, the kind which God, if he were wholly good and omnipotent, would eliminate. And yet evil (2) plainly exists, and indeed most theists (in other contexts) stress its existence more than that of evil (1). We should, therefore, state the problem of evil in terms of second order evil, and against this form of the problem the present solution is useless.

An attempt might be made to use this solution again, at a higher level, to explain the occurrence of evil (2): indeed the next main solution that we shall examine does just this, with the help of some new notions. Without any fresh notions, such a solution would have little plausibility: for example, we could hardly say that the really important good was a good (3), such as the increase of benevolence in proportion to cruelty, which logically required for its occurence the occurrence of some second order evil. But even if evil (2) could be explained in this way, it is fairly clear that there would be third order evils contrasting with this third order good: and we should be well on the way to an infinite regress, where the solution of a problem of evil, stated in terms of evil (n), indicated the existence of an evil ($n + 1$), and a further problem to be solved.

4. "Evil is due to human freewill."

Perhaps the most important proposed solution of the problem of evil is that evil is not to be ascribed to God at all, but to the independent actions of human beings, supposed to have been endowed by God with freedom of the will. This solution may be combined with the preceding one: first order evil (*e.g.* pain) may be justified as a logically necessary component in second order good (*e.g.* sympathy) while second order evil (*e.g.* cruelty) is not *justified*, but is so ascribed to human beings that God cannot be held responsible for it. This combination evades my third criticism of the preceding solution.

The freewill solution also involves the preceding solution at a higher level. To explain why a wholly good God gave men freewill although it would lead to some important evils, it must be argued that it is better on the whole that men should act freely, and sometimes err, than that they should be innocent automata, acting rightly in a wholly determined way. Freedom, that is to say, is now treated as a third order good, and as being more valuable than second order goods (such as sympathy and heroism) would be if they were deterministically produced, and it is being assumed that second order evils, such as cruelty, are logically necessary accompaniments of freedom, just as pain is a logically necessary pre-condition of sympathy.

I think that this solution is unsatisfactory primarily because of the incoherence of the notion of freedom of the will: but I cannot discuss this topic adequately here, although some of my criticisms will touch upon it.

First I should query the assumption that second order evils are logically necessary accompaniments of freedom. I should ask this: if God has made men such that in their free choices they sometimes prefer what is good and sometimes what is evil, why could he not have made men such that they always freely choose the good? If there is no logical impossibility in a man's freely choosing the good on one, or on several, occasions, there cannot be a logical impossibility in his freely choosing the good on every occasion. God was not, then, faced with a choice between making innocent automata and making beings who, in acting freely, would sometimes go wrong: there was open to him the obviously better possibility of making beings who would act freely but always go right. Clearly, his failure to avail himself of this possibility is inconsistent with his being both omnipotent and wholly good.

If it is replied that this objection is absurd, that the making of some wrong choices is logically necessary for freedom, it would seem that 'freedom' must here mean complete randomness or indeterminacy, including randomness with regard to the alternatives good and evil, in other words that men's choices and consequent actions can be "free" only if they are not determined by their characters. Only on this assumption can God escape the responsibility for men's actions; for if he made them as they are, but did not determine their wrong choices, this can only be because the wrong choices are not determined by men as they are. But then if freedom is randomness how can it be a characteristic of *will*? And, still more, how can it be the most important good? What value or merit would there be in free choices if these were random actions which were not determined by the nature of the agent?

I conclude that to make this solution plausible two different senses of 'freedom' must be confused, one sense which will justify the view that freedom is a third order good, more valuable than other goods would be without it, and another sense, sheer randomness, to prevent us from ascribing to God a decision to make men such that they sometimes go wrong when he might have made them such that they would always freely go right.

This criticism is sufficient to dispose of this solution. But besides this there is a fundamental difficulty in the notion of an omnipotent God creating men with free will, for if men's wills are really free this must mean that even God cannot control them, that is, that God is no longer omnipotent. It may be objected that God's gift of freedom to men does not mean that he *cannot* control their wills, but that he always *refrains* from controlling their wills. But why, we may ask, should God refrain from controlling evil wills? Why should he not leave men free to will rightly, but intervene when he sees them beginning to will wrongly? If God could do this, but does not, and if he is wholly good, the only explanation could be that even a wrong free act of will is not really evil, that its freedom is a value which outweighs its wrongness, so that there would be a loss of value if God took away the wrongness and the freedom together. But this is utterly opposed to what theists say about sin in other contexts. The present solution of the problem of evil, then, can be maintained only in the form that God has made men so free that he *cannot* control their wills.

This leads us to what I call the Paradox of Omnipotence: can an omnipotent being make things which he cannot subsequently control? Or, what is practically equivalent to this, can an omnipotent being make rules which then bind himself? (These are practically equivalent because any such rules could be regarded as setting certain things beyond his control, and *vice versa*.) The second of these formulations is relevant to the suggestions that we have already met, that an omnipotent God creates the rules of logic or causal laws, and is then bound by them.

It is clear that this is a paradox: the questions cannot be answered satisfactorily either in the affirmative or in the negative. If we answer "Yes", it follows that if God actually makes things which he cannot control, or makes rules which bind himself, he is not omnipotent once he has made them: there are *then* things which he cannot do. But if we answer "No", we are immediately asserting that there are things which he cannot do, that is to say that he is already not omnipotent.

It cannot be replied that the question which sets this paradox is not a proper question. It would make perfectly good sense to say that a human mechanic has made a machine which he cannot control: if there is any difficulty about the question it lies in the notion of omnipotence itself.

This, incidentally, shows that although we have approached this paradox from the free will theory, it is equally a problem for a theological determinist. No one thinks that machines have free will, yet they may well be beyond the control of their makers. The determinist might reply that anyone who makes anything determines its ways of acting, and so determines its subsequent behavior: even the human mechanic does this by his *choice* of materials and structure for his machine, though he does not know all about either of these: the mechanic thus determines, though he may not foresee, his machine's actions. And since God is omniscient, and since his creation of things is total, he both determines and foresees the ways in which his creatures will act. We may grant this, but it is beside the point. The question is not whether God *originally* determined the future actions of his creatures, but whether he can *subsequently* control their actions, or whether he was able in his original creation to put things beyond his subsequent control. Even on determinist principles the answers "Yes" and "No" are equally irreconcilable with God's omnipotence.

Before suggesting a solution of this paradox, I would point out that there is a parallel Paradox of Sovereignty. Can a legal sovereign make a law restricting its own future legislative power? For example, could the British parliament make a law forbidding any future parliament to socialise banking, and also forbidding the future repeal of this law itself? Or could the British parliament, which was legally sovereign in Australia in, say, 1899, pass a valid law, or series of laws, which made it no longer sovereign in 1933? Again, neither the affirmative nor the negative answer is really satisfactory. If we were to answer "Yes", we should be admitting the validity of a law which, if it were actually made, would mean that parliament was no longer sovereign. If we were to answer "No", we should be admitting that there is a law, not logically absurd, which parliament cannot validly make, that is, that parliament is not now a legal sovereign. This paradox can be solved in the following way. We should distinguish between first order laws, that is laws governing the actions of individuals and bodies other than the legislature, and second order laws, that is laws about laws, laws governing the actions of the legislature itself. Correspondingly, we should distinguish two orders of sovereignty, first order sovereignty (sovereignty (1)) which is unlimited authority to make first order laws, and second order sovereignty (sovereignty (2)) which is unlimited authority to make second order laws. If we say that parliament is sovereign we might mean that any parliament at any time has sovereignty (1), or we might mean that parliament has both sovereignty (1) and sovereignty (2) at present, but we cannot without contradiction mean both that the present parliament has sovereignty (2) and that every parliament at every time has sovereignty (1), for if the present parliament has sovereignty (2) it may use it to take away the sovereignty (1) of later parliaments. What the paradox shows is that we cannot ascribe to any continuing institution legal sovereignty in an inclusive sense.

The analogy between omnipotence and sovereignty shows that the paradox of omnipotence can be solved in a similar way. We must distinguish between first order omnipotence (omnipotence (1)), that is unlimited power to act, and second order omnipotence (omnipotence (2)), that is unlimited power to determine what powers to act things shall have. Then we could consistently say that God all the time has omnipotence (1), but if so no beings at any time have powers to act independently of God. Or we could say that God at one time had omnipotence (2), and use it to assign independent powers to act to certain things, so that God thereafter did not have omnipotence (1). But what the paradox shows is that we cannot consistently ascribe to any continuing being omnipotence in an inclusive sense.

An alternative solution of this paradox would be simply to deny that God is a continuing being, that any times can be assigned to his actions at all. But on this assumption (which also has difficulties of its own) no meaning can be given to the assertion that God made men with wills so free that he could not control them. The paradox of omnipotence can be avoided by putting God outside time, but the freewill solution of the problem of evil cannot be saved in this way, and equally it remains impossible to hold that an omnipotent God *binds himself* by causal or logical laws.

CONCLUSION

Of the proposed solutions of the problem of evil which we have examined, none has stood up to criticism. There may be other solutions which require examination, but this study strongly suggests that there is no valid solution of the problem which does not modify at least one of the constituent propositions in a way which would seriously affect the essential core of the theistic position.

Quite apart from the problem of evil, the paradox of omnipotence has shown that God's omnipotence must in any case be restricted in one way or another, that unqualified omnipotence cannot be ascribed to any being that continues through time. And if God and his actions are not in time, can omnipotence, or power of any sort, be meaningfully ascribed to him?

THE FREE WILL DEFENCE

Alvin Plantinga

Since the days of Epicurus many philosophers have suggested that the existence of evil constitutes a problem for those who accept theistic belief.[1] Those contemporaries who follow Epicurus here claim, for the most part, to detect logical inconsistency in such belief. So McCloskey:

> Evil is a problem for the theist in that a *contradiction* is involved in the fact of evil, on the one hand, and the belief in the omnipotence and perfection of God on the other.[2]

and Mackie:

> I think, however, that a more telling criticism can be made by way of the traditional problem of evil. Here it can be shown, not that religious beliefs lack rational support, but that they are positively irrational, that the several parts of the essential theological doctrine áre *inconsistent* with one another . . .[3]

and essentially the same charge is made by Professor Aiken in an article entitled 'God and Evil'.[4]

These philosophers, then, and many others besides, hold that traditional theistic belief is self-contradictory and that the problem of evil, for the theist, is that of deciding which of the relevant propositions he is to abandon. But just which propositions are involved? What is the set of theistic beliefs whose conjunction yields a contradiction? The authors referred to above take the following five propositions to be essential to traditional theism: (*a*) that God exists, (*b*) that God is omnipotent, (*c*) that God is omniscient, (*d*) that God is wholly good, and (*e*) that evil exists. Here they are certainly right: each of these propositions is indeed an essential feature of orthodox theism. And it is just these five propositions whose conjunction is said, by our atheologians,[5] to be self-contradictory.

Apologists for theism, of course, have been quick to repel the charge. A line of resistance they have often employed is called *The Free Will Defence*; in this paper I shall discuss and develop that idea.

First of all, a distinction must be made between *moral evil* and *physical evil*. The former, roughly, is the evil which results from human choice or volition; the latter is that which does not. Suffering due to an earthquake, for example, would be a case of physical evil; suffering resulting from human cruelty would be a case of moral evil. This distinction, of course, is not very clear and many questions could be raised about it; but perhaps it is not necessary to deal with these questions here. Given this distinction, the Free Will Defence is usually stated in something like the following way. A world containing creatures who freely perform both good and evil actions—and do more good than evil—is more valuable than a world containing quasi-automata who always do what is right because they are unable to do otherwise. Now God can create free creatures, but He cannot causally or otherwise determine them to do only what is right; for if he does so then they do not do what is right *freely*. To create creatures capable of moral good, therefore, he must create creatures capable of moral evil; but he cannot create the possibility of moral evil and at the same time prohibit its actuality. And as it turned out, some of the free creatures God created exercised their freedom to do what is wrong: hence moral evil. The fact that free creatures sometimes err, however, in no way tells against God's omnipotence or against his goodness; for he could forestall the occurrence of moral evil only by removing the possibility of moral good.

In this way some traditional theists have tried to explain or justify part of the evil that occurs by ascribing it to the will of man rather than to the will of God. At least three kinds of objections to this idea are to be found both in the tradition and in the current literature. I shall try to develop and clarify the Free Will Defence by restating it in the face of these objections.

I

The first objection challenges the assumption, implicit in the above statement of the Free Will Defence, that free will and causal determinism are logically incompatible. So Flew:

> . . . to say that a person could have helped doing something is not to say that what he did was in principle unpredictable nor that there were no causes anywhere which determined that he would as a matter of fact act in this way. It is to say that if he had chosen to do otherwise he would have been able to do so; that there were alternatives, within the capacities of one of his physical strength, of his I.Q., of his knowledge, open to a person in his situation.
>
> . . . There is no contradiction involved in saying that a particular action or choice was: *both* free, and could have been helped, and so on; *and* predictable, or even foreknown, and explicable in terms of caused causes.
>
> . . . if it is really logically possible for an action to be both freely chosen and yet fully determined by caused causes, then the keystone argument of the Free Will Defence, that there is contradiction in speaking of God so arranging the laws of nature that all men always as a matter of fact freely choose to do the right, cannot hold.[6]

Flew's objection, I think, can be dealt with in a fairly summary fashion. He does not, in the paper in question, explain what he means by 'causal determination' (and of course in that paper this omission is quite proper and justifiable). But presumably he means to use the locution in question in such a way that to say of Jones' action A that it is *causally determined* is to say that the action in question has causes and that given these causes, Jones could not have refrained from doing A. That is to say, Flew's use of 'causally determined', presumably, is such that one or both of the following sentences, or some sentences very much like them, express necessarily true propositions:

(a) If Jones' action A is causally determined, then a set S of events has occurred prior to Jones' doing A such that, given S, it is causally impossible for Jones to refrain from doing A.

(b) If Jones' action A is causally determined, then there is a set S of propositions describing events occurring before A and a set L of propositions expressing natural laws such that

(1) the conjunction of S's members does not entail that Jones does A, and
(2) the conjunction of the members of S with the members of L does entail that Jones does A.

And Flew's thesis, then, is that there is no contradiction in saying of a man, both that all of his actions are causally determined (in the sense just explained) and that some of them are free.

Now it seems to me altogether paradoxical to say of anyone all of whose actions are causally determined, that on some occasions he acts freely. When we say that Jones acts freely on a given occasion, what we say entails, I should think, that either his action on that occasion is not causally determined, or else he has previously performed an undetermined action which is causal ancestor of the one in question. But this is a difficult and debatable issue; fortunately we need not settle it in order to assess the force of Flew's objection to the Free Will Defence. The Free Will Defender claims that the sentence 'Not all free actions are causally determined' expresses a necessary truth; Flew denies this claim. This strongly suggests that Flew and the Free Will Defender are not using the words 'free' and 'freedom' in the same way. The Free Will Defender, apparently, uses the words in question in such a way that sentences 'Some of Jones' actions are free' and 'Jones did action A freely' express propositions which are inconsistent with the proposition that all of Jones' actions are causally determined, Flew, on the other hand, claims that with respect to the ordinary use of these words, there is no such inconsistency. It is my opinion that Flew is mistaken here; I think it is he who is using these words in a non-standard, unordinary way. But we need not try to resolve that issue; for the Free Will Defender can simply make Flew a present of the word 'freedom' and state his case using other locutions. He might now hold, for example, not that God made men free and that a world in which men freely do both good and evil is more valuable than a world in which they unfreely do only what is good; but rather that God made men such that some of their actions are *unfettered* (both free in Flew's sense and also causally undetermined) and that a world in which men perform both good and evil unfettered actions is superior to one in which they perform only good, but fettered, actions. By substituting 'unfettered' for 'free' throughout this account, the Free Will Defender can elude Flew's objection altogether.[7] So whether Flew is right or wrong about the ordinary sense of 'freedom' is of no consequence; his objection is in an important sense merely verbal and thus altogether fails to damage the Free Will Defence.

II

Flew's objection, in essence, is the claim that an omnipotent being could have created men in such a way that although free they would be *causally determined* to perform only right actions. According to a closely allied objection an omnipotent being could have made men in such a way that although free, and free from any such causal determination, they would nonetheless *freely refrain* from performing any evil actions. Here the contemporary spokesman is Mackie:

> . . . if God has made men such that in their free choices they sometimes prefer what is good and sometimes what is evil, why could he not have made men such that they always freely choose the good? If there is not logical impossibility in a man's freely choosing the good on one, or on several occasions, there cannot be a logical impossibility in his freely choosing the good on every occasion. God was not, then, faced with a choice between making innocent automata and making beings who, in acting freely, would sometimes go wrong; there was open to him the obviously better possibility of making beings who would act freely but always go right. Clearly, his failure to avail himself of this possibility is inconsistent with his being both omnipotent and wholly good.[8]

The objection is more serious than Flew's and must be dealt with more fully. Now the Free Will Defence is an argument for the conclusion that (a) is not contradictory or necessarily false:[9]

(a) God is omnipotent, omniscient, and all-good and God creates free men who sometimes perform morally evil actions.

What Mackie says, I think, may best be construed as an argument for the conclusion that (a) *is* necessarily false; in other words, that *God is omnipotent, omniscient and all good* entails *no free men He creates ever perform morally evil actions.* Mackie's argument seems to have the following structure:

(1) God is omnipotent and omniscient and all-good.
(2) If God is omnipotent. He can create any logically possible state of affairs.
∴(3) God can create any logically possible state of affairs. (1, 2)

(4) That all free men do what is right on every occasion is a logically possible state of affairs.

∴(5) God can create free men such that they always do what is right. (4, 3)

(6) If God can create free men such that they always do what is right and God is all-good, then any free men created by God always do what is right.

∴(7) Any free men created by God always do what is right. (1, 5, 6)

∴(8) No free men created by God ever perform morally evil actions. (7)

Doubtless the Free Will Defender will concede the truth of (4); there is a difficulty with (2), however; for

(a) that there are men who are not created by God is a logically possible state of affairs

is clearly true. But (2) and (a) entail

(b) If God is omnipotent, God can create men who are not created by God.

And (b), of course, is false; (2) must be revised. The obvious way to repair it seems to be something like the following:

(2') If God is omnipotent, then God can create any state of affairs S such that *God creates S* is consistent.

Similarly, (3) must be revised:

(3') God can create any state of affairs S such that *God creates S* is consistent.

(1') and (3') do not seem to suffer from the faults besetting (1) and (3); but now it is not at all evident that (3') and (4) entail

(5) God can create free men such that they always do what is right

as the original argument claims. To see this, we must note that (5) is true only if

(5a) God creates free men such that they always do what is right

is consistent. But (5a), one might think, is equivalent to:

(5b) God creates free men and brings it about that they always freely do what is right.

And (5b), of course, is *not* consistent; for if God *brings it about* that the men He creates always do what is right, then they do not do what is right *freely*. So if (5a) is taken to express (5b), then (5) is clearly false and clearly not entailed by (3') and (4).

On the other hand, (5a) could conceivably be used to express:

(5c) God creates free men and these free men always do what is right. (5c) is surely consistent; it is indeed logically possible that God creates free men and that the free men created by Him always do what is right. And conceivably the objector is using (5) to express this possibility—i.e., it may be that (5) is meant to express:

(5d) the proposition *God creates free men and the free men created by God always do what is right* is consistent.

If (5) is equivalent to (5d), then (5) is true—in fact necessarily true (and hence trivially entailed by (3') and (4)). But now the difficulty crops up with respect to (6) which, given the equivalence of (5) and (5d) is equivalent to

(6') If God is all-good and the proposition *God creates free men and the free men He creates always do what is right* is consistent, then any free men created by God always do what is right.

Now Mackie's aim is to show that the proposition *God is omnipotent, omniscient and all-good* entails the proposition *no free men created by God ever perform morally evil actions*. His attempt, as I outlined it, is to show this by constructing a valid argument whose premise is the former and whose conclusion is the latter. But then any additional premise appealed to in the deduction must be necessarily true if Mackie's argument is to succeed. (6') is one such additional premise; but there seems to be no reason for supposing that (6') is true at all, let alone necessarily true. Whether the free men created by God would always do what is right would presumably be up to them; for all we know they might sometimes exercise their freedom to do what is wrong. Put in a nutshell the difficulty with the argument is the following. (5a) (God creates free men such that they always do what is right) is susceptible of two interpretations ((5b) and (5c)). Under one of these interpretations (5) turns out to be false and the argument therefore fails. Under the other interpretation (6) turns out to be utterly groundless and question begging, and again the argument fails.

So far, then, the Free Will Defence has emerged unscathed from Mackie's objection. One has the feeling, however, that more can be said here; that there is something to Mackie's argument. What more? Well, perhaps something along the following lines. It is agreed that it is logically possible that all men always do only what is right. Now God is said to be omniscient and hence knows, with respect to any person he proposes to create, whether that person would or would not commit morally evil acts. For every person *P* who in fact performs morally evil actions, there is, evidently, a possible person *P'* who is exactly like *P* in every respect except that *P'* never performs any evil actions. If God is omnipotent, He could have created these possible persons instead of the persons He in fact did create. And if He is also all-good, He *would*, presumably, have created them, since they differ from the persons He did create only in being morally better than they are.

Can we make coherent sense out of this revised version of Mackie's objection? What, in particular, could the objector mean by 'possible person'? and what are we to make of the suggestion that God could have created possible persons? I think these questions can be answered. Let us consider first the set of all those properties it is logically possible for human beings to have. Examples of properties *not* in this set are the properties of *being over a mile long; being a hippotamous; being a prime number; being divisible by four;* and the like. Included in the set are such properties as *having red hair; being present at the Battle of Waterloo; being the President of the United States; being born in 1889;* and *being a pipe-smoker.* Also included are such moral properties as *being kind to one's maiden aunt, being a scoundrel, performing at least one morally wrong action,* and so on. Let us call the properties in this set *H* properties. The complement $\overline{P}$ of an *H* property *P* is the property a thing has just in case it does not have *P*. And a *consistent set of H* properties is a set of *H* properties such that it is logically possible that there be a human being having every property in the set. Now we can define 'possible person' in the following way:

> *x* is a possible person *X* is a consistent set of *H* properties such that for every *H* property *P*, either *P* or $\overline{P}$ is a member of *x*.

To *instantiate* a possible person *P* is to create a human being having every property in *P*. And a set *S* of possible persons is a *co-possible set of possible persons* just in case it is logically possible that every member of *S* is instantiated.[10]

Given this technical terminology, Mackie's objection can be summarily restated. It is granted by everyone that there is no absurdity in the claim that some man who is free to do what is wrong never, in fact, performs any wrong action. It follows that there are many possible persons containing the property *is free to do wrong but always does right.* And since it is logically possible that all men always freely do what is right, there are presumably several co-possible sets of possible persons such that each member of each set contains the property in question. Now God, if he is omnipotent, can instantiate any possible person and any co-possible set of possible persons he chooses. Hence, if He were all-good, He would have instantiated one of the sets of co-possible persons all of whose members freely do only what is right.

In spite of its imposing paraphernalia the argument, thus restated, suffers from substantially the same defect that afflicts Mackie's original version. There are *some* possible persons God obviously cannot instantiate—those, for example, containing the property *is not created by God.* Accordingly it is *false* that God can instantiate just any possible person He chooses. But of course the interesting question is whether

(1) God can instantiate possible persons containing the property of always freely doing what is right is true; for perhaps Mackie could substitute (1) for the premise just shown to be false.

Is (1) true? Perhaps we can approach this question in the following way. Let *P* be any possible person containing the property *always freely does what is right.* Then there must be some action *A* such that *P* contains the property of being free with respect to *A* (i.e., the property of being free to perform *A* and free to refrain from performing *A*). The *instantiation* of a possible person. *S*, I shall say, is a person having every property in *S*; and let us suppose that if *P* were instantiated, its instantiation would be doing something morally wrong in performing *A*. And finally, let us suppose that God wishes to instantiate *P*. Now *P* contains many properties in addition to the ones already mentioned. Among them, for example, we might find the following: *is born in 1910, has red hair, is born in Stuttgart, has feeble-minded ancestors, is six feet tall at the age of fourteen*, and the like. And there is no difficulty in God's creating a person with these properties. Further, there is no difficulty in God's bringing it about that this person (let's call him Smith) is free with respect to *A*. But if God *also* brings it about that Smith refrains from performing *A* (as he must to be the instantiation of *P*) then Smith is no longer free with respect to *A* and is hence not the instantiation of *P* after all. God cannot cause Smith to refrain from performing *A*, while allowing him to be free with respect to *A*; and therefore whether or not Smith does *A* will be entirely up to Smith; it will be a matter of free choice for him. Accordingly, whether God can instantiate *P* depends upon what Smith would freely decide to do.

This point may be put more accurately as follows: First, we shall say that an *H* property *Q* is *indeterminate* if God *creates a person and causes him to have Q* is necessarily false; an *H* property is *determinate* if it is not indeterminate. Of the properties we ascribed to *P*, all are determinate except *freely refrains from doing A* and *always freely does what is right*. Now consider P_1, the subset of *P* containing just the determinate members of *P*. In order to instantiate *P* God must instantiate P_1. It is evident that there is at most one instantiation of P_1, for among the members of P_1 will be some such individuating properties as for example, *is the third son of Richard and Lena Dykstra*. P_1 also contains the property of being free with respect to *A*; and if *P* is instantiated, its instantiation will either perform *A* or refrain from performing *A*. It is, of course, possible that P_1 is such that if it is instantiated its instantiation *I* will perform *A*. If so, then if God allows *I* to remain free with respect to *A*, *I* will do *A*; and if God prevents *I* from doing *A*, then *I* is not free with respect to *A* and hence not the instantiation of *P* after all. Hence in neither case does God succeed in instantiating *P*. And accordingly God can instantiate *P* only if P_1 is *not* such that if it is instantiated, its instantiation will perform *A*. Hence it is possible that God cannot instantiate *P*. And evidently it is also possible, further, that *every* possible person containing the property *always freely does what is right* is such that neither God nor anyone else can instantiate it.

Now we merely supposed that P_1 is such that if it is instantiated, its instantiation will perform *A*. And this supposition, if true at all, is merely contingently true. It might be suggested, therefore, that God could instantiate *P* instantiating P_1 and bringing it about that P_1 is *not* such that if it is instantiated, its instantiation will perform *A*. But to do this God must instantiate P_1 and bring it about that P_1 is such that if it is instantiated, its instantiation I will *refrain* from performing A. And if God does this then God brings it about that I will not perform A. But then I is not free to perform A and hence once more is not the instantiation of P.

It is possible, then, that God cannot instantiate any possible person containing the property *always freely does what is right*. It is also possible, of course, that He *can* instantiate some such possible persons. But *that* He can, if indeed He can, is a contingent truth. And since Mackie's project is to prove an entailment, he cannot employ any contingent propositions as added premises. Hence the reconstructed argument fails.

Now the difficulty with the reconstructed argument is the fact that God cannot instantiate just any possible person he chooses, and the possibility that God cannot instantiate any possible persons containing the property of always freely doing what is right. But perhaps the objector can circumvent this difficulty.

The H properties that make trouble for the objector are the indeterminate properties—those which God cannot cause anyone to have. It is because possible persons contain indeterminate properties that God cannot instantiate just any possible person He wishes. And so perhaps the objector can reformulate his definition of 'possible person' in such a way that a possible person in a consistent set S of *determinate* properties such that for any determinate H property P, either P or $\overline{P}$ is a member of S. Unfortunately the following difficulty arises. Where I is any indeterminate H property and D a determinate H property, D or I (the property a person has if he has either D or I) is determinate. And so, of course, is $\overline{D}$. The same difficulty, accordingly, arises all over again—there will be some possible persons God can't instantiate (those containing the properties *is not created by God or has red hair* and *does not have red hair*, for example). We must add, therefore, that no possible person *entails* an indeterminate property.[11]

Even so our difficulties are not at an end. For the definition as so stated entails that there are no *possible free persons*, i.e., possible persons containing the property *on some occasions free to do what is right and free to do what is wrong*.[12] We may see this as follows: Let P be any possible free person. P then contains the property of being free with respect to some action A. Furthermore, P would contain either the property of performing A (since that is a determinate property) or the property of refraining from performing A. But if P contains the property of performing A and the property of being free with respect to A, then P entails the property of freely performing A—which is an indeterminate property. And the same holds in case P contains the property of refraining from performing A. Hence in either case P entails an indeterminate property and accordingly is not a possible person.

Clearly the objector must revise the definition of 'possible person' in such a way that for any action with respect to which a given possible person *P* is free, *P* contains neither the property of performing that action nor the property of refraining from performing it. This may be accomplished in the following way. Let us say that a person *S* is *free with respect to a property P* just in case there is some action *A* with respect to which *S* is free and which is such that *S* has *P* if and only if he performs *A*. So, for example, if a person is free to leave town and free to stay, then he is free with respect to the property *leaves town*. And let us say that a set of properties is free with respect to a given property *P* just in case it contains the property is *free with respect to P*. Now we can restate the definition of 'possible person' as follows:

> *x* is a possible person = *x* is a consistent set of determinate *H* properties such that (1) for every determinate *H* property *P* with respect to which *x* is not free, either *P* or $\overline{P}$ is a member of *x*, and (2) *x* does not entail any indeterminate property.

Now let us add the following new definition:

> Possibly person *P* has indeterminate property *I* = if *P* were instantiated, *P's* instantiation would have *I*.

Under the revised definition of 'possible person' it seems apparent that God, if he is omnipotent, can instantiate any possible person, and any co-possible set of possible persons, he chooses. But, the objector continues, if God is also all-good. He will, presumably, instantiate only those possible persons who have some such indeterminate *H* property as that of *always freely doing what is right*. And here the Free Will Defender can no longer make the objection which held against the previous versions of Mackie's argument. For if God can instantiate any possible person he chooses, he can instantiate any possible free person he chooses.

The Free Will Defender can, however, raise what is essentially the same difficulty in a new guise: what reason is there for supposing that there are *any* possible persons, in the present sense of 'possible person', having the indeterminate property in question? For it is clear that, given any indeterminate *H* property *I*, the proposition *no possible person has I* is a contingent proposition. Further, the proposition *every possible free person freely performs at least one morally wrong action* is possibly true. But if every *possible* free person performs at least one wrong action, then every *actual* free person also freely performs at least one wrong action; hence if every possible free person performs at least one wrong action, God could create a universe without moral evil only by refusing to create any free persons at all. And, the Free Will Defender adds, a world containing free persons and moral evil (provided that it contained more moral good than moral evil) would be superior to one lacking both free persons and moral good and evil. Once again, then, the objection seems to fail.

The definitions offered during the discussion of Mackie's objection afford the opportunity of stating the Free Will Defence more formally. I said above that the Free Will Defence is in essence an argument for the conclusion that (a) is consistent:

(a) God is omnipotent, omniscient, and all-good and God creates persons who sometimes perform morally evil actions.

One way of showing (a) to be consistent is to show that its first conjunct does not entail the negation of its second conjunct, i.e., that
    (b) God is omnipotent, omniscient and all-good does not entail
    (c) God does not create persons who perform morally evil actions.

Now one can show that a given proposition p does not entail another proposition q by producing a third proposition r which is such that (1) the conjunction of p and r is consistent and (2) the conjunction of p and r entails the negation of q. What we need here, then, is a proposition whose conjunction with (b) is both logically consistent and a logically sufficient condition of the denial of (c).

Consider the following argument:

    (b)   God is omnipotent, omniscient and all-good.
    (r1)   God creates some free persons.
    (r2)   Every possible free person performs at least one wrong action.
∴(d)   Every actual free person performs at least one wrong action. (r2)
∴(e)   God creates persons who perform morally evil actions. ((r1), (d))

This argument is valid (and can easily be expanded so that it is *formally* valid). Furthermore, the conjunction of (b), (r1) and (r2) is evidently consistent. And as the argument shows, (b), (r1) and (r2) *jointly entail* (e). But (e) is the denial of (c); hence (b) and (r) jointly entail the denial of (c). Accordingly (b) does not entail (c), and (a) (God is omnipotent, omniscient and all-good and God creates persons who perform morally evil acts) is shown to be consistent. So stated, therefore, the Free Will Defence appears to be successful.

At this juncture it might be objected that even if the Free Will Defence, as explained above, shows that there is no contradiction in the supposition that God, who is all-good, omnipotent and omniscient, creates persons who engage in moral evil, it does nothing to show that an all-good, omnipotent and omniscient Being could create a universe containing as *much* moral evil as this one seems to contain. The objection has a point, although the fact that there seems to be no way of measuring or specifying amounts of moral evil makes it exceedingly hard to state the objection in any way which does not leave it vague and merely suggestive. But let us suppose, for purposes of argument, that there is a way of measuring moral evil (and moral good) and that the moral evil present in the universe amounts to φ. The problem then is to show that

(b) God is omnipresent, omniscient and all-good is consistent with

(f) God creates a set of free persons who produce φ moral evil. Here the Free Will Defender can produce an argument to show that (b) is consistent with (f) which exactly parallels the argument for the consistency of (b) with (c):

(b) God is omnipotent, omniscient and all-good.

(r3) God creates a set S of free persons such that there is a balance of moral good over moral evil with respect to the members of S.

(r4) There is exactly one co-possible set S' of free possible persons such that there is a balance of moral good over moral evil with respect to its members; and the members of S' produce φ moral evil.

Set S is evidently the instantiation of S' (i.e. every member of S is an instantation of some member of S' and every member of S' is instantiated by some member of S); hence the members of S produce φ moral evil. Accordingly, (b), (r3) and (r4) jointly entail (f); but the conjunction of (b), (r3) and (r4) is consistent; hence (b) is consistent with (f).

III

The preceding discussion enables us to conclude, I believe, that the Free Will Defence succeeds in showing that there is no inconsistency in the assertion that God creates a universe containing as much moral evil as the universe in fact contains. There remains but one objection to be considered. McCloskey, Flew and others charge that the Free Will Defence, even if it is successful, accounts for only *part* of the evil we find; it accounts only for moral evil, leaving physical evil as intractable as before. The atheologian can therefore restate his position, maintaining that the existence of *physical evil*, evil which cannot be ascribed to the free actions of human beings, is inconsistent with the existence of an omniscient, omnipotent and all-good Deity.

To make this claim, however, is to overlook an important part of traditional theistic belief; it is part of much traditional belief to attribute a good deal of the evil we find to Satan, or to Satan and his cohorts. Satan, so the traditional doctrine goes, is a mighty non-human spirit, who, along with many other angels, was created long before God created men. Unlike most of his (c) colleagues, Satan rebelled against God and has since been creating whatever havoc he could; the result, of course, is physical evil. But now we see that the moves available to the Free Will Defender in the case of moral evil are equally available to him in the case of physical evil. First he provides definitions of 'possible non-human spirit', 'free non-human spirit', etc., which exactly parallel their counterparts where it was moral evil that was at stake. Then he points out that it is logically possible that

(r5) God creates a set S of free non-human spirits such that the members of S do more good than evil,
and

(r6) there is exactly one co-possible set S' of possible free non-human spirits such that the members of S' do more good than evil, and

(r7) all of the physical evil in the world is due to the actions of the members of S.

He points out further that (r5), (r6), and (r7) are jointly consistent and that their conjunction is consistent with the proposition that God is omnipotent, omniscient and all-good. But (r5) through (r7) jointly entail that God creates a universe containing as much physical evil as the universe in fact contains; it follows then, that the existence of physical evil is not inconsistent with the existence of an omniscient, omnipotent, all-good Deity.

Now it must be conceded that views involving devils and other non-human spirits do not at present enjoy either the extensive popularity or the high esteem of (say) the Theory of Relativity. Flew, for example, has this to say about the view in question:

> To make this more than just another desperate *ad hoc* expedient of apologetic it is necessary to produce independent evidence for launching such an hypothesis (if 'hypothesis' is not too flattering a term for it).[13]

But in the present context this claim is surely incorrect; to rebut the charge of contradiction the theist need not hold that the hypothesis in question is probable or even true. He need hold only that it is not inconsistent with the proposition that God exists. Flew suspects that 'hypothesis' may be too flattering a term for the sort of view in question. Perhaps this suspicion reflects his doubts as to the meaningfulness of the proposed view. But it is hard to see how one could plausibly argue that the views in question are nonsensical (in the requisite sense) without invoking some version of the Verifiability Criterion, a doctrine whose harrowing vicissitudes are well known. Furthermore, it is likely that any premises worth considering which yield the conclusion that hypotheses about devils are nonsensical will yield the same conclusion about the hypothesis that God exists. And if *God exists* is nonsensical, then presumably theism is not self-contradictory after all.

We may therefore conclude that the Free Will Defence successfully rebuts the charge of contradiction brought against the theist. The Problem of Evil (if indeed evil constitutes a problem for the theist) does not lie in any inconsistency in the belief that God, who is omniscient, omnipotent and all-good, has created a world containing moral and physical evil.

NOTES

1. David Hume and some of the French encyclopedists, for example, as well as F. H. Bradley, J. McTaggart, and J. S. Mill.

2. H. J. McCloskey, 'God and Evil'. *The Philosophical Quarterly*, Vol. 10 (April 1960), p. 97. [The article may be found on p. 23 in this book.]

3. 'Evil and Omnipotence.' J. L. Mackie, *Mind*, Vol. 64, No. 254 (April 1955), p. 200. [The article may be found on p. 7 in this book.]

4. *Ethics*, Vol. 48 (1957–58), p. 79.

5. *Natural* theology is the attempt to infer central religious beliefs from premises that are either obvious to common sense (e.g., *that some things are in motion*) or logically necessary. *Natural atheology* is the attempt to infer the falsity of such religious beliefs from premises of the same sort.

6. 'Divine Omnipotence and Human Freedom', in *New Essays in Philosophical Theology*, ed. A. Flew and A. MacIntyre, London 1955, pp. 150, 151, 153.

7. And since this is so in what follows I shall continue to use the words 'free' and 'freedom' in the way the Free Will Defender uses them.

8. *Op. cit.*, p. 17.

9. And of course if (*a*) is consistent, so is the set (*a*)–(*e*) mentioned above for (*a*) entails each member of that set.

10. The definiens must not be confused with: For every member M of S, it is logically possible that M is instantiated.

11. Where a set S of properties entails a property P if and only if it is necessarily true that anything having every property in S also has P.

12. This was pointed out to me by Mr. Lewis Creary.

13. *Op. cit.*, p. 17.

ADVERSUS HAERESES (EXCERPTS)

St. Irenaeus

The Father of all is far removed from the emotions and passions which are common to men. He is simple, uncompounded, without diversity of parts; wholly identical and consistent; since he is all understanding, all spirit, all thought, all hearing, all seeing, all light, and the whole source of all that is good . . . .

It is best for us to begin with the first and greatest principle, that is with God the Creator . . . and to show that there is nothing above him or beyond him. It was of his own decision and free act that he made all things, not moved by anything; since he is the only God, the only Lord, the only Creator, the only Father, the only Sovereign, and it is he who bestows existence on all things. How could there be any other Totality [*plerôma*] beyond him: or another Principle or Power or another God? For God who is the totality of all these must needs include all things in his infinite being, while he himself cannot be included by any other thing. If there is anything outside him he is then not the totality of all things, nor does he contain all things . . . .

In the beginning God fashioned Adam, not because he had need of man, but that he might have a being on whom to bestow his benefits . . . . Nor did he order us to follow him because he needed our service, but because he thus conferred on us salvation . . . . Our service of God does not afford God anything, nor has he need of human obedience; but he has granted, to those who follow him and serve him, life and incorruption and eternal glory. He confers benefits on his servants because of their service, and on his followers because of their following. But he receives no benefit from them; for he is rich and complete, lacking nothing.

So also God from the beginning fashioned man with a view to displaying his bounty. He chose the patriarchs with a view to their salvation: he prepared a people, teaching them, obstinate as they were, to follow God; he set up prophets on the earth, thus accustoming man to hear his Spirit and have fellowship with God. He indeed had need of none; but to those who had need of him he granted his fellowship; and for those who were pleasing to him he drafted a plan of salvation, like an architect; and to those who saw him not in Egypt he gave guidance; to those who were restless in the wilderness he gave the Law which suited their needs; to those who entered into the good land he presented a worthy inheritance; for those who return to the Father he kills the fatted calf and gives them the best robe;[1] in many different ways he restores man to harmony and salvation. For this reason John says in the Apocalypse: 'His voice was like the voice of many waters.'[2] The 'many waters' represent the Spirit of God; and in truth they are many, because the Father is rich and great. Through all these waters the Word passed and gave assistance ungrudgingly to those who submitted to him, prescribing laws suitable for every condition . . . .

'Could not God have displayed man perfect from the beginning?' If anyone asks this, he must be told that God is absolute and eternal, and in respect of himself all things are within his power. But contingent things have their beginning of being in the course of time, and for this reason they must needs fall short of their maker's perfection; for things which have recently come to birth cannot be eternal; and, not being eternal, they fall short of perfection for that very reason. And being newly created they are therefore childish, and immature, and not yet fully trained for an adult way of life. And so, just as a mother is able to offer adult food to an infant, but the infant is not yet able to receive food unsuited to its age; so God himself could have offered perfection to man at the beginning, but man, being yet an infant, could not have taken it . . . .

All created things which through the bountiful goodness of God receive increase and persist on and on, shall gain the glory of the Eternal, for God bestows what is good without stint. In that they have a beginning they are not eternal; but in that they endure through long ages they shall gain the quality of eternity, God freely granting them to endure for ever.

And thus God is first in all respects: he only is eternal, and before all and the cause of the being of all things; all other things remain in subjection to God. And subjection to God is incorruptibility; and continuance in incorruptibility is the glory of eternity. Through such obedience and discipline and training man, who is contingent and created, grows into the image and likeness of the eternal God. This process the Father approves and commands; the Son carries out the Father's plan, the Spirit supports and hastens the process: while man gradually advances and mounts towards perfection; that is, he approaches the eternal. The eternal is perfect; and this is God. Man has first to come into being, then to progress, and by progressing come to manhood, and having reached manhood to increase, and thus increasing to persevere, and by persevering be glorified, and thus see his Lord. For it is God's intention that he should be seen: and the vision of God is the acquisition of immortality; and immortality brings man near to God . . . .

We were not made gods at our beginning, but first we were made men, then, in the end, gods. God does this out of the purity of his goodness so that none may think him envious or ungenerous. 'I have said, You are gods, and all of you children of the Highest.³ So he speaks, but since we are not able to bear the power of divinity, he goes on to say, 'But you will die like men.' Thus he expresses both the generosity of his giving, and our weakness, and the fact that we are possessed of free will. For because of his kindness he bestowed his gift upon us, and made men free, as he is free. Because of his foresight he knew men's weakness, and the results of that weakness; but because of his love and his goodness he will overcome [*the weakness of*] the nature of created man. It was necessary that [*the weakness of men's*] nature should first be shown and afterwards be overcome, and mortality be swallowed up by immortality, corruptibility by incorruptibility,⁴ and man become conformed to the image and likeness of God, having received the knowledge of good and evil . . . .

Man received the knowledge of good and evil. Now this is good: to obey God, to believe in him, and keep his commandments; and this is the life of man. Just as not to obey him is evil; and this is the death of man. Thus when God showed his kindness, man learnt the good of obedience and the evil of disobedience; his mind perceived by experience the distinction between good and evil, so that he might exercise his own decision in the choice of the better course. . . . How could he be trained in the good, without the knowledge of its contrary? For an object apprehended by experience has a surer effect than any theoretical inference. For just as the tongue by means of taste gains experience of sweet and bitter, and the eye by vision distinguishes black and white, and the ear through hearing learns to distinguish sounds; so the mind experiences good and evil, and by accepting the discipline of the good becomes more determined in preserving the good by obedience to God. First the mind discovers that disobedience is evil and bitter; and by penitence it spits it out. Then it learns by realization what sort of thing is contrary to goodness and sweetness; and thereafter it does not attempt even to taste of disobedience to God. But if a man shuns this acquaintance with good and evil, and this two-fold apprehension, he causes his own death although he does not know it.

How then will any be a god, if he has not first been made a man? How can any be perfect when he has only lately been made man? How immortal, if he has not in his mortal nature obeyed his Maker? For one's duty is first to observe the discipline of man and thereafter to share in the glory of God . . . .

It was for our benefit that the Lord allowed all these things [*sc. evil and opposition to his purposes*], that we may be trained by means of them, and learn to be circumspect, and so persevere in complete love of God when we have been taught by reason to love him. God shows his kindness in dealing with man's rebellion; for man is educated by means of it, as the prophet says: 'Your desertion shall correct you.'⁵ God directs all things to achieve the end of man's perfection and man's edification; and to display his own character, so that his goodness may be demonstrated and his righteousness fulfilled, and that the Church may be conformed to the image of his Son, and man may at length reach maturity, becoming ripe, through these experiences, for the vision and enjoyment of God . . . .

God suffered Jonah to be swallowed by a whale, not that he should thus utterly perish, but that he should be vomited out and be the more obedient to God and glorify him the more for this unlooked-for deliverance, and that he should bring the Ninevites to sincere repentance. . . . In the same way God suffered man to be swallowed by a great whale, namely the author of man's transgression, not that he should thereby perish, but because he designed and made ready for him a scheme of salvation . . . that receiving from God unlooked-for salvation man may rise from the dead and glorify God . . . and not consider his immortality as his own by nature, as if he were naturally like God . . . and that he may always be thankful to God because from him he has obtained the gift of immortality.

There are three elements of which, as we have shown, the complete man is made up, flesh, soul, and spirit; one of these preserves and fashions the man, and this is the spirit; another is given unity and form by the first, and this is the flesh; the third, the soul, is midway between the first two, and sometimes it is subservient to the spirit and is raised by it: while sometimes it allies itself with the flesh and descends to earthly passions . . . . All who fear God and believe in the coming of his Son, and through faith establish in their hearts the Spirit of God, are rightly given the name of men. They are purified and spiritual, and live for God, because they have the Spirit of the Father, who cleanses man and lifts him up to the life of God . . . .

Soul and spirit can be constituents of man; but they certainly cannot be the whole man. The complete man is a mixture and union, consisting of a soul which takes to itself the Spirit of the Father, to which is united the flesh which was fashioned in the image of God . . . men are spiritual not by the abolition of the flesh . . . there would then be the spirit of man, or the Spirit of God, not a spiritual man. But when this spirit is mingled with soul and united with created matter, then through the outpouring of the Spirit the complete man is produced; this is man made in the image and likeness of God. A man with soul only, lacking spirit [?Spirit], is 'psychic'; such a man is carnal, unfinished, incomplete; he has, in his created body, the image of God, but he has not acquired the likeness to God through the spirit . . . .

'How often did I wish to gather together your sons and you refused?' In saying this the Lord made plain the ancient law of man's freedom; for God from the beginning made man free. Man had his own power of decision, just as he had his own life, so that he might freely fall in with God's intention, without compulsion from God. For God does not use force, but his intention is at all times for man's good; and therefore his design for all is good. He equipped man with the power of choice, as he also equipped the angels (for angels are rational beings); that those who obey might deservedly possess good, the good which is given by God but whose retention depends on themselves . . . . If it was by nature that some are bad and others good, the latter would not be praiseworthy for their goodness, which would be their natural equipment; nor would the bad be responsible, having been so created. But in fact all have the same nature, with the power of accepting and achieving good, and the power likewise of spurning it and failing to achieve it. Therefore it is just that among men in a well-ordered community the good are praised . . . and the evil are called to account; and this is all the more true in respect of God's dealings with men . . . . If it were not in our power to do, or refrain from doing, what cause had the Apostle, and, which is more important, what cause had the Lord himself, to counsel to do some things and refrain from others? But because man is from the first possessed of free decision, and God, in whose likeness he was made, is also free, man is counselled to lay hold of the good, the good which is achieved in fullness as a result of obedience to God. And not only in actions but in faith also God has preserved man's free and unconstrained choice. For he says, 'Let it happen to you according to your faith',[6] thus showing that faith is something which a man has as his own, as he has his own power of decision . . . .

In the first Adam we offended God by not performing his command; in the second Adam we have been reconciled, becoming 'obedient unto death' . . . . [7]

As through a conquered man our race went down to death, so through a conqueror we ascend to life . . . .

As through a tree we were made debtors to God, so through a tree we receive the cancellation of our debt . . . .

Light does not fail because men have blinded themselves; it remains, with its own properties, while the blinded are plunged in darkness through their own fault. The light does not force itself on any man against his will; nor does God constrain a man, if he refuses to accept God's working [i.e. by which God brings man to perfection]. Therefore all who revolt from the Father's light, and who transgress the law of liberty, have removed themselves through their own fault, since they were created free and self-determining. God, with his perfect foreknowledge, has prepared for each class a fitting habitation; to those who seek the light of immortality and hasten towards it he graciously grants the light for which they long: for the others who spurn the light . . . and, as it were, blind themselves, he has prepared darkness . . . . Submission to God is eternal rest . . . those who flee from it have a habitation which their flight deserves. Now since all good things are with God, those who of their own decision flee from God defraud themselves of every good . . . and incur a just judgement . . . .

Fellowship with God is light and life . . . separation from God is death . . . .

Men, being created by God, are by nature sons of God; but they are not sons in their deeds. (3) For as among men disobedient sons, disowned by their fathers, are by nature their sons but are alienated in law, since they are no longer heirs of their natural parents: in the same way, with God, those who disobey him are disowned and have ceased to be sons . . . .

God questions Adam and Eve [*after their disobedience*] in such a way that the guilt might be brought home to the woman; and goes on to examine her so that the guilt might be transferred to the serpent . . . . The serpent he did not question, knowing him to be the prime mover in the transgression; but he first pronounced a curse on the serpent, to proceed to a milder rebuke of the man. For God detested man's seducer; but he showed a gentle pity for the man who had been seduced; and this was the reason why he cast man out of Paradise and removed him far from the tree of life; not, as some do not scruple to assert, that he grudged him the tree of life, but because he pitied him. Therefore he sought to prevent him continuing in transgression for ever, and to prevent the sin in which he was involved from being eternal, and the evil without end or remedy. So he put a stop to his wickedness by interposing death and making his sin to cease . . . so that man by dying to sin should begin to live to God . . . .

The devil was jealous of the man, God's creation, and tried to create enmity between man and God. Therefore God removed from his company him . . . who introduced sin; but man he pitied, who had thoughtlessly, though wickedly, allowed himself to disobey. And in pity God turned the enmity on the devil himself.

. . . It was the ground that God cursed, not Adam. And he cursed the serpent; and the fire was 'prepared for the devil and his angels', not originally for man . . . .

NOTES

1. Luke xv. 22 ff.
2. Rev. i. 16.
3. Ps. lxxxi (82). 6, 7.
4. 2 Cor. v. 4; 1 Cor. xv. 53–54.
5. Jer. ii. 19.
6. Matt. ix. 29.
7. Phil. ii. 8.

THE ENCHIRIDION (EXCERPTS)

St. Augustine

X. THE SUPREMELY GOOD CREATOR MADE ALL THINGS GOOD

By the Trinity, thus supremely and equally and unchangeably good, all things were created; and these are not supremely and equally and unchangeably good, but yet they are good, even taken separately. Taken as a whole, however, they are very good, because their *ensemble* constitutes the universe in all its wonderful order and beauty.

XI. WHAT IS CALLED EVIL IN THE UNIVERSE IS BUT THE ABSENCE OF GOOD

And in the universe, even that which is called evil, when it is regulated and put in its own place, only enhances our admiration of the good; for we enjoy and value the good more when we compare it with the evil. For the Almighty God, who, as even the heathen acknowledge, has supreme power over all things, being Himself supremely good, would never permit the existence of anything evil among His works, if He were not so omnipotent and good that He can bring good even out of evil. For what is that which we call evil but the absence of good? In the bodies of animals, disease and wounds mean nothing but the absence of health; for when a cure is effected, that does not mean that the evils which were present—namely, the diseases and wounds—go away from the body and dwell elsewhere: they altogether cease to exist; for the wound or disease is not a substance, but a defect in the fleshly substance—the flesh itself being a substance, and therefore something good, of which those evils—that is, privations of the good which we call health—are accidents. Just in the same way, what are called vices in the soul are nothing but privations of natural good. And when they are cured, they are not transferred elsewhere: when they cease to exist in the healthy soul, they cannot exist anywhere else.

XII. ALL BEINGS WERE MADE GOOD, BUT NOT BEING MADE PERFECTLY GOOD, ARE LIABLE TO CORRUPTION

All things that exist, therefore, seeing that the Creator of them all is supremely good, are themselves good. But because they are not, like their Creator, supremely and unchangeably good, their good may be diminished and increased. But for good to be diminished is an evil, although, however much it may be diminished, it is necessary, if the being is to continue, that some good should remain to constitute the being. For however small or of whatever kind the being may be, the good which makes it a being cannot be destroyed without destroying the being itself. An uncorrupted nature is justly held in esteem. But if, still further, it be incorruptible, it is undoubtedly considered of still higher value. When it is corrupted, however, its corruption is an evil, because it is deprived of some sort of good. For if it be deprived of no good, it receives no injury; but it does receive injury, therefore it is deprived of good. Therefore, so long as a being is in process of corruption, there is in it some good of which it is being deprived; and if a part of the being should remain which cannot be corrupted, this will certainly be an incorruptible being, and accordingly the process of corruption will result in the manifestation of this great good. But if it do not cease to be corrupted, neither can it cease to possess good of which corruption may deprive it. But if it should be thoroughly and completely consumed by corruption, there will then be no good left, because there will be no being. Wherefore corruption can consume the good only by consuming the being. Every being, therefore, is a good; a great good, if it cannot be corrupted; a little good, if it can: but in any case, only the foolish or ignorant will deny that it is a good. And if it be wholly consumed by corruption, then the corruption itself must cease to exist, as there is no being left in which it can dwell.

XIII. THERE CAN BE NO EVIL WHERE THERE IS NO GOOD; AND AN EVIL MAN IS AN EVIL GOOD

Accordingly, there is nothing of what we call evil, if there be nothing good. But a good which is wholly without evil is a perfect good. A good, on the other hand, which contains evil is a faulty or imperfect good; and there can be no evil where there is no good. From all this we arrive at the curious result: that since every being, so far as it is a being, is good, when we say that a faulty being is an evil being, we just seem to say that what is good is evil, and that nothing but what is good can be evil, seeing that every being is good, and that no evil can exist except in a being. Nothing, then, can be evil except something which is good. And although this, when stated, seems to be a contradiction, yet the strictness of reasoning leaves us no escape from the conclusion. We must, however, beware of incurring the prophetic condemnation: "Woe unto them that call evil good, and good evil: that put darkness for light, and light for darkness: that put bitter for sweet, and sweet for bitter."[1] And yet our Lord says: "An evil man out of the evil treasure of his heart bringeth forth that which is evil."[2] Now, what is an evil man but an evil being? for a man is a being. Now, if a man is a good thing because he is a being, what is an evil man but an evil good? Yet, when we accurately distinguish these two things, we find that it is not because he is a man that he is an evil, or because he is wicked that he is a good; but that he is a good because he is a man, and an evil because he is wicked. Whoever, then, says "To be a man is an evil," or, "To be wicked is a good," falls under the prophetic denunciation: "Woe unto them that call evil good, and good evil!" For he condemns the work of God, which is the man, and praises the defect of man, which is the wickedness. Therefore every being, even if it be a defective one, in so far as it is a being is good, and in so far as it is defective is evil.

XIV. GOOD AND EVIL ARE AN EXCEPTION TO THE RULE THAT CONTRARY ATTRIBUTES CANNOT BE PREDICATED OF THE SAME SUBJECT. EVIL SPRINGS UP IN WHAT IS GOOD, AND CANNOT EXIST EXCEPT IN WHAT IS GOOD

Accordingly, in the case of these contraries which we call good and evil, the rule of the logicians, that two contraries cannot be predicated at the same time of the same thing, does not hold. No weather is at the same time dark and bright: no food or drink is at the same time sweet and bitter: no body is at the same time and in the same place black and white: none is at the same time and in the same place deformed and beautiful. And this rule is found to hold in regard to many, indeed nearly all, contraries, that they cannot exist at the same time in any one thing. But although no one can doubt that good and evil are contraries, not only can they exist at the same time, but evil cannot exist without good, or in anything that is not good. Good, however, can exist without evil. For a man or an angel can exist without being wicked; but nothing can be wicked except a man or an angel: and so far as he is a man or an angel, he is good; so far as he is wicked, he is an evil. And these two contraries are so far co-existent, that if good did not exist in what is evil, neither could evil exist; because corruption could not have either a place to dwell in, or a source to spring from, if there were nothing that could be corrupted; and nothing can be corrupted except what is good, for corruption is nothing else but the destruction of good. From what is good, then, evils arose, and except in what is good they do not exist; nor was there any other source from which any evil nature could arise. For if there were, then, in so far as this was a being, it was certainly a good: and a being which was incorruptible would be a great good; and even one which was corruptible must be to some extent a good, for only by corrupting what was good in it could corruption do it harm.

XV. THE PRECEDING ARGUMENT IS IN NO WISE INCONSISTENT WITH THE SAYING OF OUR LORD: "A GOOD TREE CANNOT BRING FORTH EVIL FRUIT"

But when we say that evil springs out of good, let it not be thought that this contradicts our Lord's saying: "A good tree cannot bring forth evil fruit."[3] For, as the Truth says, you cannot gather grapes of thorns,[4] because grapes do not grow on thorns. But we see that on good soil both vines and thorns may be grown. And in the same way, just as an evil tree cannot bring forth good fruit, so an evil will cannot produce good works. But from the nature of man, which is good, may spring either a good or an evil will. And certainly there was at first no source from which an evil will could spring, except the nature of angel or of man, which was good. And our Lord Himself clearly shows this is the very same place where He speaks about the tree and its fruit. For He says: "Either make the tree good, and his fruit good; or else make the tree corrupt, and his fruit corrupt"[5]—clearly enough warning us that evil fruits do not grow on a good tree, nor good fruits on an evil tree; but that nevertheless the ground itself, by which He meant those whom He was then addressing, might grow either kind of trees.

XVI. IT IS NOT ESSENTIAL TO MAN'S HAPPINESS THAT HE SHOULD KNOW THE CAUSES OF PHYSICAL CONVULSIONS; BUT IT IS, THAT HE SHOULD KNOW THE CAUSES OF GOOD AND EVIL

Now, in view of these considerations, when we are pleased with that line of Maro, "Happy the man who has attained to the knowledge of the causes of things,"[6] we should not suppose that it is necessary to happiness to know the causes of the great physical convulsions, causes which lie hid in the most secret recesses of nature's kingdom, "whence comes the earthquake whose force makes the deep seas to swell and burst their barriers, and again to return upon themselves and settle down."[7] But we ought to know the causes of good and evil as far as man may in this life know them, in order to avoid the mistakes and troubles of which this life is so full. For our aim must always be to reach that state of happiness in which no trouble shall distress us, and no error mislead us. If we must know the causes of physical convulsions, there are none which it concerns us more to know than those which affect our own health. But seeing that, in our ignorance of these, we are fain to resort to physicians, it would seem that we might bear with considerable patience our ignorance of the secrets that lie hid in the earth and heavens.

NOTES

1. Isa. v. 20
2. Luke vi. 45
3. Matt. vii. 18
4. Matt. vii. 16
5. Matt. xii. 33
6. Virgil, *Georgics*, ii. 490
7. *Ibid.*

Questions for Part VIII

1. J. L. Mackie notes that the problem of evil is a problem only if you believe in the existence of the Christian god, that is, a God that is both all-powerful and wholly good. Explain why this is so.

2. Mackie discusses a number of what he calls fallacious solutions to the problem of evil. Three of these have in common the attempt to justify the existence of some evil in the universe because it enhances the good by contrast. Is Mackie's identification of reasons why these solutions are fallacious persuasive?

3. What is the Free-Will Defence and does it lead to what Mackie calls the Paradox of Omnipotence? Explain that paradox and relate it to the Paradox of Sovereignty.

4. Alvin Plantinga attacks Mackie's challenge that the proposition that God is omnipotent, omniscient, and all-good entails that no free persons created by God ever perform morally evil actions. Plantinga concentrates on some of the additional premises Mackie must use to make the entailment work. What is Plantinga's response to Mackie?

5. We all know that the people on earth do not always act in the morally best ways. Some are downright wicked. Surely God could have created a world in which there are only those who never commit morally evil acts. That is a possible world. God is omniscient and omnipotent, so why did God not actualize that possible world rather than the one God did actualize? Explain Plantinga's response to this way of putting the problem of evil.

6. Does his view that "it is *false* that God can instantiate just any possible person" involve Plantinga in limiting a supposedly omnipotent God's effective power in a way that falls prey to Mackie's criticisms?

7. In 1902 Mont Pelee erupted on the island of Martinique killing approximately 30,000 inhabitants of the town of St. Pierre. What is Plantinga's explanation of how there can be such physical or natural evils in the world even though God is omnipotent, omniscient, and morally all-good? Is Plantinga really committed to a belief in the existence of Satan?

8. St. Irenaeus's conception of the creation of human beings and the beginnings of sin differs radically from that of St. Augustine. What are the most distinctive differences between the two?

9. St. Irenaeus's theodicy could be described as utopian in the sense that it promises a bright future achieved through gradual steps of human improvement. St. Augustine's view is far less utopian as its focus is more on the loss of paradise and the burden of original sin. Think of how holding one or the other of these views might effect a spectrum of political and social action views and related theories about progress and human history.

10. On St. Irenaeus's account evil seems to be necessary for humans to gain knowledge and achieve perfection. Explain why he thinks this is so.

11. St. Augustine is persuaded that God made everything good and that evil is the corruption of things originally good. What are his reasons for holding this view?

12. Is St. Augustine's view that evil is merely the absence of good a viable response to Mackie's attack on the inconsistency of the Christian doctrines with the fact of evil?

Part IX. Character or Duty

Since the very beginning of philosophy, one of the philosopher's main concerns has been the study of values, and especially of moral values. We are all accustomed to making moral judgments about people; the philosopher is interested in the nature of such judgments: What exactly do they mean? What sort of facts make them true or false? What sort of evidence should or could we have in support of our moral judgments?

Moral judgments concern matters both great and small, but perhaps the small ones strike closest to home. One of the editors of the present volume once worked with a man—let us call him "Fred"—who had some interesting pastimes, about which he loved to talk. One of Fred's many stories involved the time he and several friends found a nest of baby birds. They began "teaching the birds to fly" by hurling them high into the air in the direction of a nearby barn. But the birds, too young to fly, would simply come crashing down into the side of the barn. When Fred and his friends had in this manner "used up" all the birds but one, they tied the remaining bird inside the barn by its feet and threw rocks at it from far enough away to make hitting the bird a challenge. This engaged them for some time, until finally a large rock struck the bird and put an end to the game. Fred had many similar tales—about putting on a Halloween mask in the middle of the night and knocking on the window of a sleeping friend, throwing lit firecrackers at people, and many more—but perhaps this is enough to give the flavor of these stories.

This is clearly small-time stuff. Compared to gang wars, the activities of drug dealers, or atrocities committed in Iron Curtain prisons, much less the unbelievably shocking and horrible slaughter in Nazi Germany, these actions may seem trivial. But surely they are activities which lead us to make a moral assessment. Indeed, they lead us to make moral judgments of two kinds. We want to judge, first, that Fred's actions were morally *wrong*. He had a moral obligation not to do many of the things he enjoyed, and he failed to meet this obligation. But second, we want to judge not only Fred's actions but also his *character*. Fred may have been a good person in very many respects (certainly he was a good worker), but in some respects his character was deficient. A better person would not have enjoyed the sort of sadistic behavior in which Fred loved to engage and about which he loved to talk. He lacked a certain kind of sympathy which the people we look up to and admire most have.

There are two very different traditions in ethics, each of which focuses on one of these two sorts of evaluation. It is characteristic of modern philosophy to be concerned with the evaluation of actions, with the determination of which actions are right and which wrong and, more generally, what moral principles make those actions right or wrong. This modern tradition is sometimes called the "ethics of conduct," and among the most powerful and influential investigations in this tradition is Immanuel Kant's *Fundamental Principles of the Metaphysic of Morals*, excerpted in this section.

This modern tradition stands in marked contrast to the tradition of ancient and medieval philosophy. The ancient philosophers were interested more in what makes someone a good person than in what makes an action right, and for this reason these philosophers are sometimes described as engaged in the "ethics of character." The most influential representative of this tradition is the ancient Greek philosopher Aristotle, whose principal work on ethics, the *Nicomachean Ethics*, is excerpted here.

To some extent, Aristotle and Kant are not asking the same question. For Aristotle and other Greek philosophers the fundamental moral question was "What is the good life?" They wanted to discover what kind of person one needed to be in order to live the most fulfilling life. Aristotle's specific moral advice, then, consists of describing those traits of character which will enable someone to live the best sort of life. These character traits, which Aristotle calls *virtues*, are dispositions to act in certain ways and also to feel certain emotions in certain circumstances.

For Kant, on the other hand, the central moral question is "What is my moral duty?" That is, Kant wants to know what actions we ought morally to perform or abstain from, and he sees the main function of moral philosophy as formulating the moral rules which will enable us to determine what our duty is (and which, at the same time, explain why it is our duty).

The questions Aristotle and Kant ask are so different that we might be tempted to treat their discussions as complementary rather than conflicting. And indeed much that each says is compatible with the other's views. But there is also some conflict between their views—conflict which has given rise to disagreements between contemporary Aristoteleans and contemporary Kantians.

One such disagreement concerns which sort of question is more fundamental. If we answer Kant's question first, then we will say that the virtuous or moral person is first and foremost one who does his duty by following the correct moral rules. If we answer Aristotle's question first, we will say that the right thing to do is simply the thing which the virtuous person would do; in that case when we need help deciding how to act we will be less inclined to consult a moral rulebook than to ask ourselves how the people we most admire would handle this situation. Aristoteleans, then, tend to think of moral rules and principles as less important and fundamental than Kantians do.

The contemporary selections in this section explore moral situations in which considerations about character and about duty intertwine. Jonathan Bennett discusses the way in which a good character can overcome, or be overcome by, one's belief in an inadequate set of moral rules. But he does not advocate simply following one's feelings rather than one's moral code; rather, he argues that we need moral codes, but should keep them open to revision if they offend our sympathies too deeply. Gregory Kavka, in "Some Paradoxes of Deterrence," argues that nuclear deterrence creates a number of paradoxes about the relations between character and duty—for example, that one may sometimes have a duty to do something which no morally good person could do. Both contemporary selections, then, raise questions about the relation between Kant's and Aristotle's conceptions of the bases of ethics.

THE CONSCIENCE OF HUCKLEBERRY FINN

Jonathan Bennett

In this paper, I shall present not just the conscience of Huckleberry Finn but two others as well. One of them is the conscience of Heinrich Himmler. He became a Nazi in 1923; he served drably and quietly, but well, and was rewarded with increasing responsibility and power. At the peak of his career he held many offices and commands, of which the most powerful was that of leader of the S.S.—the principal police force of the Nazi regime. In this capacity, Himmler commanded the whole concentration-camp system, and was responsible for the execution of the so-called 'final solution of the Jewish problem'. It is important for my purposes that this piece of social engineering should be thought of not abstractly but in concrete terms of Jewish families being marched to what they think are bath-houses, to the accompaniment of loud-speaker renditions of extracts from *The Merry Widow* and *Tales of Hoffman*, there to be choked to death by poisonous gases. Altogether, Himmler succeeded in murdering about four and a half million of them, as well as several million gentiles, mainly Poles and Russians.

The other conscience to be discussed is that of the Calvinist theologian and philosopher Jonathan Edwards. He lived in the first half of the eighteenth century, and has a good claim to be considered America's first serious and considerable philosophical thinker. He was for many years a widely-renowned preacher and Congregationalist minister in New England; in 1748 a dispute with his congregation led him to resign (he couldn't accept their view that unbelievers should be admitted to the Lord's Supper in the hope that it would convert them); for some years after that he worked as a missionary, preaching to Indians through an interpreter; then in 1758 he accepted the presidency of what is now Princeton University, and within two months died from a smallpox inoculation. Along the way he wrote some first-rate philosophy: his book attacking the notion of free will is still sometimes read. Why I should be interested in Edwards' *conscience* will be explained in due course.

I shall use Heinrich Himmler, Jonathan Edwards and Huckleberry Finn to illustrate different aspects of a single theme, namely the relationship between *sympathy* on the one hand and *bad morality* on the other.

* * *

All that I can mean by a 'bad morality' is a morality whose principles I deeply disapprove of. When I call a morality bad, I cannot prove that mine is better; but when I here call any morality bad, I think you will agree with me that it is bad; and that is all I need.

There could be dispute as to whether the springs of someone's actions constitute a *morality*. I think, though, that we must admit that someone who acts in ways which conflict grossly with our morality may nevertheless have a morality of his own—a set of principles of action which he sincerely assents to, so that for him the problem of acting well or rightly or in obedience to conscience is the problem of conforming to *those* principles. The problem of conscientiousness can arise as acutely for a bad morality as for any other: rotten principles may be as different to keep as decent ones.

As for 'sympathy': I use this term to cover every sort of fellow-feeling, as when one feels pity over someone's loneliness, or horrified compassion over his pain, and when one feels a shrinking reluctance to act in a way which will bring misfortune to someone else. These *feelings* must not be confused with *moral judgments*. My sympathy for someone in distress may lead me to help him, or even to think that I ought to help him; but in itself it is not a judgment about what I ought to do but just a *feeling* for him in his plight. We shall get some light on the difference between feelings and moral judgments when we consider Huckleberry Finn.

Obviously, feelings can impel one to action, and so can moral judgments; and in a particular case sympathy and morality may pull in opposite directions. This can happen not just with bad moralities, but also with good ones like yours and mine. For example, a small child, sick and miserable, clings tightly to his mother and screams in terror when she tries to pass him over to the doctor to be examined. If the mother gave way to her sympathy, that is to her feeling for the child's misery and fright, she would hold it close and not let the doctor come near; but don't we agree that it might be wrong for her to act on such a feeling? Quite generally, then, anyone's moral principles may apply to a particular situation in a way which runs contrary to the particular thrusts of fellow-feeling that he has in that situation. My immediate concern is with sympathy in relation to bad morality, but not because such conflicts occur only when the morality is bad.

Now, suppose that someone who accepts a bad morality is struggling to make himself act in accordance with it in a particular situation where his sympathies pull him another way. He sees the struggle as one between doing the right, conscientious thing, and acting wrongly and weakly, like the mother who won't let the doctor come near her sick, frightened baby. Since we don't accept this person's morality, we may see the situation very differently, thoroughly disapproving of the action he regards as the right one, and endorsing the action which from his point of view constitutes weakness and backsliding.

Conflicts between sympathy and bad morality won't always be like this, for we won't disagree with every single dictate of a bad morality.

Still, it can happen in the way I have described, with the agent's right action being our wrong one, and vice versa. That is just what happens in a certain episode in chapter 16 of *The Adventures of Huckleberry Finn*, an episode which brilliantly illustrates how fiction can be instructive about real life.

* * *

Huck Finn has been helping his slave friend Jim to run away from Miss Watson, who is Jim's owner. In their raft-journey down the Mississippi river, they are near to the place at which Jim will become legally free. Now let Huck take over the story:

> Jim said it made him all over trembly and feverish to be so close to freedom. Well, I can tell you it made me all over trembly and feverish, too, to hear him, because I begun to get it through my head that he *was* most free—and who was to blame for it? Why, *me*. I couldn't get that out of my conscience, no how nor no way. . . . It hadn't ever come home to me, before, what this thing was that I was doing. But now it did; and it stayed with me, and scorched me more and more. I tried to make out to myself that *I* warn't to blame, because *I* didn't run Jim off from his rightful owner; but it warn't no use, conscience up and say, every time: 'But you knowed he was running for his freedom, and you could a paddled ashore and told somebody.' That was so—I couldn't get around that, no way. That was where it pinched. Conscience says to me: 'What had poor Miss Watson done to you, that you could see her nigger go off right under your eyes and never say one single word? What did that poor old woman do to you, that you could treat her so mean? . . .' I got to feeling so mean and so miserable I most wished I was dead.

Jim speaks of his plan to save up to buy his wife, and then his children, out of slavery; and he adds that if the children cannot be bought he will arrange to steal them. Huck is horrified:

> Thinks I, this is what comes of my not thinking. Here was this nigger which I had as good as helped to run away, coming right out flat-footed and saying he would steal his children—children that belonged to a man I didn't even know; a man that hadn't ever done me no harm.
>
> I was sorry to hear Jim say that, it was such a lowering of him. My conscience got to stirring me up hotter than ever, until at last I says to it: 'Let up on me—it ain't too late, yet—I'll paddle ashore at first light, and tell.' I felt easy, and happy, and light as a feather, right off. All my troubles was gone.

This is bad morality all right. In his earliest years Huck wasn't taught any principles, and the only ones he has encountered since then are those of rural Missouri, in which slave-owning is just one kind of ownership and is not subject to critical pressure. It hasn't occurred to Huck to question those principles. So the action, to us abhorrent, of turning Jim in to the authorities presents itself *clearly* to Huck as the right thing to do.

For us, morality and sympathy would both dictate helping Jim to escape. If we felt any conflict, it would have both these on one side and something else on the other—greed for a reward, or fear of punishment.

But Huck's morality conflicts with his sympathy, that is, with his un-
argued, natural feeling for his friend. The conflict starts when Huck sets
off in the canoe towards the shore, pretending that he is going to recon-
noitre, but really planning to turn Jim in:

> As I shoved off, [Jim] says: 'Pooty soon I'll be a-shout'n for joy, en I'll say, it's
> all on accounts o' Huck I's a free man . . . Jim won't ever forget you, Huck;
> you's de bes' fren' Jim's ever had; en you's de *only* fren' old Jim's got now.'
> I was paddling off, all in a sweat to tell on him; but when he says this, it
> seemed to kind of take the tuck all out of me. I went along slow then, and I
> warn't right down certain whether I was glad I started or whether I warn't.
> When I was fifty yards off, Jim says:
> 'Dah you goes, de ole true Huck; de on'y white genlman dat ever kep' his
> promise to ole Jim.' Well, I just felt sick. But I says, I *got* to do it—I can't get *out*
> of it.

In the upshot, sympathy wins over morality. Huck hasn't the strength of
will to do what he sincerely thinks he ought to do. Two men hunting for
runaway slaves ask him whether the man on his raft is black or white:

> I didn't answer up prompt. I tried to, but the words wouldn't come. I tried, for
> a second or two, to brace up and out with it, but I warn't man enough—hadn't
> the spunk of a rabbit. I see I was weakening; so I just give up trying, and up
> and says: 'He's white.'

So Huck enables Jim to escape, thus acting weakly and wickedly—he
thinks. In this conflict between sympathy and morality, sympathy wins.
     One critic has cited this episode in support of the statement that Huck
suffers 'excruciating moments of wavering between honesty and respect-
ability'. That is hopelessly wrong, and I agree with the perceptive comment on it by another critic, who says:

> The conflict waged in Huck is much more serious: he scarcely cares for respect-
> ability and never hesitates to relinquish it, but he does care for honesty and
> gratitude—and both honesty and gratitude require that he should give Jim up.
> It is not, in Huck, honesty at war with respectability but love and compassion
> for Jim struggling against his conscience. His decision is for Jim and hell: a right
> decision made in the mental chains that Huck never breaks. His concern for Jim
> is and remains *irrational*. Huck finds many reasons for giving Jim up and none
> for stealing him. To the end Huck sees his compassion for Jim as a weak,
> ignorant, and wicked felony.[1]

That is precisely correct—and it can have that virtue only because Mark
Twain wrote the episode with such unerring precision. The crucial point
concerns *reasons*, which all occur on one side of the conflict. On the side
of conscience we have principles, arguments, considerations, ways of
looking at things:

> 'It hadn't ever come home to me before what I was doing'
> 'I tried to make out that I warn't to blame'
> 'Conscience said "But you knowed . . ."—I couldn't get around that'

'What had poor Miss Watson done to you?'
'This is what comes of my not thinking'
'. . . children that belonged to a man I didn't even know'.

On the other side, the side of feeling, we get nothing like that. When Jim rejoices in Huck, as his only friend, Huck doesn't consider the claims of friendship or have the situation 'come home' to him in a different light. All that happens is: 'When he says this, it seemed to kind of take the tuck all out of me. I went along slow then, and I warn't right down certain whether I was glad I started or whether I warn't.' Again, Jim's words about Huck's 'promise' to him don't give Huck any *reason* for changing his plan: in his morality promises to slaves probably don't count. Their effect on him is of a different kind: 'Well, I just felt sick.' And when the moment for final decision comes, Huck doesn't weigh up pros and cons: he simply *fails* to do what he believes to be right—he isn't strong enough, hasn't 'the spunk of a rabbit'. This passage in the novel is notable not just for its finely wrought irony, with Huck's weakness of will leading him to do the right thing, but also for its masterly handling of the difference between general moral principles and particular unreasoned emotional pulls.

* * *

Consider now another case of bad morality in conflict with human sympathy the case of the odious Himmler. Here, from a speech he made to some S.S. generals, is an indication of the content of his morality:

> What happens to a Russian, to a Czech, does not interest me in the slightest. What the nations can offer in the way of good blood of our type, we will take, if necessary by kidnapping their children and raising them here with us. Whether nations live in prosperity or starve to death like cattle interests me only in so far as we need them as slaves to our *Kultur;* otherwise it is of no interest to me. Whether 10,000 Russian females fall down from exhaustion while digging an antitank ditch interests me only in so far as the antitank ditch for Germany is finished.[2]

But has this a moral basis at all? And if it has, was there in Himmler's own mind any conflict between morality and sympathy? Yes there was. Here is more from the same speech:

> . . . I also want to talk to you quite frankly on a very grave matter . . . I mean . . . the extermination of the Jewish race. . . . Most of you must know what it means when 100 corpses are lying side by side, or 500, or 1,000. To have stuck it out and at the same time—apart from exceptions caused by human weakness—to have remained decent fellows, that is what has made us hard. This is a page of glory in our history which has never been written and is never to be written.

Himmler saw his policies as being hard to implement while still retaining one's human sympathies—while still remaining a 'decent fellow.' He is saying that only the weak take the easy way out and just squelch their sympathies, and is praising the stronger and more glorious course of retaining one's sympathies while acting in violation of them. In the same spirit, he ordered that when executions were carried out in concentration camps, those responsible 'are to be influenced in such a way as to suffer no ill effect in their character and mental attitude'. A year later he boasted that the S.S. had wiped out the Jews

> without our leaders and their men suffering any damage in their minds and souls. The danger was considerable, for there was only a narrow path between the Scylla of their becoming heartless ruffians unable any longer to treasure life, and the Charybdis of their becoming soft and suffering nervous breakdowns.

And there really can't be any doubt that the basis of Himmler's policies was a set of principles which constituted his morality—a sick, bad, wicked *morality*. He described himself as caught in 'the old tragic conflict between will and obligation'. And when his physician Kersten protested at the intention to destroy the Jews, saying that the suffering involved was 'not to be contemplated', Kersten reports that Himmler replied:

> He knew that it would mean much suffering for the Jews. . . . 'It is the curse of greatness that it must step over dead bodies to create new life. Yet we must . . . cleanse the soil or it will never bear fruit. It will be a great burden for me to bear.'

This, I submit, is the language of morality.

So in this case, tragically, bad morality won out over sympathy. I am sure that many of Himmler's killers did extinguish their sympathies, becoming 'heartless ruffians' rather than 'decent fellows'; but not Himmler himself. Although his policies ran against the human grain to a horrible degree, he did not sandpaper down his emotional surfaces so that there was no grain there, allowing his actions to slide along smoothly and easily. He did, after all, bear his hideous burden, and even paid a price for it. He suffered a variety of nervous and physical disabilities, including nausea and stomach-convulsions, and Kersten was doubtless right in saying that these were 'the expression of a psychic division which extended over his whole life'.

This same division must have been present in some of those officials of the Church who ordered heretics to be tortured so as to change their theological opinions. Along with the brutes and the cold careerists, there must have been some who cared, and who suffered from the conflict between their sympathies and their bad morality.

* * *

In the conflict between sympathy and bad morality, then, the victory may go to sympathy as in the case of Huck Finn, or to morality as in the case of Himmler.

Another possibility is that the conflict may be avoided by giving up, or not ever having, those sympathies which might interfere with one's principles. That seems to have been the case with Jonathan Edwards. I am afraid that I shall be doing an injustice to Edwards' many virtues, and to his great intellectual energy and inventiveness; for my concern is only with the worst thing about him—namely his morality, which was worse than Himmler's.

According to Edwards, God condemns some men to an eternity of unimaginably awful pain, though he arbitrarily spares others—'arbitrarily' because none deserve to be spared:

> Natural men are held in the hand of God over the pit of hell; they have deserved the fiery pit, and are already sentenced to it; and God is dreadfully provoked, his anger is as great towards them as to those that are actually suffering the executions of the fierceness of his wrath in hell . . . ; the devil is waiting for them, hell is gaping for them, the flames gather and flash about them, and would fain lay hold on them . . . ; and . . . there are no means within reach that can be any security to them. . . . All that preserves them is the mere arbitrary will, and uncovenanted unobliged forebearance of an incensed God.[3]

Notice that he says 'they have deserved the fiery pit.' Edwards insists that men *ought* to be condemned to eternal pain; and his position isn't that this is right because God wants it, but rather that God wants it because it is right. For him, moral standards exist independently of God, and God can be assessed in the light of them (and of course found to be perfect). For example, he says:

> They deserve to be cast into hell; so that . . . justice never stands in the way, it makes no objection against God's using his power at any moment to destroy them. Yea, on the contrary, justice calls aloud for an infinite punishment of their sins.

Elsewhere, he gives elaborate arguments to show that God is acting justly in damning sinners. For example, he argues that a punishment should be exactly as bad as the crime being punished; God is infinitely excellent; so any crime against him infinitely bad; and so eternal damnation is exactly right as a punishment—it is infinite, but, as Edwards is careful also to say, it is 'no more than infinite.'

Of course, Edwards himself didn't torment the damned; but the question still arises of whether his sympathies didn't conflict with his *approval* of eternal torment. Didn't he find it painful to contemplate any fellow-human's being tortured for ever? Apparently not:

> The God that holds you over the pit of hell, much as one holds a spider or some loathsome insect over the fire, abhors you, and is dreadfully provoked; . . . he is of purer eyes than to bear to have you in his sight; you are ten thousand times so abominable in his eyes as the most hateful venomous serpent is in ours.

When God is presented as being as misanthropic as that, one suspects misanthropy in the theologian. This suspicion is increased when Edwards claims that 'the saints in glory will . . . understand how terrible the sufferings of the damned are; yet . . . will not be sorry for [them].'[4] He bases this partly on a view of human nature whose ugliness he seems not to notice:

> The seeing of the calamities of others tends to heighten the sense of our own enjoyments. When the saints in glory, therefore, shall see the doleful state of the damned, how will this heighten their sense of the blessedness of their own state. . . . When they shall see how miserable others of their fellow-creatures are . . . ; when they shall see the smoke of their torment, . . . and hear their dolorous shrieks and cries, and consider that they in the mean time are in the most blissful state, and shall surely be in it to all eternity; how they will rejoice!

I hope this is less than the whole truth! His other main point about why the saints will rejoice to see the torments of the damned is that it is *right* that they should do so:

> The heavenly inhabitants . . . will have no love nor pity to the damned. . . . [This will not show] a want of a spirit of love in them . . . ; for the heavenly inhabitants will know that it is not fit that they should love [the damned] because they will know then, that God has no love to them, nor pity for them.

The implication that *of course* one can adjust one's feelings of pity so that they conform to the dictates of some authority—doesn't this suggest that ordinary human sympathies played only a small part in Edwards' life?

* * *

Huck Finn, whose sympathies are wide and deep, could never avoid the conflict in that way; but he is determined to avoid it, and so he opts for the only other alternative he can see—to give up morality altogether. After he has tricked the slave-hunters, he returns to the raft and undergoes a peculiar crisis:

> I got aboard the raft, feeling bad and low, because I knowed very well I had done wrong, and I see it warn't no use for me to try to learn to do right; a body that don't get *started* right when he's little, ain't got no show—when the pinch comes there ain't nothing to back him up and keep him to his work, and so he gets beat. Then I thought a minute, and says to myself, hold on—s'pose you'd a done right and give Jim up; would you feel better than what you do now? No, says I, I'd feel bad—I'd feel just the same way I do now. Well, then, says I, what's the use you learning to do right, when it's troublesome to do right and ain't no trouble to do wrong, and the wages is just the same? I was stuck. I couldn't answer that. So I reckoned I wouldn't bother no more about it, but after this always do whichever come handiest at the time.

Huck clearly cannot conceive of having any morality except the one he has learned—too late, he thinks—from his society. He is not entirely a prisoner of that morality, because he does after all reject it; but for him that is a decision to relinquish morality as such; he cannot envisage revising his morality, altering its content in face of the various pressures to which it is subject, including pressures from his sympathies. For example, he does not begin to approach the thought that slavery should be rejected on moral grounds, or the thought that what he is doing is not theft because a person cannot be owned and therefore cannot be stolen.

The basic trouble is that he cannot or will not engage in abstract intellectual operations of any sort. In chapter 33 he finds himself 'feeling to blame, somehow' for something he knows he had no hand in; he assumes that this feeling is a deliverance of conscience; and this confirms him in his belief that conscience shouldn't be listened to:

> It don't make no difference whether you do right or wrong, a person's conscience ain't got no sense, and just goes for him *anyway*. If I had a yaller dog that didn't know no more than a person's conscience does, I would pison him. It takes up more room than all the rest of a person's insides, and yet ain't no good, nohow.

That brisk, incurious dismissiveness fits well with the comprehensive rejection of morality back on the raft. But this is a digression.

On the raft, Huck decides not to live by principles, but just to do whatever 'comes handiest at the time'—always acting according to the mood of the moment. Since the morality he is rejecting is narrow and cruel, and his sympathies are broad and kind, the results will be good. But moral principles are good to have, because they help to protect one from acting badly at moments when one's sympathies happen to be in abeyance. On the highest possible estimate of the role one's sympathies should have, one can still allow for principles as embodiments of one's best feelings, one's broadest and keenest sympathies. On that view, principles can help one across intervals when one's feelings are at less than their best, i.e. through periods of misanthropy or meanness or self-centredness or depression or anger.

What Huck didn't see is that one can live by principles and yet have ultimate control over their content. And one way such control can be exercised is by checking of one's principles in the light of one's sympathies. This is sometimes a pretty straightforward matter. It can happen that a certain moral principle becomes untenable—meaning literally that one cannot hold it any longer—because it conflicts intolerably with the pity or revulsion or whatever that one feels when one sees what the principle leads to. One's experience may play a large part here: experiences evoke feelings, and feelings force one to modify principles. Something like this happened to the English poet Wilfred Owen, whose experiences in the First World War transformed him from an enthusiastic soldier into a virtual pacifist. I can't document his change of conscience in detail; but I want to present something which he wrote about the way experience can put pressure on morality.

The Latin poet Horace wrote that it is sweet and fitting (or right) to die for one's country—*dulce et decorum est pro patria mori*—and Owen wrote a fine poem about how experience could lead one to relinquish that particu-

lar moral principle.[5] He describes a man who is too slow donning his gas
mask during a gas attack—'As under a green sea I saw him drowning,'
Owen says. The poem ends like this:

In all my dreams before my helpless sight
He plunges at me, guttering, choking, drowning.
If in some smothering dreams, you too could pace
Behind the wagon that we flung him in,
And watch the white eyes writhing in his face,
His hanging face, like a devil's sick of sin;
If you could hear, at every jolt, the blood
Come gargling from the froth-corrupted lungs,
Bitter as the cud
Of vile, incurable sores on innocent tongues,—
My friend, you would not tell with such high zest
To children ardent for some desperate glory,
The old Lie: Dulce et decorum est
pro patria mori.

* * *

There is a difficulty about drawing from all this a moral for ourselves. I
imagine that we agree in our rejection of slavery, eternal damnation,
genocide, and uncritical patriotic self-abnegation; so we shall agree that
Huck Finn, Jonathan Edwards, Heinrich Himmler, and the poet Horace
would all have done well to bring certain of their principles under severe
pressure from ordinary human sympathies. But then we can say this
because we can say that all those are bad moralities, whereas we cannot
look at our own moralities and declare them bad. This is not arrogance: it
is obviously incoherent for someone to declare the system of moral principles that he *accepts* to be *bad*, just as one cannot coherently say of anything that one *believes* it but it is *false*.

Still, although I can't point to any of my beliefs and say 'That is false', I
don't doubt that some of my beliefs *are* false; and so I should try to
remain open to correction. Similarly, I accept every single item in my
morality—that is inevitable—but I am sure that my morality could be
improved, which is to say that it could undergo changes which I should
be glad of once I had made them. So I must try to keep my morality open
to revision, exposing it to whatever valid pressures there are—including
pressures from my sympathies.

I don't give my sympathies a blank cheque in advance. In a conflict
between principle and sympathy, principles ought sometimes to win. For
example, I think it was right to take part in the Second World War on the
allied side; there were many ghastly individual incidents which might
have led someone to doubt the rightness of his participation in that war;
and I think it would have been right for such a person to keep his
sympathies in a subordinate place on those occasions, not allowing them
to modify his principles in such a way as to make a pacifist of him.

Still, one's sympathies should be kept as sharp and sensitive and aware as possible, and not only because they can sometimes affect one's principles or one's conduct or both. Owen, at any rate, says that feelings and sympathies are vital even when they can do nothing but bring pain and distress. In another poem he speaks of the blessings of being numb in one's feelings: 'Happy are the men who yet before they are killed/Can let their veins run cold,' he says. These are the ones who do not suffer from any compassion which, as Owen puts it, 'makes their feet/Sore on the alleys cobbled with their brothers.' He contrasts these 'happy' ones, who 'lose all imagination', with himself and others 'who with a thought besmirch/Blood over all our soul.' Yet the poem's verdict goes against the 'happy' ones. Owen does not say that they will act worse than the others whose souls are besmirched with blood because of their keen awareness of human suffering. He merely says that they are the losers because they have cut themselves off from the human condition:

By choice they made themselves immune
To pity and whatever moans in man
Before the last sea and the hapless stars;
Whatever mourns when many leave these shores;
Whatever shares
The eternal reciprocity of tears.[6]

NOTES

1. M. J. Sidnell, 'Huck Finn and Jim', *The Cambridge Quarterly*, vol. 2, pp. 205–206.

2. Quoted in William L. Shirer, *The Rise and Fall of the Third Reich* (New York, 1960), pp. 937–938. Next quotation: Ibid., p. 966. All further quotations relating to Himmler are from Roger Manwell and Heinrich Fraenkel, *Heinrich Himmler* (London, 1965), pp. 132, 197, 184 (twice), 187.

3. Vergilius Ferm (ed.), *Puritan Sage: Collected Writings of Jonathan Edwards* (New York, 1953), p. 370. Next three quotations: Ibid, p. 366, p. 294 ('no more than infinite'), p. 372.

4. This and the next two quotations are from 'The End of the Wicked Contemplated by the Righteous: or, The Torments of the Wicked in Hell, no Occasion of Grief to the Saints in Heaven', from *The Works of President Edwards* (London, 1817), vol. IV, pp. 507–508, 511–512, and 509 respectively.

5. I am grateful to the Executors of the Estate of Harold Owen, and to Chatto and Windus Ltd., for permission to quote from Wilfred Owen's 'Dulce et Decorum Est' and 'Insensibility'.

6. This paper began life as the Potter Memorial Lecture, given at Washington State University in Pullman, Washington, in 1972.

SOME PARADOXES OF DETERRENCE*

Gregory S. Kavka

Deterrence is a parent of paradox. Conflict theorists, notably Thomas Schelling, have pointed out several paradoxes of deterrence: that it may be to the advantage of someone who is trying to deter another to be irrational, to have fewer available options, or to lack relevant information.[1] I shall describe certain new paradoxes that emerge when one attempts to analyze deterrence from a moral rather than a strategic perspective. These paradoxes are presented in the form of statements that appear absurd or incredible on first inspection, but can be supported by quite convincing arguments.

Consider a typical situation involving deterrence. A potential wrong-doer is about to commit an offense that would unjustly harm someone. A defender intends, and threatens, to retaliate should the wrongdoer commit the offense. Carrying out retaliation, if the offense is committed, could well be morally wrong. (The wrongdoer could be insane, or the retaliation could be out of proportion with the offense, or could seriously harm others besides the wrongdoer.) The moral paradoxes of deterrence arise out of the attempt to determine the moral status of the defender's *intention* to retaliate in such cases. If the defender knows retaliation to be wrong, it would appear that this intention is evil. Yet such "evil" intentions may pave the road to heaven, by preventing serious offenses and by doing so without actually harming anyone.

Scrutiny of such morally ambiguous retaliatory intentions reveals paradoxes that call into question certain significant and widely accepted moral doctrines. These doctrines are what I call *bridge principles*. They attempt to link together the moral evaluation of actions and the moral evaluation of agents (and their states) in certain simple and apparently natural ways. The general acceptance, and intuitive appeal, of such principles, lends credibility to the project of constructing a consistent moral system that accurately reflects our firmest moral beliefs about both agents and actions. By raising doubts about the validity of certain popular bridge principles, the paradoxes presented here pose new difficulties for this important project.

*An earlier version of this paper was presented at Stanford University. I am grateful to several, especially Robert Merrihew Adams, Tyler Burge, Warren Quinn, and Virginia Warren, for helpful comments on previous drafts. My work was supported, in part, by a Regents' Faculty Research Fellowship from the University of California.

I

In this section, a certain class of situations involving deterrence is characterized, and a plausible normative assumption is presented. In the following three sections, we shall see how application of this assumption to these situations yields paradoxes.

The class of paradox-producing situations is best introduced by means of an example. Consider the balance of nuclear terror as viewed from the perspective of one of its superpower participants, nation N. N sees the threat of nuclear retaliation as its only reliable means of preventing nuclear attack (or nuclear blackmail leading to world domination) by its superpower rival. N is confident such a threat will succeed in deterring its adversary, provided it really intends to carry out that threat. (N fears that, if it bluffs, its adversary is likely to learn this through leaks or espionage.) Finally, N recognizes it would have conclusive moral reasons *not* to carry out the threatened retaliation, if its opponent were to obliterate N with a surprise attack. For although retaliation would punish the leaders who committed this unprecedented crime and would prevent them from dominating the postwar world, N knows it would also destroy many millions of innocent civilians in the attacking nation (and in other nations), would set back postwar economic recovery for the world immeasurably, and might add enough fallout to the atmosphere to destroy the human race.

Let us call situations of the sort that nation N perceives itself as being in, *Special Deterrent Situations* (SDSs). More precisely, an agent is in an SDS when he reasonably and correctly believes that the following conditions hold. First, it is likely he must intend (conditionally) to apply a harmful sanction to innocent people, if an extremely harmful and unjust offense is to be prevented. Second, such an intention would very likely deter the offense. Third, the amounts of harm involved in the offense and the threatened sanction are very large and of roughly similar quantity (or the latter amount is smaller than the former). Finally, he would have conclusive moral reasons not to apply the sanction if the offense were to occur.

The first condition in this definition requires some comment. Deterrence depends only on the potential wrongdoer's *beliefs* about the prospects of the sanction being applied. Hence, the first condition will be satisfied only if attempts by the defender to bluff would likely be perceived as such by the wrongdoer. This may be the case if the defender is an unconvincing liar, or is a group with a collective decision procedure, or if the wrongdoer is shrewd and knows the defender quite well. Generally, however, bluffing will be a promising course of action. Hence, although it is surely logically and physically possible for an SDS to occur, there will be few actual SDSs. It may be noted, though, that writers on strategic policy frequently assert that nuclear deterrence will be effective only if the defending nation really intends to retaliate.[2] If this is so, the balance of terror may fit the definition of an SDS, and the paradoxes developed here could have significant practical implications.[3] Further, were there no actual SDSs, these paradoxes would still be of considerable theoretical interest. For they indicate that the validity of some widely accepted moral doctrines rests on the presupposition that certain situations that could arise (i.e., SDSs) will not.

Turning to our normative assumption, we begin by noting that any reasonable system of ethics must have substantial utilitarian elements. The assumption that produces the paradoxes of deterrence concerns the role of utilitarian considerations in determining one's moral duty in a narrowly limited class of situations. Let the *most useful* act in a given choice situation be that with the highest expected utility. Our assumption says that the most useful act should be performed whenever a very great deal of utility is at stake. This means that, if the difference in expected utility between the most useful act and its alternatives is extremely large (e.g., equivalent to the difference between life and death for a very large number of people), other moral considerations are overridden by utilitarian considerations.

This assumption may be substantially weakened by restricting in various ways its range of application. I restrict the assumption to apply only when (i) a great deal of *negative* utility is at stake, and (ii) people will likely suffer serious injustices if the agent fails to perform the most useful act. This makes the assumption more plausible, since the propriety of doing one person a serious injustice, in order to produce positive benefits for others, is highly questionable. The justifiability of doing the same injustice to prevent a utilitarian disaster which itself involves grave injustices, seems more in accordance with our moral intuitions.

The above restrictions appear to bring our assumption into line with the views of philosophers such as Robert Nozick, Thomas Nagel, and Richard Brandt, who portray moral rules as "absolutely" forbidding certain kinds of acts, but acknowledge that exceptions might have to be allowed in cases in which such acts are necessary to prevent catastrophe.[4] Even with these restrictions, however, the proposed assumption would be rejected by supporters of genuine Absolutism, the doctrine that there are certain acts (such as vicarious punishment and deliberate killing of the innocent) that are always wrong, whatever the consequences of not performing them. (Call such acts *inherently evil*.) We can, though, accommodate the Absolutists. To do so, let us further qualify our assumption by limiting its application to cases in which (iii) performing the most useful act involves, at most, a small *risk* of performing an inherently evil act. With this restriction, the assumption still leads to paradoxes, yet is consistent with Absolutism (unless that doctrine is extended to include absolute prohibitions on something other than doing acts of the sort usually regarded as inherently evil).[5] The triply qualified assumption is quite plausible; so the fact that it produces paradoxes is both interesting and disturbing.

II

The first moral paradox of deterrence is:

(P1)   There are cases in which, although it would be wrong for an agent to perform a certain act in a certain situation, it would nonetheless be right for him, knowing this, to form the intention to perform that act in that situation.

At first, this strikes one as absurd. If it is wrong and he is aware that it is wrong, how could it be right for him to form the intention to do it? (P1) is the direct denial of a simple moral thesis, the Wrongful Intentions Principle (WIP): *To intend to do what one knows to be wrong is itself wrong.*[6] WIP seems so obvious that, although philosophers never call it into question, they rarely bother to assert it or argue for it. Nevertheless, it appears that Abelard, Aquinas, Butler, Bentham, Kant, and Sidgwick, as well as recent writers such as Anthony Kenny and Jan Narveson, have accepted the principle, at least implicitly.[7]

Why does WIP seem so obviously true? First, we regard the man who fully intends to perform a wrongful act and is prevented from doing so solely by external circumstances (e.g., a man whose murder plan is interrupted by the victim's fatal heart attack) as being just as bad as the man who performs a like wrongful act. Second, we view the man who intends to do what is wrong, and then changes his mind, as having corrected a moral failing or error. Third, it is convenient, for many purposes, to treat a prior intention to perform an act, as the beginning of the act itself. Hence, we are inclined to view intentions as parts of actions and to ascribe to each intention the moral status ascribed to the act "containing" it.

It is essential to note that WIP appears to apply to conditional intentions in the same manner as it applies to nonconditional ones. Suppose I form the intention to kill my neighbor if he insults me again, and fail to kill him only because, fortuitously, he refrains from doing so. I am as bad, or nearly as bad, as if he had insulted me and I had killed him. My failure to perform the act no more erases the wrongness of my intention, than my neighbor's dropping dead as I load my gun would negate the wrongness of the simple intention to kill him. Thus the same considerations adduced above in support of WIP seem to support the formulation: If it would be wrong to perform an act in certain circumstances, then it is wrong to intend to perform that act on the condition that those circumstances arise.

Having noted the source of the strong feeling that (P1) should be rejected, we must consider an instantiation of (P1):

(P1′) In an SDS, it would be wrong for the defender to apply the sanction if the wrongdoer were to commit the offense, but it is right for the defender to form the (conditional) intention to apply the sanction if the wrongdoer commits the offense.

The first half of (P1′), the wrongness of applying the sanction, follows directly from the last part of the definition of an SDS, which says that the defender would have conclusive moral reasons not to apply the sanction. The latter half of (P1′), which asserts the rightness of forming the intention to apply the sanction, follows from the definition of an SDS and our normative assumption. According to the definition, the defender's forming this intention is likely necessary, and very likely sufficient, to prevent a seriously harmful and unjust offense. Further, the offense and the sanction would each produce very large and roughly commensurate amounts of negative utility (or the latter would produce a smaller amount). It follows that utilitarian considerations heavily favor forming the intention to apply the sanction, and that doing so involves only a small risk of performing an inherently evil act.[8] Applying our normative assumption yields the conclusion that it is right for the defender to form the intention in question.

This argument, if sound, would establish the truth of (P1′), and hence (P1), in contradiction with WIP. It suggests that WIP should not be applied to *deterrent intentions*, i.e., those conditional intentions whose existence is based on the agent's desire to thereby deter others from actualizing the antecedent condition of the intention. Such intentions are rather strange. They are, by nature, self-stultifying: if a deterrent intention fulfills the agent's purpose, it ensures that the intended (and possibly evil) act is not performed, by preventing the circumstances of performance from arising. The unique nature of such intentions can be further explicated by noting the distinction between intending to do something, and desiring (or intending) to intend to do it. Normally, an agent will form the intention to do something because he either desires doing that thing as an end in itself, or as a means to other ends. In such cases, little importance attaches to the distinction between intending and desiring to intend. But, in the case of deterrent intentions, the ground of the desire to form the intention is entirely distinct from any desire to carry it out. Thus, what may be inferred about the agent who seeks to form such an intention is this. He desires *having the intention* as a means of deterrence. Also, he is willing, in order to prevent the offense, to accept a certain *risk* that, in the end, he will apply the sanction. But this is entirely consistent with his having a strong desire not to apply the sanction, and no desire at all to apply it. Thus, while the object of his deterrent intention might be an evil act, it does not follow that, in desiring to adopt that intention, he desires to do evil, either as an end or as a means.

WIP ties the morality of an intention exclusively to the moral qualities of its object (i.e., the intended act). This is not unreasonable since, typi-

408   Gregory S. Kavka

cally, the only significant effects of intentions are the acts of the agent (and the consequences of these acts) which flow from these intentions. However, in certain cases, intentions may have *autonomous effects* that are independent of the intended act's actually being performed. In particular, intentions to act may influence the conduct of other agents. When an intention has important autonomous effects, these effects must be incorporated into any adequate moral analysis of it. The first paradox arises because the autonomous effects of the relevant deterrent intention are dominant in the moral analysis of an SDS, but the extremely plausible WIP ignores such effects.[9]

III

(P1') implies that a rational moral agent in an SDS should want to form the conditional intention to apply the sanction if the offense is committed, in order to deter the offense. But will he be able to do so? Paradoxically, he will not be. He is a captive in the prison of his own virtue, able to form the requisite intention only by bending the bars of his cell out of shape. Consider the preliminary formulation of this new paradox:

(P2')   In an SDS, a rational and morally good agent cannot (as a matter of logic) have (or form) the intention to apply the sanction if the offense is committed.[10]

The argument for (P2') is as follows. An agent in an SDS recognizes that there would be conclusive moral reasons not to apply the sanction if the offense were committed. If he does not regard these admittedly conclusive moral reasons as conclusive reasons for him not to apply the sanction, then he is not moral. Suppose, on the other hand, that he does regard himself as having conclusive reasons not to apply the sanction if the offense is committed. If, nonetheless, he is disposed to apply it, because the reasons for applying it motivate him more strongly than do the conclusive reasons not to apply it, then he is irrational.

But couldn't our rational moral agent recognize, in accordance with (P1'), that he ought to form the intention to apply the sanction? And couldn't he then simply grit his teeth and pledge to himself that he will apply the sanction if the offense is committed? No doubt he could, and this would amount to trying to form the intention to apply the sanction. But the question remains whether he can succeed in forming that intention, by this or any other process, while remaining rational and moral. And it appears he cannot. There are, first of all, psychological difficulties. Being rational, how can he dispose himself to do something that he knows he would have conclusive reasons not to do, when and if the time comes to do it? Perhaps, though, some exceptional people can produce in themselves dispositions to act merely by pledging to act. But even if one could, in an SDS, produce a disposition to apply the sanction in this manner, such a disposition would not count as a *rational intention* to apply the sanction. This is because, as recent writers on intentions have suggested, it is part of the concept of rationally intending to do something, that the disposition to do the intended act be caused (or justified) in an appropriate way by the agent's view of reasons for doing the act.[11] And the disposition in question does not stand in such a relation to the agent's reasons for action.

It might be objected to this that people sometimes intend to do things (and do them) for no reason at all, without being irrational. This is true, and indicates that the connections between the concepts of intending and reasons for action are not so simple as the above formula implies. But it is also true that intending to do something for no reason at all, in the face of recognized significant reasons not to do it, would be irrational. Similarly, a disposition to act in the face of the acknowledged preponderance of reasons, whether called an "intention" or not, could not qualify as rational. It may be claimed that such a disposition, in an SDS, is rational in the sense that the agent knows it would further his aims to form (and have) it. This is not to deny the second paradox, but simply to express one of its paradoxical features. For the point of (P2') is that the very disposition that *is* rational in the sense just mentioned, is at the same time irrational in an equally important sense. It is a disposition to act in conflict with the agent's own view of the balance of reasons for action.

We can achieve some insight into this by noting that an intention that is deliberately formed, resides at the intersection of two distinguishable actions. It is the beginning of the act that is its object and is the end of the act that is its formation. As such, it may be assessed as rational (or moral) or not, according to whether either of two different acts promotes the agent's (or morality's) ends. Generally, the assessments will agree. But, as Schelling and others have noted, it may sometimes promote one's aims *not* to be disposed to act to promote one's aims should certain contingencies arise. For example, a small country may deter invasion by a larger country if it is disposed to resist any invasion, even when resistance would be suicidal. In such situations, the assessment of the rationality (or morality) of the agent's intentions will depend upon whether these intentions are treated as components of their object-acts or their formation-acts. If treated as both, conflicts can occur. It is usual and proper to assess the practical rationality of an agent, at a given time, according to the degree of correspondence between his intentions and the reasons he has for performing the acts that are the objects of those intentions. As a result, puzzles such as (P2') emerge when, for purposes of moral analysis, an agent's intentions are viewed partly as components of their formation-acts.

Let us return to the main path of our discussion by briefly summarizing the argument for (P2'). A morally good agent regards conclusive moral reasons for action as conclusive reasons for action *simpliciter*. But the intentions of a rational agent are not out of line with his assessment of the reasons for and against acting. Consequently, a rational moral agent cannot intend to do something that he recognizes there are conclusive moral reasons not to do. Nor can he intend conditionally to do what he recognizes he would have conclusive reasons not to do were that condition to be fulfilled. Therefore, in an SDS, where one has conclusive moral reasons not to apply the sanction, an originally rational and moral agent cannot have the intention to apply it without ceasing to be fully rational or moral; nor can he form the intention (as this entails having it).

We have observed that forming an intention is a process that may generally be regarded as an action. Thus, the second paradox can be reformulated as:

(P2)   There are situations (namely SDSs) in which it would be right for agents to perform certain actions (namely forming the intention to apply the sanction) and in which it is possible for some agents to perform such actions, but impossible for rational and morally good agents to perform them.

(P2), with the exception of the middle clause, is derived from the conjunction of (P1') and (P2') by existential generalization. The truth of the middle clause follows from consideration of the vengeful agent, who desires to punish those who commit seriously harmful and unjust offenses, no matter what the cost to others.

(P2) is paradoxical because it says that there are situations in which rationality and virtue preclude the possibility of right action. And this contravenes our usual assumption about the close logical ties between the concepts of right action and agent goodness. Consider the following claim. *Doing something is right if and only if a morally good man would do the same thing in the given situation.* Call this the Right-Good Principle. One suspects that, aside from qualifications concerning the good man's possible imperfections or factual ignorance, most people regard this principle, which directly contradicts (P2), as being virtually analytic. Yet the plight of the good man described in the second paradox does not arise out of an insufficiency of either knowledge or goodness. (P2) says there are conceivable situations in which virtue and knowledge combine with rationality to preclude right action, in which virtue is an obstacle to doing the right thing. If (P2) is true, our views about the close logical connection between right action and agent goodness, as embodied in the Right-Good Principle, require modifications of a sort not previously envisioned.

IV

A rational moral agent in an SDS faces a cruel dilemma. His reasons for intending to apply the sanction if the offense is committed are, according to (P1'), conclusive. But they outrun his reasons for doing it. Wishing to do what is right, he wants to form the intention. However, unless he can substantially alter the basic facts of the situation or his beliefs about those facts, he can do so only by making himself less morally good; that is, by becoming a person who attaches grossly mistaken weights to certain reasons for and against action (e.g., one who prefers retribution to the protection of the vital interests of innocent people).[12] We have arrived at a third paradox:

(P3)   In certain situations, it would be morally right for a rational and morally good agent to deliberately (attempt to) corrupt himself.[13]

(P3) may be viewed in light of a point about the credibility of threats which has been made by conflict theorists. Suppose a defender is worried about the credibility of his deterrent threat, because he thinks the wrongdoer (rightly) regards him as unwilling to apply the threatened sanction. He may make the threat more credible by passing control of the sanction to some *retaliation-agent*. Conflict theorists consider two sorts of retaliation-agents: people known to be highly motivated to punish the offense in question, and machines programmed to retaliate automatically if the offense occurs. What I wish to note is that future selves of the defender himself are a third class of retaliation-agents. If the other kinds are unavailable, a defender may have to create an agent of this third sort (i.e., an altered self willing to apply the sanction), in order to deter the offense. In cases in which applying the sanction would be wrong, this could require self-corruption.

How would a rational and moral agent in an SDS, who seeks to have the intention to apply the sanction, go about corrupting himself so that he may have it? He cannot form the intention simply by pledging to apply the sanction; for, according to the second paradox, his rationality and morality preclude this. Instead, he must seek to initiate a causal process (e.g., a reeducation program) that he hopes will result in his beliefs, attitudes, and values changing in such a way that he can and will have the intention to apply the sanction should the offense be committed. Initiating such a process involves taking a rather odd, though not uncommon attitude toward oneself: viewing oneself as an object to be molded in certain respects by outside influences rather than by inner choices. This is, for example, the attitude of the lazy but ambitious student who enrolls in a fine college, hoping that some of the habits and values of his highly motivated fellow students will "rub off" on him.

We can now better understand the notion of "risking doing X" which was introduced in section *I*. For convenience, let "X" be "killing." Deliberately risking killing is different from risking deliberately killing. One does the former when one rushes an ill person to the hospital in one's car at unsafe speed, having noted the danger of causing a fatal accident. One has deliberately accepted the risk of killing by accident. One (knowingly) risks deliberately killing, on the other hand, when one undertakes a course of action that one knows may, by various causal processes, lead to one's later performing a deliberate killing. The mild-mannered youth who joins a violent street gang is an example. Similarly, the agent in an SDS, who undertakes a plan of self-corruption in order to develop the requisite deterrent intention, knowlingly risks deliberately performing the wrongful act of applying the sanction.

The above description of what is required of the rational moral agent in an SDS, leads to a natural objection to the argument that supports (P3). According to this objection, an attempt at self-corruption by a rational moral agent is very likely to fail. Hence, bluffing would surely be a more promising strategy for deterrence than trying to form retaliatory intentions by self-corruption. Three replies may be given to this objection. First, it is certainly *conceivable* that, in a particular SDS, undertaking a process of self-corruption would be more likely to result in effective deterrence than would bluffing. Second, and more important, bluffing and attempting to form retaliatory intentions by self-corruption will generally not be mutually exclusive alternatives. An agent in an SDS may attempt to form the retaliatory intention while bluffing, and plan to continue bluffing as a "fall-back" strategy, should he fail. If the offense to be prevented is disastrous enough, the additional expected utility generated by following such a combined strategy (as opposed to simply bluffing) will be very large, even if his attempts to form the intention are unlikely to succeed. Hence, (P3) would still follow from our normative assumption. Finally, consider the rational and *partly corrupt* agent in an SDS who already has the intention to retaliate. (The nations participating in the balance of terror may be examples.) The relevant question about him is whether he ought to act to become less corrupt, with the result that he would lose the intention to retaliate. The present objection does not apply in this case, since the agent already has the requisite corrupt features. Yet, essentially the same argument that produces (P3) leads, when this case is considered, to a slightly different, but equally puzzling, version of our third paradox:

(P3*)   In certain situations, it would be morally wrong for a rational and partly corrupt agent to (attempt to) reform himself and eliminate his corruption.

A rather different objection to (P3) is the claim that its central notion is incoherent. This claim is made, apparently, by Thomas Nagel, who writes:

The notion that one might sacrifice one's moral integrity justifiably, in the service of a sufficiently worthy end, is an incoherent notion. For if one were justified in making such a sacrifice (or even morally required to make it), then one would not be sacrificing one's moral integrity by adopting that course: one would be preserving it (132/3).

Now the notion of a justified sacrifice of moral virtue (integrity) would be incoherent, as Nagel suggests, if one could sacrifice one's virtue only by doing something wrong. For the same act cannot be both morally justified and morally wrong. But one may also be said to sacrifice one's virtue when one deliberately initiates a causal process that one expects to result, and does result, in one's later becoming a less virtuous person. And, as the analysis of SDSs embodied in (P1′) and (P2′) implies, one may, in certain cases, be justified in initiating such a process (or even be obligated to initiate it). Hence, it would be a mistake to deny (P3) on the grounds advanced in Nagel's argument.

There is, though, a good reason for *wanting* to reject (P3). It conflicts with some of our firmest beliefs about virtue and duty. We regard the promotion and preservation of one's own virtue as a vital responsibility of each moral agent, and self-corruption as among the vilest of enterprises. Further, we do not view the duty to promote one's virtue as simply one duty among others, to be weighed and balanced against the rest, but rather as a special duty that encompasses the other moral duties. Thus, we assent to the Virtue Preservation Principle: *It is wrong to deliberately lose (or reduce the degree of) one's moral virtue.* To many, this principle seems fundamental to our very conception of morality.[14] Hence the suggestion that duty could require the abandonment of virtue seems quite unacceptable. The fact that this suggestion can be supported by strong arguments produces a paradox.

This paradox is reflected in the ambivalent attitudes that emerge when we attempt to evaluate three hypothetical agents who respond to the demands of SDSs in various ways. The first agent refuses to try to corrupt himself and allows the disastrous offense to occur. We respect the love of virtue he displays, but are inclined to suspect him of too great a devotion to his own purity relative to his concern for the well-being of others. The second agent does corrupt himself to prevent disaster in an SDS. Though we do not approve of his new corrupt aspects, we admire the person that he *was* for his willingness to sacrifice what he loved—part of his own virtue—in the service of others. At the same time, the fact that he succeeded in corrupting himself may make us wonder whether he was entirely virtuous in the first place. Corruption, we feel, does not come easily to a good man. The third agent reluctantly but sincerely tries his best to corrupt himself to prevent disaster, but fails. He may be admired both for his willingness to make such a sacrifice and for having virtue so deeply engrained in his character that his attempts at self-corruption do not succeed. It is perhaps characteristic of the paradoxical nature of the envisioned situation, that we are inclined to admire most the only one of these three agents who fails in the course of action he undertakes.

V

It is natural to think of the evaluation of agents, and of actions, as being two sides of the same moral coin. The moral paradoxes of deterrence suggest they are more like two separate coins that can be fused

together only by significantly deforming one or the other. In this concluding section, I shall briefly explain this.

Our shared assortment of moral beliefs may be viewed as consisting of
three relatively distinct groups: beliefs about the evaluation of actions,
beliefs about the evaluation of agents and their states (e.g., motives,
intentions, and character traits), and beliefs about the relationship between the two. An important part of this last group of beliefs is represented by the three bridge principles introduced above: the Wrongful
Intentions, Right-Good, and Virtue Preservation principles. Given an
agreed-upon set of bridge principles, one could go about constructing a
moral system meant to express coherently our moral beliefs in either of
two ways: by developing principles that express our beliefs about act
evaluation and then using the bridge principles to derive principles of
agent evaluation—or vice versa. If our bridge principles are sound and
our beliefs about agent and act evaluation are mutually consistent, the
resulting systems would, in theory, be the same. If, however, there are
underlying incompatibilities between the principles we use to evaluate
acts and agents, there may be significant differences between moral systems that are *act-oriented* and those which are *agent-oriented*. And these
differences may manifest themselves as paradoxes which exert pressure
upon the bridge principles that attempt to link the divergent systems, and
the divergent aspects of each system, together.

It seems natural to us to evaluate acts at least partly in terms of their
consequences. Hence, act-oriented moral systems tend to involve significant utilitarian elements. The principle of act evaluation usually employed
in utilitarian systems is: in a given situation, one ought to perform the
most useful act, that which will (or is expected to) produce the most
utility. What will maximize utility depends upon the facts of the particular situation. Hence, as various philosophers have pointed out, the above
principle could conceivably recommend one's (i) acting from nonutilitarian motives, (ii) advocating some nonutilitarian moral theory, or even (iii)
becoming a genuine adherent of some nonutilitarian theory.[15] Related
quandaries arise when one considers, from an act-utilitarian viewpoint,
the deterrent intention of a defender in an SDS. Here is an intention
whose object-act is anti-utilitarian and whose formation-act is a utilitarian
duty that cannot be performed by a rational utilitarian.

A utilitarian might seek relief from these quandaries in either of two
ways. First, he could defend some form of rule-utilitarianism. But then he
would face a problem. Shall he include, among the rules of his system,
our normative assumption that requires the performance of the most
useful act, whenever an enormous amount of utility is at stake (and
certain other conditions are satisfied)? If he does, the moral paradoxes of
deterrence will appear within his system. If he does not, it would seem
that his system fails to attach the importance to the consequences of
particular momentous acts that any reasonable moral, much less utilitar-

ian, system should. An alternative reaction would be to stick by the utilitarian principle of act evaluation, and simply accept (P1)−(P3), and related oddities, as true. Taking this line would require the abandonment of the plausible and familiar bridge principles that contradict (P1)−(P3). But this need not bother the act-utilitarian, who perceives his task as the modification, as well as codification, of our moral beliefs.

Agent-oriented (as opposed to act-oriented) moral systems rest on the premise that what primarily matters for morality are the internal states of a person: his character traits, his intentions, and the condition of his will. The doctrines about intentions and virtue expressed in our three bridge principles are generally incorporated into such systems. The paradoxes of deterrence may pose serious problems for some agent-oriented systems. It may be, for example, that an adequate analysis of the moral virtues of justice, selflessness, and benevolence, would imply that the truly virtuous man would feel obligated to make whatever personal sacrifice is necessary to prevent a catastrophe. If so, the moral paradoxes of deterrence would arise within agent-oriented systems committed to these virtues.

There are, however, agent-oriented systems that would not be affected by our paradoxes. One such system could be called Extreme Kantianism. According to this view, the only things having moral significance are such features of a person as his character and the state of his will. The Extreme Kantian accepts Kant's dictum that morality requires treating oneself and others as ends rather than means. He interprets this to imply strict duties to preserve one's virtue and not to deliberately impose serious harms or risks on innocent people. Thus, the Extreme Kantian would simply reject (P1)−(P3) without qualm.

Although act-utilitarians and Extreme Kantians can view the paradoxes of deterrence without concern, one doubts that the rest of us can. The adherents of these extreme conceptions of morality are untroubled by the paradoxes because their viewpoints are too one-sided to represent our moral beliefs accurately. Each of them is closely attentive to certain standard principles of agent *or* act evaluation, but seems too little concerned with traditional principles of the other sort. For a system of morality to reflect our firmest and deepest convictions adequately, it must represent a middle ground between these extremes by seeking to accommodate the valid insights of both act-oriented and agent-oriented perspectives. The normative assumption set out in section *I* was chosen as a representative principle that might be incorporated into such a system. It treats utilitarian considerations as relevant and potentially decisive, while allowing for the importance of other factors. Though consistent with the absolute prohibition of certain sorts of acts, it treats the distinction between harms and risks as significant and rules out absolute prohibitions on the latter as unreasonable. It is an extremely plausible middle-ground principle; but, disturbingly, it leads to paradoxes.

That these paradoxes reflect conflicts between commonly accepted principles of agent and act evaluation, is further indicated by the following observation. Consider what initially appears a natural way of viewing the evaluation of acts and agents as coordinated parts of a single moral system. According to this view, reasons for action determine the moral status of acts, agents, and intentions. A right act is an act that accords with the preponderance of moral reasons for action. To have the right intention is to be disposed to perform the act supported by the preponderance of such reasons, because of those reasons. The virtuous agent is the rational agent who has the proper substantive values, i.e., the person whose intentions and actions accord with the preponderance of moral reasons for action. Given these considerations, it appears that it should always be possible for an agent to go along intending, and acting, in accordance with the preponderance of moral reasons; thus ensuring both his own virtue and the rightness of his intentions and actions. Unfortunately, this conception of harmonious coordination between virtue, right intention, and right action, is shown to be untenable by the paradoxes of deterrence. For they demonstrate that, in any system that takes consequences plausibly into account, situations can arise in which the rational use of moral principles leads to certain paradoxical recommendations: that the principles used, and part of the agent's virtue, be abandoned, and that wrongful intentions be formed.

One could seek to avoid these paradoxes by moving in the direction of Extreme Kantianism and rejecting our normative assumption. But to do so would be to overlook the plausible core of act-utilitarianism. This is the claim that, in the moral evaluation of acts, how those acts affect human happiness often is important—the more so as more happiness is at stake—and sometimes is decisive. Conversely, one could move toward accommodation with act-utilitarianism. This would involve qualifying, so that they do not apply in SDSs, the traditional moral doctrines that contradict (P1)–(P3). And, in fact, viewed in isolation, the considerations adduced in section II indicate that the Wrongful Intentions Principle ought to be so qualified. However, the claims of (P2) and (P3): that virtue may preclude right action and that morality may require self-corruption, are not so easily accepted. These notions remain unpalatable even when one considers the arguments that support them.

Thus, tinkering with our normative assumption or with traditional moral doctrines would indeed enable us to avoid the paradoxes, at least in their present form. But his would require rejecting certain significant and deeply entrenched beliefs concerning the evaluation either of agents or of actions. Hence, such tinkering would not go far toward solving the fundamental problem of which the paradoxes are symptoms: the apparent incompatibility of the moral principles we use to evaluate acts and agents. Perhaps this problem can be solved. Perhaps the coins of agent and act evaluation can be successfully fused. But it is not apparent how this is to be done. And I, for one, do not presently see an entirely satisfactory way out of the perplexities that the paradoxes engender.

NOTES

1. *The Strategy of Conflict* (New York: Oxford, 1960), Chaps. 1–2; and *Arms and Influence* (New Haven, Conn.: Yale, 1966), chap. 2.

2. See, e.g., Herman Kahn, *On Thermonuclear War*, 2nd ed. (Princeton, N.J.: University Press, 1960), p. 185; and Anthony Kenny, "Counterforce and Countervalue," in Walter Stein, ed., *Nuclear Weapons: A Catholic Response* (London: Merlin Press, 1965), pp. 162–164.

3. See, e.g., n. 9, below.

4. Nozick, *Anarchy, State, and Utopia* (New York: Basic Books, 1974), pp.30/1 n; Nagel, "War and Massacre," *Philosophy and Public Affairs*, I, 2 (Winter 1972): 123–144, p. 126; Brandt, "Utilitarianism and the Rules of War," *ibid.*, 145–165, p. 147, especially n. 3.

5. Extensions of Absolutism that would block some or all the paradoxes include those which forbid intending to do what is wrong, deliberately making oneself less virtuous, or intentionally risking performing an inherently evil act. (An explanation of the relevant sense of 'risking performing an act' will be offered in section IV.)

6. I assume henceforth that, if it would be wrong to do something, the agent knows this. (The agent, discussed in section IV, who has become corrupt may be an exception). This keeps the discussion of the paradoxes from getting tangled up with the separate problem of whether an agent's duty is to do what is actually right, or what he believes is right.

7. See *Peter Abelard's Ethics*, D. E. Luscombe, trans. (New York: Oxford, 1971), pp. 5–37; Thomas Aquinas, *Summa Theologica*, 1a2ae. 18–20; Joseph Butler, "A Dissertation on the Nature of Virtue," in *Five Sermons* (Indianapolis: Bobbs-Merrill, 1950), p. 83; Immanuel Kant, *Foundations of the Metaphysics of Morals*, first section; Jeremy Bentham, *An Introduction to the Principles of Morals and Legislation*, chap. 9, secs. 13–16; Henry Sidgwick, *The Methods of Ethics* (New York: Dover, 1907), pp. 60/1, 201–204; Kenny, pp. 159, 162; and Jan Narveson, *Morality and Utility* (Baltimore: Johns Hopkins, 1967), pp. 106–108.

8. A qualification is necessary. Although having the intention involves only a small risk of applying the threatened sanction to innocent people, it follows, from points made in section IV, that forming the intention might also involve risks of performing *other* inherently evil acts. Hence, what really follows is that forming the intention is right in those SDSs in which the composite risk is small. This limitation in the scope of (P1') is to be henceforth understood. It does not affect (P1), (P2), or (P3), since each is governed by an existential quantifier.

9. In *Nuclear Weapons*, Kenny and others use WIP to argue that nuclear deterrence is immoral because it involves having the conditional intention to kill innocent people. The considerations advanced in this section suggest that this argument, at best, is inconclusive, since it presents only one side of a moral paradox, and, at worst, is mistaken, since it applies WIP in just the sort of situation in which its applicability is most questionable.

10. 'Rational and morally good' in this and later statements of the second and third paradoxes, means rational and moral in the given situation. A person who

usually is rational and moral, but fails to be in the situation in question, could, of course, have the intention to apply the sanction. (P2') is quite similar to a paradox concerning utilitarianism and deterrence developed by D. H. Hodgson in *Consequences of Utilitarianism* (Oxford: Clarendon Press, 1967), chap. 4.

11. See, e.g., S. Hampshire and H. L. A. Hart, "Decision, Intention and Certainty," *Mind*, LXVII.1, 265 (January 1958): 1–12; and G. E. M. Anscombe, *Intention* (Ithaca, N.Y.: Cornell, 1966).

12. Alternatively, the agent could undertake to make himself into an *irrational* person whose intentions are quite out of line with his reasons for action. However, trying to become irrational, in these circumstances, is less likely to succeed than trying to change one's moral beliefs, and, furthermore, might itself constitute self-corruption. Hence, this point does not affect the paradox stated below.

13. As Donald Regan has suggested to me, (P3) can be derived directly from our normative assumption: imagine a villain credibly threatening to kill very many hostages unless a certain good man corrupts himself. I prefer the indirect route to (P3) given in the text, because (P1) and (P2) are interesting in their own right and because viewing the three paradoxes together makes it easier to see what produces them.

14. Its supporters might, of course, allow exceptions to the principle in cases in which only the agent's feelings, and not his acts or dispositions to act, are corrupted. (For example, a doctor "corrupts himself" by suppressing normal sympathy for patients in unavoidable pain, in order to treat them more effectively.) Further, advocates of the doctrine of double-effect might consider self-corruption permissible when it is a "side effect" of action rather than a means to an end. For example, they might approve of a social worker's joining a gang to reform it, even though he expects to assimilate some of the gang's distorted values. Note, however, that neither of these possible exceptions to the Virtue Preservation Principle (brought to my attention by Robert Adams) applies to the agent in an SDS who corrupts his *intentions* as a chosen *means* of preventing an offense.

15. See Hodgson, *Consequences*. Also, Adams, "Motive Utilitarianism," this JOURNAL, LXXIII, 14 (Aug. 12, 1976): 467–81; and Bernard Williams, "A Critique of Utilitarianism," in J. J. C. Smart and Williams, *Utilitarianism: For and Against* (New York: Cambridge, 1973), sec. 6.

NICOMACHEAN ETHICS (EXCERPTS)

Aristotle

BOOK I

1 Every art and every inquiry, and similarly every action and pursuit, is thought to aim at some good; and for this reason the good has rightly been declared to be that at which all things aim. But a certain difference is found among ends; some are activities, others are products apart from the activities that produce them. Where there are ends apart from the actions, it is the nature of the products to be better than the activities. Now, as there are many actions, arts, and sciences, their ends also are many; the end of the medical art is health, that of shipbuilding a vessel, that of strategy victory, that of economics wealth. But where such arts fall under a single capacity—as bridle-making and the other arts concerned with the equipment of horses fall under the art of riding, and this and every military action under strategy, in the same way other arts fall under yet others—in all of these the ends of the master arts are to be preferred to all the subordinate ends; for it is for the sake of the former that the latter are pursued. It makes no difference whether the activities themselves are the ends of the actions, or something else apart from the activities, as in the case of the sciences just mentioned.

2 If, then, there is some end of the things we do, which we desire for its own sake (everything else being desired for the sake of this), and if we do not choose everything for the sake of something else (for at that rate the process would go on to infinity, so that our desire would be empty and vain), clearly this must be the good and the chief good. . . .

3 Our discussion will be adequate if it has as much clearness as the subject-matter admits of, for precision is not to be sought for alike in all discussions, any more than in all the products of the crafts. Now fine and just actions, which political science investigates, admit of much variety and fluctuation of opinion, so that they may be thought to exist only by convention, and not by nature. And goods also give rise to a similar fluctuation because they bring harm to many people; for before now men have been undone by reason of their wealth, and others by reason of their courage. We must be content, then, in speaking of such subjects and with such premises to indicate the truth roughly and in outline, and in speaking about things which are only for the most part true and with premises of the same kind to reach conclusions that are no better. In the same spirit, therefore, should each type of statement be *received;* for it is the mark of an educated man to look for precision in each class of things just so far as the nature of the subject admits; it is evidently equally foolish to accept probable reasoning from a mathematician and to demand from a rhetorician scientific proofs. . . .

4 Let us resume our inquiry and state, in view of the fact that all knowledge and every pursuit aims at some good, what is the highest of all good achievable by action. Verbally there is very general agreement; for both the general run of men and people of superior refinement say that it is happiness, and identify living well and doing well with being happy; but with regard to what happiness is they differ, and the many do not give the same account as the wise. For the former think it is some plain and obvious thing, like pleasure, wealth, or honour; they differ, however, from one another—and often even the same man identifies it with different things, with health when he is ill, with wealth when he is poor; but, conscious of their ignorance, they admire those who proclaim some great ideal that is above their comprehension. Now some thought that apart from these many goods there is another which is self-subsistent and causes the goodness of all these as well. To examine all the opinions that have been held were perhaps somewhat fruitless; enough to examine those that are most prevalent or that seem to be arguable. . . .

5 To judge from the lives that men lead, most men, and men of the most vulgar type, seem (not without some ground) to identify the good, or happiness, with pleasure; which is the reason why they love the life of enjoyment. For there are, we may say, three prominent types of life—that just mentioned, the political, and thirdly the contemplative life. Now the mass of mankind are evidently quite slavish in their tastes, preferring a life suitable to beasts, but they get some ground for their view from the fact that many of those in high places share the tastes of Sardanapallus. A consideration of the prominent types of life shows that people of superior refinement and of active disposition identify happiness with honour; for this is, roughly speaking, the end of the political life. But it seems too superficial to be what we are looking for, since it is thought to depend on those who bestow honour rather than on him who receives it, but the good we divine to be something proper to a man and not easily taken from him. Further, men seem to pursue honour in order that they may be assured of their goodness; at least it is by men of practical wisdom that they seek to be honoured, and among those who know them, and on the ground of their virtue; clearly, then, according to them, at any rate, virtue is better. And perhaps one might even suppose this to be, rather than honour, the end of the political life. But even this appears somewhat incomplete; for possession of virtue seems actually compatible with being asleep, or with lifelong inactivity, and, further, with the greatest sufferings and misfortunes; but a man who was living so no one would call happy, unless he were maintaining a thesis at all costs. But enough of this; for the subject has been sufficiently treated even in the current discussions. Third comes the contemplative life, which we shall consider later.

The life of money-making is one undertaken under compulsion, and wealth is evidently not the good we are seeking, for it is merely useful and for the sake of something else. And so one might rather take the aforenamed objects to be ends; for they are loved for themselves. But it is evident that not even these are ends; yet many arguments have been thrown away in support of them. Let us leave this subject, then. . . .

7 Let us again return to the good we are seeking, and ask what it can be. It seems different in different actions and arts; it is different in medicine, in strategy, and in the other arts likewise. What then is the good of each? Surely that for whose sake everything else is done. In medicine this is health, in strategy victory, in architecture a house, in any other sphere something else, and in every action and pursuit the end; for it is for the sake of this that all men do whatever else they do. Therefore, if there is an end for all that we do, this will be the good achievable by action, and if there are more than one, these will be the goods achievable by action.

So the argument has by a different course reached the same point; but we must try to state this even more clearly. Since there are evidently more than one end, and we choose some of these (e. g. wealth, flutes, and in general instruments) for the sake of something else, clearly not all ends are final ends; but the chief good is evidently something final. Therefore, if there is only one final end, this will be what we are seeking, and if there are more than one, the most final of these will be what we are seeking. Now we call that which is in itself worthy of pursuit more final than that which is worthy of pursuit for the sake of something else, and that which is never desirable for the sake of something else more final than the things that are desirable both in themselves and for the sake of that other thing, and therefore we call final without qualification that which is always desirable in itself and never for the sake of something else.

Now such a thing happiness, above all else, is held to be; for this we choose always for itself and never for the sake of something else, but honour, pleasure, reason, and every virtue we choose indeed for themselves (for if nothing resulted from them we should still choose each of them), but we choose them also for the sake of happiness, judging that by means of them we shall be happy. Happiness, on the other hand, no one chooses for the sake of these, nor, in general, for anything other than itself.

From the point of view of self-sufficiency the same result seems to follow; for the final good is thought to be self-sufficient. Now by self-sufficient we do not mean that which is sufficient for a man by himself, for one who lives a solitary life, but also for parents, children, wife, and in general for his friends and fellow citizens, since man is born for citizenship. But some limit must be set to this; for if we extend our requirement to ancestors and descendants and friends' friends we are in for an infinite series. Let us examine this question, however, on another occasion; the self-sufficient we now define as that which when isolated makes life desirable and lacking in nothing; and such we think happiness to be; and further we think it most desirable of all things, without being counted as one good thing among others—if it were so counted it would clearly be made more desirable by the addition of even the least of goods; for that which is added becomes an excess of goods, and of goods the greater is always more desirable. Happiness, then, is something final and self-sufficient, and is the end of action.

Presumably, however, to say that happiness is the chief good seems a platitude, and a clearer account of what it is is still desired. This might perhaps be given, if we could first ascertain the function of man. For just as for a flute-player, a sculptor, or any artist, and, in general, for all things that have a function or activity, the good and the 'well' is thought to reside in the function, so would it seem to be for man, if he has a function. Have the carpenter, then, and the tanner certain functions or activities, and has man none? Is he born without a function? Or as eye, hand, foot, and in general each of the parts evidently has a function, may one lay it down that man similarly has a function apart from all these? What then can this be? Life seems to be common even to plants, but we are seeking what is peculiar to man. Let us exclude, therefore, the life of nutrition and growth. Next there would be a life of perception, but *it* also seems to be common even to the horse, the ox, and every animal. There remains, then, an active life of the element that has a rational principle; of this, one part has such a principle in the sense of being obedient to one, the other in the sense of possessing one and exercising thought. And, as 'life of the rational element' also has two meanings, we must state that life in the sense of activity is what we mean; for this seems to be the more proper sense of the term. Now if the function of man is an activity of soul which follows or implies a rational principle, and if we say 'a so-and-so' and 'a good so-and-so' have a function which is the same in kind, e. g. a lyre-player and a good lyre-player, and so without qualification in all cases, eminence in respect of goodness being added to the name of the function (for the function of a lyre-player is to play the lyre, and that of a good lyre-player is to do so well): if this is the case, [and we state the function of man to be a certain kind of life, and this to be an activity or actions of the soul implying a rational principle, and the function of a good man to be the good and noble performance of these, and if any action is well performed when it is performed in accordance with the appropriate excellence: if this is the case,] human good turns out to be activity of soul in accordance with virtue, and if there are more than one virtue, in accordance with the best and most complete.

But we must add 'in a complete life'. For one swallow does not make a summer, nor does one day; and so too one day, or a short time, does not make a man blessed and happy. . . .

13 Since happiness is an activity of soul in accordance with perfect virtue, we must consider the nature of virtue; for perhaps we shall thus see better the nature of happiness. . . . By human virtue we mean not that of the body but that of the soul. . . .

Some things are said about it, [the soul] adequately enough, even in the discussions outside our school, and we must use these; e. g. that one element in the soul is irrational and one has a rational principle. Whether these are separated as the parts of the body or of anything divisible are, or are distinct by definition but by nature inseparable, like convex and concave in the circumference of a circle, does not affect the present question.

Of the irrational element one division seems to be widely distributed, and vegetative in its nature, I mean that which causes nutrition and growth; for it is this kind of power of the soul that one must assign to all nurslings and to embryos, and this same power to full-grown creatures; this is more reasonable than to assign some different power to them. Now the excellence of this seems to be common to all species and not specifically human; for this part or faculty seems to function most in sleep, while goodness and badness are least manifest in sleep (whence comes the saying that the happy are no better off than the wretched for half their lives; and this happens naturally enough, since sleep is an inactivity of the soul in that respect in which it is called good or bad), unless perhaps to a small extent some of the movements actually penetrate to the soul, and in this respect the dreams of good men are better than those of ordinary people. Enough of this subject, however; let us leave the nutritive faculty alone, since it has by its nature no share in human excellence.

There seems to be also another irrational element in the soul—one which in a sense, however, shares in a rational principle. For we praise the rational principle of the continent man and of the incontinent, and the part of their soul that has such a principle, since it urges them aright and towards the best objects; but there is found in them also another element naturally opposed to the rational principle, which fights against and resists that principle. For exactly as paralysed limbs when we intend to move them to the right turn on the contrary to the left, so is it with the soul; the impulses of incontinent people move in contrary directions. But while in the body we see that which moves astray, in the soul we do not. No doubt, however, we must none the less suppose that in the soul too there is something contrary to the rational principle, resisting and opposing it. In what sense it is distinct from the other elements does not concern us. Now even this seems to have a share in a rational principle, as we said; at any rate in the continent man it obeys the rational principle—and presumably in the temperate and brave man it is still more obedient; for in him it speaks, on all matters, with the same voice as the rational principle.

Therefore the irrational element also appears to be twofold. For the vegetative element in no way shares in a rational principle, but the appetitive, and in general the desiring element in a sense shares in it, in so far as it listens to and obeys it; this is the sense in which we speak of 'taking account' of one's father or one's friends, not that in which we speak of 'accounting' for a mathematical property. That the irrational element is in some sense persuaded by a rational principle is indicated also by the giving of advice and by all reproof and exhortation. And if this element also must be said to have a rational principle, that which has a rational principle (as well as that which has not) will be twofold, one subdivision having it in the strict sense and in itself, and the other having a tendency to obey as one does one's father.

Virtue too is distinguished into kinds in accordance with this difference; for we say that some of the virtues are intellectual and others moral, philosophic wisdom and understanding and practical wisdom being intellectual, liberality and temperance moral. For in speaking about a man's character we do not say that he is wise or has understanding but that he is good-tempered or temperate; yet we praise the wise man also with respect to his state of mind; and of states of mind we call those which merit praise virtues.

BOOK II

1 Virtue, then, being of two kinds, intellectual and moral, intellectual virtue in the main owes both its birth and its growth to teaching (for which reason it requires experience and time), while moral virtue comes about as a result of habit, whence also its name *ethike* is one that is formed by a slight variation from the word *ethos* (habit). From this it is also plain that none of the moral virtues arises in us by nature; for nothing that exists by nature can form a habit contrary to its nature. For instance the stone which by nature moves downwards cannot be habituated to move upwards, not even if one tries to train it by throwing it up ten thousand times; nor can fire be habituated to move downwards, nor can anything else that by nature behaves in one way be trained to behave in another. Neither by nature, then, nor contrary to nature do the virtues arise in us;

rather we are adapted by nature to receive them, and are made perfect by habit.

Again, of all the things that come to us by nature we first acquire the potentiality and later exhibit the activity (this is plain in the case of the senses; for it was not by often seeing or often hearing that we got these senses, but on the contrary we had them before we used them, and did not come to have them by using them); but the virtues we get by first exercising them, as also happens in the case of the arts as well. For the things we have to learn before we can do them, we learn by doing them, e. g. men become builders by building and lyre-players by playing the lyre; so too we become just by doing just acts, temperate by doing temperate acts, brave by doing brave acts.

This is confirmed by what happens in states; for legislators make the citizens good by forming habits in them, and this is the wish of every legislator, and those who do not effect it miss their mark, and it is in this that a good constitution differs from a bad one.

Again, it is from the same causes and by the same means that every virtue is both produced and destroyed, and similarly every art; for it is from playing the lyre that both good and bad lyre-players are produced. And the corresponding statement is true of builders and of all the rest; men will be good or bad builders as a result of building well or badly. For if this were not so, there would have been no need of a teacher, but all men would have been born good or bad at their craft. This, then, is the case with the virtues also; by doing the acts that we do in our transactions with other men we become just or unjust, and by doing the acts that we do in the presence of danger, and being habituated to feel fear or confidence, we become brave or cowardly. The same is true of appetites and feelings of anger; some men become temperate and good-tempered, others self-indulgent and irascible, by behaving in one way or the other in the appropriate circumstances. Thus, in one word, states of character arise out of like activities. This is why the activities we exhibit must be of a certain kind; it is because the states of character correspond to the differences between these. It makes no small difference, then, whether we form habits of one kind or of another from our very youth; it makes a very great difference, or rather *all* the difference. . . .

4 The question might be asked, what we mean by saying that we must become just by doing just acts, and temperate by doing temperate acts; for if men do just and temperate acts, they are already just and temperate, exactly as, if they do what is in accordance with the laws of grammar and of music, they are grammarians and musicians.

Or is this not true even of the arts? It is possible to do something that is in accordance with the laws of grammar, either by chance or at the suggestion of another. A man will be a grammarian, then, only when he has both done something grammatical and done it grammatically; and this means doing it in accordance with the grammatical knowledge in himself.

Again, the case of the arts and that of the virtues are not similar; for the products of the arts have their goodness in themselves, so that it is enough that they should have a certain character, but if the acts that are in accordance with the virtues have themselves a certain character it does not follow that they are done justly or temperately. The agent also must be in a certain condition when he does them; in the first place he must have knowledge, secondly he must choose the acts, and choose them for their own sakes, and thirdly his action must proceed from a firm and unchangeable character. These are not reckoned in as conditions of the possession of the arts, except the bare knowledge; but as a condition of the possession of the virtues knowledge has little or no weight, while the other conditions count not for a little but for everything, i. e. the very conditions which result from often doing just and temperate acts.

Actions, then, are called just and temperate when they are such as the just or the temperate man would do; but it is not the man who does these that is just and temperate, but the man who also does them *as* just and temperate men do them. It is well said, then, that it is by doing just acts that the just man is produced, and by doing temperate acts the temperate man; without doing these no one would have even a prospect of becoming good.

But most people do not do these, but take refuge in theory and think they are being philosophers and will become good in this way, behaving somewhat like patients who listen attentively to their doctors, but do none of the things they are ordered to do. As the latter will not be made well in body by such a course of treatment, the former will not be made well in soul by such a course of philosophy. . . .

6 We must, . . . not only describe virtue as a state of character, but also say what sort of state it is. We may remark, then, that every virtue or excellence both brings into good condition the thing of which it is the excellence and makes the work of that thing be done well; e. g. the excellence of the eye makes both the eye and its work good; for it is by the excellence of the eye that we see well. Similarly the excellence of the horse makes a horse both good in itself and good at running and at carrying its rider and at awaiting the attack of the enemy. Therefore, if this is true in every case, the virtue of man also will be the state of character which makes a man good and which makes him do his own work well.

How this is to happen we have stated already, but it will be made plain also by the following consideration of the specific nature of virtue. In everything that is continuous and divisible it is possible to take more, less, or an equal amount, and that either in terms of the thing itself or relatively to us; and the equal is an intermediate between excess and defect. By the intermediate in the object I mean that which is equidistant from each of the extremes, which is one and the same for all men; by the intermediate relatively to us that which is neither too much nor too little—and this is not one, nor the same for all. For instance, if ten is many and two is few, six is the intermediate, taken in terms of the object; for it exceeds and is exceeded by an equal amount; this is intermediate according to arithmetical proportion. But the intermediate relatively to us is not to be taken so; if ten pounds are too much for a particular person to eat and two too little, it does not follow that the trainer will order six pounds; for this also is perhaps too much for the person who is to take it, or too little—too little for Milo, too much for the beginner in athletic exercises. The same is true of running and wrestling. Thus a master of any art avoids excess and defect, but seeks the intermediate and chooses this—the intermediate not in the object but relatively to us.

If it is thus, then, that every art does its work well—by looking to the intermediate and judging its works by this standard (so that we often say of good works of art that it is not possible either to take away or to add anything, implying that excess and defect destroy the goodness of works of art, while the mean preserves it; and good artists, as we say, look to this in their work), and if, further, virtue is more exact and better than any art, as nature also is, then virtue must have the quality of aiming at the intermediate. I mean moral virtue; for it is this that is concerned with passions and actions, and in these there is excess, defect, and the intermediate. For instance, both fear and confidence and appetite and anger and pity and in general pleasure and pain may be felt both too much and too little, and in both cases not well; but to feel them at the right times, with reference to the right objects, towards the right people, with the right motive, and in the right way, is what is both intermediate and best, and this is characteristic of virtue. Similarly with regard to actions also there is excess, defect, and the intermediate. Now virtue is concerned with passions and actions, in which excess is a form of failure, and so is defect, while the intermediate is praised and is a form of success; and being praised and being successful are both characteristics of virtue. Therefore virtue is a kind of mean, since, as we have seen, it aims at what is intermediate.

Again, it is possible to fail in many ways (for evil belongs to the class of the unlimited, as the Pythagoreans conjectured, and good to that of the limited), while to succeed is possible only in one way (for which reason also one is easy and the other difficult—to miss the mark easy, to hit it difficult); for these reasons also, then, excess and defect are characteristic of vice, and the mean of virtue;

For men are good in but one way, but bad in many.

Virtue, then, is a state of character concerned with choice, lying in a mean, i. e. the mean relative to us, this being determined by a rational principle, and by that principle by which the man of practical wisdom would determine it. Now it is a mean between two vices, that which depends on excess and that which depends on defect; and again it is a mean because the vices respectively fall short of or exceed what is right in both passions and actions, while virtue both finds and chooses that which is intermediate. Hence in respect of its substance and the definition which states its essence virtue is a mean, with regard to what is best and right an extreme.

But not every action nor every passion admits of a mean; for some have names that already imply badness, e. g. spite, shamelessness, envy, and in the case of actions adultery, theft, murder; for all of these and suchlike things imply by their names that they are themselves bad, and not the excesses or deficiencies of them. It is not possible, then, ever to be right with regard to them; one must always be wrong. Nor does goodness or badness with regard to such things depend on committing adultery with the right woman, at the right time, and in the right way, but simply to do any of them is to go wrong. It would be equally absurd, then, to expect that in unjust, cowardly, and voluptuous action there should be a mean, an excess, and a deficiency; for at that rate there would be a mean of excess and of deficiency, an excess of excess, and a deficiency of deficiency. But as there is no excess and deficiency of temperance and courage because what is intermediate is in a sense an extreme, so too of the actions we have mentioned there is no mean nor any excess and deficiency, but however they are done they are wrong; for in general there is neither a mean of excess and deficiency, nor excess and deficiency of a mean.

7 We must, however, not only make this general statement, but also apply it to the individual facts. For among statements about conduct those which are general apply more widely, but those which are particular are more genuine, since conduct has to do with individual cases, and our statements must harmonize with the facts in these cases. We may take these cases from our table. With regard to feelings of fear and confidence courage is the mean; of the people who exceed, he who exceeds in fearlessness has no name (many of the states have no name), while the man who exceeds in confidence is rash, and he who exceeds in fear and falls short in confidence is a coward. With regard to pleasures and pains—not all of them, and not so much with regard to the pains—the mean is temperance, the excess self-indulgence. Persons deficient with regard to the pleasures are not often found; hence such persons also have received no name. But let us call them 'insensible'.

With regard to giving and taking of money the mean is liberality, the excess and the defect prodigality and meanness. In these actions people exceed and fall short in contrary ways; the prodigal exceeds in spending and falls short in taking, while the mean man exceeds in taking and falls short in spending. (At present we are giving a mere outline or summary, and are satisfied with this; later these states will be more exactly determined.) With regard to money there are also other dispositions—a mean, magnificence (for the magnificent man differs from the liberal man; the former deals with large sums, the latter with small ones), and excess, tastelessness and vulgarity, and a deficiency, niggardliness; these differ from the states opposed to liberality, and the mode of their difference will be stated later.

With regard to honour and dishonour the mean is proper pride, the excess is known as a sort of 'empty vanity', and the deficiency is undue humility; and as we said liberality was related to magnificence, differing from it by dealing with small sums, so there is a state similarly related to proper pride, being concerned with small honours while that is concerned with great. For it is possible to desire honour as one ought, and more than one ought, and less, and the man who exceeds in his desires is called ambitious, the man who falls short unambitious, while the intermediate person has no name. . . .

With regard to anger also there is an excess, a deficiency, and a mean. Although they can scarcely be said to have names, yet since we call the intermediate person good-tempered let us call the mean good temper; of the persons at the extremes let the one who exceeds be called irascible, and his vice irascibility, and the man who falls short an inirascible sort of person, and the deficiency inirascibility.

There are also three other means, which have a certain likeness to one another, but differ from one another: for they are all concerned with intercourse in words and actions, but differ in that one is concerned with truth in this sphere, the other two with pleasantness; and of this one kind is exhibited in giving amusement, the other in all the circumstances of life. We must therefore speak of these too, that we may the better see that in all things the mean is praiseworthy, and the extremes neither praiseworthy nor right, but worthy of blame. Now most of these states also have no names, but we must try, as in the other cases, to invent names ourselves so that we may be clear and easy to follow. With regard to truth, then, the intermediate is a truthful sort of person and the mean may be called truthfulness, while the pretence which exaggerates is boastfulness and the person characterized by it a boaster, and that which understates is mock modesty and the person characterized by it mockmodest. With regard to pleasantness in the giving of amusement the intermediate person is ready-witted and the disposition ready wit, the excess is buffoonery and the person characterized by it a buffoon, while the man who falls short is a sort of boor and his state is boorishness. With regard to the remaining kind of pleasantness, that which is exhibited in life in general, the man who is pleasant in the right way is friendly and the mean is friendliness, while the man who exceeds is an obsequious person if he has no end in view, a flatterer if he is aiming at his own advantage, and the man who falls short and is unpleasant in all circumstances is a quarrelsome and surly sort of person.

There are also means in the passions and concerned with the passions; since shame is not a virtue, and yet praise is extended to the modest man. For even in these matters one man is said to be intermediate, and another to exceed, as for instance the bashful man who is ashamed of everything; while he who falls short or is not ashamed of anything at all is shameless, and the intermediate person is modest. Righteous indignation is a mean between envy and spite, and these states are concerned with the pain and pleasures that are felt at the fortunes of our neighbours; the man who is characterized by righteous indignation is pained at undeserved good fortune, the envious man, going beyond him, is pained at all good fortune, and the spiteful man falls so far short of being pained that he even rejoices. . . .

9 That moral virtue is a mean, then, and in what sense it is so, and that it is a mean between two vices, the one involving excess, the other deficiency, and that it is such because its character is to aim at what is intermediate in passions and in actions, has been sufficiently stated. Hence also it is no easy task to be good. For in everything it is no easy task to find the middle, e. g. to find the middle of a circle is not for every one but for him who knows; so, too, any one can get angry—that is easy—or give or spend money; but to do this to the right person, to the right extent, at the right time, with the right motive, and in the right way, *that* is not for every one, nor is it easy; wherefore goodness is both rare and laudable and noble.

FUNDAMENTAL PRINCIPLES OF THE METAPHYSIC OF MORALS

Immanuel Kant

FIRST SECTION. TRANSITION FROM THE COMMON RATIONAL KNOWLEDGE OF MORALITY TO THE PHILOSOPHICAL.

Nothing can possibly be conceived in the world, or even out of it, which can be called good, without qualification, except a Good Will. Intelligence, wit, judgment, and the other *talents* of the mind, however they may be named, or courage, resolution, perseverance, as qualities of temperament, are undoubtedly good and desirable in many respects; but these gifts of nature may also become extremely bad and mischievous if the will which is to make use of them, and which, therefore, constitutes what is called *character*, is not good. It is the same with the *gifts of fortune*. Power, riches, honour, even health, and the general well-being and contentment with one's condition which is called *happiness,* inspire pride, and often presumption, if there is not a good will to correct the influence of these on the mind, and with this also to rectify the whole principle of acting, and adapt it to its end. The sight of a being who is not adorned with a single feature of a pure and good will, enjoying unbroken prosperity, can never give pleasure to an impartial rational spectator (12). Thus a good will appears to constitute the indispensable condition even of being worthy of happiness.

There are even some qualities which are of service to this good will itself, and may facilitate its action, yet which have no intrinsic unconditional value, but always presuppose a good will, and this qualifies the esteem that we justly have for them, and does not permit us to regard them as absolutely good. Moderation in the affections and passions, self-control, and calm deliberation are not only good in many respects, but even seem to constitute part of the intrinsic worth of the person; but they are far from deserving to be called good without qualification, although they have been so unconditionally praised by the ancients. For without the principles of a good will, they may become extremely bad; and the coolness of a villain not only makes him far more dangerous, but also directly makes him more abominable in our eyes than he would have been without it.

A good will is good not because of what it performs or effects, not by its aptness for the attainment of some proposed end, but simply by virtue of the volition, that is, it is good in itself, and considered by itself is to be esteemed much higher than all that can be brought about by it in favour of any inclination, nay, even of the sum-total of all inclinations. Even if it should happen that, owing to special disfavour of fortune, or the nig-gardly provision of a step-motherly nature, this will should wholly lack power to accomplish its purpose, if with its greatest efforts it should yet achieve nothing, and there should remain only the good will (not, to be sure, a mere wish, but the summoning of all means in our power), then, like a jewel, it would still shine by its own light, as a thing which has its whole value in itself (13). Its usefulness or fruitlessness can neither add to nor take away anything from this value. It would be, as it were, only the setting to enable us to handle it the more conveniently in common com-merce, or to attract to it the attention of those who are not yet connois-seurs, but not to recommend it to true connoisseurs, or to determine its value. . . .

We have then to develop the notion of a will which deserves to be highly esteemed for itself, and is good without a view to anything fur-ther, a notion which exists already in the sound natural understanding, requiring rather to be cleared up than to be taught, and which in estimat-ing the value of our actions always takes the first place, and constitutes the condition of all the rest. In order to do this, we will take the notion of duty, which includes that of a good will, although implying certain sub-jective restrictions and hindrances. These, however, far from concealing it, or rendering it unrecognizable, rather bring it out by contrast, and make it shine forth so much the brighter.

I omit here all actions which are already recognized as inconsistent with duty, although they may be useful for this or that purpose, for with these the question whether they are done *from duty* cannot arise at all, since they even conflict with it. I also set aside those actions which really conform to duty, but to which men have *no* direct *inclination*, performing them because they are impelled thereto by some other inclination. For in this case we can readily distinguish whether the action which agrees with duty is done *from duty*, or from a selfish view. It is much harder to make this distinction when the action accords with duty, and the subject has besides a *direct* inclination to it. For example, it is always a matter of duty that a dealer should not overcharge an inexperienced purchaser; and wherever there is much commerce the prudent tradesman does not over-charge, but keeps a fixed price for everyone, so that a child buys of him as well as any other. Men are thus *honestly* served; but this is not enough to make us believe that the tradesman has so acted from duty and from principles of honesty: his own advantage required it; it is out of the question in this case to suppose that he might besides have a direct inclination in favour of the buyers, so that (17), as it were, from love he should give no advantage to one over another. Accordingly the action was done neither from duty nor from direct inclination, but merely with a selfish view.

On the other hand, it is a duty to maintain one's life; and, in addition, everyone has also a direct inclination to do so. But on this account the often anxious care which most men take for it has no intrinsic worth, and their maxim has no moral import. They preserve their life *as duty requires*, no doubt, but not *because duty requires*. On the other hand, if adversity and hopeless sorrow have completely taken away the relish for life; if the unfortunate one, strong in mind, indignant at his fate rather than desponding or dejected, wishes for death, and yet preserves his life without loving it—not from inclination or fear, but from duty—then his maxim has a moral worth. . . .

SECOND SECTION. TRANSITION FROM POPULAR MORAL PHILOSOPHY TO THE METAPHYSIC OF MORALS.

We cannot better serve the wishes of those who ridicule all morality as a mere chimera of human imagination overstepping itself from vanity, than by conceding to them that notions of duty must be drawn only from experience (as from indolence, people are ready to think is also the case with all other notions); for this is to prepare for them a certain triumph. I am willing to admit out of love of humanity that even most of our actions are correct, but if we look closer at them we everywhere come upon the dear self which is always prominent, and it is this they have in view, and not the strict command of duty which would often require self-denial (30). Without being an enemy of virtue, a cool observer, one that does not mistake the wish for good, however lively, for its reality, may sometimes doubt whether true virtue is actually found anywhere in the world, and this especially as years increase and the judgment is partly made wiser by experience, and partly also more acute in observation. This being so, nothing can secure us from falling away altogether from our ideas of duty, or maintain in the soul a well-grounded respect for its law, but the clear conviction that although there should never have been actions which really sprang from such pure sources, yet whether this or that takes place is not at all the question; but that reason of itself, independent on all experience, ordains what ought to take place, that accordingly actions of which perhaps the world has hitherto never given an example, the feasibility even of which might be very much doubted by one who founds everything on experience, are nevertheless inflexibly commanded by reason; that, *ex. gr.*, even though there might never yet have been a sincere friend, yet not a whit the less is pure sincerity in friendship required of every man, because, prior to all experience, this duty is involved as duty in the idea of a reason determining the will by *à priori* principles.

When we add further that, unless we deny that the notion of morality has any truth or reference to any possible object, we must admit that its law must be valid, not merely for men, but for all *rational creatures generally*, not merely under certain contingent conditions or with exceptions, but *with absolute necessity*, then it is clear that no experience could enable us to infer even the possibility of such apodictic laws (31). For with what right could we bring into unbounded respect as a universal precept for every rational nature that which perhaps holds only under the contingent conditions of humanity? Or how could laws of the determination of *our* will be regarded as laws of the determination of the will of rational beings generally, and for us only as such, if they were merely empirical, and did not take their origin wholly *à priori* from pure but practical reason?

Nor could anything be more fatal to morality than that we should wish to derive it from examples. For every example of it that is set before me must be first itself tested by principles of morality, whether it is worthy to serve as an original example, *i.e.* as a pattern, but by no means can it authoritatively furnish the conception of morality. Even the Holy One of the Gospels must first be compared with our ideal of moral perfection before we can recognize Him as such; and so He says of Himself, "Why call ye Me [whom you see] good; none is good [the model of good] but God only [whom ye do not see]?" But whence have we the conception of God as the supreme good? Simply from the *idea* of moral perfection, which reason frames *à priori*, and connects inseparably with the notion of a free will. Imitation finds no place at all in morality, and examples serve only for encouragement, *i.e.* they put beyond doubt the feasibility of what the law commands, they make visible that which the practical rule expresses more generally, but they can never authorize us to set aside the true original which lies in reason, and to guide ourselves by examples. . . .

From what has been said, it is clear that all moral conceptions have their seat and origin completely *à priori* in the reason, and that, moreover, in the commonest reason just as truly as in that which is in the highest degree speculative; that they cannot be obtained by abstraction from any empirical, and therefore merely contingent knowledge; that it is just this purity of their origin that makes them worthy to serve as our supreme practical principle (35), and that just in proportion as we add anything empirical, we detract from their genuine influence, and from the absolute value of actions; that it is not only of the greatest necessity, in a purely speculative point of view, but is also of the greatest practical importance, to derive these notions and laws from pure reason, to present them pure and unmixed, and even to determine the compass of this practical or pure rational knowledge, *i.e.* to determine the whole faculty of pure practical reason; and, in doing so, we must not make its principles dependent on the particular nature of human reason, though in speculative philosophy this may be permitted, or may even at times be necessary; but since moral laws ought to hold good for every rational creature, we must derive them from the general concept of a rational being. In this way, although for its *application* to man morality has need of anthropology, yet, in the first instance, we must treat it independently as pure philosophy, *i.e.* as metaphysic, complete in itself (a thing which in such distinct branches of science is easily done); knowing well that unless we are in possession of this, it would not only be vain to determine the moral element of duty in right actions for purposes of speculative criticism, but it would be impossible to base morals on their genuine principles, even for common practical purposes, especially of moral instruction, so as to produce pure moral dispositions, and to engraft them on men's minds to the promotion of the greatest possible good in the world.

But in order that in this study we may not merely advance by the natural steps from the common moral judgment (in this case very worthy of respect) to the philosophical, as has been already done, but also from a popular philosophy, which goes no further than it can reach by groping with the help of examples, to metaphysic (which does not allow itself to be checked by anything empirical (36), and as it must measure the whole extent of this kind of rational knowledge, goes as far as ideal conceptions, where even examples fail us), we must follow and clearly describe the practical faculty of reason, from the general rules of its determination to the point where the notion of duty springs from it.

Everything in nature works according to laws. Rational beings alone have the faculty of acting according *to the conception* of laws, that is according to principles, *i.e.* have a *will*. Since the deduction of actions from principles requires *reason*, the will is nothing but practical reason. If reason infallibly determines the will, then the actions of such a being which are recognized as objectively necessary are subjectively necessary also, *i.e.* the will is a faculty to choose *that only* which reason independent on inclination recognizes as practically necessary, *i.e.* as good. But if reason of itself does not sufficiently determine the will, if the latter is subject also to subjective conditions (particular impulses) which do not always coincide with the objective conditions; in a word, if the will does not *in itself* completely accord with reason (which is actually the case with men), then the actions which objectively are recognized as necessary are subjectively contingent, and the determination of such a will according to objective laws is *obligation*, that is to say, the relation of the objective laws to a will that is not thoroughly good is conceived as the determination of the will of a rational being by principles of reason, but which the will from its nature does not of necessity follow.

The conception of an objective principle, in so far as it is obligatory for a will, is called a command (of reason), and the formula of the command is called an Imperative.

All imperatives are expressed by the word *ought* [or *shall*], and thereby indicate the relation of an objective law (37) of reason to a will, which from its subjective constitution is not necessarily determined by it (an obligation). They say that something woud be good to do or to forbear, but they say it to a will which does not always do a thing because it is conceived to be good to do it. That is practically *good*, however, which determines the will by means of the conceptions of reason, and consequently not from subjective causes, but objectively, that is on principles which are valid for every rational being as such. It is distinguished from the *pleasant*, as that which influences the will only by means of sensation from merely subjective causes, valid only for the sense of this or that one, and not as a principle of reason, which holds for every one.[1]

A perfectly good will would therefore be equally subject to objective laws (viz. laws of good), but could not be conceived as *obliged* thereby to act lawfully, because of itself from its subjective constitution it can only be determined by the conception of good (38). Therefore no imperatives hold for the Divine will, or in general for a *holy* will; *ought* is here out of place, because the volition is already of itself necessarily in unison with the law. Therefore imperatives are only formulæ to express the relation of objective laws of all volition to the subjective imperfection of the will of this or that rational being, *e.g.* the human will.

Now all *imperatives* command either *hypothetically* or *categorically*. The former represent the practical necessity of a possible action as means to something else that is willed (or at least which one might possibly will). The categorical imperative would be that which represented an action as necessary of itself without reference to another end, *i.e.*, as objectively necessary.

Since every practical law represents a possible action as good, and on this account, for a subject who is practically determinable by reason, necessary, all imperatives are formulæ determining an action which is necessary according to the principle of a will good in some respects. If now the action is good only as a means *to something else*, then the imperative is *hypothetical*; if it is conceived as good *in itself* and consequently as being necessarily the principle of a will which of itself conforms to reason, then it is *categorical*.

Thus the imperative declares what action possible by me would be good, and presents the practical rule in relation to a will which does not forthwith perform an action simply because it is good, whether because the subject does not always know that it is good, or because, even if it know this, yet its maxims might be opposed to the objective principles of practical reason.

Accordingly the hypothetical imperative only says that the action is good for some purpose, *possible* or *actual* (39). In the first case it is a Problematical, in the second an Assertorial practical principle. The categorical imperative which declares an action to be objectively necessary in itself without reference to any purpose, *i.e.* without any other end, is valid as an Apodictic (practical) principle.

Whatever is possible only by the power of some rational being may also be conceived as a possible purpose of some will; and therefore the principles of action as regards the means necessary to attain some possible purpose are in fact infinitely numerous. All sciences have a practical part, consisting of problems expressing that some end is possible for us, and of imperatives directing how it may be attained. These may, therefore, be called in general imperatives of Skill. Here there is no question whether the end is rational and good, but only what one must do in order to attain it. The precepts for the physician to make his patient thoroughly healthy, and for a poisoner to ensure certain death, are of equal value in this respect, that each serves to effect its purpose perfectly. Since in early youth it cannot be known what ends are likely to occur to us in the course of life, parents seek to have their children taught a *great many things*, and provide for their *skill* in the use of means for all sorts of arbitrary ends, of none of which can they determine whether it may not perhaps hereafter be an object to their pupil, but which it is at all events *possible* that he might aim at; and this anxiety is so great that they commonly neglect to form and correct their judgment on the value of the things which may be chosen as ends (40).

There is *one* end, however, which may be assumed to be actually such to all rational beings (so far as imperatives apply to them, viz. as dependent beings), and, therefore, one purpose which they not merely *may* have, but which we may with certainty assume that they all actually *have* by a natural necessity, and this is *happiness*. The hypothetical imperative which expresses the practical necessity of an action as means to the advancement of happiness is Assertorial. We are not to present it as necessary for an uncertain and merely possible purpose, but for a purpose which we may presuppose with certainty and *à priori* in every man, because it belongs to his being. Now skill in the choice of means to his own greatest well-being may be called *prudence*,[2] in the narrowest sense. And thus the imperative which refers to the choice of means to one's own happiness, *i.e.* the precept of prudence, is still always *hypothetical*; the action is not commanded absolutely, but only as means to another purpose.

Finally, there is an imperative which commands a certain conduct immediately, without having as its condition any other purpose to be attained by it. This imperative is Categorical. It concerns not the matter of the action, or its intended result, but its form and the principle of which it is itself a result (41); and what is essentially good in it consists in the mental disposition, let the consequence be what it may. This imperative may be called that of Morality.

There is a marked distinction also between the volitions on these three sorts of principles in the *dissimilarity* of the obligation of the will. In order to mark this difference more clearly, I think they would be most suitably named in their order if we said they are either *rules* of skill, or *counsels* of prudence, or *commands* (*laws*) of morality. For it is *law* only that involves the conception of an *unconditional* and objective necessity, which is consequently universally valid; and commands are laws which must be obeyed, that is, must be followed, even in opposition to inclination. *Counsels*, indeed, involve necessity, but one which can only hold under a contingent subjective condition, viz. they depend on whether this or that man reckons this or that as part of his happiness; the categorical imperative, on the contrary, is not limited by any condition, and as being absolutely, although practically, necessary, may be quite properly called a command. We might also call the first kind of imperatives *technical* (belonging to art), the second *pragmatic*[3] (to welfare), the third *moral* (belonging to free conduct generally, that is, to morals). . . .

When I conceive a hypothetical imperative, in general I do not know beforehand what it will contain until I am given the condition. But when I conceive a categorical imperative, I know at once what it contains. For as the imperative contains besides the law only the necessity that the maxims[4] shall conform to this law, while the law contains no conditions restricting it, there remains nothing but the general statement that the maxim of the action should conform to a universal law (47), and it is this conformity alone that the imperative properly represents as necessary.

There is therefore but one categorical imperative, namely, this: *Act only on that maxim whereby thou canst at the same time will that it should become a universal law*.

Now if all imperatives of duty can be deduced from this one imperative as from their principle, then, although it should remain undecided whether what is called duty is not merely a vain notion, yet at least we shall be able to show what we understand by it and what this notion means.

Since the universality of the law according to which effects are produced constitutes what is properly called *nature* in the most general sense (as to form), that is the existence of things so far as it is determined by general laws, the imperative of duty may be expressed thus: *Act as if the maxim of thy action were to become by thy will a universal law of nature*.

We will now enumerate a few duties, adopting the usual division of them into duties to ourselves and to others, and into perfect and imperfect duties.[5](48)

1. A man reduced to despair by a series of misfortunes feels wearied of life, but is still so far in possession of his reason that he can ask himself whether it would not be contrary to his duty to himself to take his own life. Now he inquires whether the maxim of his action could become a universal law of nature. His maxim is: From self-love I adopt it as a principle to shorten my life when its longer duration is likely to bring more evil than satisfaction. It is asked then simply whether this principle

founded on self-love can become a universal law of nature. Now we see at once that a system of nature of which it should be a law to destroy life by means of the very feeling whose special nature it is to impel to the improvement of life would contradict itself, and therefore could not exist as a system of nature; hence that maxim cannot possibly exist as a universal law of nature, and consequently would be wholly inconsistent with the supreme principle of all duty.

2. Another finds himself forced by necessity to borrow money. He knows that he will not be able to repay it, but sees also that nothing will be lent to him, unless he promises stoutly to repay it in a definite time. He desires to make this promise, but he has still so much conscience as to ask himself: Is it not unlawful and inconsistent with duty to get out of a difficulty in this way? Suppose, however, that he resolves to do so, then the maxim of his action would be expressed thus: When I think myself in want of money, I will borrow money and promise to repay it, although I know that I never can do so. Now this principle of self-love or of one's own advantage may perhaps be consistent with my whole future welfare; but the question now is, Is it right? I change then the suggestion of self-love into a universal law, and state the question thus (49): How would it be if my maxim were a universal law? Then I see at once that it could never hold as a universal law of nature, but would necessarily contradict itself. For supposing it to be a universal law that everyone when he thinks himself in a difficulty should be able to promise whatever he pleases, with the purpose of not keeping his promise, the promise itself would become impossible, as well as the end that one might have in view in it, since no one would consider that anything was promised to him, but would ridicule all such statements as vain pretences.

3. A third finds in himself a talent which with the help of some culture might make him a useful man in many respects. But he finds himself in comfortable circumstances, and prefers to indulge in pleasure rather than to take pains in enlarging and improving his happy natural capacities. He asks, however, whether his maxim of neglect of his natural gifts, besides agreeing with his inclination to indulgence, agrees also with what is called duty. He sees then that a system of nature could indeed subsist with such a universal law although men (like the South Sea islanders) should let their talents rest, and resolve to devote their lives merely to idleness, amusement, and propagation of their species—in a word, to enjoyment; but he cannot possibly *will* that this should be a universal law of nature, or be implanted in us as such by a natural instinct. For, as a rational being, he necessarily wills that his faculties be developed, since they serve him, and have been given him, for all sorts of possible purposes.

4. A fourth, who is in prosperity, while he sees that others have to contend with great wretchedness and that he could help them, thinks: What concern is it of mine? Let everyone be as happy (50) as Heaven

pleases, or as he can make himself; I will take nothing from him nor even envy him, only I do not wish to contribute anything to his welfare or to his assistance in distress! Now no doubt if such a mode of thinking were a universal law, the human race might very well subsist, and doubtless even better than in a state in which everyone talks of sympathy and good-will, or even takes care occasionally to put it into practice, but, on the other side, also cheats when he can, betrays the rights of men, or otherwise violates them. But although it is possible that a universal law of nature might exist in accordance with that maxim, it is impossible to *will* that such a principle should have the universal validity of a law of nature. For a will which resolved this would contradict itself, inasmuch as many cases might occur in which one would have need of the love and sympathy of others, and in which, by such a law of nature, sprung from his own will, he would deprive himself of all hope of the aid he desires.

These are a few of the many actual duties, or at least what we regard as such, which obviously fall into two classes on the one principle that we have laid down. We must be *able to will* that a maxim of our action should be a universal law. This is the canon of the moral appreciation of the action generally. Some actions are of such a character that their maxim cannot without contradiction be even *conceived* as a universal law of nature, far from it being possible that we should *will* that it *should* be so. In others this intrinsic impossibility is not found, but still it is impossible to *will* that their maxim should be raised to the universality of a law of nature, since such a will would contradict itself. It is easily seen that the former violate strict or rigorous (inflexible) duty (51); the latter only laxer (meritorious) duty. Thus it has been completely shown by these examples how all duties depend as regards the nature of the obligation (not the object of the action) on the same principle.

If now we attend to ourselves on occasion of any transgression of duty, we shall find that we in fact do not will that our maxim should be a universal law, for that is impossible for us; on the contrary, we will that the opposite should remain a universal law, only we assume the liberty of making an *exception* in our own favour or (just for this time only) in favour of our inclination. Consequently if we considered all cases from one and the same point of view, namely, that of reason, we should find a contradiction in our own will, namely, that a certain principle should be objectively necessary as a universal law, and yet subjectively should not be universal, but admit of exceptions. As, however, we at one moment regard our action from the point of view of a will wholly conformed to reason, and then again look at the same action from the point of view of a will affected by inclination, there is not really any contradiction, but an antagonism of inclination to the precept of reason, whereby the universality of the principle is changed into a mere generality, so that the practical principle of reason shall meet the maxim half way. Now, although this cannot be justified in our own impartial judgment, yet it proves that we do really recognize the validity of the categorical imperative and (with all respect for it) only allow ourselves a few exceptions, which we think unimportant and forced from us. . . .

Now I say: man and generally any rational being *exists* as an end in himself, *not merely as a means* to be arbitrarily used by this or that will, but in all his actions, whether they concern himself or other rational beings, must be always regarded at the same time as an end. All objects of the inclinations have only a conditional worth; for if the inclinations and the wants founded on them did not exist, then their object would be without value. But the inclinations themselves being sources of want are so far from having an absolute worth for which they should be desired, that, on the contrary, it must be the universal wish of every rational being to be wholly free from them. Thus the worth of any object which is *to be acquired* by our action is always conditional. Beings whose existence depends not on our will but on nature's, have nevertheless, if they are rational beings, only a relative value as means, and are therefore called *things;* rational beings, on the contrary, are called *persons,* because their very nature points them out as ends in themselves, that is as something which must not be used merely as means, and so far therefore restricts freedom of action (and is an object of respect). These, therefore, are not merely subjective ends whose existence has a worth *for us* as an effect of our action, but *objective ends,* that is things whose existence is an end in itself: an end moreover for which no other can be substituted, which they should subserve *merely* as means, for otherwise nothing whatever would possess *absolute worth;* but if all worth were conditioned and therefore contingent, then there would be no supreme practical principle of reason whatever.

If then there is a supreme practical principle or, in respect of the human will, a categorical imperative, it must be one which (57), being drawn from the conception of that which is necessarily an end for everyone because it is *an end in itself,* constitutes an *objective* principle of will, and can therefore serve as a universal practical law. The foundation of this principle is: *rational nature exists as an end in itself.* Man necessarily conceives his own existence as being so: so far then this is a *subjective* principle of human actions. But every other rational being regards its existence similarly, just on the same rational principle that holds for me[6]: so that it is at the same time an objective principle, from which as a supreme practical law all laws of the will must be capable of being deduced. Accordingly the practical imperative will be as follows: *So act as to treat humanity, whether in thine own person or in that of any other, in every case as an end withal, never as means only.* We will now inquire whether this can be practically carried out.

To abide by the previous examples:

Firstly, under the head of necessary duty to oneself: He who contemplates suicide should ask himself whether his action can be consistent with the idea of humanity *as an end in itself.* If he destroys himself in order to escape from painful circumstances, he uses a person merely as *a mean* to maintain a tolerable condition up to the end of life. But a man is not a thing, that is to say, something which can be used merely as means, but must in all his actions be always considered as an end in himself. I cannot, therefore, dispose in any way of a man in my own person so as to mutilate him, to damage or kill him (58). (It belongs to ethics proper to define this principle more precisely, so as to avoid all misunderstanding, *e.g.* as to the amputation of the limbs in order to preserve myself; as to exposing my life to danger with a view to preserve it, &c. This question is therefore omitted here.)

Secondly, as regards necessary duties, or those of strict obligation, towards others; he who is thinking of making a lying promise to others will see at once that he would be using another man *merely as a mean*, without the latter containing at the same time the end in himself. For he whom I propose by such a promise to use for my own purposes cannot possibly assent to my mode of acting towards him, and therefore cannot himself contain the end of this action. This violation of the principle of humanity in other men is more obvious if we take in examples of attacks on the freedom and property of others. For then it is clear that he who transgresses the rights of men intends to use the person of others merely as means, without considering that as rational beings they ought always to be esteemed also as ends, that is, as beings who must be capable of containing in themselves the end of the very same action.[7]

Thirdly, as regards contingent (meritorious) duties to oneself; it is not enough that the action does not violate humanity in our own person as an end in itself, it must also *harmonize with* it (59). Now there are in humanity capacities of greater perfection which belong to the end that nature has in view in regard to humanity in ourselves as the subject: to neglect these might perhaps be consistent with the *maintenance* of humanity as an end in itself, but not with the *advancement* of this end.

Fourthly, as regards meritorious duties towards others: the natural end which all men have is their own happiness. Now humanity might indeed subsist, although no one should contribute anything to the happiness of others, provided he did not intentionally withdraw anything from it; but after all, this would only harmonize negatively, not positively, with *humanity, as an end in itself*, if everyone does not also endeavour, as far as in him lies, to forward the ends of others. For the ends of any subject which is an end in himself, ought as far as possible to be *my* ends also, if that conception is to have its *full* effect with me.

This principle, that humanity and generally every rational nature is *an end in itself* (which is the supreme limiting condition of every man's freedom of action), is not borrowed from experience, *firstly*, because it is universal, applying as it does to all rational beings whatever, and experience is not capable of determining anything about them; *secondly*, because it does not present humanity as an end to men (subjectively), that is as an object which men do of themselves actually adopt as an end; but as an objective end, which must as a law constitute the supreme limiting condition of all our subjective ends, let them be what we will; it must therefore spring from pure reason. In fact the objective principle of all practical legislation lies (according to the first principle) in *the rule* and its form of universality which makes it capable of being a law (say, *e.g.*, a law of nature); but the *subjective* principle is in the *end*; now by the second principle the subject of all ends is each rational being (60) inasmuch as it is an end in itself. Hence follows the third practical principle of the will, which is the ultimate condition of its harmony with the universal practical reason, viz.: the idea of *the will of every rational being as a universally legislative will*.

On this principle all maxims are rejected which are inconsistent with the will being itself universal legislator. Thus the will is not subject simply to the law, but so subject that it must be regarded *as itself giving the law*, and on this ground only, subject to the law (of which it can regard itself as the author). . . .

The conception of every rational being as one which must consider itself as giving in all the maxims of its will universal laws, so as to judge itself and its actions from this point of view—this conception leads to another which depends on it and is very fruitful, namely, that of a *kingdom of ends*.

By a *kingdom* I understand the union of different rational beings in a system by common laws. Now since it is by laws that ends are determined as regards their universal validity, hence, if we abstract from the personal differences of rational beings, and likewise from all the content of their private ends, we shall be able to conceive all ends combined in a systematic whole (including both rational beings as ends in themselves, and also the special ends which each may propose to himself), that is to say, we can conceive a kingdom of ends, which on the preceding principles is possible.

(63) For all rational beings come under the *law* that each of them must treat itself and all others *never merely as means*, but in every case *at the same time as ends in themselves*. Hence results a systematic union of rational beings by common objective laws, *i.e.*, a kingdom which may be called a kingdom of ends, since what these laws have in view is just the relation of these beings to one another as ends and means. It is certainly only an ideal.

A rational being belongs as a *member* to the kingdom of ends when, although giving universal laws in it, he is also himself subject to these laws. He belongs to it *as sovereign* when, while giving laws, he is not subject to the will of any other.

A rational being must always regard himself as giving laws either as member or as sovereign in a kingdom of ends which is rendered possible by the freedom of will. He cannot, however, maintain the latter position merely by the maxims of his will, but only in case he is a completely independent being without wants and with unrestricted power adequate to his will.

Morality consists then in the reference of all action to the legislation which alone can render a kingdom of ends possible. This legislation must be capable of existing in every rational being, and of emanating from his will, so that the principle of this will is, never to act on any maxim which could not without contradiction be also a universal law, and accordingly always so to act *that the will could at the same time regard itself as giving in its maxims universal laws.* If now the maxims of rational beings are not by their own nature coincident with this objective principle, then the necessity of acting on it is called practical necessitation (64), i.e. *duty.* Duty does not apply to the sovereign in the kingdom of ends, but it does to every member of it and to all in the same degree.

The practical necessity of acting on this principle, *i.e.* duty, does not rest at all on feelings, impulses, or inclinations, but solely on the relation of rational beings to one another, a relation in which the will of a rational being must always be regarded as *legislative,* since otherwise it could not be conceived as *an end in itself.* Reason then refers every maxim of the will, regarding it as legislating universally, to every other will and also to every action towards oneself; and this not on account of any other practical motive or any future advantage, but from the idea of the *dignity* of a rational being, obeying no law but that which he himself also gives. . . .

In the kingdom of ends everything has either Value or Dignity. Whatever has a value can be replaced by something else which is *equivalent;* whatever, on the other hand, is above all value, and therefore admits of no equivalent, has a dignity.

We can now end where we started at the beginning, namely, with the conception of a will unconditionally good. *That will* is *absolutely good* which cannot be evil—in other words, whose maxim, if made a universal law, could never contradict itself. This principle, then, is its supreme law: Act always on such a maxim as thou canst at the same time will to be a universal law; this is the sole condition under which a will can never contradict itself; and such an imperative is categorical. Since the validity of the will as a universal law for possible actions is analogous to the universal connexion of the existence of things by general laws, which is the formal notion of nature in general, the categorical imperative can be expressed thus: *Act on maxims which can at the same time have for their object themselves as universal laws of nature.* Such then is the formula of an absolutely good will.

NOTES

1. The dependence of the desires on sensations is called inclination, and this accordingly always indicates a *want.* The dependence of a contingently determinable will on principles of reason is called an *interest.* This, therefore, is found only in the case of a dependent will which does not always of itself conform to reason; in the Divine will we cannot conceive any interest. But the human will can also

take an interest in a thing without therefore acting *from interest*. The former signifies the *practical* interest in the action, the latter the *pathological* in the object of the action. The former indicates only dependence of the will on principles of reason in themselves; the second, dependence on principles of reason for the sake of inclination, reason supplying only the practical rules how the requirement of the inclination may be satisfied. In the first case the action interests me; in the second the object of the action (because it is pleasant to me). We have seen in the first section that in an action done from duty we must look not to the interest in the object, but only to that in the action itself, and in its rational principle (viz. the law).

2. The word *prudence* is taken in two senses: in the one it may bear the name of knowledge of the world, in the other that of private prudence. The former is a man's ability to influence others so as to use them for his own purposes. The latter is the sagacity to combine all these purposes for his own lasting benefit. This latter is properly that to which the value even of the former is reduced, and when a man is prudent in the former sense, but not in the latter, we might better say of him that he is clever and cunning, but, on the whole, imprudent.

3. It seems to me that the proper signification of the word *pragmatic* may be most accurately defined in this way. For *sanctions* are called pragmatic which flow properly, not from the law of the states as necessary enactments, but from *precaution* for the general welfare. A history is composed pragmatically when it teaches *prudence*, i.e. instructs the world how it can provide for its interests better, or at least as well as the men of former time.

4. A MAXIM is a subjective principle of action, and must be distinguished from the *objective principle*, namely, practical law. The former contains the practical rule set by reason according to the conditions of the subject (often its ignorance or its inclinations), so that it is the principle on which the subject *acts*; but the law is the objective principle valid for every rational being, and is the principle on which it *ought to act* that is an imperative.

5. It must be noted here that I reserve the division of duties for a future *metaphysic of morals*; so that I give it here only as an arbitrary one (in order to arrange my examples). For the rest, I understand by a perfect duty one that admits no exception in favour of inclination, and then I have not merely external but also internal perfect duties. This is contrary to the use of the word adopted in the schools; but I do not intend to justify it here, as it is all one for my purpose whether it is admitted or not.

6. This proposition is here stated as a postulate. The ground of it will be found in the concluding section.

7. Let it not be thought that the common: *quod tibi non vis fieri, &c.*, could serve here as the rule or principle. For it is only a deduction from the former, though with several limitations; it cannot be a universal law, for it does not contain the principle of duties to oneself, nor of the duties of benevolence to others (for many a one would gladly consent that others should not benefit him, provided only that he might be excused from showing benevolence to them), nor finally that of duties of strict obligation to one another, for on this principle the criminal might argue against the judge who punishes him, and so on.

446   Character or Duty

Questions for Part IX

1. In his discussion of conflicts between bad morality and human sympathy, Jonathan Bennett suggests three ways of responding to such conflicts. One is to eliminate one's human sympathies; one is to abandon one's morality. Explain what Bennett's third possibility is and why he favors it.

2. Gregory S. Kavka offers an argument that deterrence produces situations in which it is right to *intend* to do something which you know would be wrong. But how can it be right to intend to do something wrong? Explain Kavka's argument. Does the argument really show that it can be right to intend a wrong action, or just that it can be right to *pretend* to intend a wrong action? Can you think of other examples which might make the same point as Kavka's?

3. Kavka argues that in deterrence situations it can happen that the right thing to do is something which a good person will be unable to do. Explain and evaluate Kavka's reasons.

4. Kavka's overall conclusion is that our standards for evaluating actions and our standards for evaluating people do not fit together very well. Are you persuaded? If not, where does Kavka go wrong? If so, how might we get them to fit together better?

5. Aristotle supposes that "there is some end of the things we do, which we desire for its own sake (everything else being desired for the sake of this)." Is this correct? Or do we desire many different things for their own sakes?

6. When Aristotle speaks of happiness, he means something different from what we typically mean. (Indeed some scholars prefer to translate the Greek word *eudaimonea* as "human flourishing" rather than "happiness.") What are some of the differences between Aristotle's conception of happiness and ours?

7. A good knife is one which cuts well; a good carpenter is one who builds houses well. Aristotle thinks similarly that a good person is one who performs the human function well. Is there really a human function? Is Aristotle right to associate the human function with whatever is peculiar to humanity? If there turned out to be intelligent and rational Martians would Aristotle have to change his mind about the human function?

8. What does Aristotle mean by a *virtue*? What is the role of the emotions in the virtuous person? Of actions? How does one become virtuous?

9. Aristotle describes virtue as a mean between two extremes. What does he mean by this? Does this provide us with a rule which we can apply straightforwardly to determine what we ought to do?

10. What is the difference Kant points to between acting "as duty requires" and acting "because duty requires"? Why does Kant say that merely doing what we ought has no moral worth unless we do it because we know it is our duty? Does Kant think that an action cannot have moral worth if we enjoy doing it?

11. What does Kant mean by a hypothetical imperative? By a categorical imperative? Why does he deny that morality can consist of hypothetical imperatives?

12. What does Kant think is the only categorical imperative? What is a maxim? Give some examples. What is it to will that a maxim should become a universal law? Study Kant's four applications of the categorical imperative; then apply it to an example of your own.

13. What is it to treat someone as a means? To treat someone as an end in her-

or himself? Why should we treat others as ends rather than means? Is it possible to never treat others as means?

14. Compare and contrast Aristotle's and Kant's views on the relation between morality and rationality.

15. Compare what Aristotle's and Kant's attitudes would be toward the kind of conflict between emotions and moral principles discussed by Bennett.

Part X. Property: Rights and Distribution Problems

A number of American Indian tribes have recently brought multi-million dollar lawsuits against the states in which their reservations are located. The keystone of their cases is the claim that their lands were illegitimately wrested from them centuries ago by chicanery or military force. The land, they argue, should rightfully be restored to them, or, failing that, because much of it has been settled and developed for generations by non-Indians, they should be compensated by the government in a substantial monetary settlement. Do these Indian suits have much merit?

You might think that property that was stolen or gained by force of arms cannot properly belong to its possessor. To have a right to property one must come into possession of it in some acceptable, respectable way. You can't just take it. But what are the acceptable ways of acquiring property? Purchase and barter are, of course, common enough forms of legitimate exchange, at least when both parties to the exchange freely enter into the transfer. Inheritance and gift are other acceptable methods.

Suppose you have a car that I would like to own. We agree to a purchase price and money is exchanged for the vehicle. In the transaction (or as a result of it) each of us has transferred his or her rights to certain property. I own the car. You have the money. Each of us then is entitled to do what he or she will with the objects in question. In effect, we have redistributed property and, prima facie, the new arrangement of goods and persons is fair.

But, suppose we ask how you came by the car in the first place? What if you stole it? Do I, its innocent purchaser, now have a right to the car? I surely paid for it. You have my money. What if the original owner shows up? Ought she to be able to dispossess me of the car? If she can, then I am out the money and I have no car either. That does not seem fair. What if I had the car repainted and had extensive work done on the engine? Will that improve the status of my right to it?

Imagine that the car had not been stolen by you, but it was stolen by the person from whom you purchased it. Again the original owner discovers that I have her car and insists on its return. Do I have a right to keep it or does it rightfully belong to her? Does the situation with respect to my rights to the car alter at all if a number of legitimate transfers have ensued since the theft? How could such a history of exchange cause the original owner to forfeit her rights? Why should what other people do with a piece of stolen property affect the rights of possession of the original victimized owner?

Think again of the Indian claims. How did nonnative Americans come to have rights to the lands on which the tribes had lived and hunted for centuries? We have already mentioned legitimate ways by which property is acquired; do any of them cover the transfers of the American country-side? Let us focus on those kinds of cases where the lands were taken by brute force of arms. Many generations have passed since the Indians lost their lands. In the interim the property has been extensively developed and inhabited by non-Indians. Does justice really require that those who now live, work, and play on the former Indian lands compensate the descendants of the Indians who were dispossessed of the property? Must the government that sanctioned the settling of the lands now pay the tribes reasonable value for them? After all, it will be pointed out that contemporary Indians, though arguably not as well off as non-Indians, are so far removed from the time of the unjust transfer that it is difficult to prove real damages to individuals as a direct result of the tribal dispos-session. Too much water has flowed under the bridge and if the property were now to be restored to the tribes or a compensation paid to them that is commensurate with the current value of the land, those non-Indians who have invested their lives and fortunes in the land would be grossly disadvantaged. After all, the tribes seldom improved the property in any calculable way. The non-Indian settlers, on the other hand, worked the land, mingled their blood, sweat, and tears with it, and transformed it from wilderness to farms, ranches, and cities. Are not those marks of true ownership? The tribes merely lived on or from the lands.

It has been argued by some philosophers and economic theorists, and recently most prominently and persuasively by Robert Nozick, that ques-tions of property rights are basically historical questions. Whether or not a particular person has a right to a certain piece of property should be resolved on the basis of tracing the history of the property's transfers. If acquisitions and transfers have been in accord with certain principles of distributive justice, Nozick maintains, the right to the property resides with its possessor.

Certain constraints on acquisitions must, however, be imposed to sat-isfy our intuitions about justice. Thefts and forced transfers cannot be allowed without rectification to the victims. Also, not every kind of thing can become personal property. No one, for example, should be allowed to acquire all of the drinkable water in the world and so have the right to prevent others from using it unless they pay whatever exorbitant price the possessor fancies. A historical entitlement theory (like Nozick's) also needs to set boundaries on how much of anything any individual can legitimately own.

Other theories of property distribution, such as that of John Rawls, emphasize moral principles of justice and tend to focus on the limits of ownership. Utilitarians, like John Stuart Mill, those who adhere to the principle that distributions of goods should benefit the greatest number of people, and egalitarians, who believe in equal shares (at least in the end-state of distributions) and Marxists, who want property doled according to needs, defend various versions of what may be called "pattern theories of property distribution." The basic formula, as Nozick notes, for all of these theories is "to each according to his _____." Different pattern theories fill in the blank differently, but in each case the idea is that the concept of justice requires that property in a society should only be held by persons in accord with some ideal pattern of distribution.

The right to own property is clearly one of the most important elements in the structure of our society. When limited and desirable resources, of which land is one example, are involved, the very peace and security of the society may be at stake. Some controls on ownership and acquisition may be essential to the preservation of the institution of private property in a free market economy. Nozick defends a proviso on free acquisition of property that he attributes to John Locke. The effect of the proviso is that the conditions of others are not to be worsened by an acquisition. What is meant by "worsening a situation" is a complex matter for it implies that a baseline for comparison can be fixed. Once that is settled, we may still ask whether an acquisition that worsens the situation of others can still be allowed if those others are compensated for their losses. Compensation might come in various ways. It might be argued that common ownership is not as productive as private ownership and so those of us who are now barred from property to which we might have had access are compensated by being able to participate in a vibrant economic system. It might be maintained in a way that does not seem inconsistent with Rawls' principles of justice that certain property in certain specific hands (rather than others) has a better effect on the standard of living for all, or on the standard of living of the least well-off than some other arrangement, such as equal distribution or community ownership, might have. In any event, the Indian tribes might use the baseline-driven proviso to argue that they are owed compensation for the lands of which they have been deprived.

Sometimes, however, there is no adequate compensation for the deprivation of property and then the right to own it, or to press one's ownership claims to it, even as a staunch rights theorist like Nozick will argue, must be relinquished. Suppose that you are the sole owner of an island in the middle of a vast sea. I am shipwrecked and swept up on your beach. Would you be justified in ordering me off as a trespasser? Most of us would think your actions indefensible if you were to drive me back into the sea.

Our intuitions about the limits of your control of the island, Nozick urges, should not, however, be interpreted as an overriding of your rights in order to avoid a catastrophic occurrence in my life. Considerations built into the notion of justifiable property rights govern the case. Contrast the island case with one in which you synthesize a new substance from readily available chemicals and your creation effectively cures a fatal disease from which I suffer. You refuse to give me the cure unless I will pay a very high price, a sum I cannot possibly afford. Your appropriation of the chemicals to produce your cure in no way makes them a scarce commodity, and anyone else might try to produce your results. I am no worse off because you will not give me the cure than I was before you created it. Hence, you have a property right to the cure and so can sell it for whatever the market will bear. I'm just out of luck and justice in distribution, at least in Nozick's account, is not offended. Does such an outcome, however, not seem unjust?

Surely I have a need that is as undeniable as it is great. But why should the needs of people override the rights of acquisition of possessions by other people? Would not the very institution of private property be severely threatened if overridings of this type were to be required to satisfy a principle of distributive justice?

DISTRIBUTIVE JUSTICE
Robert Nozick

The term "distributive justice" is not a neutral one. Hearing the term "distribution," most people presume that some thing or mechanism uses some principle or criterion to give out a supply of things. Into this process of distributing shares some error may have crept. So it is an open question, at least, whether *re*distribution should take place; whether we should do again what has already been done once, though poorly. However, we are not in the position of children who have been given portions of pie by someone who now makes last minute adjustments to rectify careless cutting. There is no *central* distribution, no person or group entitled to control all the resources, jointly deciding how they are to be doled out. What each person gets, he gets from others who give to him in exchange for something, or as a gift. In a free society, diverse persons control different resources, and new holdings arise out of the voluntary exchanges and actions of persons. There is no more a distributing or distribution of shares than there is a distributing of mates in a society in which persons choose whom they shall marry. The total result is the product of many individual decisions which the different individuals involved are entitled to make. Some uses of the term "distribution," it is true, do not imply a previous distributing appropriately judged by some criterion (for example, "probability distribution"); nevertheless, it would be best to use a terminology that clearly is neutral. We shall speak of people's holdings; a principle of justice in holdings describes (part of) what justice tells us (requires) about holdings. I shall state first what I take to be the correct view about justice in holdings, and then turn to the discussion of alternate views.

THE ENTITLEMENT THEORY

The subject of justice in holdings consists of three major topics. The first is the *original acquisition of holdings,* the appropriation of unheld things. This includes the issues of how unheld things may come to be held, the process, or processes, by which unheld things may come to be held, the things that may come to be held by these processes, the extent of what comes to be held by a particular process, and so on. We shall refer to the complicated truth about this topic, which we shall not formulate here, as the principle of justice in acquisition. The second topic concerns the *transfer of holdings* from one person to another. By what processes may a person transfer holdings to another? How may a person acquire a holding from another who holds it? Under this topic come general descriptions of voluntary exchange, and gift and (on the other hand) fraud, as well as reference to particular conventional details fixed upon in a given society. The complicated truth about this subject (with placeholders for conventional details) we shall call the principle of justice in transfer. (And we shall suppose it also includes principles governing how a person may divest himself of a holding, passing it into an unheld state.)

If the world were wholly just, the following inductive definition would exhaustively cover the subject of justice in holdings.

1. A person who acquires a holding in accordance with the principle of justice in acquisition is entitled to that holding.

2. A person who acquires a holding in accordance with the principle of justice in transfer, from someone else entitled to the holding, is entitled to the holding.

3. No one is entitled to a holding except by (repeated) applications of 1 and 2.

The complete principle of distributive justice would say simply that a distribution is just if everyone is entitled to the holdings they possess under the distribution.

A distribution is just if it arises from another just distribution by legitimate means. The legitimate means of moving from one distribution to another are specified by the principle of justice in transfer. The legitimate first "moves" are specified by the principle of justice in acquisition.[1] Whatever arises from a just situation by just steps is itself just. The means of change specified by the principle of justice in transfer preserve justice. As correct rules of inference are truth-preserving, and any conclusion deduced via repeated application of such rules from only true premises is itself true, so the means of transition from one situation to another specified by the principle of justice in transfer are justice-preserving, and any situation actually arising from repeated transitions in accordance with the principle from a just situation is itself just. The parallel between justice-preserving transformations and truth-preserving transformations illuminates where it fails as well as where it holds. That a conclusion could have been deduced by truth-preserving means from premises that are true suffices to show its truth. That from a just situation a situation *could* have arisen via justice-preserving means does *not* suffice to show its justice. The fact that a thief's victims voluntarily *could* have presented him with gifts does not entitle the thief to his ill-gotten gains. Justice in holdings is historical; it depends upon what actually has happened. We shall return to this point later.

Not all actual situations are generated in accordance with the two principles of justice in holdings: the principle of justice in acquisition and the principle of justice in transfer. Some people steal from others, or defraud them, or enslave them, seizing their product and preventing them from living as they choose, or forcibly exclude others from competing in exchanges. None of these are permissible modes of transition from one situation to another. And some persons acquire holdings by means not sanctioned by the principle of justice in acquisition. The existence of past injustice (previous violations of the first two principles of justice in holdings) raises the third major topic under justice in holdings: the rectification of injustice in holdings. If past injustice has shaped present holdings in various ways, some identifiable and some not, what now, if anything, ought to be done to rectify these injustices? What obligations do the performers of injustice have toward those whose position is worse than it would have been had the injustice not been done? Or, than it would have been had compensation been paid promptly? How, if at all, do things change if the beneficiaries and those made worse off are not the direct parties in the act of injustice, but, for example, their descendants? Is an injustice done to someone whose holding was itself based upon an unrectified injustice? How far back must one go in wiping clean the historical slate of injustices? What may victims of injustice permissibly do in order to rectify the injustices being done to them, including the many injustices done by persons acting through their government? I do not know of a thorough or theoretically sophisticated treatment of such issues. Idealizing greatly, let us suppose theoretical investigation will produce a principle of rectification. This principle uses historical information about previous situations and injustices done in them (as defined by the first two principles of justice and rights against interference), and information about the actual course of events that flowed from these injustices, until the present, and it yields a description (or descriptions) of holdings in the society. The principle of rectification presumably will make use of its best estimate of subjunctive information about what would have occurred (or a probability distribution over what might have occurred, using the expected value) if the injustice had not taken place. If the actual description of holdings turns out not to be one of the descriptions yielded by the principle, then one of the descriptions yielded must be realized.[2]

The general outlines of the theory of justice in holdings are that the holdings of a person are just if he is entitled to them by the principles of justice in acquisition and transfer, or by the principle of rectification of injustice (as specified by the first two principles). If each person's holdings are just, then the total set (distribution) of holdings is just. To turn these general outlines into a specific theory we would have to specify the details of each of the three principles of justice in holdings: the principle of acquisition of holdings, the principle of transfer of holdings, and the principle of rectification of violations of the first two principles. I shall not attempt that task here. (Locke's principle of justice in acquisition is discussed below.)

HISTORICAL PRINCIPLES AND END-RESULT PRINCIPLES

The general outlines of the entitlement theory illuminate the nature and defects of other conceptions of distributive justice. The entitlement theory of justice in distribution is *historical;* whether a distribution is just depends upon how it came about. In contrast, *current time-slice principles* of justice hold that the justice of a distribution is determined by how things are distributed (who has what) as judged by some *structural* principle(s) of just distribution. A utilitarian who judges between any two distributions by seeing which has the greater sum of utility and, if the sums tie, applies some fixed equality criterion to choose the more equal distribution, would hold a current time-slice principle of justice. As would someone who had a fixed schedule of trade-offs between the sum of happiness and equality. According to a current time-slice principle, all that needs to be looked at, in judging the justice of a distribution, is who ends up with what; in comparing any two distributions one need look only at the matrix presenting the distributions. No further information need be fed into a principle of justice. It is a consequence of such principles of justice that any two structurally identical distributions are equally just. (Two distributions are structurally identical if they present the same profile, but perhaps have different persons occupying the particular slots. My having ten and your having five, and my having five and your having ten are structurally identical distributions.) Welfare economics is the theory of current time-slice principles of justice. The subject is conceived as operating on matrices representing only current information about distribution. This, as well as some of the usual conditions (for example, the choice of distribution is invariant under relabeling of columns), guarantees that welfare economics will be a current time-slice theory, with all of its inadequacies.

Most persons do not accept current time-slice principles as constituting the whole story about distributive shares. They think it relevant in assessing the justice of a situation to consider not only the distribution it embodies, but also how that distribution came about. If some persons are in prison for murder or war crimes, we do not say that to assess the justice of the distribution in the society we must look only at what this person has, and that person has, and that person has, . . . at the current time. We think it relevant to ask whether someone did something so that he *deserved* to be punished, deserved to have a lower share. Most will agree to the relevance of further information with regard to punishments and penalties. Consider also desired things. One traditional socialist view is that workers are entitled to the product and full fruits of their labor; they have earned it; a distribution is unjust if it does not give the workers what they are entitled to. Such entitlements are based upon some past history. No socialist holding this view would find it comforting to be told that because the actual distribution *A* happens to coincide structurally with the one he desires *D*, *A* therefore is no less just than *D*; it differs only in that the "parasitic" owners of capital receive under *A* what the workers are entitled to under *D*, and the workers receive under *A* what the owners are entitled to under *D*, namely very little. This socialist rightly, in my view, holds onto the notions of earning, producing, entitlement, desert, and so forth, and he rejects current time-slice principles that look only to the structure of the resulting set of holdings. (The set of holdings resulting from what? Isn't it implausible that how holdings are produced and come to exist has no effect at all on who should hold what?) His mistake lies in his view of what entitlements arise out of what sorts of productive processes.

We construe the position we discuss too narrowly by speaking of *current* time-slice principles. Nothing is changed if structural principles operate upon a time sequence of current time-slice profiles and, for example, give someone more now to counterbalance the less he has had earlier. A utilitarian or an egalitarian or any mixture of the two over time will inherit the difficulties of his more myopic comrades. He is not helped by the fact that *some* of the information others consider relevant in assessing a distribution is reflected, unrecoverably, in past matrices. Henceforth, we shall refer to such unhistorical principles of distributive justice, including the current time-slice principles, as *end-result principles* or *end-state principles*.

In contrast to end-result principles of justice, *historical principles* of justice hold that past circumstances or actions of people can create differential entitlements or differential deserts to things. An injustice can be worked by moving from one distribution to another structurally identical one, for the second, in profile the same, may violate people's entitlements or deserts; it may not fit the actual history.

PATTERNING

The entitlement principles of justice in holdings that we have sketched are historical principles of justice. To better understand their precise character, we shall distinguish them from another subclass of the historical principles. Consider, as an example, the principle of distribution according to moral merit. This principle requires that total distributive shares vary directly with moral merit; no person should have a greater share than anyone whose moral merit is greater. (If moral merit could be not merely ordered but measured on an interval or ratio scale, stronger principles could be formulated.) Or consider the principle that results by substituting "usefulness to society" for "moral merit" in the previous principle. Or instead of "distribute according to moral merit," or "distribute according to usefulness to society," we might consider "distribute according to the weighted sum of moral merit, usefulness to society, and need," with the weights of the different dimensions equal. Let us call a principle of distribution *patterned* if it specifies that a distribution is to vary along with some natural dimension, weighted sum of natural dimensions, or lexicographic ordering of natural dimensions. And let us say a distribution is patterned if it accords with some patterned principle. (I speak of natural dimensions, admittedly without a general criterion for them, because for any set of holdings some artificial dimensions can be gimmicked up to vary along with the distribution of the set.) The principle of distribution in accordance with moral merit is a patterned historical principle, which specifies a patterned distribution. "Distribute according to I.Q." is a patterned principle that looks to information not contained in distributional matrices. It is not historical, however, in that it does not look to any past actions creating differential entitlements to evaluate a distribution; it requires only distributional matrices whose columns are labeled by I.Q. scores. The distribution in a society, however, may be composed of such simple patterned distributions, without itself being simply patterned. Different sectors may operate different patterns, or some combination of patterns may operate in different proportions across a society. A distribution composed in this manner, from a small number of patterned distributions, we also shall term "patterned." And we extend the use of "pattern" to include the overall designs put forth by combinations of end-state principles.

Almost every suggested principle of distributive justice is patterned: to each according to his moral merit, or needs, or marginal product, or how hard he tries, or the weighted sum of the foregoing, and so on. The principle of entitlement we have sketched is *not* patterned.[3] There is no one natural dimension or weighted sum or combination of a small number of natural dimensions that yields the distributions generated in accordance with the principle of entitlement. The set of holdings that results when some persons receive their marginal products, others win at gambling, others receive a share of their mate's income, others receive gifts from foundations, others receive interest on loans, others receive gifts from admirers, others receive returns on investment, others make for themselves much of what they have, others find things, and so on, will not be patterned. Heavy strands of patterns will run through it; significant portions of the variance in holdings will be accounted for by pattern-variables. If most people most of the time choose to transfer some of their entitlements to others only in exchange for something from them, then a large part of what many people hold will vary with what they held that others wanted. More details are provided by the theory of marginal productivity. But gifts to relatives, charitable donations, bequests to children, and the like, are not best conceived, in the first instance, in this manner.

Ignoring the strands of pattern, let us suppose for the moment that a distribution actually arrived at by the operation of the principle of entitlement is random with respect to any pattern. Though the resulting set of holdings will be unpatterned, it will not be incomprehensible, for it can be seen as arising from the operation of a small number of principles. These principles specify how an initial distribution may arise (the principle of acquisition of holdings) and how distributions may be transformed into others (the principle of transfer of holdings). The process whereby the set of holdings is generated will be intelligible, though the set of holdings itself that results from this process will be unpatterned.

The writings of F. A. Hayek focus less than is usually done upon what patterning distributive justice requires. Hayek argues that we cannot know enough about each person's situation to distribute to each according to his moral merit (but would justice demand we do so if we did have this knowledge?); and he goes on to say, "our objection is against all attempts to impress upon society a deliberately chosen pattern of distribution, whether it be an order of equality or of inequality." However, Hayek concludes that in a free society there will be distribution in accordance with value rather than moral merit; that is, in accordance with the perceived value of a person's actions and services to others. Despite his rejection of a patterned conception of distributive justice, Hayek himself suggests a pattern he thinks justifiable: distribution in accordance with the perceived benefits given to others, leaving room for the complaint that a free society does not realize exactly this pattern. Stating this patterned strand of a free capitalist society more precisely, we get "To each according to how much he benefits others who have the resources for benefiting those who benefit them." This will seem arbitrary unless some acceptable initial set of holdings is specified, or unless it is held that the operation of the system over time washes out any significant effects from the initial set of holdings. As an example of the latter, if almost anyone would have bought a car from Henry Ford, the supposition that it was an arbitrary matter who held the money then (and so bought) would not place Henry Ford's earnings under a cloud. In any event, *his* coming to hold it is not arbitrary. Distribution according to benefits to others *is* a major patterned strand in a free capitalist society, as Hayek correctly points out, but it is only a strand and does not constitute the whole pattern of a system of entitlements (namely, inheritance, gifts for arbitrary reasons, charity, and so on) or a standard that one should insist a society fit. Will people tolerate for long a system yielding distributions that they believe are unpatterned? No doubt people will not long accept a distribution they believe is *unjust*. People want their society to be and to look just. But must the look of justice reside in a resulting pattern rather than in the underlying generating principles? We are in no position to conclude that the inhabitants of a society embodying an entitlement conception of justice in holdings will find it unacceptable. Still, it must be granted that were people's reasons for transferring some of their holdings to others always irrational or arbitrary, we would find this disturbing. (Suppose people always determined what holdings they would transfer, and to whom, by using a random device.) We feel more comfortable upholding the justice of an entitlement system if most of the transfers under it are done for reasons. This does not mean necessarily that all deserve what holdings they receive. It means only that there is a purpose or point to someone's transferring a holding to one person rather than to another; that usually we can see what the transferrer thinks he's gaining, what cause he thinks he's serving, what goals he thinks he's helping to achieve, and so forth. Since in a capitalist society people often transfer holdings to others in accordance with how much they perceive these others benefiting them, the fabric constituted by the individual transactions and transfers is largely reasonable and intelligible.[5] (Gifts to loved ones, bequests to children, charity to the needy also are nonarbitrary components of the fabric.) In stressing the large strand of distribution in accordance with benefit to others, Hayek shows the point of many transfers, and so shows that the system of transfer of entitlements is not just spinning its gears aimlessly. The system of entitlements is defensible when constituted by the individual aims of individual transactions. No overarching aim is needed, no distributional pattern is required.

To think that the task of a theory of distributive justice is to fill in the blank in "to each according to his_____" is to be predisposed to search for a pattern; and the separate treatment of "from each according to his_____" treats production and distribution as two separate and independent issues. On an entitlement view these are *not* two separate questions. Whoever makes something, having bought or contracted for all other held resources used in the process (transferring some of his holdings for these cooperating factors), is entitled to it. The situation is *not* one of something's getting made, and there being an open question of who is to get it. Things come into the world already attached to people having entitlements over them. From the point of view of the historical entitlement conception of justice in holdings, those who start afresh to complete "to each according to his_____" treat objects as if they appeared from nowhere, out of nothing. A complete theory of justice might cover this limit case as well; perhaps here is a use for the usual conceptions of distributive justice.

So entrenched are maxims of the usual form that perhaps we should present the entitlement conception as a competitor. Ignoring acquisition and rectification, we might say:

> From each according to what he chooses to do, to each according to what he makes for himself (perhaps with the contracted aid of others) and what others choose to do for him and choose to give him of what they've been given previously (under this maxim) and haven't yet expended or transferred.

This, the discerning reader will have noticed, has its defects as a slogan. So as a summary and great simplification (and not as a maxim with any independent meaning) we have:

From each as they choose, to each as they are chosen.

HOW LIBERTY UPSETS PATTERNS

It is not clear how those holding alternative conceptions of distributive justice can reject the entitlement conception of justice in holdings. For suppose a distribution favored by one of these nonentitlement conceptions is realized. Let us suppose it is your favorite one and let us call this distribution D_1; perhaps everyone has an equal share, perhaps shares vary in accordance with some dimension you treasure. Now suppose that Wilt Chamberlain is greatly in demand by basketball teams, being a great gate attraction. (Also suppose contracts run only for a year, with players being free agents.) He signs the following sort of contract with a team: In each home game, twenty-five cents from the price of each ticket of admission goes to him. (We ignore the question of whether he is "gouging" the owners, letting them look out for themselves.) The season starts, and people cheerfully attend his team's games; they buy their tickets, each time dropping a separate twenty-five cents of their admission price into a special box with Chamberlain's name on it. They are excited about seeing him play; it is worth the total admission price to them. Let us suppose that in one season one million persons attend his home games, and Wilt Chamberlain winds up with $250,000, a much larger sum than the average income and larger even than anyone else has. Is he entitled to this income? Is this new distribution D_2 unjust? If so, why? There is *no* question about whether each of the people was entitled to the control over the resources they held in D_1; because that was the distribution (your favorite) that (for the purposes of argument) we assumed was acceptable. Each of these persons *chose* to give twenty-five cents of their money to Chamberlain. They could have spent it on going to the movies, or on candy bars, or on copies of *Dissent* magazine, or of *Monthly Review*. But they all, at least one million of them, converged on giving it to Wilt Chamberlain in exchange for watching him play basketball. If D_1 was a just distribution, and people voluntarily moved from it to D_2, transferring parts of their shares they were given under D_1 (what was it for if not to do something with?), isn't D_2 also just? If the people were entitled to dispose of the resources to which they were entitled (under D_1), didn't this include their being entitled to give it to, or exchange it with, Wilt Chamberlain? Can anyone else complain on grounds of justice? Each other person already has his legitimate share under D_1. Under D_1, there is nothing that anyone has that anyone else has a claim of justice against. After someone transfers something to Wilt Chamberlain, third parties *still* have their legitimate shares; *their* shares are not changed. By what process could such a transfer among two persons give rise to a legitimate claim of distributive justice on a portion of what was transferred, by a third party who had no claim of justice on any holding of the others *before* the transfer?[6] To cut off objections irrelevant here, we might imagine the exchanges occurring in a socialist society, after hours. After playing what-ever basketball he does in his daily work, or doing whatever other daily work he does, Wilt Chamberlain decides to put in *overtime* to earn addi-tional money. (First his work quota is set; he works time over that.) Or imagine it is a skilled juggler people like to see, who puts on shows after hours.

Why might someone work overtime in a society in which it is assumed their needs are satisfied? Perhaps because they care about things other than needs. I like to write in books that I read, and to have easy access to books for browsing at odd hours. It would be very pleasant and conve-nient to have the resouces of Widener Library in my back yard. No society, I assume, will provide such resources close to each person who would like them as part of his regular allotment (under D_1). Thus, per-sons either must do without some extra things that they want, or be allowed to do something extra to get some of these things. On what basis could the inequalities that would eventuate be forbidden? Notice also that small factories would spring up in a socialist society, unless forbidden. I melt down some of my personal possessions (under D_1) and build a machine out of the material. I offer you, and others, a philosophy lecture once a week in exchange for your cranking the handle on my machine, whose products I exchange for yet other things, and so on. (The raw materials used by the machine are given to me by others who possess them under D_1, in exchange for hearing lectures.) Each person might participate to gain things over and above their allotment under D_1. Some persons even might want to leave their job in socialist industry and work full time in this private sector. I shall say something more about these issues in the next chapter. Here I wish merely to note how private prop-erty even in means of production would occur in a socialist society that did not forbid people to use as they wished some of the resources they are given under the socialist distribution D_1. The socialist society would have to forbid capitalist acts between consenting adults.

The general point illustrated by the Wilt Chamberlain example and the example of the entrepreneur in a socialist society is that no end-state principle or distributional patterned principle of justice can be continu-ously realized without continuous interference with people's lives. Any favored pattern would be transformed into one unfavored by the princi-ple, by people choosing to act in various ways; for example, by people exchanging goods and services with other people, or giving things to other people, things the transferrers are entitled to under the favored distributional pattern. To maintain a pattern one must either continually interfere to stop people from transferring resources as they wish to, or continually (or periodically) interfere to take from some persons resources that others for some reason chose to transfer to them. (But if some time limit is to be set on how long people may keep resources others voluntarily transfer to them, why let them keep these resources for *any* period of time? Why not have immediate confiscation?) It might be objected that all persons voluntarily will choose to refrain from actions which would upset the pattern. This presupposes unrealistically (1) that all will most want to maintain the pattern (are those who don't, to be "reeducated" or forced to undergo "self-criticism"?), (2) that each can gather enough information about his own actions and the ongoing activities of others to discover which of his actions will upset the pattern, and (3) that diverse and far-flung persons can coordinate their actions to dovetail into the pattern. Compare the manner in which the market is neutral among persons' desires, as it reflects and transmits widely scattered information via prices, and coordinates persons' activities.

It puts things perhaps a bit too strongly to say that every patterned (or end-state) principle is liable to be thwarted by the voluntary actions of the individual parties transferring some of their shares they receive under the principle. For perhaps some *very* weak patterns are not so thwarted. Any distributional pattern with any egalitarian component is overturnable by the voluntary actions of individual persons over time; as is every patterned condition with sufficient content so as actually to have been proposed as presenting the central core of distributive justice. Still, given the possibility that some weak conditions or patterns may not be unstable in this way, it would be better to formulate an explicit description of the kind of interesting and contentful patterns under discussion, and to prove a theorem about their instability. Since the weaker the patterning, the more likely it is that the entitlement system itself satisfies it, a plausible conjecture is that any patterning either is unstable or is satisfied by the entitlement system. . . .

NOTES

1. Applications of the principle of justice in acquisition may also occur as part of the move from one distribution to another. You may find an unheld thing now and appropriate it. Acquisitions also are to be understood as included when, to simplify, I speak only of transitions by transfers.

2. If the principle of rectification of violations of the first two principles yields more than one description of holdings, then some choice must be made as to which of these is to be realized. Perhaps the sort of considerations about distributive justice and equality that I argue against play a legitimate role in *this* subsidiary choice. Similarly, there may be room for such considerations in deciding which otherwise arbitrary features a statute will embody, when such features are unavoidable because other considerations do not specify a precise line; yet a line must be drawn.

3. One might try to squeeze a patterned conception of distributive justice into the framework of the entitlement conception, by formulating a gimmicky obligatory "principle of transfer" that would lead to the pattern. For example, the principle that if one has more than the mean income one must transfer everything one holds above the mean to persons below the mean so as to bring them up to (but not over) the mean. We can formulate a criterion for a "principle of transfer" to rule out such obligatory transfers, or we can say that no correct principle of transfer, no principle of transfer in a free society will be like this. The former is probably the better course, though the latter also is true.

Alternatively, one might think to make the entitlement conception instantiate a pattern, by using matrix entries that express the relative strength of a person's entitlements as measured by some real-valued function. But even if the limitation to natural dimensions failed to exclude this function, the resulting edifice would *not* capture our system of entitlements to *particular* things.

4. F. A. Hayek, *The Constitution of Liberty* (Chicago: University of Chicago Press, 1960), p. 87.

5. We certainly benefit because great economic incentives operate to get others to spend much time and energy to figure out how to serve us by providing things we will want to pay for. It is not mere paradox mongering to wonder whether capitalism should be criticized for most rewarding and hence encouraging, not individualists like Thoreau who go about their own lives, but people who are occupied with serving others and winning them as customers. But to defend capitalism one need not think businessmen are the finest human types. (I do not mean to join here the general maligning of businessmen, either.) Those who think the finest should acquire the most can try to convince their fellows to transfer resources in accordance with *that* principle.

6. Might not a transfer have instrumental effects on a third party, changing his feasible options? (But what if the two parties to the transfer independently had used their holdings in this fashion?) I discuss this question below, but note here that this question concedes the point for distributions of ultimate intrinsic noninstrumental goods (pure utility experiences, so to speak) that are transferrable. It also might be objected that the transfer might make a third party more envious because it worsens his position relative to someone else. I find it incomprehensible how this can be thought to involve a claim of justice. On envy, see Chapter 8 [not reprinted here].

Here and elsewhere in this chapter, a theory which incorporates elements of pure procedural justice might find what I say acceptable, *if* kept in its proper place; that is, if background institutions exist to ensure the satisfaction of certain conditions on distributive shares. But if these institutions are not themselves the sum or invisible-hand result of people's voluntary (nonaggressive) actions, the constraints they impose require justification. At no point does *our* argument assume any background institutions more extensive than those of the minimal night-watchman state, a state limited to protecting persons against murder, assault, theft, fraud, and so forth.

TWO PRINCIPLES OF JUSTICE

John Rawls

Justice as fairness begins . . . with one of the most general of all choices which persons might make together, namely, with the choice of the first principles of a conception of justice which is to regulate all subsequent criticism and reform of institutions. Then, having chosen a conception of justice, we can suppose that they are to choose a constitution and a legislature to enact laws, and so on, all in accordance with the principles of justice initially agreed upon. Our social situation is just if it is such that by this sequence of hypothetical agreements we would have contracted into the general system of rules which defines it. Moreover, assuming that the original position does determine a set of principles (that is, that a particular conception of justice would be chosen), it will then be true that whenever social institutions satisfy these principles those engaged in them can say to one another that they are cooperating on terms to which they would agree if they were free and equal persons whose relations with respect to one another were fair. They could all view their arrangements as meeting the stipulations which they would acknowledge in an initial situation that embodies widely accepted and reasonable constraints on the choice of principles. The general recognition of this fact would provide the basis for a public acceptance of the corresponding principles of justice. No society can, of course, be a scheme of cooperation which men enter voluntarily in a literal sense; each person finds himself placed at birth in some particular position in some particular society, and the nature of this position materially affects his life prospects. Yet a society satisfying the principles of justice as fairness comes as close as a society can to being a voluntary scheme, for it meets the principles which free and equal persons would assent to under circumstances that are fair. In this sense its members are autonomous and the obligations they recognize self-imposed.

One feature of justice as fairness is to think of the parties in the initial situation as rational and mutually disinterested. This does not mean that the parties are egoists, that is, individuals with only certain kinds of interests, say in wealth, prestige, and domination. But they are conceived as not taking an interest in one another's interests. They are to presume that even their spiritual aims may be opposed, in the way that the aims of those of different religions may be opposed. Moreover, the concept of rationality must be interpreted as far as possible in the narrow sense, standard in economic theory, of taking the most effective means to given ends. I shall modify this concept to some extent, as explained later, but one must try to avoid introducing into it any controversial ethical elements. The initial situation must be characterized by stipulations that are widely accepted. . . .

I shall maintain that the persons in the initial situation would choose two rather different principles: the first requires equality in the assignment of basic rights and duties, while the second holds that social and economic inequalities, for example inequalities of wealth and authority, are just only if they result in compensating benefits for everyone, and in particular for the least advantaged members of society. These principles rule out justifying institutions on the grounds that the hardships of some are offset by a greater good in the aggregate. It may be expedient but it is not just that some should have less in order that others may prosper. But there is no injustice in the greater benefits earned by a few provided that the situation of persons not so fortunate is thereby improved. The intuitive idea is that since everyone's well-being depends upon a scheme of cooperation without which no one could have a satisfactory life, the division of advantages should be such as to draw forth the willing cooperation of everyone taking part in it, including those less well situated. Yet this can be expected only if reasonable terms are proposed. The two principles mentioned seem to be a fair agreement on the basis of which those better endowed, or more fortunate in their social position, neither of which we can be said to deserve, could expect the willing cooperation of others when some workable scheme is a necessary condition of the welfare of all. Once we decide to look for a conception of justice that nullifies the accidents of natural endowment and the contingencies of social circumstance as counters in quest for political and economic advantage, we are led to these principles. They express the result of leaving aside those aspects of the social world that seem arbitrary from a moral point of view. . . .

The idea of the original position is to set up a fair procedure so that any principles agreed to will be just. The aim is to use the notion of pure procedural justice as a basis of theory. Somehow we must nullify the effects of specific contingencies which put men at odds and tempt them to exploit social and natural circumstances to their own advantage. Now in order to do this I assume that the parties are situated behind a veil of ignorance. They do not know how the various alternatives will affect their own particular case and they are obliged to evaluate principles solely on the basis of general considerations.

It is assumed, then, that the parties do not know certain kinds of particular facts. First of all, no one knows his place in society, his class position or social status; nor does he know his fortune in the distribution of natural assets and abilities; his intelligence and strength, and the like. Nor, again, does anyone know his conception of the good, the particulars of his rational plan of life, or even the special features of his psychology such as his aversion to risk or liability to optimism or pessimism. More than this, I assume that the parties do not know the particular circumstances of their own society. That is, they do not know its economic or political situation, or the level of civilization and culture it has been able to achieve. The persons in the original position have no information as to which generation they belong. These broader restrictions on knowledge are appropriate in part because questions of social justice arise between generations as well as within them, for example, the question of the appropriate rate of capital saving and of the conservation of natural resources and the environment of nature. There is also, theoretically anyway, the question of a reasonable genetic policy. In these cases too, in order to carry through the idea of the original position, the parties must not know the contingencies that set them in opposition. They must choose principles the consequences of which they are prepared to live with whatever generation they turn out to belong to.

As far as possible, then, the only particular facts which the parties know is that their society is subject to the circumstances of justice and whatever this implies. It is taken for granted, however, that they know the general facts about human society. They understand political affairs and the principles of economic theory; they know the basis of social organization and the laws of human psychology. Indeed, the parties are presumed to know whatever general facts affect the choice of the principles of justice. There are no limitations on general information, that is, on general laws and theories, since conceptions of justice must be adjusted to the characteristics of the systems of social cooperation which they are to regulate, and there is no reason to rule out these facts. It is, for example, a consideration against a conception of justice that in view of the laws of moral psychology, men would not acquire a desire to act upon it even when the institutions of their society satisfied it. For in this case there would be difficulty in securing the stability of social cooperation. It is an important feature of a conception of justice that it should generate its own support. That is, its principles should be such that when they are embodied in the basic structure of society men tend to acquire the corresponding sense of justice. Given the principles of moral learning, men develop a desire to act in accordance with its principles. In this case a conception of justice is stable. This kind of general information is admissible in the original position. . . .

Thus there follows the very important consequence that the parties have no basis for bargaining in the usual sense. No one knows his situation in society nor his natural assets, and therefore no one is in a position to tailor principles to his advantage. We might imagine that one of the contractees threatens to hold out unless the others agree to principles favorable to him. But how does he know which principles are especially in his interests? The same holds for the formation of coalitions: if a group were to decide to band together to the disadvantage of the others, they would not know how to favor themselves in the choice of principles. Even if they could get everyone to agree to their proposal, they would have no assurance that it was to their advantage, since they cannot identify themselves either by name or description. . . .

The restrictions on particular information in the original position are, then, of fundamental importance. Without them we would not be able to work out any definite theory of justice at all. We would have to be content with a vague formula stating that justice is what would be agreed to without being able to say much, if anything, about the substance of the agreement itself. The formal constraints of the concept of right, those applying to principles directly, are not sufficient for our purpose. The veil of ignorance makes possible a unanimous choice of a particular conception of justice. Without these limitations on knowledge the bargaining problem of the original position would be hopelessly complicated. Even if theoretically a solution were to exist, we would not, at present anyway, be able to determine it. . . .

I shall now state in a provisional form the two principles of justice that I believe would be chosen in the original position. . . .

The first statement of the two principles reads as follows.

> First: each person is to have an equal right to the most extensive basic liberty compatible with a similar liberty for others.
>
> Second: social and economic inequalities are to be arranged so that they are both (a) reasonably expected to be to everyone's advantage, and (b) attached to positions and offices open to all.

Our common sense intuitions for the former may be a poor guide to the latter. There are two ambiguous phrases in the second principle, namely "everyone's advantage" and "equally open to all." Determining their sense more exactly will lead to a second formulation of the principle. . . .

By way of general comment, these principles primarily apply, as I have said, to the basic structure of society. They are to govern the assignment of rights and duties and to regulate the distribution of social and economic advantages. As their formulation suggests, these principles presuppose that the social structure can be divided into two more or less distinct parts, the first principle applying to the one, the second to the other. They distinguish between those aspects of the social system that define and secure the equal liberties of citizenship and those that specify and establish social and economic inequalities. The basic liberties of citizens are, roughly speaking, political liberty (the right to vote and to be eligible for public office) together with freedom of speech and assembly; liberty of conscience and freedom of thought; freedom of the person along with the right to hold (personal) property; and freedom from arbitrary arrest and seizure as defined by the concept of the rule of law. These liberties are all required to be equal by the first principle, since citizens of a just society are to have the same basic rights.

The second principle applies, in the first approximation, to the distribution of income and wealth and to the design of organizations that make use of differences in authority and responsibility, or chains of command. While the distribution of wealth and income need not be equal, it must be to everyone's advantage, and at the same time, positions of authority and offices of command must be accessible to all. One applies the second principle by holding positions open, and then, subject to this constraint, arranges social and economic inequalities so that everyone benefits.

These principles are to be arranged in a serial order with the first principle prior to the second. This ordering means that a departure from the institutions of equal liberty required by the first principle cannot be justified by, or compensated for, by greater social and economic advantages. The distribution of wealth and income, and the hierarchies of authority, must be consistent with both the liberties of equal citizenship and equality of opportunity.

It is clear that these principles are rather specific in their content, and their acceptance rests on certain assumptions that I must eventually try to explain and justify. A theory of justice depends upon a theory of society in ways that will become evident as we proceed. For the present, it should be observed that the two principles (and this holds for all formulations) are a special case of a more general conception of justice that can be expressed as follows.

> All social values—liberty and opportunity, income and wealth, and the bases of self-respect—are to be distributed equally unless an unequal distribution of any, or all, of these values is to everyone's advantage.

Injustice, then, is simply inequalities that are not to the benefit of all. Of course, this conception is extremely vague and requires interpretation.

As a first step, suppose that the basic structure of society distributes certain primary goods, that is, things that every rational man is presumed to want. These goods normally have a use whatever a person's rational plan of life. For simplicity, assume that the chief primary goods at the disposition of society are rights and liberties, powers and opportunities, income and wealth. These are the social primary goods. Other primary goods such as health and vigor, intelligence and imagination, are natural goods; although their possession is influenced by the basic structure, they are not so directly under its control. Imagine, then, a hypothetical initial arrangement in which all the social primary goods are equally distributed: everyone has similar rights and duties, and income and wealth are evenly shared. This state of affairs provides a benchmark for judging improvements. If certain inequalities of wealth and organizational powers would make everyone better off than in this hypothetical starting situation, then they accord with the general conception.

Now it is possible, at least theoretically, that by giving up some of their fundamental liberties men are sufficiently compensated by the resulting social and economic gains. The general conception of justice imposes no restrictions on what sort of inequalities are permissible; it only requires that everyone's position be improved. We need not suppose anything so drastic as consenting to a condition of slavery. Imagine instead that men forego certain political rights when the economic returns are significant and their capacity to influence the course of policy by the exercise of these rights would be marginal in any case. It is this kind of exchange which the two principles as stated rule out; being arranged in serial order they do not permit exchanges between basic liberties and economic and social gains. The serial ordering of principles expresses an underlying preference among primary social goods. When this preference is rational so likewise is the choice of these principles in this order. . . .

The fact that the two principles apply to institutions has certain consequences. Several points illustrate this. First of all, the rights and liberties referred to by these principles are those which are defined by the public rules of the basic structure. Whether men are free is determined by the rights and duties established by the major institutions of society. Liberty is a certain pattern of social forms. The first principle simply requires that certain sorts of rules, those defining basic liberties, apply to everyone equally and that they allow the most extensive liberty compatible with a like liberty for all. The only reason for circumscribing the rights defining liberty and making men's freedom less extensive than it might otherwise be is that these equal rights as institutionally defined would interfere with one another.

Another thing to bear in mind is that when principles mention persons, or require that everyone gain from an inequality, the reference is to representative persons holding the various social positions, or offices, or whatever, established by the basic structure. Thus in applying the second principle I assume that it is possible to assign an expectation of well-being to representative individuals holding these positions. This expectation indicates their life prospects as viewed from their social station. In general, the expectations of representative persons depend upon the distribution of rights and duties throughout the basic structure. When this changes, expectations change. I assume, then, that expectations are connected: by raising the prospects of the representative man in one position we presumably increase or decrease the prospects of representative men in other positions. Since it applies to institutional forms, the second principle (or rather the first part of it) refers to the expectations of representative individuals. As I shall discuss below, neither principle applies to distributions of particular goods to particular individuals who may be identified by their proper names. The situation where someone is considering how to allocate certain commodities to needy persons who are known to him is not within the scope of the principles. They are meant to regulate basic institutional arrangements. We must not assume that there is much similarity from the standpoint of justice between an administrative allotment of goods to specific persons and the appropriate design of society.

Now the second principle insists that each person benefit from permissible inequalities in the basic structure. This means that it must be reasonable for each relevant representative man defined by this structure, when he views it as a going concern, to prefer his prospects with the inequality to his prospects without it. One is not allowed to justify differences in income or organizational powers on the ground that the disadvantages of those in one position are outweighed by the greater advantages of those in another. Much less can infringements of liberty be counterbalanced in this way. Applied to the basic structure, the principle of utility would have us maximize the sum of expectations of representative men (weighted by the number of persons they represent, on the classical view); and this would permit us to compensate for the losses of some by the gains of others. Instead, the two principles require that everyone benefit from economic and social inequalities. . . .

To illustrate the difference principle, consider the distribution of income among social classes. Let us suppose that the various income groups correlate with representative individuals by reference to whose expectations we can judge the distribution. Now those starting out as members of the entrepreneurial class in property-owning democracy, say, have a better prospect than those who begin in the class of unskilled laborers. It seems likely that this will be true even when the social injustices which now exist are removed. What, then, can possibly justify this kind of initial inequality in life prospects? According to the difference principle, it is justifiable only if the difference in expectation is to the advantage of the representative man who is worse off, in this case the representative unskilled worker. The inequality in expectation is permissible only if lowering it would make the working class even more worse off. Supposedly, given the rider in the second principle concerning open positions, and the principle of liberty generally, the greater expectations allowed to entrepreneurs encourages them to do things which raise the long-term prospects of the laboring class. Their better prospects act as incentives so that the economic process is more efficient, innovation proceeds at a faster pace, and so on. Eventually the resulting material benefits spread throughout the system and to the least advantaged. I shall not consider how far these things are true. The point is that something of this kind must be argued if these inequalities are to be just by the difference principle.

I shall now make a few remarks about this principle. First of all, in applying it, one should distinguish between two cases. The first case is that in which the expectations of the least advantaged are indeed maximized (subject, of course, to the mentioned constraints). No changes in the expectations of those better off can improve the situation of those worst off. The best arrangement obtains, what I shall call a perfectly just scheme. The second case is that in which the expectations of all those better off at least contribute to the welfare of the more unfortunate. That is, if their expectations were decreased, the prospects of the least advantaged would likewise fall. Yet the maximum is not yet achieved. Even higher expectations for the more advantaged would raise the expectations of those in the lowest position. Such a scheme is, I shall say, just throughout, but not the best just arrangement. A scheme is unjust when the higher expectations, one or more of them, are excessive. If these expectations were decreased, the situation of the least favored would be improved. How unjust an arrangement is depends on how excessive the higher expectations are and to what extent they depend upon the violation of the other principles of justice, for example, fair equality of opportunity; but I shall not attempt to measure in any exact way the degrees of injustice. The point to note here is that while the difference principle is, strictly speaking, a maximizing principle, there is a significant distinction between the cases that fall short of the best arrangement. A society should try to avoid the region where the marginal contributions of those better off are negative, since, other things equal, this seems a greater fault than falling short of the best scheme when these contributions are positive. The even larger difference between rich and poor makes the latter even worse off, and this violates the principle of mutual advantage as well as democratic equality. . . .

. . . . And therefore the second principle is to read as follows.

> Social and economic inequalities are to be arranged so that they are both (a) to the greatest benefit of the least advantaged and (b) attached to offices and positions open to all under conditions of fair equality of opportunity.

Finally, it should be observed that the difference principle, or the idea expressed by it, can easily be accommodated to the general conception of justice. In fact, the general conception is simply the difference principle applied to all primary goods including liberty and opportunity and so no longer constrained by other parts of the special conception.

MARGINAL NOTES TO THE PROGRAMME OF THE GERMAN WORKERS' PARTY

Karl Marx

I

1. "Labour is the source of all wealth and all culture, *and since* useful labour is possible only in society and through society, the proceeds of labour belong undiminished with equal rights to all members of society."

First Part of the Paragraph: "Labour is the source of all wealth and all culture."

Labour is *not the source* of all wealth. *Nature* is just as much the source of use values (and it is surely of such that material wealth consists!) as labour, which itself is only the manifestation of a force of nature, human labour power. The above phrase is to be found in all children's primers and is correct in so far as it is *implied* that labour is performed with the appurtenant subjects and instruments. But a socialist programme cannot allow such bourgeois phrases to pass over in silence the *conditions* that alone give them meaning. And in so far as man from the beginning behaves toward nature, the primary source of all instruments and subjects of labour, as an owner, treats her as belonging to him, his labour becomes the source of use values, therefore also of wealth. The bourgeois have very good grounds for falsely ascribing *supernatural creative power* to labour; since precisely from the fact that labour depends on nature it follows that the man who possesses no other property than his labour power must, in all conditions of society and culture, be the slave of other men who have made themselves the owners of the material conditions of labour. He can work only with their permission, hence live only with their permission.

Let us now leave the sentence as it stands, or rather limps. What would one have expected in conclusion? Obviously this:

"Since labour is the source of all wealth, no one in society can appropriate wealth except as the product of labour. Therefore, if he himself does not work, he lives by the labour of others and also acquires his culture at the expense of the labour of others."

Instead of this, by means of the verbal rivet *"and since"* a second proposition is added in order to draw a conclusion from this and not from the first one.

Second Part of the Paragraph: "Useful labour is possible only in society and through society."

According to the first proposition, labour was the source of all wealth and all culture; therefore no society is possible without labour. Now we learn, conversely, that no "useful" labour is possible without society.

One could just as well have said that only in society can useless and even socially harmful labour become a branch of gainful occupation, that only in society can one live by being idle, etc., etc.—in short, one could just as well have copied the whole of Rousseau.

And what is "useful" labour? Surely only labour which produces the intended useful result. A savage—and man was a savage after he had ceased to be an ape—who kills an animal with a stone, who collects fruits, etc., performs "useful" labour.

Thirdly. The Conclusion: "And since useful labour is possible only in society and through society, the proceeds of labour belong undiminished with equal right to all members of society."

A fine conclusion! If useful labour is possible only in society and through society, the proceeds of labour belong to society—and only so much therefrom accrues to the individual worker as is not required to maintain the "condition" of labour, society.

In fact, this proposition has at all times been made use of by the champions of the *state of society prevailing at any given time.* First come the claims of the government and everything that sticks to it, since it is the social organ for the maintenance of the social order; then come the claims of the various kinds of private property, for the various kinds of private property are the foundations of society, etc. One sees that such hollow phrases can be twisted and turned as desired.

The first and second parts of the paragraph have some intelligible connection only in the following wording:

"Labour becomes the source of wealth and culture only as social labour," or, what is the same thing, "in and through society."

This proposition is incontestably correct, for although isolated labour (its material conditions presupposed) can create use values, it can create neither wealth nor culture.

But equally incontestable is this other proposition:

"In proportion as labour develops socially, and becomes thereby a source of wealth and culture, poverty and destitution develop among the workers, and wealth and culture among the non-workers."

This is the law of all history hitherto. What, therefore, had to be done here, instead of setting down general phrases about "labour" and "society," was to prove concretely how in present capitalist society the material, etc., conditions have at last been created which enable and compel the workers to lift this social curse.

In fact, however, the whole paragraph, bungled in style and content, is only there in order to inscribe the Lassallean catchword of the "undiminished proceeds of labour" as a slogan at the top of the party banner. I shall return later to the "proceeds of labour," "equal right," etc., since the same thing recurs in a somewhat different form further on.

2. "In present-day society, the instruments of labour are the monopoly of the capitalist class; the resulting dependence of the working class is the cause of misery and servitude in all its forms."

This sentence, borrowed from the Rules of the International, is incorrect in this "improved" edition.

In present-day society the instruments of labour are the monopoly of the landowners (the monopoly of property in land is even the basis of the monopoly of capital) *and* the capitalists. In the passage in question, the Rules of the International do not mention either the one or the other class of monopolists. They speak of the *"monopoliser of the means of labour, that is, the sources of life."* The addition, *"sources of life,"* makes it sufficiently clear that land is included in the instruments of labour.

The correction was introduced because Lassalle, for reasons now generally known, attacked *only* the capitalist class and not the landowners. In England, the capitalist is usually not even the owner of the land on which his factory stands.

3. "The emancipation of labour demands the promotion of the instruments of labour to the common property of society and the co-operative regulation of the total labour with a fair distribution of the proceeds of labour."

"Promotion of the instruments of labour to the common property" ought obviously to read their "conversion into the common property"; but this only in passing.

What are "proceeds of labour"? The product of labour or its value? And in the latter case, is it the total value of the product or only that part of the value which labour has newly added to the value of the means of production consumed?

"Proceeds of labour" is a loose notion which Lassalle has put in the place of definite economic conceptions.

What is "a fair distribution"?

Do not the bourgeois assert that the present-day distribution is "fair"? And is it not, in fact, the only "fair" distribution on the basis of the present-day mode of production? Are economic relations regulated by legal conceptions or do not, on the contrary, legal relations arise from economic ones? Have not also the socialist sectarians the most varied notions about "fair" distribution?

To understand what is implied in this connection by the phrase "fair distribution," we must take the first paragraph and this one together. The latter presupposes a society wherein "the instruments of labour are common property and the total labour is co-operatively regulated," and from the first paragraph we learn that "the proceeds of labour belong undiminished with equal right to all members of society."

"To all members of society"? To those who do not work as well? What remains then of the "undiminished proceeds of labour?" Only to those members of society who work? What remains then of the "equal right" of all members of society?

But "all members of society" and "equal right" are obviously mere phrases. The kernel consists in this, that in this communist society every worker must receive the "undiminished" Lassallean "proceeds of labour."

Let us take first of all the words "proceeds of labour" in the sense of the product of labour; then the co-operative proceeds of labour are the *total social product*.

From this must now be deducted:

First, cover for replacement of the means of production used up.

Secondly, additional portion for expansion of production.

Thirdly, reserve or insurance funds to provide against accidents, dislocations caused by natural calamities, etc.

These deductions from the "undiminished proceeds of labour" are an economic necessity and their magnitude is to be determined according to available means and forces, and partly by computation of probabilities, but they are in no way calculable by equity.

There remains the other part of the total product, intended to serve as means of consumption.

Before this is divided among the individuals, there has to be deducted again, from it:

First, the general costs of administration not belonging to production.

This part will, from the outset, be very considerably restricted in comparison with present-day society and it diminishes in proportion as the new society develops.

Secondly, that which is intended for the common satisfaction of needs, such as schools, health services, etc.

From the outset this part grows considerably in comparison with present-day society and it grows in proportion as the new society develops.

Thirdly, funds for those unable to work, etc., in short, for what is included under so-called official poor relief today.

Only now do we come to the "distribution" which the programme, under Lassallean influence, alone has in view in its narrow fashion, namely, to that part of the means of consumption which is divided among the individual producers of the cooperative society.

The "undiminished proceeds of labour" have already unnoticeably become converted into the "diminished" proceeds, although what the producer is deprived of in his capacity as a private individual benefits him directly or indirectly in his capacity as a member of society.

Just as the phrase of the "undiminished proceeds of labour" has disappeared, so now does the phrase of the "proceeds of labour" disappear altogether.

Within the co-operative society based on common ownership of the means of production, the producers do not exchange their products; just as little does the labour employed on the products appear here *as the value* of these products, as a material quality possessed by them, since now, in contrast to capitalist society, individual labour no longer exists in an indirect fashion but directly as a component part of the total labour. The phrase "proceeds of labour," objectionable also today on account of its ambiguity, thus loses all meaning.

What we have to deal with here is a communist society, not as it has *developed* on its own foundations, but, on the contrary, just as it *emerges* from capitalist society; which is thus in every respect, economically, morally and intellectually, still stamped with the birth marks of the old society from whose womb it emerges. Accordingly, the individual producer receives back from society—after the deductions have been made—exactly what he gives to it. What he has given to it is his individual quantum of labour. For example, the social working day consists of the sum of the individual hours of work; the individual labour time of the individual producer is the part of the social working day contributed by him, his share in it. He receives a certificate from society that he has furnished such and such an amount of labour (after deducting his labour for the common funds), and with this certificate he draws from the social stock of means of consumption as much as costs the same amount of labour. The same amount of labour which he has given to society in one form he receives back in another.

Here obviously the same principle prevails as that which regulates the exchange of commodities, as far as this is exchange of equal values. Content and form are changed, because under the altered circumstances no one can give anything except his labour, and because, on the other hand, nothing can pass to the ownership of individuals except individual means of consumption. But, as far as the distribution of the latter among the individual producers is concerned, the same principle prevails as in the exchange of commodity-equivalents: a given amount of labour in one form is exchanged for an equal amount of labour in another form.

Hence, *equal right* here is still in principle—*bourgeois right*, although principle and practice are no longer at loggerheads, while the exchange of equivalents in commodity exchange only exists *on the average* and not in the individual case.

In spite of this advance, this *equal right* is still constantly stigmatised by a bourgeois limitation. The right of the producers is *proportional* to the labour they supply; the equality consists in the fact that measurement is made with an *equal standard*, labour.

But one man is superior to another physically or mentally and so supplies more labour in the same time, or can labour for a longer time; and labour, to serve as a measure, must be defined by its duration or intensity, otherwise it ceases to be a standard of measurement. This *equal* right is an unequal right for unequal labour. It recognises no class differences, because everyone is only a worker like everyone else; but it tacitly recognises unequal individual endowment and thus productive capacity as natural privileges. *It is, therefore, a right of inequality, in its content, like every right.* Right by its very nature can consist only in the application of an equal standard; but unequal individuals (and they would not be different individuals if they were not unequal) are measurable only by an equal standard in so far as they are brought under an equal point of view, are taken from one *definite* side only, for instance, in the present case, are regarded *only as workers* and nothing more is seen in them, everything else being ignored. Further, one worker is married, another not; one has more children than another, and so on and so forth. Thus, with an equal performance of labour, and hence an equal share in the social consumption fund, one will in fact receive more than another, one will be richer than another, and so on. To avoid all these defects, right instead of being equal would have to be unequal.

But these defects are inevitable in the first phase of communist society as it is when it has just emerged after prolonged birth pangs from capitalist society. Right can never be higher than the economic structure of society and its cultural development conditioned thereby.

In a higher phase of communist society, after the enslaving subordination of the individual to the division of labour, and therewith also the antithesis between mental and physical labour, has vanished; after labour has become not only a means of life but life's prime want; after the productive forces have also increased with the all-round development of the individual, and all the springs of co-operative wealth flow more abundantly—only then can the narrow horizon of bourgeois right be crossed in its entirety and society inscribe on its banners: From each according to his ability, to each according to his needs!

I have dealt more at length with the "undiminished proceeds of labour," on the one hand, and with "equal right" and "fair distribution," on the other, in order to show what a crime it is to attempt, on the one hand, to force on our Party again, as dogmas, ideas which in a certain period had some meaning but have now become obsolete verbal rubbish, while again perverting, on the other, the realistic outlook, which it cost so much effort to instil into the Party but which has now taken root in it, by means of ideological nonsense about right and other trash so common among the democrats and French Socialists.

Quite apart from the analysis so far given, it was in general a mistake to make a fuss about so-called *distribution* and put the principal stress on it.

Any distribution whatever of the means of consumption is only a consequence of the distribution of the conditions of production themselves. The latter distribution, however, is a feature of the mode of production itself. The capitalist mode of production, for example, rests on the fact that the material conditions of production are in the hands of non-workers in the form of property in capital and land, while the masses are only owners of the personal condition of production, of labour power. If the elements of production are so distributed, then the present-day distribution of the means of consumption results automatically. If the material conditions of production are the co-operative property of the workers themselves, then there likewise results a distribution of the means of consumption different from the present one. Vulgar socialism (and from it in turn a section of the democracy) has taken over from the bourgeois economists the consideration and treatment of distribution as independent of the mode of production and hence the presentation of socialism as turning principally on distribution. After the real relation has long been made clear, why retrogress again?

DISTRIBUTION
John Stuart Mill

The laws and conditions of the production of wealth, partake of the character of physical truths. There is nothing optional, or arbitrary in them. Whatever mankind produce, must be produced in the modes, and under the conditions, imposed by the constitution of external things, and by the inherent properties of their own bodily and mental structure. Whether they like it or not, their productions will be limited by the amount of their previous accumulation, and, that being given, it will be proportional to their energy, their skill, the perfection of their machinery, and their judicious use of the advantages of combined labor. Whether they like it or not, a double quantity of labor will not raise, on the same land, a double quantity of food, unless some improvement takes place in the process of cultivation. Whether they like it or not, the unproductive expenditure of individuals will *pro tanto* tend to impoverish the community, and only their productive expenditure will enrich it. . . . But howsoever we may succeed in making for ourselves more space within the limits set by the constitution of things, we know that there must be limits. We cannot alter the ultimate properties either of matter or mind, but can only employ those properties more or less successfully, to bring about the events in which we are interested.

It is not so with the Distribution of Wealth. That is a matter of human institution solely. The things once there, mankind, individually or collectively, can do with them as they like. They can place them at the disposal of whomsoever they please, and on whatever terms. Further, in the social state, in every state except total solitude, any disposal whatever of them can only take place by the consent of society, or rather of those who dispose of its active force. Even what a person has produced by his individual toil, unaided by anyone, he cannot keep, unless by the permission of society. Not only can society take it from him, but individuals could and would take it from him, if society only remained passive; if it did not either interfere *en masse*, or employ and pay people for the purpose of preventing him from being disturbed in the possession. The distribution of wealth, therefore, depends on the laws and customs of society. The rules by which it is determined, are what the opinions and feelings of the ruling portion of the community make them, and are very different in different ages and countries; and might be still more different, if mankind so chose.

Private property, as an institution, did not owe its origin to any of those considerations of utility, which plead for the maintenance of it when established. Enough is known of rude ages, both from history and from analogous states of society in our own time, to show, that tribunals (which always precede laws) were originally established, not to determine rights, but to repress violence and terminate quarrels. With this object chiefly in view, they naturally enough gave legal effect to first occupancy, by treating as the aggressor the person who first commenced violence, by turning, or attempting to turn, another out of possession. The preservation of the peace, which was the original object of civil government, was thus attained; while by confirming, to those who already possessed it, even what was not the fruit of personal exertion, a guarantee was incidentally given to them and others that they would be protected in what was so. . . .

In considering the institution of property we may suppose a community unhampered by any previous possession; a body of colonists, occupying for the first time an uninhabited country; bringing nothing with them but what belonged to them in common, and having a clear field for the adoption of the institutions and polity which they judged most expedient; required, therefore, to choose whether they would conduct the work of production on the principle of individual property, or on some system of common ownership and collective agency.

If private property were adopted, we must presume that it would be accompanied by none of the initial inequalities and injustices which obstruct the beneficial operation of the principle in old societies. Every full-grown man or woman, we must suppose, would be secured in the unfettered use and disposal of his or her bodily and mental faculties; and the instruments of production, the land and tools, would be divided fairly among them, so that all might start, in respect to outward appliances, on equal terms. It is possible also to conceive that in this original apportionment, compensation might be made for the injuries of nature, and the balance redressed by assigning to the less robust members of the community advantages in the distribution, sufficient to put them on a par with the rest. But the division, once made, would not again be interfered with; individuals would be left to their own exertions and to the ordinary chances, for making an advantageous use of what was assigned to them. If individual property, on the contrary, were excluded, the plan which must be adopted would be to hold the land and all instruments of production as the joint property of the community, and to carry on the operations of industry on the common account. The direction of the labor of the community would devolve upon a magistrate or magistrates, whom we may suppose elected by the suffrages of the community, and whom we must assume to be voluntarily obeyed by them. The division of the produce would in like manner be a public act. The principle might either be that of complete equality, or of apportionment to the necessities or deserts of individuals, in whatever manner might be conformable to the ideas of justice or policy prevailing in the community. . . .

The assailants of the principle of individual property may be divided into two classes: those whose scheme implies absolute equality in the distribution of the physical means of life and enjoyment, and those who admit inequality, but grounded on some principle, or supposed principle, of justice or general expediency, and not, like so many of the existing social inequalities, dependent on accident alone. At the head of the first class, as the earliest of those belonging to the present generation, must be placed Mr. Owen and his followers. . . . The characteristic name for this economical system is Communism. . . .

Whatever may be the merits or defects of these various schemes, they cannot be truly said to be impracticable. No reasonable person can doubt that a village community, composed of a few thousand inhabitants cultivating in joint ownership the same extent of land which at present feeds that number of people, and producing by combined labor and the most improved processes the manufactured articles which they required, could raise an amount of productions sufficient to maintain them in comfort; and would find the means of obtaining, and if need be, exacting the quantity of labor necessary for this purpose, from every member of the association who was capable of work.

The objection ordinarily made to a system of community of property and equal distribution of the produce, that each person would be incessantly occupied in evading his fair share of the work, points, undoubtedly, to a real difficulty. But those who urge this objection, forget to how great an extent the same difficulty exists under the system on which nine-tenths of the business of society is now conducted. The objection supposes, that honest and efficient labor is only to be had from those who are themselves individually to reap the benefit of their own exertions. But how small a part of all . . . labor . . . , from the lowest paid to the highest, is done by persons working for their own benefit. . . . Nearly all the work of society is remunerated by day wages or fixed salaries. A factory operative has less personal interest in his work than a member of a Communist association, since he is not, like him, working for a partnership of which he is himself a member. It will no doubt be said, that though the laborers themselves have not, in most cases, a personal interest in their work, they are watched and superintended, and their labor directed, and the mental part of the labor performed, by persons who have. Even this, however, is far from being universally the fact. . . . If Communistic labor might be less vigorous than that of a peasant proprietor, or a workman laboring on his own account, it would probably be more energetic than that of a laborer for hire, who has no personal interest in the matter at all. . . .

A more real difficulty is that of fairly apportioning the labor of the community among its members. There are many kinds of work, and by what standard are they to be measured one against another? Who is to judge how much cotton spinning, or distributing goods from the stores, or bricklaying, or chimney sweeping, is equivalent to so much ploughing? The difficulty of making the adjustment between different qualities of labor is so strongly felt by Communist writers, that they have usually thought it necessary to provide that all should work by turns at every description of useful labor: an arrangement which by putting an end to the division of employments, would sacrifice so much of the advantage of co-operative production as greatly to diminish the productiveness of labor. Besides, even in the same kind of work, nominal equality of labor would be so great a real inequality, that the feeling of justice would revolt against its being enforced. All persons are not equally fit for all labor; and the same quantity of labor is an unequal burden on the weak and the strong, the hardy and the delicate, the quick and the slow, the dull and the intelligent.

But these difficulties, though real, are not necessarily insuperable. The apportionment of work to the strength and capacities of individuals, the mitigation of a general rule to provide for cases in which it would operate harshly, are not problems to which human intelligence, guided by a sense of justice, would be inadequate. And the worst and most unjust arrangement which could be made of these points, under a system aiming at equality, would be so far short of the inequality and injustice with which labor (not to speak of remuneration) is now apportioned, as to be scarcely worth counting in the comparison. . . .

Private property, in every defence made of it, is supposed to mean, the guarantee to individuals, of the fruits of their own labor and abstinence. The guarantee to them of the fruits of the labor and abstinence of others, transmitted to them without any merit or exertion of their own, is not of the essence of the institution, but a mere incidental consequence, which when it reaches a certain height, does not promote, but conflicts with the ends which render private property legitimate. To judge of the final destination of the institution of property, we must suppose everything rectified, which causes the institution to work in a manner opposed to that equitable principle, of proportion between remuneration and exertion, on which in every vindication of it that will bear the light, it is assumed to be grounded. We must also suppose two conditions realized, without which neither Communism nor any other laws or institutions could make the condition of the mass of mankind other than degraded and miserable. One of these conditions is, universal education; the other, a due limitation of the numbers of the community. With these, there could be no poverty even under the present social institutions: . . .

After the means of subsistence are assured, the next in strength of the personal wants of human beings is liberty; and (unlike the physical wants, which as civilization advances become more moderate and more amenable to control) it increases instead of diminishing in intensity, as the intelligence and the moral faculties are more developed. The perfection both of social arrangements and of practical morality would be, to secure to all persons complete independence and freedom of action, subject to no restriction but that of not doing injury to others: and the education which taught or the social institutions which required them to exchange the control of their own actions for any amount of comfort or affluence, or to renounce liberty for the sake of equality, would deprive them of one of the most elevated characteristics of human nature. It remains to be discovered how far the preservation of this characteristic would be found compatible with the communistic organization of society. No doubt, this, like all the other objections to the Socialist schemes, is vastly exaggerated. The members of the association need not be required to live together more than they do now, nor need they be controlled in the disposal of their individual share of the produce, and of the probably large amount of leisure which, if they limited their production to things really worth producing, they would possess. Individuals need not be chained to an occupation, or to a particular locality. . . . The question is whether there would be any asylum left for individuality of character; whether public opinion would not be a tyrannical yoke; whether the absolute dependence of each on all, and surveillance of each by all, would not grind all down into a tame uniformity of thoughts, feelings, and actions. . . . No society in which eccentricity is a matter of reproach, can be in a wholesome state. . . .

It is next to be considered, what is included in the idea of private property, and by what considerations the application of the principle should be bounded.

The institution of property, when limited to its essential elements, consists in the recognition, in each person, of a right to the exclusive disposal of what he or she have produced by their own exertions, or received either by gift or by fair agreement, without force or fraud, from those who produced it. The foundation of the whole is, the right of producers to what they themselves have produced. It may be objected, therefore, to the institution as it now exists, that it recognizes rights of property in individuals over things which they have not produced. For example (it may be said) the operatives in a manufactory create, by their labor and skill, the whole produce; yet, instead of its belonging to them, the law gives them only their stipulated hire, and transfers the produce to some one who has merely supplied the funds, without perhaps contributing anything to the work itself, even in the form of superintendence. The answer to this is, that the labor of manufacture is only one of the conditions which must combine for the production of the commodity. The labor cannot be carried on without materials and machinery, nor without a stock of necessaries provided in advance, to maintain the laborers during the production. All these things are the fruits of previous labor. If the laborers were possessed of them, they would not need to divide the produce with any one; but while they have them not, an equivalent must be given to those who have, both for the antecedent labor, and for the abstinence by which the produce of that labor, instead of being expended on indulgences, has been reserved for this use. The capital may not have been, and in most cases was not, created by the labor and abstinence of the present possessor; but it was created by the labor and abstinence of some former person, who may indeed have been wrongfully dispossessed of it, but who, in the present age of the world, much more probably transferred his claims to the present capitalist by gift or voluntary contract: and the abstinence at least must have been continued by each successive owner, down to the present. If it be said, as it may with truth, that those who have inherited the savings of others have an advantage which they may have in no way deserved, over the industrious whose predecessors have not left them anything; I not only admit, but strenuously contend, that this unearned advantage should be curtailed, as much as is consistent with justice to those who thought fit to dispose of their savings by giving them to their descendants. But while it is true that the laborers are at a disadvantage compared with those whose predecessors have saved, it is also true that the laborers are far better off than if those predecessors had not saved. They share in the advantage, though not to an equal extent with the inheritors. The terms of co-operation between present labor and the fruits of past labor and saving, are subject for adjustment between the two parties. Each is necessary to the other. The capitalists can do nothing without laborers, not the laborers without capital. If the laborers compete for employment, the capitalists on their part compete for labor, to the full extent of the circulating capital of the country. Competition is often spoken of as if it were necessarily a cause of misery and degradation to the laboring class; as if high wages were not precisely as much a product of competition as low wages. . . .

The right of property includes, then, the freedom of acquiring by contract. The right of each to what he has produced, implies a right to what has been produced by others, if obtained by their free consent; since the producers must either have given it from good will, or exchanged it for what they esteemed an equivalent, and to prevent them from doing so would be to infringe their right of property in the product of their own industry.

Before proceeding to consider the things which the principle of individual property does not include, we must specify one more thing which it does include: and this is, that a title, after a certain period, should be given by prescription. According to the fundamental idea of property, indeed, nothing ought to be treated as such, which has been acquired by force or fraud, or appropriated in ignorance of a prior title vested in some other person; but it is necessary to the security of rightful possessors, that they should not be molested by charges of wrongful acquisition, when by the lapse of time witnesses must have perished or been lost sight of, and the real character of the transaction can no longer be cleared up. Possession which has not been legally questioned within a moderate number of years, ought to be, as by the laws of all nations it is, a complete title. Even when the acquisition was wrongful, the dispossession, after a generation has elapsed, of the probably *bonâ fide* possessors, by the revival of a claim which had been long dormant, would generally be a greater injustice, and almost always a greater private and public mischief, than leaving the original wrong without atonement. It may seem hard, that a claim, originally just, should be defeated by mere lapse of time; but there is a time after which, (even looking at the individual case, and without regard to the general effect on the security of possessors,) the balance of hardship turns the other way. With the injustices of men, as with the convulsions and disasters of nature, the longer they remain unrepaired, the greater become the obstacles to repairing them, arising from the aftergrowths which would have to be torn up or broken through. In no human transactions, not even in the simplest and clearest, does it follow that a thing is fit to be done now, because it was fit to be done sixty years ago. It is scarcely needful to remark, that these reasons for not disturbing acts of injustice of old date, cannot apply to unjust systems or institutions; since a bad law or usage is not one bad act, in the remote past, but a perpetual repetition of bad acts, as long as the law or usage lasts. . . .

Nothing is implied in property but the right of each to his (or her) own faculties, to what he can produce by them, and to whatever he can get for them in a fair market: together with his right to give this to any other person if he chooses, and the right of that other to receive and enjoy it.

It follows, therefore, that although the right of bequest, or gift after death, forms part of the idea of private property, the right of inheritance, as distinguished from bequest, does not. That the property of persons who have made no disposition of it during their lifetime, should pass first to their children, and failing them, to the nearest relations, may be a proper arrangement or not, but is no consequence of the principle of private property. . . .

The duties of parents to their children are those which are indissolubly attached to the fact of causing the existence of a human being. The parent owes to society to endeavor to make the child a good and valuable member of it, and owes to the children to provide, so far as depends on him, such education, and such appliances and means, as will enable them to start with a fair chance of achieving by their own exertions a successful life. To this every child has a claim; and I cannot admit, that as a child he has a claim to more. There is a case in which these obligations present themselves in their true light, without any extrinsic circumstances to disguise or confuse them: it is that of an illegitimate child. To such a child it is generally felt that there is due from the parent, the amount of provision for his welfare which will enable him to make his life on the whole a desirable one. I hold that to no child, merely as such, anything more is due, than what is admitted to be due to an illegitimate child: and that no child for whom thus much has been done, has, unless on the score of previously raised expectations, any grievance, if the remainder of the parent's fortune is devoted to public uses, or to the benefit of individuals on whom in the parent's opinion it is better bestowed.

In order to give the children that fair chance of a desirable existence, to which they are entitled, it is generally necessary that they should not be brought up from childhood in habits of luxury which they will not have the means of indulging in after life. This, again, is a duty often flagrantly violated by possessors of terminable incomes, who have little property to leave. When the children of rich parents have lived, as it is natural they should do, in habits corresponding to the scale of expenditure in which the parents indulge, it is generally the duty of the parents to make a greater provision for them, than would suffice for children otherwise brought up. I say generally, because even here there is another side to the question. It is a proposition quite capable of being maintained, that to a strong nature which has to make its way against narrow circumstances, to have known early some of the feelings and experiences of wealth, is an advantage both in the formation of character and in the happiness of life. But allowing that children have a just ground of complaint, who have been brought up to require luxuries which they are not afterwards likely to obtain, and that their claim, therefore, is good to a provision bearing some relation to the mode of their bringing up; this, too, is a claim which is particularly liable to be stretched further than its reasons warrant. The case is exactly that of the younger children of the nobility and landed gentry, the bulk of whose fortune passes to the eldest son. The other sons, who are usually numerous, are brought up in the same habits of luxury as the future heir, and they receive, as a younger brother's portion, generally what the reason of the case dictates, namely, enough to support, in the habits of life to which they are accustomed, themselves, but not a wife or children. It really is no grievance to any man, that for the means of marrying and of supporting a family, he has to depend on his own exertions.

A provision, then, such as is admitted to be reasonable in the case of illegitimate children, of younger children, wherever in short the justice of the case, and the real interests of the individuals and of society, are the only things considered, is, I conceive, all that parents owe to their children, and all, therefore, which the state owes to the children of those who die intestate. The surplus, if any, I hold that it may rightfully appropriate to the general purposes of the community. I would not, however, be supposed to recommend that parents should never do more for their children than what, merely as children, they have a moral right to. In some cases it is imperative, in many laudable, and in all allowable, to do much more. For this, however, the means are afforded by the liberty of bequest. It is due, not to the children but to the parents, that they should have the power of showing marks of affection, of requiting services and sacrifices, and of bestowing their wealth according to their own preferences, or their own judgment of fitness. . . .

The next point to be considered is, whether the reasons on which the institution of property rests, are applicable to all things in which a right of exclusive ownership is at present recognized; and if not, on what other grounds the recognition is defensible.

The essential principle of property being to assure to all persons what they have produced by their labor and accumulated by their abstinence, this principle cannot apply to what is not the produce of labor, the raw material of the earth. If the land derived its productive power wholly from nature, and not at all from industry, or if there were any means of discriminating what is derived from each source, it not only would not be necessary, but it would be the height of injustice, to let the gift of nature be engrossed by individuals. The use of the land in agriculture must indeed, for the time being, be of necessity exclusive; the same person who has ploughed and sown must be permitted to reap: but the land might be occupied for one season only, . . . or might be periodically redivided as population increased: or the State might be the universal landlord, and the cultivators tenants under it, either on lease or at will.

But though land is not the produce of industry, most of its valuable qualities are so. Labor is not only requisite for using, but almost equally so for fashioning the instrument. Considerable labor is often required at the commencement, to clear the land for cultivation. In many cases, even when cleared, its productiveness is wholly the effect of labor and art. The Bedford Level produced little or nothing until artificially drained. The bogs of Ireland, until the same thing is done to them, can produce little besides fuel. One of the barrenest soils in the world, composed of the material of the Goodwin Sands, the Pays de Waes in Flanders, has been so fertilized by industry, as to have become one of the most productive in Europe. Cultivation also requires buildings and fences, which are wholly the produce of labor. The fruits of this industry cannot be reaped in a short period. The labor and outlay are immediate, the benefit is spread over many years, perhaps over all future time. A holder will not incur this labor and outlay when strangers and not himself will be benefited by it. If he undertakes such improvements, he must have a sufficient period before him in which to profit by them; and he is in no way so sure of having always a sufficient period as when his tenure is perpetual.

These are the reasons which form the justification, in an economical point of view, of property in land. It is seen that they are only valid, in so far as the proprietor of land is its improver. Whenever, in any country, the proprietor, generally speaking, ceases to be the improver, political economy has nothing to say in defence of landed property, as there established. In no sound theory of private property was it ever contemplated that the proprietor of land should be merely a sinecurist quartered on it. . . .

When the "sacredness of property" is talked of, it should always be remembered, that any such sacredness does not belong in the same degree to landed property. No man made the land. It is the original inheritance of the whole species. Its appropriation is wholly a question of general expediency. When private property in lands is not expedient, it is unjust. It is no hardship to any one, to be excluded from what others have produced: they were not bound to produce it for his use, and he loses nothing by not sharing in what otherwise would not have existed at all. But it is some hardship to be born into the world and to find all nature's gifts previously engrossed, and no place left for the new-comer. To reconcile people to this, after they have once admitted into their minds the idea that any moral rights belong to them as human beings, it will always be necessary to convince them that the exclusive appropriation is good for mankind on the whole, themselves included. But this is what no sane human being could be persuaded of, if the relation between the landowner and the cultivator were the same everywhere as it has been in Ireland.

Landed property is felt even by those most tenacious of its rights, to be a different thing from other property; and where the bulk of the community have been disinherited of their share of it, and it has become the exclusive attribute of a small minority, men have generally tried to reconcile it, at least in theory, to their sense of justice, by endeavoring to attach duties to it, and erecting it into a sort of magistracy, either moral or legal. But if the state is at liberty to treat the possessors of land as public functionaries, it is only going one step further to say, that it is at liberty to discard them. The claim of the landowners to the land is altogether subordinate to the general policy of the state. The principle of property gives them no right to the land, but only a right to compensation for whatever portion of their interest in the land it may be the policy of the state to deprive them of. To that, their claim is indefeasible. It is due to landowners, and to owners of any property whatever, recognized as such by the state, that they should not be dispossessed of it without receiving its pecuniary value, or an annual income equal to what they derived from it. This is due on the general principles on which property rests. If the land was bought with the produce of the labor and abstinence of themselves or their ancestors, compensation is due to them on that ground; even if otherwise, it is still due on the ground of prescription. Nor can it ever be necessary for accomplishing an object by which the community altogether will gain, that a particular portion of the community should be immolated. When the property is of a kind to which peculiar affections attach themselves, the compensation ought to exceed a bare pecuniary equivalent. But, subject to this proviso, the state is at liberty to deal with landed property as the general interests of the community may require, even to the extent, if it so happen, of doing with the whole, what is done with a part whenever a bill is passed for a railroad or a new street. The community has too much at stake in the proper cultivation of the land, and in the conditions annexed to the occupancy of it, to leave these things to the discretion of a class of persons called landlords, when they have shown themselves unfit for the trust. The legislature, which if it pleased might convert the whole body of landlords into fund-holders or pensioners, might, *à fortiori,* commute the average receipts of Irish landowners into a fixed rent charge, and raise the tenants into proprietors; supposing always that the full market value of the land was tendered to the landlords, in case they preferred that to accepting the conditions proposed. . . .

. . . To me it seems almost an axiom that property in land should be interpreted strictly, and that the balance in all cases of doubt should incline against the proprietor. The reverse is the case with property in movables, and in all things the product of labor; over these, the owner's power both of use and of exclusion should be absolute, except where positive evil to others would result from it; but in the case of land, no exclusive right should be permitted in any individual, which cannot be shown to be productive of positive good. To be allowed any exclusive right at all, over a portion of the common inheritance, while there are others who have no portion, is already a privilege. No quantity of movable goods which a person can acquire by his labor, prevents others from acquiring the like by the same means; but from the very nature of the case, whoever owns land, keeps others out of the enjoyment of it. The privilege, or monopoly, is only defensible as a necessary evil; it becomes an injustice when carried to any point to which the compensating good does not follow it.

For instance, the exclusive right to the land for purposes of cultivation does not imply an exclusive right to it for purposes of access; and no such right ought to be recognized, except to the extent necessary to protect the produce against damage, and the owner's privacy against invasion. The pretension of two Dukes to shut up a part of the Highlands, and exclude the rest of mankind from many square miles of mountain scenery to prevent disturbance to wild animals, is an abuse; it exceeds the legitimate bounds of the right of landed property. When land is not intended to be cultivated, no good reason can in general be given for its being private property at all; and if any one is permitted to call it his, he ought to know that he holds it by sufferance of the community, and on an implied condition that his ownership, since it cannot possibly do them any good, at least shall not deprive them of any, which they could have derived from the land if it had been unappropriated. Even in the case of cultivated land, a man whom, though only one among millions, the law permits to hold thousands of acres as his single share, is not entitled to think that all this is given to him to use and abuse, and deal with as if it concerned nobody but himself. The rents or profits which he can obtain from it are at his sole disposal; but with regard to the land, in everything which he does with it, and in everything which he abstains from doing, he is morally bound, and should whenever the case admits be legally compelled, to make his interest and pleasure consistent with the public good. The species at large still retains, of its original claim to the soil of the planet which it inhabits, as much as is compatible with the purposes for which it has parted with the remainder.

Besides property in the produce of labor, and property in land, there are other things which are or have been subjects of property, in which no proprietary rights ought to exist at all. . . . At the head of them, is property in human beings. It is almost superfluous to observe, that this institution can have no place in any society even pretending to be founded on justice, or on fellowship between human creatures. But, iniquitous as it is, yet when the state has expressly legalized it, and human beings, for generations, have been bought, sold, and inherited under sanction of law, it is another wrong, in abolishing the property, not to make full compensation.

Questions for Part X

1. Discuss the Wilt Chamberlain problem in Robert Nozick's article and its implications for a theory of distributive justice in a state.

2. Suppose Dr. X, by combining relatively abundant chemicals, synthesizes a cure for certain kinds of cancer and that a great number of people of varying incomes contract that form of cancer regularly. Dr. X offers his cure at a price that only the very wealthy can afford. Should Dr. X be forced to give his cure to those diseased persons who cannot pay his price? Explain fully in terms of Robert Nozick's entitlement theory and the Lockean proviso.

3. What is the purpose of the original position and the veil of ignorance in John Rawls's account of distributive justice?

4. Contrast historical principles of justice in distribution of property with end-result principles. Nozick's theory is a historical one, while Rawls, Marx, and Mill represent different forms of end-result theories.

5. Discuss and evaluate Nozick's analysis of taxation on the earnings of labor. Is he right that the tax system places an unfair burden on the person who chooses to work to gain a more than sufficient income and rewards those whose pleasures are satisfied by looking at sunsets?

6. Discuss the emigration problem in patterned distribution systems. Should people be allowed to emigrate from a country that forces contributions for the aid of the needy, such as taxes used for social welfare projects, to one that has no such compulsory system? If a person is allowed to emigrate, why can't they stay and opt out of the contribution scheme? Discuss fully.

7. Does the current American socio-economic system reflect Rawlsian or Nozickian principles of distributive justice?

8. Explain why Karl Marx opposes the sentence "Labour is the source of all wealth and all culture" in the Programme of the German Workers' Party.

9. Marx carefully examines the Programme's account of the proceeds of labor and fair distribution. What is Marx's analysis of the latter notion and how does it compare to those of Rawls and Nozick?

10. What are the characteristics of the various phases of a communist society according to Marx?

11. Examine John Stuart Mill's criticisms of communism. Does he believe that a communistic system of distribution is impractical or does he provide a more philosophical (or conceptual) attack on its basic principles?

12. Contrast Mill's account of acquisition to that propounded by Nozick.

13. What is Mill's position on inheritance?

14. For Mill the right to property, to exclusive individual ownership, does not extend to all things. To what does it not extend? What principle or principles govern his refusal to extend the right of exclusive ownership to all things? Are those principles similar to those espoused by Nozick, who also restricts the rights of ownership?

Part XI. The Sceptical Challenge

At some time or other you have made a discovery which forced you to reinterpret a very great deal of evidence whose explanation you had felt certain you understood. For example, there may have been someone whom, on what seemed to be compelling evidence, you took to be a good friend. Everything the person did seemed to confirm you in this—he or she would talk with you at length, smile when you appeared, invite you to do things, take an interest in your affairs. Yet despite all this evidence it may one day have become perfectly clear that this person did not care about you at all, but was using you as a tool in order to obtain something—acceptance into a certain group, or money, or information, perhaps. Suddenly you saw everything the person did in a new light: actions that had seemed spontaneous you now saw as calculated and scheming, actions that had seemed signs of affection you now saw as deliberately deceptive expressions of pure self-interest, actions that had seemed generous or selfless now seemed greedy and grasping.

This sort of experience can be profoundly unsettling. It can lead you to wonder whether *any* of your friends really like you. For it may be that your evidence that this person liked you was as good as or even better than the evidence you now have that the rest of your friends like you. If you could be mistaken in this one case, it seems that you could be mistaken in any and every similar case. You may become convinced that you do not and cannot know that any of your supposed friends actually cares about you.

Such an experience might be described as an *epistemological crisis.*[1] It brings home in a forceful way the fact that the available evidence is susceptible of more than one interpretation, and the interpretation you have taken for granted, no matter how plausible, may turn out to be mistaken. After such an experience, we are likely to become much less confident in our claims to know things.

Philosophers have long been troubled by whether we can legitimately claim to know things when we could turn out to be mistaken; the examples they consider are typically more general and their conclusions more sweeping than the ones just considered, but the point remains much the same. In the case just considered, you were led to doubt whether you could know that you had any genuine friends; we will now consider some increasingly general considerations which may lead you to doubt whether you can know anything at all.

How do you know that other people have minds? You ordinarily think that the other bodies you see wandering around, making noises, driving cars, sitting in classrooms, and so on, have minds; and in particular that they have thoughts, feel pains, have visual sensations and possess all the other characteristics of consciousness. Now suppose you see Joe cry out, grab his knee, and hobble around while grimacing fiercely. You believe that he is feeling pain. But do you *know* this? What makes you think that Joe is in pain? The fact that he is *behaving* in a certain way. You can't simply see into his mind and notice the pain; you have to infer that he is in pain from your observation of his behavior. But now it seems that your observing a certain sort of behavior is only a reason to infer that Joe is in pain if you know that in general that sort of behavior is correlated with pain. But how *could* you know this? You *never* directly observe Joe's pain; you *only* observe his behavior—so you cannot, for instance, keep a record of all the times you directly observe "pain behavior" and all the times you directly observe pain, and then notice that the two usually go together.

Perahps this argument seems fishy. After all, you do know that at least in your own case certain behavior is reliably correlated with pain. It is worth considering whether that gives you reason enough to suppose that such behavior is reliably correlated with pain in other bodies which resemble yours. (One argument that it does is called the "argument from analogy," for obvious reasons—but there are notorious difficulties with this argument.) But let us consider a similar argument for scepticism about a different sort of knowledge, an argument which is not similarly fishy.

Much of what we think of as our present knowledge relies on memory. For instance, I now believe that I grew up in Montana. How do I know this? Because I remember it. But it seems that the fact that I apparently remember something is not good grounds for believing it unless I know that my memory is reliably correlated with the past. But how could I know *that*? Granted, I seem to remember my past memories turning out to be correct when I checked them. But *that* apparent memory is just as suspect as any of the rest. Perhaps I systematically misremember things, including memories about the reliability of my memory.

At their most general, arguments like these purport to show that I cannot know anything about "the external world," the world outside my own mind. It seems that ultimately my reasons for any of my beliefs about the external world rest on my experience. But do my experiences provide good reasons for any beliefs about the external world? Only, it would seem, if the way I experience the world is reliably correlated with the way it is. But how could I know that? All I have to go on is my experiences; I can't compare my experiences directly with the world, but at best with other experiences.

This argument is an argument for *scepticism,* the view that we can know very, very little—perhaps nothing at all. We might call the argument an "appearance-reality" argument for scepticism. Another kind of argument for scepticism, the "contrast-case" argument, is presented in the selections from Descartes and Peter Unger. The form of the appearance-reality argument we have been considering may be put (borrowing a specific example from Unger) like this:

(1) I can know that there are rocks only if I know that how things appear is reliably correlated with how they are

But   (2) I cannot know that how things appear is reliably correlated with how things are

Therefore, (3) I do not know that there are rocks.

Now, what are we to say about such arguments? If we accept the conclusion, we are sceptics. But presumably we do not want to be sceptics, so let us see if we can reject (3). If (3) is false, then at least one of three things must be true: *either* (3) is not really a logical consequence of (1) and (2), *or* (1) is false, *or* (2) is false. We can immediately rule out the first possibility because the argument is valid. If (1) and (2) are true, then (3) must be true also. (The argument, like the one Unger will discuss, has the form: (1) P only if Q; (2) not Q; therefore (3) not P, and any argument with this form is valid.) So if (3) is false either or both of (1) and (2) must be false.

It would be interesting to consider whether (1) is true. But let us focus on (2) instead. The sceptic says that we cannot know that appearance is systematically and reliably connected with reality. Why does the sceptic deny this?

In answering this question it is useful to have in mind the answer philosophers have traditionally given to the question, "what is knowledge?" The answer is, in a nutshell: knowledge is *justified true belief.* (Many contemporary philosophers reject this answer. But most would still agree that it is *approximately* correct.) If this is correct, then the denial that we know that appearance and reality are reliably correlated could be for three reasons: that we do not *believe* that they are correlated, that it is not *true* that they are correlated, or that we are not *justified in believing* that they are correlated.

The sceptic certainly does not make the first claim: most people do believe that appearance and reality are correlated, and the sceptic has no reason to deny that people believe this. (But he would deny that he *knows* that people believe this, and might even, if he had read Smullyan, deny that the people who believe this know that they believe it.) Nor does the sceptic want to deny that it is true that appearance and reality are reliably correlated. He believes that he cannot know whether they are correlated or not, so he certainly is not going to *assert either* that they are *or* that they are not. So the sceptic must want to deny that we are justified in believing that the two are correlated.

Whether the sceptic convinced by appearance-reality arguments is right or wrong thus depends crucially upon whether we are justified in believing that appearance and reality are reliably correlated. (Similarly, whether the Cartesian sceptic is correct depends on whether we are justified in believing that we are not being deceived by an evil demon, and whether Peter Unger's sceptic is correct depends on whether we are justified in believing that we are not brains in vats.) Several of the articles in this session center around the issue of what justifies us in holding a certain belief.

Descartes clearly holds a *foundations theory of justification*. The general idea behind the foundations theory is that we are justified in believing something only if it "follows" in some sense from other things we believe, and ultimately from truths of which we are absolutely certain. (The sense in which these beliefs must "follow" differs in different thinkers. Descartes seemed to have in mind that the justified beliefs had to be derivable from the justifying ones using only the laws of deductive logic. Others would also allow inductive principles to be used. And some thinkers add still more principles.) The term "foundations theory" is clearly appropriate for this view, since the idea is that we build up the edifice of knowledge, by reliable principles, upon the firm foundation of certain truths.

An alternative theory, the *coherence theory of justification*, is elaborated and defended in the selections by Charles Peirce and Gilbert Harman. This view is so called because it holds that our beliefs are justified by how well they cohere with all the rest of our beliefs, not by being derived from certain foundational beliefs. A bit more specifically, the coherence theory holds that we are justified in believing something unless we have some specific reason to doubt it, where a specific reason for doubting a belief might be either (a) that it conflicts with other beliefs we have, or (b) that we have acted according to the belief and things did not turn out as we were led to expect.

Which theory of justification is correct will have a great deal to do with whether the sceptic's argument is correct. Are we justified in believing that how things appear is reliably correlated with how they are? The sceptic argued that we were not by arguing that we couldn't *support* that belief by reference to other beliefs. The sceptic thus apparently presupposed that the foundations theory is correct. But a coherence theorist like Peirce would argue that we are justified in believing that appearance and reality are reliably connected because this belief has worked for us— because, that is, we have so far found no specific reason to doubt it.

NOTE

1. This notion is borrowed from Alasdair MacIntyre, "Epistemological Crisis, Dramatic Narrative, and the Philosophy of Science," *The Monist*, vol 60 (1977), 453–472.

AN EPISTEMOLOGICAL NIGHTMARE

Raymond M. Smullyan

Scene 1. Frank is in the office of an eye doctor. The doctor holds up a book and asks "What color is it?" Frank answers, "Red." The doctor says, "Aha, just as I thought! Your whole color mechanism has gone out of kilter. But fortunately your condition is curable, and I will have you in perfect shape in a couple of weeks."

Scene 2. (A few weeks later.) Frank is in a laboratory in the home of an experimental epistemologist. (You will soon find out what that means!) The epistemologist holds up a book and also asks, "What color is this book?" Now, Frank has been earlier dismissed by the eye doctor as "cured." However, he is now of a very analytical and cautious temperament, and will not make any statement that can possibly be refuted. So Frank answers, "It seems red to me."

EPISTEMOLOGIST: Wrong!

FRANK: I don't think you heard what I said. I merely said that it *seems* red to me.

EPISTEMOLOGIST: I heard you, and you were wrong.

FRANK: Let me get this clear; did you mean that I was wrong that this book *is* red, or that I was wrong that it *seems* red to me?

EPISTEMOLOGIST: I obviously couldn't have meant that you were wrong in that it *is* red, since you did not say that it is red. All you said was that it *seems* red to you, and it is *this* statement which is wrong.

FRANK: But you can't say that the statement "It *seems* red to me" is wrong.

EPISTEMOLOGIST: If I *can't* say it, how come I did?

FRANK: I mean you can't *mean* it.

EPISTEMOLOGIST: Why not?

FRANK: But surely *I* know what color the book *seems* to me!

EPISTEMOLOGIST: Again you are wrong.

FRANK: But nobody knows better than I how things seem to *me*.

EPISTEMOLOGIST: I am sorry, but again you are wrong.

FRANK: But who knows better than I?

EPISTEMOLOGIST: I do.

FRANK: But how could you have access to my private mental states?

EPISTEMOLOGIST: Private mental states! Metaphysical hogwash! Look, I am a *practical* epistemologist. Metaphysical problems about "mind" versus "matter" arise only from epistemological confusions. Epistemology is the true foundation of philosophy. But the trouble with all past epistemologists is that they have been using wholly theoretical methods, and much of their discussion degenerates into mere word games. While other epistemologists have been solemnly arguing such questions as whether a man can be wrong when he asserts that he believes such and such, I have discovered how to settle such questions *experimentally*.

FRANK: How could you possibly decide such things empirically?

EPISTEMOLOGIST: By reading a person's thoughts directly.

FRANK: You mean you are telepathic?

EPISTEMOLOGIST: Of course not. I simply did the one obvious thing which should be done, *viz.* I have constructed a brain-reading machine— known technically as a cerebrescope—that is operative right now in this room and is scanning every nerve cell in your brain. I thus can read your every sensation and thought, and it is a simple objective truth that this book does *not* seem red to you.

FRANK (thoroughly subdued): Goodness gracious, I really could have sworn that the book seemed red to me; it sure *seems* that it seems red to me!

EPISTEMOLOGIST: I'm sorry, but you are wrong again.

FRANK: Really? It doesn't even *seem* that it seems red to me? It sure *seems* like it seems like it seems red to me!

EPISTEMOLOGIST: Wrong again! And no matter how many times you reiterate the phrase "it seems like" and follow it by "the book is red" you will be wrong.

FRANK: This is fantastic! Suppose instead of the phrase "it seems like" I would say "I believe that." So let us start again at ground level. I retract the statement "It seems red to me" and instead I assert "I *believe* that this book is red." Is this statement true or false?

EPISTEMOLOGIST: Just a moment while I scan the dials of the brain-reading machine—no, the statement is false.

FRANK: And what about "I believe that I believe that the book is red"?

EPISTEMOLOGIST (consulting his dials): Also false. And again, no matter how many times you iterate "I believe," all these belief sentences are false.

FRANK: Well, this has been a most enlightening experience. However, you must admit that it is a *little* hard on me to realize that I am entertaining infinitely many erroneous beliefs!

EPISTEMOLOGIST: Why do you say that your beliefs are erroneous?

FRANK: But you have been telling me this all the while!

EPISTEMOLOGIST: I most certainly have not!

FRANK: Good God, I was prepared to admit all my errors, and now you tell me that my beliefs are *not* errors; what are you trying to do, drive me crazy?

EPISTEMOLOGIST: Hey, take it easy! Please try to recall: When did I say or imply that any of your beliefs are erroneous?

FRANK: Just simply recall the infinite sequence of sentences: (1) I believe this book is red; (2) I believe that I believe this book is red; and so forth. You told me that every one of those statements is false.

EPISTEMOLOGIST: True.

FRANK: Then how can you consistently maintain that my *beliefs* in all these false statements are not erroneous?

EPISTEMOLOGIST: Because, as I told you, you don't believe any of them.

FRANK: I think I see, yet I am not absolutely sure.

EPISTEMOLOGIST: Look, let me put it another way. Don't you see that the very falsity of each of the statements that you assert *saves* you from an erroneous belief in the preceding one? The first statement is, as I told you, false. Very well! Now the second statement is simply to the effect that you believe the first statement. If the second statement were *true*, then you would believe the first statement, and hence your belief about the first statement would indeed be in error. But fortunately the second statement is false, hence you don't really believe the first statement, so your belief in the first statement is not in error. Thus the falsity of the second statement implies you do *not* have an erroneous belief about the first; the falsity of the third likewise saves you from an erroneous belief about the second, etc.

FRANK: Now I see perfectly! So none of my *beliefs* were erroneous, only the statements were erroneous.

EPISTEMOLOGIST: Exactly.

FRANK: Most remarkable! Incidentally, what color is the book really?

EPISTEMOLOGIST: It is red.

FRANK: What!

EPISTEMOLOGIST: Exactly! Of course the book is red. What's the matter with you, don't you have eyes?

FRANK: But didn't I in effect keep saying that the book is red all along?

EPISTEMOLOGIST: Of course not! You kept saying it *seems* red to you, it *seems* like it seems red to you, you *believe* it is red, you *believe* that you believe it is red, and so forth. Not once did you say that it *is* red. When I originally asked you "What color is the book?" if you had simply answered "red," this whole painful discussion would have been avoided.

Scene 3. Frank comes back several months later to the home of the epistemologist.

EPISTEMOLOGIST: How delightful to see you! Please sit down.

FRANK (seated): I have been thinking of our last discussion, and there is much I wish to clear up. To begin with, I discovered an inconsistency in some of the things you said.

EPISTEMOLOGIST: Delightful! I love inconsistencies. Pray tell!

FRANK: Well, you claimed that although my belief sentences were false, I did not have any actual *beliefs* that are false. If you had not admitted that the book actually is red, you would have been consistent. But your very admission that the book *is* red, leads to an inconsistency.

EPISTEMOLOGIST: How so?

FRANK: Look, as you correctly pointed out, in each of my belief sentences "I believe it is red," "I believe that I believe it is red," the falsity of each one other than the first saves me from an erroneous belief in the preceding one. However, you neglected to take into consideration the first sentence itself! The falsity of the first sentence "I believe it is red," in conjunction with the fact that it *is* red, *does* imply that I do have a false belief.

EPISTEMOLOGIST: I don't see why.

FRANK: It is obvious! Since the sentence "I believe it is red" is false, then I in fact believe it is not red, and since it really is red, then I *do* have a false belief. So there!

EPISTEMOLOGIST (disappointed): I am sorry, but your proof obviously fails. Of course the falsity of the fact that you believe it is red implies that you *don't* believe it is red. But this does not mean that you believe it is *not* red!

FRANK: But obviously I know that it either is red or it isn't, so if I don't believe it is, then I must believe that it isn't.

EPISTEMOLOGIST: Not at all. I believe that either Jupiter has life or it doesn't. But I neither believe that it does, nor do I believe that it doesn't. I have no evidence one way or the other.

FRANK: Oh well, I guess you are right. But let us come to more important matters. I honestly find it impossible that I can be in error concerning my own beliefs.

EPISTEMOLOGIST: Must we go through this again? I have already patiently explained to you that you (in the sense of your beliefs, not your statements) are *not* in error.

FRANK: Oh, all right then, I simply do not believe that even the *statements* are in error. Yes, according to the machine they are in error, but why should I trust the machine?

EPISTEMOLOGIST: Whoever said you should trust the machine?

FRANK: Well, *should* I trust the machine?

EPISTEMOLOGIST That question involving the word "should" is out of my domain. However, if you like, I can refer you to a colleague who is an excellent moralist—he may be able to answer this for you.

FRANK: Oh come on now, I obviously didn't mean "should" in a moralistic sense. I simply meant "Do I have any evidence that this machine is reliable?"

EPISTEMOLOGIST: Well, do you?

FRANK: Don't ask *me!* What I mean is should *you* trust the machine?

EPISTEMOLOGIST: *Should* I trust it? I have no idea, and I couldn't care less what I *should* do.

FRANK: Oh, your moralistic hangup again. I mean, do *you* have evidence that the machine is reliable?

EPISTEMOLOGIST: Well of course!

FRANK: Then let's get down to brass tacks. What is your evidence?

EPISTEMOLOGIST: You hardly can expect that I can answer this for you in an hour, a day, or a week. If you wish to study this machine with me, we can do so, but I assure you this is a matter of several years. At the end of that time, however, you would certainly not have the slightest doubts about the reliability of the machine.

FRANK: Well, possibly I could believe that it is reliable in the sense that its measurements are accurate, but then I would doubt that what it actually measures is very significant. It seems that all it measures is one's physiological states and activities.

EPISTEMOLOGIST: But of course, what else would you expect it to measure?

FRANK: I doubt that it measures my psychological states, my actual *beliefs.*

EPISTEMOLOGIST: Are we back to that again? The machine *does* measure those physiological states and processes that you call psychological states, beliefs, sensations, and so forth.

FRANK: At this point I am becoming convinced that our entire difference is purely semantical. All right, I will grant that your machine does correctly measure beliefs in *your* sense of the word "belief," but I don't believe that it has any possibility of measuring beliefs in *my* sense of the word "believe." In other words I claim that our entire deadlock is simply due to the fact that you and I mean different things by the word "belief."

EPISTEMOLOGIST: Fortunately, the correctness of your claim can be decided experimentally. It so happens that I now have two brain-reading machines in my office, so I now direct one to *your* brain to find out what *you* mean by "believe" and now I direct the other to my own brain to find out what *I* mean by "believe," and now I shall compare the two readings. Nope, I'm sorry, but it turns out that we mean *exactly* the same thing by the word "believe."

FRANK: Oh, hang your machine! Do *you* believe we mean the same thing by the word "believe"?

EPISTEMOLOGIST: Do *I* believe it? Just a moment while I check with the machine. Yes, it turns out I do believe it.

FRANK: My goodness, do you mean to say that you can't even tell me what *you* believe without consulting the machine?

EPISTEMOLOGIST: Of course not.

FRANK: But most people when asked what they believe simply *tell* you. Why do you, in order to find out your beliefs, go through the fantastically roundabout process of directing a thought-reading machine to your own brain and then finding out what you believe on the basis of the machine readings?

EPISTEMOLOGIST: What other scientific, objective way is there of finding out what I believe?

FRANK: Oh, come now, why don't you just ask yourself?

EPISTEMOLOGIST (sadly): It doesn't work. Whenever I ask myself what I believe, I never get any answer!

FRANK: Well, why don't you just *state* what you believe?

EPISTEMOLOGIST: How can I state what I believe before I know what I believe?

FRANK: Oh, to hell with your *knowledge* of what you believe; surely you have some *idea* or *belief* as to what you believe, don't you?

EPISTEMOLOGIST: Of course I have such a belief. But how do I find out what this belief is?

FRANK: I am afraid we are getting into another infinite regress. Look, at this point I am honestly beginning to wonder whether you may be going crazy.

EPISTEMOLOGIST: Let me consult the machine. Yes, it turns out that I may be going crazy.

FRANK: Good God, man, doesn't this frighten you?

EPISTEMOLOGIST: Let me check! Yes, it turns out that it does frighten me.

FRANK: Oh please, can't you forget this damned machine and just tell me whether you are frightened or not?

EPISTEMOLOGIST: I just told you that I am. However, I only learned of this from the machine.

FRANK: I can see that it is utterly hopeless to wean you away from the mahcine. Very well, then, let us play along with the machine some more. Why don't you ask the machine whether your sanity can be saved?

EPISTEMOLOGIST: Good idea! Yes, it turns out that it can be saved.

FRANK: And how can it be saved?

EPISTEMOLOGIST: I don't know, I haven't asked the machine.

FRANK: Well, for God's sake, ask it!

EPISTEMOLOGIST: Good idea. It turns out that . . .

FRANK: It turns out what?

EPISTEMOLOGIST: It turns out that . . .

FRANK: Come on now, it turns out what?

EPISTEMOLOGIST: This is the most fantastic thing I have ever come across! According to the machine the best thing I can do is to cease to trust the machine!

FRANK: Good! What will you do about it?

EPISTEMOLOGIST: How do I know what I *will* do about it, I can't read the future?

FRANK: I mean, what do you *presently* intend to do about it?

EPISTEMOLOGIST: Good question, let me consult the machine. According to the machine, my current intentions are in complete conflict. And I can see why! I am caught in a terrible paradox! If the machine is trustworthy, then I had better accept its suggestion to distrust it. But if I distrust it, then I also distrust its suggestion to distrust it, so I am really in a total quandary.

FRANK: Look, I know of someone who I think might be really of help in this problem. I'll leave you for a while to consult him. *Au revoir!*

Scene 4. (Later in the day at a psychiatrist's office.)

FRANK: Doctor, I am terribly worried about a friend of mine. He calls himself an "experimental epistemologist."

DOCTOR: Oh, the experimental epistemologist. There is only one in the world. I know him well!

FRANK: That is a relief. But do you realize that he has constructed a mind-reading device that he now directs to his own brain, and whenever one asks him what he thinks, believes, feels, is afraid of, and so on, he has to consult the machine first before answering? Don't you think this is pretty serious?

DOCTOR: Not as serious as it might seem. My prognosis for him is actually quite good.

FRANK: Well, if you are a friend of his, couldn't you sort of keep an eye on him?

DOCTOR: I do see him quite frequently, and I do observe him much. However, I don't think he can be helped by so-called "psychiatric treatment." His problem is an unusual one, the sort that has to work itself out. And I believe it will.

FRANK: Well, I hope your optimism is justified. At any rate I sure think *I* need some help at this point!

DOCTOR: How so?

FRANK: My experiences with the epistemologist have been thoroughly unnerving! At this point I wonder if *I* may be going crazy; I can't even have confidence in how things *appear* to me. I think maybe *you* could be helpful here.

DOCTOR: I would be happy to but cannot for a while. For the next three months I am unbelievably overloaded with work. After that, unfortunately, I must go on a three-month vacation. So in six months come back and we can talk this over.

Scene 5. (Same office, six months later.)

DOCTOR: Before we go into your problems, you will be happy to hear that your friend the epistemologist is now completely recovered.

FRANK: Marvelous, how did it happen?

DOCTOR: Almost, as it were, by a stroke of fate—and yet his very mental activities were, so to speak, part of the "fate." What happened was this: For months after you last saw him, he went around worrying "should I trust the machine, shouldn't I trust the machine, should I, shouldn't I, should I, shouldn't I." (He decided to use the word "should" in your empirical sense.) He got nowhere! So he then decided to "formalize" the whole argument. He reviewed his study of symbolic logic, took the axioms of first-order logic, and added as nonlogical axioms certain relevant facts about the machine. Of course the resulting system was inconsistent—he formally proved that he should trust the machine if and only if he shouldn't, and hence that he both should and should not trust the machine. Now, as you may know, in a system based on classical logic (which is the logic he used), if one can prove so much as a single contradictory proposition, then one can prove any proposition, hence the whole system breaks down. So he decided to use a logic weaker than classical logic—a logic close to what is known as "minimal logic"—in which the proof of one contradiction does not necessarily entail the proof of every proposition. However, this system turned out too weak to decide the question of whether or not he should trust the machine. Then he had the following bright idea. Why not use classical logic in his system even though the resulting system is inconsistent? Is an inconsistent system necessarily useless? Not at all! Even though given any proposition, there exists a proof that it is true and another proof that it is false, it may be the case that for any such pair of proofs, one of them is simply more psychologically convincing than the other, so simply pick the proof you actually believe! Theoretically the idea turned out very well—the actual system he obtained really did have the property that given any such pair of proofs, one of them was always psychologically *far* more convincing than the other. Better yet, given any pair of contradictory propositions, *all* proofs of one were more convincing than *any* proof of the other. Indeed, anyone *except the epistemologist* could have used the system to decide whether the machine could be trusted. But with the epistemologist, what happened was this: He obtained one proof that he should trust the machine and another proof that he should not. Which proof was more convincing to him, which proof did he really "believe"? The only way *he* could find out was to consult the machine! But he realized that this would be begging the question, since his consulting the machine would be a tacit admission that he did in fact trust the machine. So he still remained in a quandary.

FRANK: So how did he get out of it?

DOCTOR: Well, here is where fate kindly interceded. Due to his absolute absorption in the theory of this problem, which consumed about his every waking hour, he became for the first time in his life experimentally negligent. As a result, quite unknown to him, a few minor units of his machine blew out! Then, for the first time, the machine started giving contradictory information—not merely subtle paradoxes, but blatant contradictions. In particular, the machine one day claimed that the epistemologist believed a certain proposition and a few days later claimed that he did *not* believe that proposition. And to add insult to injury, the machine claimed that he had not changed his belief in the last few days. This was enough to simply make him totally distrust the machine. Now he is fit as a fiddle.

FRANK: This is certainly the most amazing thing I have ever heard! I guess the machine was really dangerous and unreliable all along.

DOCTOR: Oh, not at all; the machine used to be excellent before the epistemologist's experimental carelessness put it out of whack.

FRANK: Well, surely when *I* knew it, it couldn't have been very reliable.

DOCTOR: Not so, Frank, and this brings us to your problem. I know about your entire conversation with the epistemologist—it was all tape-recorded.

FRANK: Then surely you realize the machine could not have been right when it denied that I *believed* the book was red.

DOCTOR: Why not?

FRANK: Good God, do I have to go through all this nightmare again? I can understand that a person can be wrong if he claims that a certain physical object has a certain property, but have you ever known a single case when a person can be mistaken when he claims to have or not have a certain sensation?

DOCTOR: Why, certainly! I once knew a Christian Scientist who had a raging toothache; he was frantically groaning and moaning all over the place. When asked whether a dentist might not cure him, he replied that there was nothing to be cured. Then he was asked, "But do you not feel pain?" He replied, "No, I do not feel pain; nobody feels pain, there is no such thing as pain, pain is only an illusion." So here is a case of a man who claimed not to feel pain, yet everyone present knew perfectly well that he did feel pain. I certainly don't believe he was lying, he was just simply mistaken.

FRANK: Well, all right, in a case like that. But how can one be mistaken if one asserts his belief about the color of a book?

DOCTOR: I can assure you that without access to any machine, if I asked someone what color is this book, and he answered, "I believe it is red," I would be very doubtful that he really believed it. It seems to me that if he really believed it, he would answer, "It is red" and not "I believe it is red" or "It seems red to me." The very timidity of his response would be indicative of his doubts.

FRANK: But why on earth should I have doubted that it was red?

DOCTOR: You should know better than I. Let us see now, have you ever in the past had reason to doubt the accuracy of your sense perception?

FRANK: Why, yes. A few weeks before visiting the epistemologist, I suffered from an eye disease, which did make me see colors falsely. But I was cured before my visit.

DOCTOR: Oh, so no wonder you doubted it was red! True enough, your eye perceived the correct color of the book, but your earlier experience lingered in your mind and made it impossible for you to really believe it was red. So the machine *was* right!

FRANK: Well, all right, but then why did I doubt that I *believed* it was true?

DOCTOR: Because you *didn't* believe it was true, and unconsciously you were smart enough to realize the fact. Besides, when one starts doubting one's own sense perceptions, the doubt spreads like an infection to higher and higher levels of abstraction until finally the whole belief system becomes one doubting mass of insecurity. I bet that if you went to the epistemologist's office *now*, and if the machine were repaired, and you now claimed that you believe the book is red, the machine would concur.

No, Frank, the machine is—or, rather, was—a good one. The epistemologist learned much from it, but misused it when he applied it to his own brain. He really should have known better than to create such an unstable situation. The combination of his brain and the machine each scrutinizing and influencing the behavior of the other led to serious problems in feedback. Finally the whole system went into a cybernetic wobble. Something was bound to give sooner or later. Fortunately, it was the machine.

FRANK: I see. One last question, though. How could the machine be trustworthy when it claimed to be untrustworthy?

DOCTOR: The machine never claimed to be untrustworthy, it only claimed that the epistemologist would be better off not trusting it. And the machine was right.

A CLASSICAL FORM OF SCEPTICAL ARGUMENT

Peter Unger

There are certain arguments for scepticism which conform to a familiar, if not often explicitly articulated, pattern or form. These arguments rely, at least for their psychological power, on vivid descriptions of exotic *contrast cases*. The following is one such rough argument, this one in support of scepticism regarding any alleged knowledge of an external world. The exotic contrast case here concerns an evil scientist, and is described to be in line with the most up to date developments of science, or science fiction. We begin by arbitrarily choosing something concerning an external world which might conceivably, we suppose, be *known*, in one way or another, e.g. that there are rocks or, as we will understand it, that there is at least one rock. Now, first, *if* someone, anyone, *knows* that there are rocks, then the person *can know* the following quite exotic thing: there is *no* evil scientist deceiving him into *falsely* believing that there are rocks. This scientist uses electrodes to induce experiences and thus carries out his deceptions, concerning the existence of rocks or anything else. He first drills holes painlessly in the variously coloured skulls, or shells, of his subjects and then implants his electrodes into the appropriate parts of their brains, or protoplasm, or systems. He sends patterns of electrical impulses into them through the electrodes, which are themselves connected by wires to a laboratory console on which he plays, punching various keys and buttons in accordance with his ideas of how the whole thing works and with his deceptive designs. The scientist's delight is intense, and it is caused not so much by his exercising his scientific and intellectual gifts as by the thought that he is deceiving various subjects about all sorts of things. Part of that delight is caused, on this supposition, by his thought that he is deceiving a certain person, perhaps yourself, into falsely believing that there are rocks. He is, then, an evil scientist, and he lives in a world which is entirely bereft of rocks. Now, as we have agreed, *if you know* that there are rocks, then you *can know* that there is no such scientist doing this to you. But, no one *can* ever *know* that this exotic situation does *not obtain;* no one *can* ever *know* that there is *no* evil scientist who is, by means of electrodes, deceiving him into falsely believing there to be rocks. That is our second premiss, and it is also very difficult to deny. So, thirdly, as a consequence of these two premisses, we have our sceptical conclusion: you never *know* that there are rocks. But of course we have chosen our person, and the matter of there being rocks, quite arbitrarily, and this argument, it surely seems, may be generalized to cover any external matter at all. From this, we may conclude, finally, that nobody ever *knows* anything about the external world.

This argument is the same in form as the 'evil demon' argument in Descartes's *Meditations*; it is but a more modern, scientific counter-part, with its domain of application confined to matters concerning the external world.[1] Taking the *Meditations* as our source of the most compelling sceptical argument the philosophical literature has to offer, we may call any argument of this form *the classical argument* for scepticism. Arguments of this form may be called merely different presentations of *the* argument, at least when they share the same sceptical conclusion. An argument of the same classical form may also be offered for the conclusion that nobody ever knows anything about the future or even the past, in brief, about other times. And arguments of the same form may also be offered for sceptical conclusions about having reasons for believing certain things, and thus being reasonable in believing them. For example, such an argument may be offered for the conclusion that nobody is ever reasonable in believing anything about the external world, even if Descartes himself might not be much concerned (in any explicit way) with anything so apparently weak as reasonable believing.

These arguments are exceedingly compelling. They tend to make sceptics of us all if only for a brief while. Anyone who would try to further scepticism, as I will try to do, will do well to link his own ideas to these arguments. For, then, the very notable feelings and intuitions which they arouse may serve as support for the theses he would advance.

Unfortunately, I think, these arguments are soon ignored, and the inclinations towards scepticism which they arouse disappear shortly after. On the other hand, they are perennially capable of stirring up again feelings which seem to support the sceptical view. Their being ignored has nothing to do with anyone's finding any serious fault with the arguments, for none has ever been exposed. Nor, then, can anyone's abandoning his sceptical views, however briefly held, be due to that. But though that cannot be the explanation for scepticism's rejection, the explanation is, I think, still quite a simple one: we don't connect the arguments with enough other things of interest to hold our prolonged attention, not even our attention in pursuing our philosophical interests. Lacking any larger connected discussion which favours scepticism, our sceptical inclinations do not remain active and we easily fall back on the comfortable, habitual thinking of 'common sense'. We easily return to think confidently that we *know* all sorts of things, and that we have *reasons* for believing many others, at least quite often then being *reasonable* in believing these latter things.

Being a sceptic, I of course think that we then return to ways of continued error. In every bit of my sceptical work, I will try to do something to remedy this situation. Being much like other people, I too return quickly to supposing that I know quite a fair amount. I do this almost as soon as I cease to think actively about what seems the deeper aspects of these issues. Perhaps even, I must always despair of doing otherwise, not just for fear of losing common ground with others in society, but for fear of disrupting my habitual patterns of thought to the point where my thought itself slows to a halt. Even so, if a sceptical philosophy is the only alternative to massive error, as I suspect it to be, then, at least as a philosopher, I must try to examine our sceptical arguments, and to follow out the implications of their sceptical conclusions. If my suspicions are correct, that will place me, as we are wont to say, in the service of truth. In any case, be they correct or incorrect, this attempt may help us all take scepticism seriously for more than just a moment. Perhaps, then, we will even demand from ourselves a reasonable explanation of those feelings and intuitions which certain sceptical arguments so forcefully and so perennially arouse.

NOTE

1. Rene Descartes, *Meditations on First Philosophy*, 2nd ed., 1642, in *The Philosophical Works of Descartes*, trans. by E. S. Haldane and G. R. T. Ross, vol. I (Cambridge, 1972), Meditation I, pp. 144–9. The crux of what I take to be the main argument occurs near the end of Meditation I. During sections which follow I try to convey the spirit of Descartes's sceptical reasonings, and to extend this reasoning along lines which further convey that spirit. I nowhere claim any expertise on interpreting the works of this great philosopher, nor have I any intention of making a contribution to Cartesian scholarship. Rather, in those sections, I will try to be, or to pretend to be, a latter-day Descartes.

POSITIVE VERSUS NEGATIVE UNDERMINING IN BELIEF REVISION

Gilbert Harman

I am going to compare two competing theories of reasoned belief revision. I will call the theories I am concerned with the "foundations theory of belief revision" and the "coherence theory of belief revision," respectively, since there are similarities between these theories and certain philosophical theories of justification sometimes called "foundation" and "coherence" theories [Sosa 1980, Pollock 1980]. But the theories I am concerned with are not precisely the same as the corresponding philosophical theories of justification, which are not normally presented as theories of belief revision. So, although I will be using the *term* "justification" in what follows, as well as the terms "coherence" and "foundations," I do not claim that my use of any of these terms is the same as its use in these theories of justification. I mean to be raising a new issue, not discussing an old one.

The key point in what I am calling the *foundations* theory is that some of one's beliefs "depend on" others for their "justification"; these other beliefs may depend on still others, until one gets to foundational beliefs that do not depend on any further beliefs for their justification. In this theory, reasoning or belief revision should consist, first, in subtracting any of one's beliefs that do not now have a satisfactory justification and, second, in adding new beliefs that either need no justification or are justified on the basis of other justified beliefs one has.

On the other hand, according to what I am calling the *coherence* theory, it is not true that one's beliefs have, or ought to have, the sort of justificational structure required by the foundations theory. In this view beliefs do not usually require any sort of justification at all. Justification is taken to be required only if one has a special reason to doubt a particular belief. Such a reason might consist in a conflicting belief or in the observation that one's beliefs could be made more "coherent," that is, more organized or simpler or less ad hoc, if the given belief were abandoned (and perhaps certain other changes were made). According to the coherence theory, belief revision should involve minimal changes in one's beliefs in a way that sufficiently increases overall coherence.

It turns out that the theories are most easily distinguished by the conflicting advice they occasionally give concerning whether one should *give up* a belief P from which many other of one's beliefs have been inferred, when P's original justification has to be abandoned. Here a surprising contrast seems to emerge—"is" and "ought" seem to come apart. The foundations theory seems, at least at first, to be more in line with our intuitions about how people *ought* to revise their beliefs; the coherence theory is more in line with what people *actually do* in such situations. Intuition seems strongly to support the foundations theory over the coherence theory as an account of what one is *justified* in doing in such cases; but *in fact* one will tend to act as the coherence theory advises.

After I explain this, I will go on to consider how this apparent discrepancy might be resolved. I will conclude by suggesting that the coherence theory is normatively correct after all, despite initial appearances.

Taking each of these theories in turn, I begin with the foundations theory.

THE FOUNDATIONS THEORY OF BELIEF REVISION

The basic principle of the foundations theory is that one's beliefs have a justificational structure, some serving as reasons or justifications for others, these justifying beliefs being more basic or fundamental for justification than the beliefs they justify.

The justifications are *prima facie* or defeasible. The foundations theory allows, indeed insists, that one can be justified in believing something P and then come to believe something else that undermines one's justification for believing P. In that case one should stop believing P, unless one has some further justification that is not undermined.

I say "unless one has some further justification," because, in this view, a belief may have more than one justification. To be justified, a belief must have *at least* one justification, but it may have more than one. That is, if a belief in P is to be justified, it is required, either that P be a foundational belief whose intrinsic justification is not defeated, or that there be at least one undefeated justification of P from other beliefs one is justified in believing. If one believes P and it happens that all of one's justifications for believing P come to be defeated, one is no longer justified in continuing to believe P and one should subtract P from one's beliefs.

Furthermore, and this is very important, if one comes not to be justified in continuing to believe P in this way, then not only is it true that one must abandon belief in P but justifications one has for other beliefs are also affected if these justifications appeal to one's belief in P. Justifications appealing to P must be abandoned when P is abandoned. If that means further beliefs are left without justification, then these beliefs too must be dropped, along with any justifications appealing to them. So there will be a chain reaction when one loses justification for a belief on which other beliefs depend for their justification. (This is worked out in more detail for an artificial intelligence system in Doyle [2], [3].)

So much then for the foundations theory. Let me turn now to the coherence theory.

THE COHERENCE THEORY OF BELIEF REVISION

The coherence theory is a *conservative* theory in a way the foundations theory is not. The coherence theory supposes one's present beliefs are justified just as they are in the absence of special reasons to change them. Given such special reasons, changes are allowed only to the extent that they yield sufficient increases in coherence. Note that where the foundations theory takes one to be justified in continuing to believe something only if one has a special reason to continue to believe it, the coherence theory takes one to be justified in continuing to believe something as long as one has no special reason to stop believing it.

For our purposes, we do not need to be too specific as to exactly what coherence involves, except to say it includes not only consistency but also a network of relations among one's beliefs, especially relations of implication and explanation.

It is important that in this view coherence competes with conservatism. It is as if there are two aims or tendencies of reasoned revision, one being to maximize coherence, the other to minimize change. Both tendencies are important. Without conservatism, one would be led to reduce one's beliefs to the single Parmenidean thought that all is one. Without the tendency toward coherence, we would have what Peirce ([9]) called "the method of tenacity," in which one holds to one's initial convictions no matter what evidence may accumulate against them.

According to the coherence theory, the assessment of a challenged belief is always holistic. Whether such a belief is justified depends on how well it fits together with everything else one believes. If one's beliefs are coherent, they are mutually supporting. All of one's beliefs are, in a sense, equally fundamental. In the coherence theory there are not the assymmetical justification relations among one's beliefs that there are in the foundations theory.

Here then is a brief sketch of the coherence theory. I turn now to testing these theories against our intuitions about cases. This raises an immediate problem for the coherence theory.

AN OBJECTION TO THE COHERENCE THEORY: KAREN'S APTITUDE TEST

The problem is that, contrary to what is assumed in the coherence theory, there do seem to be assymmetrical justification relations among one's beliefs.

Consider Karen, who has taken an aptitude test and has just been told her results show she has a considerable aptitude for science and music, but little aptitude for history and philosophy. This news does not correlate perfectly with her previous grades. She had previously done very well, not only in physics, for which her aptitude scores are reported to be high, but also in history, for which her aptitude scores are reported to be low. Furthermore, she had previously done poorly, not only in philosophy, for which her aptitude scores are reported to be low, but also in music, for which her aptitude scores are reported to be high.

After carefully thinking over these discrepancies, Karen concludes (1) her reported aptitude scores accurately reflect and are explained by her actual aptitudes, so (2) she has an aptitude for science and music and no aptitude for history and philosophy, so (3) her history course must have been an easy one, and (4) she did not work hard enough in the music course. She decides (5) to take another music course but not take any more history.

It seems quite clear that, after Karen reaches these conclusions, some of her beliefs are based on others. Her belief that the history course was very easy depends for its justification on her belief that she has no aptitude for history, a belief which depends in turn for its justification on her belief that she got a low score for history aptitude in her aptitude test. There is not a dependence in the other direction. Her belief about her aptitude test score in history is not based on her belief that she has no aptitude for history or on her belief that the history course was an easy one.

This assymmetry would seem to conflict with the coherence theory which denies there are such relations of assymmetrical dependency among one's beliefs.

It might be suggested on behalf of the coherence theory, that the relevant relations here are merely *temporal* or *causal*. One can agree that Karen's belief about the outcome of her aptitude test precedes and is an important cause of her belief that the history course she took was a very easy one, without having to agree that a relation of dependence or justification holds or ought to hold among these two beliefs once the new belief has been accepted.

In order to test this suggestion, it is sufficient to tell more of Karen's story. Some days later she is informed that the report about her aptitude scores was incorrect! The scores reported were those of someone else whose name was confused with hers. Unfortunately, her own scores have now been lost. How should Karen revise her views, given this new information?

Let us assume that, if Karen had not been given the false information about her aptitude test scores, she could not have reasonably reached any of the conclusions she did reach about her aptitudes in physics, history, philosophy, and music; and let us also assume that without those beliefs, Karen could not have reached any of her further conclusions about the courses she has already taken. Then, according to the foundations theory, Karen should abandon her beliefs about her relative aptitudes in these subjects; and she should give up her belief that the history course she took was very easy, as well as her belief that she did not work hard enough in the music course. She should also reconsider her decisions to take another course in music and not take any more history courses.

The coherence theory does not automatically yield the same advice. Karen's new information does produce a loss of overall coherence in her beliefs, since she can no longer coherently suppose that her aptitudes in science, music, philosophy, and history are in any way responsible for the original report she received about the results of her aptitude test. So she must abandon that particular supposition about the explanation of the original report of her scores. Still, there is considerable coherence among the beliefs she inferred from this false report. For example, there is a connection between her belief that she has little aptitude for history, her belief that her high grade on the history course was the result of the course's being an easy one, and her belief that she will not take any more courses in history. There are similar connections between her beliefs about her aptitudes in other subjects, how well she did in courses in those subjects, and her plans for the future in those areas. Let us suppose Karen inferred a great many other things that we have not mentioned from that original report so there are a great many beliefs involved here. Abandoning all of these beliefs would be costly from the point of view of conservatism, which says to minimize change. Let us suppose it turns out that there are so many of these beliefs, and they are so connected with each other and with other things Karen believes, that the coherence theory implies Karen should retain all these new beliefs even though she must give up her beliefs about the explanation of the report of her aptitude scores.

Then the foundations theory says Karen should give up all these beliefs, while the coherence theory says Karen should retain them. Which theory is right about what Karen ought to do? Almost everyone who has considered this sort of example sides with the foundations theory: Karen should not retain any beliefs she inferred from the false report of her aptitude test scores that she would not have been justified in believing in the absence of that false report. That does seem to be the intuitively right answer. The foundations theory is in accordance with our intuitions about what Karen *ought* to do in a case like this. The coherence theory is not.

BELIEF PERSEVERANCE

But now I must remark on an important complication, to which I have already referred. In fact, Karen would almost certainly keep her new beliefs! That is what people actually do in situations like this. Although the foundations theory gives intuitively satisfying advice about what Karen *ought* to do in such a situation, the coherence theory is more in accord with what people actually do!

Lack of space prevents me from fully documenting the rather surprising facts here. I can only say that there is a considerable psychological literature on "belief perseverance" initially deriving from difficulties psychologists have in "debriefing" subjects who have been exposed to experimental deception. It has proved to be very difficult to eliminate the erroneous beliefs induced during psychological experiments, some of which involve situations much like Karen's ([11]: 147–49).

Why should this be so? It might be suggested that belief is like a habit in that, once a belief has become established, considerable effort may be required to get rid of it, even if one should come to see one ought to get rid of it, just as it is hard to get rid of other bad habits. Often, one cannot simply decide to get rid of a bad habit; one must take active steps to ensure that the habit does not reassert itself. Perhaps it is just as difficult to get rid of a bad belief. If so, foundationalism could be normatively correct as an ideal, even though the ideal is one it takes considerable effort to live up to.

But this suggestion does not provide an adequate explanation of the phenomenon of belief perseverance. Of course, there are cases in which one has to struggle in order to abandon a belief one takes to be discredited. One finds oneself coming back to thoughts one realizes one should no longer accept. There are such habits of thought. But this does not seem to be what is happening in the debriefing studies. Subjects in these studies are not struggling to abandon beliefs they see are discredited. On the contrary, the problem is that subjects do not see that the beliefs they have acquired have been discredited. They see all sorts of reasons for the beliefs, where the reasons consist in connections with other beliefs of a sort that the coherence theory might approve, but not the foundations theory. So the correct explanation of belief perseverance in these studies is not that beliefs that have lost their evidential grounding are like bad habits.

POSITIVE VERSUS NEGATIVE UNDERMINING

A more plausible hypothesis as to why beliefs might survive after the evidence for them has been discredited is that people simply do not keep track of the justification relations among their beliefs. They continue to believe things after the evidence for them has been discredited because they do not realize what they are doing.

This is to suppose people do not in fact proceed in accordance with the advice of the foundations theory. The foundations theory says people should keep track of their reasons for believing as they do and should stop believing anything that is not associated with adequate evidence. So the foundations theory implies that, if Karen has not kept track of her reason for believing her history course to have been an easy one, she should have abandoned her belief even before she was told about the mix up with her aptitude test scores.

This implication of the foundations theory is implausible. If, as I have just suggested, people rarely keep track of their reasons, the implication would be that people are unjustified in almost all their beliefs, an absurd result. In this case, foundationalism seems clearly wrong even as a normative theory. So let us see whether we cannot defend the coherence theory as a normative theory.

Now, although justification in a coherence theory is always "holistic" in that whether one is justified in coming to adopt a new belief depends on how that belief would fit in with everything else one believes, we have already seen how appeal might be made to a nonholistic *causal* notion of "local justification" by means of a limited number of one's prior beliefs, namely those prior beliefs that are most crucial to one's justification for adding the new belief. To be sure, the coherence theory must not suppose there are *continuing* links of justification dependency among beliefs that can be consulted when revising one's beliefs. But the theory can admit that Karen's coming to believe certain things depended on certain of her prior beliefs in a way that it did not depend on others, where this dependence represents a kind of local justification, even though in another respect whether Karen was justified in coming to believe those things depended on everything she then believed.

Given this point, I suggest that the coherence theory might incorporate something like the principle that it is incoherent to believe both P and also that one would not be justified in believing P if one had relied only on true beliefs. Within the coherence theory, this implies, roughly speaking

Principle of Positive Undermining: One should stop believing P whenever one positively believes one's reasons for believing P are no good.

I want to compare this with the analogous principle within a foundations theory:

Principle of Negative Undermining: One should stop believing P whenever one does not associate one's belief in P with an adequate justification (either intrinsic or extrinsic).

It seems clear to me that the principle of positive undermining is much more plausible than the principle of negative undermining. The principle of negative undermining implies that, as one loses track of the justifications of one's beliefs, one should give up those beliefs. If one does not keep track of one's justifications for most of one's beliefs, the principle of negative undermining would say one should stop believing almost everything one believes, which is absurd. On the other hand, the principle of positive undermining does not have this absurd implication. The principle of positive undermining does not suppose the absence of a justification is a reason to stop believing something. It only supposes one's belief in P is undermined by the *positive* belief that one's reasons for P are no good.

In this connection it is relevant that subjects *can* be successfully debriefed after experiments involving deception, if the subjects are made vividly aware of this very phenomenon, that is, if they are made vividly aware of this very tendency for people to retain false beliefs after the evidence for them has been undercut and are also made vividly aware of how this phenomenon has acted in their own case ([8]). This further phenomenon seems clearly to support the coherence theory, with its principle of positive undermining, over the foundations theory, with its principle of negative undermining. The so-called "full debriefing" cannot merely undermine the evidence for the conclusions subjects have reached but must also directly attack each of these conclusions themselves. The full debriefing works, not just by getting subjects to give up the beliefs that originally served as evidence for the conclusions they have reached, but by getting them to accept certain further positive beliefs about their lack of good reasons for each of these conclusions.

CLUTTER AVOIDANCE

I now want to suggest that there are practical considerations that tell against keeping track of justifications.

In particular, there is a practical reason to avoid too much clutter in one's beliefs. There is a limit to what one can remember, a limit to the number of things one can put into long term storage, and a limit to what one can retrieve. It is important to save room for important things and not clutter one's mind with a lot of unimportant matters. This is one very important reason why one does not try to believe all sorts of logical consequences of one's beliefs. One should not try to infer all one can from one's beliefs. One should try not to retain too much trivial information. Furthermore, one should try to store in long term memory only the key matters that one will later need to recall. When one reaches a significant conclusion from one's other beliefs, one needs to remember the conclusion but does not normally need to remember all the intermediate steps involved in reaching that conclusion. Indeed, one should not try to remember those intermediate steps; one should try to avoid too much clutter in one's mind.

Similarly, even if much of one's knowledge of the world is inferred ultimately from what one believes oneself to be immediately perceiving at one or another time, one does not normally need to remember these original perceptual beliefs or many of the various intermediate conclusions drawn from them. It is enough to recall the more important of one's conclusions about the location of the furniture, etc.

This means one should not be disposed to try to keep track of the local justifications of one's beliefs. One could keep track of these justifications only by remembering an incredible number of mostly perceptual original premises, along with many, many intermediate steps which one does not want and has little need to remember. One will not want to link one's beliefs to such justifications because one will not in general want to try to retain the prior beliefs from which one reached one's current beliefs.

The practical reason for not keeping track of the justifications of one's beliefs is not as severe as the reason that prevents one from operating purely probabilistically, namely a combinatorial explosion ([5]). Still, there are important practical constraints. It is more efficient not to try to retain these justifications and the accompanying justifying beliefs. This leaves more room in memory for important matters.

SUMMARY AND FINAL CONCLUSIONS

To sum up: I have discussed two theories of belief revision, the foundations theory and the coherence theory. The foundations theory says one's beliefs are to be linked by relations of justification that one is to make use of in deciding whether to stop believing something. The coherence theory denies that there should be this sort of justificational structure to one's beliefs. The coherence theory takes conservatism to be an important principle—one's beliefs are justified in the absence of a special reason to doubt them. The foundations theory rejects any such conservatism.

When we consider a case like Karen's, our intuitive judgments may seem to support foundationalism. But it is important to distinguish two different principles, the coherence theory's principle of positive undermining and the foundations theory's much stronger principle of negative undermining. Once we distinguish these principles we see it is really the foundations theory that is counterintuitive, since that theory would have one give up almost everything one believes, if, as I have argued, one does not keep track of one's justifications. Furthermore, there is a very good practical reason not to keep track of justifications, namely that in the interests of clutter avoidance one should not normally even try to retain the beliefs from which one's more important beliefs were inferred.[1]

REFERENCES

[1] J. R. Anderson and G. H. Bower, *Human Associative Memory* (Washington, DC: Winston, 1973).
[2] Jon Doyle, "A Truth Maintenance System," *Artificial Intelligence* 12(1979): 231–272.

[3] ——, *A Model for Deliberation, Action, and Introspection* (Cambridge, MA: MIT Artificial Intelligence Laboratory Technical Report #561, 1980).

[4] Alvin I. Goldman, "Epistemology and the Psychology of Belief," *Monist* 61(1978): 525–535.

[5] Gilbert Harman, *Change in View: Principles of Reasoned Revision*, forthcoming.

[6] Richard C. Jeffrey, *The Logic of Decision*, second edition (Chicago, IL: University of Chicago Press, 1983).

[7] Daniel Kahneman, Paul Slovic, and Amos Tversky, *Judgment under Uncertainty: Heuristics and Biases* (Cambridge, England: Cambridge University Press, 1982).

[8] Richard Nisbett and Lee Ross, *Human Inference: Strategies and Shortcomings of Social Judgment* (Englewood Cliffs, NJ: Prentice-Hall, 1980).

[9] C. S. Peirce (1877), *Popular Science Monthly*, reprinted in *Philosophical Writings of Peirce*, edited by Justice Buchler (New York, NY: Dover).

[10] John Pollock, "A Plethora of Epistemological Theories," in *Justification and Knowledge*, edited by George Pappas (Dordrecht, Holland: Reidel, 1979).

[11] Lee Ross and Craig A. Anderson, "Shortcomings in the Attribution Process: On the Origins and Maintenance of Erroneous Social Assessments," in Kahneman, Slovic, and Tversky (1982).

[12] Ernest Sosa, "The Raft and the Pyramid: Coherence Versus Foundations in the Theory of Knowledge," *Midwest Studies in Philosophy* 5(1980): 3–25.

NOTE

1. This paper is excerpted from [5]. I am indebted to Jens Kulenkampff and John Pollock for helpful comments on an earlier draft.

MEDITATIONS I

Rene Descartes

OF THE THINGS WHICH MAY BE BROUGHT WITHIN THE SPHERE OF THE DOUBTFUL

It is now some years since I detected how many were the false beliefs that I had from my earliest youth admitted as true, and how doubtful was everything I had since constructed on this basis; and from that time I was convinced that I must once for all seriously undertake to rid myself of all the opinions which I had formerly accepted, and commence to build anew from the foundation, if I wanted to establish any firm and permanent structure in the sciences. But as this enterprise appeared to be a very great one, I waited until I had attained an age so mature that I could not hope that at any later date I should be better fitted to execute my design. This reason caused me to delay so long that I should feel that I was doing wrong were I to occupy in deliberation the time that yet remains to me for action. Today, then, since very opportunely for the plan I have in view I have delivered my mind from every care [and am happily agitated by no passions] and since I have procured for myself an assured leisure in a peaceable retirement, I shall at last seriously and freely address myself to the general upheaval of all my former opinions.

Now for this object it is not necessary that I should show that all of these are false—I shall perhaps never arrive at this end. But inasmuch as reason already persuades me that I ought no less carefully to withhold my assent from matters which are not entirely certain and indubitable than from those which appear to me manifestly to be false, if I am able to find in each one some reason to doubt, this will suffice to justify my rejecting the whole. And for that end it will not be requisite that I should examine each in particular, which would be an endless undertaking; for owing to the fact that the destruction of the foundations of necessity brings with it the downfall of the rest of the edifice, I shall only in the first place attack those principles upon which all my former opinions rested.

All that up to the present time I have accepted as most true and certain I have learned either from the senses or through the senses; but it is sometimes proved to me that these senses are deceptive, and it is wiser not to trust entirely to any thing by which we have once been deceived.

But it may be that, although the senses sometimes deceive us concerning things which are hardly perceptible, or very far away, there are yet many others to be met with as to which we cannot reasonably have any doubt, although we recognize them by their means. For example, there is the fact that I am here, seated by the fire, attired in a dressing gown, having this paper in my hands, and other similar matters. And how could I deny that these hands and this body are mine, were it not perhaps that I compare myself to certain persons, devoid of sense, whose cerebella are so troubled and clouded by the violent vapors of black bile, that they constantly assure us that they think they are kings when they are really quite poor, or that they are clothed in purple when they are really without covering, or who imagine that they have an earthenware head or are nothing but pumpkins or are made of glass. But they are mad, and I should not be any the less insane were I to follow examples so extravagant.

At the same time I must remember that I am a man, and that consequently I am in the habit of sleeping, and in my dreams representing to myself the same things or sometimes even less probable things, than do those who are insane in their waking moments. How often has it happened to me that in the night I dreamt that I found myself in this particular place, that I was dressed and seated near the fire, whilst in reality I was lying undressed in bed! At this moment it does indeed seem to me that it is with eyes awake that I am looking at this paper; that this head which I move is not asleep, that it is deliberately and of set purpose that I extend my hand and perceive it; what happens in sleep does not appear so clear nor so distinct as does all this. But in thinking over this I remind myself that on many occasions I have in sleep been deceived by similar illusions, and in dwelling carefully on this reflection I see so manifestly that there are no certain indications by which we may clearly distinguish wakefulness from sleep that I am lost in astonishment. And my astonishment is such that it is almost capable of persuading me that I now dream.

Now let us assume that we are asleep and that all these particulars, e.g., that we open our eyes, shake our head, extend our hands, and so on, are but false delusions; and let us reflect that possibly neither our hands nor our whole body are such as they appear to us to be. At the same time we must at least confess that the things which are represented to us in sleep are like painted representations which can only have been formed as the counterparts of something real and true, and that in this way those general things at least, i.e., eyes, a head, hands, and a whole body, are not imaginary things, but things really existent. For, as a matter of fact, painters, even when they study with the greatest skill to represent sirens and satyrs by forms the most strange and extraordinary, cannot give them natures which are entirely new, but merely make a certain medley of the members of different animals; or if their imagination is extravagant enough to invent something so novel that nothing similar has ever before been seen, and that their work represents a thing purely fictitious and absolutely false, it is certain all the same that the colors of which this is composed are necessarily real. And for the same reason, although these general things, to wit, [a body], eyes, a head, and such like, may be imaginary, we are bound at the same time to confess that there are at least some other objects yet more simple and more universal, which are real and true; and of these just in the same way as with certain real colors, all these images of things which dwell in our thoughts, whether true and real or false and fantastic, are formed.

To such a class of things pertains corporeal nature in general, and its extension, the figure of extended things, their quantity or magnitude and number, as also the place in which they are, the time which measures their duration, and so on.

That is possibly why our reasoning is not unjust when we conclude from this that Physics, Astronomy, Medicine, and all other sciences which have as their end the consideration of composite things, are very dubious and uncertain; but that Arithmetic, Geometry, and other sciences of that kind which only treat of things that are very simple and very general, without taking great trouble to ascertain whether they are actually existent or not, contain some measure of certainty and an element of the indubitable. For whether I am awake or asleep, two and three together always form five, and the square can never have more than four sides, and it does not seem possible that truths so clear and apparent can be suspected of any falsity [or uncertainty].

Nevertheless, I have long had fixed in my mind the belief that an all-powerful God existed by whom I have been created such as I am. But how do I know that He has not brought it to pass that there is no earth, no heaven, no extended body, no magnitude, no place, and that nevertheless [I possess the perceptions of all these things and that] they seem to me to exist just exactly as I now see them? And besides, as I sometimes imagine that others deceive themselves in the things which they think they know best, how do I know that I am not deceived every time that I add two and three, or count the sides of a square, or judge of things yet simpler, if anything simpler can be imagined? But possibly God has not desired that I should be thus deceived, for He is said to be supremely good. If, however, it is contrary to His goodness to have made me such that I constantly deceive myself, it would also appear to be contrary to His goodness to permit me to be sometimes deceived, and nevertheless I cannot doubt that He does permit this.

There may, indeed, be those who would prefer to deny the existence of a God so powerful, rather than believe that all other things are uncertain. But let us not oppose them for the present, and grant that all that is said of a God is a fable; nevertheless, in whatever way they suppose that I have arrived at the state of being that I have reached—whether they attribute it to fate or to accident, or make out that it is by a continual succession of antecedents, or by some other method—since to err and deceive oneself is a defect, it is clear that the greater will be the probability of my being so imperfect as to deceive myself ever, as is the Author to whom they assign my origin the less powerful. To these reasons I have certainly nothing to reply, but at the end I feel constrained to confess that there is nothing in all that I formerly believed to be true, of which I cannot in some measure doubt, and that not merely through want of thought or through levity, but for reasons which are very powerful and maturely considered; so that henceforth I ought not the less carefully to refrain from giving credence to these opinions than to that which is manifestly false, if I desire to arrive at any certainty [in the sciences].

But it is not sufficient to have made these remarks; we must also be careful to keep them in mind. For these ancient and commonly held opinions still revert frequently to my mind, long and familiar custom having given them the right to occupy my mind against my inclination and rendered them almost masters of my belief; nor will I ever lose the habit of deferring to them or of placing my confidence in them, so long as I consider them as they really are, i.e., opinions in some measure doubtful, as I have just shown, and at the same time highly probable, so that there is much more reason to believe than to deny them. That is why I consider that I shall not be acting amiss, if, taking of set purpose a contrary belief, I allow myself to be deceived, and for a certain time pretend that all these opinions are entirely false and imaginary, until at last, having thus balanced my former prejudices with my latter [so that they cannot divert my opinions more to one side than to the other], my judgment will no longer be dominated by bad usage or turned away from the right knowledge of the truth. For I am assured that there can be neither peril nor error in this course, and that I cannot at present yield too much to distrust, since I am not considering the question of action, but only of knowledge.

I shall then suppose, not that God, who is supremely good and the fountain of truth, but some evil genius not less powerful than deceitful, has employed his whole energies in deceiving me; I shall consider that the heavens, the earth, colors, figures, sound, and all other external things are nought but the illusions and dreams of which this genius has availed himself in order to lay traps for my credulity; I shall consider myself as having no hands, no eyes, no flesh, no blood, nor any senses, yet falsely believing myself to possess all these things; I shall remain obstinately attached to this idea, and if by this means it is not in my power to arrive at the knowledge of any truth, I may at least do what is in my power [i.e., suspend my judgment], and with firm purpose avoid giving credence to any false thing, or being imposed upon by this arch deceiver, however powerful and deceptive he may be. But this task is a laborious one, and insensibly a certain lassitude leads me into the course of my ordinary life. And just as a captive who in sleep enjoys imaginary liberty, when he begins to suspect that his liberty is but a dream, fears to awaken, and conspires with these agreeable illusions that the deception may be prolonged, so insensibly of my own accord I fall back into my former opinions, and I dread awakening from this slumber, lest the laborious wakefulness which would follow the tranquillity of this repose should have to be spent, not in daylight, but in the excessive darkness of the difficulties which have just been discussed.

THE FIXATION OF BELIEF

C. S. Peirce

I

Few persons care to study logic, because everybody conceives himself to be proficient enough in the art of reasoning already. But I observe that this satisfaction is limited to one's own ratiocination, and does not extend to that of other men. . . .

II

The object of reasoning is to find out, from the consideration of what we already know, something else which we do not know. Consequently, reasoning is good if it be such as to give a true conclusion from true premises, and not otherwise. Thus, the question of its validity is purely one of fact and not of thinking. A being the premises and B the conclusion, the question is, whether these facts are really so related that if A is B is. If so, the inference is valid; if not, not. It is not in the least the question whether, when the premises are accepted by the mind, we feel an impulse to accept the conclusion also. It is true that we do generally reason correctly by nature. But that is an accident; the true conclusion would remain true if we had no impulse to accept it; and the false one would remain false, though we could not resist the tendency to believe in it.

We are, doubtless, in the main logical animals, but we are not perfectly so. Most of us, for example, are naturally more sanguine and hopeful than logic would justify. We seem to be so constituted that in the absence of any facts to go upon we are happy and self-satisfied; so that the effect of experience is continually to contract our hopes and aspirations. Yet a lifetime of the application of this corrective does not usually eradicate our sanguine disposition. Where hope is unchecked by any experience, it is likely that our optimism is extravagant. Logicality in regard to practical matters is the most useful quality an animal can possess, and might, therefore, result from the action of natural selection; but outside of these it is probably of more advantage to the animal to have his mind filled with pleasing and encouraging visions, independently of their truth; and thus, upon unpractical subjects, natural selection might occasion a fallacious tendency of thought.

That which determines us, from given premises, to draw one inference rather than another, is some habit of mind, whether it be constitutional or acquired. The habit is good or otherwise, according as it produces true conclusions from true premises or not; and an inference is regarded as valid or not, without reference to the truth or falsity of its conclusion specially, but according as the habit which determines it is such as to produce true conclusions in general or not. The particular habit of mind which governs this or that inference may be formulated in a proposition whose truth depends on the validity of the inferences which the habit determines; and such a formula is called a *guiding principle* of inference. Suppose, for example, that we observe that a rotating disk of copper quickly comes to rest when placed between the poles of a magnet, and we infer that this will happen with every disk of copper. The guiding principle is, that what is true of one piece of copper is true of another. Such a guiding principle with regard to copper would be much safer than with regard to many other substances—brass, for example.

A book might be written to signalize all the most important of these guiding principles of reasoning. . . .

The subject could hardly be treated, however, without being first limited; since almost any fact may serve as a guiding principle. But it so happens that there exists a division among facts, such that in one class are all those which are absolutely essential as guiding principles, while in the others are all which have any other interest as objects of research. This division is between those which are necessarily taken for granted in asking whether a certain conclusion follows from certain premises, and those which are not implied in that question. A moment's thought will show that a variety of facts are already assumed when the logical question is first asked. It is implied, for instance, that there are such states of mind as doubt and belief—that a passage from one to the other is possible, the object of thought remaining the same, and that this transition is subject to some rules which all minds are alike bound by. As these are facts which we must already know before we can have any clear conception of reasoning at all, it cannot be supposed to be any longer of much interest to inquire into their truth or falsity. . . .

III

We generally know when we wish to ask a question and when we wish to pronounce a judgment, for there is a dissimilarity between the sensation of doubting and that of believing.

But this is not all which distinguishes doubt from belief. There is a practical difference. Our beliefs guide our desires and shape our actions.

The Assassins, or followers of the Old Man of the Mountain, used to rush into death at his least command, because they believed that obedience to him would insure everlasting felicity. Had they doubted this, they would not have acted as they did. So it is with every belief, according to its degree. The feeling of believing is a more or less sure indication of there being established in our nature some habit which will determine our actions. Doubt never has such an effect.

Nor must we overlook a third point of difference. Doubt is an uneasy and dissatisfied state from which we struggle to free ourselves and pass into the state of belief; while the latter is a calm and satisfactory state which we do not wish to avoid, or to change to a belief in anything else.[1] On the contrary, we cling tenaciously, not merely to believing, but to believing just what we do believe.

Thus, both doubt and belief have positive effects upon us, though very different ones. Belief does not make us act at once, but puts us into such a condition that we shall behave in a certain way, when the occasion arises. Doubt has not the least effect of this sort, but stimulates us to action until it is destroyed. This reminds us of the irritation of a nerve and the reflex action produced thereby; while for the analogue of belief, in the nervous system, we must look to what are called nervous associations— for example, to that habit of the nerves in consequence of which the smell of a peach will make the mouth water.

IV

The irritation of doubt causes a struggle to attain a state of belief. I shall term this struggle *inquiry*, though it must be admitted that this is sometimes not a very apt designation.

The irritation of doubt is the only immediate motive for the struggle to attain belief. It is certainly best for us that our beliefs should be such as may truly guide our actions so as to satisfy our desires; and this reflection will make us reject any belief which does not seem to have been so formed as to insure this result. But it will only do so by creating a doubt in the place of that belief. With the doubt, therefore, the struggle begins, and with the cessation of doubt it ends. Hence, the sole object of inquiry is the settlement of opinion. We may fancy that this is not enough for us, and that we seek, not merely an opinion, but a true opinion. But put this fancy to the test, and it proves groundless; for as soon as a firm belief is reached we are entirely satisfied, whether the belief be true or false. And it is clear that nothing out of the sphere of our knowledge can be our object, for nothing which does not affect the mind can be the motive for a mental effort. The most that can be maintained is, that we seek for a belief that we shall *think* to be true. But we think each one of our beliefs to be true, and, indeed, it is mere tautology to say so.

That the settlement of opinion is the sole end of inquiry is a very important proposition. It sweeps away at once, various vague and erroneous conceptions of proof. A few of these may be noticed here.

1. Some philosophers have imagined that to start an inquiry it was only necessary to utter a question or set it down upon paper, and have even recommended us to begin our studies with questioning everything! But the mere putting of a proposition into the interrogative form does not stimulate the mind to any struggle after belief. There must be a real and living doubt, and without this all discussion is idle.

2. It is a very common idea that a demonstration must rest on some ultimate and absolutely indubitable propositions. These, according to one school, are first principles of a general nature; according to another, are first sensations. But, in point of fact, an inquiry, to have that completely satisfactory result called demonstration, has only to start with propositions perfectly free from all actual doubt. If the premises are not in fact doubted at all, they cannot be more satisfactory than they are.

3. Some people seem to love to argue a point after all the world is fully convinced of it. But no further advance can be made. When doubt ceases, mental action on the subject comes to an end; and, if it did go on, it would be without a purpose. . . .

To satisfy our doubts, therefore, it is necessary that a method should be found by which our beliefs may be caused by nothing human, but by some external permanency—by something upon which our thinking has no effect. . . . Such is the method of science. Its fundamental hypothesis, restated in more familiar language, is this: There are real things, whose characters are entirely independent of our opinions about them; those realities affect our senses according to regular laws, and, though our sensations are as different as our relations to the objects, yet, by taking advantage of the laws of perception, we can ascertain by reasoning how things really are, and any man, if he have sufficient experience and reason enough about it, will be led to the one true conclusion. The new conception here involved is that of reality. It may be asked how I know that there are any realities. If this hypothesis is the sole support of my method of inquiry, my method of inquiry must not be used to support my hypothesis. The reply is this: 1. If investigation cannot be regarded as proving that there are real things, it at least does not lead to a contrary conclusion; but the method and the conception on which it is based remain ever in harmony. No doubts of the method, therefore, necessarily arise from its practice, as is the case with all the others. 2. The feeling which gives rise to any method of fixing belief is a dissatisfaction at two repugnant propositions. But here already is a vague concession that there is some *one* thing to which a proposition should conform. Nobody, therefore, can really doubt that there are realities, or, if he did, doubt would not be a source of dissatisfaction. The hypothesis, therefore, is one which every minds admits. So that the social impulse does not cause me to doubt it. 3. Everybody uses the scientific method about a great many things, and only ceases to use it when he does not know how to apply it. 4. Experience of the method has not led me to doubt it, but, on the contrary, scientific investigation has had the most wonderful triumphs in the way of settling opinion. These afford the explanation of my not doubting the method or the hypothesis which it supposes; and not having any doubt, nor believing that anybody else whom I could influence has, it would be the merest babble for me to say more about it. If there be anybody with a living doubt upon the subject, let him consider it.

NOTE

1. I am not speaking of secondary effect occasionally produced by the interference of other impulses.

SOME CONSEQUENCES OF FOUR INCAPACITIES

C. S. Peirce

Descartes is the father of modern philosophy, and the spirit of Cartesianism—that which principally distinguishes it from the scholasticism which it displaced—may be compendiously stated as follows:

1. It teaches that philosophy must begin with universal doubt; whereas scholasticism had never questioned fundamentals.

2. It teaches that the ultimate test of certainty is to be found in the individual consciousness; whereas scholasticism had rested on the testimony of sages and of the Catholic Church.

3. The multiform argumentation of the middle ages is replaced by a single thread of inference depending often upon inconspicuous premises.

4. Scholasticism had its mysteries of faith, but undertook to explain all created things. But there are many facts which Cartesianism not only does not explain, but renders absolutely inexplicable, unless to say that "God makes them so" is to be regarded as an explanation.

In some, or all of these respects, most modern philosophers have been, in effect, Cartesians. Now without wishing to return to scholasticism, it seems to me that modern science and modern logic require us to stand upon a very different platform from this.

1. We cannot begin with complete doubt. We must begin with all the prejudices which we actually have when we enter upon the study of philosophy. These prejudices are not to be dispelled by a maxim, for they are things which it does not occur to us *can* be questioned. Hence this initial scepticism will be a mere self-deception, and not real doubt; and no one who follows the Cartesian method will ever be satisfied until he has formally recovered all those beliefs which in form he has given up. It is, therefore, as useless a preliminary as going to the North Pole would be in order to get to Constantinople by coming down regularly upon a meridian. A person may, it is true, in the course of his studies, find reason to doubt what he began by believing; but in that case he doubts because he has a positive reason for it, and not on account of the Cartesian maxim. Let us not pretend to doubt in philosophy what we do not doubt in our hearts.

2. The same formalism appears in the Cartesian criterion, which amounts to this: "Whatever I am clearly convinced of, is true." If I were

really convinced, I should have done with reasoning, and should require no test of certainty. But thus to make single individuals absolute judges of truth is most pernicious. The result is that metaphysicians will all agree that metaphysics has reached a pitch of certainty far beyond that of the physical sciences;—only they can agree upon nothing else. In sciences in which men come to agreement, when a theory has been broached, it is considered to be on probation until this agreement is reached. After it is reached, the question of certainty becomes an idle one, because there is no one left who doubts it. We individually cannot reasonably hope to attain the ultimate philosophy which we pursue; we can only seek it, therefore, for the *community* of philosophers. Hence, if disciplined and candid minds carefully examine a theory and refuse to accept it, this ought to create doubts in the mind of the author of the theory himself.

3. Philosophy ought to imitate the successful sciences in its methods, so far as to proceed only from tangible premisses which can be subjected to careful scrutiny, and to trust rather to the multitude and variety of its arguments than to the conclusiveness of any one. Its reasoning should not form a chain which is no stronger than its weakest link, but a cable whose fibres may be ever so slender, provided they are sufficiently numerous and intimately connected.

4. Every unidealistic philosophy supposes some absolutely inexplicable, unanalyzable ultimate; in short, something resulting from mediation itself not susceptible of mediation. Now that anything *is* thus inexplicable can only be known by reasoning from signs. But the only justification of an inference from signs is that the conclusion explains the fact. To suppose the fact absolutely inexplicable, is not to explain it, and hence this supposition is never allowable. . . .

Questions for Part XI

1. In Smullyan's dialogue, the experimental epistemologist has a machine which can tell him, by examining his brain, what he believes. Could there be such a machine? Why or why not? (You may want to link your answer to material in Part I, Mind-Body Puzzles.)

2. Could a person really make sincere claims about his or her own beliefs and yet be mistaken? Consider the Doctor's discussion of the Christian Scientist and of Frank himself at the end of "An Epistemological Nightmare."

3. Unger asks you to consider the possibility that you are really a brain in a vat. Describe evidence which would convince you that you were a brain in a vat. Can you describe evidence which would show that you are not a brain in a vat? If you can, do; if you cannot, explain why not.

4. Can you know that you are not a brain in a vat? Can you know that there are rocks? Why does Unger claim that you cannot answer "no" to the first question and "yes" to the second? Is he right?

5. Why does Harman describe the Coherence Theory of justification as "conservative"?

6. The Coherence Theory says, roughly, that you are justified in believing something so long as you have no reason to doubt it. Suppose that you wake up one morning firmly convinced, for no particular reason, that the star the twentieth-furthest from the sun will go nova next July. You have no evidence against this belief. Does the Coherence Theory say that you are justified in continuing to believe it? Why or why not?

7. Harman argues that keeping track of all our justifications for our beliefs is unwise, since it would require too much time and money. What would he say about keeping track of our justification for unusual or surprising beliefs for which we have a limited number of sources—such as remembering where you read that the earth was once visited by aliens from outer space?

8. Descartes writes: "Owing to the fact that the destruction of the foundations of necessity brings with it the downfall of the rest of the edifice, I shall only in the first place attack those principles upon which all my former opinions rested." What would Peirce or Harman say about this?

9. Descartes seems to argue that if my senses do sometimes deceive me, then they *could always* deceive me. Is this a legitimate inference? (Compare the following inference mentioned in Bernard Williams' book *Descartes:* some men are younger brothers, so it *could* be that *all* men are younger brothers.)

10. Is Descartes correct in thinking that I cannot be sure I am not dreaming? Why does he introduce the possibility of my being deceived by an "evil genius"?

11. Descartes concludes that "there is nothing in all that I formerly believed to be true, of which I cannot in some measure doubt." Evaluate this claim in light of Peirce's discussion of doubt.

12. Compare Peirce's discussion of how he knows "that there are any realities" with Descartes's and Unger's arguments that we cannot know anything about the external world. Would Peirce's reasons persuade Descartes or Unger? Should they?

Acknowledgments (continued from p. iv)

"Dr. Who and the Philosophers or Time-Travel for Beginners," by Jonathan Harrison. From *The Proceedings of The Aristotelian Society*, supplementary vol. XLV (1971), pp. 1–24. Reprinted by courtesy of the Editor of the Aristotelian Society. © 1971 The Aristotelian Society.

"The Paradoxes of Time Travel," by David Lewis. In the *American Philosophical Quarterly*, vol. 13, no. 2 (1976), pp. 145–52.

"Confessions," by St. Augustine, from Book Eleven, Chapters XIII, XIV, XV, XVIII, XIX, XXIII, XXIV, XXVIII of *Confessions*, translated by J.G. Pilkington (1876).

"Of Time," by Immanuel Kant, from *Kant's Critique of Pure Reason* (Second Edition), translated by J. M. D. Meiklejohn (1901).

"Bringing About the Past," by Michael Dummett. In *Philosophical Review* (1964), pp. 338–59.

"Leaving the Past Alone," by Samuel Gorovitz, In *Philosophical Review*, vol. LXXIII, no. 3 (1964), pp. 360–371.

"Of the Idea of Necessary Connection," by David Hume, from sections VII and V of *An Inquiry Concerning Human Understanding* (1748).

"Of the Words Cause and Effect, Action, and Active Power," by Thomas Reid, from Essay Four, Chapter 2 of *Essays on the Active Powers* in *The Works of Thomas Reid*, ed., William Hamilton, 6th ed. (1863).

"It Was to Be," by Gilbert Ryle, from *Dilemmas* by Gilbert Ryle, New York: Cambridge University Press, 1954. Reprinted by permission of Cambridge University Press.

"Freedom and Necessity," by A. J. Ayer. From *Philosophical Essays*, London: Macmillan, 1954. Reprinted by permission of Macmillan London Ltd.

"The System of Nature," by Baron Holbach, from Vol. 1, Chapters 11 and 12 of *The System of Nature*, translated by H. D. Robinson (1853).

"Are Human Actions Subject to the Law of Causality," by John Stuart Mill, from Chapter 2, Book VI, of *A System of Logic* (1843).

"The Dilemma of Determinism," by William James, from "The Dilemma of Determinism," *Unitarian Review* (September, 1884).

"Evil and Omnipotence," by J. L. Mackie. From *Mind* (1955), vol. 64, no. 254. Reprinted by permission of Oxford University Press.

"The Free Will Defense," by Alvin Plantinga. In Max Black, *Philosophy in America*, (1965). Copyright under the Berne Convention by George Allen and Unwin Ltd. Reprinted by permission of George Allan and Unwin Ltd.

"Adversus Haereses," by St. Irenaeus, from *Adversus Haereses*, translated by W. W. Harvey (1857).

"The Enchiridion X–XVI," by St. Augustine, from The Enchiridion on Faith, Hope and Love. Edited by Henry Paolucci.

"The Conscience of Huckleberry Finn," by Jonathan Bennett. Reprinted from *Philosophy* vol. 49, no. 188 (1974), pp. 123–134, by permission of Cambridge University Press.

"Some Paradoxes of Deterrence," by Gregory S. Kavka. In the *Journal of Philosophy* (1978), vol. LXXV, no. 6, pp. 285–302.

"Nicomachean Ethics," by Aristotle, from Book I, Sections 1–4, 7, 13; Book II, Sections 1, 4, 6, 7, 9 of *Nicomachean Ethics*, translated by W. D. Ross (1925).

"Fundamental Principles of the Metaphysics of Morals," by Immanuel Kant, from the First and Second Sections of *Fundamental Principles of the Metaphysics of Morals*, translated by T. K. Abbott (1873).

"Distributive Justice," by Robert Nozick, from *Anarchy, State and Utopia* by Robert Nozick. © 1974 by Basic Books, Inc., Publishers. Reprinted by permission of the publisher.

"Two Principles of Justice," by John Rawls, from *A Theory of Justice* by John Rawls. © Copyright 1971 by the President and Fellows of Harvard College. All rights reserved. Reprinted by permission of Harvard University Press.

"Marginal Notes to the Programme of the German Workers' Party," by Karl Marx, from the translation in Karl Marx and Frederick Engels, *Selected Works* (Moscow, 1970).

"Distribution," by John Stuart Mill, from Book II of *Principles of Political Economy* (1848).

"An Epistemological Nightmare," by Raymond M. Smullyan, from *5000 B.C. and Other Philosophical Fantasies* by Raymond M. Smullyan. Copyright © 1983 by Raymond Smullyan. Reprinted by permission of St. Martin's Press, Inc., New York.

Index